Construction Safety Auditing Made Easy

☑ **A Checklist Approach to OSHA Compliance**

Kathleen Hess

Government Institutes
Rockville, Maryland

Government Institutes, Inc., 4 Research Place, Suite 200
Rockville, Maryland 20850, USA.
Phone: (301) 921-2300
Fax: (301) 921-0373
Email: giinfo@govinst.com
Internet address: http://www.govinst.com
Government Institutes, Inc., is an ABS Group Company: http://www.abs-group.com/main.htm

Library of Congress Cataloging-in-Publication Data

Hess, Kathleen.
    Construction safety auditing made easy : a checklist approach to OSHA compliance / by Kathleen Hess.
        p.   cm.
    Includes index.
    ISBN: 0-86587-635-5
    1. Building–safety measures. 2. Industrial safety–Auditing.
    I. Title.
TH443.H473   1998
 690' .22--dc21
                     98-35545
                     CIP

Printed in the United States of America

Summary Contents

Expanded Contents

List of Figures and Tables

Preface

The task of performing a safety audit may be likened to that of training an elephant to cross a tight wire above the Grand Canyon, and rifling through mountains of regulations and deciphering their hieroglyphics can add further confusion and frustration.

Those daring enough to attempt the task alone may spend hours developing some variation of an internal audit checklist, while others may use the shotgun approach, addressing those areas they are familiar with and hoping to pick up information in other areas along the way. Some of the larger corporations have developed a checklist or generalized approach to auditing. OSHA has created a question-and-answer checklist.

However, most audits should be performed by a person who has a basic understanding of the subject matter under investigation, such as a Certified Safety Professional performing the safety audit. But sometimes even the safety professionals overlook discrepancies, not out of incompetence, but due to the complexity of some of the mandates. The intent of this book is to minimize the organizing time and provide an easy-to-follow path to completing a thorough audit.

The following pages present a methodical process for performing an effective audit using a series of checklists and supporting data. The checklists are based on federal OSHA regulatory requirements and on commonly used, recommended practices. Many examples have been included, and supporting information is presented in the form of figures and tables.

The reader is introduced to a quick and easy approach to auditing which is intended to free the auditor from the need to carry along a veritable reference library. The book also sets up a rating system that allows the auditor to determine compliance with the regulations and the effectiveness of the various programs.

The topics chosen are the standards which are most commonly cited, those most frequently overlooked, and workplace activities where accidents and injuries are most likely to occur. (See appendix A.)

Although many of the checklists were derived from *Environmental Health and Safety Auditing Made Simple: A Checklist Approach for Industry*, an effort was made to identify differences between industry and construction standards or areas where they overlap. Although construction standards are not as thorough as those of industry, OSHA compliance officers may cite the General Duty Clause of the Occupational Safety and Health Act and the General Safety and Health Provisions for Construction in cases where the construction standards are insufficient to protect the workers from injury. These provisions mandate that employers provide a safe and healthy work environment for their workers. Thus, items which are not found with the construction standards but are commonly accepted as good practice are provided herein—presented in italic print for easy identification.

Firms wanting to enter the OSHA Voluntary Protection Program must have exemplary safety and health programs and must demonstrate an exceptional worker incident record. The audit checklist can be used to determine regulatory competence relative to the basic regulatory requirements which must be met and exceeded in order for a firm to be admitted to the program. (See Appendix B.)

There are several places where additional regulatory and compliance assistance may be obtained. OSHA statistics and updated regulations may be accessed on the World Wide Web at **osha.gov** and assistance may be obtained by telephone from the state consulting agencies. (See Appendix C.)

Dangers caused by hazardous building materials in existing structures is discussed in Part IV, immediately following the checklists. During renovation and demolition projects, building contractors may disturb these materials, potentially exposing their workers, building occupants, and the environment to health hazards. Although abbreviated, this part of the book is a heads-up warning to contractors not trained in the management of these materials.

Use the checklists as a basic tool. Allow for bonuses and the spirit of competition between construction sites and/or regions. The possibilities for making your safety and health program the best it can be starts here!

Part I

Introduction

An audit is a methodical approach to evaluating records, procedures, and practices for accuracy and completeness. Although some prefer to perform an audit without a checklist, itemizing discrepancies as they go, a simplified checklist approach allows for easy identification of topics which require corrective actions. This helps to ensure all considerations have been covered.

In planning an audit, one should consider the goals and composition of the audit team, its approach, and a rating system. Each of these components is important for getting a good start along the path to a successful audit.

Purpose of an Audit

A safety audit is driven by a single event or a combination of factors. Although the results may not be immediately evident, a proactive response to discrepancies has historically resulted in reduction in costs, positive employee morale, and improved public relations. Some of the reasons for performing an audit and correcting discrepancies are as follows:

▶ **Loss prevention program**

▶ **Reduction and/or control of losses**

☐ **Protect Workers**

- Injuries and illnesses

- Lost time and wages

☐ **Control insurance costs**

- Workers' compensation

- General liability

- Pollution liability

☐ **Prevent property damage due to physical hazards** *(e.g., fires and explosions)*

- Company property
- Surrounding property (commercial and residential)

☐ **Prevent environmental pollution** *(e.g., groundwater contamination)*

- Company property
- Surrounding property (commercial and residential)

☐ **Prevent adverse public relations**

- Community relations

☐ **Prevent emergency response costs**

- Fire and hazardous material

☐ **Prevent damage recovery costs**

- Lost production time
- Replacement of product equipment and materials
- Replacement of building structures
- Environmental cleanup

☐ **Prevent enforcement citations**

- OSHA
- EPA

☐ **Avoid criminal penalties**

► **Increased confidence**

☐ **Worker**

- Morale
- Productivity
- Comfort
- Awareness

☐ **Public trust**

☐ **Community relations**

A clearly defined purpose will assist the audit team leader in selling the program to corporate management and to others who will be asked to participate in the process. Summarizing in-house statistics and company history can further justify an audit program. This information may include costs incurred during past exposures, adverse conditions which impacted production, a recap of negative press releases, and a survey of public and employee opinion (e.g., through questionnaires). Clarity of purpose is a must!

Audit Team

Although an individual with a broad background can conduct an audit, a team leader and specialized expediters are usually more efficient. Most construction employers have a safety director who can either conduct the audit or act as the audit team leader with assistance from other safety and industrial hygiene personnel—either consultants or other safety personnel who work for the same construction firm or personnel acquired in a cooperative trade with another firm.

Where there is no in-house safety director, a team leader may be assigned to one of the superintendents or managers. The team leader does not necessarily need to have knowledge in all areas to be audited. He or she must, however, be familiar with the job activities and be able to provide direction and guidance, as well as effectively manage the flow of events.

Team participants should, however, have some degree of technical knowledge. Ideally, this should include a safety professional, an industrial hygienist, and occasionally an environmental engineer. Yet, the ideal rarely becomes reality.

The audit checklists presented in this book require minimal knowledge and understanding of the disciplines covered. It is desirable to have at least one team participant who has some general knowledge of and/or training in safety issues.

In the audit process, it may be necessary and even desirable to involve the following personnel:

- Upper level management (e.g., superintendent)
- Human resources
- Field supervisors
- Employee representatives
- Consultants

Some larger construction firms with multiple job sites managed regionally may assign a team leader and participants to perform routine audits by region. They may stay within their own region or be assigned to another region. A dedicated audit team will improve with experience, and participants will find themselves getting more involved on a daily basis in the health and safety issues. This type of team can be highly effective!

Figure I-1: Checklist for Selecting Applicable Audit Topics

Topic applicability, if unclear, may be determined by referring to the topic introduction at the beginning of each section. The safety and health issues which are most commonly used are in bold type.

- ☐ **Battery Management**
- ☐ Carcinogenic/Toxic Dusts and Fumes
- ☐ Chemical Carcinogens Not Requiring Air Monitoring
- ☐ Chemical Carcinogens Requiring Air Monitoring
- ☐ Chemical Storage Procedures
- ☐ Compressed Gases
- ☐ Confined Space Entry Procedures
- ☐ Cranes
- ☐ **Electrical Hazards**
- ☐ **Emergency Action Plan**
- ☐ Ergonomics
- ☐ Excavations and Trenching
- ☐ **Fall Protection**
- ☐ **Fire Protection and Prevention**
- ☐ Flammable and Combustible Liquids
- ☐ **Hazard Communication Program**
- ☐ Hazardous Waste and Emergency Response Activities
- ☐ Hearing Conservation Program
- ☐ Heat Stress
- ☐ Ionizing Radiation
- ☐ Laser Equipment
- ☐ Local Exhaust Ventilation
- ☐ **Lockout and Tagout Program**
- ☐ **Manual Lifting**
- ☐ Personal Protective Equipment
- ☐ Portable Power Tools/Equipment
- ☐ Powered Industrial Trucks
- ☐ Process Safety Management
- ☐ Respiratory Protection Program
- ☐ **Scaffolds**
- ☐ **Stairways and Ladders**
- ☐ Toxic Substances Exposure Monitoring
- ☐ Welding and Cutting

Some smaller firms and some of the larger firms assign an internal "audit team," personnel intimately knowledgeable in the day-to-day workings of the construction firm. A disadvantage of such an audit is that key participants may have a direct responsibility for some of the audit discrepancies and may not report all observations. They may unknowingly overlook some areas due to assumed compliance, or they may be limited as to quality comparisons.

As a means to avoid biases, small firms may benefit by using outside consultants with expertise not only in safety and health matters, but in the type of construction work typically performed by the firm. The team leader may be assigned from within or he/she may be part of a "consulting audit team."

In all cases, an internal support team should be assigned to assist with technical knowledge, ease of communication, and information gathering. Team commitment and support from top management is paramount.

Methodical Approach

With purpose defined and an audit team identified, a methodical approach to performing the audit must be set forth. This can help save time and minimize resistance.

Since an audit may be very disruptive to operations, a "letter of notification" should be the first order of business. This letter should be sent to all personnel impacted by the audit, including the personnel to be interviewed. Relevant disclosures of information include purpose, approach, schedule, required participation, and a list of records to be reviewed. The participants must be alerted as to what will be required of them—information, allocation of time, equipment, and special resources.

At the time of notification, the team leader should seek to "obtain the pre-audit records" which are to be reviewed prior to the site visit. This will allow the audit team to identify special areas of concern and trends. The pre-audit records review can also be performed prior to the letter of notification. The information derived may impact both target concerns and scheduling.

Once the preliminary notification and records review have been completed, the audit team leader will have considerable information to proceed with and effectively carry out a site audit. The team participants are briefed, updated on the records review, and assigned their specific duties.

Upon arrival on site, the team leader reviews with top management (or the team coordinator) the findings of the initial records review and adjusts the itinerary as indicated by the records review. Any changes and/or updates should, in turn, be communicated to other participants impacted by the audit. Although the easiest and most efficient method is the written memo, oral communication may be necessary for expediency. A general posting of the itinerary and daily updates is helpful as well.

The steps in the site audit are best performed in the following order:
1. Site records review
2. Interviews
3. Inspection

Upon completion of the audit, a closing conference should include a generalized overview of impressions and glaring discrepancies. Disclose the anticipated turnaround time for the completed audit results and report.

The written audit report should specify all discrepancies found, summarize the problem areas and potential impact of the discrepancies, recommend corrective actions to be taken, and suggest a reasonable response time. Although the audit team recommends, top management or the project coordinator dictates the actual response time for correcting discrepancies. A follow-up visit is then scheduled to allow the original audit team to check for adequacy and completeness.

Rating System

In more elaborate programs, a rating system is used to involve participants and foster a competitive, fun-spirited work environment. A challenge between different field management teams or regional team members will encourage active participation and *esprit de corps*.

The group with the best rating receives the "Best in Safety and Health Award." This may be in the form of a plaque, a lunch or banquet, custom ball caps, special privileges, or assigned parking spaces. The sky is the limit! Let the workers suggest an award. Watch them toy with ideas, toss about wild thoughts, and plot how they might win the prize!

There are many different rating systems, most of which are fairly complicated and based on a corporate checklist of complex, oftentimes subjective, measuring devices. Some systems are designed to give points where there are discrepancies, and zero implies no discrepancies. Others provide greater numerical value to some disciplines. There is rarely a pattern or common thread between techniques of one firm verses another. The mix is a medley of mind-boggling possibilities!

There are over thirty topics in this book. Not all are applicable to each and every construction firm. Select those sections which are applicable to your firm. Then assign equal importance to each, or give a weighted value to each prior to performing the site audit. For example, scaffolding may be assigned a value of 12 points, ionizing radiation a value of 8 points. For ease of management, the total value of all sections should be 100 percent compliance.

Upon completion of each section, count the number of items audited (all check boxes and/or subtopics identified by bullets). Next, count all the nondiscrepancies identified. Then determine the percentage achieved. A perfect score is 100 percent.

$$\text{Section Score (percentage achieved)} = \frac{\text{Nondiscrepancies}}{\text{Total items}} \times 100$$

Now, let's go one step further: A bonus system can allow for additional credit where extra effort can be acknowledged. If there are more features to a program than those which are mandated (i.e., there are items "recommended as a good practice" in the checklist indicated in italics), the auditor may wish to grant additional credit. Add up to 10 percent in bonus points. This can bring an already perfect score up to 110 percent, or it may result in a bonus score of 10 percent on top of a total nondiscrepancy score of 80 percent for a final score of 90 percent.

Upon audit completion, all scores may be averaged for an overall percentage rating. If some sections have been given greater value than others, this also is taken into consideration. Multiply the value for each section by the score conferred to the same. Add the calculated scores, and divide by 100 (or the sum of all the values).

$$\text{Weighted Score} = \frac{(\text{Section Score} \times \text{Value})_1}{\text{Value}_1} + \frac{(\text{Section Score} \times \text{Value})_2}{\text{Value}_2} + \frac{(\text{Section Score} \times \text{Value})_n}{\text{Value}_n}$$

Awards are to be based upon the highest overall score. If there are no awards, section scores and overall ratings can be maintained for easy reference and comparison to past performances. A suggested interpretation of the rating results may be as follows:

101 – 110% Exceptional
If this is the total score for safety and health issues, consider filing for the OSHA "Voluntary Protection Program!" Great job. Your company deserves a pat on the back!

90 – 100% Excellent
Compliance citations are a remote possibility. The world smiles upon you!

80 – 89% Good
Compliance citations are a slight possibility. You are headed in the right direction. Keep going!

70 – 79% Marginal (or Fair)
Compliance citations are likely. "Marginal" means you are barely keeping your head above water. Time to express concern!

60 – 69% Poor
Compliance citations are highly probable. You are sinking, not down for the count, but getting there. Get with the program!

< 60% Awful!
Compliance citations are imminent. Get your head out of the sand!

Part II

General Procedures

> The general audit procedures presented herein are one of many possible audit approaches. They may be added to or adapted in accordance with special circumstances, the user's experiences, and the experiences of others. Although not required by federal statutes, an audit is a "widely used, recommended tool," and the checklist approach minimizes oversight.

▶ **Letter of notification**

☐ **Purpose of audit**

☐ **Approach**

☐ **Schedule of events**

☐ **Required participation**

☐ **List of records to be reviewed**

▶ **Pre-audit records review**

☐ **Accident history and previous inspection reports**

- Accident investigation reports
- Dispensary records
- Hospital records
- Safety inspection reports
- Industrial hygiene reports

Figure GP-1: OSHA Form 200

Log and Summary of Occupational
Injuries and Illnesses

NOTE: This form is required by Public Law 91-596 and must be kept in the establishment for 5 years. Failure to maintain and post can result in the issuance of citations and assessment of penalties. (See posting requirements on the other side of form.)		RECORDABLE CASES: You are required to record information about every occupational death; every nonfatal occupational illness; and those nonfatal occupational injuries which involve one or more of the following: loss of consciousness, restriction of work or motion, transfer to another job, or medical treatment (other than first aid. (See definitions on the other side of form.)			
Case or File Number	Date of Injury or Onset of Illness	Employee's Name	Occupation	Department	Description of Injury or Illness
Enter a nonduplicating number which will facilitate comparisons with supplementary records.	Enter Mo./day.	Enter first name or initial, middle initial, last name.	Enter regular job title, not activity employee was performing when injured or at onset of illness. In the absence of a formal title, enter a brief description of the employee's duties.	Enter department in which the employee is regularly employed or a description of normal workplace to which employee is assigned, even though temporarily working in another department at the time of injury or illness.	Enter a brief description of the injury or illness and indicate the part or parts of body affected.

Typical entries for this column might be. Amputation of 1st joint right forefinger; Strain of lower back; Contact dermatitis on both hands; Electrocution—body. |
(A)	(B)	(C)	(D)	(E)	(F)
					PREVIOUS PAGE TOTALS ➡
					TOTALS (Instructions on other side of form.) ➡

OSHA No. 200

Figure GP-1: OSHA Form 200

U.S. Department of Labor

For Calendar Year 19 _____   Page ____ of____

Company Name	Form Approved
Establishment Name	O.M.B. No. 1218-0176
Establishment Address	See OMB Disclosure Statement on reverse.

Extent of and Outcome of INJURY						Type, Extent of, and Outcome of ILLNESS												
Fatalities	Nonfatal Injuries					Type of Illness							Fatalities	Nonfatal Illnesses				
Injury Related	Injuries With Lost Workdays				Injuries Without Lost Workdays	CHECK Only One Column for Each Illness *(See other side of form for terminations or permanent transfers.)*							Illness Related	Illnesses With Lost Workdays				Illnesses Without Lost Workdays
Enter DATE of death. Mo./day/yr.	Enter a CHECK if injury involves days away from work, or days of restricted work activity, or both.	Enter a CHECK if injury involves days away from work.	Enter number of DAYS away from work.	Enter number of DAYS of restricted work activity.	Enter a CHECK if no entry was made in columns 1 or 2 but the injury is recordable as defined above.	Occupational skin diseases or disorders	Dust diseases of the lungs	Respiratory conditions due to toxic agents	Poisoning (systemic effects of toxic materials)	Disorders due to physical agents	Disorders associated with repeated trauma	All other occupational illnesses	Enter DATE of death. Mo./day/yr.	Enter a CHECK if illness involves days away from work, or days of restricted work activity, or both.	Enter a CHECK if illness involves days away from work.	Enter number of DAYS away from work.	Enter number of DAYS of restricted work activity.	Enter a CHECK if no entry was made in columns 8 or 9.
(1)	(2)	(3)	(4)	(5)	(6)	(7)							(8)	(9)	(10)	(11)	(12)	(13)
						(a)	(b)	(c)	(d)	(e)	(f)	(g)						

Certification of Annual Summary Totals By _____ Title _____ Date _____

OSHA No. 200   **POST ONLY THIS PORTION OF THE LAST PAGE NO LATER THAN FEBRUARY 1.**

Figure GP-2: Sample Schedule of Events

Cyber Kinetics, Inc., Assembly Facility, Timbucktown, Ohio

Activity	Duration (number of days relative to zero start-date)
	0 1 2 3 4 5 6 7 8 9 10 11 12 13 14 15 16 17 18 19 20 21 22 23
Pre-audit data collection and review	
Opening conference	
In-house records review	
Management interviews	
Employee interviews	
Facility walk-through	
Closing conference	
Report	
Follow-up (to be determined at a later date)	

- Accident report summaries *(e.g., OSHA Form 200)*
- Workers' compensation claims
- Compliance citations
- Follow-up reports

☐ **Safety and health meeting records**

- Minutes
- Names of participants
- Frequency

☐ **Production process documentation**

- Flow diagrams detailing end products and evolved waste
- Process descriptions
- Waste management plans

☐ **Written safety and health program**

- Policy or statement of commitment by top management
- Chain of command and participants
- Environmental, health, and/or safety director's authority

▶ **Analyze data from records review**

☐ **Summarize target problem hazards requiring special attention.**
  Be particularly alert to recurring accidents and/or previously noted problem areas.

☐ **Identify special safety and health programs and/or requirements that are pertinent to the function of activities performed at the site under evaluation.**

▶ **Employee interviews**

☐ **Routine interviews, including**

- Individual (one-on-one) interviews
- Group interviews
- Question-and-answer surveys

☐ **Information not evident by records review**

- Minor unreported accidents

Figure GP-3: Management and Employee Interviews

- Clear delineation and understanding of accountability/responsibility

- Expectations of personnel

- Actual personnel participation and contributions

- Awareness of the location of written programs and/or procedures

- Understanding of various programs and/or procedures

- Awareness of potential hazards and what to look for

- Understanding and ability to comply with procedures

- Perception of management commitment by employees

- Special observations made by personnel which are or were not reported

- Special employee concerns regarding potential exposures

- Unreported or unrecorded accidents

- Suggestions for improvement of overall programs and management issues

- Minor medical problems *(e.g., unreported skin rashes)*

- Employee understanding of safety and health programs

- Employee commitment to safety and health programs

- Employee comments and suggestions

▶ Site inspection

- *Use the appropriate programs and/or requirements checklists.*

- *Involve the plant manager, area supervisors, the site safety director(s), and operations employees as much as possible.*

- *Photographs of areas and operations are often helpful for documenting findings and for instructional purposes. Color slides are useful for presentations.*

▶ Written audit report

☐ Background

- Rationale for audit
  - ◻ Historic overview of events leading to audit *(e.g., excessive workers' comp loss ratio)*
  - ◻ Desired outcome *(e.g., workers' comp cost containment)*
- Names and titles of audit participants

☐ Inspection procedures used

- Extent of involvement *(e.g., problem process areas)*

- Sequence of events

☐ Safety evaluation results

- Records review

- Employee interviews

- Site inspections

☐ Industrial hygiene evaluation results

- Records review

- Employee interviews

- Site inspections

- Monitoring results

Figure GP-4: Sample Written Audit Report

Table of Contents

Section 1:   Background

Section 2:   Inspection Procedure

Section 3:   Records Review

      3.1:   Safety

      3.2:   Industrial Hygiene

Section 4:   Employee Interview

Section 5:   Site Inspections

      5.1:   Safety

      5.2:   Industrial Hygiene

Section 6:   Results and Discussion

Section 7:   Conclusions

Section 8:   Recommendations

☐ **Summary of results and discussion**

- Written programs and procedures

- Training programs

- Recordkeeping

- Effectiveness of programs

- Major discrepancies

☐ **Conclusion** *(e.g., numerous discrepancies which may lead to compliance citations, workers' comp losses, and increased production costs)*

☐ **Recommendations**

- Corrective actions

- Projected cost of corrective actions (optional)

- Deadline for completion of corrective actions

- Follow-up

▶ **Site inspection**

Before You Begin

Determine purpose of the audit.

The purpose may be to target a specific incident or perform a routine annual overview of a facility. Keep in mind that the topics contain issues which are primarily regulatory in nature, yet these regulations provide guidance based upon previous incidents. Good common practice entries are presented in italics or as a separate topic (e.g., Ergonomics).

Select applicable topic checklists.

Not all topics presented herein are applicable to each and every construction firm. For example, Laser Equipment is probably not applicable to the home builder who does not utilize such equipment. Some topics, however, are applicable to everyone. For example, Electrical Hazards, Hazard Communication Program, Emergency Action Plans, and Personal Protective Equipment are likely to impact every construction firm to some degree. If you are uncertain as to applicability, review the introduction to that topic in question.

Table GP-1: Summary of Administrative Requirements

	Written Program/ Procedures	Training Requirements	Medical Surveillance	Monitoring Results	Auditor Comments (other key components)
Battery Management	—	—	(occasionally)	—	
Carcinogenic/Toxic Dusts and Fumes	(compliance program)	X	X	X	
Chemical Carcinogens Requiring Air Monitoring	(compliance program)	X	X	X	
Chemical Carcinogens Not Requiring Air Monitoring	(compliance program)	X	X	—	
Chemical Storage Procedures	—	—	—	—	
Compressed Gases	—	—	—	—	
Confined Space Entry Procedures	X	X	—	X	
Cranes	—	X	—	—	
Electrical Hazards	—	X	—	—	
Emergency Action Plan	X	X	—	—	—
Ergonomics	X	X	(case dependent)	—	—
Excavations and Trenching	—	X	—	—	
Fall Protection					
Fire Protection and Prevention	X	X	—	—	
Flammable and Combustible Liquids	—	—	—	—	
Hazard Communication Program	X	X	—	—	
Hazardous Waste and Emergency Response Activities	X	X	X	X	
Hearing Conservation Program	X	X	X	X	
Heat Stress	X	X	—	X	
Ionizing Radiation	—	X	—	X	

Organize a plan of attack.

Discuss with management the audit's purpose and intent. Create a schedule and proceed in the order outlined in the General Procedures. If management chooses to include items not on each checklist, add topics, or include some of the more stringent state and local requirements. You may wish to expand the checklist provided, but be sure to detail each item prior to the site investigation! A summary of administrative requirements is provided in Table GP-1.

With your direction clearly defined, go for it!

The table on pages 18 and 20 displays a Summary of Administrative Requirements. It is another tool that the auditor may or may not choose to use. The intent is to provide the information so the auditor may know, at a glance, what paperwork and files will require review prior to physical inspection of a site. The topics that do not appear in boldface type will typically apply to all industries. The column for auditor comments is for inclusion of important key components to which the auditor may wish to have rapid access.

Table GP-1 (cont'd.): Summary of Administrative Requirements

	Written Program/ Procedures	Training Requirements	Medical Surveillance	Monitoring Results	Auditor Comments (other key components)
Laser Equipment					
Local Exhaust Ventilation	—	—	—	—	
Lockout and Tagout Program	X	X	—	—	
Manual Lifting	—	X	—	—	
Personal Protective Equipment	(exposure assessment)	X	—	—	
Portable Power Tools/Equipment	—	X	—	—	
Powered Industrial Trucks	—	X	—	—	
Process Safety Management	X	X	—	—	
Respiratory Protection Program	X	X	X	X	
Scaffolds	—	X	—	—	
Stairs and Ladders	—	—	—	—	
Toxic Substances Exposure Monitoring	—	—	—	X	
Welding and Cutting	—	X	—	—	

The Checklists

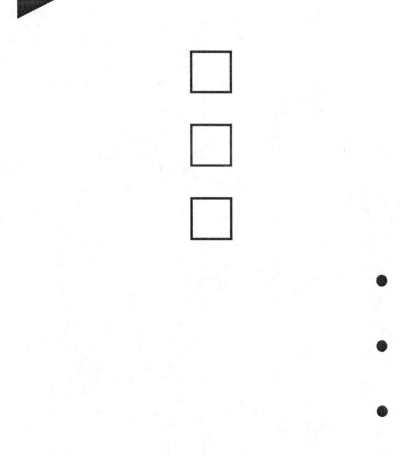

Battery Management

These standards are applicable to all battery charging and changing activities performed in the construction industry. 29 CFR 1926.441

▶ **Designated charging stations**

☐ **Ventilation provided**

- Ensure diffusion of gases from the battery
- Prevent accumulation of an explosive mixture

☐ **"No Smoking" signs**

☐ **Charging apparatus protected from damage by trucks**

☐ **Vent caps**

- Properly used so as to avoid electrolyte spray
- Properly functioning

▶ **Designated battery storage area** *(unsealed batteries)*

☐ **Location**

- Within well-ventilated rooms

  OR

- Within enclosures with outside vents

Figure 1-1: Procedures for Handling Batteries

- **Filler caps in place when batteries are being transported**

- **Parking brakes applied before batteries are charged or changed**

- **Jumper battery procedures**

    ▫ Ground lead connected away from the vehicle's battery

    ▫ Ignition, lights, and accessories of vehicle turned off prior to connecting

- **Installed to avoid physical or electrical contact with compartment walls or components**

- **No metallic objects placed on uncovered batteries**

- **Vent caps in place when batteries are being charged**

- **Chargers turned off when leads are being connected/disconnected**

- **Battery handling equipment which could contact battery terminals or cell connectors**

    ▫ Insulated

      OR

    ▫ Otherwise protected

☐ **Arranged to prevent the escape of fumes, gases, or electrolyte spray into other areas**

☐ **Racks and trays adequate**

- Resistant to electrolyte

- Sturdy

- Spark resistant

☐ **Acid protection of floors**

- Acid resistant construction

  OR

- Protected from acid accumulations

▶ **Worker protection provided when workers are handling acids or batteries**

☐ **Face shields**

☐ **Aprons**

☐ **Rubber gloves**

▶ **Emergency supplies and/or facilities in battery handling area(s)**

☐ **Worker emergency response equipment located within 25 feet of the battery handling area(s)**

- Eye wash station

- Deluge shower

☐ **Flushing and neutralizing spilled or leaked electrolyte**

☐ **Fire protection**

▶ **Overall program effectiveness**

☐ **Employee understanding of procedures**

☐ **Employee compliance with procedures**

☐ **Lack of associated incidents**

Figure 1-2: Battery Rules of Thumb

- **Properly park a truck and apply the brake before attempting to charge or change the battery.**

- **Management of battery acid**
  - Pour acid into water, never the reverse.
  - Do not allow acids to run into ordinary cast iron, lead, steel, or brass drains.

- **Use wood slat mats, rubber mats, or clean floor boards to**
  - Avoid slips and falls.
  - Protect against electric shock.

- **Charging a battery**
  - Open battery cover(s) or compartment(s) to dissipate heat.
  - Prohibit smoking.

- **Battery terminals**
  - Be sure they are clean.
  - Be sure connections are tight.

- **Never lay tools or metal parts on a battery.**

- **Aids to prevent operator strains from manual handling**
  - Roller conveyor
  - Overhead hoist
  - Equivalent

- **Chains, hooks, yokes, and other mechanical devices should be insulated to prevent shortcircuiting.**

Notes and special comments

_____

_____

_____

_____

_____

_____

_____

_____

_____

_____

_____

_____

_____

_____

_____

Score: _____

Carcinogenic and Toxic Dusts and Fumes

The carcinogenic and toxic dusts and fumes standards are similar in basic mandates and vary only in specifics. The standards of reference included here are for workplace exposures to inorganic arsenic, asbestos, cadmium, and lead. They are applicable to all occupational exposures in the construction industry. See Figure 2-5. 29 CFR 1926.1118, 29 CFR 1926.1101, 29 CFR 1926.127, and 29 CFR 1926.62

▶ Exposure monitoring

Required if exposures are above the action level for two consecutive periods at least seven days apart.

☐ **Representative air sampling performed**

- 8-hour time-weighted average (TWA)

- 30-minute excursion limit—asbestos only

☐ **Frequency of air monitoring** *(See Table 3-2.)*

- Initial

- At or above the 8-hour TWA

- At or above the "action" level and below the 8-hour TWA

- At or above the 30-minute excursion limit—asbestos only

- When there is a change in production, process, control equipment, personnel, or work practices

- During emergencies

Figure 2-1: Asbestos Work Classifications

Class I

Removal of thermal system insulation and surfacing asbestos-containing material and potential asbestos-containing material.

Class II

Removal of asbestos-containing material which is not thermal system insulation or surfacing material, including, but not limited to, the removal of asbestos-containing wallboard, floor tile and sheeting, roofing and siding shingles, and construction mastics.

Class III

Repair and maintenance operations where asbestos-containg material is likely to be disturbed.

Class IV

Maintenance and custodial activities during which employees contact but do not disturb asbestos-containing material and potential asbestos-containing material and activities to clean up dust, waste, and debris resulting from Class I, II, and III activities.

☐ **Employees understand and have been permitted to observe the air monitoring process**

☐ **Employees notified of results**

- After receipt of results (e.g., within 5 to 15 workdays)

- Written disclosure of corrective action(s) where the results exceed 8-hour exposure limits

▶ Regulated areas identified

Regulated areas must be established wherever the airborne exposures may potentially or are known to exceed the 8-hour TWA and/or excursion limit. All Class I, II, and III asbestos work must be conducted within regulated areas.

☐ **Segregated from rest of workplace** *(e.g., critical barriers and barrier tape)*

☐ **Access limited** *(e.g., entry limited to authorized persons)*

☐ **Food, beverage, and tobacco restrictions**
(Exception: Drinking water may be consumed within inorganic arsenic regulated areas.)

☐ **Properly posted signs**

- Visible

- Legible

▶ Container and material labeling—intact and legible

Container includes all contained raw materials, mixtures, scrap, waste, debris, and other products—to be shipped or stored.

☐ **Identified by name**

☐ **Warning labels** *(e.g., Cancer Hazard, Cancer and Lung Disease Hazard, etc.)*

☐ **No contradictory statements**

▶ Written compliance program

With the exception of asbestos, a compliance program is required wherever exposures exceed the 8-hour TWA. Engineering and work practice controls must be defined along with information and documentation of relevant data leading to that determination. Asbestos controls are delineated in the regulation by the class of work to be performed and potential for fiber release.

Figure 2-2: Engineering Controls and Work Practices for Asbestos

Regardless of Level of Exposure

- Vacuum cleaners equipped with HEPA filters (**Exception**: roofing material)
- Wet methods (**Exception**: employer can demonstrate reason not to, such as electrical hazards, equipment malfunction, and roofing slip hazards)
- Prompt clean-up and disposal of wastes and debris contaminated with asbestos in leak-tight containers (**Exception**: roofing material)

Exceed the TWA and/or Excursion Limits

- Local exhaust ventilation with HEPA filter
- Enclosure or isolation of processes producing asbestos dust
- Ventilation of the regulated area to move contaminated air away from breathing zone of workers

Class I Requirements (vary in accordance with the class of work to be performed, with special procedures for resilient floor tiles and roofing material)

- Supervision by a competent person (e.g., trained in accordance with EPA's Model Accreditation Plan)
- Where nonasbestos personnel are in adjacent areas, the following methods should be complied with:
  - Critical barriers over all openings (**Exception**: out-of-doors)
  - Perimeter area air monitoring
  - Double layer of 6-mil plastic or equivalent to isolate HVAC systems
  - Impermeable dropcloths on surfaces beneath all removal activity
  - All objects within the regulated area covered with impermeable dropcloths or plastic sheeting, secured by duct tape or equivalent
- Use of specified negative pressure system
- Thermal system insulation may be done by one of several prescribed glovebag methods
  - Negative pressure glove bag
  - Negative pressure glove box
  - Water spray process
- Alternative control methods may be performed under certain circumstances and where they have been approved in writing by a certified industrial hygienist or licensed professional engineer (**Exception**: competent person may sign where insulation is less than 25 linear feet or surfacing material is less than 10 square feet)

Prohibited Work Practices

- High speed abrasive disc saws without point of cut ventilator or enclosure with HEPA filtered exhaust
- Dry sweeping or shoveling
- Employee rotation to reduce employee exposures

☐ **Content**

- Description of the process, operation, or activity

- Air monitoring data that documents source

- Technological considerations

- Method of compliance

- Work practice program

- Administrative control schedule (if applicable)

- Schedule for implementation

- Description of means to inform other contractors on multi-contractor sites as to potential for exposures

- Other relevant information
  (e.g., Inspections of job sites, materials, mechanical ventilation information, and equipment)

☐ **Timely revisions and updates**

- Every 6 months—inorganic arsenic and lead

- To reflect significant changes—asbestos and cadmium

▶ **Written respiratory protection program**

Respiratory protection may be used only as a backup where engineering and work practice controls are being implemented, where other control measures are not feasible, during machine maintenance and repair activities, and in emergencies. See Section 29, "Respiratory Protection Program."

▶ **Personal protective equipment**

☐ **Proper equipment selection (situation dependent)**

- Respirators—based on dust/fume type, physical state, job description, and exposure levels

- Protective clothing

- Gloves

- Shoes, boots, and/or coverlets

- Goggles

- Face shields

Figure 2-3: Respiratory Protection Requirements for Asbestos Work

Class I

Activities involving the removal of thermal insulation, surface asbestos-containing material (ACM), and material presumed to contain asbestos.

Class II

Activities involving the removal of ACM other than thermal insulation or surfacing materials (e.g., wallboard, floor tiles/sheeting, roofing, siding shingles, and mastic).

Class III

Activities involving repair and maintenance of ACM which is likely to be disturbed.

Class IV

Activities involving custodial work where contact with ACM is possible but not likely.

All Classes

All work where employees are potentially exposed or known to be exposed above the TWA and/or excursion limits, and in all cases where there is an emergency.

Table 2-1: Minimum Respirator Fit Testing Requirements

	Qualitative Fit Test		Quantitative Fit Test		
Chemical	Initial	Biannual	Initial	Biannual	Annual
asbestos	X	X	X	X	
inorganic arsenic	X	X	X	X	
lead	X	X	X	X	
cadmium			X		X

For asbestos exposures, qualitative fit testing may be performed only for half-mask and full facepiece air purifying respirators. For inorganic arsenic exposures where more than 20 employees are wearing respirators, quantitative fit testing is required. For lead exposures, qualitative fit testing may be performed only for half-mask air purifying respirators. Qualitative fit testing may be performed, on the same schedule, where exposures to cadmium are less than 50 μg/m³.

☐ **Proper management of contaminated clothing**

- Disposable clothing

  OR

- Reusable clothing cleaned and/or laundered
  - Documented proof that the personnel/services which clean the clothing have been informed of the presence of the contaminant and its hazard(s)
  - Handling method(s) used which avoid release of contaminant into air *(e.g., no blowing or shaking of the garments)*
  - Transported in sealed impermeable bags or closed container(s)
  - Bags/containers properly labeled

☐ **Emergency respirator(s) and equipment—easily accessible**

▶ Written emergency procedures

Written emergency procedures are required by law for cadmium and recommended for asbestos, inorganic arsenic, and lead.

▶ Housekeeping

Required housekeeping practices are substance specific, itemized basic practices are mandated, and all are applicable to recommended good management practices.

Asbestos and Cadmium

☐ **No visible surface dust accumulation and waste**

☐ **No compressed air cleaning**

☐ **Spills and sudden releases cleaned immediately**

☐ **Proper clean-up of dust and debris**

- HEPA-filtered vacuum equipment

- Wet clean

- Shoveling, dry sweeping, and dry clean-up—used only when the preceding methods are not feasible

☐ **Waste disposal**

- Sealed, impermeable bags

- Other closed, impermeable containers

Figure 2-4: Restrictions on Asbestos-Containing Material

Vinyl and asphalt flooring

- Sanding is prohibited
- Stripping of finishes shall be conducted using low abrasion pads (speeds lower than 300 rpm) and wet methods
- Burnishing or dry buffing only on flooring which has sufficient finish so the pad cannot contact the flooring material

Waste and debris from areas with thermal insulation, surfacing material, or visibly deteriorated asbestos-containing material

- No dusting or dry sweeping
- HEPA filter on vacuum
- Cleaned up and disposed of in leak-tight container

Inorganic arsenic

☐ **Written housekeeping and maintenance plan**

☐ **Periodic cleaning of dust collection and ventilation equipment**

☐ **Equipment effectiveness checks**

☐ **Logs maintained and current**

- Equipment effectiveness checks

- Cleaning and maintenance activities

Lead

☐ **No visible surface dust accumulation**

☐ **No compressed air cleaning**

► **Hygiene facilities and practices in restricted areas**
Hygiene facilities and practices are mandated for all toxic/carcinogenic dusts and/or fumes.

☐ **Restrictions enforced** *(e.g., no signs nor other evidence of food)*

- Food

- Beverages

- Drinking fountains

- Cosmetics

- Smoking

- Chewing

☐ **Personal protective equipment provided AND worn properly**

☐ **Special facilities available**

- Change rooms

- Shower facilities

- Lunchroom controls
  - Separate area with air monitoring to confirm low levels of contaminants—asbestos, cadmium, and lead
  - Positive pressure area, temperature controlled with filtered make-up air—asbestos, inorganic arsenic, and lead

---

Figure 2-5: Scope and Application of 29 CFR 1926 Regulations

Asbestos

- Construction, alteration, repair, maintenance or renovation of structures, substrates or portions thereof, or painting and decorating of materials that contain asbestos
- Demolition or salvage of structures where asbestos is present
- Removal or encapsulation of materials containing asbestos
- Installation of products containing asbestos
- Asbestos spill/emergency cleanup
- Transportation, disposal, storage, containment of, and housekeeping activities involving asbestos or products containing asbestos, on the site or location at which construction activities are performed

Inorganic Arsenic

- All industrial and construction occupational exposures to inorganic arsenic except employee exposures in agriculture or resulting from pesticide application, treatment of wood with preservatives, or the utilization of arsenically preserved wood

Lead

- Construction, alteration, repair, or renovation of structures, substrates, or portions thereof, that contain lead, or materials containing lead
- Demolition or salvage of structures where lead or materials containing lead is present
- Removal or encapsulation of materials containing lead
- Installation of products containing lead
- Lead contamination/emergency cleanup
- Transportation, disposal, storage, containment of and housekeeping activities involving asbestos or products containing asbestos, on the site or location at which construction activities are performed

Cadmium

- Construction, alteration, and/or repair of materials that contain cadmium
- Wrecking, demolition, or salvage of structures where cadmium or materials containg cadmium are present
- Use of cadmium-containing paints and cutting, brazing, burning, grinding, or welding on surfaces that were painted with cadmium-containing paints
- Cadmium welding, cutting/welding of cadmium-plated steel, brazing/welding with cadmium alloys
- Installation of products containing cadmium
- Electrical grounding with cadmium welding or electrical work using cadmium-coated conduit
- Maintaining or retrofitting cadmium-coated equipment
- Cadmium contamination/emergency cleanup
- Transportation, disposal, storage, or containment of cadmium or materials containing cadmium on the site or location at which construction activities are performed

---

- Lavatories—inorganic arsenic
- *Toilets*

Employees requirements enforced

- Wash hands and face prior to eating
- Shower at the end of the workday
- Shower immediately upon skin contamination
- Class I and II asbestos work—Shower upon leaving containment
- Inorganic arsenic exposures >100 µg/m³—vacuum clothing upon leaving restricted area

▶ Employee training

☐ **Pertinent employees should receive training and records should be kept for:**

- Any potential exposures to cadmium and lead (abbreviated training)
- Exposures to inorganic arsenic or lead at or above the "action level"
- Exposures to asbestos at or above the TWA or excursion limit(s)

☐ **Content of training—records maintained and available for review**
(Asbestos training is based on class of work to be performed.)

- Toxicity and properties of toxic/carcinogenic substances
- Other hazards if applicable
- Quantity, location, manner of use, release, and storage of toxic/carcinogenic substances
- Operations and activities involving potential exposures
- Personal protective equipment
- Emergency procedures and purpose(s)
  - Employee's role
  - Recognition and situation evaluation methods
  - First aid methods
  - Application rehearsals
- Engineering and work practice controls
- Rationale for medical surveillance
- Review of the applicable standard and its appendices

Figure 2-6: Medical Surveillance Special Medical Testing Requirements

asbestos

1. 14- by 17-inch posterior/anterior chest X-ray

2. Pulmonary function—FVC and FEV(1)

inorganic arsenic

1. 14- by 17-inch posterior-anterior chest X-ray

2. Nasal and skin examination

3. Sputum cytology

lead

1. Hemoglobin and hematocrit, red cell indices, and examination of peripheral smear morphology

2. Zinc protoporphyrin in blood

3. Blood urea nitrogen

4. Serum creatine

5. Urinalysis with microscopic examination

cadmium

1. Cadmium in urine

2. Beta-2 microglobulin in urine

3. Cadmium in blood

Figure 2-7: Tasks, Operations, and Jobs Involving Cadmium Exposures That Require Medical Surveillance*

- Electrical grounding with cadmium welding
- Cutting, brazing, burning, grinding, or welding on surfaces that were painted with cadmium-containing paints
- Electrical work using cadmium-coated conduit
- Use of cadmium-containiung paints
- Cutting and welding cadmium-plated steel
- Brazing or welding with cadmium alloys
- Fusing of reinforced steel by cadmium welding
- Maintaining or retrofitting cadmium-coated equipment
- Wrecking and demolition where cadmium is present

   *   Required medical surveillance irrespective of the air monitoring results.

☐ **Frequency**

- Initial

- Annual

☐ **Documention**

- General records file

- Employee's personnel file
  - Proof of completion and date(s)
  - Proof of understanding *(e.g., written statement or test)*

▶ **Medical surveillance**

☐ **Adequate content of medical examination**

- Work and medical history

- Physical examination

- Special X-rays and laboratory tests

- Physician's written opinion

☐ **Physician provided with information**

- Standard and appendices

- Employee's duties

- Actual or representative exposure level(s)

- Personal protective equipment to be worn

- Information from previous examination, if not already provided

☐ **Frequency of employee's medical exams**

- Initial

- Annual

- Upon termination of employment

- When signs or symptoms indicate need

- When exposures occur during an emergency

Table 2-2: Minimum Records Retention

Chemical	Objective Data	Exposure Monitoring	Medical Surveillance[1]	Training Program	Other
asbestos	reliance[2]	30 years	30 years+	1 year	reliance (records of notification) life of bldg. (records of notification)
inorganic arsenic	—	40 years	40 years	—	—
lead	—	40 years	40 years	—	+ (medical removals)
cadmium	30 years	30 years	30 years+	1 year	—

Upon expiration of retention period, notify the OSHA Area Director, or if there is no successor to a terminated business, transmit records to the Director.

[1] The plus symbol indicates inclusion of employment duration.
[2] Duration of the employer's reliance on objective data.

☐ **Properly executed medical removal from job**

- Dated physician restriction order

- Physician return-to-work authorization in writing

- Protection benefit provided—same wage, seniority, etc.

☐ **Proper response actions to medical indications of elevated exposures**

▶ **Records—maintained for period mandated**

☐ **Objective data**

☐ **Exposure monitoring**

☐ **Medical surveillance**

☐ **Training program**

☐ **Medical removals**

☐ **Data demonstrating presumed asbestos-containing materials do not contain asbestos**

☐ **Records of required asbestos notification**

▶ **Multi-employer workplace communication of hazards**

☐ **Where employees of other employers may potentially become exposed**

☐ **Where office occupants may potentially become exposed**

▶ **Overall program effectiveness**

☐ **Employee understanding of procedures**

☐ **Employee compliance with procedures**

☐ **Lack of associated disease/illness**

Figure 2-8: Asbestos Hazard Communication Schedule

Information conveyance assigned to building owners and employers of potentially exposed employees:

- Identify material to be impacted during construction/renovation which contains or potentially contains asbestos.
- Prior to work, the building and facility owners must:
  - Determine the presence, location, and quantity of asbestos or potentially asbestos-containing material.
  - Notify all prospective employers applying or bidding for work in or adjacent to areas containing asbestos or potential asbestos-containing material.
  - Notify all employees who will work in or adjacent to the area(s).
  - Notify all employers of employees performing work in the area(s).
  - Notify all tenants located in areas containing such material.
- Prior to work, employers shall:
  - Inform building/facility owners, employees who will perform the work, and employees in adjacent areas as to the location and quantity of asbestos-containing material in the area and precautions to be taken to ensure airborne fibers are confined to the area.
- Within ten days of work completion, employers shall:
  - Inform building/facility owners and employees in adjacent areas as to the location and quantity of asbestos-containing material remaining in the area and the results of the final air monitoring.
- Within 24 hours of discovery, inform building/facility owners and employees in adjacent areas as to the presence, location, and quantity of newly discovered known or suspect asbestos-containing material.

Notes and special comments

_____

_____

_____

_____

_____

_____

_____

_____

_____

_____

_____

_____

_____

_____

_____

_____

Score: _____

Chemical Carcinogens Requiring Air Monitoring

Applicable to all OSHA targeted chemical carcinogens which require air monitoring. Those not requiring air monitoring can be located in a separate section. The target chemical carcinogen standards are similar in basic mandates and vary only in specifics. The standards of reference, herein, include that of acrylonitrile (AN), benzene, 1,2-dibromo-3-chloropropane (DBCP), ethylene oxide (EtO), formaldehyde, methylene chloride, methylenedianiline (MDA), and vinyl chloride. Each standard is applicable within the construction industry, some under specified conditions, and exemptions should be noted as well. See Figures 3-1 and 3-2. Sections 1926.1145, 1926.1128, 1926.1144, 1926.1147, 1926.1148, 1926.1152, 1926.60, and 1926.1117.

▶ **Exposure monitoring**

After the initial air monitoring, periodic monitoring is required if exposures are above the action level for two consecutive periods at least seven days apart (five days for vinyl chloride)

☐ **Representative air sampling performed**

- 8-Hour TWA

- 15-Minute exposure limit

- Ceiling limit—acrylonitrile only

Figure 3-1: Applications of 29 CFR 1926 Standards

Acrylonitrile (same as 1910.1045)

- Construction uses

Benzene (same as 1910.1028)

- Construction uses

1,2-Dibromo-3-chloropropane (same as 1910.1044)

- Construction uses

Ethylene oxide (same as 1910.1047)

- Construction uses

Formaldehyde (same as 1910.1048)

- Construction uses involving gaseous formaldehyde, formalin solutions, and products that off-gas formaldehyde (e.g., indoor particleboard)

Methylene chloride (same as 1910.1052)

- Construction uses

Methylenedianiline

- Construction, alteration, repair, maintenance, or renovation of structures, substrates, or portions thereof that contain MDA
- Installation of or finishing surfaces with products which contain MDA
- Spill/emergency cleanup at construction sites involving MDA
- Transportation, disposal, storage, or containment of MDA, or products containing MDA, on the site or location at which construction activities are performed

Vinyl chloride (same as 1910.1017)

- Construction uses

☐ **Frequency of air monitoring**

- Initial (two consecutive samples or one initial with an indicated need for periodic monitoring)

- At or above the 8-hour TWA

- At or above the "action" level and below the 8-hour TWA

- At or above the 15-minute exposure limit

- When there is a change in production, process, control equipment, personnel, or work practices

- During emergencies

☐ **Employees understand and have been given the opportunity to observe the air monitoring process**

☐ **Employees notified of results**

- After receipt of results *(e.g., within 5 to 15 workdays)*

- Written notice or posted

- Where the results exceed 8-hour exposure limits, written disclosure of corrective action(s)

▶ **Regulated areas identified**

Regulated areas must be established wherever the airborne levels of said carcinogen(s) are in excess of the 8-hour TWA and/or 15-minute exposure limit, OR regulated areas may be required where dermal exposures may potentially occur.

☐ **Segregated from rest of workplace**

☐ **Access limited to authorized personnel only**

☐ **Food, beverage, and tobacco restrictions**

☐ **Personal protective equipment and clothing provided**

☐ **Properly posted signs**

- Visible

- Legible

▶ **Container labeling** *(intact and legible)*

☐ **Identified by name**

Table 3-1: Target Chemical Carcinogens and Their Exposure Limits

Carcinogen(s)	Exempted Process(es), Uses and Handling Procedures	8-Hour TWA	Action Level	15-Minute Exposure	Skin Absorption[1]
acrylonitrile (AN)	yes	2 ppm	1 ppm	10 ppm[2]	yes
benzene	yes	1 ppm	0.5 ppm	5 ppm	—
1,2-dibromo-3-chloropropane (DBCP)	yes	1 ppb	—	—	yes
ethylene oxide (EtO)	yes	1 ppm	0.5 ppm	5 ppm	—
formaldehyde	no	0.75 ppm	0.5 ppm	2 ppm	—
methylene chloride	no	25 ppm	12.5 ppm	125 ppm	—
methylenedianiline (MDA)	yes	10 ppb	5 ppb	100 ppb	yes
vinyl chloride	yes	1 ppm	0.5 ppm	5 ppm	—

1   Skin absorption data extracted from American Conference of Governmental Industrial Hygienists. In all the above cases, OSHA requires measures be taken to protect from skin and eye contact.

2   The 15-minute exposure limit for acrylonitrile is referred to as a "ceiling limit" by OSHA. The others are referred to as a "short-term exposure limit" (STEL) and "excursion limit."

☐ **Warning labels** *(e.g., "Cancer and Reproductive Hazard," "Cancer-Suspect Agent," etc.)*

☐ **No contradictory statements**

▶ Written compliance program

A compliance program is required wherever exposures exceed the 8-hour TWA and/or 15-minute exposure limit. Engineering and work practice controls must be defined along with information and documentation of relevant data leading to that determination.

☐ **Content**
- Description of the process or operation
- Outline of mechanism
- Technological considerations
- Schedule for implementation
- Other

☐ **Updated**
- Every 6 months—AN, DBCP, and vinyl chloride
- Every 12 months—EtO and MDA
- During air monitoring updates—benzene and formaldehyde

▶ Written respiratory protection program

Respiratory protection may be used only as a backup where engineering and work practice controls are being implemented, where other control measures are not feasible, during machine maintenance and repair activities, and in emergencies. See Section 29, "Respiratory Protection Program."

▶ Personal protective equipment

☐ **Proper respirator selection** *(based on chemical type and exposure levels)*

☐ **"Impermeable clothing" for employees in areas where they may come in contact with the chemical** *(check permeability charts)*

☐ **Proper management of contaminated clothing**
- Disposable clothing, OR
- Reusable clothing cleaned and/or laundered *(documented proof that the personnel/services which clean the clothing have been informed of the contaminant and its hazards)*
- Emergency respirator(s) and equipment *(easily accessible)*

Table 3-2: Frequency of Air Monitoring

Carcinogen(s)	≥ 8-Hour TWA	≥ Action Level	≥ 15-Minute Exposure	Results Reported [1]
acrylonitrile	monthly	quarterly	monthly	5 days
benzene	biannually	yearly	as necessary	15 days
1,2-dibromo-3-chloropropane[2]	monthly	N.A.	N.A.	5 days
ethylene oxide	quarterly	biannually	quarterly	15 days
formaldehyde	biannually	biannually	annually	15 days
methylene chloride	quarterly	biannually	quarterly	15 days
methylenedianiline	quarterly	biannually	quarterly	15 days
vinyl chloride	monthly	quarterly	monthly	10 days

[1] Air sampling results must be made available to affected employees within a given number of days from receipt of the results.

[2] If less than the 8-hour TWA for 1,2-dibromo-3-chloropropane, "quarterly monitoring" must still be performed. PERIODIC AIR MONITORING IS NOT REQUIRED WHERE ALL POTENTIALLY EXPOSED EMPLOYEES ARE WEARING SUPPLIED-AIR RESPIRATORS.

Table 3-3: Regulated Areas Defined

Carcinogen	Engineering Practices
acrylonitrile	Area where acrylonitrile exposures exceed the PEL or 15-minute exposure limit
benzene	Area where benzene exposures exceed the PEL or 15-minute exposure limit
dibromochloropropane	Area where dibromochloropropane exposures exceed the PEL
ethylene oxide	Area where ethylene oxice exposures exceed the PEL or 15-minute exposure limit
formaldehyde	Area where formaldehyde exposures exceed the PEL or 15-minute exposure limit
methylene chloride	Area where methylene chloride exposures exceed the PEL or 15-minute exposure limit
methylenedianaline (MDA)	Area where MSA exposures exceeds the PEL or where employees are subject to dermal exposures to MDA
vinyl chloride and polyvinyl chloride	Area where vinyl chloride and/or polyvinyl chloride are manufactured, reacted, repackaged, stored, handled, or used, and exposures exceed the PEL

► ## Written emergency procedures

Emergency procedures are required for all except formaldehyde (which is recommended, not mandated).

☐ **Content**

- Evacuation procedures
- Means for alerting employees (e.g., alarm)
- Emergency response actions required
- Area decontamination procedures
- Provision to initiate medical surveillance within 24 hours *(for those present at the time of the emergency)*
- Provisions for showering as soon as possible after direct exposures have occurred
- Follow employee decontamination procedures

☐ **Operable alarm system or discrete means for alerting employees in case of an emergency**

☐ **Written procedures posted and/or accessible to employees**

► ## Housekeeping

Required housekeeping practices are chemical-specific, itemized basic practices are mandated, and all are applicable to recommended good management practices.

☐ **All surfaces free of visible accumulations**

- No dry sweeping—DBCP
- No compressed air—DBCP and MDA
- Vacuums with controlled exhaust features—DBCP
- Restriction of hose wet-washing to fine spray of DBCP only

☐ **Proper containment and cleanup of visual accumulations of contaminants**

☐ **Adequate leak and spill response actions**

☐ **Means for properly disposing of contaminated waste, debris, and other materials**

- Decontamination prior to incorporation with general waste
- Contaminated materials
  - Sealed in bags or other closed container(s)
  - Labeled
  - Disposed of as hazardous waste

Figure 3-2: Exemptions from Applicability of Standards

AN	1) Resins (e.g., ABS, SAN, nitrile barrier resins, solid nitrile elastomers, and acrylic/modacrylic fibers)
	2) Materials made from AN for which objective data can demonstrate the material is not capable of releasing AN in average concentrations in excess of 1 ppm over 8-hours
	3) Solid materials made from and/or containing AN which will not be heated to 170° F
Benzene	1) Storage, transportation, distribution, dispensing, sale or use of gasoline, motor fuels, or other fuels containing benzene (except where indoor dispensing exceeds 4 hours per day)
	2) Loading and unloading at bulk wholesale storage facilities which use vapor control
	3) Storage, transportation, distribution or sale of benzene and mixtures within intact containers or vapor-sealed pipelines
	4) Containers, pipelines, and natural gas (in processing plants) with mixtures of less than 0.1 percent benzene
	5) Liquid mixtures of less than 0.1 percent benzene
	6) Oil and gas drilling, production, and service stations
	7) Coke oven batteries
DBCP	1) Pesticide usage
	2) Storage, transportation, distribution or sale of benzene and mixtures within intact containers
EtO	1) Processing, use, or handling of products containing EtO for which objective data can demonstrate the material is not capable of releasing EtO in excess of the "action level" (0.5 ppm)
Methylene chloride	no exemptions
MDA	1) Processing, use, or handling of products containing MDA for which initial air monitoring has indicated exposures less than the "action level" (5 ppb) and no dermal exposures can occur
	2) Processing, use, or handling of products containing MDA for which objective data can demonstrate the material is not capable of releasing MDA in excess of the "action level" (5 ppb) and no dermal exposures can occur
	3) Storage, transportation, distribution, or sale of MDA in intact containers which are sealed
	4) Finished articles containing MDA
Vinyl chloride	1) Handling or use of fabricated products made of polyvinyl chloride (PVC)

* Exemptions due to air monitoring or objective data must be documented.

▶ Hygiene facilities and practices in restricted areas

Hygiene facilities and practices are mandated for all except benzene and ethylene oxide.

☐ **Restrictions enforced** *(e.g., no signs nor other evidence of food)*

- Food
- Beverages
- Drinking fountains
- Cosmetics
- Smoking
- Chewing

☐ **Personal protective equipment provided AND worn properly**

☐ **Special facilities available**

- Change rooms
- Shower facilities
  - ▫ Quick drench showers—formaldehyde
  - ▫ Eyewash station(s)—formaldehyde
- *Lunchroom controls*
  - ▫ *Separate area*
  - ▫ *Positive pressure, temperature controlled, with filtered makeup air—airborne MDA only*
  - ▫ *Outside work area—dermal MDA only*
- *Lavatories*
- *Eye wash station(s)*
- Toilets outside the regulated area(s)

☐ **Employee requirements enforced**

- Wash hands and face prior to eating
- Shower at the end of the workday
- Shower immediately upon skin contamination

▶ Employee training

☐ **Pertinent employees trained**

- Where there are potential exposures to DBCP, MDA, vinyl chloride

Figure 3-3: Checklist of Emergency Procedures

☐ Sound alarm

☐ Evacuate

☐ Shower immediately after all direct exposures

☐ Emergency responders don protective equipment

☐ Fix the source of the problem

☐ Clean-up

☐ Emergency responders remove protective equipment

☐ Emergency responders decontaminate

☐ Follow-up medical surveillance

Table 3-4: Minimum Respirator Fit Testing Requirements

Chemical	Qualitative Fit Test		Quantitative Fit Test		
	Initial	Annual	Initial	Biannual	Annual
Acrylonitrile	X	X			
Acrylonitrile[1]			X	X	
Benzene			X		X
DBCP		X		X	
Ethylene oxide			X		X
Formaldehyde			X		X
Methylene chloride			X		X
MDA		X		X	
Vinyl chloride			X		X

In all instances, qualitative fit testing may be used instead of quantitative fit testing. Quantitative fit testing is a minimum requirement.

[1]Where there are more than 10 employees wearing negative pressure respirators.

- Exposures to acrylonitrile, benzene, or ethylene oxide at or above the "action level"

- Exposure to formaldehyde greater than 0.1 ppm

☐ **Proper content**

- Toxicity and properties of chemical(s)

- Other hazards, if applicable *(e.g., flammability of benzene)*

- Quantity, location, manner of use of chemical(s)

- Operations and activities involving potential exposures

- Personal protective equipment

- Emergency procedures and purpose(s)
  - ▫ Employee's role
  - ▫ Recognition and situation evaluation methods
  - ▫ First aid methods
  - ▫ Application rehearsals

- Engineering and work practice controls

- Rationale for medical surveillance

- Review of the applicable standard and its appendices

☐ **Proper frequency**

- Initial

- Annual

► **Medical surveillance**

☐ **Adequate content of medical examination**

- Work and medical history

- Physical examination

- Special X-rays and laboratory tests

- Physician's written opinion

☐ **Physician provided with information**

- Standard and appendices

- Employee's duties

- Actual or representative exposure level(s)

- Personal protective equipment to be worn

Figure 3-4: Medical Surveillance and Laboratory Testing Requirements

AN　　　*Employees potentially exposed at or above the action level*
- 14- by 17-inch posterior-anterior chest X-ray
- Fecal occult blood screening for all workers 40 years and older

Benzene　*Employees potentially exposed at or above the action level for 30 or more days per year, exposed at or above the PEL for 10 or more days per year, and tire building operators who use greater than 0.1 percent benzene*
- Complete blood cell count

DBCP　　*All employees who work in regulated areas and those who are potentially exposed in an emergency situation*
- Serum specimen analysis by radioimmunoassay techniques, using National Institutes of Health specific antigen or an equivalent

EtO　　　*Employees potentially exposed at or above the action level for 30 or more days per year and those who are potentially exposed in an emergency situation*
- Complete blood count

Formaldehyde

　　　　　Employees potentially exposed at or above the action level or STEL, workers demonstrating signs and symptoms of overexposure, and those who are potentially exposed in an emergency situation
- Pulmonary function—FVC, FEV(1), and FEF (respirator users only)

Methylene chloride

　　　　　Employees potentially exposed at or above the action level for 30 or more days per year, above the PEL for 10 or more days per year, and those who are potentially exposed in an emergency
- Post-shift carboxyhemoglobin
- Alanine aminotransferase
- Hemoglobin and hematocrit

MDA　　　*Employees potentially exposed at or above the action level for 30 or more days per year and/or subject to dermal exposures for 15 or more days per year*
- Liver function test
- Urinalysis

Vinyl chloride

　　　　　Employees potentially exposed at or above the action level
- Serum specimen

---

* Potentially means "may be or are known to be exposed"

☐ **Proper frequency**

- Initial

- Annual *(all chemical carcinogens listed except methylene chloride if employee is more than 45 years of age)*

- Every 3 years—methylene chloride only *(employees younger than 45 years old)*

- Upon termination of employment

- When signs or symptoms indicate need

- Where exposures occur during an emergency

☐ **Properly executed medical removal decisions**

- Dated physician restriction order

- Physician return-to-work authorization in writing

- Protection benefit provided *(same wage, seniority, etc.)*

▶ **Documentation** *(maintained for period mandated)*

☐ **Objective data for exempted operations and/or exposure monitoring**

☐ **Exposure monitoring**

☐ **Medical surveillance**

☐ **Respirator fit testing**

▶ **Reports to OSHA Area Director**

☐ **Emergencies**

- Oral *(24 hours)*

- Written *(15 workdays)*

☐ **Regulated areas** *(vinyl chloride only)*

- Address and location of material

- Number of employees potentially exposed

- Written *(one month after establishment)*

Table 3-5: Minimum Records Retention

Chemical	Objective Data	Exposure Monitoring	Medical Surveillance[1]	Compliance Program	Respirator Fit Tests
Acrylonitrile	reliance**	40 years	40 years	reliance	—
Benzene	—	30 years	30 years	—	—
DBCP	—	40 years	*40 years*	—	—
Ethylene oxide	reliance	30 years	30 years	—	
Formaldehyde	30 years	30 years	30 years	—	replacement
Methylene chloride	reliance	30 years	30 years	—	—
MDA	reliance	30 years	30 years	reliance	—
Vinyl chloride	—	30 years	30 years	—	—

* Upon expiration of retention period, notify the OSHA Area Director, or if there is no successor to a terminated business, transmit records to the Director.

** Duration of the employer's reliance on objective data.

[1] Duration of employment plus.

Notes and special comments

_____

_____

_____

_____

_____

_____

_____

_____

_____

_____

_____

_____

_____

_____

_____

_____

_____

Score: _____

Chemical Carcinogens Not Requiring Air Monitoring

Applicable wherever any of the listed thirteen target carcinogens not requiring air monitoring are used in construction. These carcinogens include 2-acetyl-amino-fluorene, 4-aminodiphenyl, benzidine, bis-chloromethyl ether, 3,3'-dichlorobenzidene and its salts, 4-dimethylamino-azobenzene, ethyleneimine, alpha-naphthylamine, beta-naphthylamine, methyl chloromethyl ether, 4-nitro-biphenyl, N-nitro-sodimethylamine, and beta-propiolacetone. Although formerly referred to under separate sections, they are now grouped and regulated in a single section. Section 1910.1003.

▶ **General work practices**

☐ **Isolated, fully enclosed systems**
(e.g., glove bag)—hands and arms washed upon each task completion

☐ **Restricted access to closed systems**
(e.g., maintenance on pipe systems and sealed containers)

☐ **No open vessels**

☐ **Transfer of chemical carcinogens**

• Restricted to authorized personnel only

• Continuous local exhaust ventilation

• Decontamination of exhaust air

Figure 4-1: List of Target Carcinogens Not Requiring Air Monitoring

2-Acetylaminofluorene	1% by weight
3,3'-Dichlorobenzidine and it salts	1% by weight
4-Aminodiphenyl	0.1% by weight
4-Dimethylaminoazobenzene	1% by weight
4-Nitrobiphenyl	0.1% by weight
alpha-Naphthylamine	1% by weight
Benzidine	0.1% by weight
beta-Naphthylamine	0.1% by weight
beta-Propiolactone	1% by weight
bis-Chloromethyl ether	0.1% by weight
Ethyleneimine	1% by weight
Methyl chloromethyl ether	0.1% by weight
N-Nitrosodimethylamine	1% by weight

NOTE: *Carcinogens listed in italics* require washing hands, forearms, face, and neck when departing regulated areas, close to the exits, or before performing other activities.

☐ **Personal protective equipment**
(full body coverings and minimum of half-face, filter-type respirator for dust, fumes, and mist)

☐ **Personnel decontamination procedures**

- Clothing change area at entrance/exit

- Wash hands, forearms, face, and neck upon exit

- Required showers at end of day

- Marked garment disposal containers

☐ **Equipment/supplies decontamination procedures**

☐ **No drinking fountains in restricted areas**

► **Properly labeled containers**

☐ **Identified by name**

☐ **Warning labels** *(e.g., "Cancer-Suspect Agent")*

☐ **No contradictory statements**

► **Controls for regulated areas**

☐ **Negative pressure**

- Regulated areas to nonregulated areas

- Laboratory hoods "average" face velocity of 150 feet per minute (fpm), minimum of 125 fpm

☐ **Area decontamination procedures**

- No dry sweeping and dry mopping

- Wet wipe with special solvent/cleaning substance

☐ **Warning signs at entrance(s) and other area access locations**

☐ **Deluge shower(s) and eyewash fountains**
(within sight of and on the same level with locations where direct exposures may occur to ethyleneimine or beta-propiolactone due to equipment failure or improper work practices)

Figure 4-2: Sign Requirements for Regulated Areas

Minimum requirement for all regulated areas:

Cancer-Suspect Agent

Authorized Personnel Only

Requirement for all regulated areas where performing maintenance activities:

Cancer-Suspect Agent

Impervious Suit Including Gloves, Boots,

and Air-Supplied Hood

Required at All Times

Authorized Personnel Only

▶ **Maintenance procedures**
Where direct contact is possible (e.g., routine maintenance and nonroutine repairs)

☐ **Personal protective equipment** *(full body coverings and continuous-air-supplied respirator)*

☐ **Decontamination** *(full body shower upon removing the protective equipment)*

▶ **Emergency procedures** *(written and posted)*

☐ **Follow evacuation methods**

☐ **Use personal protective equipment** *(full body coverings and continuous-air supplied respirator)*

☐ **Correct the source of emergency**

☐ **Decontaminate the area**

☐ **Initiate medical surveillance within 24 hours for those present at the time of the emergency**

☐ **Shower as soon as possible for direct exposures**

☐ **Complete an incident report**

☐ **Follow employee decontamination procedure**
- Full body shower upon removing the protective equipment
- Instructions accessible
  - Close by
  - Within sight
  - On the same level

▶ **Hygiene facilities and practices**

☐ **Regulated area prohibitions on storage and use/application**
- Food
- Beverages
- Drinking fountains
- Cosmetics
- Smoking
- Chewing

Figure 4-3: Potential Ethyleneimine or Beta-Propiolactone Exposures

Special decontamination equipment requirements include:

☐ Emergency deluge showers

☐ Eyewash fountains

Figure 4-4: Checklist of Requirements for Operations Report(s)

☐ Description and in-plant location of area(s) regulated

☐ Name(s) and/or identifier of each carcinogen

☐ Number of employees in each regulated area

☐ Method of handling (e.g., manufacturing, repackaging, storage, etc.)

☐ **Wash facilities**

☐ **Shower facilities**

- Change rooms where employees wear protective clothing and equipment

- No toilets in regulated area(s)

▶ Employee training

☐ **Employees authorized to enter regulated area(s)**

☐ **Content**

- Toxicity and properties of carcinogenic hazard(s)

- Operations and activities involving potential exposures

- Rationale for medical surveillance

- Self-examination methods, if appropriate

- Decontamination procedures and purpose(s)

- Emergency procedures and purpose(s)
  - Employee's role
  - Recognition and situation evaluation methods
  - First aid methods
  - Application rehearsals

☐ **Proper frequency**

- Initial

- Annual

☐ **Properly documented**

- Employee's name *and social security number*

- Proof of understanding *(e.g., written exam or signed statement)*

- Date(s) of training

- Filed *(e.g., general and personnel files)*

Figure 4-5: Written Incident Report(s)

- Amount of material released and means for determination

- Amount of exposure time involved and means for determination

- Description of area involved

- Extent of known and possible employee exposure(s) and means for determination

- Medical treatment of affected employees

- Medical surveillance implemented

- Analysis of circumstances of the incident

- Corrective actions taken and date(s) of completion

▶ OSHA reports filed

☐ **Operations report(s)**

- Regulated carcinogens use and/or storage

- Completeness of content

- Frequency
  - ▫ Initial
  - ▫ Within 15 days of any changes

☐ **Incident report(s)**

- Initial communication with OSHA Area Director by telephone
  - ▫ Information should include incident occurrence, facts, and medical treatment administered
  - ▫ Communicated within 24 hours of incident

- Written report(s)
  - ▫ Completeness of content
  - ▫ Report filed with OSHA Area Director within 15 days of the incident

▶ Medical surveillance

☐ **Medical examination(s)**

- Content
  - ▫ Personal history
  - ▫ Physical examination
  - ▫ Increased risk conditions assessment by doctor *(e.g., pregnancy, steroids, cigarette smoking, etc.)*
  - ▫ Physician's statement of suitability for employment

- Proper frequency
  - ▫ Initial
  - ▫ Annual

▶ Retention of records and reports

☐ **Retained by employer for duration of employment**

☐ **Forwarded by registered mail to the OSHA Area Director**

- Death of employee or termination of employment

- Business cessation without a successor

Figure 4-6: Summary of Exposure Controls

Laboratory-type hood(s)

Average face velocity—150 feet per minute

Minimum face velocity—125 feet per minute

Clean make-up air sufficient to replace air withdrawn through local exhaust system(s)

Restricted area personal protective equipment

Full body protective clothing

Shoe covers

Gloves

Respirator requirements—employees engaged in handling target carcinogens

Minium half-face, filter-type respirator for dusts, mists, and fumes

Emergency personal protective equipment

Impervious full body protective clothing

Boots

Gloves

Continuous-air supplied respirator

▶ **Overall program effectiveness**

☐ **Employee understanding of procedures**

☐ **Employee compliance with procedures**

☐ **Lack of associated accidents**

Notes and special comments

_____

_____

_____

_____

_____

_____

_____

_____

_____

_____

_____

_____

_____

_____

_____

_____

_____

_____

Score: _____

Chemical Storage Procedures

Applicable to construction activities where chemicals and/or hazardous substances are stored in small quantities, drums, and/or above-ground storage tanks. This section is based on good common practices as well as excerpts from several regulations which are detailed in other sections of this document. See also "Flammable and Combustible Liquids," 29 CFR 1926.152; "Gas Welding and Cutting," 29 CFR 1926.350; "Blasting and Use of Explosives," 29 CFR 1926.9000; and the "Hazard Communication Program," 29 CFR 1926.59.

▶ **Containers properly labeled**

☐ **Trade and chemical name**

☐ **Manufacturer**

☐ **Hazards properly identified**

▶ **Material safety data sheet for each chemical**

☐ **Hazardous**

☐ **Nonhazardous**

☐ **Proprietary**

Figure 5-1: Some Storage Conditions to Avoid

Type of Hazard	Condition(s) to Avoid
Flammable	Heat
	Sparks and other sources of ignition
	Substances which will promote combustion
Toxic	Easy access to the area
Reactive	
Explosives	Heat
	Temperature changes
Oxidizer/reducer	Heat
	Strong sunlight
Water and air sensitive	Water and water solutions
	Moist air
	Aqueous acids and bases
Corrosive	Unprotected storage/stacking materials

Figure 5-2: Examples of Storage Class Groupings

Large Volume/Large Facility

1. Inorganic oxidizing agents
2. Inorganic corrosive oxidizing agents
3. Inorganic unstable explosive
4. Inorganic corrosive acids and bases
5. Metals
6. Flammable and combustible metals
7. General inorganics
8. Perchloric acid and perchlorates
9. Flammable organics (Class I)
10. Flammable organics (Class II)
11. Organic explosives
12. Organic corrosives
13. Organics
14. Flammable compressed gases
15. Nonflammable compressed gases
16. Halogens
17. Cryogenics

Small Volume/Small Facility

1. Flammable
2. Toxic
3. Reactive oxidizing agents
4. Corrosive

Specially constructed building(s), shed(s), rooms, sections of a warehouse, and/or areas within a single room designed and designated for each class grouping. Some organizations have had as many as 24 class groupings of the stored chemicals.

► *Limited amounts of chemicals on hand*

    ☐ *Purchase only what will be used within a reasonable time period (e.g., 6 months)*

    Actual use time for purchases: _____

    ☐ *Routine inventory and disposal of unused chemicals*

    Frequency of inventory: _____

► **Segregation of chemicals**

    ☐ **Keep away from populated areas**

    ☐ **Isolate incompatible substances from one another**

- Separate storage areas, rooms or buildings *(dependent upon the amount of chemicals involved)*

- Identify each storage site according to class
  - Flammable
  - Toxic
  - Corrosive
  - Reactive

- Place chemicals with more than one hazard characteristic
  - In area which represents its greatest hazard
  - Segregated within its storage area if possible

► **Properly posted storage areas**

    ☐ **Hazard signs at entrance to each storage site depicting the worst-case scenario** *(e.g., NFPA Flammability Code 3 and Toxic Code 2 in flammable storage where the flammable substances may include ratings 1,2, and 3 and one or some of the flammable substances have a toxicity rating of 2)*

    ☐ **Special precautions to be taken when accessing the area** *(e.g., no smoking in flammable storage area)*

► **Construction design of special storage areas**
(based on classification of material stored)

Table 5-1: Partial List of Chemical Incompatibilities

Chemical	Incompatible Chemical(s)	Chemical	Incompatible Chemical(s)
Acetaldehyde	Acetic anhydride Ethanol Acetone Acetic acid Sulfuric acid	Cyanide salts	Acids and alkalis
Acetic acid	Formaldehyde Peroxides Chromic acid Nitric acid Perchloric acid Glycols	Dimethyl sulfoxide	Perchloric acid Acetyl chloride Benzenesulfonyl chloride Acetic anhydride
Acetone	Nitric/sulfuric acids mixed	Flammable liquids	Chromic acid Peroxide Nitric acid Halogens (e.g., bromine)
Acetonitrile	Nitric acid Perchloric acid	Fluorine	Most materials
Aniline	Nitric acid Chromic acid Peroxides	Hydrocarbons (e.g., gasoline)	Halogens Chromic acid Peroxides
Bromine	Acetone Acrylonitrile Ethyl ether Hydrogen Rubber	Hydrogen peroxide (>3% in water)	Most metals
Carbon tetrachloride	Diborane Fluorine	Hydrogen peroxide (30 or 90%)	Most metals Flammable/combustible liquids Nitromethane Organics
Carbon monoxide	Oxygen Fluorine	Mercury	Acetylene Alkali metals Ammonia Nitric Acid with ethanol Oxalic acid
Chlorine	Ammonia Acetylene Propane Hydrogen Benzene	Perchloric acid	Acetic anhydride Ethanol Sulfuric Acid Paper
		Sulfuric acid	Any perchlorate Cyanide Chlorate salts

The above chemicals may react violently if allowed to come in contact with each other, resulting in an explosion or production of highly toxic and/or flammable gases/vapors. The list is incomplete and all should be checked and/or cross-referenced for completeness of information.

► **Adequate safety equipment**
(based on level of concern for worse-case scenario and types of hazards)

☐ **Fire extinguishers**

☐ **Showers**

☐ **Eye wash fountains**

☐ **Alarms**

☐ **Portable self-contained breathing apparatus**

☐ **Personal protective clothing**

► **Other programs required**

☐ **Hazard Communication Program**

☐ **Emergency Response Program** *(or Emergency Action Plan)*

☐ **Community Right-to-Know Program**
(if stocked quantities exceed the federal and state limits)

Figure 5-3: NFPA Fire Diamond

Health Hazard

4.....Deadly
3.....Extreme danger
2.....Hazardous
1.....Slightly hazardous
0.....Normal material

Fire Hazard

Flash Points
4.....Below 73°F
3.....Below 100°F
2.....Below 200°F
1.....Above 200°F
0.....Will not burn

Specific Hazard

Oxidizer ....OXY
Acid.........................ACID
Alkali ....ALK
Corrosive ....COR
Use NO WATER ......W
Radiation Hazard.....

Reactivity

4.....May detonate
3.....Shock and heat may detonate
2.....Violent chemical change
1.....Unstable if heated
0.....Stable

Notes and special comments

_____

_____

_____

_____

_____

_____

_____

_____

_____

_____

_____

_____

_____

_____

Score: _____

Section 6

Compressed Gases

Applicable where compressed gases are handled and/or stored in a pressurized container. A pressurized container may be a gas cylinder, portable tank, or cargo tank. This section is based on good common practices and regulatory requirements.

▶ **General condition of compressed gas containers**

☐ **Integrity of container(s)** *(No visible signs of damage, leaks, rust, or excessive wear)*

☐ **Properly labeled**

- Contents clearly identified

- Hazards

- Warnings

☐ **Fitted with pressure relief device(s)**

▶ **Properly transported**

☐ *Written procedures for in-house transport*

☐ *Mechanical transport equipment available*

☐ *Employees trained*

Figure 6-1: Rules for Compressed Gases Handling and Storage

- Always use a hand truck for transport, and chain cylinders to it. May roll about the bottom rim, but do not drag or slide!
- Do not transport cylinders in closed vehicles.
- Cylinders should be chained or otherwise secured in their upright position at all times.
- Do not drop cylinders or otherwise permit them to strike each other.
- Leave valve cap on cylinder until secured AND ready for use.
- Ground all cylinders containing flammable gases.
- Use compressed gases only when the cylinder is in an upright position.
- All valves should be closed when not in use.
- Always assume the cylinders are full and handle accordingly.
- Discontinue using high-pressure cylinders when the pressure approaches 30 psi, and clearly mark the cylinder "EMPTY." Then remove and/or replace it. Store separately from full containers.
- Oily (not specially cleaned) fittings should never be used with oxygen. Oxygen under *pressure will rapidly oxidize oil or grease, resulting in an explosion.*
- Avoid acetylene direct contact with copper or brass (with more than 65% copper). *An explosive compound is formed when acetylene and copper are in contact.*
- Glass equipment should not be pressurized.
- Never mix gases in a cylinder. *Explosion, contamination, corrosion, and other hazards may result.*
- Cylinders with large amounts of a flammable gas should be stored outside in protected areas and piped into the work area.
- Drain regulators and pressure-adjusting devices prior to opening the gas flow valve(s).
- Cylinders should be chained or otherwise secured in an upright position at all times.
- Replace valve cap on cylinder when it is not in use.
- Upon work completion, close all valves.
- Group cylinders by gas type (e.g., flammable or toxic).
- Old stock should be used prior to more recent shipments.
- Make sure fire extinguishers for the storage area are appropriate for the gas(es) stored.
- Do not handle oxygen when hand, gloves, or clothing are oily.
- Store compressed flammable gas cylinders in fire-protected, well-ventilated areas.
- Store all compressed gas cylinders in areas where the temperature is regulated.
- Store combustion supporting gases (e.g., oxygen and chlorine) at least 25 feet from flammable gas cylinders, preferably in another area entirely.
- When in doubt, consult the supplier.

☐ **Cylinders transported in open vehicles**

☐ **Valve caps left on cylinders when being transported**

☐ **Proper DOT labels posted on all highway transport vehicles**

▶ **Properly stored**

☐ **Written procedures**

☐ **Employees trained**

☐ **Cylinders secured (e.g., chained) in upright position at all times, not in a horizontal position**

☐ **Ensure that there are no signs of cylinder damage due to dropping or striking other surfaces**

☐ **Valve caps left on cylinders when not in use**

☐ **Flammable gas cylinders properly grounded**

☐ **Proper flammable gas storage**

- Fire-protected area(s)

- Well-ventilated area(s)

- Away from sources of ignition

- At least 25 feet away from oxygen and oxidizers

- Spark retardant lighting, equipment, and wiring

- No weeds and similar combustibles in proximity

☐ **Appropriate fire prevention**

- Fire extinguishers installed

- Appropriate for the gases/chemicals stored

☐ *Quantity limitations for different types of material posted in each storage area*

☐ **Empty cylinders labeled and stored separately from full cylinders**

☐ **Gas leak detection system—case dependent** *(e.g., required for nitrous oxide)*

Table 6-1: Oxygen Storage Limitations

Type of Proximity Material	Distance (feet)	Capacity of Material
Flammable liquid storage		
Above ground	50 feet	0 to 1,000 gallons
	90 feet	1,001 gallons or more
Below ground	15 feet to tank and 50 feet to vent or opening	0 to 1,000 gallons
	30 feet to tank and 50 feet to vent or opening	1,001 gallons or more
Combustible liquid storage		
Above ground	25 feet	0 to 1,000 gallons
	50 feet	1,001 gallons or more
Below ground	15 feet to tank and 40 feet to vent or opening	—
Flammable gas storage	50 feet	less than 5,000 cu. ft.
	90 feet	5,000 cu. ft. or more

▶ Properly used

☐ *Written procedures*

☐ *Employees trained in safety precautions*

☐ Cylinders secured (e.g., chained) in upright position at all times

☐ Valves closed when not in use

☐ Empty cylinders labeled "**EMPTY**" and removed to be stored

☐ Oily, greasy material not used around compressed oxygen

- Rags
- Clothes
- Gloves
- Hands

☐ Means for matching regulator with compressed gas type

☐ Operating instructions accessible to the worker

▶ Overall program effectiveness

☐ Employee understanding of procedures

☐ Employee compliance with procedures

☐ Lack of associated incidents

Figure 6-2: Checklist of Minimum Distances of Oxygen Containers from Flammable/Combustible Materials

☑ Combustible structures greater than 50 feet away from bulk storage

☑ At least 25 feet from fire-resistive structures

☑ At least 10 feet from openings in adjacent walls

☑ At least 50 feet from flammable liquid storage (less than 1,000 gallons) and 90 feet from storage (greater than 1,000 gallons) of above-ground material

☑ Minimum distance from flammable liquid storage below ground

☑ Minimum distance from combustible liquid storage above ground

☑ Minimum distance for combustible liquid storage below ground

☑ Minimum distance from flammable gas storage

☑ At least 50 feet from highly combustible materials (e.g., paper)

☑ At least 25 feet from solid slow-burning materials (e.g., timber)

☑ At least 75 feet in one direction and 35 feet from confining walls

☑ At least 25 feet from congested areas (e.g., lunch rooms)

Notes and special comments

_____

_____

_____

_____

_____

_____

_____

_____

_____

_____

_____

_____

_____

Score: _____

Section 7

Confined Space Entry Procedures

There is no single confined space entry regulation in the construction standards, but the General Duty Safety Clause, as well as the clarification of the construction term "repairs" to mean maintenance (which falls under the General Industry Standards) and portions of various construction standards do apply to confined space activities . 29 CFR 1910.146 [general industry], 29 CFR 1926.21 [general safety provisions], 29 CFR 1926.651(g) [excavations], 29 CFR 1926.800(j) [tunneling], 29 CFR 1926.956(b) [underground utilities], and 29 CFR 1926.350(b) [welding, cutting, and heating]

▶ **Written permitted confined space entry procedures**

☐ **Identification of all permit-required confined spaces**

☐ **Safety and personal protective equipment**

- Signs and barriers
- Light sources
- Spark-proof tools (where applicable)
- Climbing equipment (where applicable)
- Means for communication

Figure 7-1: Confined Space Entry Information Sheet

Of the more than 1.6 million workers who enter confined spaces each year, approximately 63 die from asphyxiation, burns, electrocution, drowning, and other accidents related to their work. An estimated 60 percent of those who die are untrained personnel. *

Confined Space Characteristics:

- Size and shape sufficient to allow a person to enter
- Limited openings for workers to enter and exit
- Not designated for continuous occupancy

Permit-Required Confined Space Characteristics:

- Contains or has a potential for containing a hazardous atmosphere (e.g., toxic substances and/or oxygen deficient)
- Contains a material that has the potential for trapping an entrant in liquid or solid material
- Has an internal configuration such that the entrant could be trapped or asphyxiated by inwardly converging walls or by a floor which slopes downward and tapers to a smaller cross-section
- Contains any other recognized serious safety or health hazards

Hazardous Atmosphere

- Hazardous atmosphere
  - Not enough oxygen (oxygen concentration below 19.5 percent or above 23.5 percent)
  - Flammable air components (e.g., flammable gas, vapor, or mist in excess of 10 percent of the LFL and dusts at or in excess of their LFL)
  - Toxic air components (may potentially exceed their permissible exposure limits)
- Space can trap entrant in liquid or solid material
- Potential danger from unexpected movement of machinery
- Presence electricity
- Heat stress
- Can become wedged into a narrow part of the space and suffocate
- Physical hazards of falling, tripping, and slipping

Hot Work Permit: Employer's written authorization to perform operations capable of providing a source of ignition (e.g., riveting, welding, cutting, burning, and heating).

29 CFR 1926.21

DEFINITION OF CONFINED (OR ENCLOSED) SPACE: Any space having limited means of egress, which is subject to the accumulation of toxic or flammable contaminants or has an oxygen deficient atmosphere. This includes storage tanks, process vessels, bins, boilers, ventilation or exhaust ducts, sewers, underground utility vaults, tunnels, pipelines, and open top spaces more than 4 feet in depth (e.g., pits, butts, vaults, and vessels).

---

*   Coastal: *Confined Space Rescue.* [Catalog Number CSR00H] Coastal Video Communications Corp., Virginia Beach, Virginia (1991).

- Portable air monitors for entrant(s)

- Respirators

- Other personal protective equipment (e.g., special protective coveralls)

☐ **Personnel requirements and responsibilities**

- Entry supervisor

- Attendant

- Entrant

☐ **Employee training**

- Definition and identification of permitted and nonpermitted confined space entry

- Proper equipment

- Implementation procedures

- Emergency methods

☐ **Means for preventing unauthorized employee entry**

- Signs (e.g., *danger signs at permit spaces:*
  DANGER! PERMIT-REQUIRED
  CONFINED SPACE
  DO NOT ENTER WITHOUT PERMIT)

- Oral communication or training

☐ **Detailed entry procedures**

☐ **Procedures for filling out and posting permit form(s)**

☐ **Emergency procedures**

☐ **Requirements for re-evaluation notification whenever conditions change**

☐ **Procedures for notifying contractors who may enter permit-required confined spaces**

☐ **Requirements and procedures for obtaining a hot work permit**

Figure 7-2: Sample Confined Space Entry Permit

GENERAL INFORMATION

Space to be Entered:

Location/Building:

Purpose of Entry:

Authorized Duration of Permit: Date: to

Time: to

PERMIT SPACE HAZARDS (indicate specific hazards with initials)

Oxygen deficiency (< 19.5%)
Oxygen enrichment (> 23.5%)
Flammable gases or vapors (> 10% LEL)
Airborne combustible dust (≥ LFL)
Toxic gases or vapors (> PEL)
Mechanical hazards
Electrical hazards
Materials corrosive to skin
Engulfment
Other:

PREPARATION FOR ENTRY (Check after steps taken)

☐ **Notification of affected departments**
   of service interruption

☐ **Isolation:**   ☐ Lockout/tagout ☐ Blank/blind
   ☐ Purge/clean ☐ Inert   ☐ Ventilate
   ☐ Atm. test ☐ Barriers   ☐ Other

☐ **Personnel Awareness:**
   ☐ Pre-entry briefing
   ☐ Notify contractors of permit and hazard
      conditions
   ☐ Other

☐ **Additional permits**
   ☐ Hotwork ☐ Line breaking ☐ Other

EMERGENCY SERVICE

Name of Service   Phone Number

EQUIPMENT REQUIRED

Specify as required for entry and/or work.

Personal Protective Equipment:

_____

_____

Respiratory Protection:_____

Atmospheric Testing/Monitoring Equipment:

_____

Communication Equipment:_____

Rescue Equipment:_____

Other:_____

_____

COMMUNICATION PROCEDURES

To be used by attendants and entrants:

_____

_____

AUTHORIZED ENTRANTS

_____

_____

_____

AUTHORIZED ATTENDANTS

_____

_____

_____

TESTING RECORD

	Acceptable Conditions	Testing Periods and Results					
		Time	Time	Time	Time	Time	Time
Oxygen	19.5 to 23.5%						
LEL	< 10%						
H_2S	< 10 ppm						
Toxins (specify)							
Cl2	< 0.5						
CO	< 35 ppm						
SO2	< 2						
Heat							
Other							

AUTHORIZATION BY ENTRY SUPERVISORS

I certify that all required precautions have been taken, and necessary equipment has been provided for safe entry and work in this confined space.

Printed Name   **Signature**   **Date**   **Time**

► **Designated entry supervisor(s)**

Name(s): _____

_____

_____

_____

_____

► **Proper air testing equipment**

Type(s): _____

_____

_____

_____

► **Proper entry equipment**

   ☐ **Barriers**

   ☐ **Personal protective equipment**

   ☐ **Ventilator fans/blowers**

   ☐ **Ladders/climbing equipment**

► **Proper emergency rescue equipment**

► **Hot work permits issued as required**

► **Employee training**

   ☐ **Contents**

      • Duties of entrant and attendant

      • Hazards

      • Signs, symptoms, and consequences of exposures

      • Awareness of behavioral effects of exposures—attendant

      • Use of equipment

Figure 7-3: Sample Equipment Checklist

☑ **Calibrated direct reading monitors**

- Typical four-gas confined space entry monitor
  - ▫ Oxygen
  - ▫ Combustible gases (%LEL)
  - ▫ Hydrogen sulfide
  - ▫ Carbon monoxide
- Monitor capable of detecting toxic chemicals anticipated
  - ▫ Chlorine
  - ▫ Sulfur dioxide
  - ▫ Chlorinated hydrocarbons
  - ▫ Toxic gases
- Heat stress monitor
  - ▫ Dry bulb thermometer
  - ▫ Dry/wet/globe monitor
  - ▫ Body monitors

☑ **Emergency safety equipment**

- Safety harnesses and lifelines
- Hoisting equipment
- Communications equipment
- Self-contained breathing apparatus

☑ **Personal protective equipment for entry**

- Respirator(s) rated for exposures anticipated
- Protective clothing where there is the presence of corrosives or other chemicals that are absorbed by the skin

☑ **Tools and equipment to perform the job**

- UL-approved equipment
- Nonsparking tools
- Ventilator(s)/fans/blowers
- Barrier(s) and/or barrier tape
- Ladders and/or other climbing aids

- Means of communication

- When to declare an emergency

- Rescue procedures

☐ **Personal protective equipment**

☐ **Proper frequency**

- Initial

- Prior to change in assigned duties

- Prior to change in permit space procedures

- Whenever there is reason to believe there have been deviations from the required procedures

☐ **Properly documented**

- Employee's name

- Date(s) of training

- Filed

▶ **Written nonpermitted confined space procedures**

▶ **Overall program effectiveness**

☐ **Employee understanding of procedures**

☐ **Employee compliance with procedures**

☐ **Lack of associated incidents**

Figure 7-4: Sample Confined Space Entry Program

Table of Contents

Section 1: Company Policy

Section 2: Regulatory Requirements and Practices

Section 3: Location of Permit-Required Confined Spaces

Section 4: Personnel Requirements and Responsibilities

Section 5: Safety Procedures

Section 6: Personal Protective Equipment

Section 7: Permitting Requirements

      7.1: Confined Space Entry Permits

      7.2: Hot Work Permits

Section 8: Routine Entry and Exit Procedures

Section 9: Response to Changed Conditions

Section 10: Emergency Procedures

Section 11: Training Requirements

Section 12: Contractor Confined Space Notification Requirements

Notes and special comments

_____

_____

_____

_____

_____

_____

_____

_____

_____

_____

_____

_____

_____

_____

_____

Score: _____

Cranes

Applicable to all construction activities where there are crawler, truck, and locomotive cranes. Many of the requirements are similar to that of the general industry standard for overhead and gantry cranes. 29 CFR 1926.550, ANSI B30.5-1968, and 1910.179

▶ **Written operating procedures**

- ☐ **Policy**

- ☐ **Authorized personnel**

- ☐ **Inspection procedures**

- ☐ **Operating techniques**

- ☐ **Safety practices**

- ☐ **Required personal protective equipment**

- ☐ **Training program requirements**

▶ **Specifications and limitations**

- ☐ **Proper source**

Figure 8-1: Proper Safety Features

Guarded parts and equipment
- Belts
- Shafts
- Pulleys
- Sprockets
- Spindles
- Drums
- Fly wheels
- Chains
- Other rotating, reciprocating, or moving parts

Exhaust pipes guarded or insulated—in areas of possible employee contact

Cab windows
- Safety glass or equivalent
- No visible distortion

Figure 8-2: Wire Rope Conditions Requiring Decommissioning

One lay
- Six randomly distributed broken wires
  OR
- Three broken wires in one strand

Deterioration of $\frac{1}{3}$ the original diameter of outside individual wires (e.g., kinking, crushing, and bird caging)

Evidence of heat damage

Reductions from nominal diameter
- More than $\frac{1}{64}$ inch for diameters up to $\frac{5}{16}$ inch
- $\frac{1}{32}$ inch for diameters from $\frac{3}{8}$ inch to $\frac{1}{2}$ inch
- $\frac{3}{64}$ inch for diameters from $\frac{9}{16}$ inch to $\frac{3}{4}$ inch
- $\frac{1}{16}$ inch for diameters from $\frac{7}{8}$ inch to $1\frac{1}{8}$ inch
- $\frac{3}{32}$ inch for diameters from $1\frac{1}{4}$ inch to $1\frac{1}{2}$ inch

Standing ropes
- More than 2 broken wires in one lay in sections beyond end connections
  OR
- More than 1 broken wire at an end connection

- Manufacturer

  OR

- Qualified engineer competent in this field (if not available through the manufacturer)

☐ **Posted on the equipment**

- Load capacity
  □ Crane
  □ Hoist (or its load block)
- Recommended operating speeds
- Special warnings

▶ Safety equipment

☐ **Fire extinguisher with 5BC rating or higher**

☐ **Warning device for power traveling mechanism** *(Exception: floor operated cranes)*

▶ Safety features

☐ **Guarding**

☐ **Variable angle booms equipped with a visible angle indicator**

☐ **Telescoping booms equipped with visible indicator of extension length or an accurate determination of the load radius**

☐ **Device which prevents contact between the load block or overhaul ball and the boom tip or a two-block damage prevention feature**

☐ **Controlled load lowering system or device**

▶ Operational tests

☐ **Cranes**

- New
- Altered

☐ **Records on file—test results on each crane**

☐ **Inclusion of rated load test results**

Figure 8-3: Equipment Deficiency Checks

Frequency
- Routine use—monthly
- Infrequent use—prior to use
- Standby cranes—every 6 months

Proper inclusion of equipment
- Deformed, cracked, or corroded members
- Loose bolts and/or rivets
- Cracked or worn sheaves and drums
- Worn, cracked, or distorted parts
- Excessive wear on brake system parts, linings, pawls, and ratchets
- Load, wind, and other indicator inaccuracies
- Improper performance of crane powerplant (e.g., gasoline, diesel, or electric)
- Excessive wear of chain drive sprockets
- Excessive chain stretch
- Signs of pitting or deterioration of electrical control contractors, limiting switch(s), and push-button stations

Figure 8-4: Procedures for Maintaining Clearance between Electrical Lines and Cranes/Loads

NOTE: All electrical lines shall be considered energized unless the owner has confirmed otherwise.

For ≤50 kV, use a clearance of at least 10 feet

For >50 kV, use a clearance of at least 10 feet plus 0.4 inches for each kv over 50 (or twice the length of the line insulator)

For equipment in transit without the load and boom lowered
- Use at least 4 feet for volages < 50 kV
- Use at least 10 feet for voltages between 50 and 345 kV
- Use at least 16 feet for voltages between 345 and 750 kV

Designated person to observe clearance and give warning where operator has difficulty observing it alone

When working around transmitter towers where an electrical charge can be induced
- Tower de-energized
  OR
- Tests shall be made to determine if electrical charge is induced on the crane

▶ Annual inspections

- ☐ **Hoisting machinery and equipment**

- ☐ **Performed by qualified person(s)**
  - Competent person
  - Government or private agency recognized by the U.S. Department of Labor

- ☐ **Records on file—test results and date(s)**

▶ Monthly certifications

- ☐ **Equipment**
  - Hoists
  - Hooks
  - Running ropes

- ☐ **Wear on operating mechanisms**

- ☐ **Rope revving**

- ☐ **Proper information**
  - Inspection date
  - Signature of inspector
  - Identification or serial number of specific item inspected

- ☐ **Latest record on file**

▶ Daily inspections

- ☐ **Maladjusted functional equipment**

- ☐ **Deterioration or leakage of air or hydraulic systems**
  - Lines
  - Tanks
  - Valves
  - Drain pumps

Figure 8-5: Sample Crane Operator Checklist

Daily Inspection Checklist

Crane Number _____

Crane Operator _____

Lead Hook-On Man _____

Crane Model _____ Dept. _____ Shift _____

Date _____

Highlight or circle discrepancies. Check if OK.

☐ **Monthly inspection certification**
    ☐ Hoist chains
    ☐ Hooks
    ☐ Ropes
    ☐ Fire extinguisher
    ☐ Warning device operating (if applicable)

☐ **No observed red hold tags**
    (e.g., DANGER: DO NOT OPERATE)

☐ **Operating mechanisms**
    ☐ Jerky movements
    ☐ Unusual noises

☐ **Controls**
    ☐ Labels on buttons legible
    ☐ UP button causes hook to rise
    ☐ DOWN button causes hook to lower

☐ **Deterioration or leakage**
    ☐ Lines
    ☐ Tanks
    ☐ Valves
    ☐ Drain pumps
    ☐ Air or hydraulic system

☐ **Hoist chain or wire rope**
    ☐ Excessive wear
    ☐ Twisting
    ☐ Distorted links
    ☐ Excessive stretch
    ☐ Kinked
    ☐ Damaged

☐ **Hoist limits operating**

☐ **Hooks**
    ☐ Safety latch operable
    ☐ Deformed
    ☐ Cracked
    ☐ Certified record of last monthly inspection

☐ **Obvious physical damage**
    ☐ Loose or missing parts
    ☐ Missing end stops at ends of monorail, beam, or runway

☐ **Dedicated disconnect switches**

☐ **Obstructions to path of movement**

Discrepancies attended to immediately: _____

_____

_____

Decommissioning comments: _____

_____

_____

RED HOLD TAG PLACED ON EQUIPMENT AND DISCREPANCIES REPORTED TO MAINTENANCE.

Signature of crane operator: _____

Signature of hook-on man (if applicable): _____

☐ **Cracked or deformed hooks**

☐ **Hoist chains**

▶ *Operator training*

☐ *Content*

- Daily inspection procedures
- Operating procedures
- Hand signals
- Safety practices
- Personal protective equipment requirements

☐ **Proper documentation of training**

- Written authorization
- *Proof of understanding*

▶ **Clearance minimums understood and observed**

☐ **Nonelectrical obstructions**

- Overhead—3 inches
- Lateral—2 inches
- Parallel cranes—bridges treated as obstructions

☐ **Electrical power lines**

- Power de-energized and visibly grounded at point of work

    OR

- Insulating barriers erected to maintain minimum clearance between lines and crane/load (*See Figure 8-4.*)

▶ **Overall program effectiveness**

☐ **Employee understanding of the procedures**

☐ **Employee compliance with procedures**

☐ **Lack of accidents or injuries**

Figure 8-6: Safety Tips for Overhead Crane Operators

Crane cab operator

- Only authorized operators are permitted to operate the cranes.
- Inspect the crane at the start of your shift.
- Make sure a fire extinguisher is available and fully charged.
- Check the weight of each load against the capacity of the crane, and if in doubt, seek assistance.
- When on duty, remain in the cab, ready for prompt service.
- Never go on top of the crane, or permit anyone else to do so, without first opening the main power disconnect switch and locking it "off" with a padlock.
- Before traveling the trolley or the crane bridge, be sure that the hook is high enough to clear obstacles.
- Never permit your crane to bump into another crane.
- While hoisting, you should not perform any other work. Never leave your position at the controls until the load has been properly positioned or placed on the ground.
- Do not carry a load over people on the ground and sound a warning signal to alert pedestrians.
- Do not lift a passenger riding on a load or on the crane hooks.
- If the power goes off, move the controller to the "Off" position until power becomes available again.
- Report to your supervisor if you are feeling ill or distracted. You should not attempt to operate the equipment when unable to remain alert!
- Do not drag slings, chains, or load blocks. Do not move the crane until you have lowered the hook and the hook-on man has hooked up the chain or sling.
- If asked to do something that appears to be unsafe, seek advice from your foreman or supervisor.
- If your crane fails to respond, don't force it. Stop the operation, open the power switch, and seek assistance.
- If a load appears to be out of balance or sliding, locate the nearest set-down location and carefully lower the load for readjustment.
- If operating from a cab, know and review hand signals.
- If you are working with more than one hook-on man, obey the signal of the head hooker or all emergency stop signals given from any of the other hook-on men.
- Wait until hook-on men and others are out of the way when raising and lowering a load.
- Watch out for obstacles, machinery, and vertical surfaces when raising and lowering a load.
- NEVER leave a load suspended!

Hook-on man

- At the start of your shift, inspect all slings and hooks to be used. Pay particular attention to sling attachments.
- Make sure each load does not exceed the rated load capacity of the crane.
- Never use a sling that has a stretched or deformed hook. Decommission and tag inadequate equipment.
- If one sling in a set needs repair, decommission the entire set.
- Know the capacity of each sling, and stay within its limits.
- Distribute loads equally between the legs with as small an angle as possible between the legs and the vertical.
- Make sure slings are not kinked, twisted, or knotted when positioning a load. If necessary, use an adjuster or wooden wedge.
- Load compressed gas cylinders and acid carboys ONLY in a cradle or similar device.
- Center the crane block directly over the load to prevent the load from swinging during lifting.
- Set load in the bowl of a hook, never on or toward the point (unless the hook has been so designed).
- When hooking and/or unhooking a load, avoid pinch points.
- Do not leave separator blocks or short lengths of steel loose on top of a load.
- Before signaling for the crane operator to lift, clear the area and warn people to stay clear.
- Stand where the operator can see you signal and use standard signals.
- If possible, move ahead of the load to assure adequate obstacle clearances.
- Never walk under a raised load or permit others to do so!
- Free slings from the load before attempting to release them.
- Hook both ends of an empty sling to the block before signaling the operator to move the crane.
- Do not drag, throw, or drop slings.
- Pile and block material so it will not slip or overbalance.
- Use hardwood separator blocks in piles of steel stock or dies.

Notes and special comments

_____

_____

_____

_____

_____

_____

_____

_____

_____

_____

_____

_____

_____

_____

_____

Score: _____

Section 9

Electrical Hazards

Applicable to electrical equipment, supplies, and installations which are to provide electric power to a job site—both temporary and permanent. OSHA recommends that wherever electrical hazards are not addressed by the Construction Standards, the General Industry Standards should be followed. 29 CFR 1926.402 through 1926.408, 29 CFR 1910.301 through 1910.308, 29 CFR 1910.332 through 1910.335, and 1910.399

▶ **Cords, cables, and raceways** *(e.g., electrical wiring, power lines, and conduit)*
The following precautions should be taken:

☐ **Inaccessible energized components**

- Out of reach

- Connections properly covered

- Guarded against damage and/or easy access

- Insulation repaired immediately when frayed or deteriorated

☐ **No potential for water contact**

☐ **No splices or taps**

☐ **Properly grounded cords and cables**

Figure 9-1: Installations Not Covered under the Construction Standards

- Existing permanent installations that had been placed there prior to the start of construction activity(ies)
- Installations used for generation, transmission, and distribution of electricity, including communications, metering, controls, and transformations*

* Portable and vehicle-mounted generators are covered.

Figure 9-2: Major Causes of Job-Related Electrocution

Electrocution rates are historically higher among electrical workers and construction trades, especially when erecting steel. One study (1988) indicated about 60 percent of all electrocution deaths were caused by accidental contact with live power lines.

- Accidentally slipping with tools in hand while working on or near electrical equipment with "live" parts (over 50 volts)
- Switching off the wrong circuit and failing to verify the circuit was de-energized before beginning work
- Failing to implement lockout/tagout procedures
- Failure to use adequate protective equipment
- Using noninsulated tools
- Wearing metal jewelry while working on live circuits
- Using instruments/meters/tools not designated for the system voltage
- Nonelectrical personnel working too close to live equipment (e.g., power lines), usually with cranes or lifting equipment or while handling metal materials

DOE: *Occupational Safety and Health Technical Reference Manual.* Government Institutes, Inc., Rockville, Maryland. Chapter 2, p. 1.

Figure 9-3: Flexible Cords and Cable

- Permitted Uses
  - Pendants
  - Wiring of fixtures
  - Connection of portable lamps or appliances
  - Elevator cables
  - Wiring of cranes and hoists
  - Connection of stationary equipment to facilitate their frequent interchange
  - Prevention of the transmission of noise or vibration
  - Appliances where the fastening means and mechanical connections are designed to permit removal for maintenance and repair
- Prohibited Uses
  - As a substitute for fixed wiring of a structure
  - Where run through holes in walls, ceilings, or floors
  - Where run through doorways, windows, or similar openings
  - Where attached to building surfaces
  - Where concealed behind building walls, ceilings, or floors

☐ **No visible damage**

- Cut wires

- Frayed insulation

- Exposed terminals

- Loose connections

☐ **Properly secured**

- No staples or nails into wires

- No hanging wires

- No trip hazards

☐ **Proper use of flexible cords and cables**

☐ **Special wiring for areas where there are hazardous gases, vapors, and dusts**

▶ **Electrical conductors and equipment**

☐ **Readily accessible for operations and maintenance**

☐ **Covered openings and fittings** (*e.g., wall plug plates*)

☐ **Confirmed suitability of equipment for the job**
(*e.g., equipment in combustible storage unit*)

- Listing

- Labeling

- Certification

☐ **Confirmed suitability of insulation for the job**

- Environmental conditions (*e.g., temperature, rain, high humidity, submerged in water, oil and grease, corrosives, flammable chemicals, etc.*)

- Proper voltage

☐ **Electrical ratings (e.g., voltage) clearly marked and visible on the equipment**

☐ **Properly grounded live components of 50 volts or more**

☐ **Low voltage protection with control for motors driving machines and equipment**

Table 9-1: Safe Work Clearance Distances for Energized Equipment Components

Nominal Voltage to Ground (volts)	Minimum Clearance Distance (feet)		

Workspace clearances for qualified persons working on energized electrical components at ground level.

	Conditions		
	A	B	C
	not less than 30 inches wide in front		
150 or less	3	3	3
151 to 600	3	3½	4
	not less than 36 inches wide in front		
601 to 2,500	3	4	5
2,501 to 9,000	4	5	6
9,001 to 25,000	5	6	9
25,001 to 75 k	6	8	10
more than 75 k	8	10	12

Condition A: Exposed live parts on one side and no live or grounded parts on the other side of the working space, or exposed live parts on both sides effectively guarded by suitable wood or other insulating materials.

Condition B: Exposed live parts on one side and grounded parts on the other side. Concrete, brick, or tile walls may be considered grounded.

Condition C: Exposed live parts on both sides of the work space not guarded.

Nominal Voltage Between Phases	Minimum Elevation
Elevation requirements of energized electrical components above ground level.	
601 to 7,000	8 feet 6 inches
7,501 to 35,000	9 feet
more than 35 k	9 feet plus 0.37 inches per kV above 35 kV

☐ **Insulation intact**

- Not damaged *(crushed, torn, or removed)*

- Installed by the manufacturer

☐ **Equipment firmly mounted and secured**

☐ **Routine maintenance checks for recognized hazards**

☐ **Inspected prior to job start-up**

- No cracks in insulation

- Clean

- Dry

- No oily film or carbon deposits

☐ **Proper work clearance distance(s)**

☐ **Special designs for areas where there are flammable vapors, liquids, or gases or where combustible dusts or fibers may be present**

- Clearly marked "HAZARDOUS LOCATION CLASSIFICATION"
  - Class
  - Operating temperature

- Classification adequate for the hazard
  (e.g., no changes in anticipated exposures have been made since installation)

- Posted explosion properties of specific gas, vapor, or dust present

▶ **Plugs and receptacles**

☐ **Undamaged**

☐ **Secured covers**

☐ **No loose wires**

☐ **Properly grounded**

Figure 9-4: Hazardous Location Classifications

Class I Location: Flammable gases or vapors may be present in the air in quantities sufficient to produce explosive or ignitable mixtures.

Division 1: Location where hazardous conditions exist: 1) under normal operating conditions; 2) where hazardous concentrations of gases or vapors may exist frequently during repair, maintenance, or a leak; or 3) as a result of a breakdown or faulty equipment operations of equipment or processes which might release hazardous concentrations of flammable gases or vapors with the simultaneous failure of the electrical equipment, e.g., spray paint booth interiors.

Division 2: Location where hazardous conditions exist: 1) where volatile flammable liquids or flammable gases are handled, processed, or used, but where they will normally be confined within enclosed containers or systems (from which they may escape only in case of an accidental rupture/breakdown, or in case of abnormal operations); 2) where normally prevented by positive mechanical ventilation but might become hazardous upon failure or abnormal operations; or 3) which are adjacent to Class I, Division I locations and where exposures to these gases or vapors may occur, e.g., degreasing tanks (prevented by adequate positive-pressure ventilation and effective safeguards against ventilation failure).

Class II Location: Combustible dust may be present in the air in quantities sufficient to produce explosive or ignitable mixtures.

Division 1: Location where hazard conditions exist: 1) under normal operating conditions; 2) where failure or abnormal operation of machinery or equipment might result in explosive or ignitable mixtures of dust while providing a source of ignition; or 3) where electrically conducting dusts may be present, e.g., grain elevators.

Division 2: Location where hazardous conditions exist: 1) where deposits or accumulations of dust may be sufficient to interfere with the safe dissipation of heat from electrical equipment or apparatus; or 2) where such deposits or accumulations of dust on, in, or in the vicinity of electrical equipment might be ignited by arcs, sparks, or burning material from such equipment, e.g., closed bins and hoppers.

Class III Location: Ignitable fibers or flyings are handled, manufactured, or used but not likely to be suspended in the air in quantities sufficient to produce ignitable mixtures.

Division 1: Easily ignitable fibers or materials may be present in quantities sufficient to produce combustible flyings, e.g., cotton textile mills.

Division 2: Easily ignitable fibers are stored or handled (except in process manufacturing areas).

Temperature Identification Numbers (°C)

T1	450	T3	200	T5	100
T2	300	T3A	180	T6	85
T2A	280	T3B	165		
T2B	260	T3C	160		
T2C	230	T4	135		
T2D	215	T4A	120		

► **Special procedures for high risk personnel**

☐ **Restricted use of metal tools** *(e.g., measuring tapes, ladders, and hand lines)*

- Clothing *(e.g., rubber gloves)*

- Hotline tools

☐ **Restricted use of metal adornments** *(e.g., jewelry and belt buckles)*

☐ **Availability and use of electrically protected supplies**

- Clothing *(e.g., rubber gloves)*

- Hotline tools

☐ **Avoidance of working while wet**

- Dry clothing

- Towel to dry sweaty hands

- No working in rain

- No work in standing water *(e.g., puddle)*

☐ **Use of the "buddy system" when working around 600 volts or more**

☐ **Instruction in cardiopulmonary resuscitation**

☐ **Understanding and use of the "lockout and tagout" program**
(See Section 23 for details.)

► **Circuit breakers and disconnect switches**

☐ **Legibly marked and identified as to use**

- All service, feeder, and branch circuits

- Each disconnect switch

☐ **"On" and "off" positions clearly indicated**

☐ **Properly guarded** *(e.g., enclosed)*

☐ **Located within sight of the motor control(s)**

Figure 9-5: Special Requirements for Circuit Breakers

- All 120-volt, fluorescent lighting circuits—marked "SWD"
- Over 600 volts—feeders and branch circuits shall have short-circuit protection

Figure 9-6: Special Grounding Requirements

- 3-wire DC systems—neutral conductor grounded
- 2-wire DC systems, generating 50 to 300 volts—grounded unless rectifier-derived from an AC system
- AC systems, generating less than 50 volts—grounded if one of the following conditions applies:
  - If installed overhead outside a building
    OR
  - If supplied by a transformer
    AND
    - The transformer primary supply system is not grounded
      OR
    - The transformer primary supply system exceeds 150 volts to ground
- AC systems, generating 50 to 1000 volts—grounded under the following conditions:
  - If the system can be grounded so that the maximum voltage to ground on the ungrounded conductors does not exceed 150 volts
  - If the system is nominally rated 480Y/277 volt, 3-phase, 4-wire in which the neutral is used as a circuit conductor
  - If the system is nominally rated 240/120 volt, 3-phase, 4-wire in which the midpoint of one phase is used as a circuit conductor
  - If a service conductor is not insulated

Exemptions: If the system is separately derived and is supplied by a transformer that has a primary voltage rating of less than 1000 volts AND meets all of the following conditions:

  - System is used exclusively for control circuits
  - Conditions of maintenance and supervision ensure that only qualified persons will service the installation
  - Continuity of control power is required
  - Ground detectors are installed on the control system

▶ **Transformers and high voltage equipment**

☐ **Secured against unauthorized entry**

☐ **Properly labeled with warning sign(s)**

▶ **Procedure for managing hidden electric circuits**

☐ **Identification of underground electric utilities possible prior to ground or structural penetrations** *(e.g., trenching, excavating, and demolition)*

☐ **If identification is not possible, employees using jackhammers, bars, or other hand tools which may contact a line are required to wear at least insulated protective gloves**

▶ **Procedures for contract labor**

☐ **Properly informed of electrical hazards**
(Documentation of information disclosure is recommended.)

☐ **Required to comply with OSHA regulations**

▶ **Employee training program** *(classroom or on-the-job)*

☐ **All employees properly trained**

- Be able to recognize obvious electrical hazards
- Know reporting procedures for potential or known electrical hazards

☐ **Housekeeping personnel properly trained**

- Know precautions to be taken when working around electrical components
- Be aware of restricted areas
- Know that no electrically conductive supplies are to be used in the vicinity of electrical components

☐ **High risk job employees properly trained**

- Develop skills for identifying exposed live electrical components
- Know use and inspection procedures for in-house electrical test equipment and instruments
- Be aware of safe work clearance distances

Figure 9-7: Checklist of Specialty Equipment Requiring Specific Installation Procedures

29 CFR 1910.306

☑ Electric signs and outline lighting

☑ Cranes and hoists

☑ Elevators, dumbwaiters, escalators, and moving walks

☑ Data processing systems

☑ X-Ray equipment

☑ Induction and dielectric heating equipment

☑ Electrolytic cells

☑ Electrically driven or controlled irrigation machines

☑ Swimming pools, fountains, and similar installations

Figure 9-8: Electrical Hazards
General Information

- Know color coding on equipment.
  - Red—emergency cutoff switches
  - Orange—dangerous exposed machine parts or electrical shock hazards
- Water and electricity do not mix.
  - Do not handle electrical equipment while wet (e.g., rain-soaked clothes).
  - Clean up liquid spills immediately unless the liquid has come into contact or may have potentially contacted electrical components. In such cases, contact someone trained in the proper management of electrical hazards.
- Disconnect plugs at the receptacle. Do not pull the cord!
- Report electrically supplied equipment discrepancies.
  - Cracks in insulation
  - Exposed/visible wires and connections
  - Wet equipment and/or vicinity of the equipment
  - Oily film and carbon deposits

☐ **Personnel qualified to work on electrical circuits and equipment properly trained and certified**

- Have proper credentials and training in electrical work

- Know use of, and inspection procedures for, in-house electrical test equipment and instruments

- Know proper use of personal protective equipment available in-house

- Be aware of safe work clearance distances

- Know "buddy system" requirements

- Know alerting procedures
  - Signs and tags (e.g., lockout and tagout procedure)
  - Barricades
  - Requirement for backup attendant if barricades are ineffective

▶ Adequate area precautions

☐ **Proper illumination**

☐ **Securing devices used for doors and hinged panels when working in confined/ enclosed work spaces**

▶ Ground-fault protection

☐ **Ground-fault circuit interrupters**

- Required for all 120-volt, single phase, 15- and 20-amp receptacle outlets which are not part of a building or structural permanent wiring

- Not required where receptacles are on a 2-wire, single phase portable or vehicle-mounted generator rated not more than 5 kW where the circuit conductors of the generator are insulated from the generator and other ground surfaces

OR

☐ **Equipment grounding conductor program**

- Required at each construction job site where there are cord sets, receptacles (which are not part of a building or structure), and equipment connected by cord and plug which are available for employee use

Table 9-2: Safe Approach Distances to Energized Electrical Components

Voltage Range (volts)	Minimum Approach Distance	
	Feet and Inches	**Centimeters**

Applicable to <u>persons qualified</u> to work around electrical circuits and equipment and to any conductive object to be used by that person, without an approved insulating handle.

Voltage Range (volts)	Feet and Inches	Centimeters
300 or less	avoid contact	
over 300 to 750	1' 0"	30.5
over 750 to 2 k	1' 6"	46
over 2 k to 15 k	2' 0"	61
over 15 k to 37 k	3' 0"	91
over 37 k to 87.5 k	3' 6"	107
over 87.5 k to 121 k	4' 0"	122
over 121 k to 140 k	4' 6"	137

Applicable to <u>persons not qualified</u> to work around electrical circuits and equipment and working in an elevated position near overhead lines and to the longest conductive object used by that person.

50 k or less	10'	305
over 50 k	10' plus 4" for every 10 k over 50 k	

Applicable to any <u>vehicular and mechanical equipment</u> with parts which may be elevated to within reach of overhead power lines.

Not in transit

50 k or less	10'	305
over 50 k	10' plus 4" for every 10 k over 50 k	

In transit

50 k or less	4'	122
over 50 k	4' plus 4" for every 10 k over 50 k	

- Minimum program components
  - Written description of the program
  - One or more competent persons designated to implement the program
  - Inspection requirements detailed
  - Test requirements detailed
  - Protocol for removal from use and/or means to assure that inadequate electrical items are not used
  - Effective procedures for maintaining test records

▶ Electrical items used in hazardous locations

☐ **Hazardous locations properly identified** *(See Figure 9-4.)*

- Class I, Division 1
- Class I, Division 2
- Class II, Division 1
- Class II, Division 2
- Class III, Division 1
- Class III, Division 2

☐ **All electrical items identified**

- Equipment
- Wiring
- Installations of equipment

☐ **All items identified as one of the following:**

- Intrinsically safe
- Approved for the class of hazard and its properties
- Proven safe by the employer to provide protection from the hazards

☐ **All conduits threaded and wrench-tight or bonded**

- Free of corrosion
- Cap vent holes open
- Installed to avoid physical or electrical contact with compartment walls or components

Figure 9-9: Minimum Visual Inspection for Ground Fault Protection

- **Inspected frequently (at the start of each work shift)**
- **Items to be inspected**
  - Cord sets
  - Attachment caps
  - Plugs
  - Receptacles of cord sets
  - Equipment connected by cord and plug
- **Inspect for damage and defects**
  - Deformed or missing pins
  - Damage to insulation
  - Potential internal damage (e.g., crimped or signs of excessive heat)
- **All equipment found damaged shall identified and not used again until it has been repaired**

---

* Items "not requiring" inspection include cord sets and receptacles which are fixed and not openly exposed to damage.

Figure 9-10: Minimum Test Requirements for Ground Fault Protection

- **Testing frequency**
  - Before first use
  - Before equipment is returned to service following any repairs
  - Before equipment is used after an incident which can reasonably be suspected of having caused damage (e.g., cord run over by vehicle)
  - Minimum intervals not to exceed 3 months (If the cord sets and receptacles are fixed and not exposed to damage, testing intervals may be extended to 6 months.)
- **Items to be tested**
  - All equipment grounding conductors tested for continuity (must be electrically continuous)
  - Each receptacle and attachment cap or plug tested for correct attachment to the equipment grounding conductor
  - Equipment grounding conductors connected to their proper terminals
- **All tests (positive and negative) must be recorded**
  - Last date or interval tested
  - Maintained by logs, color coding, or other effective means
  - Preceding records replaced

▶ **Overall program effectiveness**

☐ **Employee understanding of procedures**

☐ **Employee compliance with procedures**

☐ **Lack of associated incidents**

Notes and special comments

_____

_____

_____

_____

_____

_____

_____

_____

_____

_____

_____

_____

_____

_____

_____

_____

_____

Score: _____

Section 10

Emergency Action Plan

Applicable wherever an emergency may develop, requiring employee evacuation and/or immediate medical assistance. An "emergency" includes, but is not limited to, fires, inclement weather (e.g., hurricanes), and chemical spills. "Immediate medical assistance" may be needed for a serious injury or an employee health problem. 29 CFR 1926.35 and 29 CFR 1926.50

▶ **Written emergency action plan** *(for companies with more than 10 employees)*

☐ **Types of emergencies**

- Fires
- Explosions
- Hazardous material releases *(e.g., toxic chemicals)*
- Weather extremes *(e.g., blizzard)*
- Floods
- Hurricanes and tornadoes
- Earthquakes
- Bomb threat
- *Civil strife*
- Sabotage

Figure 10-1: Fire Prevention
Safe Practices in the Workplace

Smoking

Cigarettes, matches, and lighters are major causes of fires.

- If your company allows smoking in the workplace, smoke only where permitted. Do not flick ashes onto floors or into wastebaskets. Use large, non-tip ashtrays and make sure everything in them is cold before they are emptied.
- Apply the same cautions to visitors and be sure no one leaves a smoldering cigarette on furniture or in a wastebasket.

Wiring

- Replace electrical cords which have cracked insulation or broken connectors.
- Never run extension cords across doorways or where they can be stepped on or chafed.
- Do not plug one extension cord into another and avoid plugging more than one extension cord into an outlet.
- Do not pinch electrical cords under or behind furniture.

Appliances

- Leave space for air to circulate around heaters and other heat-producing equipment such as copy machines and computer terminals.
- Keep appliances away from anything that might catch fire.
- Designate an employee to turn off or unplug all appliances—including coffee makers and hot plates—at the end of each work day.

Housekeeping

- Keep exits, storage areas, and stairways free from waste paper, empty boxes, dirty rags, and other fire hazards.

Arson

Arson is the leading cause of fires in general office buildings.

- Adhere to your building's security measures and keep unauthorized people out.
- Keep doors locked after business hours.
- Alleys and other areas around your building should be well lit.
- Keep clutter out of halls, lobbies, alleys, and other public areas.

- *Work accidents and rumors*
- *Emergency shutdowns*
- *Industrial civil defense (e.g., war)*

☐ **Emergency escape procedures and routes**

- Area schematic
- Easy-to-identify signs
- Exit direction markings
- Routes free of debris and clutter

☐ **Procedures for critical plant operations employees to follow prior to evacuation**

☐ **Rescue and medical duties required of emergency responders**

☐ **Preferred means for reporting emergencies**

☐ **Means to use to account for all building occupants/employees after evacuation has been completed**

☐ **Names or job titles of persons (or departments) who can be contacted for further information in case of an emergency**

☐ **Copies of emergency action plan located throughout the workplace and available to all employees**

▶ **Alarm system**

☐ **Distinct** *(specific required response action)*

☐ **Audible** *(or visually perceptible where an audible alarm may not be recognizable)*

☐ **Emergency reporting procedures**

- Building occupants/ employees properly trained
- Posted emergency telephone number(s) *(in conspicuous locations)*
- Emergency messages receive priority over nonemergency messages

☐ **Serviced, maintained and tested routinely**

- Performed by trained/knowledgeable individuals
- Tests conducted at least every 2 months

Figure 10-2: Fire Preparedness Tips

Employees

- Count the doors or desks between your work area and the nearest exit. *During a fire you may have to find your way out in the dark.*
- Learn the location of posted and alternative exits from all work areas.
- Know the location of the nearest fire alarm and learn how to use it.
- Post the fire department emergency number on or near your telephone.
- Be sure someone in authority knows about any disability that you may have which could delay escape.
- Become familiar with the use of fire extinguishers.

Employers

- Post building evacuation plans and discuss them during orientation of new employees .
- Conduct regular fire drills.
- When possible, include disabled employees in the planning process.
- Train employees in the use of fire extinguishers.

Excerpted from *Fire Safety on the Job*, National Fire Protection Association, 1993.

- Multi-actuation device systems—test different actuation devices each test period

- Backup *(e.g., employee runners)* for periods when systems are out-of-service

- Maintain power supplies *(e.g., replace batteries)*

- Supervised alarm systems
  - Installed after January 1, 1981 *(Ensure supervision of the circuitry and notification of deficiencies.)*
  - Tested annually

☐ **Voice communication only** *(for companies with 10 or fewer employees)*

☐ **Manually operated actuation devices**

- Unobstructed

- Conspicuous

- Readily accessible

▶ **Emergency evacuation team**
The recommended number of evacuation wardens is one for every 20 people.

☐ **Designated by name**

☐ **Training schedule**

- When plan is first developed

- When responsibilities or assignments change

- When the plan changes

☐ **Training material**

- Responsibilities

- Alarm signals

- Routines of evacuation

- Where to direct personnel in case of an emergency

- Use and location of fire extinguishers

- How to assist disabled employees

Figure 10-3: What to Do If Fire Strikes

- Sound the alarm and call the fire department, no matter how small the fire appears to be.

- Leave the area quickly, closing doors as you go to contain fire and smoke.

- Heat and smoke rise, leaving cleaner air near the floor. If you must escape through an area with smoke, crawl low, keeping your head 12 to 24 inches (30 to 60 cm) above the floor.

- Test doors before you open them. Kneeling or crouching at the door, reach up as high as you can and touch the door, the knob, and the space between the door and its frame with the back of your hand. If the door is hot, use another escape route. If the door is cool, open it slowly.

- Follow directions from fire and security personnel. Once outside, move away from the building, out of the way of fire fighters. Remain outside until the fire department says you may go back in.

Excerpted from *Fire Safety on the Job*, National Fire Protection Association, 1993.

► Employee training

☐ **"What-to-do" in case of an emergency** *(including how to get assistance for or assist disabled employees)*

☐ **Alarm signals**

☐ **Evacuation routes and procedures**

☐ **How to seek prompt medical assistance**

► Availability of medical assistance

☐ **Company designated medical professional for advice and consultation on matters of occupational health**

☐ **Emergency medical telephone number(s) conspicuously posted**

OR

☐ **Reasonably accessible distance and time period in case of a serious injury**

• Medical professionals *(e.g., infirmary, clinic, hospital, or physician)*

• Sufficient number of employees with a current first aid training certificate so there will be someone available at all times, during all work shifts.

☐ **Available during work hours—especially for 24-hour operations**

☐ **Prearranged means for seeking medical assistance**

• Point of initial contact *(e.g., security)*

• Response action prearranged *(e.g., security calls EMS)*

• *Medical facility identified and administrative arrangements understood with facility prior to any incidents in order to expedite admission for injured employees.*

► Emergency supplies and equipment properly maintained

☐ **First aid kit**

• Approved by consulting physician

• Weatherproof container

• Individually sealed packages for each item

• Contents checked prior to each new job site

• Checked weekly on each job for expended items

Figure 10-4: Sample Emergency Action Plan

Table of Contents

Figure 10-5: Classification of Fire Extinguishers

Class A

Typically consists of a solution of water for fighting fires caused and propagated by ordinary combustible materials such as paper, wood, rags, and general trash.

Class B

Dry chemical, carbon dioxide, foam, and halogenated hydrocarbon components for fighting fires caused and propagated by flammable liquids such as gasoline, oil, grease, and paint.

Class C

Dry chemical, carbon dioxide, compressed gas, and vaporizing liquid components for fighting fires in or near electrical equipment or any other potential electrical hazard situation.

Class D

Special extinguishing components for fighting fires caused and propagated by combustible metals such as magnesium, lithium, and sodium. WARNING: May pose a hazard when used on other types of fires.

- Transport system
    - Equipment for prompt transport of injured person to a physician or hospital
    OR
    - Communication system for contacting necessary ambulance services

☐ **Where there are corrosive materials**

- Eye wash stations

- Deluge shower(s)

▶ **Routine emergency evacuation drills**

☐ **Frequency:** _____

▶ **Overall program effectiveness**

☐ **Employee understanding of procedures**

☐ **Employee ability to efficiently respond to procedures**

Notes and special comments

_____

_____

_____

_____

_____

_____

_____

_____

_____

_____

_____

_____

Score: _____

Section 11

Ergonomics

Applicable in all workplace environments where employees may develop either OSHA recordable musculoskeletal disorders or have daily exposures to "signal risk factors" for musculoskeletal disorders.

Musculoskeletal disorders may be determined by evaluating past performances (e.g., OSHA 200 logs and workers' compensation data). Signal risk factors include jobs which require performance of the same motions or motion patterns every few seconds, fixed or awkward work postures (e.g., twisted or bent back), use of vibrating or impact tools or equipment, use of forceful hand exertions, and unassisted frequent or forceful manual handling (e.g., lifting). The latter is covered Section 24, "Manual Lifting."

This topic is yet to be regulated by any specific regulations. However, the requirements are implied under the General Duty Clause of the Occupational Safety and Health Act which requires an employer to provide a safe and healthy work environment for its personnel.

▶ **Written ergonomics program**

☐ **Work site analysis**

☐ **Job improvement processes**

☐ **Employee training**

☐ **Employee medical management logs worksite analysis**

Figure 11-1: Types of Ergonomic Injuries

Cumulative trauma disorder (CTD)

Injury to the tissues, nerves, tendons, tendon sheaths, and muscles (predominantly of the upper extremities) which is the result of repeated forceful actions. CTD may be caused by one or a combination of the following:
- Repetitive motion
- Forceful exertions
- Vibration
- Hard and sharp edges
- Sustained or awkward postures
- Exposure to noise over extended periods

Carpal tunnel syndrome (CTS)

A form of cumulative trauma disorder which affects one's hands and wrists. The symptoms are tingling, numbness, and severe pain in the wrist and/or hand, reduced hand strength, and an inability to make a fist or hold objects. These problems are typically not noticeable until after work, in the evening. The more advanced cases may result in permanent loss of sensation and partial paralysis of the hand and wrist.

Back disorders

Injury to the back involving pulled/strained muscles, ligaments, tendons, and disks. Most result from chronic injury, not by a single incident. They may be caused by one or a combination of the following:
- Excessive/repetitive twisting, bending, and/or reaching
- Carrying, moving, and/or lifting loads that are either too heavy or too large
- Staying in one position for too long
- Poor physical condition
- Poor posture
- Prolonged sitting
- Back degeneration due to age
- Excessive activity without the benefit of prior physical conditioning
- Stress
- Vibration

Contributing factors to CTD and back disorders
- Routine, repetitive tasks
- Awkward postures
- Forceful exertions
- Temperature extremes
- Inappropriate hand tools
- Restrictive workstations
- Vibration from power tools
- Poor body mechanics
- Lifting heavy or awkward objects

▶ **Work site analysis**

☐ **Identify problem jobs**

- Identify recordable musculoskeletal disorders

- Note signal risk factors

☐ **Risk factors analysis of problem jobs**

- Job description

- Identification and description of each workplace risk factor

- Analysis of manual handling tasks

- Employee input as to problems they are, or have been, experiencing while performing the job

▶ **Hazard prevention and control**
(e.g., effective design of a job or job site and the tools or equipment used in the job)

☐ **Initial improvement and exposure controls**

- Engineering

- Administrative

- Work practice

☐ **Ongoing, continuous improvements**

▶ **Means for identifying and controlling new or changed jobs**

☐ **Employee training**

☐ **All employees in potentially problem jobs**

☐ **Cumulative trauma and back disorders**

- Define

- Causes

- Contributing factors

- Signs and symptoms

- Prevention

- Early intervention

Figure 11-2: Prevention and Controls for Cumulative Trauma and Back Disorders

Design of Work Station
- Accommodate full range of movements
- Enough space for knees and feet
- Able to adjust the height of work tables and chairs
- Able to reach machine controls with ease

Design of Tools and/or Equipment
- Position of use
- Vibration
- Grip strength required
- Awkwardness
- Force required
- Repetitive motion
- Handle sizes and adequacy of grip for gloved hands
- Accommodations for both right- and left-handed workers
- Balance
- Center of gravity
- Weight of the tool
- Appropriateness for the job

Administrative Controls
- Reduce duration
- Reduce frequency
- Reduce severity

Work Practice Controls
- Instruction in proper work practices
- Employee conditioning
- Regular monitoring
- Feedback with signs and symptoms
- Adjustments
- Modifications
- Maintenance

► **Medical management**

☐ **Physical examination**

- Medical and occupational history
- Physical examination

☐ **Frequency**

- Initial
- Upon first symptoms of medical condition

☐ **Treatment**

☐ **Follow-up**

► **Overall program effectiveness**

☐ **Employee understanding of program**

☐ **Employee compliance with work practice controls**

☐ **Lack of associated injuries**

Notes and special comments

_____

_____

_____

_____

_____

_____

_____

_____

_____

Score: _____

Excavations and Trenching

Applies to construction activities involving excavating and trenching activities in the earth's surface. 29 CFR 1926.650 through 1926.652

▶ **Supported surface encumbrances** *(if present)*

▶ **Method for locating all underground utilities and pipelines**
(e.g., written or oral request to locate)

▶ **Access and egress**

☐ **Designed by competent person**

☐ **Structurally sound**

☐ **Trenches with stairway, ladder, ramp, or other means of egress**
(wherever the trench is 4 feet or more in depth and at least one form of egress every 25 feet)

▶ **High visibility vests/clothes** *(wherever there is public vehicle traffic)*

▶ **Distance maintained from loading/unloading activities**

▶ **Approach warning system for mobile equipment**

Figure 12-1: Sample Excavation Summary Worksheet

Project name: _____

Project number: _____

Client: _____

Location of excavation: _____

City: _____ County: _____

Name and title of site supervisor: _____

Start date: _____ Estimated completion date: _____

Project description: _____
_____
_____

Underground structures investigated (See attached log): _____

Gas: _____ Pipeline: _____

Electric: _____ Telephone: _____

Water: _____ Other: _____

Sewer: _____

Site characteristics: _____

Anticipated depth: _____ width: _____ length: _____

Soil type: _____ Water : _____

Ground protection method(s): _____
_____
_____

Required air monitoring: _____

Oxygen: _____ Toxic substance(s): _____

Combustible gases: _____

Other: _____

Required special equipment: _____
_____
_____

Approved by (competent person or registered professional engineer): _____

Name: _____ Date: _____

Signature: _____

Site supervisor review: _____

Name: _____ Date: _____

Signature: _____

State notification (if required): _____

Name of contact: _____ Date: _____

Permit number issued: _____

▶ **Hazardous atmospheres**

☐ **Testing for oxygen deficiency** *(wherever greater than 4 feet in depth)*

☐ **Flammable gas testing**

☐ **Routine toxic substance testing** *(where applicable)*

☐ **Dedicated emergency rescue equipment**
(e.g., self-contained breathing apparatus and safety harness)

▶ **Water hazards**

☐ **Protected from cave-ins**

☐ **Water removal equipment monitored** *(where applicable)*

☐ **Diversion of surface waters** *(e.g., natural streams)* **from excavation**

▶ **Adjacent structures**
Applicable where the structure is below the level of the base or footing of any foundation or retaining wall and where there are sidewalks, pavements, and/or similar structures.

☐ **Protected from cave-ins**

☐ **Design or response approved by registered professional engineer**
(if there is anything other than stable rock)

▶ **Loose rock and soil protection**
(e.g., scaling to remove loose material and barricades)

▶ **Fall protection**

☐ **Standard guardrails on excavation walkways**

☐ **Open hole(s)**
  • Barrier
  • Covered
  • Backfilled

Figure 12-2: Sample Notification Log

Underground Structure(s)

Project name: _____ Project number: _____

Location of excavation: _____

Start date: _____ Estimated completion date: _____

Gas

Contact name	Date of contact	Type contact (e.g., phone)
Comments		
Contact name/title/signature		

Sewer

Contact name	Date of contact	Type contact (e.g., phone)
Comments		
Contact name/signature		

Electric

Contact name	Date of contact	Type contact (e.g., phone)
Comments		
Contact name/title/signature		

Water

Contact name	Date of contact	Type contact (e.g., phone)
Comments		
Contact name/title/signature		

Telephone

Contact name	Date of contact	Type contact (e.g., phone)
Comments		
Contact name/title/signature		

Pipeline

Contact name	Date of contact	Type contact (e.g., phone)
Comments		
Contact name/title/signature		

Other

Contact name	Date of contact	Type contact (e.g., phone)
Comments		
Contact name/title/signature		

▶ **Daily inspection logs**

☐ **Performed by competent person**

☐ **Prior to entry into the hole(s)**

☐ **After every rainstorm or other hazard increasing occurrence**

▶ **Proper protective systems**
Applicable every time except where there are stable rock formations and where excavations are less than 5 feet deep with no indication of a potential cave-in.

☐ **Sloping and benching design**

- Allowable configurations *(at or greater than one horizontal to 1½ vertical)*

- Calculated configurations

- Other tabulated data
  - Written
  - Approved by registered professional engineer
  - Maintained at job site during construction and use

- Designed by registered professional engineer
  - Written
  - Maintained at job site during construction and use

☐ **Shield(s) and other protection**

- Allowable design

- Manufacturer's design

- Other tabulated data
  - Identified parameters
  - Identified limits
  - Selection explanation

- Designed by registered professional engineer
  - Written
  - Maintained at job site during construction and use

☐ **Materials and equipment**

- No compromising damage or defects

- Consistent with manufacturer recommendations

Figure 12-3: Maximum Allowed Sloping

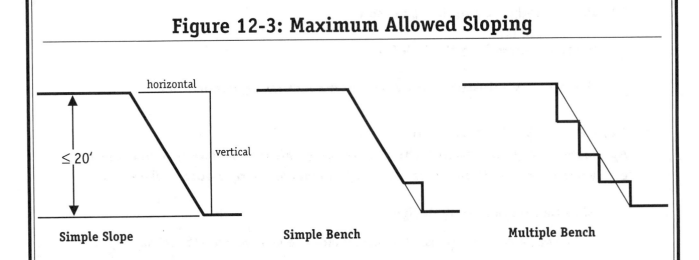

Soil or rock type	Sloping (horizontal : vertical) for excavations less than 20 feet deep
Stable rock	straight up or 90°
Type A soil	¾ : 1 or 53°
Type B soil	1 : 1 or 45°
Type C soil	1½ : 1 or 34°

Soil Definitions

Type A

Cohesive soils with an undisturbed, unconfined compressive strength of 1.5 tons per square foot or greater. Examples include clay, silty clay, sandy clay, clay loam, caliche, and hardpan). Exceptions are addressed in the other soil type definitions.

Type B

Cohesive soil with an unconfined compressive strength of greater than 0.5 and less than 1.5 tons per square foot; granular cohesionless soils; previously disturbed soil (unless the cohesion is less than 0.5 tons per square foot); Type A soils which are fissured or subject to vibration; and material that is part of a sloped layered system where the layers dip into the excavation on a slope less steep than four horizontal to one vertical within the cohesive soil requirements for Type B. Examples include crushed rock, silt, silt loam, and sandy loam.

Type C

Cohesive soil with an unconfined compressive strength of 0.5 tons per square foot or less; granule soils; submerged soil (e.g., soil with seeping water); unstable submerged rock; and material that is part of a sloped layered system where the layers dip into the excavation on a slope of four horizontal to one vertical or steeper. Examples include gravel, sand, loamy sand, and water saturated sandy clay.

☐ **Installation and removal**

- Secure connections

- Avoid cave-ins

- *Load limits posted*

- Backup precautions/supports

- Begin and progress from bottom of excavation

- Backfill immediately upon removal of supports

▶ **Employees not permitted to work above other employees**
Applicable on the faces of benched/sloped excavations and where the person in the hole is not adequately protected.

▶ **Proper shielding**
Applicable where lateral loading is protected by these "trench boxes."

▶ **Overall program effectiveness**

☐ **Employee understanding of procedures**

☐ **Employee compliance with procedures**

☐ **Lack of associated disease/illness**

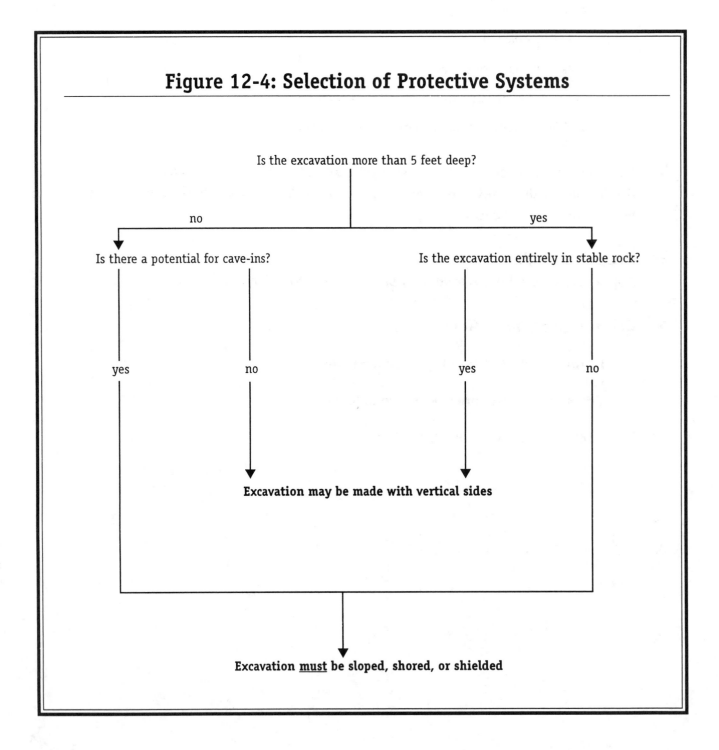

Figure 12-4: Selection of Protective Systems

Is the excavation more than 5 feet deep?

no | yes

Is there a potential for cave-ins? | Is the excavation entirely in stable rock?

yes | no | yes | no

Excavation may be made with vertical sides

Excavation <u>must</u> be sloped, shored, or shielded

Notes and special comments

_____

_____

_____

_____

_____

_____

_____

_____

_____

_____

_____

_____

_____

Score: _____

Fall Protection

Applicable to fall protection systems within construction where there is a potential for employ-ees to be injured from a fall greater than 6 feet above a lower level or from falling objects. Some of the activities which require fall protection include, but are not limited to, excavations, hoisting work, steel erection, leading edge work, bricklaying, precast concrete erection, roofing, work on scaffolds, and residential construction. 29 CFR 1926.502 and 1926.503

▶ **Guardrails**

☐ **Top edge 42 inches ± 3 inches above walking/working surface**
Where stilts are used, the top edge height shall include the height of the stilts.

☐ **Prevention of punctures, lacerations, or other injuries**

- Smooth rail surfaces

- Top rails and mid rails at least ¼ inch diameter or thickness

- Ends of top rails and mid rails not overhand

☐ **Intermediate structure members *(if no wall or parapet exists)* at least 21 inches high**

- Mid rails—midway

- Screens (or mesh)—entire opening

- Intermediate vertical members—no opening greater than 19 inches

- Other structural members less than 19 inches wide

Figure 13-1: Fall Protection Definitions

FALL PROTECTION SYSTEMS

- **Guardrail system:** a barrier erected to prevent employees from falling to lower levels.
- **Personal fall arrest system:** a system including, but not limited to, an anchorage, connectors, and a body harness used to stop an employee in a fall from a working level.
- **Positioning device system:** a body harness system rigged to allow an employee to be supported on an elevated vertical surface (e.g., a wall) and work with both hands free while leaning backwards.
- **Safety-monitoring system:** a safety system in which a competent person is responsible for recognizing and warning employees of fall hazards.
- **Safety net system:** system for installing safety nets below workers to break a fall or to catch falling objects.
- **Warning line system:** a barrier erected on a roof to warn employees that they are approaching an unprotected roof side or edge and to designate an area in which roofing work may take place without the use of a guardrail, body belt, or safety net system.

IMPORTANT TERMS

- **Anchorage:** a secure point of attachment for lifelines, lanyards, or deceleration devices.
- **Body harness:** straps that may be secured about the person in a manner that distributes the fall-arrest forces over at least the thighs, pelvis, waist, chest, and shoulders with a means for attaching the harness to other components of a personal fall arrest system.
- **Connector:** a device that is used to connect parts of a personal fall arrest system or positioning device system together.
- **Controlled access zone:** a work area designated and clearly marked in which certain types of work may take place without the use of conventional fall protection systems.
- **Deceleration device:** any mechanism which serves to dissipate a substantial amount of energy during a fall arrest, or otherwise limits the energy imposed on an employee during fall arrest.
- **Hole:** a void or gap 2 inches or more in the least dimension in a floor, roof, or other walking/working surface.
- **Lanyard:** a flexible line of rope, wire rope, or strap that generally has a connector at each end for connecting the body harness to a deceleration device, lifeline, or anchorage.
- **Leading edge:** the edge of a floor, roof, or formwork for a floor or other walking/working surface which changes location as additional floor, roof, decking, or formwork sections are placed, formed, or constructed.
- **Lifeline:** a component of a flexible line for connection to an anchorage at one end to stretch vertically or for connection to anchorages at both ends to stretch horizontally and that serves as a means for connecting other components of a personal fall arrest system to the anchorage.
- **Opening:** a gap or void 30 inches or more high and 18 inches or more wide in a wall or partition.

(continued on page 156)

☐ **Able to withstand force of 200 pounds within 2 inches of the top edge**

☐ **Handrails and top rails**

- No snags or exposed nails

- Hoisting area openings
  - Chain
  - Gate
  - Removable guardrail section

- Around openings in floors and holes in ground
  - Materials handling holes provided with no more than 2 sides
  - Not-in-use protection
    - ◆ Cover
      OR
    - ◆ Guardrail along all unprotected sides

- Precautions at access holes *(e.g., hole with ladder)*
  - Provided with a gate
  - Offset so a person cannot walk directly into the hole

- Erected along unprotected sides/edges of ramps and runways

- Plastic, synthetic, or manila rope used for top rails inspected routinely for continued strength

▶ **Safety net systems**

☐ **No more than 30 feet below walking/working surface(s)**

☐ **Adequate horizontal net coverage** *(See Table 13-1.)*

☐ **Adequate clearance below net to prevent contact with surface or structures below should the drop test force impact the net**

☐ **Drop test certification by employer**

- Method
  - A 400 pound bag, 29 to 32 inches in diameter
  - Dropped into net from highest walking/working surface
  - Not less than 42 inches above the highest level
  - If unreasonable to perform the test, the employer or a designated competent person may certify the installation

Figure 13-1 (cont'd): Fall Protection Definitions

- **Rope grab**: a deceleration device that travels on a lifeline and automatically, by friction, engages the lifeline and locks to arrest a fall.

- **Self-retracting lifeline/lanyard**: a deceleration device containing a drum-wound line which can be slowly extracted from, or retracted onto, the drum under minimal tension during normal employee movement and which, after onset of a fall, automatically locks the drum and arrests the fall.

- **Snap hook**: a connector consisting of a hook-shaped member with a normally closed keeper, or similar arrangement, which may be opened to permit the hook to receive an object and, when released, automatically closes to retain the object.

- **Toeboard**: a low protective barrier that prevents material and equipment from falling to lower levels and which protects personnel from falling.

- **Unprotected sides and edges**: any side or edge of a walking/working surface where there is no wall or guardrail system at least 39 inches high. This does not include entrances to points of access.

- **Walking/working surface**: any horizontal or vertical surface on which an employee walks or works including, but not limited to, floors, roofs, ramps, bridges, runways, formwork, and concrete reinforcing steel. Does not include ladders, vehicles, or trailers on which employees must be located to perform their work duties.

Table 13-1: Safety Net Coverage

Vertical Distance from Working Level to Horizontal Plane of Net	Minimum Required Horizontal Distance of Outer Edge of Net from the Edge of the Working Surface
Up to 5 feet	8 feet
Between 5 feet and 10 feet	10 feet
Greater than 10 feet	13 feet

- Frequency
  - After initial installation and before use
  - Whenever relocated
  - After a major repair
  - Every 6 months
- Certification record
  - Net identified
  - Type of installation
  - Date
  - Signature of competent person
  - Available at job site

☐ **Size of net openings and connections**

- At or less than 36 inches

- At or less than 6 inches on each side

☐ **Fallen items removed from net before end of work shift**

☐ **Border rope with at least 5,000 pounds breaking strength**

▶ **Personal fall arrest systems**
(e.g., safety body harnesses)

☐ **Steel connectors**

- Corrosion resistant finish

- Smooth edges

☐ **"D" rings and snap hooks**

- Minimum tensile strength: 5,000 pounds

- Minimum tensile load: 3,500 pounds proof tested

- Locking type snap hooks

- Work platforms with horizontal lifelines which may become vertical lifelines with snap hook(s) capable of locking in both directions

☐ **Horizontal lifelines with a safety factor of 2**

Figure 13-2: Personal Fall Arrest Systems
Exceptions to Lanyards and Vertical Lifelines

- Self-retracting lanyards and lifelines should automatically limit falls to 2 feet or less with minimum breaking strength of 3,000 pounds.

- Construction of elevator shafts should permit two persons per lifeline in the hoistway while working atop a false car that is equipped with guardrails and the lifeline strength is 10,000 pounds.

Figure 13-3: Personal Fall Arrest System Requirements

- Limit maximum arresting force on an employee to 1,800 pounds when used with body harness.

- Rigged so an employee cannot fall more than 6 feet or contact any lower level.

- Bring an employee to a complete stop and limit maximum deceleration distance an employee travels to 3.5 feet.

- Have sufficient strength to withstand 2 times the potential impact energy of an employee free falling a distance of 6 feet or the free fall distance permitted by the system, whichever is less.

- Not attached to guardrail systems or hoists.

- Rigged to allow movement only as far as the walking/working surface.

☐ **Lanyards and vertical lifelines**

- Minimum breaking strength of 5,000 pounds *(See Figure 13-2 for exception.)*

- Separate line for each person *(See Figure 13-2 for exception.)*

☐ **Lifelines protected from cutting and abrasion**

☐ **Ropes and straps made of synthetic fibers**

☐ **Anchorages**

- Independent of any anchorage being use to support or suspend platforms

- Support at least 5,000 pounds per employee attached or specially designed

☐ **Body harnesses only**

- Body belts prohibited as of January 1998

- Not used for hoisting materials

☐ **Inspection of system**

- Conducted by competent person after impact loading

- Prior to use
    □ Inspect for damage and deterioration
    □ Defective components decommissioned

▶ **Positioning device systems**

☐ **Rigged so person cannot fall more than 2 feet**

☐ **Secured to anchorage which is capable of supporting at least twice the potential impact load of an employee's fall or 3,000 pounds, whichever is greater**

☐ **Connectors**

- Steel

- Corrosion-resistant finish

- Surfaces and edges smooth

- Tensile strength of 5,000 pounds

Figure 13-4: Proper Placement of Warning Lines When Mechanical Equipment Is in Use

- At least 6 feet from roof edge which is parallel to the direction of the mechanical equipment operation

- At least 10 feet from the roof edge which is perpendicular to the direction of mechanical equipment operation

☐ **"D" rings and snap hooks**

- Minimum tensile strength 5,000 pounds

- Minimum tensile load 3,500 pounds proof tested

- Locking type snap hooks

- Work platforms with horizontal lifelines which may become vertical lifelines with snap hook(s) capable of locking in both directions

☐ **Inspected prior to use**

☐ **Not used for hoisting materials**

▶ **Warning line systems**
Typically used in roofing operations.

☐ **Around all sides of the roof work area**

☐ **Proper placement around mechanical equipment** (See Figure 13-4.)

☐ **Point(s) of access**

- Access path formed by two warning lines

- Barricaded when not in use

☐ **Ropes, wires, and chains**

- Flagged at more than 6 foot intervals with highly visible material

- Between 34 inches and 39 inches above the walking/working surface

- Capable of withstanding at least 16 pounds of force

- Minimum tensile strength of 500 pounds

☐ **Mechanical equipment stored within work area**

▶ **Controlled access zones**

☐ **Control line(s)**

- Define access zone

- May use other means to restrict access

Figure 13-5: Controlled Access Zone for Bricklaying

- Zone is defined by a control line erected between 10 to 15 feet from the working edge.

- Control line extends a sufficient distance for the controlled access zone to enclose all employees performing overhand bricklaying and related work at the working edge.

- Control line approximately parallel to the working edge.

- Zone is enclosed at each end.

- Only employees engaged in overhand bricklaying and related work are permitted in the area.

- Erected between 6 to 25 feet from unprotected or leading edge (**Exception**: *precast concrete members*)

- Precast concrete members: zones erected between 6 to 60 feet or half the length of the member being erected from the leading edge, whichever is less

- Must extend parallel along entire length of unprotected or leading edge

- Connected to guardrail or wall on each side

☐ **Ropes, wires, and chains**

- Flagged at more than 6 foot intervals with highly visible material

- Between 39 to 45 inches above the walking/working surface

- Minimum breaking strength at least 200 pounds

☐ **Area of inclusion**

- Where no guardrails exist

- Work area

- All points of access

- Material handling areas

- Storage areas

▶ **Safety monitoring systems**

☐ **Safety monitor requirements met** *(See Figure 13-6.)*

☐ **No mechanical equipment used or stored**

☐ **No employees allowed in area unless**

- Engaged in low-sloped roofing work *(at or less than 4° to 12° slope)*
  OR

- Employees are trained in Fall Protection Plan

▶ **Surface/ground covers**

☐ **Road covers capable of supporting twice maximum axle load of largest vehicle anticipated**

Figure 13-6: Safety Monitor Requirements

- Competent to recognize fall hazards.

- Warns each employee when it appears that employee is unaware of a fall hazard or is acting in an unsafe manner.

- Located on same walking/working surface and within sight of the employee being monitored.

- Close enough to communicate orally with the employees being monitored.

- No other responsibilities assigned to distract from the monitoring function.

☐ Floor, roof, walking/working surface covers capable of supporting at least twice the weight that may be imposed

☐ Properly secured to prevent accidental displacement

☐ Color coded or marked "HOLE" or "COVER"

▶ Protection from falling objects
By means of toeboards, guardrails, and procedures intended to minimize danger of falling objects.

▶ Fall protection plan
This is only required for contractors engaged in leading edge work, precast concrete erection work, and residential construction work and who can demonstrate that it is not feasible or creates a greater hazard to use conventional fall protection equipment.

☐ Prepared and implemented by a qualified person

☐ Written plan maintained at the job site

☐ Content of written plan

- Reasons that the use of conventional fall protection systems are not feasible or would create a greater hazard

- Discussion of other measures that will be taken to reduce or eliminate the fall hazard(s)

- Identification of "control access zone(s)" *(locations where conventional fall protection methods cannot be used)*

- Description of the safety monitoring system to be implemented

- List of employees designated to work in the control access zone(s)

☐ Specifically written for the job site where it is to be used

☐ Fall events and falling object incidents

- Investigated

- Changes in plan implemented as needed

Figure 13-7: Protection from Falling Objects in Special Cases

Toeboards

- Able to withstand a force of at least 50 pounds
- Minimum of 3½ inches vertical height from top edge to the level of the walking/working surface
- Solid or with openings not greater than 1 inch at greatest dimension

Overhand bricklaying and related work

- With the exception of masonry and mortar, no materials stored within 4 feet of working edge
- Routine removal of excess mortar, broken/scattered masonry units, and all other materials/debris

Roofing work

- Materials and equipment stored within 6 feet of roof edge (**Exception:** guardrails present)
- Materials piled, grouped, or stacked near roof edge shall be stable and self-supporting.

▶ Employee training

- ☐ **Content of training**

  - Nature of fall hazards

  - Correct procedures for erecting, maintaining, disassembling, and inspecting the fall protection systems

  - Use and operation of fall protection systems

  - Role of each employee
    - ▫ In the fall protection plan
    - ▫ In the safety monitoring system, if applicable

  - Limitations on the use of mechanical equipment

  - Procedures for handling and storing equipment and materials

  - Methods for erecting overhead protection

- ☐ **Certificate of training**

  - Employee's name

  - Date of training

  - Signature of trainer

- ☐ **Frequency**

  - Initial

  - Changes in the workplace

  - Changes in types of fall protection systems or equipment

  - Inadequate previous training

▶ Overall program effectiveness

- ☐ **Employee understanding of procedures**

- ☐ **Employee compliance with procedures**

- ☐ **Lack of associated incidents**

Figure 13-8: Sample Fall Protection Plan

SPECIFIC PROJECT: _____

Location: _____

Erecting Company: _____

Date Plan Prepared or Modified: _____

Plan Prepared by: _____

Plan Approved by: _____

Plan Supervised by: _____

Table of Contents

Section 1:   Statement of Company Policy

Section 2:   Fall Protection Systems to be Used on This Project

Section 3:   Implementation of Fall Protection

Section 4:   Conventional Fall Protection

Section 5:   Other Fall Protection Measures Considered for This Job

Section 6:   Changes to the Plan

Notes and special comments

_____

_____

_____

_____

_____

_____

_____

_____

_____

_____

_____

_____

_____

_____

_____

Score: _____

Section 14

Fire Protection and Prevention

Applicable to all construction activities, including the construction of new structures and renovation/demolition of old structures. The term "fire protection" refers to the provision on a job site for a means to respond to fire hazards without delay. "Fire prevention" is directed toward avoiding fires. It does not provide for a means whereby workers must respond to fires and other emergency situations. The latter is detailed within Section 10, "Emergency Action Plans." 29 CFR 1926.150 (protection), 1926.151 (prevention), and 1926.159 (fire alarms)

▶ **Fire protection program**
A written program recommended for construction and mandated for industry

☐ **Major workplace fire hazards**

- Proper handling and storage procedures

- Potential ignition sources *(e.g., welding sparks)*

- Fire prevention controls *(e.g., control sources of ignition, fuel, and oxygen)*

- Firefighting equipment and/or systems *(e.g., portable fire extinguishers)*

Figure 14-1: Sample Fire Prevention Plan for Industry

Table of Contents

☐ Housekeeping practices for controlling accumulations of flammable and combustible waste materials/residues *(e.g., housekeeping requirements)*

☐ Names/job titles of personnel responsible for maintenance of fire protection equipment and/or systems

☐ Names/job titles of personnel responsible for fire prevention controls

▶ **Fire fighting equipment**

☐ **Available at all times**

☐ **Conspicuously located**

☐ **Periodic inspection and maintenance checks**

- Date recorded
  - Within company files, or
  - Entered on an attached tag

- Records kept for at least one year after the last entry or the life of the shell, whichever is less

- Exempted stored pressure dry chemical extinguishers require checks every 6 years

☐ **Last hydrostatic testing within proper interval for the type of extinguisher being inspected**

- Performed by qualified personnel *(typically an outside contracting service)*

- Variable test intervals

- Whenever evidence of corrosion or mechanical injury appears

- Hose assemblies which are equipped with a shut-off nozzle at the discharge end of the hose

▶ **Fire brigade**
A fire brigade is an organized group of employees who are knowledgeable, trained, and skilled in at least basic fire fighting. This includes private fire departments and organized industrial fire respondents.

☐ **Assigned positions and responsibilities**

☐ **Initial training**

Figure 14-2: Major Causes of Fire and How to Deal with Them

Cigarettes, matches, and lighters

- If your company allows smoking in the workplace, smoke only where permitted. Do not flick ashes onto floors or into wastebaskets. Use large, non-tip ashtrays and make sure everything in them is cold before they are emptied.
- Ensure that visitors follow these same precautions and be sure no one leaves a smoldering cigarette on furniture or in a wastebasket.

Flammable liquids

- Comply with company rules for safe handling of flammable liquids.
- Ensure that there are no ignition sources within the vicinity of flammable liquids.

Electrical wiring

- Replace electrical cords which have cracked insulation or broken connectors.
- Never run extension cords across doorways or where they can be stepped on or chafed.
- Do not plug one extension cord into another and avoid plugging more than one extension cord into an outlet.
- Do not pinch electrical cords under or behind furniture.

Appliances

- Leave space for air to circulate around heaters and other heat-producing equipment such as copy machines and computer terminals.
- Keep appliances away from anything that might catch fire.
- Designate an employee to turn off or unplug all appliances—including coffee makers and hot plates—at the end of each work day.

Housekeeping

- Keep exits, storage areas, and stairways free of waste paper, empty boxes, dirty rags, and other fire hazards.

Arson and malicious mischief

- Adhere to your building's security measures and keep unauthorized people out.
- Keep doors locked after business hours.
- Alleys and other areas around your building should be well lit.
- Keep clutter out of halls, lobbies, alleys, and other public areas.

Gas fires and explosions

- Ensure that suspected gas leaks are checked immediately.
- Conduct routine checks for gases escaping from piping, storage tanks, and equipment.

▶ **Adequate water supplied for fire fighting**
Required under certain circumstances only

☐ **Where combustible materials are stored**

☐ **During construction of buildings** *(Underground water mains are installed, completed, and made available as soon as possible.)*

▶ **Portable fire fighting equipment**

☐ **Fire extinguishers and small hose lines**

- Appropriate type of fire extinguisher

- Appropriate number per area

- Within given travel distance limits

☐ **Fire hose connected and operable**
An installed fire hose may be used instead of fire extinguishers given the same area and travel distance coverage.

- At least 1½ inch diameter hose

- Nozzle capable of discharging water at 25 gallons per minute

- Hose line not greater than 100 feet in length

- Connections compatible with local firefighting equipment OR adaptor provided for hook-ups

☐ **Demolition involving combustible materials**

- Charged hose lines to hydrants

  OR

- Water tank trucks with pumps

  OR

- Alternative equivalent to one of the above

▶ **Fixed fire fighting equipment**

☐ **Construction**
(Automatic sprinkler systems are placed in service in a timely fashion.)

- As soon as permitted by applicable laws

- Upon completion of each building level

Table 14-1: Portable Fire Fighting Equipment Requirements

Type of Area Requiring Protection	Fire Extinguisher Rating	Extinguisher per Area	Minimum Travel Distance
Protected building area	≥ 2A[1]	3000 square feet	100 feet
Multistory building	≥ 2A[1]	each floor and adjacent to stairway	—
Greater than 5 gallons of flammable/combustible liquids OR more than 5 lbs. of flammable gases	≥ 10B[2]	—	50 feet
Yard area	≥ 2A[1]	—	100 feet

[1] May use one 55-gallon open drum of water with 2 fire pails instead of a 2A rating OR a ½ inch diameter garden-type hose equipped with a nozzle and a hose that does not exceed 100 feet in length and is capable of discharging at least 5 gallons/minute with a minimum hose stream range of 30 feet horizontally. The hose lines must be mounted on conventional racks or reels, and the number and location of the hose racks or reels at least one hose stream away from all points in the area.

[2] Not applicable to integral fuel tanks of motor vehicles.

SPECIAL PRECAUTIONS

Fire extinguishers must be suitable for the type of fire(s) that might occur.

Extinguishers and water drums shall be protected from freezing given foul weather conditions.

Carbon tetrachloride and other toxic vaporizing liquid fire extinguishers are prohibited.

☐ **Demolition**

(Automatic sprinkler systems remain in service as long as reasonably possible.)

☐ **Renovations and alterations**

- Automatic sprinkler systems which are undergoing modifications
  □ Returned to service as soon as possible
  □ Valves checked at close of each workday to assure the system is in service
- Standpipes, where required or pre-existing
  □ Returned to service as soon as possible
  □ Siamese fire department connections provided outside the structure at street level
  □ At least one hose outlet per floor

► Fire alarm system

☐ **Distinct** *(different alarms for different types of hazards)*

☐ **Audible**

(or visually perceptible where an audible alarm may not be heard over the ambient background noise)

☐ **Emergency reporting procedures**

- Employees properly trained
- Posted emergency telephone number(s) *(in conspicuous locations)*
- Method for emergency messages to receive priority over nonemergency messages

☐ **Serviced, maintained, and tested routinely**

- Performed by trained/knowledgeable individual
- Tests conducted at least every 2 months
- Multi-actuation device systems—test different actuation devices each test period
- Backup *(e.g., employee runners)* for periods when systems are out-of-service
- Maintain power supplies *(e.g., replace batteries)*
- Supervised
  □ Installed after January 1, 1981—assure supervision of the circuitry and notification of deficiencies
  □ Tested annually

Figure 14-3: Types of Fire Alarm Systems

- Voice communication (e.g., telephone)

- Visual signals (e.g., flashing lights)

- Tactile signals (e.g., vibrating devices)

- Audible (e.g., alarm bells and alert sounding devices)

Note: *Do not forget to take into account employees with vision and hearing impairments.*

Figure 14-4: List of Fire Cutoffs

- Fire walls

- Exit stairways

- Fire doors with automatic closing devices

☐ **Manually operated actuation devices**

- Unobstructed

- Conspicuous

- Readily accessible

☐ **Voice communication only**

▶ Fire cutoffs

☐ **Construction** *(Top priority given to cutoffs.)*

☐ **Renovation and demolition** *(Cutoffs retained as long as possible.)*

▶ Fire prevention procedures

☐ **Ignition hazard controls**

- Proper wiring and equipment for light, heat, and power

- Location of exhaust outlets for equipment operated by internal combustion engine

- "No Smoking or Open Flames" signs

- Portable battery powered lights around flammable gases and/or liquids—approved for hazardous locations

- Bonding to tanks and vessel shells that contain flammable gases or vapors
  - Nozzle or hoses to air, inert gas, and steam lines
  - During cleaning and/or ventilating activities
  - NOT ATTACHED OR DETACHED IN HAZARDOUS CONCENTRATIONS OF FLAMMABLE GASES OR VAPORS

☐ **Temporary buildings**

- Must not impact ability to exit an area

- Within another building or structure
  - Noncombustible construction
    OR
  - Fire resistance of not less than one hour

- Outside another building or structure
  - Greater than 10 feet from the nearest structure
  - Not used for hazardous materials storage or handling

Figure 14-5: Checklist of Fixed Extinguishing System Inspection and Maintenance Records

☑ **Refillable containers**

- Semiannual checks

- Maintenance and refill
  - If pressure loss was greater than 10 percent
  - If weight loss was greater than 5 percent

☑ **Containers without pressure gauges**

- Semiannual checks

- Maintenance and refill—if weight loss was greater than 5 percent

Figure 14-6: Acceptable Locations for Internal Combustion Engine Exhausts

- Away from combustible materials

- Exhausts piped outside building—at least 6 inches between pipe and combustible materials

☐ **Open yard storage**

- Free of accumulation of unnecessary combustible materials (*e.g., dry grass and paper*)
  - ▫ Weeds and grass periodically mowed or cleared
  - ▫ Periodic cleanups of area

- Combustible materials storage
  - ▫ No higher than 20 feet
  - ▫ Not within 10 feet of building or structure
  - ▫ Stable

- Driveways between and around combustible storage piles properly designed and maintained

- No flammable/combustible storage where danger of underground fires and/or explosions exists

☐ **Indoor storage**

- Must not impact ability to exit an area

- Arranged according to fire characteristics

- Incompatible materials separated by at least a one-hour fire-resistant barrier

- Storage piles
  - ▫ Minimized spread of fire
  - ▫ Permit convenient access
  - ▫ Stable
  - ▫ Aisles maintained to safely accommodate the widest vehicle to be used in the area for fire fighting

- Clearance from top of storage piles
  - ▫ At least 36 inches to the sprinkler deflectors
  - ▫ Not so close to lights and heating units so as to result in ignition of combustibles

- Clearance for fire doors
  - ▫ At least 24 inches around the path of door travel if there is no provision for barricade
  - ▫ Not stored within 36 inches of fire door opening

▶ Overall program effectiveness

☐ **Employee understanding of procedures**

☐ **Lack of associated mismanagement of incidents**

Figure 14-7: Proper Design and Maintenance of Driveways between and around Combustible Storage Areas

- At least 15 feet wide

- Free from rubbish, equipment, and other articles or materials

- Maximum grid system unit of 50 feet by 150 feet

Figure 14-8: Hazardous Materials Requiring Special Structures

- Flammable and combustible liquids

- Flammable gases

- Explosives

- Blasting agents

Notes and special comments

_____

_____

_____

_____

_____

_____

_____

_____

_____

_____

_____

_____

_____

_____

_____

_____

_____

Score: _____

Section 15

Flammable and Combustible Liquids

Applicable to occupational exposures in construction where there are flammable and/or combustible liquids in use and/or being stored. A flammable liquid is any liquid having a flash point below 100° F that makes up 99 percent or more of the total volume of a mixture. A combustible liquid is any liquid having a flash point at or above 100° F and at or below 200°F. Herein is a subsection on general procedures for portable containers/tanks and for container/ tank storage areas. Although most of the references are to construction, some of the more extensive industry requirements are deferred to for more concise direction. 29 CFR 1926.152.

General Procedures for Portable Containers and Tanks

This subsection applies to all cans, drums, and other containers which do not exceed the capacity of 60 gallons and all portable tanks which do not exceed the capacity of 660 gallons. Exceptions include: (1) storage containers in bulk plants, service stations, refineries, chemical plants, and distilleries; (2) Class I or II liquids in the fuel tanks of motor vehicles, aircraft, boats, or portable/stationary engines; (3) flammable/ combustible paints, oils, varnishes, and similar mixtures used for painting or maintenance when not kept for a period in excess of 30 days; and (4) beverages when packaged in individual containers not exceeding one gallon.

Table 15-1: Definition of Flammable and Combustible Liquids

Classes	Flash point range(s)	Boiling point range(s)
Flammable		
Class I liquids	<100°F	—
Class IA	<73°F	<100°F
Class IB	<73°F	≥100°F
Class IC	≥73°F	<100°F
Combustible		
Class II liquids	≥100°F and <140°F	>200°F
Class III liquids	≥140°F	—
Class IIIA	≥140°F and <200°F	—
Class IIIB	≥200°F	—

▶ **Proper container usage**

☐ **Container composition** *(e.g., glass or metal)*

☐ **Maximum container sizing requirements not exceeded** *(See Table 15-2.)*

☐ **Specially marked Class I flammable liquid containers**

- Painted red with yellow band around the container

  OR

  Name of contents stenciled or painted in yellow

- Properly identified

- Hazard warning(s)

☐ **Emergency venting system** *(e.g., spring-loaded safety can)*

▶ **Placement**

☐ **Not in aisles/walkways, at exits, and under stairways**

☐ **Away from sources of heat**

- Stoves

- Heated pipes

- Sun

☐ **Not stored in office spaces** *(except where there is maintenance being performed)*

☐ **Compliance with storage requirements for exceptions to office space storage of flammable/combustible liquids**

- Storage cabinets

- Safety cans

- Closable storage room

▶ **Transfer**

☐ **Transfer of more than 5 gallons of flammable/combustible liquids**

- Separation from other work activities
  - At least 25 feet
    OR
  - Fire resistance of at least one hour

Figure 15-1: Bonding and Grounding

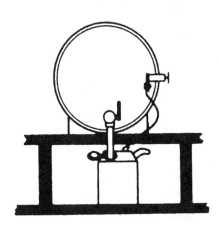 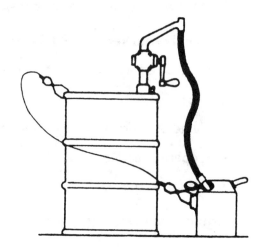

Bonding

Process of connecting two or more conductive objects together by means of a conductor so that they possess the same electrical potential. This is accomplished by connecting two objects by bonding wire or by maintaining direct contact between both objects at all times. They should also be grounded. Containers should be kept closed until after bonding has taken place, and bonding wires should not be disconnected until finished with chemical transference and closure of the containers.

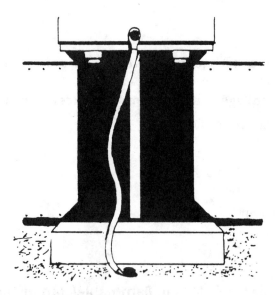

Grounding

Process of connecting one or more conductive objects to an electrical or earth ground so that electrical charges are allowed to dissipate. This is a means of "bonding" to the ground and may be accomplished by extending an insulated wire from the point of contact to the ground.

- Spill controls

- Adequate ventilation *(able to maintain airborne concentrations at or below 10 percent LEL)*

☐ **Dispensing units protected from collision**
(e.g., steel posts to prevent vehicles from accidentally running into the units)

☐ **Adequate transfer system(s)**

- Closed piping system

- Safety cans

- Device which draws through the top

- Gravity or pump with self-closing valve

- Air pressure prohibited

☐ **Bonding and grounding devices**

- Equipment available

- Properly used

☐ **Dispensing devices and nozzles approved for type of hazard**

☐ **"No Smoking" signs**

▶ **Handling procedures**

☐ **Containers kept closed until actually used**

☐ **No open flames or other sources of ignition within 50 feet**
(Conditions may warrant greater distances.)

▶ **Housekeeping**

☐ **Spills cleaned up promptly**

☐ **Unobstructed aisles**

☐ **Covered metal receptacles for waste and residue**

☐ **Daily disposal of contents of flammable/combustible waste receptacles**

☐ **No weeds, trash, and other debris**

Figure 15-2: Fire Safety Can

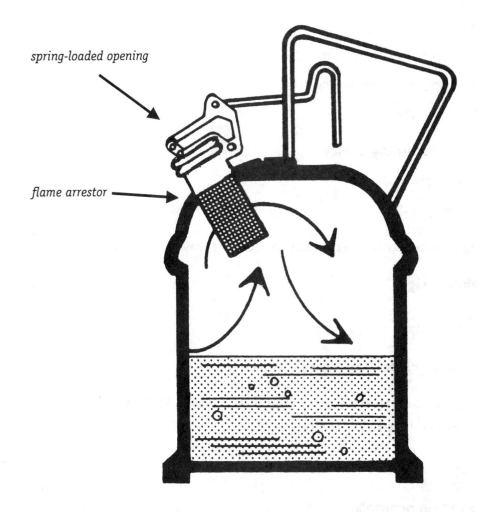

spring-loaded opening

flame arrestor

Spring-loaded covers are designed to open in order to relieve vapor pressure built up in the can, and the flame arrestor operates to cool hot air, keeping the vapor temperature below its flash point. Solvent compatibility with the can must also be considered, and the most commonly compatible material is stainless steel. However, compatibility charts should be referred to. For example, toluene is compatible with most all materials, including stainless steel, polyethylene, and galvanized steel. Cyclohexane is only compatible with galvanized steel, and cyclohexanone is only compatible with stainless steel.

▶ **Leak and spill controls**

☐ **Drainage, dikes, and berms**

☐ **Hazardous materials cleanup program**

☐ **Method for disposal of waste**

▶ **Integrity of containers/tanks**

☐ **Good condition**

☐ **Periodically inspected**

Container/Tank Storage Area(s)

This subsection applies to fire hazard controls in and around flammable/combustible storage areas and specific requirements for flammable storage cabinets, flammable/combustible storage inside buildings, flammable/combustible outdoor storage buildings, and nonstructure flammable/combustible storage areas.

▶ **Fire hazard controls**

☐ **Fire extinguishers**

- Storage buildings and rooms
  - At least one 20B fire extinguisher outside each entrance
  - Not more than 10 feet from the entrance(s) and/or area(s) where there is more than 60 gallons of flammable/ combustible liquids

- Outside storage area
  - At least one 20B fire extinguisher outside each entrance
  - Not less than 10 feet nor more than 25 feet from the storage area(s)

- Tank trucks and other vehicles used for transporting and/or dispensing *(at least one 20B-C fire extinguisher on the vehicle)*

☐ **Smoking prohibited** *(e.g., signs)*

☐ **No water reactive materials in vicinity** *(e.g., powered potassium)*

Table 15-2: Maximum Allowable Container Sizes

Container type	Flammable liquids			Combustible liquids	
	Class IA	Class IB	Class IC	Class II	Class III
Glass or approved plastic	1 pint	1 quart	1 gallon	1 gallon	1 gallon
Metal (other than DOT drums)	1 gallon	5 gallons	5 gallons	5 gallons	5 gallons
Safety cans	2 gallons	5 gallons	5 gallons	5 gallons	5 gallons

Metal drums (DOT drums) .... 60 gallons

Approved portable tanks .... 660 gallons

Note: Only approved metal safety cans for handling and use of flammable liquids in quantities greater than one gallon with the exception of hard-to-pour liquids which may be used and handled in their original containers.

Table 15-3: Quantities Permitted Outside Designated Storage Area

29 CFR 1910

Flammable/combustible substance	Maximum quantities allowed
Class IA liquids (in containers)	25 gallons
Class IB, IC, II, and III liquids (in containers)	120 gallons
Class IB, IC, II, and III liquids (single portable tank)	660 gallons

► **Flammable storage cabinets**

☐ **Capacity limitations not exceeded**

- Class I and Class II liquids—60 gallons per storage unit

- Class III liquids—120 gallons per storage unit

☐ **Fire retardant construction** *(e.g., metal cabinet with tight joints and seams)*

☐ **Vented according to manufacturer's directions**

☐ **Properly labeled** *(e.g., "FLAMMABLE—KEEP FIRE AWAY")*

► **Indoor storage rooms**

☐ **No more than 25 gallons stored outside a flammable storage cabinet**
(Exception: liquefied petroleum gas, 29 CFR 1926.153)

☐ **Fire resistant rating suitable for size and quantities stored** *(See Table 15-4.)*

☐ **Spark retardant electrical wiring and equipment** *(e.g., light fixtures)*

☐ **Proper ventilation of room**

- At least 6 room changes per hour

- Mechanical exhaust venting
  - Exhausting commences less than 12 inches above the floor
  - Air exhausted at rate of 6 room changes per hour
  - Control switch outside door
  - Venting equipment and lighting fixtures operated by same switch
  - Pilot light adjacent to venting equipment in room
    (if Class I flammable liquids are dispensed inside the room)

- Where gravity ventilation is provided—fresh air intake and exhaust to exterior of building

☐ **No containers over 30 gallons stacked upon one another**

☐ **One clear aisle at least 3 feet wide in each room**

☐ **No storage of materials which will react with water and create a fire hazard**

☐ **Vicinity of spraying operations**
(Quantity of flammable/combustible liquids not to exceed needs for one shift.)

Table 15-4: Indoor Storage Room Requirements and Limits

Fire protection required*	Fire resistance (hours)	Maximum size (square feet)	Allowable quantities (gallons/square feet per floor area)
yes	2	500	10
no	2	500	5
yes	1	150	4
no	1	150	2

* Fire protection system shall be sprinkler, water spray, carbon dioxide, or other.

Excerpted from 29 CFR 1926.152, Table F-2

Table 15-5: Outdoor Storage Area Limits and Requirements

29 CFR 1910

	Maximum per pile	Distance between piles	Distance to build line	Distance to street, alley, etc.
Portable Containers				
Class IA	1,100 gallons	5 feet	20 feet	10 feet
Class IB	2,200 gallons	5 feet	20 feet	10 feet
Class IC	4,400 gallons	5 feet	20 feet	10 feet
Class II	8,800 gallons	5 feet	10 feet	5 feet
Class III	22,000 gallons	5 feet	10 feet	5 feet
Portable Tanks				
Class IA	2,200 gallons	5 feet	20 feet	10 feet
Class IB	4,400 gallons	5 feet	20 feet	10 feet
Class IC	8,800 gallons	5 feet	20 feet	10 feet
Class II	17,600 gallons	5 feet	10 feet	5 feet
Class III	44,000 gallons	5 feet	10 feet	5 feet

Excerpted from 29 CFR 1910. 106, Tables H-16 AND H-17.

► **Outside storage building(s)**

☐ **Greater than 50 feet from an occupied building**

OR

☐ **Exposed wall with fire-resistance rating of at least 2 hours**

☐ **Portable tanks over one tier high**
- Secured
- Safely accessible

☐ **Storage area exterior**
- Graded to divert spills

  OR

- Surrounded by curb or dike
  □ At least 12 inches high
  □ Provision for draining accumulations of ground or rain water or spills of flammable/combustible liquids
  □ Drains terminate at safe location and accessible

☐ **Storage level limits observed**

☐ **Pile capacity restrictions observed**
- At least 3 feet below sprinkler deflectors
- At least 3 feet from nearest obstruction *(e.g., beam, chord, or girder)*
- Maximums per pile not exceeded
  □ Up to 1100 gallons in one pile or area
  □ Not more than 60 gallons per container
- Greater than 20 feet from a building
- Pile separations observed
  □ At least 5-foot-wide clearance between each pile or group
  □ At least 12-foot-wide access way within 200 feet of each pile of containers

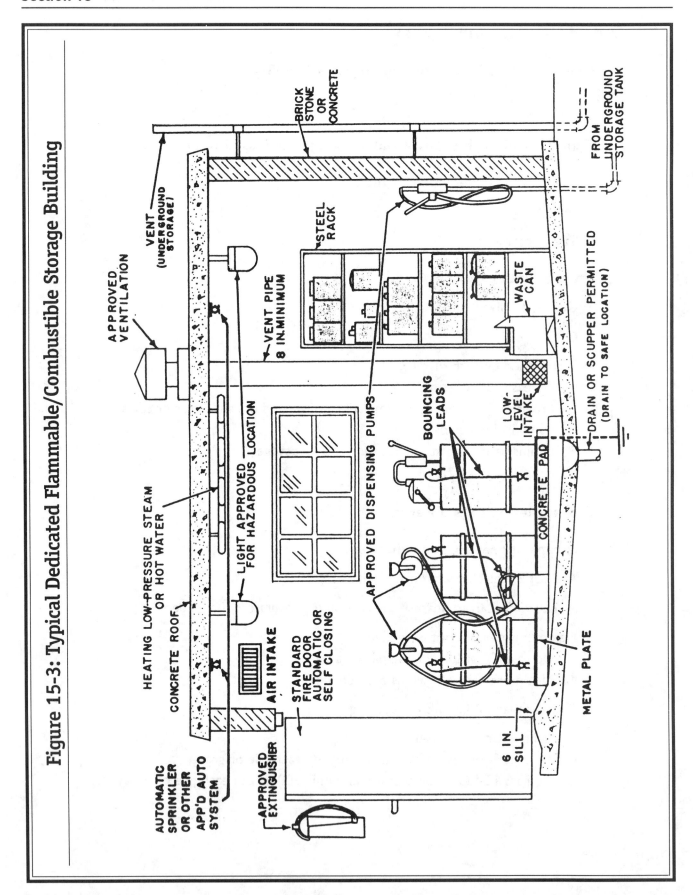

Figure 15-3: Typical Dedicated Flammable/Combustible Storage Building

☐ **Minimum 3-foot-wide aisles for access**

- Doors

- Windows

- Standpipe connections

▶ Outside storage area

☐ **Pile capacity restrictions observed**

- Minimum of 3 feet below sprinkler deflectors

- Minimum of 3 feet from nearest obstruction *(e.g., beam, chord, or girder)*

- Maximum gallons *(or drums)* per pile not exceeded *(See Table 15-5.)*

☐ **Minimum 3-foot-wide aisles for access**

- Doors

- Windows

- Standpipe connections

☐ **Proper distance to building line** *(See Table 15-5.)*

☐ **Proper distance to alley, street, etc.**

☐ **Secured against tampering or trespassing** *(e.g., locked within a fenced-in area)*

☐ **Spill containment measures**

- Grading

  OR

- Minimum 6-inch-high curbing

▶ Overall program effectiveness

☐ **Employee understanding of procedures**

☐ **Lack of associated incidents**

Figure 15-4: Fire Facts

According to the National Safety Council figures, losses due to workplace fires in 1991 totaled $2.2 billion. Of the 4,200 persons who lost their lives due to fires in 1991, the National Safety Council estimates 327 were workplace deaths. Fires and burns accounted for 3.3 percent of all occupational fatalities.

There is a long and tragic history of workplace fires in this country. One of the most notable was the fire at the Triangle Shirtwaist Factory in New York City in 1911 in which nearly 150 women and young girls died because of locked fire exits and inadequate fire extinguishing systems.

History repeated itself several years ago in the fire in Hamlet, North Carolina, where 25 workers died in a fire in a poultry processing plant. It appears that here, too, there were problems with fire exits and extinguishing systems. *

Fire-resistive structural components—materials which will not contribute fuel to a fire and will withstand most fires without structural failure. Examples include:

- Masonry load-bearing walls
- Reinforced concrete
- Protected steel columns
- Poured or precast concrete floors and roofs

Ignition sources for fires—sources of ignition which are known causes of fires are listed in order of frequency of occurrence. These include:

- Electrical (e.g., wiring and motors)
- Smoking
- Friction (e.g., poor adjustment of power drives)
- Overheated materials (e.g., high process temperatures)
- Hot surfaces (e.g., furnaces and electric lamps)
- Burner flames (e.g., ovens and dryers)
- Combustion sparks (e.g., fire boxes and industrial trucks)
- Spontaneous ignition (e.g., oily waste and deposits in dryers)
- Cutting and welding (e.g., arcs and hot metal)
- Open fires
- Arson
- Mechanical sparks (e.g., foreign metal in machines and grinding)
- Molten substances (e.g., ruptured furnaces)
- Chemically (e.g., decomposition of unstable chemicals)
- Static sparks (e.g., discharge of accumulated static electricity)
- Lightning

---

* *Workplace Fire Safety* [Fact Sheet #93-41], OSHA, U.S. Department of Labor, 1993.

Notes and special comments

_____

_____

_____

_____

_____

_____

_____

_____

_____

_____

_____

_____

_____

_____

_____

Score: _____

Hazard Communication Program

Applicable to construction environments where potentially hazardous chemicals are known to be present in the workplace. Where offices are maintained at the workplace, certain office supplies are also included in "chemicals known to be present in the workplace." 29 CFR 1926.59 (same as 29 CFR 1910.1200)

▶ **Written hazard communication program**

☐ List of all the hazardous materials in the workplace

☐ Procedures for proper labeling

☐ Location of material safety data sheets (MSDSs)

☐ Training requirements

☐ Identification method for hazards associated with unlabeled pipes

☐ Procedure for identification of hazards associated with nonroutine tasks

Figure 16-1: Sample Hazard Communication Program

Table of Contents

Figure 16-2: Sample Manufacturer's Label

LIQUID DETERGENT
HAZARD INFORMATION

NFPA HAZARD RATINGS - Toxicity: 0; Flammability: 0; Reactivity: 0

Excessive exposures, particularly through ingestion, may cause gastrointestinal disturbances. This product may also be slightly irritating to the nose, throat, lungs, and/or eyes. **CONTACT LENS USAGE SHOULD BE PROHIBITED.** WHEN IMMERSING HANDS IN THIS PRODUCT, THE USER SHOULD WEAR WATER-IMPERVIOUS GLOVES. WHERE SPLASHING MAY OCCUR, THE USER SHOULD WEAR CHEMICAL GOGGLES OR A FACE SHIELD.

First Aid

Ingestion: Drink large amounts of water and consult a physician.

Inhalation: Remove from the source of exposure.

Eyes: Flush with large amounts of water for 15 minutes.

Skin: Flush with large amounts of water.

DO NOT MIX OR STORE WITH ACIDS OR STRONG OXIDIZERS.

▶ Hazard communication training

☐ **Explanation of the standard**

- Federal standard

- In-house procedures
  - ▫ Location of MSDSs *(e.g., central to each work area)*
  - ▫ Training requirements and frequency

☐ **Finding and understanding MSDSs**

- In-house index system *(e.g., alphabetically by location)*

- How to read MSDSs

☐ **Potential chemical exposures in each work area**

- Trade name

- *In-house name—as referred to by the employees*

- Significant physical and health hazards associated with each

- Exposure control requirements
  - ▫ Engineering design *(e.g., local exhaust ventilation)*
  - ▫ Administrative controls *(e.g., reduced duration of exposure)*
  - ▫ Respiratory protection
  - ▫ Gloves
  - ▫ Body coverings
  - ▫ Eye protection

- Emergency practices

☐ **How to detect the release of hazardous chemicals**

- Odor

- Visual appearance *(e.g., fluorine gas is pale yellow)*

- Personal air monitoring

- Continuous monitoring devices

- Symptoms of exposure

Figure 16-3: Material Safety Data Sheet

TRADE NAME: **NFPA Codes:**

I. PRODUCT IDENTIFICATION

Manufacturer: Telephone: Emergency Phone:

Address: Chemical Name:

II. HAZARDOUS INGREDIENTS AND EXPOSURE LIMITS

III. PHYSICAL/CHEMICAL CHARACTERISTICS

Boiling Point: Specific Gravity:

Vapor Pressure: Melting Point:

Vapor Density: Evaporation Rate:

Solubility in Water:

Appearance and Odor:

IV. FIRE AND EXPLOSION HAZARDS

Flash Point: Flammable Limits:

Extinguishing Media:

Special Fire Fighting Procedures:

Unusual Fire and Explosion Hazard:

V. HEALTH HAZARDS

Routes of Entry:

Toxicity:

Symptoms of Overexposure:

First Aid Emergency Procedures:

Suspected Cancer Agent in Accordance with OSHA, IARC, or NTP   Yes ☐   No ☐

VI. REACTIVITY HAZARD DATA

Stability: Stable ☐ Unstable ☐

Conditions to Avoid:

Incompatibility:

Hazardous Decomposition Products:

Hazardous Polymerization: May Occur ☐   Will Not Occur ☐

VII. SPILL PRECAUTIONS AND WASTE DISPOSAL

Spill Response Procedures:

Waste Disposal Methods:

VIII. PROTECTIVE EQUIPMENT AND CONTROL MEASURES

Ventilation:

Respiratory Protection:

Protective Gloves:

Eye Protection:

Other Protective Equipment:

IX. ENVIRONMENTAL REGULATORY DATA

DOT -	TSCA -	CERCLA -
EPCRA -	SARA 302 & 304 -	RCRA -

X. SPECIAL PRECAUTIONS

☐ **Documentation**

- General records file

- Employees' personnel files
  - ▫ Proof of completion and date
  - ▫ Proof of understanding *(e.g., written statement or test)*

▶ **Properly labeled containers**

☐ **Designation of person(s) responsible**

- New shipments *(e.g., shipping and receiving)*

- In-house containers *(e.g., department heads)*

- Containers to be shipped *(e.g., shipping and receiving)*

☐ **Minimum information on in-house container(s)**

- Legible trade name or other form of identification

- Hazard warnings

☐ **Labels on portable containers**

- Legible

- Prominently displayed

☐ **Alternatives for stationary process containers**

- Placards

- Signs

- Process sheets

- Batch tickets

- Operating procedures

☐ **Same as names on the MSDSs**

☐ **Routine audits**

Figure 16-4: Summary of Responsibilities

Trainer(s)

Departments/Job Descriptions Requiring Training

Responsible for Maintaining MSDSs

Responsible for Proper Labels

Responsible for Overall Program

▶ **Maintenance and review of MSDSs**

☐ **Delineation of person(s) responsible**

• First time shipments

• Updates

☐ **Routine audits**

Frequency: _____

▶ **Overall program effectiveness**

☐ **Employee understanding of program**

☐ **Employee compliance with program**

☐ **Lack of associated accidents**

Notes and special comments

_____

_____

_____

_____

_____

_____

_____

_____

_____

_____

_____

Score: _____

Hazardous Waste and Emergency Response Activities

The Hazardous Waste Operations and Emergency Response standard (HAZWOPER) is applicable to cleanup of uncontrolled hazardous waste sites and the investigations thereof when the presence of hazardous substances has been ascertained (state and federal National Priority List sites and those recommended for the federal listing). It is also applicable to corrective actions involving cleanup of RCRA sites; voluntary cleanup operations of uncontrolled hazardous waste sites; operations involving hazardous wastes that are conducted at treatment, storage, and disposal facilities; and emergency response operations for releases, or substantial threats of releases, of hazardous substances without regard to the location. 29 CFR 1926.65

General Requirements

(**Exception**: Not all components of the General Requirements subsection are required of treatment, storage, and disposal sites. There is a separate subsection for these sites: RCRA Site Requirements, p. 231.)

Figure 17-1: Sample General Safety and Health Plan

Table of Contents

▶ Written safety and health plan

☐ **General contents**

- Organizational structure
- Comprehensive work plan
- Site-specific safety and health plan
- Safety and health training program
- Standard operating procedures for safety and health
- Training program—safety and health
- Medical surveillance program
- Interface with site-specific activities—as needed

☐ **Periodically updated**

☐ **Workplace accessibility of written document**

☐ **Method for informing contractors and subcontractors of hazards and in-house procedures**

☐ **Site excavation procedures** *(where applicable)*

▶ Organizational structure
Line(s) of authority, responsibility, and communication.

☐ **General supervisor**

☐ **Site safety and health supervisor**

☐ **Job functions and responsibilities of other personnel**

☐ **Current information**

▶ Comprehensive work plan
Tasks and objectives of the site operations and the logistics/resources required to reach those tasks and objectives.

☐ **Anticipated cleanup activities and operating procedures**

☐ **Work tasks and objectives**

☐ **Means for performing work tasks and objectives**

Figure 17-2: Types of Hazardous Substance Risks

- Toxic chemical exposures exceeding the permissible exposure limits and other published exposure limits

- Anticipated potential of chemical exposures which may be immediately dangerous to life and health concentrations (IDLH)

- Chemicals which may pose a potential for skin absorption and/or irritation

- Chemicals which may potentially cause eye damage or severe eye irritation

- Substances which are explosion sensitive

- Substances which are highly flammable

- Oxygen-deficient environments

☐ **Personnel requirements**

☐ **Worker training requirements**

☐ **Information program**

☐ **Implementation procedures for medical surveillance program**

☐ **Means for implementing informal programs to inform outside employees, contractors, and subcontractors likely to be exposed to hazardous wastes**

▶ **Site-specific safety and health program**
Required for each unique, separate site task and operation, this plan is based on the "site characterization and analysis" for each specific site.

☐ **Pre-entry briefing(s) provision**

☐ **Safety and health risks and/or hazard analyses**

- Identify type of hazard
- Determine quantity of hazardous substance(s)
- Identify defined health hazards
- Identify chemical and physical properties

☐ **Employee training assignments**

☐ **Personal protective equipment requirements**

- Assignment of appropriate equipment
- Emergency backup equipment *(e.g., minimum 5-minute escape self-contained breathing apparatus)*
- If there is insufficient information on initial evaluation, minimum required protection is Level B protection and a direct reading instrument

☐ **Medical surveillance requirements**

☐ **Exposure monitoring requirements**

- Frequency
- Type(s)
- Methods
- Equipment

Figure 17-3: Example of Posted Phone Numbers

— EMERGENCIES —

Ambulance 911

Doctor 703-666-9000

Minor Emergency Center 703-666-9001

Hospital 703-666-9003

Fire Department 911

Police 911

Sheriff 703-666-9007

Regional Poison Control Center 911

U.S. EPA (24-hour hotline) 800/424-8802

Chemtrec (chemical transportation emergencies) 800/424-9300

— UTILITIES —

Electric Company 703-666-1000

Water Company 703-666-1001

Gas Company 703-555-1003

☐ **Site information and controls**
Developed during the planning stages of hazardous waste cleanup operations.

- Site map

- Site work zones

- A "buddy system" approach

- Communication system

- Emergency alert system

- Standard work practices

- Identification of nearest medical facility

  ▫ *Name*

  ▫ *Location*

  ▫ *Phone number*

- Pre-emergency coordination with outside emergency response organization (*e.g., fire departments and emergency medical services*)

☐ **Decontamination procedures**

☐ **Emergency response plan**

☐ *Alert system*

- *Proper alarm system*

- *Location of the emergency*

- *Type of emergency*

- *Direction of evacuation*

- *Special escape equipment*

☐ **Confined space entry procedures**

☐ **Spill containment program**

☐ **Plan effectiveness routinely evaluated and plan updated by the designated safety and health person**

Figure 17-4: Written Program Requirements

	General	RCRA Sites	Hazardous Substance Releases
Similar to the General Requirements			
Written Hazard Communication Program	X	X	X
Medical Surveillance Program	X	X	X
Decontamination Program	X	X	—
New Technology Procedures	X	X	—
Site Characterization and Analysis	X	(as appropriate)	—
Different Details for Each Response Type			
Written Safety and Health Program	X	X	—
Emergency Response Program	X	X	X
Training Program	X	X	X
Materials Handling Procedures	X	X	X
Handling Emergency Incidents	—	X	—

▶ Standard operating procedures

☐ **Engineering controls** *(e.g., remotely operated material handling equipment)*

☐ **Work practices** *(e.g., wetting down dusty operations and locating employees upwind of possible hazards)* *May include conduct during weather extremes, biological hazards (e.g., snakes), and other issues which may pose a threat to the health and safety of the workers.*

☐ **Special protective equipment**

- Respiratory protection

- Body protection *(e.g., wherever hazardous substances may be absorbed by the skin and result in a substantial possibility of immediate death, immediate serious illness or injury, or impaired ability to escape)*
  - ▫ Substance-specific for hazards identified during site characterization and analysis
  - ▫ Positive air pressure in suits
  - ▫ Capable of preventing inward test gas leakage of more than 0.5 percent

- *Hand protection*

- *Foot protection*

- *Head protection*

- *Hearing protection*

▶ Training program
All management, supervisors, and employees on site who are potentially exposed to hazardous substances and/or health and safety hazards.

☐ **Content of classroom training**

- Names of personnel and alternates responsible for site safety and health

- Hazard identification

- Risk minimization practices

- Safe use of engineering controls and equipment

- Personal protective equipment

- Medical surveillance requirements

- Sections of the Site Safety and Health Plan
  - ▫ Decontamination procedures
  - ▫ Emergency response plan
  - ▫ Confined space entry procedures
  - ▫ Spill containment program

Figure 17-5: Training Requirements for Onsite Emergency Responders

Job function	Training required
General site workers (e.g., general laborers and equipment operators where there is an excessive exposure potential)	40 hours of classroom training 3 days of field training Annual refresher
Occasional workers (e.g., limited tasks such as groundwater monitor where there is minimal exposure potential)	24 hours of classroom training 1 day of field training Annual refresher
Minimal exposure workers (e.g., general laborers and equipment operators where there is minimal exposure potential)	24 hours of classroom training 1 day of field training Annual refresher
General site management and supervisors (e.g., on-site management where there is an excessive exposure potential)	40 hours of classroom training 3 days of field training 8 hours specialized training Annual refresher
Minimal exposure management and supervisors (e.g., on-site management where there is a minimal exposure potential)	24 hours of classroom training 3 days of field training 8 hours specialized training Annual refresher

☐ **Field experience under trained, experienced supervisor**

☐ **Training records**

- Certification of training
  - ▫ Trainer or head instructor
  - ▫ Field training supervisor

- Accessible written training materials *(if training is performed in-house)*

- Appropriate number of training hours for the job *(e.g., 40 hours offsite training and 3 days on-the-job training for site workers)*

- Frequency of training
  - ▫ Initial
  - ▫ Annual refresher

► **Medical surveillance program**

☐ **All applicable employees are covered**

☐ **Frequency**

- Initial

- Annual

- Upon termination

- Development of signs or symptoms

- Special circumstances

☐ **Records of medical examinations**

- Information provided to physician by employer
  - ▫ Employee's duties
  - ▫ Employee's known or anticipated exposure levels
  - ▫ Description of personal protective equipment to be used
  - ▫ Information from previous medical examinations

- Each employee's name and social security number

- Physician's written opinion, recommended limitations, and results of examinations and tests

- Any employee medical statements related to hazardous substance exposures

- *Signature indicating review completed by supervisor*

Figure 17-6: Employees Affected by Medical Surveillance Program

- All workers potentially exposed for 30 days or more per year

- All workers exposed to hazardous substances or health hazards at or above the exposure limits for 30 days or more

- Those required to wear a respirator for 30 days or more per year

- Those who become injured, ill, or develop signs or symptoms due to possible overexposure

- All members of a HAZMAT team

► ## Site characterization and analysis
Required to identify specific site hazards and determine the appropriate safety and health controls needed to protect the workers.

☐ **Preliminary evaluation**

☐ **Hazardous substances identified**

- Identification

- Associated health hazards

- Chemical and physical properties

☐ **Required site information**

- Location of site

- Size of the site

- Site topography *(if applicable)*

- Safety and health hazards anticipated

- Site accessibility by roads and air

- Pathways for hazardous substance dispersion

- Present status and capabilities of emergency responders

- Response activity and/or job task
  - Description of activities/job tasks
  - Duration of planned activities/job tasks

- Hazardous substances and health hazards anticipated at the site—physical and chemical properties

☐ **Personal protective equipment for initial entry**

- Based on preliminary evaluation

- Level B equipment, if uncertain

- Maintain backup of 5-minute escape, self-contained breathing apparatus
  - If evaluation indicates a potential exposure hazard
  - If a positive pressure self-contained breathing apparatus is not used

☐ **Exposure monitoring for initial entry**

- Direct reading equipment

- Observations

☐ **Risk determination of identified hazardous substance and health hazards**

Figure 17-7: Level B Equipment Checklist

Level B requires the highest level of respiratory protection but a lesser level of skin protection than that required for Level A.

☐ Pressure-demand, full-facepiece, self-contained breathing (SCBA) apparatus or pressure-demand supplied air respirator with escape SCBA

☐ Hooded chemical-resistant clothing

☐ Outer and inner chemical-resistant gloves

☐ Chemical-resistant, steel toe and shank boots

☐ Hard hat

☐ Two-way radio

☐ Optional gear

Figure 17-8: Hazards Which Require Exposure Monitoring

- Ionizing radiation

- Immediate dangers to life and health

- Oxygen deficiency

- Combustible or explosive atmospheres

- High levels of extremely toxic substances

- *Heat stress*

► **Personal protective equipment program**
May be included in the Safety and Health Program.

☐ **Selection**

☐ **Use and limitations**

☐ **Durability**

☐ **Maintenance and storage**

☐ **Decontamination and disposal**

☐ **Training and proper fitting**

☐ **Donning and doffing procedures**

☐ **Inspection procedures**

☐ **Limitations during temperature extremes and other appropriate medical considerations**

☐ **Method for evaluating the effectiveness of the program**

► **Exposure monitoring**
Air monitoring shall be performed to identify and quantify airborne exposures to hazardous substances and safety and health hazards to determine the proper protection needed.

☐ **Adequate frequency and type of monitoring**

- Initial
  - Identify conditions immediately dangerous to life and health
  - Identify exposures over permissible *(or published)* exposure limits
  - Identify excessive radioactive levels
  - Identify dangerous conditions *(e.g., oxygen deficiency or flammable atmospheres)*

- Periodic—whenever there is an indication that exposures may have increased
  - Different portion of the site
  - Not previously monitored exposures
  - Different activity initiated
  - Activities involving increased exposure risks *(e.g., handling leaking drums)*

- If exposures exceed the acceptable limits when commencing the cleanup phase, "high risk employee" monitoring should be performed often enough to characterize each employee's exposure level.

Figure 17-9: Special Handling Precautions

Shock Sensitive Waste

All drums/containers holding packaged laboratory wastes shall be considered shock-sensitive or explosive until they have been characterized otherwise.

- Evacuate all nonessential employees.

- Material handling equipment provided with explosive containment devices or protective shields.

- Continuous use of employee alarm system capable of being recognized above surrounding light and/or noise conditions for the duration of the handling activities.

- Continuous communication between handling team and the site safety and health supervisor and command post.

- Bulging and swelling drums/containers shall not be moved until the cause for excess pressure is determined and appropriate containment procedures have been implemented to protect employees from an explosive relief which may result when opening/penetrating the drum/container.

CAUTION: Shock sensitive wastes may be prohibited under the U.S. Department of Transportation regulations. See 49 CFR 173.21.

Opening Drums and Containers

- Where airline respirator system is used, source of air shall be protected from contamination and the entire system protected from physical damage.

- Nonessential employees shall be kept at a safe distance.

- Suitable shield that does not interfere with the work operation shall be placed between the employee and a drum/container being opened.

- Controls for drum or container equipment used during opening, monitoring, and fire suppression shall be located behind the explosion-resistant barrier.

- When there is a reasonable possibility of flammable atmospheres, material-handling equipment and hand tools shall be nonsparking.

- Drums/containers shall be opened so that excess interior pressure will be relieved at a remote location or beyond a shield.

- Employees shall neither stand on nor work on drums/containers.

Laboratory Waste Packs

- These shall be opened only when necessary and by an individual knowledgeable in the inspection, classification, and segregation of containers within the pack.

- If crystalline material is noted on any container, the contents shall be handled as shock-sensitive waste until proven otherwise.

▶ ## Materials handling program

Applicable to the management of all hazardous substances and contaminated soils, liquids, and other residues to be contained in drums/containers.

- ☐ **Comply with DOT, OSHA, and EPA labeling and handling requirements**

- ☐ **Drums and containers routinely inspected for integrity**

- ☐ **Sites organized to minimize amount of drum/container movement**

- ☐ **Transfer personnel warned of potential hazards of each drum/container**

- ☐ **Unlabeled drums and containers handled as hazardous material until identification and labeling has been completed**

- ☐ **DOT salvage drums or containers and absorbent available in case of spills, leaks, or ruptures**

- ☐ **Spill containment program**

- ☐ **Drums/containers unable to be moved without rupture, leakage, or spillage are transferred to an appropriate container**

- ☐ **Method for handling covered/buried drums and containers**
  - Ground-penetrating system (or other detection device) to estimate location and depth
  - Use of caution when removing soil or other covering material

- ☐ **Fire extinguishers available**

- ☐ **Drum and container opening procedures**

- ☐ **Material handling equipment methods to minimize sources of ignition**

- ☐ **Radioactive wastes assessed prior to handling**

- ☐ **Special precautions and shipping procedures for "shock sensitive wastes"**

- ☐ **Special laboratory waste handling procedures**

- ☐ **Drum/container staging areas for purposes of identification and classification**
  - Kept to a minimum number
  - Adequate access and egress routes

Figure 17-10: Hazardous Materials/Waste Transportation Checklist

☑ **Shipping information**

- Proper shipping name
  Based on listings provided by DOT in the Hazardous Materials Table (49 CFR 172.101).

- Hazard class

- Identification number
  Must correspond to the proper shipping name and hazard class.

☑ **Shipping label(s) on container(s)**

☑ **Packaging**

- Within volume and weight limitations for mode of transport

- DOT and EPA markings

☑ **Placard(s)**

☑ **Shipping documentation (e.g., manifest)**

Figure 17-11: Toilet Facility Requirements*

Number of employees	Minimum number of facilities
≤ 20	One (1)
>20 and ≤ 200	One (1) toilet seat and 1 urinal/40 employees
>200	One toilet seat and 1 urinal/50 employees

* Excerpted from Table D-65.2

☐ Characterization performed prior to bulking

☐ Identification and classification performed prior to packaging for shipment

▶ **Decontamination practices**
Practices will vary and are to be specified for each site within the site-specific health and safety plan.

☐ **Written procedures**

☐ **Monitored for effectiveness**

☐ **Located to minimize exposure to other employees and/or equipment**
(e.g., site diagram)

☐ **Supplies and equipment decontamination procedures**

☐ **Waste water and solvent disposal procedures**

☐ **Procedures detailed for decontamination of protective equipment**

☐ **Notification of laundry and cleaners as to the potential exposure hazards**
(where applicable)

☐ **Showers and change rooms**

▶ **Proper sanitation**

☐ **Potable and nonpotable water**

☐ **Toilets**

☐ **Food handling**

☐ **Washing facilities**

☐ **Showers and change rooms**

▶ **Proper illumination**

Figure 17-12: Minimum Illumination Intensities*

Footcandles	Area or operation(s)
5	General area
3	Excavation and waste areas, access ways, active storage areas, loading platforms, refueling, and field maintenance areas
5	Indoors: warehouses, corridors, hallways, and exit ways
5	Tunnels, shafts, and general underground work areas (exception: minimum of 10 footcandles is required at tunnel and shaft heading during drilling, mucking, and scaling. Mine Safety and Health Administration approved cap lights shall be acceptable for use in the tunnel heading)
10	General shops (e.g., mechanical and electrical equipment rooms, active storerooms, barracks or living quarters, locker or dressing rooms, dining areas, and indoor toilets and workrooms)
30	First aid stations, infirmaries, and offices

* Excerpted from Table D-65.1

► **Emergency response program**

An emergency response program or emergency action plan is required as part of the site specific safety and health program. Where employees are to be evacuated and not assist in the handling of an emergency, an emergency action plan may be provided. For details, see Section 10, "Emergency Action Plan."

☐ **Workplace accessibility of written plan**

☐ **General contents of plan**

- Pre-emergency planning

- Roles, lines of authority, training, and communication

- Emergency recognition and prevention

- Safe distances and places of refuge

- Site security and control

- Evacuation routes and procedures

- Emergency equipment

- Decontamination procedures *(which are not covered in the site safety and health plan)*

- Emergency medical treatment and first aid

- Emergency alerting and response procedures

- Critique of response and follow-up

- Personal protective equipment

☐ **Procedures for handling emergency incidents**

- Site information
  - Topography
  - Site layout
  - Prevailing weather conditions

- Procedures for reporting incidents to local, state, and federal agencies

☐ **Plan compatible with disaster, fire, and/or emergency response plans of local, state, and federal agencies**

☐ **Routine drills**

☐ **Plans reviewed periodically**

Figure 17-13: Procedures for Handling Emergency Response Activities at Treatment, Storage, and Disposal Facilities

Senior emergency response person (may change with arrival of others at the site)

- Center for communications
- Identify hazardous substances and/or conditions
- Implement appropriate emergency activities
- Ensure that personal protective equipment is appropriate for hazards to be encountered
- Designate a safety official
- Limit the number of response personnel
- Ensure the use of the buddy system
- Ensure that emergency response team is decontaminated upon completion of response activities

Safety official

- May alter, suspend, or terminate activities when the activities are judged to be immediately dangerous to life and health and/or to involve an imminent danger
- Keep the senior emergency response person informed of all activities

Emergency response team

- Where hazard(s) involve potential or known inhalation of hazardous substances, team must wear a positive pressure self-contained breathing apparatus until told otherwise by senior emergency response person
- Decontamination upon completion of response activities

Backup emergency response personnel

- Emergency response personnel must be on standby, ready to provide assistance or rescue
- First aid support personnel with medical equipment and transportation capabilities

Skilled support personnel (e.g., heavy equipment operators) not trained in emergency response procedures must be briefed on site prior to participation

Procedures for reporting incidents to local, state, and federal agencies

☐ **Emergency alarm system**

- Effective

- Employees trained

▶ **New technology program**

☐ **Method developed whereby new technologies, equipment, and control measures may be evaluated by the employer or employer's designated representative prior to introduction to the workplace**

☐ **Verification that the procedures are being implemented**

RCRA Site Requirements

(Hazardous waste operations that are conducted at treatment, storage, and disposal sites)

▶ **Written safety and health program**

☐ **Emergency response plan**

☐ **Site analysis**

☐ **Engineering controls**

☐ **Maximum exposure limits**

☐ **Hazardous waste handling procedures**

☐ **Uses of new technology**

▶ **Written hazard communication program**
See details in Section 16, "Hazard Communication Program."

▶ **Medical surveillance program**
See details under "General Requirements" at the beginning of Section 17.

▶ **Decontamination program**
See details under "General Requirements."

Figure 17-14: Abbreviated Definitions

Buddy System: A system of organizing employees into work groups of two or three personnel for the purpose of providing rapid assistance to one another in an emergency.

Cleanup Operation: An operation where hazardous substances are removed, contained, incinerated, neutralized, stabilized, cleared from the area, or in some manner processed/handled with the ultimate goal of making the site safer for people or the environment.

Decontamination: The removal of hazardous substances from employees and their equipment.

Emergency Response: A response effort by employees from outside the immediate release area or by designated responders (e.g., fire departments) to an occurrence which results, or is likely to result, in an uncontrolled release of a hazardous substance.

Facility: Any building, structure, installation, equipment, pipe or pipeline, well, pit, pond, lagoon, impoundment, ditch, storage container, motor vehicle, rolling stock, or aircraft. May also refer to any site or area where a hazardous substance has been deposited, stored, disposed of, placed, or come to be located. The term does not include any consumer product in consumer use or any waterborne vessel.

Hazardous Materials Response Team (HAZMAT): An organized group of employees, designated to perform work to handle and control actual or potential leaks or spills of hazardous substances requiring proximity to the hazard.

Hazardous Substance: Any substance designated or listed under CERCLA, any biological agent or other disease-causing agent which may cause health effects, any substance designated as hazardous by the U.S. Department of Transportation, and any hazardous waste. (Defined in 40 CFR 261.3 or 49 CFR 171.8.)

Hazardous Waste Site: Any facility or location at which hazardous waste operations take place.

Health Hazard: A chemical, mixture of chemicals, or a pathogen for which there is statistically significant evidence, based on at least one study conducted in accordance with scientific principles, that acute or chronic health effects may occur in exposed employees. This includes chemicals, biological agents, and heat stress.

Published Exposure Levels: Exposure limits published by NIOSH or the ACGIH.

Post Emergency Response: That part of an emergency response which is performed after the immediate threat of a release has been stabilized or eliminated and cleanup of the site has begun.

Qualified Person: A person who has specific training, knowledge, and experience in the area for which he/she has the responsibility and the authority to control.

▶ **New technology program**
See details under "General Requirements."

▶ **Materials handling program**
Applicable to the management of all hazardous substances and contaminated soils, liquids, and other residues to be contained in drums/containers.

- ☐ **Comply with DOT, OSHA, and EPA labeling and handling requirements**

- ☐ **Drums and containers routinely inspected for integrity**

- ☐ **Sites organized to minimize amount of drum/container movement**

- ☐ **Transfer personnel warned of potential hazards of each drum/container**

- ☐ **Unlabeled drums and containers handled as hazardous material until identification and labeling has been completed**

- ☐ **DOT salvage drums or containers and absorbent available in case of spills, leaks, or ruptures**

- ☐ **Spill containment program**

- ☐ **Method for handling buried/covered drums and containers**
  - Ground-penetrating system (or other detection device) to estimate location and depth
  - Use of caution when removing soil or other covering material

- ☐ **Material handling equipment methods to minimize sources of ignition**

- ☐ **Drum/container staging areas for purposes of identification and classification**
  - Kept to a minimum number
  - Adequate access and egress routes

- ☐ **Characterization performed prior to bulking**

- ☐ **Identification and classification performed prior to packaging for shipment**

Figure 17-15: Checklist for an Emergency Response Program

☐ **Written plan**

- Pre-emergency planning
- Roles, lines of authority, training, and means for communication
- Emergency recognition and prevention
- Safe distances and places of refuge
- Site security and control
- Evacuation routes and procedures
- Emergency equipment
- Decontamination procedures (not covered in the site safety and health plan)
- Emergency medical treatment and first aid
- Emergency alerting and response procedures
- Critique of response and follow-up
- Personal protective equipment

☐ **Procedures for handling emergency incidents**

- Site information
- Procedures for reporting incidents to local, state, and federal agencies

☐ **Plan compatible with disaster, fire, and/or emergency response plans of local, state, and federal agencies**

☐ **Routine drills**

☐ **Plans reviewed periodically**

☐ **Emergency alarm system**

- Effective
- Employees trained

► **Emergency response program**

An emergency response program or emergency action plan is required as part of the site-specific safety and health program. Where employees are to be evacuated and not assist in the handling of an emergency, an emergency action plan may be provided. For details, see Section 10, "Emergency Action Plan."

- ☐ **Workplace accessibility of written plan**

- ☐ **General contents of plan**
  See details under "General Requirements" at the beginning of Section 17.

► **Procedures for handling emergency incidents**

Contained within the emergency response plan wherever information is not being repeated in the plan.

- ☐ **Site topography and layout**

- ☐ **Prevailing weather conditions**

- ☐ **Procedures for reporting incidents to local, state, and federal agencies**

- ☐ **Plan compatible with disaster, fire, and/or emergency response plans of local, state, and federal agencies**

- ☐ **Routine drills**

- ☐ **Plans reviewed periodically**

- ☐ **Emergency alarm system**
  - Effective
  - Employees trained

Emergency Response to Hazardous Substance Releases Requirement without Regard for Location

► **Emergency response plan**

An emergency response program or emergency action plan is required as part of the site-specific safety and health program. Where employees are to be evacuated and not assist in the handling of an emergency, an emergency action plan may be provided. For details, see Section 10, "Emergency Action Plan."

Figure 17-16: Training Requirements for Emergency Response Activities at a Treatment, Storage, and Disposal Facility

Job function	Training required
Emergence response team*	**Minimum: 24 hours**
(e.g., laborers in the facility designated as response personnel)	Recognition of health and safety hazards Procedures to minimize risks Use of control equipment Selection and use of appropriate personal protective equipment Safe operating procedures at the scene of an incident Techniques of coordination with other employees to minimize risks Appropriate response to overexposures from health hazards and/or injury to self and others Recognition of subsequent symptoms resulting from overexposure
	Annual refresher
First responder	**Minimum: none**
Awareness training (e.g., all employees who are not part of the emergency response team)	Sufficient training to recognize an emergency response situation, summon trained personnel, and not attempt to manage emergencies on their own
	Annual refresher

* Emergency response team may be an outside, fully-trained emergency response team which is able to respond to emergencies within a reasonable period of time. For instance, some city fire departments have a HAZMAT team which is available to industry for a small annual fee.

☐ **Workplace accessibility of written plan**

☐ **General contents**
See details under "General Requirements" at the beginning of Section 17.

☐ **Means for identifying the senior emergency response person**
This person may be relieved as others arrive at the site.

- In charge of emergency activities

- Communicates, coordinates, and controls emergencies

- Identifies hazardous substances or conditions

- Implements appropriate response actions

- Ensures appropriate personal protective equipment is used

- Ensures positive-pressure, self-contained breathing apparatuses are worn

- Determines prevailing weather conditions

☐ **Procedures for reporting incidents to local, state, and federal agencies**

☐ **Plan compatible with disaster, fire, and/or emergency response plans of local, state, and federal agencies**

☐ **Routine drills**

☐ **Plans reviewed periodically**

☐ **Emergency alarm system**

- Effective

- Employees trained

► **Training program**
For details, see Figure 17-17.

► **Medical surveillance program**
Applicable to all members of the HAZMAT team. See details under "General Requirements."

► **Personal protective equipment**

☐ **Proper type and amount**

☐ **Respiratory protection program provided where respirators are to be worn**

Figure 17-17: Training Requirements for Emergency Response to Hazardous Substance Releases (Not Location Dependent)

First responders, awareness level

Persons likely to witness or discover a hazardous substance release and who have been trained to initiate an emergency response by notifying the proper authorities.

- Understand hazards involved and the risks associated with them
- Understand the potential outcomes associated with an emergency created when hazardous substances are present
- Able to recognize presence of hazardous substances in an emergency
- Able to identify the hazardous substances
- Understand the role of the first responder in the employer's emergency response plan (e.g., site security and control and the U.S. DOT Emergency Response Guidebook)
- Familiar with the means of communicating an emergency
- Familiar with instructions to depart/withdraw from the emergency (not attempt to respond or assist the actual responders)

Emergency responders, operations level

Individuals who respond to a release or potential release of a hazardous substance as part of the initial response to the site for the purpose of protecting nearby personnel, property, or the environment from the effects of the release(s) and who are trained to protect against, not stop the release.

- Know the basic hazard and risk assessment techniques
- Know how to select and use proper personal protective equipment
- Understand basic hazardous materials terms
- Know how to perform basic control, containment and/or confinement operations
- Know how to implement basic decontamination procedures
- Understand the relevant standard operating procedures and termination procedures
- Familiar with personal protective equipment required
- Familiar with procedures for handling an emergency

Hazardous materials (HAZMAT) technicians

Individuals who respond to releases or potential releases for the purpose of stopping the release.

- Possess knowledge equivalent to "emergency responder, operations level"
- Know how to implement the employer's emergency response plan
- Know the classification, identification, and verification of known/unknown materials by using field survey instruments/equipment

(continued on page 240)

▶ **Site cleanup** *(post-emergency response operations)*
If the HAZMAT team is to clean up the site, it must comply with the requirements as presented under "General Requirements" if off site. Otherwise, cleanup performed on plant property using plant or workplace employees must comply with requirements listed in 29 CFR 1926.35, 1926.59, and 1926.103.

☐ **Supplies and equipment**

- Maintained in serviceable condition

- Inspected prior to use

☐ **All regulatory requirements met**

▶ **Overall program effectiveness**

☐ **Employee understanding of procedures**

☐ **Employee compliance with procedures**

☐ **Lack of and/or proper management of associated incidents**

Figure 17-17 (cont'd.): Training Requirements

- Able to function within an assigned role in the incident command system
- Know how to select and use proper specialized chemical personal protective equipment
- Understand hazard and risk assessment techniques
- Able to perform advanced control, containment, and/or confinement operations
- Understand and are able to implement decontamination procedures
- Understand termination procedures
- Understand basic chemical and toxicological terminology and behavior

Hazardous materials (HAZMAT) specialist

Individuals who respond to releases or potential releases for the purpose of stopping the release.

- Possess knowledge equivalent to "HAZMAT technician"
- Know how to implement the local emergency response plan
- Understand classification, identification, and verification of known/unknown materials by using advanced survey instruments/equipment
- Know the state emergency response plan
- Able to select and use proper specialized chemical personal protective equipment provided to the HAZMAT specialist
- Understand in-depth hazard and risk techniques
- Able to perform specialized control, containment, and/or confinement operations
- Able to determine and implement decontamination procedures
- Have the ability to develop a site safety and control plan
- Understand chemical, radiological, and toxicological terminology and behavior

On-scene incident commander

Individuals who assume control of the incident scene beyond the first responder awareness level.

- Possess knowledge equivalent to "first responder, operations level"
- Know and are able to implement the employer's "incident command system"
- Know how to implement the employer's emergency response plan
- Know and understand the hazards and risks associated with employees working in chemical protective clothing
- Know how to implement the local emergency response plan.
- Know the state emergency response plan
- Know the Federal Regional Response Team
- Know and understand the importance of decontamination procedures

Notes and special comments

_____

_____

_____

_____

_____

_____

_____

_____

_____

_____

_____

_____

_____

_____

Score: _____

Hearing Conservation Program

Applicable where noise exposures are equal to or greater than an 8-hour time-weighted average of 90dBA. 29 CFR 1926.52

▶ **Written hearing conservation program**

☐ **Employee exposure monitoring**

- Monitoring performed
- *Work conditions and/or locations clearly identified*
- Excessive noise level notification process implemented
- Employees permitted to observe monitoring process

☐ **Work conditions and exposures requiring the use of hearing protection**

☐ **Audiometric testing requirements**

- Baseline
- Annual testing
- Follow-up procedures
- *End-of-employment provision*

Table 18-1: Permissible Noise Exposures

Duration of exposure (hours/day)	Sound level (dBA)
8	90
6	92
4	95
3	97
2	100
1.5	102
1	105
0.5	110
≤ 0.25	115

Note: Impact or impulse noise level exposure limit: 140 DB

☐ **Training schedule**

▶ **Employee training**

☐ **Physical examination requirements**

☐ **Exposure health hazards**

☐ **Types of hearing protection**

- Description of different types
- Uses and limitations of each type

☐ **Fitting procedures**

☐ **Maintenance and cleaning of reusable hearing protection**

☐ **Storage requirements for reusable hearing protection**

▶ **Availability of information to employees**

☐ **Noise standard posted in workplace**

☐ **Exposure monitoring results**

☐ **Training and education records**

▶ **Noise exposure monitoring**

☐ **Initial noise level readings**

☐ **Records of noise levels following changes in production, process, equipment, or controls**

▶ **Proper placement of warning signs and delineation of areas**
(where hearing protection is required)

▶ **Engineered noise controls**

☐ **Evaluated for feasibility**

☐ **Documented effectiveness**

Figure 18-1: Types of Hearing Protection

EARPLUGS

PREMOLDED

V-51 R   2-FLANGE   3-FLANGE

FORMABLE

FOAM   FIBERGLASS   SILICONE

CUSTOM MOLDED

PORTION THAT
ENTERS CANAL

SEMI-INSERT

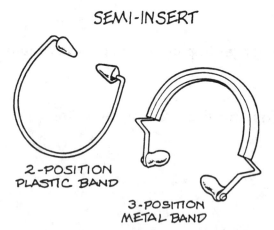

2-POSITION
PLASTIC BAND

3-POSITION
METAL BAND

EARMUFFS

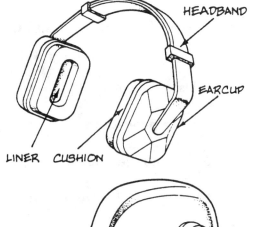

HEADBAND

EARCUP

LINER   CUSHION

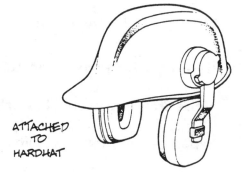

ATTACHED
TO
HARDHAT

HELMETS

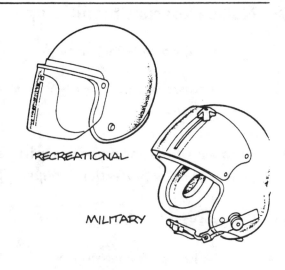

RECREATIONAL

MILITARY

Reprinted from C.W. Nixon and E.H. Berger, "Hearing Protection Devices," in C.M. Harris (ed.), *Handbook of Acoustical Measurements and Noise Control*, McGraw-Hill, New York, 1991, pp. 21.1–21.24.

▶ Documentation

☐ **Noise exposure monitoring records** *(maintained for at least 2 years)*

☐ **Employee audiometric records** *(maintained for duration of worker's employment)*

▶ Overall program effectiveness

☐ **Employee understanding of program**

☐ **Employee compliance with program**

☐ **No hearing loss claims**

Notes and special comments

_____

_____

_____

_____

_____

_____

_____

_____

_____

_____

Score: _____

Heat Stress

Applicable to all occupational exposures where there is a potential for employees to develop health problems due to heat stress (e.g., outdoor construction work in the summer). Although this topic is yet to be regulated by any specific regulations, employee monitoring and exposure controls are implied under the General Duty Clause of the Occupational Safety and Health Act. The approach herein has been excerpted from several sources, including the ACGIH recommended practices for heat stress evaluation and controls.

► **Written heat stress program**

☐ **Worksite analysis**

☐ **Prevention and controls**

☐ **Employee training**

► **Worksite evaluation**

☐ **Identify jobs at risk**

☐ **Perform monitoring**

Type (e.g., WBGT): _____

Frequency: _____

Table 19-1: Heat Exposure Calculations and Recommended Work-Rest Regimens

Outdoors with solar load: WBGT = 0.7 NWB + 0.2 GT + 0.1 DB

Indoors or outdoors (with no solar load): WBGT = 0.7 NWB + 0.3 GT

where: WBGT = Wet Bulb Globe Temperature Index

NWB = Natural Wet Bulb Temperature

DB = Dry Bulb Temperature

GT = Globe Temperature

Work Load Based on WBGT*

Work-Rest Regimen	Light	Moderate	Heavy
Continuous work	30.0 (86)	26.7 (80)	25.0 (77)
75% work/25% rest, each hour	30.6 (87)	28.0 (82)	27.9 (82)
50% work/50% rest, each hour	31.4 (89)	29.4 (85)	27.9 (82)
25% work/75% rest, each hour	32.9 (90)	31.1 (88)	30.0 (86)

* WBGT values given in °C (°F)

☐ Determine work load categories for each job

☐ Compare monitoring results with a published threshold

▶ **Enforcement of precaution and control measures**

☐ **Work-rest regimen**

☐ **Water and salt substitutes**

☐ **Lightweight clothing**

☐ **Acclimatization schedule**

▶ **Employee training**
All employees in problem jobs

☐ **Jobs impacted**

☐ **Monitoring results**

☐ **Factors which may affect heat stress**

☐ **Recognition of early symptoms**

☐ **First aid treatment**

☐ **Reporting procedures**

▶ **Overall program effectiveness**

☐ **Employee understanding of procedures**

☐ **Employee compliance with procedures**

☐ **Lack of heat stress incidents**

Figure 19-1: Heat Stress Disorders

heat cramps	**Warning sign for heat exhaustion!**
Cause:	excessive sweating water replacement without salt
Symptoms:	hot, moist skin slightly elevated body temperature cramping of the muscles (e.g., arms, legs, or stomach)
Treatment:	move into cooler area loosen clothing drink lightly salted liquids (e.g., 0.1% saline) if symptoms persist, seek medical aid
heat exhaustion	**Higher risk to older employees or those with coronary artery disease or emphysema.**
Cause:	enlarged surface blood vessels collapse from loss of body fluids and minerals
Symptoms:	heavy sweating intense thirst and cool, moist skin weak and rapid pulse, low to normal blood pressure fatigue, weakness or loss of coordination
Advanced Symptoms:	anxiety or agitation clouded senses, impaired judgment or fainting tingling in hands and feet and/or headache loss of appetite, nausea, or vomiting hyperventilation, oral temperature low
Treatment:	move into the cooler area loosen clothing provide additional cooling (i.e., ice, fan, water, etc.) elevate legs and massage the limbs drink water with salt seek medical aid
heat stroke	**Collapse is often misinterpreted as a heart attack or head injury!**
Cause:	body depleted of salt and water, stop sweating and failure of body temperature regulatory mechanisms
Symptoms:	absence of sweating body temperature above 103°F hot, red, or flushed dry skin rapid pulse, difficulty breathing constricted pupils, high blood pressure headache, dizziness, confusion, delirium, bizarre behavior weakness, nausea, vomiting
Advanced Symptoms:	seizure or convulsions collapse, loss of consciousness deep coma no detectable pulse, body temperature above 108°F
Treatment:	immerse in water massage body with ice do not give liquids if unconscious get victim to the hospital immediately

Notes and special comments

_____

_____

_____

_____

_____

_____

_____

_____

_____

_____

_____

_____

_____

Score: _____

Ionizing Radiation

Applicable to where there is potential for employee exposure to alpha rays, beta rays, gamma rays, X-rays, neutrons, high-speed electrons, high-speed protons, and other atomic particles. This does not include nonionizing electromagnetic radiation, licensing, certification, receipt, disposal, production utilization reporting requirements, medical administration received by patients, voluntary participation in medical research, or background levels of radiation. 29 CFR 1910.1096 and 1926.53

▶ **Exposure monitoring**

☐ **Records maintained for all employees working in restricted area(s)**

- Past

- Current

☐ **Monitoring properly applied**

- All employees exposed to over 25 percent of the calendar and quarter-calendar limits

- All employees under the age of 18, exposed to over 5 percent of the calendar and quarter-calendar limits

- Each employee who enters a "high radiation area"

Table 20-1: Exposure Limits for Ionizing Radiation

Employee Dose Limits*

Body part(s)	Rems per calendar year
Whole body (head and trunk, active blood-forming organs, lens of eyes, or gonads)	1.25
Hands and forearms; feet and ankles	18.75
Skin of whole body	7.50

* Employees under the age of 18 years shall not be permitted a dose in excess of 10 percent of these exposure limits.

Exceptions to Exposure Limits
1. Whole body < 3 rems/calendar quarter
2. Whole body, when added to the accumulated whole body dose does not exceed 5(N–18) where N is the employee's age in years at the last birthday
3. Adequate past and current exposure records

Airborne Exposure Limits

(Sample from 10 CFR 20, Appendix B)

Atomic Number	Radionuclide	Class	Table 1 Occupational Values			Table 2 Effluent Concentrations	
			Oral ALI (μCi)	Inhalation ALI (μCi)	DAC (μCi/ml)	Air (μCi/ml)	Water (μCi/ml)
38	Strontium-90	D	3E+1	2E+1	8E-9	—	—
86	Radon-220	Daughters removed	—	2E+4	7E-6	2E-8	—

ALI = Annual Limit on Intake
DAC = Derived air concentration = ALI/[2.4 X 109]μCi/ml

☐ Performed and documented daily

☐ *Records of employees having been notified of results*

▶ Airborne exposure monitoring in restricted area(s)

☐ **Records maintained**

☐ **Exposures acceptable**

- Within exposure limits for general work force
  See Table 1 of Appendix B to 10 CFR Part 20

- Within exposure limits for workers under the age of 18 years
  See Table 2 of Appendix B to 10 CFR Part 20

▶ Radioactive hazards evaluation performed

☐ **Physical location/point source survey**

- Production

- Use

- Release

- Disposal

- Presence of radioactive materials or sources of ionizing radiation

☐ **Employee dose exposure monitoring**

☐ **Airborne exposure monitoring in restricted areas**

▶ Radioactive area signs

☐ **Appropriate caution sign(s)**

- **Radiation Area**
  An area where the dose potential is greater than 5 millirem in 1 hour or an accumulation of greater than 100 millirem in 5 consecutive days

- **High Radiation Area**
  An area where the dose potential is greater than 100 millirem in 1 hour

Figure 20-1: Radiation Symbol*

RADIATION HAZARD

* Magenta or purple on yellow

Restricted area

An area accessible to employees where radiation levels may result in a major portion of the body receiving, in a 1-hour time period, a dose in excess of 5 millirem, OR in a 5-consecutive-day time period, a dose in excess of 100 millirem.

High radiation area

An area accessible to employees where radiation levels may result in a major portion of the body receiving, in a 1-hour time period, a dose in excess of 100 millirem.

Airborne radioactivity area

An area accessible to employees where airborne radiation may result in levels which exceed 25 percent of the amounts specified in Column 1, Table 1, Appendix B in 10 CFR Part 20 and averaged over the number of hours in any week during which individuals are in the area, OR levels which exceed the amounts specified in Column 1 for any time period.

- **Airborne Radiation Area**

  Any room, enclosure, or operation area in which airborne radioactive materials exist in concentrations in excess of Column 1, Table 1, Appendix B, 10 CFR Part 20

  Any room, enclosure, or operation area in which airborne radioactive materials exist in concentrations which exceed 25 percent of the amounts specified in Column 1, Table 1, Appendix B, 10 CFR Part 20

☐ **All signs conspicuously posted at entrance**

☐ **High radiation area control device**

A control device is required where area is established as a high radiation area for a period greater than 30 days.

- Radiation reduction device

- Conspicuously visible warning light

- Audible alarm

▶ Radioactive material(s) storage areas

☐ **Appropriate caution sign(s)**

- Area or room where radioactive material (other than natural uranium or thorium) is used or stored in any amount exceeding 10 times the quantity specified in Appendix C, 10 CFR Part 20

- Area or room where radioactive natural uranium or thorium is used or stored in any amount exceeding 100 times the quantity specified in 10 CFR Part 20

☐ **All signs conspicuously posted at entrance**

☐ **Secured area for radioactive materials stored in area which has no caution sign(s)**

▶ Radioactive material(s) containers

☐ **Containers where radioactive material (other than natural uranium or thorium) is transported, used, or stored in any amount exceeding the quantity specified in Appendix C to 10 CFR Part 20**

☐ **Containers where radioactive natural uranium or thorium is transported, used, or stored in any amount exceeding 10 times the quantity specified in 10 CFR Part 20**

Figure 20-2: Evacuation Warning Signal Characteristics

- **Frequency**: 450 to 500 Hertz

- **Modulation**: 4 to 5 Hertz

- **Signal generator**: ≥ 75 decibels

- **Employee/occupant locations**

► Radioactive material storage containers

☐ **Caution signs**

☐ **Radioactive material caution labels**

☐ **Recorded contents**

- Quantities

- Type of radioactive materials

- Date of quantities last measured

☐ **Materials packaged for shipment may be labeled in accordance with DOT requirements**

► Radioactive materials in nonradiation areas
Secured against unauthorized removal from the area

► Evacuation warning signal

☐ **Characteristics**

☐ **Tested and inspected**

- Initially

- Routinely

☐ **Actual inspection schedule(s):**

► Employee training

☐ **Training applicable to all individuals working in or frequenting any portion of a radiation area unless their training is regulated by:**

- The Atomic Energy Commission (10 CFR Part 20)

- A state which has developed an agreement with the Atomic Energy Commission

☐ **Appropriate regulatory requirements**

☐ **Health hazards**

☐ **Precautions and devices to minimize exposures**

Figure 20-3: Radiation Caution Signs

CAUTION

RADIATION AREA

CAUTION

HIGH RADIATION AREA

CAUTION

AIRBORNE RADIOACTIVITY AREA

CAUTION

RADIATIVE MATERIALS

☐ **Exposure records**

▶ **Posting requirements**

☐ **Appropriate signs and placards**

☐ **Operating procedures**

▶ **Waste management procedures**

☐ **Proper disposal methods**

☐ **Incident notification** *(exposure level dependent)*

- Immediate
- 24-hour

▶ **Excessive exposure reporting procedures**

☐ **Employee notification**

☐ **Agency notification** *(in accordance with appropriate controlling agency)*

▶ **Recordkeeping**

☐ **Radiation personnel monitoring records** *(maintained for at least one year)*

☐ **Area/airborne exposure monitoring records**

▶ **Overall program effectiveness**

☐ **Employee understanding of procedures**

☐ **Employee compliance with procedures**

☐ **Lack of associated incidents**

Figure 20-4: Restricted Area
Radiation Exposure Limits

Definition of REM

> A measure of the dose of any ionizing radiation to body tissue in terms of its estimated biological effect relative to a dose of 1 roentgen of X-rays.

1 REM equivalent dose

> X-ray or gamma radiation: .... 1 roentgen

> X-ray, gamma radiation, or beta radiation: .... 1 rad (energy absorbed per unit of tissue mass)

> neutrons or high energy protons: .... 0.1 rad

> particles heavier than protons and with sufficient energy to reach the lens of the eye: .... 0.05 rad

Notes and special comments

Score: _____

Section 21

Laser Equipment

Applicable where there is a potential for employee exposures to direct or reflected laser light in excess of 0.005 watts. 29 CFR 1926.54

▶ **Warning placards posted**

▶ **Qualification of employees**

☐ All workers assigned to install, adjust, or operate laser equipment

☐ Properly trained

☐ Proof of qualification in possession of operator at all times

▶ **Employee exposure limits monitored and observed**

☐ Light intensities

☐ Power densities

Figure 21-1: Laser Exposure Limits

Light Intensity

Direct staring .... 1 µwatt/square inch

Incidental observing .... 1 mwatt/square cm

Diffused reflected light .... 2¹/₂ watts/square cm

Power density: 10 mwatts/square cm

▶ Proper exposure controls

☐ **Eye protection provided**

Areas where potential exposure to direct or reflected laser light is greater than 0.005 watts

☐ **When laser transmission not required**

- Beam shutters or caps in place

  OR

- Laser turned off

☐ **Laser turned off when left unattended**

- Lunch
- Overnight
- Change of shifts

☐ **Only mechanical or electronic detection used for guiding internal alignment**

☐ **Laser beam never directed at employees**

☐ **Prohibited use or restricted employee access to area during inclement weather**

☐ **All equipment labeled as to maximum output**

☐ **Operating equipment set above heads of employees where possible**

▶ Overall program effectiveness

☐ **Employee understanding of procedures**

☐ **Procedures complied with**

☐ **No reported injuries or mishaps**

Figure 21-2: Weather Conditions Requiring Restrictions on Laser Use

Rain

Snow

Dust

Fog

Notes and special comments

_____

_____

_____

_____

_____

_____

_____

_____

_____

_____

_____

_____

_____

_____

Score: _____

Local Exhaust Ventilation

Applicable to all activities where there is a potential to exceed the employee permissible exposure limit(s) for dusts, fumes, mists, vapors, and gases and where local exhaust ventilation has been the chosen method of exposure controls. Installation and operation details are included for the following: general exhaust ventilation systems, abrasive blasting, grinding/polishing/ buffing, spray finishing, and open surface tanks. 29 CFR 1926.57

▶ General exhaust ventilation systems

☐ **Adequate capture velocity**

- Type of contaminant

- Air movement conditions

☐ **Proper conveyance of contaminants after capture**

- No return of contaminants into general work area *(unless the concentrations which may accumulate result in excessive exposures to the workers)*

- Contaminants exhausted away from general public *(e.g., not to a public walkway)*

- Not exhausted around air intake for general work area

Table 22-1: Local Exhaust Ventilation Systems
Regulatory Tables and Figures

	Table	Figure
Grinding, Polishing, and Buffing		
Grinding and abrasive cutting-off wheels	D–57.1	
Buffing and polishing wheels	D–57.2	
Horizontal single-spindle disc grinder	D–57.3	
Horizontal double-spindle disc grinder	D–57.4	
Vertical spindle disc grinder	D–57.5	
Grinding and polishing belts	D–57.6	
Vertical spindle disc grinder exhaust hood and branch pipe connections		D–57.1
Standard grinder hood		D–57.2
Method for applying an exhaust enclosure to swing-frame grinders		D–57.3
Standard buffing and polishing hood		D–57.4
Cradle polishing or grinding enclosure		D–57.5
Horizontal single-spindle disc grinder exhaust hood and branch pipe connections		D–57.6
Horizontal double-spindle disc grinder exhaust hood and branch pipe connections		D–57.7
Typical hood for a belt operation		D–57.8
Spray-Finishing		
Minimum maintained velocities into spray booths	D–57.7	
Lower explosive limit of some commonly used solvents	D–57.8	
Open-Surface Tanks		
Determination of hazard potential	D–57.9	
Determination of rate of gas, vapor, or mist evolution	D–57.10	
Control velocities in feet per minute for undisturbed locations	D–57.11	
Minimum ventilation rate in cubic feet of air per minute per square foot of tank area for lateral exhaust	D–57.12	

☐ **Duration of exhaust operation**

- While work activities are in progress

- System shall continue operating until all contaminants have been removed
  - When worker remains in area after work complete
  - When highly hazardous contaminants remain or potentially remain suspended in the air after work activities

☐ ***Activities should not be transferred outside the capture velocity range***

☐ ***Operators consistent in materials handling***
(e.g., turning up the degreasing spray or moving material to finish area prior to drying)

☐ ***No external booster fans***
(e.g., pedestal fans directed at the exhaust system which will likely compromise the system design)

☐ **Appropriate type of air cleaning device(s)**

- Designed for type of contaminant(s) being discharged

- Not required where concentrations exhausted may not exceed acceptable OSHA and EPA limits

☐ **Proper management of accumulated material**

- *Collection device(s) checked routinely for load*

- *Cleaning procedures established to avoid excessive employee exposures to accumulated contaminants*

- *Accumulated material contained and properly disposed of*

☐ ***Established routine evaluation(s)***

Frequency: _____

☐ ***Established routine maintenance program***

Frequency: _____

☐ ***Procedures for reporting signs of improper functioning***
(e.g., operator smells chemicals or experiences exposure symptoms and/or visible dust accumulations)

Figure 22-1: Personal Protective Equipment Requirements When Local Exhaust Is Used

Respiratory protection when:

- Working inside blast-cleaning rooms
- Using silica sand in manual blasting operations where the nozzle is not within the enclosure
- Concentrations of toxic dust dispersed by the abrasive blasting may exceed exposure limits and the nozzle and blast are not physically separated from the operator in an enclosure

Heavy canvas or leather gloves and aprons

Safety shoes—when working with heavy work products

Eye and face protection—when respirator does not provide it

Figure 22–2: Checklist of Requirements for Air Supply Units and Air Compressors

☐ **Trap and carbon filter**

- Installed
- Regularly maintained
- Removes oil, water, scale, and odor

☐ **Pressure reducing diaphragm or valve**

☐ **Automatic control to either sound alarm or shut down the compressor in case of overheating**

▶ **Abrasive blasting operations** *(e.g., sand blasting)*

☐ **When dust leaks are noted, repairs are made "as soon as possible"**

☐ **Routine pressure-drop checks, maintenance, and cleaning**
(documentation not required but recommended)

☐ **A separator where the abrasive is recirculated**

☐ **Exhaust dust collection system** *(e.g., cyclone)*

☐ **Procedure for emptying accumulated dust from collectors**

- Fully contained

- Personnel exposures not allowed

- Area contamination not allowed

- Operator who is emptying the dust is properly protected *(e.g., respiratory protection)*

☐ **Special equipment provided for combustible organic abrasives**

☐ **No dust accumulation on floor or ledges outside of enclosure**

☐ **No accumulation of steel abrasives in aisles or walkways**

☐ **Immediate cleanup of dust spills**

☐ **Blast-cleaning enclosures**

- Proper rate of exhaust

- Enclosure not opened prior to completion of work

- Small access openings
  □ Fitted with slit abrasive-resistant baffles
  □ Inspected regularly
  □ Replaced when needed

- Doors to enclosure
  □ Flanged and tight when closed
  □ Operable from inside and outside *(exception: work access door where there is a small operator access door)*

- Continuous inward flow of air maintained

- Baffled air inlets and access openings

Table 22–2: Minimum Exhaust Air Volumes

Grinding and Abrasive Cutting-Off Wheels

Wheel diameter (inches)		Wheel width (inches)	Minimum exhaust volume (CFM)
Over	Up To		
0	9	1½	220
9	16	2	390
16	19	3	500
19	24	4	610
24	30	5	880
30	36	6	1,200

Excerpted from Table D–57.1

Buffing and Polishing Wheels

Wheel diameter (inches)		Wheel width (inches)	Minimum exhaust volume (CFM)
Over	Up To		
0	9	2	300
9	16	3	500
16	19	4	610
19	24	5	740
24	30	6	1,040
30	36	6	1,200

Excerpted from Table D–57.2

Horizontal Spindle Disc Grinder

Wheel diameter (inches)		Minimum exhaust volume (CFM)
Over	Up To	
Single Spindle		
0	12	220
12	19	390
19	30	610
30	36	880
Double Spindle		
0	19	610
19	25	880
25	30	1,200
30	53	1,770
53	72	6,280

Excerpted from Tables D–57.3 and D–57.4

(continued on page 280)

- Upon work completion, enclosure remains closed and exhaust system remains in operation until dusty air is removed

- Where deep-cutting abrasives are used, screening is installed over safety glass

☐ **Air supply and compressors free of dust, mist, and noxious gas accumulations**

☐ **Controls for combustible organic abrasives if used**

- Automatic systems

- Specially designed for flammable materials

- Blast nozzle bonded and grounded

- Enclosure, ducts, and dust collector constructed of loose panels or explosion venting areas

☐ **Personal protective equipment worn** *(See Figure 22-1.)*

- Respiratory protection
  - Based on exposure monitoring performed in the worker's breathing zone for toxic substances
  - Based on size composition and toxicity

- Body and foot protection

- Eye protection

▶ Grinding, polishing, and buffing operations
Generally applicable when performed "dry."

☐ **Proper hood and branch design**

- Wheel movement toward exhaust and away from operator

- Minimum exhaust volumes

- Minimum duct velocity (4,500 fpm in branch)

☐ **Adequate system design**

- Tested upon installation

- Suitable dust collector(s)

☐ **Adequate structural strength of hood and enclosures**
(Such that the structures do not collapse or become damaged.)

☐ **Proximity sufficient for dust capture**
(Visible material not collected is indication of inadequacy of placement and/or design.)

Table 22–2 (cont'd.): Minimum Exhaust Air Volumes

Vertical Spindle Disc Grinder

| Wheel diameter (inches) | | Half or more of disc covered | | Disc not covered | |
Over	Up To	Number	Exhaust (CFM)	Number	Exhaust (CFM)
0	20	1	500	2	780
20	30	2	780	2	1,480
30	53	2	1,770	4	3,530
53	72	2	3,140	5	6,010

Excerpted from Table D–57.5

Grinding and Polishing Belts

| Wheel diameter (inches) | | Minimum exhaust volume (CFM) |
Over	Up To	
0	3	220
3	5	300
5	7	390
7	9	500
9	11	610
11	13	740

Excerpted from Table D–57.6

Table 22-3: Minimum Air Velocities in Spray Booths

| Operating conditions for objects completely inside booth | Airflow velocities (fpm) | | |
	Crossdraft (fpm)	Design	Range
Electrostatic and automatic airless operation contained in booth without operator	negligible	large booth—50	50 - 75
		small booth—100	75 - 125
Air-operated guns, manual or automatic	up to 50	large booth—100	75 - 125
		small booth—150	125 - 175
Air-operated guns, manual or automatic	up to 100	large booth—150	125 - 175
		small booth—200	150 - 250

Excerpted from Table D-57.7

▶ Spray finishing operations *(e.g., spray painting)*

☐ **Minimum face velocity(ies)**

☐ **Minimum air volume exhausted**
(Down to at least 25 percent of the lower explosion limit of the solvent being sprayed.)

☐ **Sufficient makeup air**

- Not contaminated or recycled

- Provision for heated air *(where outdoor temperature is expected to remain below 55°F or is more than 10°F below room temperature)*

- Heaters evaluated

- Does not yield greater than 200 ppm of carbon monoxide

- Does not yield greater than 2,000 ppm of total combustible gases

☐ **Proper design characteristics** *(See Figure 22-3.)*

- Spray room

- Spray booth

- Ventilation

- Velocity and air flow requirements

- Makeup air

▶ Open surface tanks

☐ **Minimum face velocity(ies)**

- Hazard potential index and rating determined

- Face (or control) velocity(ies) requirements determined

- Face (or control) velocity(ies) measured
  - ▫ Measured
  - ▫ Recorded

☐ **Air flow past the worker's breathing zone**

☐ **Air flow undisturbed by environmental factors** *(e.g., wind from open windows)*

Figure 22-3: Spray Finishing Operations Design Checklist

Spray Booth

☐ Special considerations
- Lights, motors, electrical equipment, and other ignition sources
- Spray booth or ducting not constructed of combustible materials

☐ Unobstructed walkways
- At least 6½ feet high
- Clear of obstructions

☐ Proper escape exits
- Open front only exit—at least 3 feet wide
- Multiple exits—at least 2 feet wide with no more than 25 feet from work location to exit
- All doors open outward

☐ Proper baffles, distribution plates, and dry-type overspray collectors

☐ Water chamber enclosures—constructed of steel
- At least 18 gage or more
- Protected against corrosion

☐ Chambers (e.g., spray nozzles and troughs)—means for creating and maintaining scrubbing action

☐ Pump manifolds, raisers, and headers—sized to discourage accumulation of hazardous deposits

☐ Collecting equipment
- Tanks—welded steel or other noncombustible material and designed to discourage accumulation of hazardous deposits
- Pits—concrete, masonry, or other similar materials

Spray Room Designs

☐ Constructed of masonry, concrete, or other noncombustible material

☐ Noncombustible fire doors and shutters

☐ Ventilated to bring air below 25% of the LEL

☐ Conform with requirement for Spray Booth Designs

(continued on page 284)

---

* See also NFPA No. 33-1969 and ANSI Z9.2-1960.

The above are not applicable to spraying building exteriors, fixed tanks, or similar structures, and also not to infrequently used small portable spraying apparatus.

☐ **Air flow undisturbed by mechanical factors**

- Pedestal fans

- Wall fans

- Heater blowers

- Moving machinery

☐ **Proper design of overhead hood** *(located above the tank)*

☐ **Proper design of lateral exhaust hoods** *(or horizontal flow hoods)*

☐ **Proper design for associated spray cleaning and degreasing activities**

☐ **Proper use of alternative controls** *(e.g., tank lids and surface beads)*

- *Air monitoring (with and without controls) to prove effectiveness*

- *Documented substantiating information (e.g., manufacturer's spec sheet)*

☐ **Proper system design**

- Two or more operations not connected where a hazardous mix may result *(e.g., fire, explosion, or chemical reaction hazards)*

- Condensate traps (or other devices) prevent drainage of material back into tank

- Measured air flow
  - Pitot traverse in exhaust duct
  - Corrective action(s) taken
  - Final measurement recorded

- Hoods and duct system inspected for corrosion or damage
  - At least every 3 months
  - After a prolonged shutdown

- Effluent discharged away from air return and/or air intake for building OR properly cleaned prior to recycling into the building

- Makeup air
  - Measured and documented to between 90% and 110% of the exhaust volume
  - Uncontaminated

Figure 22–3 (cont'd.): Spray Finishing Operations Design Checklist

Ventilation
- ☐ Air plenum
  - Sufficient strength and rigidity to withstand differential air pressure
  - Can be accessed for cleaning
- ☐ Supply duct for makeup air—noncombustible materials
- ☐ All seams and joints must be sealed
- ☐ Sized for design requirements
- ☐ Ducting adequately supported
- ☐ Longitudinal joints in sheet metal ducting lock-seamed, riveted, or welded
- ☐ Circumferential joints
  - Fastened together
  - Lapped in the direction of airflow
  - Every fourth joint with connecting flanges bolted together, or equivalent security
- ☐ Inspection or clean-out doors
  - Ducts up to 12 inches diameter—every 9 to 12 feet
  - Ducts in excess of 12 inches diameter—less frequently
  - Provided for servicing fan and drain (if necessary)
- ☐ Fire-protected ducting
  - Open space or fire-resistant material—when penetrating combustible roof or wall
  - Automatic fire dampers on both sides of penetration—when penetrating fire-resistant material (**Exception:** Ducts less than 18 inches in diameter may have 3 to 8 inch steel plates.)
- ☐ Ducts not connected to chimney, flue, or other device used for conveying products of combustion

Velocity and air flow requirements
- ☐ Minimum velocities maintained for spray booths
- ☐ If solvent is flammable, air diluted to a less than 25% LEL
- ☐ Where operator inside booth on downstream flow of air—must wear air supplied respirator
- ☐ Downdraft booths with doors—doors closed during work activities

Makeup air
- ☐ Clean and fresh
- ☐ Source kept open at all times
- ☐ Fan static pressure calculation—presumption that filters need replacing
- ☐ Pressure gage installed
  - Shows drop in pressure across filters
  - Marked to show when filters must be cleaned or replaced
- ☐ Means for conditioning booth or room
  - Maintained at not less than 65°F
  - General building heat or conditioned outside air
  - No heat supply inside booth
  - If heated by coal, oil, or gas products, must be exhausted away from the makeup air intake (**Exception:** Gas may meet other combustible product requirements, such as a strong odor, limited carbon monoxide production, and a fan for delivery of heated air and products to the spray booth.)

☐ **Personal protection provided**

- Rubber or impervious footwear—feet may become wet

- Impervious gloves
    - When handling liquid other than water
    - No corrosive or irritating contaminants on interior of gloves

- Impervious clothing—when and wherever street clothes may become wet

- Goggles
    - Danger of splashing
    - Additions made manually to tanks
    - Acids and chemicals removed from tanks

- Respirators
    - Emergencies
    - Airborne levels exceed exposure limits

☐ **Lockers (or storage area) provide for street clothing where applicable**

☐ **Emergency equipment provided**

- Clean cold water (*e.g., deluge showers and eye flushes*)

- Washing facilities where liquids may burn, irritate, or corrode—one basin with hot water per 10 employees

- Respirator and one trained standby where chemical may cause dermatitis or be absorbed through the skin

☐ **Means for maintenance personnel to effectively work on equipment**

- Tanks cleaned thoroughly prior to welding or other open flames near solvent cleaning equipment

- Special ventilation where working with cadmium, chromium, or lead

☐ **Proper design and use of vapor degreasing tanks**

Figure 22-4: Open Surface Tanks

Alkaline cleaning
Anodizing
Bleaching
Degreasing
Digesting
Dipping
Dressing
Dyeing
Electroplating
Pickling
Quenching
Rinsing
Stripping
Tanning
Washing
Other similar operations

Table 22-4: Hazard Potential and Rating for Open Surface Tanks

| Hazard Potential | Toxicity Group | | |
	Gas or Vapor (ppm)	Mist (mg/m3)	Flash Point (degrees F)
A	0 - 10	0 - 0.1	—
B	11 - 100	0.11 - 1.0	< 100
C	101 - 500	1.1 - 10	100 - 200
D	> 500	> 10	> 200

Excerpted from Table D–57.9

	Liquid Temperature Rating(degrees F)	Degrees Below Boiling Point	Relative Evaporation	Gassing
1	> 200	0 - 20	fast	high
2	150 - 200	21 - 50	medium	medium
3	94 - 149	51 - 100	slow	low
4	< 94	> 100	nil	nil

Excerpted from Table D–57.10

Table 22-5: Minimum Ventilation Rate for Lateral Exhaust Hoods

Required minimum capture velocity (fpm—above table)	Rate (cfm/sq. ft.) to maintain required minimum velocities at following ratios (tank width:tank length; W:L)				
	0.0-0.09	0.1-0.24	0.25-0.49	0.5-0.99	1.0-2.0
Hood along one side or two parallel sides of tank when one hood is against a wall or baffle. Also for a manifold along tank centerline.					
50	50	60	75	90	100
75	75	90	110	110	150
100	100	125	150	175	200
150	150	190	225	260	300
Hood along one side or two parallel sides of free-standing tank not against a wall or baffle.					
50	75	90	100	110	125
75	110	130	150	170	190
100	150	175	200	225	250
150	225	260	300	340	375

Excerpted from Table D-57.12

[1] Not practicable to ventilate across the long dimension of a tank whose W:L ratio exceeds 2.0. It is also undesirable to do so when the W:L radio exceeds 1.0. For circular tanks with lateral exhaust of half the circumference, use W:L = 1.0. For over half the circumference, use W:L = 0.5.

[2] Baffle is a vertical plate the same length as the tank with the top of the plate as high as the tank is wide. If the exhaust hood is on the side of a tank, against a wall, or close to it, it is considered "baffled."

[3] Use $^W/_2$ as tank width in computing when manifold is along the centerline or hoods are used on two parallel sides of the tank.

Figure 22-5: Open Surface Tank Design Checklist

Proper design of hood located over the tank
- ☐ Hood covers the entire space above the tank
- ☐ Fixed in position where head of operator clears and is in front of hood openings
- ☐ Completely enclosed on at least two sides
- ☐ Air quantity not less than capture velocity times the area of all openings in the enclosure through which air can flow
- ☐ Where the determined rate of vapor evaporation is 10% or greater than the exhaust volume, the exhaust volume must have been increased accordingly

Proper design of lateral exhaust hoods (or horizontal flow hoods)
- • Hood exceeds 42 inches in width, OR
- • It is desirable to reduce the amount of air removed from the workroom
- ☐ Adequate quantity of air movement
- ☐ Air supply slots (or orifices) along the side or center, opposite the exhaust slots where:
- ☐ Supply air and entrained air do not exceed 50% of the exhaust volume
- ☐ Velocity of supply is not less than effective velocity over the exhaust slot
- ☐ Vertical height of receiving hood (including baffles) is not less than ¼ the width of the tank
- ☐ Supply not allowed to impinge on obstructions to exhaust slot
- ☐ Method established to measure and adjust supply air
- ☐ Where the determined rate of vapor evaporation is 10% or greater than the exhaust volume, the exhaust volume must have been increased accordingly

Proper design for associated spray cleaning and degreasing activities
- ☐ Controls for airborne spray
- ☐ Enclosed as much as possible
- ☐ Capture velocity sufficient to prevent discharge into work area—may be assisted by the use of mechanical baffles

Use of other controls to reduce concentrations of hazardous materials
- • Tank covers
- • Foams
- • Beads
- • Chips
- • Surface tension depressive agents
- • Other floating materials

Proper system design
- ☐ Entrance losses into hood
- ☐ Resistance to air flow in branch pipe
- ☐ Entrance loss into the main pipe
- ☐ Resistance to air flow in main pipe
- ☐ Resistance of mechanical equipment
- ☐ Resistance in outlet duct and discharge stack
- ☐ Avoidance of mixtures which may be hazardous
- ☐ Condensate traps

Vapor degreasing tanks
- ☐ Condenser or thermostat kept below the top edge of the tank at minimum distance of half the tank width or 36 inches (whichever is shorter)
- ☐ Combustion chamber with tight construction (**Exception:** exhaust and make-up air)
- ☐ Heating elements maintained to prevent decomposition, breakdown, or conversion of vapor
- ☐ Wherever tanks are more than 4 square feet
  - • Cleanout or sludge doors near bottom of each tank or still
  - • Door gaskets do not leak

Notes and special comments

_____

_____

_____

_____

_____

_____

_____

_____

_____

_____

_____

_____

_____

Score: _____

Lockout and Tagout Program

This is a recommended practice to be used in construction activities where the servicing and maintaining of machines and equipment may result in employee injuries from an unexpected start-up (e.g., mechanical movement of parts) OR release of stored energy (e.g., electricity). 29 CFR 1910.47 (italics) and 1926.417 (normal)

▶ **Written lockout/tagout program**

☐ *Summary "when and how" procedural statement*

☐ *Procedural steps*

- *Shut down*

- *Isolation*

- *Mechanism to prevent start-up*

- *Secure machine(s) and/or equipment*

☐ *Approach for designating the safe placement, removal, and transfer of lockout/tagout devices*

☐ *Responsible personnel designated*

☐ *Specific requirements for testing machines or equipment to determine and verify the effectiveness of locks, tags, and other energy control measures*

Figure 23-1: Checklist of Energy Sources

- ☑ Electrical
- ☑ Hydraulic
- ☑ Pneumatic
- ☑ Chemical
- ☑ Thermal

Figure 23-2: Lockout and Tagout Devices

A *tagout device* is any prominent warning device, such as a tag and means of attachment, that can be securely fastened to an energy-isolating device in accordance with an established procedure. The tag indicates that the machine or equipment to which it is attached is not to be operated until the tagout device is removed by an authorized person (usually the person who installed the tag). It should be noted, however, that a lockout device is preferred to a tagout and should be the method of choice, unless the employer can show that the tagout system provides full employee protection.

A *lockout device* is any device that uses a physical means of control, such as a lock (either key or combination), to hold an energy-isolating device in a safe position, thereby preventing the energizing of machinery or equipment. When properly installed, either a blank flange or a bolted slip blind is considered to be an appropriate lockout device.

DANGER

**DO NOT
THROW
SWITCH**

MEN AT WORK ON CIRCUIT

Signature: _____

Date: _____

DANGER

**DO NOT
REMOVE THIS TAG**

**TO DO SO WITHOUT
AUTHORIZATION WILL MEAN
IMMEDIATE DISCHARGE
IT IS HERE FOR A PURPOSE**

SEE OTHER SIDE

☐ *Steps to re-energize equipment after work completion*

☐ *Periodic inspections (minimum frequency: annually)*

▶ **Lockout/tagout devices**

☐ **Durable**

☐ **Standardized**

☐ **Substantial enough to minimize early or accidental removal**

☐ **Identifies employee who affixed the device**

☐ **Warning(s) associated with tags**

▶ *Employee training*

☐ *Contents of training*
- *Lockout and tagout program*
- *Specific job responsibilities*

☐ *Proper frequency*
- *Initial*
- *Change in job assignments*
- *Change in machines*
- *Equipment or processes that present a new hazard*

☐ *Proper documentation*
- *Change in the procedures*
- *Proof of understanding (e.g., written exam or signed statement)*
- *Date(s) of training*
- *Filed (e.g., general and personnel files)*

▶ **Contract labor procedures**

☐ *Contract employees should be properly informed of management procedures*

☐ *They should understand the lockout and tagout program*

Figure 23-3: Sample Lockout and Tagout Program

Table of Contents

Section 1:   Purpose

Section 2:   General Information

Section 3:   Worksite Analysis of Potential Hazardous
Energy Sources

Section 4:   Lockout and Tagout Procedures

4.1:   Preparation

4.2:   Sequence of Events

4.3:   Re-energizing Machines and/or Equipment

Section 5:   Procedures for Re-energizing Equipment

Section 6:   Authorized Personnel

Section 7:   Employee Training Requirements

Section 8:   Inspections Schedule

☐ *Written approval on file for all contract labor*

▶ **Overall program effectiveness**

☐ **Employee understanding of procedures**

☐ **Employee compliance with procedures**

☐ **Lack of associated accidents**

Notes and special comments

_____

_____

_____

_____

_____

_____

_____

_____

_____

_____

_____

_____

_____

_____

_____

_____

_____

Score: _____

Section 24

Manual Lifting

> *Applicable to all construction, industrial, and commercial activities where lifting heavy objects is a component of the job. Although there are no regulatory mandates, manual lifting is a source of numerous back injuries and having a prevention program is implied under the General Duty Clause of the Occupational Safety and Health Act.*

► **Employee training**

☐ **Anatomy and physiology of the spine**

☐ **Causes of back problems**
  - Back pain
  - Back strain
  - Back sprain
  - Ruptured disc

☐ **Individual limitations**
  - Weight
  - Age
  - Physical condition
  - Exercise habits
  - Smoking
  - Proper standing and sitting techniques

Figure 24-1: Method for Lifting

Can you lift it alone, or will you require assistance?

Get lifting aid by any one or a combination of the following:

- Other workers
- Special lifting tool
- Special lifting equipment

Face the object squarely, get a firm stance, bend at the knees, and get a firm grip on the box.

(continued on page 300)

☐ **Proper lifting techniques**

- *Individual*
- *Two or more people*

☐ **Management of variously shaped objects**

- *Cartons and boxes*
- *Sacks*
- *Drums and barrels*
- *Scrap metal*
- *Heavy, round, flat objects*
- *Large objects*
- *Sharp-edged objects (e.g., glass and metal)*
- *Irregular shapes*

☐ **Injury prevention exercises**

☐ **Jobs most likely to be impacted**

☐ **When personal protective equipment is required**
(e.g., heavy gloves with sharp objects)

▶ **Jobs requiring manual lifting**

☐ **Identified**

- *Amount*
- *Frequency*

☐ **Preplacement physical**

▶ **Clarification of situations where personal protective equipment should be worn** (e.g., scrap metal workers should wear goggles, leather gloves or mittens, safety shoes, safety hats, and protection for the legs and body)

▶ **Availability and use of special equipment**

☐ **Hand tools**

- *Rubber suction cups with handles (e.g., glass)*
- *Hooks*
- *Bars*
- *Rollers*
- *Drum lifter*

Figure 24-1 (cont'd.): Method for Lifting

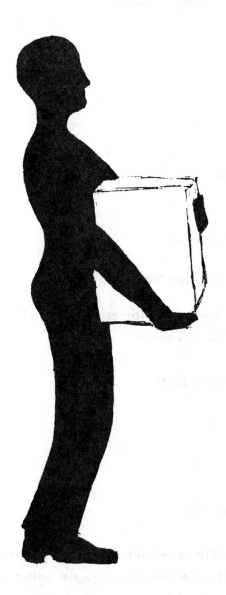

Keep your back straight, load close to your body, weight centered over your feet, and lift straight up using the power of your legs!

Arms and elbows should be positioned close to your body and your chin tucked to allow your neck and head to remain in a straight line with your spine.

☐ *Jacks*

☐ *Hand trucks and wheelbarrows*

☐ *Powered industrial trucks*

☐ *Cranes, derricks, hoists, and conveyors*

▶ **Overall program effectiveness**

☐ **Employee understanding of the procedures**

☐ **Employee compliance with procedures**

☐ **Lack of accidents or injuries**

Notes and special comments

_____

_____

_____

_____

_____

_____

_____

_____

_____

_____

_____

_____

_____

_____

Score: _____

Personal Protective Equipment

Applicable to occupational exposures where protective equipment is required and/or supplied by an employer or where an employee chooses to supply his or her own equipment. 29 CFR 1926.95, 1926.96, 1926.100 through 1926.106, American National Standards Institute (ANSI), and American Society for Testing and Materials (ASTM)

▶ **Written hazard assessment**

☐ *Type(s) of exposure(s)*

☐ *Type(s) of hazard(s)*

☐ **Documented exposure levels**
(where applicable, such as noise or chemical exposure levels)

☐ **Identification and clear delineation of exposure area(s) and/or job types**

☐ *Type(s) of equipment required for each exposure area or job type*

▶ **Assignment of proper equipment type(s)**
(e.g., outdoors electrical workers should wear at least Class B head protection and rubber-soled foot protection)

Figure 25-1: Head Protection

Type 1

Helmets with full brim, not less than 1¼ inches wide

Type 2

Brimless helmets with a peak extending forward from the crown

Class A

General service, limited voltage protection
- Mining
- Construction
- Shipbuilding
- Tunneling
- Lumbering
- Manufacturing

Class B

Utility service, high-voltage protection
- Electrical workers

Class C

Special service, no voltage protection
- Oil fields
- Refineries
- Chemical plants

Figure 25-2: Eye and Face Protection Requirements

- Provide adequate protection against the particular hazards for which they are designed (e.g., shielded metal arc welding: 7 to 11 minimum protective shade)

- Reasonable comfort when worn under the designated conditions

- Fit snugly without interfering with the movements or vision of the wearer

- Durable

- Capable of being disinfected

- Easily cleaned

- Kept clean and in good repair

- Special eye protection for corrective eyeglass wearers

► **Appropriateness and adequacy of equipment**

☐ **Head protection**

- ANSI designation and class on each head protector
- Worn properly *(e.g., head strap fitted)*
- Routine inspection and maintenance program

☐ **Eye and face protection** *(e.g., face shields)*

- Meet minimum requirements based on the exposure(s) *(e.g., chemicals, flying objects, and ultraviolet radiation)*
- Acceptable provision(s) for corrective lenses
- Proper fitting by someone skilled
- Routine inspection and maintenance program

☐ **Torso protection** *(e.g., aprons and disposable coveralls)*

- Exposures to skin-absorbed toxic substances
- Adequacy of material *(e.g., polypropylene, which provides good to excellent protection against sulfuric acid)*
- Adequate body coverage
- Reusable torso protection inspected routinely for wear and tear of material

☐ **Hand and arm protection** *(e.g., gloves and arm sleeves)*

- Exposures to skin-absorbed toxic substances
- Adequacy of material
- Adequate body coverage
- Reusable hand/arm protection inspected routinely for wear and tear of material

☐ **Foot and leg protection**
(e.g., steel-toed shoes and leather leg protection for welders)

- Meet requirements based on exposures *(e.g., rubber boots/shoes for electrical workers and safety footwear for heavy construction work)*
- Routinely inspected and maintained

Table 25-1: Eye and Face Protection Selection Guide

Operation	Hazards	Recommended Protection
Acetylene-burning • cutting • welding	sparks, harmful rays, molten metal, and flying particles	7,8,9
Chemical handling	splash, acid burns, fumes	2,10 severe exposures: both
Chipping	flying particles	1, 3, 4, 5, 6, 7A, 8
Electric (arc) welding	sparks, intense rays, molten metal	9,11 (recommended: 11 with 4,5,6, in tinted lenses)
Furnace operations	glare, heat, molten metal	7,8,9 severe exposures: add 10
Grinding (light)	flying particles	1,3,4,5,6,10
Grinding (heavy)	flying particles	1, 3, 7A, 8A severe exposures: add 10
Laboratory	chemical splash, glass breakage	2 or 10 with 4,5,6
Machining	flying particles	1,3,4,5,6,10
Molten metals	heat, glare, sparks, splash	7,8 or 10 with 4,5,6, in tinted lenses
Spot welding	flying particles, sparks	1,3,4,5,6,10

1   Goggles, flexible fittings with regular ventilation
2   Goggles, flexible fittings with hooded ventilation
3   Goggles, cushioned fitting with rigid body
4   Spectacles, metal frame with side shields (side shields not required with limited hazard use requiring only frontal protection)
5   Spectacles, plastic frame with side shields (same as above)
6   Spectacles, metal-plastic frame with side shields (same as above)
7   Welding goggles, eyecup type with tinted lenses
7A Chipping goggles, eyecup type with clear safety lenses
8   Welding goggles, coverspec type with tinted lenses
8A Chipping goggles, coverspec type with clear safety lenses
9   Welding goggles, coverspec type with tinted plate lens
10 Face shield (available with plastic or mesh window)
11 Welding helmets

☐ **Goggles**

- Required where machines or operations may cause eye or face injury
  - Chemical substances
  - Physical agents
  - Radiation

- Corrected vision
  - Lenses with vision correction built in
  - Corrective lenses mounted behind
  - Corrective lenses mounted within

- Limitations understood

- Properly worn and maintained

☐ **Safety nets**

- Required when workplaces exceed 25 feet above the ground or water surface

- Required for other surfaces where it is impractical to use ladders, scaffolds, catch platforms, temporary floors, safety lines, or safety belts

☐ **Safety belts, lifelines, lanyards**

- Used only for employee safeguarding, not to be used for in-service loading

- Secured above the point of operation to an anchorage or structural member capable of supporting at least 5,400 pounds

- Wire core manila rope with minimum 5,400 pounds breaking strength
  - Normal use: minimum ¾ inch
  - Rock climbing use: minimum ⅞ inch

- Hardware—smooth and free of sharp edges

- Capable of withstanding tensile loading of 4,000 pounds without cracking, breaking, or taking a permanent deformation

☐ **Ear protection** *(e.g., ear plugs and muffs)*
(See Section 18, "Hearing Conservation Program.")

☐ **Respirator protection**
(See Section 29, "Respiratory Protection Program.")

Figure 25-3: Safety Net Requirements

- Extend 8 feet beyond the edge of the work surface and as close beneath as possible but in no case greater than 25 feet below

- Tested prior to use

- Sufficient clearance to prevent user's contact with the surfaces or structures below (Distance determined by impact load testing)

- Net mesh size not in excess of 6" by 6"

- Nets meet accepted performance standards of 17,500 foot-pounds minimum impact resistance

- Edge ropes shall provide a minimum breaking strength of 5,000 pounds

- Forged steel safety hooks or shackles used to fasten the net to its supports

- Connections between net panels develop full strength of the net

---

Figure 25-4: Safety Belt Classifications

Class I: Body Belts

For limited movement and positioning to restrict the worker to a safe area to help prevent a fall

Class II: Chest Harness

For use where freedom of movement is important and only limited fall hazards exist (Not recommended for use where vertical free fall hazards may occur.)

Class III: Body Harness

For use where the worker must move at dangerous heights (In a fall, the harness distributes impact forces over a wider body area than a belt, reducing the possibility of injury to the wearer during a fall)

Class IV: Suspension Belt

Used where it is not possible to work from a fixed surface, and the worker must be totally supported by a suspension harness (e.g., shipboard painting, stack maintenance, and tree trimming)

▶ **Overall program effectiveness**

☐ **Employee understanding of rationale for wearing required personal protective equipment**

☐ **Employee compliance with equipment use and maintenance**

☐ **Lack of associated accidents**

Notes and special comments

_____

_____

_____

_____

_____

_____

_____

_____

_____

_____

_____

_____

_____

_____

Score: _____

Portable Power Tools and Equipment

Applicable to all workplaces where portable power tools are used either in the production process or incidental to the job. Tools and equipment which are the responsibility of the employer include those which are provided by an employee as well as the employer. 29 CFR 1926.300, 29 CFR 1926.302, and 29 CFR 1910.242 to 1910.243

▶ **Proper guarding**

☐ **Protects from associated components/debris**

- Sparks, wood chips, and shavings

- Power transmission components

- Electrical connections

☐ **Point of operation design**

- *Prevents hands, arms, and other body parts from making contact with moving parts*

- *Firmly secured*

- *Not easily removed*

- *Permits safe, comfortable, easy operation*

- *Can be oiled without removing guard(s)*

- *No openings/holes where objects may fall into moving parts*

Figure 26-1: Power Tools and Equipment Requiring Additional Regulatory Research

Pneumatic power tools	1926.302(b)
Fuel powered tools	1926.302(c)
Hydraulic powered tools	1926.302(d)
Power-actuated tools	1926.302(e)
Radial saws	1926.304(g)
Hand-fed crosscut table saws	1926.304(h)
Hand-fed rip saws	1926.304 (f)
Portable abrasive wheels *	1910.243(c)
Explosive-actuated fastening tools *	1910.243(d)
Power lawnmowers *	1910.243(e)
Portable circular saws*	1910.243(a)
Abrasive wheels	1926.303(a-e)
Power-transmission apparatus	1926.307(a-p)
Air receivers	1926.306(a-b)
Jacks	1926.305(a-d)

* Those indicated with an asterisk may require a little extra research under the general industry standard.

Figure 26-2: Checklist for Nonelectric Hand Tools

☑ **Wrenches**

Not sprung to point that slippage occurs

☑ **Impact tools**

Free of mushroom heads

☑ **Wooden handles (e.g., hammers)**

Free of splinters or cracks with a snug, tight fit of the implement

---

☐ **Designed to avoid electrical hazards**

▶ **Adequately designed control(s)**

☐ **Constant pressure switches and/or controls shut off when pressure is released**

☐ **Operating controls not accessible for accidental start-up**

☐ **Lock-on controls provided with easy access turnoff**

▶ **Proper grounding**

☐ *Ground wire fastener(s)*

- *Available*

- *Properly used*

☐ *Three-prong plug/extension cord(s)*

▶ *Proper use of tools/equipment*

☐ *Operating instructions available*
(e.g., posted or filed in work area)

☐ *Proper procedures followed*

☐ *Properly replaced in storage area after use*

☐ *Placed where they cannot fall or get snagged*

☐ *Placement of extension cords away from and/or secured against foot traffic tripping and displacement of tools/equipment*

☐ *Electric cords not used for hoisting or lowering tools*

▶ **Routine inspections of personal tools and equipment**

☐ **Performed daily and/or prior to use**

☐ *Operator(s) capable of detailing inspection procedures*

☐ *Operator(s) capable of minor adjustments and lubrication*

Figure 26-3: Safety Rules

Saws

- Before cutting, inspect the material which is to be cut for nails and other foreign objects.
- Be sure the blade guards are in place and operating properly.
- Stay alert! Noisy operations may drown out audible warnings of danger.
- Wear goggles or a face shield.
- Inspect blade routinely by turning off the saw and unplugging it.
- Don't use dull or loose saw blades.
- Don't overload the motor by pushing it beyond its capability to cut (e.g., through dense wood with a lot of knots).
- Establish firm footing and balance during operation to avoid slips and falls with the power tool in hand.

Portable Drills and Routers

- Select the correct bit to suit the job, and use only sharpened cutting surfaces.
- Make sure the material being drilled/routed is secured or firmly clamped.
- Hold the drill/router firmly and level (or at a predetermined angle).
- Don't force or lean into the work.
- Use a jig or guide for routing.
- *Always* remove the bit from the drill when finished!

Grinding Wheels

- Wear ear and eye protection.
- Inspect wheels to assure they are firmly in place and the work rests are tight.
- Stand to one side when starting the motor.
- Use light pressure when grinding.

Portable Sanders

- Arrange the cord so it can't be damaged by the abrasive belt.
- Keep both hands on the sander.
- Hold the sander when plugging it in.
- Routinely clean dust and chips from the motor and vent holes and lubricate when necessary.

Impact Wrenches

- Do not force a wrench to handle a job larger than it is designed to handle.
- Do not use standard hand sockets or driver parts with an impact tool.
- Do not reverse direction of rotation while the trigger is depressed.

▶ *Scheduled inspections and maintenance of all tools and equipment*

Frequency: _____

☐ *Performed by someone knowledgeable in equipment troubleshooting and repairs*

☐ *Scheduled inspection dates recorded*

- *On the tools/equipment,*

- *Posted, or*

- *Filed in the work area*

☐ *Inspections completed by scheduled inspection dates*

▶ *Training provided for authorized personnel*

☐ *Proper operating procedures*

☐ *Inspection and minor maintenance procedures*

☐ *Procedures to be use for preventing unauthorized use of tools*

☐ *When to take tools/equipment out of service and/or replace parts* (e.g., cracked saw blades)

☐ *Procedures for avoiding unintentional actuation*

☐ *Proper personal protective equipment required*

☐ *Condition requirements and placement*

- *Proper use conditions (e.g., away from edge of table)*

- *Upon storage (e.g., disassemble jigs and drill bits)*

☐ *Limitations of tools/equipment*

☐ *Written record of training*

▶ **Procedures for limiting tool access to authorized personnel only**

☐ **Established** (e.g., written or understood)

☐ **Complied with**

Figure 26-4: Routine Inspection Checklist

- ☑ Condition of electrical cords
  - • Insulation and plugs intact
  - • Protected against trucks and oil
  - • Not located in aisles
- ☑ Integrity of operable parts
- ☑ Free of debris
- ☑ Guard(s) in place
- ☑ Moveable guards operate freely
- ☑ All external screws and bolts secured
- ☑ Easy movement of sliding/turning/swivel components
- ☑ Free of cracks and/or signs of damage to casing
- ☑ Adequately lubricated
- ☑ Eye protection not scratched, cracked, and/or unusable

Figure 26-5: Sample Certificate of Training
(enlarged from wallet card)

QUALIFIED OPERATOR OF POWER-ACTUATED TOOLS

Make(s) and model(s) _____

_____

_____

This certifies that _____
                                              (name of operator)

Card number _____   Social Security number _____

has received the prescribed training in the operation of power-actuated tools.

Trainer's signature _____

I have received instruction in the safe operation and maintenance of power-actuated fastening tools of the makes and models specified and agree to conform to all rules and regulations governing their use. I understand that failure to comply shall be cause for immediate revocation of this card.

_____   _____
      (signature of operator)   (date)

▶ **Proper use of compressed air for cleaning**

  ☐ **Pressure reduced to less than 30 pounds per square inch**

  ☐ **Chip guard installed**

  ☐ **Eye protection required and complied with**

  • Operator

  • Personnel in the vicinity

▶ *Special spark-resistant tool/equipment requirements around flammable/ combustible chemicals*

▶ **Overall program effectiveness**

  ☐ **Employee understanding of procedures**

  ☐ **Employee compliance with procedures**

  ☐ **Lack of associated accidents**

Notes and special comments

_____

_____

_____

_____

_____

_____

_____

_____

_____

_____

Score: _____

Section 27

Powered Industrial Trucks

Applicable to all construction, industrial, and commercial activities where lifting heavy objects is a component of the job. Although there are no regulatory mandates under the construction standards, the industrial standards provide direction for safety applications to forklifts, platform lift trucks, motorized hand trucks, tractors, and other specialized industrial trucks which are powered by electric motor or internal combustion engine. 29 CFR 1910.178

▶ **Proper use of equipment**

☐ **Ground surface**

☐ **Type of material handled**

☐ **Equipment capabilities and/or limitations**

▶ **Safety equipment provided**

☐ **Overhead protection**

☐ **Locking chocks and brakes for loading/unloading**

Figure 27-1: Safety Features and Proper Position for Forklift Storage

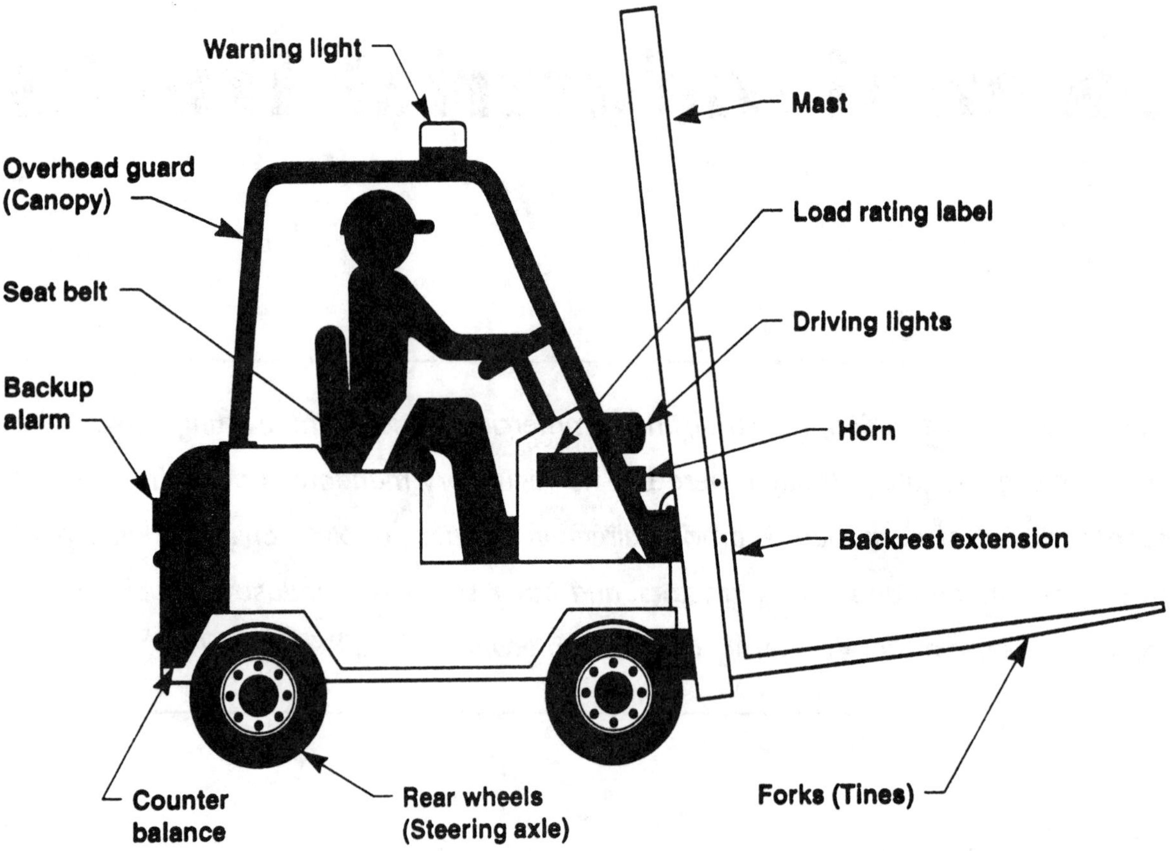

Warning light

Mast

Overhead guard (Canopy)

Load rating label

Seat belt

Driving lights

Backup alarm

Horn

Backrest extension

Counter balance

Rear wheels (Steering axle)

Forks (Tines)

Properly Set Forklift

- Carriage fully lowered
- Engine off
- Parking brake set

☐ **Wheel plates**

☐ **Fire extinguisher**

☐ **Audible warning device** *(e.g., backup alarm)*

▶ **Load limit signs**

☐ **Visible and legible to operators**

☐ **Weight limits observed**

▶ **Operator training**

☐ **Personnel**

- Authorized operators

- Inspectors

- Maintenance workers

☐ **Contents**

- Proper operating procedures

- Types of trucks and environments

- Operation hazards

- Physical and mental condition, attitude, and aptitude

- Operating rules

- Inspection procedures *(e.g., daily checklist)*

- Procedure for taking truck out of service for maintenance and repairs

- Supervised practice

☐ **Documented proof of completion**

- Classroom training

- Performance skills

▶ **Passenger prohibitions enforced**

Figure 27-2: Operating a Forklift Safely

General Rules

- Always keep arms and legs inside the vehicle.
- Face direction of travel. Keep your mind focused, and never travel with the load blocking your view.
- Keep three vehicle lengths away from other vehicles.
- No horseplay or stunt driving!
- Be aware of overhead clearances, such as pipes, sprinklers, and jambs.
- Know your weight limits. They are posted on the equipment.
- Do not exceed the load and extension limits.
- Do not allow passengers or unauthorized personnel to drive.
- Never drive a truck up to someone standing in front of a bench or other fixed object.

Picking Up the Load

- Make sure the load does not exceed the capacity of the equipment.
- If loading a truck, trailer, or rail car, make sure the brakes are set and wheel blocks in place on the vehicle being loaded.
- Make sure the forks are positioned, balanced, and secured properly for lifting.
- Check for overhead obstructions.
- Raise the forks to proper height.
- Place the forks all the way into the pallet, and tilt the mast back to stabilize the load.
- Back out. Stop completely, and lower the load.
- Pedestrians and emergency vehicles always have the right-of-way.
- Never allow anyone to ride on your forklift or pass under a raised load!
- Always watch where you are going. If the load obstructs visibility, travel with the load trailing.
- Keep the forks low during travel.
- Always have the unloaded forks as low as possible, but high enough to clear bumps and curbs. Never travel with a raised load!
- Know the position of the forks at all times.
- Keep your load tilted back slightly.
- Obey speed limits.
- Slow down at intersections, and always sound your horn at cross aisles.

Traveling with a Load

- Always drive with the load against the backrest. Drive a loaded forklift with the load on the uphill side. Going downhill, back down!
- Always drive an unloaded forklift with the forks on the downhill side. Go down in the forward position and up in the backward position.
- Never turn a forklift sideways on a ramp!
- Avoid sudden braking.
- Lift and lower the load only when stopped.
- Watch out for oil, grease, and slippery areas.
- Make sure the load is balanced and secure at all times.
- Pass other trucks which are traveling in the same direction only where there are no intersections, blind spots, or other potentially dangerous locations.
- Reduce speed when negotiating turns.
- Cross railroad tracks at a diagonal, and never park within 8 feet of the center of the tracks.
- Avoid drop-offs and edges of loading docks, ramps, and platforms.
- Enter elevators, or other confined spaces, with the load forward.

(continued on page 324)

▶ Adequate ventilation

☐ **During operation of fuel operated trucks**

- Avoid excessive carbon monoxide exposures

- Well ventilated—not in confined area

- *Confirmatory personnel air monitoring for carbon monoxide levels*

☐ **Around battery charge stations**

- Controlled evolution of flammable hydrogen gas
  - ▫ Ventilated to unconfined outside area

    OR
  - ▫ Local exhaust

- *Confirmatory area air monitoring for combustible gases within acceptable limits—may involve constant readout equipment with a warning alarm*

▶ Routine inspection and maintenance program

☐ **Operator checklist**

- Completed at beginning of each work shift

- Form properly filled out and signed

- Minor discrepancies rectified

- Equipment decommissioned when requiring repair

☐ **Routine maintenance evaluation**

- Scheduled inspection and maintenance checks by qualified person

- Completed in a timely fashion

▶ Overall program effectiveness

☐ **Employee understanding of the procedures**

☐ **Employee compliance with procedures**

☐ **Lack of accidents or injuries**

Figure 27-2 (cont'd.): Operating a Forklift Safely

Placing a Load

- Stop the forklift completely before raising the load.
- Move slowly to position the raised load.
- Never allow anyone to walk or stand under a raised load.
- Tilt the load forward only when over a stack or rack.
- Be certain the forks are clear of the pallet before turning or changing height.
- Always stack the load square and straight.
- Before backing up, check behind you and on both sides for pedestrians or other traffic.

Leaving the Forklift Unattended

- Lower the carriage, neutralize the controls, and set the brakes.
- If greater than 25 feet from, or out of viewing range of the vehicle, lower the carriage, neutralize the controls, set the brakes, and turn the power off.
- On an incline, always block the wheels.

Figure 27-3: Sample Daily Inspection and Maintenance Checklist

Gas Operated Forklift

Truck Number _____   Operator _____

Truck Model _____   Dept. _____ Shift _____

Date _____   Meter Reading _____

Item	O.K.	Adjusted (initials)	Addition of Components (amount)
1. Gasoline/propane			
2. Water (or antifreeze)			
3. Engine oil			
4. Hydraulic fluid			
5. Steering mechanism			
6. Horn			
7. Brakes			
8. Wheels and tires			
9. Hoist cylinder			
10. Tilt cylinders			
11. Air cleaner			
12. Fork pins and stops			
13. Battery water level			
14. Lights			
15. Fire extinguisher			
16. Water level			
17. Broken/loose parts			
18. Hydraulic controls			
19. Clutch operation			
20. Proper storage position			

Signature of Operator _____

Notes and special comments

_____

_____

_____

_____

_____

_____

_____

_____

_____

_____

_____

_____

_____

_____

_____

Score: _____

Process Safety Management

Applicable to construction activities where there exists a potential for a catastrophic release of: 1) toxic; 2) reactive; 3) flammable; and/or 4) explosive chemicals. This includes those sites which store/use "highly hazardous chemicals" which are listed in the standard, AND where the stored quantity of these chemicals exceeds a published threshold. Excluded are retail facilities, oil or gas well-drilling/servicing operations, and normally unoccupied remote facilities. 29 CFR 1926.64

▶ **Written process safety information**

☐ **Hazards**
Material safety data sheets may be used to meet this requirement.

- Toxicity and exposure limits

- Physical data

- Reactivity data

- Corrosivity data

- Thermal and chemical stability

- Hazardous effects of inadvertent mixing of different materials

Table 28-1: Highly Hazardous Chemicals

Chemical	Threshold Quantity	Chemical	Threshold Quantity
Acetaldehyde	2,500	Hydrogen selenide	150
Acrolein	150	Hydrogen sulfide	1,500
Acrylyl chloride	250	Hdroxlamine	2,500
Allyl chloride	1,000	Iron, pentacarbonyl	250
Allylamine	1,000	Isopropylamine	5,000
Alkylaluminums	5,000	Ketene	100
Ammonia, anhydrous	10,000	Methacrylaldehyde	1,000
Ammonia solutions (> 44% ammonia by weight)	15,000	Methacryloyl chloride	150
Ammonium perchlorate	7,500	Methyl acrylonitrile	250
Ammonium permanganate	7,500	Methylamine, anhydrous	1,000
Arsine	100	Methyl bromide	2,500
Bis(chloromethyl) ether	100	Methyl chloride	15,000
Boron trichloride	2,500	Methyl chloroformate	500
Boron trifluoride	250	Methyl ethyl ketone peroxide (concentration > 60%)	5,000
Bromine	1,500	Methyl fluoroacetate	100
Bromine chloride	1,500	Methyl fluorosulfate	100
Bromine pentafluoride	15,000	Methyl hydrazine	100
3-Bromopropyne	100	Methyl iodide	7,500
Butyl hydroperoxide (tertiary)	5,000	Methyl isocyanate	250
Butyl perbenzoate (tertiary)	7,500	Methyl mercaptan	5,000
Carbonyl chloride	100	Methyl vinyl ketone	100
Carbonyl fluoride	2,500	Methyltrichlorosilane	500
Cellulose nitrate (concentration > 12.6% nitrogen)	2,500	Nickel carbonyl	150
Chlorine	1,500	Nitric acid (94.5% by weight or greater)	500
Chlorine dioxide	1,000	Nitric oxide	250
Chlorine pentrafluoride	1,000	Nitroaniline	5,000
Chlorine trifluoride	1,000	Nitromethane	2,500
Chlorodiethylaluminum	5,000	Nitrogen dioxide	250
1-Chloro-2,4-dinitrobenzene	5,000	Nitrogen tetroxide	250
Chloromethyl methyl ether	500	Nitrogen trifluoride	5,000
Chloropicrin	500	Nitrogen trioxide	250
Chloropicrin and methyl bromide mixture	1,500	Osmium tetroxide	100
Chloropicrin and methyl chloride mixture	1,500	Oxygen difluoride	100
Cumene hydroperoxide	5,000	Ozone	100
Cyanogen	2,500	Pentaborane	100
Cyanogen chloride	500	Paracetic acid (> 60% acetic acid)	1,000
Cyanuric fluoride	100	Perchloric acid (concentration > 60% by weight)	5,000
Diacetyl peroxide (concentration > 70%)	5,000	Perchloromethyl mercaptan	150
Diazomethane	500	Perchloryl fluoride	5,000
Dibenzoyl peroxide	7,500	Peroxyacetic acid (concentration > 60% acetic acid)	1,000
Diborane	100	Phosgene	100
Dibutyl peroxide (tertiary)	5,000	Phosphine	100
Dichloro acetylene	250	Phosphorus oxychloride	1,000
Dichlorosilane	2,500	Phosphorus trichloride	1,000
Diethylzinc	10,000	Phosphoryl chloride	1,000
Diisopropyl peroxydicarbonate	7,500	Propargyl bromide	100
Dialuroyl peroxide	7,500	Propyl nitrate	100
Dimethyldichlorosilane	1,000	Sarin	100
Dimethylhydrazine, 1,1-	1,000	Stibine	500
Ethyl methyl ketone peroxide (concentration > 60%)	5,000	Sulfur dioxide (liquid)	1,000
Ethyl nitrite	5,000	Sulfur pentafluoride	250
Ethylamine	7,500	Sulfur tetrafluoride	250
Ethylene fluorohydrin	100	Sulfur trioxide	1,000
Ethylene oxide	5,000	Sulfuric acid, fuming (65% to 80% by weight)	1,000
Ethyleneimine	1,000	Sulfuric anhydride	1,000
Fluorine	100	Tellurium hexafluoride	250
Formaldehyde	1,000	Tetrafluoroethylene	5,000
Furan	500	Tetrafluorohydrazine	5,000
Hexafluoroacetone	5,000	Tetramethyl lead	1,000
Hydrochloric acid, anhydrous	5,000	Thionyl chloride	250
Hydrofluoric acid, anhydrous	1,000	Trichloro (chloromethyl) silane	100
Hydrogen bromide	5,000	Trichloro (dichlorophenyl) silane	2,500
Hydrogen chloride	5,000	Trichlorosilane	5,000
Hydrogen cyanide, anhydrous	1,000	Triflurochloroethylene	10,000
Hydrogen fluoride	1,000	Trimethyloxysilane	1,500
Hydrogen peroxide (52% by weight or greater)	7,500		

Threshold quantity is in terms of pounds.

☐ **Technology**

- Temperatures

- Pressures

- Flow compositions

- Evaluation of consequences of deviations
  (**Exception**: *Where original technical information no longer exists, information may be developed with the process hazard analysis in sufficient detail to support the analysis.*)

☐ **Equipment**

- Materials of construction

- Piping and instrument diagrams

- Electrical classification

- Relief system design and design basis

- Ventilation system design

- Design codes and standards employed

- Material and energy balances for processes built after May 26, 1992

- Safety systems

- Document stating that "equipment complies with recognized and generally accepted good engineering practices"

▶ **Written process hazard analysis**

Method of analysis used: _____

_____

_____

☐ **Appropriate to complexity of the process**

☐ **Identification, evaluation, and control for each of the hazards**

☐ **Involve one of, or combination of, methods shown in Figure 28-1**

☐ **Hazards of each process**

☐ **All previous incidents identified which had a potential for catastrophic consequences**

Figure 28-1: Methods for Performing a Process Hazards Analysis

What-if

Evaluate effects of component failures or procedural errors on the process.

Checklist

A more complex variety of the "what-if" method.
- Audit operator practices and job knowledge
- Suitability of equipment and materials of construction
- Review chemistry of the process(es) and controls
- Audit the operating and maintenance records

What-if/Checklist

Combination of creative "what-if" method with the more methodical checklist approach.

Hazard and Operability Study (HAZOP)

A formal method for systematically investigating each element of a system for parameter deviation from the intended design conditions which may result in hazards and operability problems.

Failure Mode and Effect Analysis (FMEA)

Methodical study involving the review of a diagram of the operation and all components that could fail and conceivably affect the safety of the operation.
- Potential mode of failure
- Consequence of the failure
- Effect on the other components and whole system
- Hazard class
- Probability of failure
- Detection methods
- Remarks/compensation provisions

Fault Tree Analysis

A qualitative or quantitative model of all the undesirable outcomes that could result from a specific initiating event.

☐ **Engineering and administrative controls applicable to the hazards and their relationships** *(e.g., hydrocarbon detectors)*

- Consequences of control failures

- Facility siting

- Human factors

- Qualitative evaluation of possible safety and health effects due to a control failure

☐ **Performed by qualified team**

☐ **Provision for analysis updates at least once every 5 years**

▶ **Written operating procedures**

☐ **Operating phases**
(e.g., initial start-up, normal operations, temporary operations, emergency shutdown, emergency operations, normal shutdown, and start-up after turnaround or emergency shutdown)

☐ **Operating limits**

☐ **Safety and health considerations**

☐ **Operating procedures accessible to employees**

☐ **Procedures reviewed to assure they reflect current operating practices**

- As frequently as needed

- Certified annually by employer
  - Current
  - Accurate

☐ **Develop and implement safe work practices to control hazards**

▶ **Employee training**

☐ **Contents**

- Specific safety and health hazards

- Emergency and shutdown procedures

- Safe work practices applicable to the employee's job task(s)

+---+
| ## Figure 28-2: Process Hazard Analysis Team Requirements |
| |
| • Expertise in engineering and process operations |
| |
| • Experience and knowledge specific to the process under evaluation |
| |
| • Knowledgeable in specific process hazard analysis methodology |
+---+

Figure 28-3: Important Definitions

Catastrophic release

Major uncontrolled emission, fire, or explosion, involving one or more highly hazardous chemicals, that may present a serious danger to employees in the workplace.

Highly hazardous chemical

A chemical which is toxic, reactive, flammable, or explosive which is either listed with a specified threshold quantity or meets certain standards of a flammable liquid or gas with a given quantity.

Hot work

Work involving electric or gas welding, cutting, brazing, or similar flame or spark-producing operations. A permit must be issued for all hot work operations on or near a covered process.

Process

Any activity which involves a highly hazardous chemical, including use, storage, manufacturing, handling, or on-site movement/transport of these chemicals. Any group of vessels which are interconnected and located such that a highly hazardous chemical could be involved in a potential release are also considered part of a process.

☐ **Proper frequency**

- Initial

- New job assignments *(e.g., recent hire)*

- Refresher employee training *(minimum of at least once every 3 years)*

- Change in job assignments

☐ **Properly documented**

- Employee's name

- Proof of understanding
  - Written exam
  - Signed statement

- Date(s) of training

- Filed
  - Written exam
  - Signed statement

▶ **Contract labor procedures**

☐ **Method for evaluating their safety programs and performance**

- Written procedures

- Documentation of employee training in regards to process(es) with which they will be involved

- Written assurance by contract employer that each contract employee will follow the safety rules

☐ **Procedure for identifying unique or newly identified hazards not normally incident to or known by the contracting employer**

☐ **Method for informing all contract labor of the processes and hazards associated with their job**

☐ **Method for evaluating contract labor's performance/compliance with procedures during the job** *(e.g., checklist of potential discrepancies to be completed by the Safety Director)*

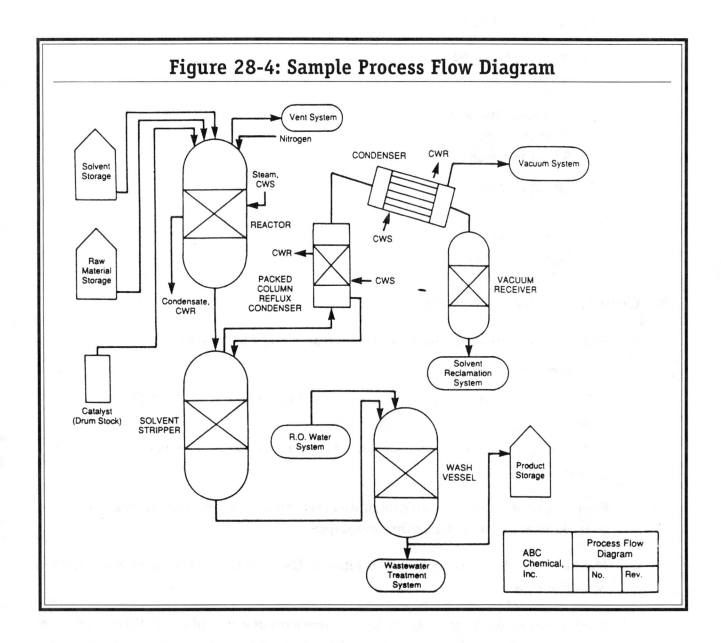

Figure 28-4: Sample Process Flow Diagram

▶ **Pre-start-up safety review**
To be performed for new and modified facilities which may impact the process safety information.

☐ **Prior to hazardous chemical introduction to a process**

- Construction and equipment is in accordance with design specs

- Safety, operating, maintenance, and emergency procedures are in place and adequate

- In new processes, ensure that process hazard analysis has been performed and recommendations resolved or implemented prior to start-up

- In modified facilities, requirements within the management of change have been met

☐ **Employee training for each process**

- Completed

- Documented for each process

☐ **Site injury and illness log maintained on each contractor when the contractor's employees are working in and/or around the process area(s)**

▶ **Written procedures for maintaining process equipment**

☐ **Maintenance requirements**

☐ **Means for training maintenance employees**

☐ **Inspection and testing procedures**

☐ **Method for identifying equipment deficiencies**

☐ **Quality assurance approach**

▶ **Hot work permits**

☐ **Required for work conducted on OR near a hazardous process**

☐ **Maintained on file until work is completed**

☐ **Statement that "The fire prevention and protection requirements of 29 CFR 1910.252 (a) have been implemented prior to beginning the hot work operations."**

Figure 28-5: Sample Notification of Process Change Form

Process Change Notification

Notification by: _____ Date of Notification: _____

_____ Date of Proposed Change: _____

Area of Process Change: _____

Temporary Inclusion Dates: _____

Scope of Change

_____

_____

_____

Technical Basis for Change

_____

_____

_____

_____

Anticipated Impact

☐ Safety   ☐ Health   ☐ Environment   ☐ Loss Prevention

Type of Change

☐ Alarm   ☐ Shutdown Point   ☐ Addition/Removal of Equipment

☐ Piping Modification   ☐ Chemical   ☐ Process Computer Control

☐ Job Procedures   ☐ Instrument   ☐ Equipment/Material

☐ Other

Premodification Checklist

☐ Attached   ☐ Requested

To Be Completed by (date): _____

Post Modification Checklist (prior to start-up)

☐ Attached   ☐ Requested

To Be Completed by (date): _____

Approvals	Name	Title	Signature	Date
Notifier				
Reviewer				
Dept. Head				

► **Written procedures for management of change**
Items which may impact hazardous processes

☐ **Technical basis for the proposed change**

☐ **Impact of the change on safety and health**

☐ **Modifications to operating procedures**

☐ **Necessary time period for the change**

☐ **Authorization requirements**

► **Incident investigation procedures**

☐ **Method used to assign an investigator or team of investigators**

☐ **Implemented within 48 hours of an incident**

☐ **Contents of an incident investigation report**

- Date of incident

- Date of investigation

- Description of the incident

- Factors that contributed to the incident

- Recommendations

► **Written emergency response plan**
(See "Written emergency action plan," p. 127.)

☐ **Releases which may impact the entire plant**

☐ **Small releases**

► **Routine compliance audits** *(at least once every 3 years)*

Actual in-house frequency:_____

Figure 28-6: Example of an Incident Investigation Report Checklist

☑ **Dates and times indicated**
- Incident
- Investigation Report

☑ **Description of the incident**
- Circumstance(s)
- Cause(s)
- Contributing factors

☑ **Recommended corrective actions**

☑ **Filed and retained for 5 years**

Figure 28-7: Checklist of Written Report Requirements

☐ **Process Safety Information**

☐ **Process Hazard Analysis**

☐ **Operating Procedures**

☐ **Contract Labor Procedures**

☐ **Pre-start-up Safety Review Procedures**

☐ **Maintenance of Process Equipment Procedures**

☐ **Management of Change Procedures**

☐ **Emergency Response Plan**

► **Records retained**

☐ Process analysis updates and incident investigation reports—5 years

☐ Hot work permits—until permitted work has been completed

☐ Compliance audits—latest 2 audits

☐ Employee training records—3 years

► **Overall program effectiveness**

☐ Employee understanding of procedures

☐ Employee compliance with procedures

☐ Lack of associated incidents

Notes and special comments

_____

_____

_____

_____

_____

_____

_____

_____

_____

_____

_____

_____

Score: _____

Respiratory Protection Program

> *Applicable to occupational exposures in general industry, shipyards, longshoring, and construction where a respirator is either mandated or worn due to employee preference. 29 CFR 1910.134 (28 April 1998)*

▶ **Written respiratory protection program**
Employers are not required to provide a written respiratory protection program for those employees whose only use of a respirator involves the "voluntary use" of filtering air purifying respirators.

☐ **Potential exposure health hazards**

- Routine

- Emergency

☐ **Work conditions and exposures requiring the use of respirators**

☐ **Physical examination requirements**

☐ **Procedures for selection**

☐ **Fit testing procedures**

Figure 29-1: Sample Respiratory Protection Program

Table of Contents

Section 1:   Company Policy

Section 2:   Health Hazards

Section 3:   Exposure Standards

Section 4:   Air Monitoring Procedures and Results

Section 5:   Physical Examination Requirements

Section 6:   Respiratory Protection Training

    6.1:   Types of Respirators

    6.2:   Selection

    6.3:   Usage

    6.4:   Fit Testing

    6.5:   Limitations

    6.6:   Cleaning Procedures

    6.7:   Storage

    6.8:   Inspection and Maintenance

    6.9:   Respirator Effectiveness Checks

Section 7:   Frequency of Training

Section 8:   Recordkeeping Requirements

Section 9:   Designated Program Administrator

☐ **Use and limitations of respirators**

- Routine

- Emergency

☐ **Training schedule**

☐ **Maintenance schedule**

☐ **Emergency-use respirator inspections schedule**

☐ **Updated to reflect changes in workplace conditions which may affect respirator requirements**

☐ **Routine evaluations scheduled to determine the continued effectiveness of the program**

▶ **Designated program administrator**

☐ **Administers and/or oversees respiratory protection program**

☐ **Conducts required evaluations for program effectiveness**

☐ **Qualified through training and/or experience**

▶ **Employee training**

☐ **Physical examination requirements**

☐ **Exposure health hazards**

- Types of chemicals/substances

- Toxicological concerns

- Exposure air monitoring procedures

- Documented air monitoring exposure levels

☐ **Types of respirators**

- Description of different types

- Use and limitations of each type (e.g., no beards)

Figure 29-2: Checklist of Special Problems Associated with Poor Respirator Seal

☑ **Facial hair**
- Beards
- Five-o'clock shadow
- Sideburns
- Moustaches

☑ **Eyeglasses (with full-facepiece respirators)**

☑ **Facial deformities**
- Deep skin creases
- Prominent cheekbones
- Severe acne
- Lack of teeth
- Dentures

☑ **Attempts to communicate by breaking the seal**

☑ **Refusal to wear properly**
- Psychological concerns
- Discomfort

☑ **Claustrophobia**

☑ **Excessive perspiration**

☐ **Fit testing procedures**

- When to test for fit

- How to test for fit

- Different types of fit testing and when each is used

☐ **Maintenance and cleaning**

- Procedures

- Schedule

☐ **Storage requirements**

▶ **Emergency-use respirator inspections**

☐ **Logged inspections and use**

- Date(s)

- Finding(s)

- Circumstance(s) of use

☐ **Frequency**

- After each use

- At least once a month

☐ **Actual inspection schedule(s):**

▶ **Medical surveillance**

☐ **Frequency**

- Initial

- Annual

☐ **Physician aware of potential exposures and their effects**

☐ **Appropriate to the exposures**

☐ **Psychological considerations** *(e.g., claustrophobia)*

☐ **Statement by the physician that employee is approved/not approved to wear a respirator**

Figure 29-3: Air Purifying Cartridge/Canister Codes

Airborne Contaminant(s)	Color Code Assigned
Acid gases (general)	White
Hydrocyanic acid	White with ½ inch green stripe completely around the cartridge/canister
Chlorine gas	White with ½ inch yellow stripe completely around the cartridge/canister
Acid gases and organic vapors (both)	Yellow
Hydrocyanic acid gas and chloropicrin vapor	Yellow with ½ inch blue stripe completely around the cartridge/canister
Organic vapors	Black
Ammonia gas	Green
Acid and ammonia gases (both)	Green with ½ inch white stripe completely around the cartridge/canister
Carbon monoxide	Blue
Acid gases, organic vapors, and ammonia gases	Brown
Radioactive materials and asbestos	Purple (or magenta)
Particlulates	Color for type of airborne contaminant with a ½ inch gray strip stripe completely around the cartridge/canister
All of the above in combination	Red with a ½ inch gray strip stripe completely around the cartridge/canister

► **Fit testing**

☐ **Employees tested for fit with same make, model, style, and size of respirator that is to be used**

☐ **Appropriate procedures used**

- Quantitative fit testing
  □ Negative pressure air-purifying respirators with a fit factor of greater than 100
  □ Fit factor of 500 or more for full facepieces
- Qualitative fit testing
  □ Negative pressure air-purifying respirators with a fit factor of up to 100
- User seal check—positive/negative pressure checks with daily use

☐ **Proper frequency**

- Prior to initial use of respirator

- Prior to use of different make, model, style, and/or size

- Upon any noted changes in an employee's physical condition
  □ Facial scarring
  □ Dentures
  □ Cosmetic surgery
  □ Body weight

- Annually

☐ **When an employee feels a fitted respirator is unacceptable (for whatever reason), that employee is given the opportunity to select a different respirator and again fit tested**

► **Overall program effectiveness**

☐ **Employee understanding of procedures**

☐ **Employee compliance with procedures**

☐ **Lack of associated incidents, illness, and/or disease**

Figure 29-4: Respirator Fit Testing Procedures

Respirator shall be worn for 5 minutes prior to start of fit testing, and the test shall be performed while the subject is wearing equipment which will be worn during actual respirator use AND can potentially interfere with respirator fit. During testing the following shall be performed:

- Normal breathing
- Deep breathing
- Turning head side to side
- Moving head up and down
- Talking

QUANTITATIVE FIT TESTING

- Isoamyl acetate protocol
  - Not appropriate for particulate respirators
  - Respirator must be equipped with an organic vapor filter during testing
  - Performed within a clear 55-gallon drum liner inverted over a 2-foot diameter frame, the top of the chamber at least 6 inches above the subject's head, or similar chamber
- Saccharin solution aerosol protocol
  - Subject not permitted to eat, drink, smoke, or chew gum 15 minutes prior to the test
  - Enclosure about the head and shoulders that is about 12 inches in diameter by 14 inches tall with front clear, allowing for head movement
- Irritant smoke protocol
  - Fit respirator with HEPA or P100 series filter
  - No test enclosure shall be used

QUANTITATIVE FIT TESTING
(Both methods require an enclosure and special equipment.)

- Generated aerosol fit testing protocol
- Ambient aerosol condensation nuclei counter fit testing protocol (Portacount Test)

Notes and special comments

_____

_____

_____

_____

_____

_____

_____

_____

_____

_____

_____

_____

_____

_____

Score: _____

Section 30

Scaffolds

> *Applicable to the installation and use of scaffolds within construction. A scaffold is any temporary elevated platform—supported or suspended—and its supporting structure, including points of anchorage, used for supporting employees, materials, or both. 29 CFR 1926.450 through 1926.452*

▶ General condition

☐ **Posted safety rules**

- Visible
- Legible

☐ **Means of access** *(e.g., ladder, ramp, or stairway)*

☐ **No deterioration or damage**

☐ **No rust**

▶ Railings and toeboards

☐ **Guarded where greater than 10 feet**

- Top rail
- Mid rail
- Toeboard

Table 30-1: Scaffold Limitations

Type of Scaffold	Maximum Height Allowed

Single pole
- Light duty .... 20 to 60 feet *
- Medium duty .... 60 feet
- Heavy duty .... 60 feet

Independent pole
- Light duty .... 20 to 60 feet *
- Medium duty .... 60 feet
- Heavy duty .... 60 feet

Tube and coupler

Light duty
- 1-2 working levels .... 125 feet
- 3 working levels .... 91 feet

Medium duty
- 1 working level .... 125 feet
- 2 working levels .... 78 feet

Heavy duty—1 working level .... 125 feet

Mobile tubular welded sectional folding .... 50 feet

Mobile tube and coupler .... 50 feet

Note: *Types which have dimension requirements only*

Outrigger	Needle beam
Mason's adjustable multiple-point suspension	Plasterer's, decorator's, and large area
Two-point suspension/swinging	Interior hung
Stone setter's adjustable multiple-point suspension	Ladder jack
Single-point adjustable suspension	Window jack
Boatswain's chair	Roofing brackets
Carpenter's bracket	Crawling boards (or chicken ladders)
Bricklayer's square	Float (or ship)
Horse	Mobile work platforms
	Mobile ladder stands

* Ranges are based on structural members defined in 29 CFR 1910.28, Safety Requirements for Scaffolding. Any scaffolds in excess of the above maximum allowed height must undergo special considerations (e.g., designed by a registered professional engineer) which are based on the type of scaffold to be erected. All scaffolds have dimensional and structural requirements which must be met.

Design Loads Defined
- Light duty: Working load of 25 pounds per square foot.
- Medium duty: Working load of 50 pounds per square foot.
- Heavy duty: Working load of 75 pounds per square foot.

☐ **Screened toeboards where greater than 10 feet and above walks or work areas**

▶ **Planks (or decks) and platforms**

☐ **General conditions**

- Rigid

- Secured from movement

- Nonslip surface

- Fully planked from front uprights to guardrail supports

- Capable of supporting at least 4 times the maximum intended load

☐ **Posted design and specification limitations** *(e.g., weight limit)*

▶ **Supported scaffolds**

☐ **Special restraints where greater than a four to one height to width ratio**

☐ **Rigid poles, legs, posts, frames, and uprights**

- Firm foundation

- Plumb

- Braced to prevent swaying and displacement

▶ **Suspended scaffolds**

☐ **Support devices**

- Rest on adequate surfaces
  - Capable of supporting 4 times the load imposed on them by the scaffold operating at the rated load of the hoist
    OR
  - At least 1.5 times the load imposed on them by the scaffold at the stall capacity of the hoist

- Strong

- Supported by bearing blocks

- Secured against movement

- Tiebacks as strong as hoisting rope

Table 30-2: Resources for Information Regarding Specific Types of Scaffolds

Pole scaffolds .... 1926.452(a)

Tube and coupler scaffolds .... 1926.452(b)

Fabricated frame scaffolds .... 1926.452(c)

Tubular welded frame scaffolds .... 1926.452(c)

Plasterers' scaffolds .... 1926.452(d)

Decorators' scaffolds .... 1926.452(d)

Large area scaffolds .... 1926.452(d)

Bricklayers' square scaffolds .... 1926.452(e)

Horse scaffolds .... 1926.452(f)

Form scaffolds .... 1926.452(g)

Carpenters' bracket scaffolds .... 1926.452(g)

Road bracket scaffolds .... 1926.452(h)

Outrigger scaffolds .... 1926.452(i)

Pump jack scaffolds .... 1926.452(j)

Ladder jack scaffolds .... 1926.452(k)

Window jack scaffolds .... 1926.452(l)

Crawling boards .... 1926.452(m)

Chicken ladders .... 1926.452(m)

Step ladder scaffolds .... 1926.452(n)

Platform ladder scaffolds .... 1926.452(n)

Trestle ladder scaffolds .... 1926.452(n)

Single-point adjustable suspension scaffolds .... 1926.452(o)

Two-point adjustable suspension scaffolds .... 1926.452(p)

Swing stages .... 1926.452(p)

Multi-point adjustable suspension scaffolds .... 1926.452(q)

Stonesetters' multi-point adjustable
    suspension scaffolds .... 1926.452(q)

Masons' multi-point adjustable
    suspension scaffolds .... 1926.452(q)

Catenary scaffolds .... 1926.452(r)

Float scaffolds .... 1926.452(s)

Ship scaffolds .... 1926.452(s)

Interior hung scaffolds .... 1926.452(t)

Needle beam scaffolds .... 1926.452(u)

Multi-level suspended scaffolds .... 1926.452(v)

Mobile scaffolds .... 1926.452(w)

Repair bracket scaffolds .... 1926.452(x)

Stilts .... 1926.452(y)

Aerial lifts 1926.453

---

* Scaffold specifications for all of the above can be found in 29 CFR 1926, Subpart L, Appendix A.

☐ **Suspension scaffold outrigger beams**

- Structural metal or equivalent

- Restrained to prevent movement

- Inboard ends
  - ▫ Secured by bolts or equivalent
    OR
  - ▫ Stabilized by counterbalances

- Provided with stop bolts or shackles at both ends

- Securely fastened

- Bearing supports perpendicular to the beam center line

- Web in vertical position

- Shackle or clevis to road directly over the center line of the stirrup

☐ **Winding drum hoists not less than four wraps of rope at lowest point of scaffold travel**

☐ **Wire suspension ropes**

- Repaired ropes not used

- Joined together properly
  - ▫ Through the use of eye splice thimbles connected with shackles
    OR
  - ▫ Cover plates and bolts

- Load end secured by splicing or equivalent means

- Routinely inspected
  - ▫ Prior to each work shift
  - ▫ After an incident

☐ **Limitations and inspection of wire rope clips—if used**

- Known

- Observed

☐ **Testing performed by qualified testing laboratory**

- Power-operated hoists

- Manual hoists

- *Gasoline-powered equipment not permitted with suspension scaffolds*

Figure 30-1: Wire Suspension Rope Inspection Items

- Any physical damage which impairs the function and strength of the rope.
- Kinks that might impair the tracking or wrapping of rope around the drum(s) and sheave(s).
- Six randomly distributed broken wires in one rope lay or three broken wires in one strand in one rope lay.
- Abrasion, corrosion, scrubbing, flattening, or peening causing loss of more than one-third of the original diameter of the outside wires.
- Heat damage caused by a torch or any damage caused by contact with electrical wires.
- Evidence that the secondary brake has been activated during an overspeed condition and has engaged the suspension rope.

Figure 30-2: Use of Wire Suspension Rope Clips

- A minimum of 3 wire rope clips installed, with the clips a minimum of 6 rope diameters apart.
- Clips installed according to the manufacturer's recommendations.
- Clips retightened to the manufacturer's recommendations after the initial loading.
- Clips inspected and retightened to the manufacturer's recommendations at the start of each work shift.
- U-bolt clips not used at the point of suspension for any scaffold hoist.
- U-bolts placed over the dead end and saddle placed over the live end of the rope.

Table 30-3: Clearance Distances from Power Lines

Voltage	Minimum distance	Alternatives
Insulated Lines		
Less than 300 volts	3 feet	
0.3 to 50 kvolts	10 feet	
Greater than 50 kvolts	10 feet + 0.4 inches	2 Xs the length of the line insulator,
	0.4 inches for each kv over 50 kv	but never less than 10 feet
Uninsulated Lines		
Less than 50 kvolts	10 feet	
Greater than 50 kvolts	10 feet + 0.4 inches	2 Xs the length of the line insulator,
	0.4 inches for each kv over 50 kv	but never less than 10 feet

* Clearance distances need not be observed if lines have been de-energized or relocated, or if protective coverings have been installed to prevent accidental contact.

☐ **Enclosed gears and brakes**

☐ **Appropriate automatic braking device or locking pawl**

- Normal operating brake

- Safety brake
    - Instantaneous change in momentum
    - Accelerated overspeed

☐ **Positive crank force—manually operated hoists**

☐ **Sway prevention for two-point and multi-point suspension scaffolds**

▶ **Proper use of equipment**

☐ **Maximum intended load and/or rated capacity limits—not exceeded**

☐ **Components inspected for visible defects by competent person**

- Prior to each work shift

- After an event

☐ **Decommissioning procedure for damaged/weakened components**

☐ **Horizontal mobility limited to special design features only**

☐ **Proper clearance from energized power lines** *(See Table 30-3.)*

▶ **Falling object protection procedures**

☐ **Hard hats required**

☐ **Potential for tools, materials, or equipment to fall from scaffold to traffic below**

- Backup system
    - Area barricaded below the scaffold(s), OR
    - A canopy structure, debris net, or catch platform above employees—strong enough to withstand potential falling objects

- Required equipment
    - Toeboard along the edge of platform when greater than 10 feet above ground level
    - Paneling or screening extending to top of guardrail where tools are piled higher than the top edge of the toeboard
    - Guardrail system small enough to prevent passage of smallest potential falling objects

Figure 30-3: Fall Protection Equipment

Fall protection should be provided for each employee on a scaffold greater than 10 feet above the lower level.

Personal fall arrest system only

- Boatswain's chair
- Catenary scaffold
- Float scaffold
- Needle beam scaffold
- Ladder jack

Single-point or two-point adjustable suspension scaffold

- Personal fall arrest system
- Guardrail system

Crawling board or chicken ladder

- Personal fall arrest system
- Guardrail system with minimum 200 pound top rail capacity, ¾ inch diameter grab line or equivalent

Self-contained adjustable scaffold

- Personal fall arrest system
- Guardrail system with minimum 200 pound top rail capacity when the platform is supported by ropes
- Guardrail system with minimum 200 pound top rail capacity when the platform is supported by the frame structure

Walkway within a scaffold

- Guardrail with minimum 200 pound top rail capacity installed within 9½ inches of and along at least one side of the walkway

Overhand bricklaying operations from a supported scaffold

- Personal fall arrest system
  OR
- Guardrail system with minimum 200 pound top rail capacity

Other scaffolds not mentioned above

- Personal fall arrest system
  OR
- Special guardrail systems based on scaffold type (29 CFR 1926, Subpart L, Appendix A)

Note: After September 2, 1997, employers shall have a competent person determine the feasibility and safety of providing fall protection for employees erecting and dismantling supported scaffolds. Employers are required to provide fall protection for employees erecting or dismantling supported scaffolds where the installation and use of such protection is feasible and DOES NOT create a greater hazard.

☐ **Potential for tools, materials, or equipment to fall from above the scaffold**

- Backup system
  - ▫ A canopy structure, debris net, or catch platform above employees—strong enough to withstand potential falling objects

- Equipment on higher work activities
  - ▫ Toeboard along the edge of platform when greater than 10 feet above ground level
  - ▫ Paneling or screening extending to top of guardrail where tools are piled higher than the top edge of the toeboard
  - ▫ Guardrail system small enough to prevent passage of smallest potential falling objects

► **Employee training**

☐ **Pertinent employees** *(anyone required to erect, move, dismantle, or alter a scaffold)*

☐ **Content of training**

- Regulations
- Procedures for erecting and dismantling
- Personal protective equipment
- Fall protection
- Materials handling
- Access procedures
- Walking platforms
- Foundations
- Guys, ties, and braces
- Routine inspection procedures
- Method for decommissioning equipment/components
- Special conditions to be aware of
- Safety precautions
- Special welding precautions, if applicable

☐ **Records of training maintained**

Figure 30-4: Some Scaffolding Training Items

Special Conditions
- Managing swinging loads
- Shielding ropes from heat-producing processes
- Protecting ropes from corrosives and acids
- Storms and high winds
- Debris accumulation
- Ice, rain, and snow

Safety Precautions
- Do not use makeshift devices (e.g., boxes)
- No ladders on scaffolds
- Adjacent ladder—secured from sideways thrust exerted by ladder
- Platform units—secured to prevent movement
- Ladder legs
  - On same platform or other means provided to stabilize the ladder against unequal platform deflection
  - Secured to prevent them from slipping or being pushed off the platform

Welding from Suspended Scaffolds
- Use an insulated thimble to attach each suspension wire rope to its hanging support
- Insulate excess suspension wire rope and additional independent lines from grounding
- Suspension wire rope covered with insulating material extending at least 4 feet above the hoist
- Any tail lines below the hoist shall be insulated to prevent contact with the platform
- Tail line that hangs free below the scaffold shall be guided or retained so it does not become grounded
- Each hoist covered with insulated protective covers
- In addition to the work lead-attachment required for welding, a grounding conductor shall be connected from the scaffold to the structure—at least the size of the welding work lead—and the conductor shall not be in series with the welding work or process
- Should the scaffold grounding lead be disconnected, turn off the welding machine
- Do not allow an active welding rod or uninsulated welding lead contact the scaffold or its suspension system

▶ **Fall protection plan**

☐ **Written plan properly applied**

- When installing suspension scaffold support systems on floors, roof, and other elevated surfaces

- When engaged in leading edge work, precast concrete construction work, and residential construction work and when one can demonstrate that it is not feasible or it creates a greater hazard to use conventional fall protection systems

☐ **Implemented and enforced**

▶ **Overall program effectiveness**

☐ **Employee understanding of procedures**

☐ **Employee compliance with procedures**

☐ **Lack of associated incidents**

Notes and special comments

Score: _____

Section 31

Stairways and Ladders

Applicable to the installation and use of stairways and ladders in construction. Employers are required to ensure the necessary installation and use of stairways, ladders, and their respective fall protection systems. 29 CFR 1926.1051 through 1926.1053 and 1926.1060

▶ **General requirements**

☐ **Provided where elevation is greater than 19 inches**

☐ **Double cleated or more than one ladder**

- Only means of access to or egress from a working area for 25 employees or more

  OR

- When a ladder serves as simultaneous two-way traffic

☐ **If area access is blocked by work, another access point is provided**

▶ **Stairways**

☐ **Slope—30 to 50 degrees from the horizontal**

☐ **Landing**

- Equal to or greater than 30 inches in the direction of travel

- Equal to or greater than 22-inch width

- Every 12 feet or less

Figure 31-1: Preferred Angles and Limits for Fixed Ladders, Stairs, and Ramps

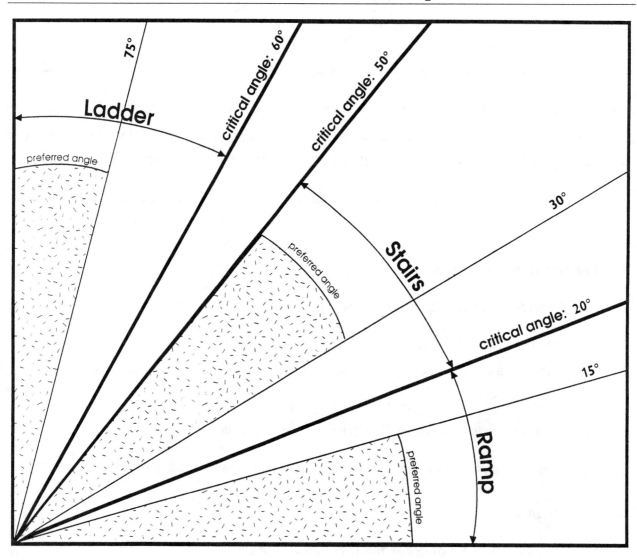

☐ **Uniform risers** *(not greater than ¼ inch variation)*

☐ **Platform where doors and/or gates open onto the stairway**
(should not reduce effective width of the platform to less than 20 inches)

☐ **No protruding nails**

☐ **Nonslip surfaces**

☐ **At least one hand rail and stair rail system along unprotected edge**
(if more than 4 risers or greater than 30 inches)

☐ **Height of stair rail**

- At least 36 inches (installed after March 15, 1991)

- At least 30 inches (installed before March 15, 1991)

☐ **Intermediate structure members**

- Mid rails—midway

- Screens (or mesh)—entire opening

- Intermediate vertical members—no opening greater than 19 inches

☐ **Hand rails and top rails**

- At least 30 to 37 inches from surface of stair

- Top edge of stair rail 36 to 37 inches

- No snags or exposed nails

- Adequate hand hold to prevent falls

- Clearance of at least 3 inches from the wall or other objects

- Able to withstand force of 200 pounds within 2 inches of the top edge

☐ **Landings provided with protected sides or guardrails**

▶ **Portable ladders**

☐ **General condition and use**

- Fiberglass and wood only around electrical hazards

- Metal ladders
  - Posted with electrical caution label at eye level
  - Ends fitted with insulating nonslip material
  - Special precautions taken near electric circuits

Figure 31-2: Condemned Ladder Tag

Dangerous—Do Not Use

This ladder is not to be used until it has been properly repaired.

Repairs needed: _____

_____

Date:_____ Date to be repaired by: _____

Inspected/condemned by: _____

This tag shall be removed by the Safety Department only.

Table 31-1: Ladder Specifications

Type of Ladder	Maximum Length	Minimum Section Overlap
Portable stepladders		
Industrial	20 feet	
Commercial	12 feet	
Household	6 feet	
Portable rung ladders		
Single	30 feet	
Two-section		
Wood	60 feet	
Metal	48 feet	
All section wood/metal	≥ 36 feet	3 feet
	> 36 feet and ≤ 48 feet	4 feet
	> 48 feet and ≤ 60 feet	5 feet
Three-section (wood and metal)	60 feet	
Trestle	20 feet	
Extension trestle	20 feet	
Mason's	40 feet	
Trolley ladders	20 feet	

Uniform spacing between rungs and rails. Wood with 11.5 inches (inside to inside) and metal with 12-inch centers.

- Sturdy (*e.g., does not shake*)

- Steps, cleats, and rungs intact

- No loose nails, screws, bolts, or other metal parts

- No cracked, split, or broken uprights, braces, or rungs

- No slivers or dents on uprights, rungs, or steps

- Not damaged or worn

- Top and bottom areas kept clear of tools, equipment, and debris

- Nonslip base or some form of slip prevention (*e.g., held or tied down*)

- Free of oil and grease

- Frequent lubrication of metal bearings

- Used for climbing only (*not as a brace skid, gangway, or other*)

- Used on stable, level surfaces

- Structurally defective ladders decommissioned on a timely basis

☐ **Adequate work procedures**

- Clear door blockages

- Face the ladder when ascending and descending

- Place ladder where there is usable space

- Check amount ladder is required to extend above upper landing surface

- Prevent displacement of ladder by traffic and workplace activities
  - Secure ladder to prevent inadvertent knocking over OR
  - Barricade area around the ladder(s)

- Know ladder design limitations
  - Design purpose understood
  - Manufacturer's rated capacity posted

☐ **Condition of stepladders**

- Not wobbly

- No loose or bent hinge spreaders

- No broken, split, or worn steps

- No loose hinges

- Proper length, based on use (*e.g., heavy duty industrial use*)

- Uniform step spacing

- Minimum width between side rails 11.5 inches

Figure 31-3: Types of Ladders

Extension Ladder

Decorator Ladder

Sectional Painter's Ladder

Platform Ladder

Tripod Ladder

☐ **Condition of extension ladders**

- Tight joints

- Secure hardware and fittings *(e.g., locks)*

- Free and unrestricted movable parts

- No deteriorated rope(s)

- Proper length, based on type

☐ **Condition of trestle ladders**

- No loose hinges

- Not wobbly

- No loose or bent hinge spreaders

- No broken stop on hinge spreader

- Center section guide for extension in proper alignment

- No defective locks for extension

☐ **Condition of sectional ladders**

- No worn or loose metal parts

- Not wobbly

☐ **Condition of fixed ladders**

- No loose, worn, or damaged rungs or side rails

- No damage, rust, or corrosion

- No corroded bolts and rivet heads on inside of metal stacks

- No weakened or damaged rungs on brick or concrete slabs

- Base of ladder unobstructed

- Pitch not greater than 90 degrees

- Proper safety equipment where greater than 24 feet
  - Ladder safety device
    OR
  - Self-retracting lifeline and rest platforms at intervals not to exceed 150 feet
    OR
  - Cage/well and multiple sections not to exceed 50 feet

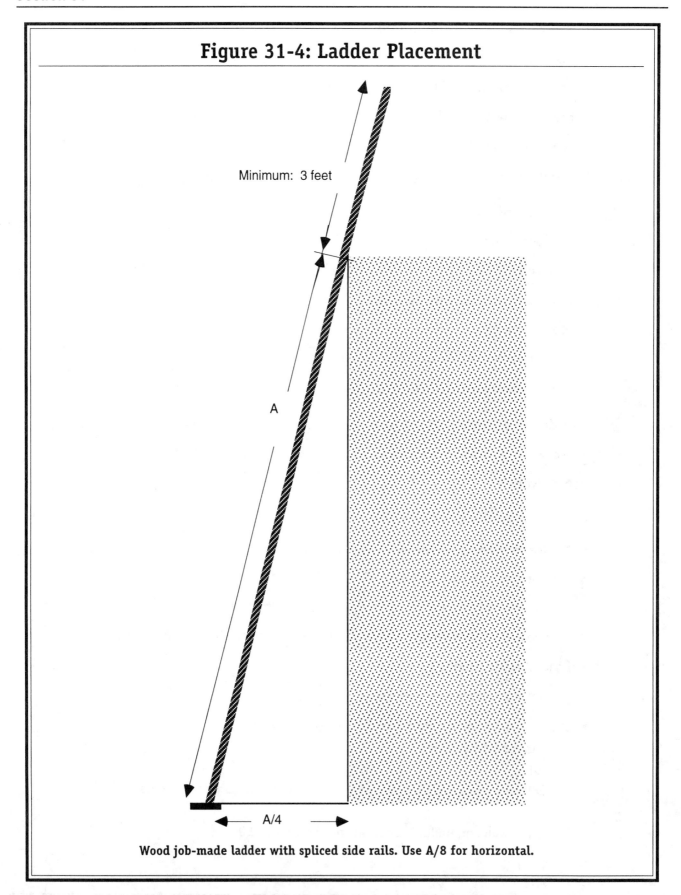

Figure 31-4: Ladder Placement

Minimum: 3 feet

A

A/4

Wood job-made ladder with spliced side rails. Use A/8 for horizontal.

☐   Routine inspections for defects performed by competent person

▶ **Training program for the use of stairs and ladders**

☐   **Content of training**

- Recognize fall hazards

- Know correct procedures for erecting, maintaining, and disassembling

- Know proper construction, use, placement, and care in handling

- Understand maximum intended load-carrying capacities of ladders

- Know standards contained within 29 CFR 1926.1060

☐   **Frequency**

- Initial

- As necessary to maintain knowledge

☐   **Training documented**

▶ **Overall program effectiveness**

☐   **Employee understanding of procedures**

☐   **Employee compliance with procedures**

☐   **Lack of associated incidents**

Figure 31-5: Source List of ANSI Standards for Ladders

Manufactured portable wood ladders .... ANSI A14.1-1982

Manufactured portable metal ladders .... ANSI A14.2-1982

Manufactured fixed ladders .... ANSI A14.3-1982

Job-made ladders .... ANSI A14.4-1982

Plastic ladders .... ANSI A14.5-1982

Notes and special comments

_____

_____

_____

_____

_____

_____

_____

_____

_____

_____

_____

_____

_____

_____

Score: _____

Toxic Substance Exposure Monitoring

Applicable to occupational exposures in construction where there is a potential for airborne exposures to toxic substances. This includes a list of about 450 chemicals which have a specified acceptable 8 hour and 15 minute exposure limit, as well as specific toxic substances which require more detailed management and control measures. 29 CFR 1926.55

▶ **Toxic substances properly identified**

☐ **Chemicals listed in the "Threshold Limit Values of Airborne Contaminants for 1970" and Appendix A of 29 CFR 1926.55** *(See Figure 32-1.)*

_____

_____

_____

_____

_____

_____

_____

_____

_____

_____

Figure 32-1: List of Toxic Substances

Acetaldehyde
Acetic acid
Acetic anhydride
Acetone
Acetonitrile
Acetylene—Asphyxiant
Acetylene tetrabromide
Acrolein
Acrylamide—Skin
Aldrin—Skin
Allyl alcohol—Skin
Allyl chloride
Allyl glycidyl ether—C
Allyl propyl disulfide
2-Aminoethanol
2-Aminopyridine
Ammonia
Ammonium sulfamate
n-Amyl acetate
sec-Amyl acetate
Aniline and homologs—Skin
Anisidine (o, p-isomers)—Skin
Antimony and compounds (as Sb)
ANTU
Arsenic—organic and inorganic
    compounds
Arsine
Azinphos methyl—Skin
Barium (soluble compounds)
Benzene
Benzyl peroxide
Beryllium and compounds
Boron oxide
Boron tribromide
Boron trifluoride
Bromine
Bromine pentafluoride
Bromoform—Skin
1-Butanone (Methyl ethyl ketone)
1,3-Butadiene
2-Butanone (MEK)
2-Butoxyethanol—Skin
Butyl acetate
Butyl alcohol
Butylamine—Skin—C
tert-Butyl chromate (as CrO^3)—Skin—C
n-Butyl glicidyl ether
Butyl mercaptan
p-tert-Butyltoluene
Cadmium
Calcium carbonate
Calcium oxide
Camphor, synthetic
Carbaryl (Sevin®)
Carbon black
Carbon dioxide
Carbon disulfide

Carbon monoxide
Carbon tetrachloride
Cellulose
Chlordane—Skin
Chlorinated camphene—Skin
Chlorinated diphenyl oxide
Chlorine—C
Chlorine dioxide
Chlorine trifluoride—C
Chloroacealdehyde—C
a-Chloroacetophenone
Chlorobenzene
o-Chlorobenzylidene malononitrile
Chlorobromomethane
Chlorodiphenyl —Skin
2-Chloroethanol
Chloroethylene
Chloroform (trichloromethane)
bis (Chloromethyl) ether
Chloromethyl methyl ether
1-Chloro-1-nitropropane
Chloropicrin
beta-Chloroprene—Skin
Chromic acid and chromates
Chromium (II and III) as compounds
Chromium (metal and insoluble salts)
Chrysene
Coal tar pitch volatiles (benzene
    soluble fraction)
Cobalt (metal fume and dust)
Coke oven emissions
CopperCotton dust
Crag® herbicide
Cresol (all isomers)—Skin
Crotonaldehyde
Cumene—Skin
Cyanides (as CN)—Skin
Cyanogen
Cyclohexane
Cyclohexanol
Cyclohexanone
Cyclohexene
Cylclonite
Cyclopentadiene
2,4-D
DDT—Skin
DDVP—Skin
Decaborane—Skin
Demeton® (Systox)—Skin
Diacetone alcohol
1,2-Diaminoethane
Diazomethane
Diborane
Dibromo-3-chloroethane
1,2-Diaminoethane
Dibutyl phosphate
Dibutyl phthalate

Dichloroacetylene
Dichlorobenzene—C
Dichlorodifluoromethane
1,3-Dichloro-5,5-dimethyl hydrantoin
1,1-Dichloroethane
1,2-Dichloroethylene
Dichloroethyl ether—Skin—C
Dichloromonofluoromethane
1,1-Dichloro-1-nitroethane—C
Dichlorotetrafluoroethane
Dieldrin—Skin
Diethylamine
Diethylamino ethanol—Skin
Diethylene triamine
Difluorodibromomethane
Diglycidyl ether—C
Diisobutyl ketone
Diisopropylamine—Skin
4-Dimethylaminoazobenzene
Dimethyl acetamide—Skin
Dimethylamine
Dimethylaniline—Skin
Dimethyl-1,2-dibromo-2,2-dichloroethyl
    phosphate
Dimethylformamide—Skin
1,1-Dimethylhydrazine—Skin
Dimethylphthalate
Dimethylsulfate—Skin
Dinitrobenzene (all isomers)—Skin
Dinitro-o-cresol—Skin
Dinitrotoluene—Skin
Dioxane—Skin
Diphenylamine
Dipropylene glycol methyl ether—Skin
Di-sec, octyl phthalate
Emery
Endosulfan
Endrin—Skin
Epichlorohydrin—Skin
EPN—Skin
1,2-Epoxypropane
Ethane—asphixiant
Ethanolamine
2-Ethoxyethanol—Skin
2-Ethoxyethyl acetate—Skin
Ethyl acetate
Ethyl acrylate—Skin
Ethyl alcohol
Ethylamine
Ethyl amyl ketone
Ethyl benzene
Ethyl bromide
Ethyl butyl ketone
Ethyl chloride
Ethyl ether
Ethyl formate
Ethyl mercaptan—C

(continued on page 378)

☐ **Chemicals listed as toxic substances with short-term exposure limits**

_____

_____

_____

_____

_____

_____

_____

_____

_____

☐ **Substances listed in Mineral Dust Exposures** *(See Figure 32-2.)*

_____

_____

_____

_____

_____

_____

_____

_____

☐ **Unlisted toxic substances**
(Substances indicated by research/published literature to be toxic and which don't have an established exposure limit, such as the listing published by the ACGIH, which is generally stricter and more inclusive than OSHA)

_____

_____

_____

_____

_____

_____

_____

Figure 32-1 (cont'd.): List of Toxic Substances

Ethyl silicate
Ethylene
Ethylene chlorohydrin—Skin
Ethylene diamine
Ethylene dibromide
Etrhylene dichloride
Ethylene glycol dinitrate—Skin
Ethyleneimine—Skin
Ethylene oxide
N-Ethylmorpholine—Skin
Ferbam
Ferrovanadium dust
Fluorides (as F)
Fluorine
Fluorotrichloromethane
Formaldehyde
Formic acid
Furfural—Skin
Furfuryl alcohol
Gasoline
Glycerin
Glycidol
Glycol monoethyl ether
Graphite
Gypsum
Hafnium
Helium—Asphyxiant
Heptachlor—Skin
n-Heptane
Hexachloroethane—Skin
Hexachloronaphthalene—Skin
n-Hexane
2-Hexanone
Hexone
sec-Hexyl acetate
Hydrazine—Skin
Hydrogen
Hydrogen bromide
Hydrogen chloride—C
Hydrogen cyanide—Skin
Hydrogen fluoride
Hydrogen peroxide
Hydrogen sulfide
Hydrogen selenide
Hydroquinone
Indene
Indium and compounds (as In)
Iodine—C
Iron oxide fume
Iron salts (soluble) (as Fe)
Isoamyl acetate
Isoamyl alcohol
Isobutyl acetate
Isobutyl alcohol
Isophorone
Isopropyl acetate
Isopropyl alcohol

Isopropylamine
Isopropyl ether
Isopropyl glycidyl ether
Kaolin
Ketene
Lead
Limestone
Lindane—Skin
Lithium hydride
Liquified petroleum gas
Magnesite
Magnesium oxide
Malathion—Skin
Maleic anhydride
Manganese—C
Mercury—Skin
Marble
Mesityl oxide
Methane—Asphyxiant
Methoxychlor
2-Methoxyethanol—Skin
2-Methoxyethyl acetate
Methyl acetate
Methyl acetylene
Methyl acetylene-propadiene mix
Methyl acrylate
Methylal
Methyl alcohol
Methylamine
Methyl n-amyl ketone
Methyl bromide—Skin
Methyl chloride
Methyl chloroform
Methylcyclohexane
Methylcyclohexanol
o-Methylcyclohexanone—Skin
Methylene chloride
Methyl formate
Methyl hydrazine—Skin—C
Methyl iodide—Skin
Methyl isoamyl ketone
Methyl isobutyl carbinol—Skin
Methyl isocyanate—Skin
Methyl mercaptan—C
Methyl methacrylate
Methyl silicate
Methyl styrene—C
Methylene bisphenyl isocyanate (MDI)
Methylenedianiline (MDA)
Molybdenum
Monomethyl aniline—Skin
Morpholine—Skin
Naphtha (coal tar)
Naphthalene
Naphthylamine
Neon
Nickel carbonyl

Nickel
Nicotine—Skin
Nitric acid
Nitric oxide
p-Nitroaniline—Skin
Nitrobenzene—Skin
Nitrochlorobenzene—Skin
4-Nitrodiphenyl
Nitroethane
Nitrogen
Nitrogen dioxide
Nitrogen trifluoride
Nitroglycerin—Skin
Nitromethane
1-Nitropropane
2-Nitropropane
N-Nitrosodimethylamine
Nitrotoluene (all isomers)
Nitrous oxide
Octachloronaphthalene—Skin
Octane
Oil mist, mineral
Osmium tetroxide (as Os)
Oxalic acid
Oxygen difluoride
Ozone
Paraquat—Skin
Parathion—Skin
Pentaborane
Pentachloronaphthalene—Skin
Pentachlorophenol—Skin
Pentaerythritol
Pentane
2-Pentanone
Perchloroethylene
Perchloromethyl mercaptan
Perchloryl fluoride
Phenol—Skin
p-Phenylene diamine—Skin
Phenyl ether (vapor)
Phenyl ether-biphenyl mixture (vapor)
Phenylethylene ether
Phenylhydrazine—Skin
Phosdrin (Mevinphos®)—Skin
Phosgene
Phosphine
Phosphoric acid
Phosphorus (yellow)
Phosphorus pentachloride
Phosphorus pentasulfide
Phosphorus trichloride
Phthalic anhydride
Picric acid—Skin
Pindone
Plaster of Paris
Platinum (as Pt)
Polytetrafluoroethylene

(continued on page 380)

▶ **Exposure monitoring performed properly**

☐ **Employees given the opportunity to observe air monitoring**

☐ **Proper frequency**

- Initial

- Routine

- Process and/or condition changes

☐ **Proper type(s) of monitoring completed**

- Time-weighted average (TWA)–full shift or duration of job performance (where this is less than a full shift) air monitoring

- Short term exposure (STEL)—15-minute exposure monitoring

- Ceiling (C)

☐ **Proper documentation**

- Type of exposure

- Sample exposure location

- Sample date

- Employee name and social security number

- Number, duration, and results of sampling

- *Process description for activities performed during monitoring*

- Results *and conclusions*

- *Recommendations (if applicable)*

☐ **Employees notified of results**

- Written notice

  OR

- Posted in the workplace

Figure 32-1 (cont'd.): List of Toxic Substances

Propane—Asphyxiant
Propargyl alchol
n-Propyl acetate
n-Propyl alcohol
n-Propyl nitrate
Propylene dichloride
Propylene imine—Skin
Propylene oxide
Pyrethrum
Pyridine
Quinone
Rhodium (as Rh)
Rotenone
Selenium compounds (as Se)
Selenium hexafluoride
Silica
Silicates
Soapstone
Silicon carbide
Silver
Sodium fluoroacetate—Skin
Sodium hydroxide
Starch
Stibine
Stoddard solvent
Strychnine
Styrene
Sucrose
Sulfur dioxide

Sulfur hexafluoride
Sulfuric acid
Sulfur monochloride
Sulfuryl pentafluoride
Sulfur fluoride
Systox
2,4,5-T
Tantalum
Teflon decomposition products
Tellurium (as Te)
Tellurium hexafluoride (as Te)
Temephos
TEPP—Skin
Terphenylis
1,1,1,2-Tetrachloro-2,2-difluoroethane
1,1,2,2-Tetrachloro-1,2-difluoroethane
1,1,2,2-Tetrachloroethane—Skin
Tetrachloronaphthalene—Skin
Tetraethyl lead (as Pb)
Tetrahydrofuran
Tetramethyl lead (as Pb)—Skin
Tetramethyl succinonitrile—Skin
Tetranitromethane
Tetranitromethyl succinonitrile—Skin
Tetryl (2,4,6-trinitrophenyl-methyl-
    nitramine)—Skin
Thallium (as Tl)—Skin
Thiram
Tin (as Sn)

Titanium dioxide
Toluene—Skin
Toluene—2,4-diisocyanate (TCI)—C
o-Toluidine—Skin
Tributyl phosphate
1,1,2-Trichloroethane—Skin
Trichloroethylene
Trichloromethane
Trichloronaphthalene—Skin
1,2,3-Trichloropropane
1,1,2-Trichloro-1,2,2-trifluoroethane
Triethylamine
Trifluoromonobromomethane
2,4,6-Trinitrotoluene (TNT)—Skin
Triothocresyl phosphate
Triphenyl phosphate
Tungsten
Turpentine
Uranium
Vanadium
Vinyl chloride
Vinyl toluene
Warfarin
Xylene (all isomers)
Xylidine—Skin
Yttrium
Zinc chloride fume
Zinc oxide fume
Zirconium (as Zr)

C = Ceiling limit
Skin = Skin absorption
List extracted from 29 CFR 1926.55, Appendix A (January 10, 1997)

Figure 32-2 Mineral Dusts Which Have Exposure Limits

Silica
    Crystalline Quartz
    Cristobalite
        Amorphous, including Diatomaceous earth

Silicates (less than 1% crystallin silica)
    Mica
    Soapstone
    Talc (non-asbestos form)—asbestos-containing talc is restricted to the asbestos standard
    Portland cement

Graphite (natural)

Inert or Nuisance Particulates (A partial list of nuisance particulates is included below.)

Aluminina	*Fibrous glass*	*Plaster of paris*
Ammonium sulfamate	*Glycerin mist*	*Portland cement*
Calcium carbonate	*Kaolin*	*Rouge (e.g., jeweler's rouge)*
Calcium sulfate	*Limestone*	*Silicon carbide*
Cellulose (e.g., paper and wood chips)	*Magnesite*	*Starch*
Crag herbicide (Sesone)	*Marble*	*Sucrose (e.g., sugar)*
Emery	*Pentaerythritol*	*Temphos*

☐ **Documentation of operations exempted from exposure monitoring**

- Type of exposure

- Exposure location

- Rationale for exemption *(e.g., source of information)*

- Process description

- Within 15 days of written disclosure *(e.g., laboratory results or industrial hygiene report)*

- Written notice to individuals or posted notice

- Corrective action(s) to be taken

☐ *Performed by an experienced professional*

Notes and special comments

_____

_____

_____

_____

_____

_____

_____

_____

_____

_____

_____

_____

_____

_____

Score: _____

Welding and Cutting

Applicable to gas and arc welding/cutting in construction. Details for handling some of the "Compressed Gases" which are required for welding and cutting may be excerpted from said section. 29 CFR 1926.350 through 1926.354

▶ **Compressed gas cylinders**

☐ **Management of cylinders not in use**

- Valves closed

- Valve caps secured

- Not used as rollers or supports

- Damaged and defective cylinders decommissioned

- Gases not mixed in the cylinders themselves

☐ **Hoisted in cradle, slingboard, or pallet only**
(manual tilting and rolling on bottom edge is acceptable for short distances)

☐ **Kept in vertical position at all times unless rolling to move**

☐ **Secured when in use**

☐ **Oxygen cylinders stored away from fuel gases *(e.g., acetylene)* and highly combustible materials *(e.g., oil)***

Figure 33-1: Safe Handling of Fuel Gas Cylinders during Use

- Before the regulator is connected, the valve shall be opened slightly and closed immediately while standing to one side of the outlet.. This is referred to as "cracking" and is intended to clear the valve of dust and dirt.

- Do not crack valves where the cylinder contents may reach welding work, sparks, flames, or other possible sources of ignition.

- Open the valve slowly to prevent damage to the regulator and not more than 1½ turns—in case there should be a need to close the valve in an emergency. If a special wrench is used to open/close the valve, leave it in position while the cylinder is in use for quick shut off. One wrench should always be available for immediate use where there are manifolded and/or coupled cylinders.

- Do not place anything on top of the fuel gas cylinder when it is in use. The intent should be to avoid damage and allow for quick access.

- Do not turn off torches or other such devices until you reduce the pressure through the regulator attached to the valve or manifold.

- Purge the cylinder valve regulator(s) prior to removal from the cylinder.

- Should a leak be observed around the valve stem, upon valve opening, close the valve and tighten the gland nut. It the tightened gland nut does not stop the leak, the cylinder shall be tagged and decommissioned.

- Should a leak be observed around the cylinder valve and it cannot be stopped, turn off the cylinder, tag it, and remove it from the work area.

- Should a leak develop at a fuse plug or other safety device, the cylinder shall be tagged and decommissioned.

- At least 20 feet of separation

  OR

- Noncombustible barrier at least 5 feet high with a fire-resistance rating of a minimum of ½ hour

☐ **Cylinder storage areas inside a building**

- At least 20 feet away from highly combustible materials

- Protected from damage *(e.g., forklift impact)*

- Ventilated

- Dry

- Away from elevators, stairs, and gangways

- Away from vehicle and foot traffic

- Inaccessible to unauthorized persons

☐ **Relative placement for hazards**

- Away from welding and cutting sparks, slag, and flames
  - ▫ Distance
  - ▫ Fire-resistant shield

- Away from potential electrical arcing

- Away from open flames, hot metal, and other sources of artificial heat

- Oxygen and fuel gases not taken into confined spaces

▶ Gas welding/cutting devices

☐ **Manifolds**

- Clearly identified as to substance they are used for

- Stored where well ventilated

- Connections kept free of grease and oil

- No objects other than that intended for the equipment is placed on top surface

☐ **Hose(s)**

- Clearly identified use *(e.g., fuel gas or oxygen)*

- Fuel gas and oxygen hoses not used interchangeably

- Taped hose sections of not more than 4 inches for every 12 inches of hose

Figure 33-2: Storage of Gas Cylinders

- Store cylinders in a protected, well-ventilated place specifically designated for that purpose.

- Do not store gas cylinders near elevators, gangways, stairs, lanes of traffic, or other places where they can be knocked down or damaged.

- Do not store oxygen cylinders within 20 feet of flammable gas cylinders or highly combustible materials if not separated by a fire-resistive partition.

- Acetylene and liquefied fuel gas cylinders should be stored with the valve end up.

- Limit indoor storage of acetylene cylinders to 2000 cubic feet of gas. If greater than 2000 cubic feet of acetylene must be stored, it should be stored either in a special indoor room, separate building, or outside.

- Storage rooms must be well-ventilated, open flames should be prohibited, and rooms must be dedicated to storage only (no other occupancy).

- Outdoor storage areas should be protected from contact with the ground and from extremes in weather (e.g., continuous direct sun in the summer and accumulations of ice and snow in the winter).

- Keep storage away from heat sources and highly flammable substances (e.g., diesel, above-ground storage tanks).

- Use cylinders in the order they were received.

- Store empty and full cylinders separately.

- Smoking must be prohibited around storage areas.

- Electrical wiring in storage areas shall be in conduit.

- Electrical lights in storage areas should be enclosed in glass or another transparent material to prevent gas from contacting light sockets or lamps, and the enclosure should be protected from breakage with a guard (e.g., wire protector).

- Electrical switches should be located outside the storage area.

- Inspected for defects at start of work shift

- Hose with prior flashback—tested to twice the normal pressure

- Defective, questionable hoses decommissioned

- Disconnect and locking mechanisms on hose coupling(s) by rotary motion only (*not straight pull only*)

- Hose-storage boxes ventilated

☐ **Hoses, cables, and other equipment clear of passageways, ladders, and stairs**

☐ **Torches**

- Clogged tip openings cleaned properly

- Inspected at beginning of each work shift

- Defective, questionable torches decommissioned

☐ **Strike device for torches**
   (*e.g., friction lighter, not matches or hot work*)

☐ **Regulators and gauges—proper working order**

▶ **Arc welding/cutting devices**

☐ **Manual electrode holders**

- Capacity capable of handling the maximum rated current required by the electrodes

- Fully insulated for maximum voltage where hand grips the holders

☐ **Welding cables and connectors**

- Completely insulated—flexible with no breaks

- No repaired or spliced cables within a distance of 10 feet from the cable end

- Connected/spliced lengths completely insulated

- Worn or exposed bare connectors properly repaired or decommissioned

☐ **Ground returns and machine grounding**

- Current carrying capacity at least the specified maximum output capacity

- Proper grounding
  - Not to pipelines containing gases or flammable liquids
  - Not to electrical conduits

Figure 33-3: Definitions

Gas Welding

Process which unites metals by heating with a flame from the combustion of a fuel gas or gases and sometimes includes the use of pressure and a filler metal.

Resistance Welding

Process which unites metals by using electric current to melt the components.

Spot Welding

Process which applies heat and pressure, usually on overlapped parts.

Seam Welding

Process which involves overlapping spot welds, spaced close enough to make a single continuous joint.

Flash Welding

Process wherein coalescence is produced, simultaneously over the entire area of abutting surfaces, by the heat obtained from resistance to the flow of electric current between the two surfaces, and by the application of pressure after heating is substantially completed. Flashing and upsetting are accompanied by expulsion of metal from the joint.

Percussion Welding

A welding process wherein coalescence is produced simultaneously over the entire abutting surfaces by the heat obtained from an arc. This arc is produced by a rapid discharge of electrical energy. It is extinguished by pressure percussively applied during the discharge.

Projection Welding

A welding process wherein coalescence is produced by the heat obtained from resistance to the flow of electric current through the work parts held together under pressure by electrodes. The resulting welds are localized at predetermined pointed by the design of the parts to be welded. The localization is usually accomplished by projections, embossments, or intersections.

Upset Welding

A welding process wherein coalescence is produced, simultaneously over the entire area of abutting surfaces or progressively along a joint, by the heat obtained from resistance to the flow of electric current through the area of contact of those surfaces. Pressure is applied before heating is started and is maintained throughout the heating period.

Arc Welding

Process which unites metals by using an electric arc within an inert gas or a solid flux.

- Structural pipeline ground
  - Has required electrical contact at all joints *(e.g., no arc, sparks, or heat at any point)*
  - All joints are bonded
  - Periodic inspections for conditions of electrolysis or fire hazards
- Frame(s) grounded properly
- Routine inspections of ground connections

☐ **Shielding whenever practicable**

- Noncombustible or flameproof screens
- Protect employees and other persons in the vicinity from the direct rays of the arc

▶ **Fire prevention**
(See also Section 14: "Fire Protection and Prevention.")

☐ **No fire hazards in vicinity** *(e.g., combustible paper waste)*

☐ **Sparks, heat, and slag confined**

☐ **No flammable paints on product**

☐ **No flammable compounds or heavy dust in the area** *(e.g., airborne acetone)*

☐ **Fire extinguishers**

☐ **Take special precautions**

- Backup procedure to assign additional personnel to guard against fire during and after the work performance where other precautions are not feasible or sufficient
- When work is being done on walls, floors, and ceilings

☐ **Confined space procedures**

- Shut off gas supply at point outside enclosed space when torch not in use or left unattended for an abbreviated period of time *(e.g., lunch)*
- Remove torch and hose at end of shift
- Open-end fuel gas and oxygen hoses removed when disconnected

☐ **Flammable liquid containers**

- Kept closed if not being used
- Removed from area when empty

Table 33-1: Eye Protection for Welders

Operation	Electrode Size (1.32 inch diameter standard)	Arc Current (amps)	Minimum Protective Shade
Shielded metal arc welding	< $^3/_{32}$	< 60	7
	$^3/_{32}$ - $^5/_{32}$	60 - 160	8
	$^5/_{32}$ - $^8/_{32}$	160 - 250	10
	> $^8/_{32}$	250 - 500	11
Gas metal arc welding and flux cored arc welding	—	< 60	7
	—	60 - 160	10
	—	160 - 250	10
	—	250 - 500	10
Gas tungsten arc welding	—	< 50	8
	—	50 - 150	8
	—	150 - 500	10
Air carbon arc cutting	(light)	< 500	10
	(heavy)	500 - 1000	10
Plasma arc welding	—	< 20	6
	—	20 - 100	8
	—	100 - 400	10
	—	400 - 800	11
Plasma arc cutting	(light)	< 300	8 *
	(medium)	300 - 400	9 *
	(heavy)	400 - 800	10 *
Torch brazing	—	—	3
Torch soldering	—	—	2
Carbon arc welding	—	—	14

* Values applicable where the actual arc is clearly seen. Lighter filters may be used when the arc is hidden by the workpiece.

Operation	Plate Thickness		Minimum Protective Shade
	inches	millimeters	
Gas welding			
light	< $^1/_8$	< 3.2	4
medium	$^1/_8$ - $^1/_2$	3.2 - 12.5	5
heavy	> $^1/_2$	> 12.7	6
Oxygen cutting			
light	< 1	< 25	3
medium	1 - 6	25 - 150	4
heavy	> 6	> 150	5

☐ **Empty toxic or flammable containers/tanks prior to welding, cutting, or heating them**

- Filled with water

- Thoroughly cleaned, ventilated, and tested

- Special precautions for steel pipelines containing natural gas *(See 49 CFR 192.)*

☐ **Empty nontoxic or nonflammable containers/drums/tanks prior to applying heat**

- Vented

  OR

- Opening

► Ventilation
(See 29 CFR 1926.353.)

☐ **Mechanical ventilation** *(See also Section 22, "Local Exhaust Ventilation.")*

☐ **Confined spaces** *(See also Section 7, "Confined Space Entry Procedures.")*

☐ **Toxic metals** *(See also Section 32, "Toxic Substance Exposure Monitoring.")*

☐ **Inert gas metal-arc welding**

► Special management of preservative coatings

► Employees trained

☐ **All employees who weld, cut, or otherwise use gas and/or arc welding equipment**

☐ **Content of training**

- Technical

- Safe management of equipment

- Personal protective equipment

- Fire protection and prevention

☐ **Documented**

Figure 33-4: Special Precautions When Welding, Cutting, or Heating Preservative Coatings

- Prior to work on preservative coatings, determine flammability by scraping off a portion and attempting to ignite it.

- Preservative coatings shall be determined highly flammable when the scrapings are found to burn rapidly.

- Strip coatings that are highly flammable from the area to be heated.

- In an enclosed space, when working with toxic-generating preservative coatings, strip out at least 4 inches from the area of heat application, or wear an air line respirator.

- Determine and take proper precautions against toxic vapors/fumes *(e.g., respirator)*.

Figure 33-5: Special Hazards and Precautions Common to Welding

Hazards	Engineering Controls	Personal Protective Equipment
Fire	Dilution ventilation	Eye protection
Ultraviolet light—eye injury	Mechanical ventilation	Respiratory protection
Infrared rays—heating effect	Area shield(s)	Fire-resistant gloves
Toxic gases, vapors, and fumes		Flame-resistant aprons
Heat		Fire-resistant leggings and high boots
Skin burns		Safety shoes
Heavy objects		Ear protection for sparks
		Safety hats

▶ **Overall program effectiveness**

☐ **Employee understanding of procedures**

☐ **Employee compliance with procedures**

☐ **Lack of associated incidents**

Notes and special comments

_____

_____

_____

_____

_____

_____

_____

_____

_____

_____

_____

_____

_____

_____

_____

_____

Score: _____

Hazardous Building Materials

Many buildings contain hazardous substances which pose a potential health hazard to a contractor's workers and people in the vicinity (e.g., building occupants) when those substances are mismanaged and inadvertently released into the environment. Although there is a duty to inform a contractor as to the existence of these materials, the building owners do not always comply for one reason or another.

Often the building owner is not informed and/or does not know any better, or he thinks it unlikely that the contractor's work activities will disturb the hazardous building materials. Some owners may fail to recognize that work in the vicinity of contained hazards may result in damage and subsequent release of the hazardous material.

For example, workers are installing electrical wires in the ceiling where there is asbestos-insulated pipe adjacent to the work to be performed. If not warned of the need to use caution, a worker may inadvertently damage the enclosing wrap on the asbestos pipe insulation and release disease-causing fibers into the air.

Hazardous building materials include, but are not limited to, asbestos and lead-containing paint as well as PCB-containing transformers and light ballasts. Federal mandates require all public buildings be assessed for asbestos, but there are no federal mandates for work involving residences. Lead-containing paint has been federally banned, and it must be properly managed in older structures which are occupied/used by children (e.g., schools and playgrounds). The lead-containing paint ban does not, however, include commercial buildings, bridges, and industrial equipment. Although there has been a manufacturing ban on PCBs, PCB-containing transformers and light ballasts are still in service and become a disposal concern during a renovation/demolition jobs.

Management and disposal of hazardous building materials is controlled by designated state agencies. Thus, the appropriate state agency must be consulted for details. (See Appendix D.)

Further information regarding asbestos-containing building materials, lead-containing paint, and PCBs used in structures is contained herein. This is for information only.

Figure IV-1: Date of Origin of Some Asbestos Products

1890	Roofing material
1897	Sprayed-on acoustical insulation
1902	Pipe insulation
1909	Cement cladding
1910	Corrugated paper products
1910	Roofing felts
1920	Asphalt tiles
1926	Break linings
1930	Cement
1930	Caulking putties
1935	High temperature, cement-like pipe elbows and joints
1935	Roofing shingles
1938	Transite board
1945	Theater curtains
1946	Drywall
1950	Asphalt
1950	Vinyl floor tiles
1951	Electrical insulation
1952	Paper laminate for electrical equipment
1953	Conduit
1965	Teflon

Asbestos-Containing Material

Asbestos is a fibrous rock which can cause lung disease, and it has been used extensively in building materials. According to the Environmental Protection Agency (EPA), asbestos-containing material (ACM) is any material which has greater than one percent asbestos by volume.

Background

Asbestos was used by the Greeks over 2,500 years ago to weave "stone flax." The product was used for eternal wicks, handkerchiefs, and napkins, each of which was not washed but placed in a fire to burn away the stains—magic! Yet, many of the craftsmen suffered from a "sickness of the lungs."

In the late 1800s, the industrial revolution was met head on with problems. Roofs were ignitable and dangerous. Steam engine gaskets were deteriorating as fast as they were installed, and tenders were not shielded from the sparks and heat extremes created by the steam boilers. Boiler pipe insulation (e.g., old carpet and mortar) was ineffective and deteriorated rapidly. Need became the mother of invention. Thus, an inventor and roof manufacturer stepped forward. This was Henry W. Johns.

Mr. Johns read about an Italian fireproof paper and linen. This sparked his imagination, and the future roofing magnate and asbestos zealot proceeded to develop a fireproof roofing material while expanding its use to durable gaskets, heat shields, and pipe insulation. In 1898, Mr. Johns died of a dust "phthisis pneumonitis." In 1902, C.B. Manville bought out the Johns estate, changed the name from Johns to John, and created the John-Manville Corporation.

By 1936, asbestos had become the most common construction material in the United States. Some of the uses included ceiling tiles, floor tiles, insulation on electrical wires, circuit boxes, caulking, spackling, and thermal/acoustical surfacing material. It was also used for automobile convertibles, boat and auto insulation, Christmas tree flock, papier-mache mixes, baby blankets, mattress stuffing, and theater curtains. The list goes on.

Throughout the 1920s, British medical journals published accounts of patients suffering a peculiar lung disease. By 1930, a report was published, indicating an association between the lung disease and asbestos exposures. By 1935, the U.S. legal profession had acknowledged the association, and the relationship became widely published information. Over the next 40 years, evidence mounted, and asbestos was clearly linked with lung cancer, mesothelioma, and "asbestosis"—a progressive, deadly lung disease. Public interest and concern set off a chain reaction.

In 1972, the Occupational Safety and Health Administration (OSHA) set a limit to the acceptable levels to which workers may be exposed and established proper handling procedures in 1972. The standard was modified in 1976, and OSHA published regulations to cover asbestos-removal work practices in 1986.

In 1973, the Environmental Protection Agency (EPA) issued regulations (National Emission Standards for Hazardous Air Pollutants, NESHAPS) which set forth procedures requiring asbestos removal in buildings prior to demolition. The EPA also banned the manufacture and use of asbestos-containing sprayed-on surfacing insulation in buildings.

Figure IV–2: Classification of Asbestos-Containing Materials (ACM)

Friable ACM   Crumbled, pulverized, or reduced to powder by hand pressure, and >1% asbestos.

Nonfriable ACM   When dry, cannot be crumbled, pulverized, or reduced to powder by hand pressure, and >1% asbestos.

Category I   Asbestos-containing packing, gaskets, resilient floor coverings, and asphalt roofing products.

Category II   Any nonfriable ACM not designated as Category I.

U.S. EPA: *Asbestos/NESHAP Regulated Asbestos-Containing Materials Guidance*. [Bulletin]. Office of Toxic Substances, Washington, DC, EPA 340/1-90-018. p. 12.

The 1975 and 1978 NESHAPS Amendment banned the manufacture and use of "all" types of insulating asbestos-containing materials (ACM) in new buildings and special controls/work practices for removing friable ACM from areas under renovation. In abbreviated terms, the special controls called for wet removal and no visible emissions during removal, transportation, and disposal.

In 1982, EPA promulgated guidelines for controlling "friable" ACM in school buildings under the Friable Asbestos-Containing Materials in Schools: Identification and Notification Rule. They applied a 1983 deadline for compliance.

Asbestos-containing materials are classified as friable or nonfriable. Friable asbestos-containing material poses more of a potential release problem than the nonfriable, and EPA has classified two categories to the nonfriable building materials.

In 1986, EPA promulgated guidelines for identifying and controlling "nonfriable," as well as friable, ACM in school buildings and the development of operations and management plans. This law was the Asbestos Hazard Emergency Response Act (AHERA) and was directed only at the public/private schools up to the 12th grade.

In 1994, a similar law was passed which is applicable to all public buildings, and the enforcement is left up to state governments. This law requires that all those persons who conduct asbestos inspections in public buildings and perform other services which impact the management of ACM must have been trained in accordance with the AHERA training requirements. The law is referred to as the Asbestos School Hazard Abatement Reorganization Act (ASHARA).

In July 1989, the EPA promulgated a rule providing for a seven-year phaseout plan for all asbestos-containing material. This ban was later vacated and remanded by the Fifth Circuit Court of Appeals which clarified that the decision still held for products that were not being manufactured, imported, or processed on July 1989. In 40 CFR 763, the EPA identifies those products they "believe" remain subject to the ban. As of March 1993, an attempt was being made to clarify the restrictions.

In November 1990, a clarifying rule to the NESHAPS amendment limits the 1973 requirement for removal of all ACM prior to demolition. This is discussed in greater detail in the section below.

Special Demolition Requirements Involving Asbestos-Containing Building Materials

In the past, all asbestos-containing building materials (ACBM) had to be removed prior to demolition of a building. Since 1990, however, ACM does not have to be removed before demolition if it meets one of the following criteria:

1. The ACBM is a Category I nonfriable ACM that has not become friable and is in good condition.

2. The ACBM is encased in concrete or other similarly hard material and is adequately wetted whenever exposed during demolition.

3. The ACBM was not accessible during testing, therefore, not discovered until after demolition began, and as a result of the demolition, cannot be safely removed. If not removed for safety reasons, the

exposed ACBM and any asbestos-containing debris must be treated as asbestos-containing waste material and kept adequately wet at all times until disposed of.

4. The ACBM is a Category II nonfriable ACM and the probability is low that the material will become crumbled, pulverized, or reduced to powder during demolition.

Category I nonfriable ACM is asbestos-containing packing, gaskets, resilient floor coverings, and asphalt roofing products. Category II nonfriable ACM is all other asbestos-containing material which cannot be crumbled by manual effort. An attempt should be made in all cases to minimize possible fiber release into the ambient air during demolition. This generally requires wetting the material while it is undergoing demolition. (See Figure IV-2.)

A building permit must be obtained for all demolition activities. The controlling state agency will ask for information concerning asbestos content of the building to be demolished. This must ultimately come from the owner.

Lead-Containing Paint

Paint is considered to contain lead when it consists of 0.5 percent lead by weight. Cracked and peeling paint may pose an inhalation hazard, and completely intact paint may pose an ingestion hazard to preschool children.

Background

Lead-containing paint is the most common source of lead exposure to preschool children. Containing up to 50 percent lead, the paint was in widespread use until the 1950s when it became common knowledge that exposures to lead posed a health hazard. Thereafter, exterior lead-based paint and decreased usage of interior lead-based paint continued until 1978.

About 74 percent of privately owned, occupied housing units in the United States built prior to 1980 were coated with lead-based paints. Preschool children become exposed when they ingest paint chips or paint-contaminated dust and soil. Many exposures also result when homes are remodeled or renovated without the proper precautions being taken. Lead-containing paint is typically found on kitchen and bathroom walls, doors, and wood trim of houses. It was used on children's playground equipment where small children may chew the surfaces and in house paints for interior/exterior windows. The latter poses a particular problem, because the surfaces are abraded and worn by opening and closing the windows.

In 1978, the manufacture and use of paints containing more than 0.05 percent lead by weight on the interiors and exteriors of residential surfaces, toys, and furniture were banned. With proper labeling (i.e., "Warning: Contains Lead. Dried Film of This Paint May Be Harmful if Eaten or Chewed."), the following products are exempt from the ban:

1. Agricultural and industrial equipment paints

2. Industrial/commercial buildings, maintenance equipment, and traffic/safety line paints

3. Graphic art paints (i.e., paints marketed solely for billboards, road signs, identification markings in industrial buildings, and other similar uses)

4. Touch-up paints for agricultural equipment, lawn/garden equipment, and appliances

5. Catalyzed coatings marketed solely for use on radio-controlled model powered aircraft

The following products are exempt without labeling:

1. Mirrors with lead-containing paint in the backing

2. Artists' paints and related materials

3. Metal furniture articles, not intended for use by children, and bearing factory-applied lead-containing paint

Be forewarned! Exempted paints have been used in homes on occasion. Although a residence may have been built after the ban, this fact alone is not sufficient to state with a high degree of certainty that there is no lead-containing paint.

Management of Lead-Containing Paint

HUD and some state agencies control the management and disposal of lead-containing materials around children, and OSHA controls the method for managing the release of lead-containing materials under any circumstance. Management generally involves controlling airborne exposures during removal and/or renovation. Disposal is based on TCLP sampling, the results of which determine whether the waste is to be designated hazardous or nonhazardous. This impacts the disposal cost. Then, OSHA requires air monitoring and special controls, the requirements for which can be found in Section 2, "Carcinogenic/Toxic Dusts and Fumes."

Polychlorinated Biphenyls

Polychlorinated biphenyls (PCBs) are a group of chlorinated, aromatic hydrocarbons with 209 possible structures. These synthetic compounds range from heavy oily liquids to waxy solids. They have a high boiling point, chemical stability, low solubility in water, high solubility in fat, low electrical conductivity, and are nonflammable. By law, a substance is considered a PCB if it contains PCBs in excess of 50 ppm.

Background

PCBs were manufactured in the U.S. from 1929 to 1979 for use in electrical products. Principal uses were oil-insulated transformers, capacitors, and fluorescent light ballasts. They were used in electromagnetic, heat transfer/hydraulic systems, natural gas pipeline compressors, air compressors, and industrial lubricants. Some other products they have been used in are paints, plasticizers, pesticide extenders, ceiling tiles, flame retardants, and fillers. They are also found as by-products in the production of organic chemicals.

A transformer may have as much as 800 gallons of oil, and a ballast has about 1 to 1½ ounces of oil. The life expectancy for capacitors and transformers is 10 to 30 years, although some may not last more than a month while others may last in excess of 50 years. The use of PCBs in transformers and ballasts has been banned, but it is not always clear as to the production date and/or content of the oil in those products which have not been withdrawn from use. In 1979, the EPA issued regulations prohibiting the manufacture of PCBs after July 1 of the same year, unless specifically exempted by the EPA.

Management of PCB Transformers and Ballasts

Improperly disposed of PCB-contaminated materials and leaking transformers have led to surface water contamination in the nation's water system. Measurable amounts of PCBs can be found in soils, water, fish, milk, and human tissue. Some fish in the Hudson River, Great Lakes, and other bodies of water are too contaminated for human consumption.

Problems with PCBs are minor compared to products of burned PCBs. Transformers and ballasts can catch on fire and occasionally blow up. When PCBs burn there is a chemical change. Components of the heat decomposition include dibenzofurans and dibenzo-p-dioxins. Suspected carcinogens, some of the dioxins (e.g., 2,3,7,8-tetra-chlorodibenzo-p-dioxin) are among the most toxic substances known to man. Cases involving burning PCBs, resulting in dioxin contamination of people and areas, occur more frequently than are reported.

Although PCBs do not have an odor, burned or burning ballast capacitor fluids may give off a noxious odor as well as soot and an oily liquid. This is thought to be associated with the volatilization of asphalt.

When handling burned-out ballasts, they should be managed with gloves and properly disposed of in accordance with local, state, and federal regulations. The contractor may have to investigate this within his respective state and region for disposal requirements.

Summary

If information regarding hazardous materials is not volunteered up front, ask the building owner prior to starting a job. If he is uncertain, advise him to have the materials evaluated when work is to be performed. He must understand that this request is not only for your information so that you can protect your employees, but he is ultimately responsible and would be well advised to seek a proper evaluation of all hazardous materials in or on the property that might affect occupants and visitors.

In conclusion, the following information should consistently be sought, obtained, and documented:

▶ **Written query to each building owner**

☐ **Existence of hazardous materials as might apply to the construction job to be performed**

- Asbestos-containing building materials

- Lead-containing paint
- PCB-containing light ballasts and transformers

☐ **Location relative to the area where contractor's work is to be performed**

▶ **Documented response from each building owner**

☐ **Written**

OR

☐ **Name, date, time, and witnesses recorded**

Reference

Hess, Kathleen, *Environmental Site Assessment: Phase I, A Basic Guide.* CRC Press, Boca Raton, Florida. Chapter 9, pp. 191-224. (1997)

Appendix A

OSHA Statistics

Number of Citations in Construction
The Top Twenty

	OSHA Standard	Number of Citations
1. Scaffolding	1926.451	5746
2. Fall Protection—Scope/Applications/Definitions	1926.501	3927
3. Electrical—Wiring Design and Protection	1926.404	1797
4. Excavations—General Requirements	1926.651	1793
5. Construction—General Safety and Health Provisions	1926.20	1651
6. Electric Wiring—Methods, Components, and Equipment	1926.405	1465
7. Ladders	1926.1053	1429
8. Head Protection	1926.100	1337
9. Construction—Safety Training and Education	1926.21	1187
10. Asbestos	1926.1101	1182
11. Excavations—Requirements for Protective Systems	1926.652	1180
12. Lead	1926.62	1102
13. Stairways	1926.1052	916
14. Fall Protection—Training Requirements	1926.503	832
15. Fall Protection—Systems Criteria and Practices	1926.502	817
16. Electrical—General Requirements	1926.403	716
17. Scaffolds—Training	1926.454	588
18. Cranes and Derricks	1926.550	576
19. Hazard Communication	1926.59	525
20. Gas Welding and Cutting	1926.350	500

Excerpted from Federal OSHA Statistics for October 1996 through September 1997.

As the General Duty Clause (29 CFR 5A0001) is mentioned frequently throughout the text, the penalties assessed within construction for noncompliance may be relevant to the reader. Thus, the total citations under the clause for the statistics ending September 1997 was 944. Of this number, 247 citations were issued to construction. This is 26 percent of the total of ten industry classification citations.

Penalty Costs of Citations in Construction
The Top Twenty

		OSHA Standard	Total Penalty Costs
1.	Fall Protections—Scope/Applications/Definitions	1926.501	$5,748,158
2.	Scaffolding	1926.451	5,439,847
3.	Excavations—Requirements for Protective Systems	1926.652	4,217,523
4.	Asbestos	1926.1101	2,664,181
5.	Excavations—General Requirements	1926.651	2,206,270
6.	Construction—General Safety and Health Provisions	1926.20	1,363,729
7.	Lead	1926.62	1,238,730
8.	Construction—Safety Training and Education	1926.21	1,226,341
9.	Electrical—Wiring Design and Protection	1926.404	816,854
10.	Head Protection	1926.100	748,572
11.	Cranes and Derricks	1926.550	745,796
12.	Ladders	1926.1053	728,572
13.	Fall Protection—Systems Criteria and Practices	1926.502	571,462
14.	Fall Protection—Training Requirements	1926.503	478,328
15.	Electric Wiring—Methods, Components, and Equipment	1926 405	476 445
16.	Electrical Safety-Related Work Practices	1926.41 6	435,198
17.	Materials Handling Equipment	1926.602	336,141
18.	Electrical—General Requirements	1926.403	320,518
19.	Stairways	1926.1052	299,280
20.	Scaffolds—Training	1926.454	269,787

Excerpted from Federal OSHA Statistics for October 1996 through September 1997.

The total penalty costs under the General Duty Clause for the statistics ending September 1997 was $3,908,216. Of this cost, $921,220 was the total penalty costs to construction. This is 24 percent of the total of ten industry classification penalties.

Inspections Performed
Construction and Manufacturing

Type of Work	Citations	Inspections	Penalties
All	110,270	23,225	87,821,934
Construction	38,912	11,971	36,541,468
Manufacturing	49,467	7,060	37,469,425

Period ending September 1997

Worker Fatality Statistics
The Top Four

Type of Work	Number of Fatalities
Private Industry (e.g., agriculture)	5,521
Construction	1,039
Transportation and public utilities	947
Manufacturing	715

Period ending 1996

Elements of an Effective Voluntary Protection Program

Management Commitment and Employee Involvement

- A worksite policy on safe and healthful work and working conditions clearly stated so all personnel with responsibilities at a site and personnel at other locations with responsibility for those sites understand the priority of safety and health protection in relation to other organizational values.

- A clear goal for the safety and health program and objectives for meeting goals so all members of the organization understand the results.

- Top management involvement in implementing the program so all will understand the seriousness of management's commitment.

- Employee involvement in the structure and operation of programs and decisions that affect their safety and health in order to make full use of their insight and energy.

- Assignment of responsibilities for all aspects of the program so managers, supervisors, and employees in all parts of the organization know what performance is expected of them.

- Provision of adequate authority and resources to responsible parties so assigned responsibilities can be met.

- Holding managers, supervisors, and employees accountable for meeting their responsibilities so essential tasks can be performed.

- Annual reviews of program operations to evaluate their success in meeting the goal and objectives, so deficiencies can be identified, and programs and/or objectives may be revised when the goals and objectives are not met.

Worksite Analysis

- Identification of all hazards by conducting baseline worksite surveys for safety and health, and periodic comprehensive update surveys. Also included would be an analysis of planned and new facilities, processes, materials, and equipment, as well as an analysis of routine job hazards.

- Regular site safety and health inspections so the new or previously missed hazards and failures in hazard controls can be identified.

- A reliable system to encourage employees, without fear of reprisal, to notify management personnel about conditions that appear hazardous and to ensure timely and appropriate corrective actions are taken.

- Investigation of accidents and "near misses" so their causes and means for prevention can be identified.

- Analysis of injury and illness trends over extended periods so patterns with common causes can be identified and prevented.

Hazard Prevention and Control

- Procedures that ensure all current and potential hazards are corrected in a timely manner through engineering techniques where appropriate.

- Safe work practices are understood and followed by all parties.

- Personal protective equipment is provided.

- Administrative controls are introduced, such as reducing the duration of exposures.

Safety and Health Training

- Ensure all employees understand the hazards to which they may be exposed and how to prevent harm to themselves and others.

- Ensure all supervisors and managers understand their responsibilities and the reasons for them so they can carry out their responsibilities effectively.

Note: Program "effectiveness" is given greater credence than that of elaborate written programs and procedures. Effectiveness may be measured in terms of corporate loss ratios, past experiences, and employee interviews.

Appendix C

State OSHA Consultation Services

State OSHA Consultation Services

This list provides names of state programs or offices where consulting services may be found. Personnel within each office will provide assistance and information relevant to their particular state, as well as federal requirements. The states are listed in alphabetical order.

Alabama
(205) 348-3033

Safe State Program
University of Alabama
Tuscaloosa, AL

Alaska
(907) 269-4939

Health and Safety Consultation and Training
ADOL/OSHA
Anchorage, AK

Arizona
(602) 542-5795

Consultation and Training
Division of Occupational Safety and Health
Industrial Commission of Arizona
Phoenix, AZ

Arkansas
(501) 682-4522

OSHA Consultation
Arkansas Department of Labor
Little Rock, AR

California
(415) 703-4441

CAL/OSHA Consulting
Department of Industrial Relations
San Francisco, CA

Colorado
(303) 491-6151

Occupational Safety and Health Services
Colorado State University
Fort Collins, CO

Connecticut
(203) 566-4550

Occupational Safety and Health
Connecticut Department of Labor
Wethersfield, CT

Delaware
(302) 577-3908

Occupational Safety and Health
Delaware Department of Labor
Wilmington, DE

District of Columbia
(202) 576-6339

Occupational Safety and Health
Department of Employment Services
Washington, DC

Florida
(904) 488-3044

Safety and Health Consultation Program
Florida Department of Labor and Employment Security
Tallahassee, FL

Georgia
(404) 894-2646

Safety and Health Consultation Program
Georgia Institute of Technology
Atlanta, GA

Guam
(671) 647-4202

OSHA Onsite Consultation
Department of Labor, Government of Guam
Tamuning, GU

Hawaii
(809) 586-9116

Consultation and Training Branch
Department of Labor and Industrial Relations
Honolulu, HI

Idaho
(208) 385-3283

Safety and Health Consultation Program
Department of Health Studies
Boise State University
Boise, ID

Illinois
(312) 814-2337

Industrial Services
Department of Commerce and Community Affairs
Chicago, IL

Indiana
(317) 232-2688

Safety, Education and Training
Indiana Department of Labor
Indianapolis, IN

Iowa
(515) 281-5352

Safety and Health Consultation Program
Iowa Bureau of Labor
Des Moines, IA

Kansas
(913) 296-4386

Safety and Health Consultation Program
Kansas Department of Human Resources
Topeka, KS

Kentucky
(502) 564-6895

Safety and Health Consultation and Training
Kentucky Occupational Safety and Health Program
Frankfort, KY

Louisiana
(504) 342-9601

Safety and Health Consultation Program
Louisiana Department of Labor
Baton Rouge, LA

Maine
(207) 624-6460

Safety and Health Consultation Program
Maine Department of Labor
Augusta, ME

Maryland
(410) 333-4218

Safety and Health Consultation Program
Maryland Division of Labor and Industry
Baltimore, MD

Massachusetts
(617) 969-7177

Safety and Health Consultation Program
Massachusetts Department of Labor and Industries
West Newton, MA

Michigan
(517) 332-8250 [health]
(517) 332-1809 [safety]

Division of Occupational Health (health)
Bureau of Safety and Regulation (safety)
Michigan Department of Public Health
Lansing, MI

Minnesota
(612) 297-2393

Safety and Health Consultation
Department of Labor and Industry
St. Paul, MN

Mississippi
(601) 987-3981

Safety and Health Consultation
Mississippi State University
Jackson, MS

Missouri
(314) 751-3403

Safety and Health Consultation
Department of Labor and Industrial Relations
Jefferson City, MO

Montana
(406) 444-6418

Safety Bureau
Department of Labor and Industry
Helena, MT

Nebraska
(402) 471-4717

Labor and Safety Standards
Nebraska Department of Labor
Lincoln, NE

Nevada
(702) 486-5016

Safety and Health Training and Consultation
Nevada Occupational Safety and Health
Reno, NV

New Hampshire
(603) 271-2024

Public Health Services
New Hampshire Department of Labor
Concord, NH

New Jersey
(609) 292-3923

Workplace Standards
New Jersey Department of Labor
Trenton, NJ

New Mexico
(505) 827-2877

Occupational Health and Safety
New Mexico Environment Department
Santa Fe, NM

New York
(518) 457-2481

Safety and Health Consultation
New York State Department of Labor
Albany, NY

North Carolina
(919) 662-4641

Safety and Health Consultative Services
North Carolina Department of Labor
Raleigh, NC

North Dakota
(701) 328-5188

Environmental Engineering
North Dakota State Department of Health
Bismarck, ND

Ohio
(614) 644-2631

OSHA Onsite Consultation
Bureau of Employment Services
Columbus, OH

Oklahoma
(405) 528-1500

OSHA Consulting
Oklahoma Department of Labor
Oklahoma City, OK

Oregon
(503) 378-3272

Occupational Health and Safety
Department of Insurance and Finance
Salem, OR

Pennsylvania
(412) 367-2396

Safety Sciences
Indiana University of Pennsylvania
Indiana, PA

Puerto Rico
(809) 754-2171

Occupational Safety and Health Office
Puerto Rico Department of Labor and Human Resources
Hato Rey, PR

Rhode Island
(401) 277-2438

Occupational Health Consulting
Rhode Island Department of Health
Providence, RI

South Carolina
(803) 734-9599

South Carolina Department of Labor,
Licensing and Regulations
Columbia, SC

South Dakota
(605) 688-4101

Health and Safety Onsite Technical Division
Engineering Extension
South Dakota State University
Brookings, SD

Tennessee
(615) 741-7036

OSHA Consultative Services
Tennessee Department of Labor
Nashville, TN

Texas
(512) 440-3834

Workers' Safety Division
Texas Workers' Compensation Commission
Austin, TX

Utah
(801) 530-6868

Industrial Commission Consultation Service
Salt Lake City, UT

Vermont
(802) 828-2765

Occupational Safety and Health
Vermont Department of Labor and Industry
Montpelier, VT

Virginia
(804) 786-8707

Occupational Safety and Health Training and Consultation
Virginia Department of Labor and Industry
Richmond, VA

Virgin Islands
(809) 772-1315

Occupational Safety and Health
Virgin Islands Department of Labor
St. Croix, VI

Washington
(206) 956-5443

Industrial Safety and Health
Washington Department of Labor and Industries
Olympia, WA

West Virginia
(304) 558-7890

West Virginia Department of Labor
Charleston, WV

Wisconsin
(608) 266-8579 (health)

Occupational Health
Wisconsin Department of Health and Human Services
Madison, WI

(414) 521-5188 (safety)

Bureau of Safety Inspection
Wisconsin Department of Industry Labor and
Human Relations
Waukesha, WI

Wyoming
(307) 777-7786

Safety and Compensation
Wyoming Department of Employment
Cheyenne, WY

State Environmental Regulatory Agencies

State Environmental Regulatory Agencies

This list provides contact information for environmental control agencies in each state. Personnel within these offices will provide assistance and information relevant to state environmental laws, planning, permits, and reporting requirements. The states are listed in alphabetical order.

Alabama
(205) 271-7700

Department of Environmental Management
Montgomery, AL

Alaska
(907) 465-5050

Department of Environmental Conservation
Juneau, AK

Arizona
(602) 207-2203

Department of Environmental Quality
Phoenix, AZ

Arkansas
(501) 562-4632

Pollution Control and Ecology
Little Rock, AR

California
(916) 445-3846

California Environmental Protection Agency
Sacramento, CA

Colorado
(303) 692-3099

Office of the Environment
Department of Public Health and Environment
Denver, CO

Connecticut
(203) 424-3001

Department of Environmental Protection
Hartford, CT

Delaware
(302) 739-6242

Department of Natural Resources and
Environmental Control
Dover, DE

District of Columbia
(202) 404-1136

Environmental Regulation Administration
Washington, DC

Florida
(904) 488-1554

Department of Environmental Protection
Tallahassee, FL

Georgia
(404) 656-4317

Department of Natural Resources
Atlanta, GA

Guam
(671) 646-8863

Guam Environmental Protection Agency
Harmon, GU

Hawaii
(808) 586-4424

Department of Health and Environmental Planning
Honolulu, HI

Idaho
(208) 334-5840

Department of Health and Welfare
Boise, ID

Illinois
(217) 782-9039

Illinois Environmental Protection Agency
Springfield, IL

Indiana
(317) 232-8612

Department of Environmental Management
Indianapolis, IN

Iowa
(515) 281-6284

Bureau of Natural Resources
Des Moines, IA

Kansas
(913) 296-8464

Department of Health and Environment
Topeka, KS

Kentucky
(502) 564-2150

Department of Environmental Protection
Frankfort, KY

Louisiana
(504) 765-0222

Department of Environmental Quality
Baton Rouge, LA

Maine
(207) 287-2812

Department of Environmental Protection
Augusta, ME

Maryland
(410) 631-3084

Department of Natural Resources
Baltimore, MD

Massachusetts
(617) 727-3163

Department of Environmental Protection
North Grafton, MA

Michigan
(517) 373-2329

Department of Natural Resources
Lansing, MI

Minnesota
(612) 296-2603

Environmental Quality Board
St. Paul, MN

Mississippi
(601) 961-5000

Department of Environmental Quality
Jackson, MS

Missouri
(314) 751-0763

Department of Natural Resources
Jefferson City, MO

Montana
(406) 444-2544

Department of Health and Environmental Sciences
Helena, MT

Nebraska
(402) 471-2186

Department of Environmental Quality
Lincoln, NE

Nevada
(702) 687-4670

Division of Environmental Protection
Carson City, NV

New Hampshire
(603) 271-3503

Department of Environmental Services
Concord, NH

New Jersey
(609) 292-2885

Department of Environmental Protection and Energy
Trenton, NJ

New Mexico
(505) 827-2850

Department of the Environment
Santa Fe, NM

New York
(518) 457-3446

Department of Environmental Conservation
Albany, NY

North Carolina
(919) 733-7015

Division of Environmental Management
Raleigh, NC

North Dakota
(701) 328-5150

State Department of Health
Bismarck, ND

Ohio
(614) 644-2782

Ohio Environmental Protection Agency
Columbus, OH

Oklahoma
(405) 271-8056

Department of Environmental Quality
Oklahoma City, OK

Oregon
(503) 239-5300

Department of Environmental Quality
Portland, OR

Pennsylvania
(717) 787-5028

Department of Environmental Protection
Harrisburg, PA

Puerto Rico
(809) 766-2483

Environmental Quality Board
Hato Rey, PR

Rhode Island
(401) 277-2771

Department of Environmental Management
Providence, RI

South Carolina
(803) 734-5360

Department of Health and Environmental Control
Columbia, SC

South Dakota
(605) 773-3151

Department of Water and Natural Resources
Pierre, SD

Tennessee
(615) 532-0220

Department of Environment and Conservation
Nashville, TN

Texas
(512) 458-7111

Texas Natural Resource Conservation Commission
Austin, TX

Utah
(801) 536-4402

Department of Environmental Quality
Salt Lake City, UT

Vermont
(802) 241-3808

Department of Environmental Conservation
Waterbury, VT

Virginia
(804) 762-4020

Department of Environmental Quality
Richmond, VA

Virgin Islands
(809) 774-3320

Department of Planning and Natural Resources
St. Croix, VI

Washington
(360) 407-6000

Department of Ecology
Olympia, WA

West Virginia
(304) 759-0515

Department of Commerce, Labor and Environmental
Resources
Charleston, WV

Wisconsin
(608) 266-1099

Department of Natural Resources
Madison, WI

Wyoming
(307) 777-7192

Department of Environmental Quality
Cheyenne, WY

Sample Scorekeeper's Note Pad

Sample Scorekeeper's Note Pad

Health and Safety Issues

	Applicable/ Not Applicable	Section Score Awarded	Special Credit Points	Weight of Topic	Subtotal [(score + credit) × weight]
Battery Management	yes	90	0	1.2	108
Carcinogenic/Toxic Dusts and Fumes					
Chemical Carcinogens Requiring Air Monitoring	no				
Chemical Carcinogens Not Requiring Air Monitoring	no				
Chemical Storage Procedures	yes	75	0	1.0	75
Compressed Gases	no				
Confined Space Entry Procedures	yes	80	8	1.5	132
Electrical Hazards	yes	80	8	1.5	132
Emergency Action Plan	no				
Emergency Response Program	yes	85	0	1.0	85
Ergonomics	yes	90	5	1.0	95
Excavation and Trenching	no				
Fall Protection	yes	85	10	1.2	114
Fire Protection and Prevention	yes	85	10	1.2	114
Flammable and Combustible Liquids	yes	85	0	1.0	85
Hazard Communication Program	yes	90	0	0.8	84

Score Keeper's Note Pad (*cont'd.*)

	Applicable/ Not Applicable	Section Score Awarded	Special Credit Points	Weight of Topic	Subtotal [(score + credit) x weight]
Hearing Conservation Program	yes	50	0	1.0	50
Heat Stress	no				
Ionizing Radiation	no				
Laser Equipment	no				
Local Exhaust Ventilation	yes	85	4	1.0	89
Lockout and Tagout Program	yes	100	10	1.0	110
Manual Lifting	yes	60	0	1.2	72
Personal Protective Equipment	yes	100	10	1.0	100
Portable Power Tools/Equipment	no				
Powered Industrial Trucks	no				
Process Safety Management	no				
Respiratory Protection Program	yes	90	5	1.0	95
Scaffolds	no				
Stairways and Ladders	yes	88	0	1.0	88
Toxic Substances Exposure Monitoring	yes	90	5	1.0	95
Welding and Cutting	yes	100	0	1.0	100

Totals: 18.9   1672

1672/18.9=88.5

Total Score for Health and Safety Issues: 88.5%

Glossary of Terms

abatement: Corrective action(s) to eliminate problems.

action level: The airborne exposure level to a toxic and/or carcinogenic substance which is typically within the acceptable exposure limits for a given substance yet requires special attention, such as routine air monitoring and medical surveillance.

asbestos-containing material (ACM): Material containing more than one percent of asbestos.

authorized person: A person approved or assigned by the employer to perform a specific type of duty or duties and/or be at a specific location or locations at the job site.

ballast: A device, often a resistor, that maintains the current in circuit at a constant value by varying its resistance in order to counteract changes in voltage, such as in a fluorescent light fixture.

biannual (also semiannual): Occurs once every 6 months

biohazard: A material of biological composition that constitutes a threat of death, injury, or illness to man.

carcinogenic: Able to cause cancer.

carpal tunnel syndrome (CTS): A form of cumulative trauma disorder which affects one's hands and wrists.

ceiling limit (C): An airborne exposure level which should not be exceeded for any time period, instantaneous or over a 15 to 30 minute time period.

certified: Equipment is "certified" if it has been tested and found by a nationally recognized testing laboratory to meet nationally recognized standards or to be safe for use in a specified manner, is of a kind whose production is periodically inspected by a nationally recognized testing laboratory, and bears a label, tag, or other record of certification.

circuit: A conductor or system of conductors through which an electric current is intended to flow.

closure: The process of securing a solid waste landfill or hazardous waste management facility according to state and federal EPA-specified technical and administrative procedures.

coal tar pitch volatiles: The volatile components emitted when coal tar or coal tar pitch is heated, consisting of benzo(a)pyrene and other polynuclear aromatic hydrocarbons.

coke oven: An oven in which coal is changed into coke (used in pig iron and steel production) by destructive distillation.

combustible: A substance which has a flash point at or below 100° F, such as paper, plastic, lawn clippings, leaves, and other organic materials.

confined space: A space that: (1) is large enough to allow a person to enter; (2) has limited openings for workers to enter and exit; and (3) is not designed for continuous occupancy.

corrosive: A substance that by direct action may cause damage to body tissues and/or metal.

cryogenic: Extremely low temperatures.

cumulative trauma disorder: Injury to the tissues, nerves, tendons, tendon sheaths, and muscles (predominantly of the upper extremities) which is the result of repeated forceful actions.

dielectric fluid: A fluid which can conduct current but does not store a charge.

dike: An embankment or ridge of either natural or manmade materials used to prevent the movement of liquids, sludges, solids, or other materials.

discharge: Waterborne pollutants released to a receiving stream, directly or indirectly, or to a sewage system.

dust: Fine-grain particles of undefined composition.

excursion limit: The airborne exposure limit which should not be exceeded for a given time period, based on the exposure.

explosive: A chemical that causes a sudden, almost instantaneous release of pressure, gas, and heat when subjected to sudden shock, pressure, or high temperatures.

exposure assessment: The determination or estimation of the magnitude, frequency, duration, route, and extent of exposure to a chemical.

facility: Any building, structure, installation, equipment, pipe or pipeline, well, pit, pond, lagoon, impoundment, ditch, landfill, storage container, motor vehicle, rolling stock, or aircraft; any site or area where a hazardous substance has been deposited, stored, disposed of, or placed, or otherwise come to be located; but does not include any consumer product or consumer use or any vessel.

fire brigade: An organized group of employees who are knowledgeable, trained, and skilled in the safe evacuation of employees during emergency situations and in assisting in fire fighting operations.

fires, Class A: Fires occurring in common combustible materials, such as wood, cloth, paper, rubber, and plastics.

fires, Class B: Fires occurring in flammable liquids, gases, and greases.

fires, Class C: Electrical fires which require a nonconducting extinguishing medium.

fires, Class D: Fires occurring in combustible metals, such as magnesium and sodium.

flammable: Description of a material which has a flash point of less than 100°F and ignites easily, burns intensely, or has a rapid rate of flame spread.

floor opening: An opening—measuring 12 inches or more in its least dimension, in any floor, platform, pavement, or yard—through which persons may fall.

friable: Material, which when dry, may be crushed, pulverized, or reduced to powder by hand pressure.

fumes: Solid particles less than one micron in diameter, formed as vapors condense or as chemical reactions take place, such as copper welding fumes.

hazardous: A substance which is flammable, toxic, reactive, or may potentially pose a threat to life and/or health if mismanaged.

heat cramps: Muscle cramps due to excessive sweating with no water replacement.

heat exhaustion: Occurs when the body's thermal regulatory mechanism is overactive leading to weakness and the appearance of physical exhaustion.

heat stroke: Occurs when the body's thermal regulatory mechanisms shut down completely leading to elevated body temperatures, absence of sweating, and eventual collapse.

hot work: Work involving electric or gas welding, cutting, brazing, or similar flame or spark-producing operations.

ionizing radiation: Any electromagnetic or particulate radiation capable of producing ions, directly or indirectly, by interacting with matter.

lockout device: Any device that uses a positive means of control, such as a lock (either key or combination type) to hold an energy-isolating device in a safe position, thereby preventing the energizing of machinery or equipment.

musculoskeletal disorder: Any of a number of physical problems which include back injury, carpal tunnel syndrome, and cumulative trauma disorder.

monitoring: Periodic or continuous surveillance or testing to determine the level of compliance with statutory requirements and/or pollutant levels in various media or in humans, animals, and other living things.

PCB-containing: Contains 500 ppm or greater of PCBs.

PCB-contaminated: Contains 50 ppm or greater of PCBs.

pipe system: A system of hollow cylinders and/or tubular conduit.

point of operation: That point at which cutting, shaping, or forming is accomplished upon the stock and shall include such other points as may offer a hazard to the operator in inserting or manipulating the stock in the operation of a machine.

qualified person: A person who by reason of experience or training is familiar with the operation to be performed and the hazards involved.

raceway: A metal or insulating channel designed expressly for holding wires, cables, or busbars, with additional functions.

rad: Energy absorbed per unit of tissue mass.

reactive: Substances which enter into violent reactions during which the spontaneous liberation of heat and/or gases is too rapid to be safely dissipated.

regulated area: A delineated area requiring special controls.

remediation: Permanent remedy of a problem.

REM: Measure of the dose of any ionizing radiation to body tissue in terms of its estimated biological effect relative to a dose of one roentgen of X-rays.

semiannual (also biannual): Occurs once every 6 months.

short term exposure limit: An airborne exposure limit which is based on short exposure durations, usually not longer than 15 minutes, and not to be repeated for more than a given number of times during a day, typically 4 times with 60 minutes between exposures.

surfacing material: In reference to asbestos, material that is sprayed, troweled-on, or otherwise applied to a surface. Included is acoustical plaster on ceilings, fireproofing material on structural members (vertical and horizontal) and other surfaces, and acoustical surfacing material.

tagout device: Any prominent warning device, such as a tag and means of attachment, that can be securely fastened to an energy-isolating device in accordance with an established procedure.

time-weighted average (TWA): The airborne exposure level of a worker, which is based on an 8-hour workday.

toxic: A substance which in low levels may cause harm, irreversible damage, or death.

transformer: A device that is used to step up or step down alternating current voltage.

vapor: The gaseous phase of a substance that is normally a liquid or solid at atmospheric temperature and pressure.

Index

THE  ASTRO SOLUTION

 + CENGAGENOW +  +

Special Note To Students

It is important to begin reading this text with one thing in mind: *This business course does not have to be difficult .* We have done everything possible to eliminate the problems that students encounter in a typical class. All the features in each chapter have been evaluated and recommended by instructors with years of teaching experience. In addition, business students were asked to critique each chapter component. Based on this feedback, the text includes the following features:

- *Learning objectives* appear at the beginning of each chapter.
- *Inside Business* is a chapter-opening case that highlights how successful companies do business on a day-to-day basis.
- *Margin notes* are used throughout the text to reinforce both learning objectives and key terms.
- *Boxed features* highlight how both employees and entrepreneurs can be successful.
- *Spotlight* features highlight interesting facts about business and society and often provide a real-world example of an important concept within a chapter.

Visually Engaging Textbook   **Online Study Tools**   **Tear-Out Review Cards**   **Interactive Ebook**

STUDENT RESOURCES:

- Interactive Ebook
- Flashcards
- Videos
- Auto-graded Interactive Quizzes
- Active Figures
- End-of-Chapter Exercises
- Math Reference Cards

INSTRUCTOR RESOURCES:

- Instructor's Manual
- Test Bank
- PowerPoint® Slides
- Image Library

Students sign in at **www.nelson.com/student**   Instructors sign in at **www.nelson.com/instructor**

"**The online learning is great and the review cards in the back make test review easy!**"

– Kyle McConnell, student

NELSON
EDUCATION

ASTRO, Second Canadian Edition

by Shohini Ghose, Vesna Milosevic-Zdjelar, and
L. Arthur Read

Vice President, Editorial Higher Education:
Anne Williams

Senior Publisher:
Paul Fam

Marketing Manager:
Leanne Newell

Developmental Editor:
Toni Chahley

Photo Researcher:
Lisa Brant

Permissions Coordinator:
Lisa Brant

Production Project Manager:
Wendy Yano

Production Service:
MPS Limited

Copy Editor:
Carolyn Jongeward

Proofreader:
MPS Limited

Indexer:
Edwin Durbin

Design Director:
Ken Phipps

Managing Designer:
Franca Amore

Interior Design:
Cenveo Publisher Services

Cover Design:
Cathy Mayer

Cover Image:
© Stocktrek/Getty Images

Compositor:
MPS Limited

Library and Archives Canada Cataloguing in Publication Data

Ghose, Shohini, 1974–, author

ASTRO / Ghose, Milosevic-Zdjelar, Read. — Second Canadian edition.

Includes index. Title from cover. Revision of: Astro / Backman ... [et al.]. — Canadian ed. – Toronto: Nelson Education, ©2013. ISBN 978-0-17-653214-7 (pbk.)

1. Astronomy—Textbooks. I. Milosevic-Zdjelar, Vesna, 1961–, author II. Read, L. Arthur, 1941–, author III. Title.

QB61.G56 2015   520
C2015-901315-1

ISBN 13: 978-0-17-653214-7
ISBN 10: 0-17-653214-5

We gratefully acknowledge the support and contribution of Michael Seeds and Dana Backman, upon whose considerable efforts and expertise we have built this Canadian edition. The key to writing an effective and engaging textbook is the ability to understand your audience and present concepts in an inspiring way. The work of Seeds and Backman exemplifies this skill, and their work forms the foundation of the Second Canadian Edition of *ASTRO*.

About the Cover

The International Space Station (shown on the cover) is not some faraway object that you need a telescope to see. Students may view it for themselves with the naked eye! (For sighting opportunities, see http://spaceflight.nasa.gov/realdata/sightings/.) The ISS is a remarkable symbol of humanity's achievements in science, technology, and astronomy. As an international effort involving scientists from around the world, and jointly operated by the space agencies of the United States, Russia, Japan, Europe, and Canada, the ISS reflects ASTRO's message that astronomy is a global unifying effort. At the same time, Canada's important contributions to the space station—including the innovative Canadarm—make the ISS an exciting and ideal cover image for ASTRO, Second Canadian Edition.

BRIEF CONTENTS

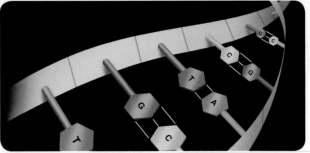

CONTENTS

Shohini Ghose is an Associate Professor of Physics and Computer Science and Director of the Centre for Women in Science at Wilfrid Laurier University. She is an adjunct professor at the University of Waterloo, a member of the Guelph-Waterloo Physics Institute, and an affiliate of the Perimeter Institute for Theoretical Physics. She is a theoretical physicist who has made important contributions in the areas of nonlinear dynamics, quantum information, and quantum optics. Shohini has taught physics and astronomy to over 2000 students enrolled in her courses, and has developed innovative online teaching and learning tools for science. Her research and teaching has earned her numerous awards, including a WOW (Women of Waterloo) Education award and a prestigious TED Fellowship. Shohini is also passionate about addressing gender issues in science and recently founded the Laurier Centre for Women in Science (WinS). Apart from physics she loves reading, travelling, and cricket (the game, not the insect).

Vesna Milosevic-Zdjelar, former astrophysicist from the National Observatory in Belgrade, Serbia, joined the University of Winnipeg's Physics Department in 2000. In Canada, she obtained a degree in science education, and has made important contributions teaching science courses to non-science and life sciences students, and creating community awareness by initiating science outreach programs. She initiated and co-created "Concepts in Science," a course that became the preferred science course choice for education and arts students, with enrollment increasing tenfold to 300 students. Vesna's passion for science education came from generations of educators in her family, especially her mother Ljiljana, a nuclear physicist, whose expertize and ideas contributed to this book. Vesna has been invited to make numerous presentations at conferences and symposia for university instructors and science teachers. She teaches a broad range of courses including Astronomy, Concepts in Science, Physics for Life Sciences, and Physics of Music.

L. Arthur (Art) Read is Professor Emeritus at Wilfrid Laurier University (WLU), Waterloo. He received both his BA and MSc (Physics) from McMaster University, and his PhD (Physics) from University of Waterloo.

At WLU, Art taught physics and served in various administrative roles including Dean of Arts & Science (1983–1999), Director of the Brantford Development Project, and was subsequently appointed as the first Dean of the Laurier Brantford campus (1999–2001).

His research interests involved microwave optics and broadband molecular spectroscopy. With a keen interest in education quality and standards development, he has served as curriculum assessor for the Ontario Postsecondary Education Quality Assessment Board. He has developed and taught a variety of physics courses, including musical acoustics, analog electronics, physics for life sciences, and introductory astronomy. In his retirement, Art is currently teaching two popular online astronomy courses for Laurier and has recently completed the development of two interactive online astronomy courses for provincial use in Ontario.

INTRODUCTION

ASTRONOMY CAN GIVE you a perspective on what it means to be here on Earth. It can help you locate yourself in space and time. Once you realize how vast our universe is, Earth seems quite small, and people on the other side of the world seem like neighbours. Furthermore, in the entire history of the universe, the human story is only a flicker of an eye blink. This may seem humbling at first, but you can be proud of how much humans have understood in such a short time.

Not only does astronomy locate you in space and time, it also places you in the physical processes that govern the universe. Gravity and atoms work together to make stars, light the universe, generate energy, and create the chemical elements in your body. By learning astronomy you can see how you fit into that cosmic process.

Although we are very small and human beings have existed in the universe for only a short time, we are an important part of something very large and very beautiful.

PART ONE

1

The Scale of the Cosmos: Space and Time

CHAPTER OUTLINE

GUIDEPOST

You are already an expert in astronomy. You have enjoyed sunsets and moonrises, have admired the stars, and may know a few constellations. You have probably read about Mars rovers and the Hubble Space Telescope. That is more than most Earthlings know about astronomy. Still, you owe it to yourself to understand where you are. You should know what it means to live on a planet that whirls around a star sailing through one galaxy in a universe full of galaxies.

It is easy to learn a few facts, but it is the relationships among facts that are important. This chapter will give you the sense of scale that you need to understand where you are in the universe.

Here, you will consider three important questions about astronomy:

- **Where are you and Earth in the universe?**
- **How does the time span of human civilization compare with the age of the universe?**
- **How does science give us a way to know about nature?**

The remaining chapters in this book will fill in the details, give evidence, describe theories, and illustrate the wonderful intricacy and beauty of the universe. That journey begins here.

You are about to go on a voyage to the limits of the known universe, travelling outward, away from your home on Earth, past the Moon and the Sun and the other planets of our solar system, past the stars you see in the night sky, and beyond billions more stars that can be seen only with the aid of telescopes. You will visit the most distant galaxies—great globes and whirlpools of stars—and continue on, carried only by experience and imagination, seeking to understand the structure of the universe. Astronomy

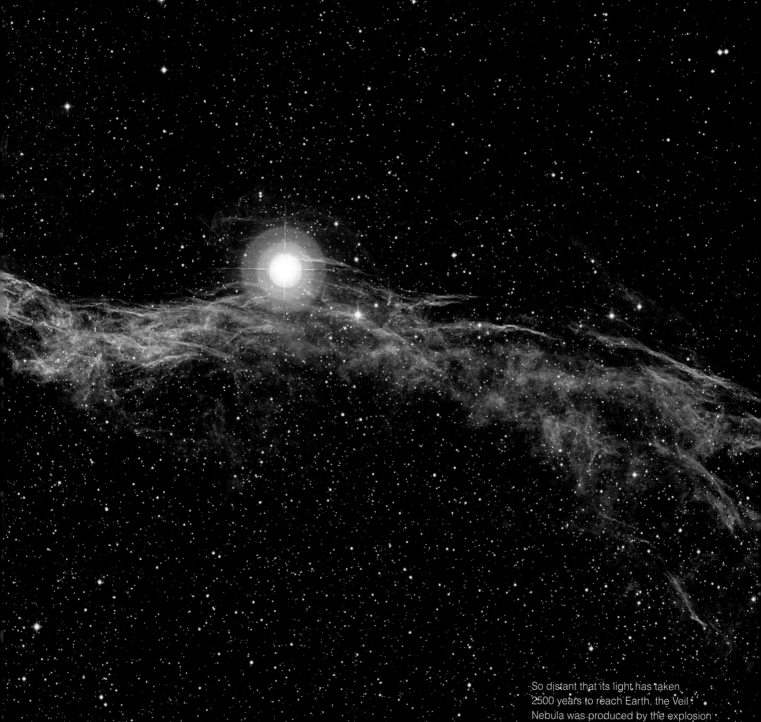

Space is big. You just won't believe how vastly, hugely, mind-bogglingly big it is. I mean, you may think it's a long way down the road to the chemist's, but that's just peanuts to space.

Douglas Adams,
The Hitchhiker's Guide to the Galaxy

So distant that its light has taken 2500 years to reach Earth, the Veil Nebula was produced by the explosion of a star 15000 years ago.

is more than the study of planets, stars, and galaxies—it is the study of the whole universe in which you live. Although humanity is confined to a small planet circling an average star, the study of astronomy can take you beyond these boundaries and help you not only see where you are but also understand *what* you are.

Your imagination is the key to discovery; it will be your scientific space-and-time machine transporting you across the universe and into the past and future. Go back in time to watch the formation of the Sun and Earth, the birth of the first stars, and ultimately the creation of the universe. Then, rush into the future to see what will happen when the Sun dies and Earth withers.

Although you will discover a beginning to the universe, you will not find an edge or an end in space. No matter how far you voyage, you will not run into a wall. In a later chapter you will discover evidence that the universe may be infinite; that is, it may extend in all directions without limit.

Astronomy will introduce you to sizes, distances, and times far beyond your usual experience on Earth. Your task in this chapter is to grasp the meaning of these unfamiliar sizes, distances, and times. The solution lies in a single word: scale. In this chapter, you will compare objects of different sizes in order to comprehend the scale of the universe.

1.1 From Solar System to Galaxy to Universe

We start with our human scale in the Universe of Particles, a museum exhibit at the Globe of Science and Innovation at CERN (Organisation Européenne pour la Recherche Nucléaire) in Geneva (see **Visualizing Astronomy 1.1, The Scale of the Very Small and Very Large: Powers of 10**). CERN is the home of the Large Hadron Collider, the largest particle accelerator in operation today, which was designed to simulate the beginning of the universe (see also Chapter 11, **Visualizing Astronomy 11.1, The Large Hadron Collider**). Not more than 100 m under the ground from the Globe of Science and Innovation, massive detectors are looking for the first signs of the big bang, microscopic black holes, and

scientific notation The system of recording very large or very small numbers by using powers of 10.

field of view The area visible in an image, usually given as the diameter of the region.

dark matter. The results might shed light on many topics in this book, and perhaps even change a few chapters. We indeed live in exciting times, when new technology can bring us closer to our origins.

Now let's use our imagination to fly out from the Globe of Science and Innovation. Along the way, study the journey described in **Visualizing Astronomy 1.1, The Scale of the Very Small and Very Large: Powers of 10**. (The following figure numbers refer to these pages.)

Our journey to the smallest realm of nature starts with the human hand on the museum exhibit (Figure 1a). To reach the scale of skin cells in our hand (Figure 1b), we have to zoom in with a microscope 100 000 times to a size that is 100-thousandth of a metre. The metre quickly becomes too large as a unit. Instead we use either prefixes (e.g., "milli," which means "one-thousandth") or **scientific notation**—the powers of 10. The information about the cell and the organism to which the cell belongs is encoded in the DNA molecule. The DNA strand shown here is a billionth of a metre thick (Figure 1c). Diving through the molecule, we encounter the main building block of matter: the atom. The size of the electron cloud surrounding the tiny nucleus of an atom is 10-billionth of a metre (Figure 1d). The nucleus of the atom is 10 000 times smaller than the atom itself. Elementary particles are roughly in the order of 10 times smaller than the nucleus. How far can we go? Large Hadron Collider achieved collisions in which a Higgs boson has been produced, on the scale of 10^{-15} m (Figure 1e). The smallest length that theoretically makes sense is the Planck length—100 billion billion times smaller than the scale of the smallest elementary particles (Figure 1f)! An understanding of these building blocks of space and matter allows us to unravel the secrets of the birth and evolution of the universe.

In the following chapters you will embark on a journey from Earth to the farthest visible extent of the universe. For those distances we use larger measures than the metre as we move outward from Earth.

You will now follow the sequence in **Visualizing Astronomy 1.1, The Scale of the Very Small and Very Large: Powers of 10,** starting again from the Globe of Science and Innovation (Figure 2a), and moving farther and farther away. Each view is made from a distance that is some power of 10 times farther away, until the distance becomes so large that we jump with higher increments. Every time we move 10 times away, our **field of view** encompasses an area 10 × 10 larger than the previous square.

Distances are first expressed in metres until they become so large that a metre becomes too small as a unit. At a distance of 10 000 m, or 10 km, the view includes about the same area as CERN's Large Hadron Collider (Figure 2b).

In the next step of the journey, we can see the entire planet Earth, which is about 13 000 kilometres in diameter. The image of Earth (Figure 2c) shows most of the daylight side of the planet, and the blurriness at the extreme right is the sunset line. The rotation of Earth on its axis each 24 hours carries us eastward, and as we cross the sunset line into darkness we say that the Sun has set. At the scale of this image, the atmosphere on which our life depends is thinner than a strand of thread.

Next we enlarge our field of view by a factor of 100 and see a region 1 000 000 km wide (Figure 2d). Earth is the small blue dot in the centre, and the Moon, with a diameter only about one-fourth that of Earth, is an even smaller dot along its orbit. If you've had a high-mileage car, it may have travelled the equivalent of a trip to the Moon, which has an average distance from Earth of 380 000 km. These numbers are so large that it is inconvenient to write them out. Astronomy is the science of big numbers, and you will use numbers much larger than these to describe the universe.

Here, we jump to another measuring unit. We enlarge a picture not 10 times or 100 times, but 150 times in order to fit a specific distance into the picture: the average distance from Earth to the Sun. This distance is called the **astronomical unit (AU)**, which is 1.5×10^8 km, or 1.5×10^{11} m. Introducing new units is another way astronomers deal with large numbers. Using that unit, we can say, for example, that the average distance from Venus to the Sun is about 0.7 AU. At this scale we find the Sun and planets of our solar system (Figure 2e). The **solar system** consists of the Sun, its family of planets, and some smaller bodies, such as moons, asteroids, and comets.

Like Earth, Venus and Mercury are **planets**—small, nonluminous bodies that shine by reflecting sunlight. Venus is about the size of Earth, and Mercury is a bit larger than Earth's moon. In this figure they are both too small to be seen as anything but tiny dots. The Sun is a **star**, a self-luminous ball of hot gas that generates its own energy (Figure 1.1). The Sun is about 110 times larger in diameter than Earth, but it, too, is nothing more than a dot in this view. Earth orbits the Sun once a year.

Now, jump 100 times farther away than the previous view, and you will see the entire solar system, all the major planets and their slightly elliptical orbits (Figure 2f). You see only the brighter, more widely separated objects as you back away. The Sun, Mercury,

Venus, and Earth are so close together that we cannot separate them at this scale.

Mars, the next outward planet, is only 1.5 AU from the Sun. In contrast, Jupiter, Saturn, Uranus, and Neptune are so far from the Sun that they are easy to find in this figure. Light from the Sun reaches Earth in only eight minutes, but it takes over four hours to reach Neptune. Pluto, which orbits mostly outside Neptune's orbit, is no longer considered a major planet.

The Sun is a fairly typical star, a bit larger than average, and it is located in a fairly normal neighbourhood in the universe. The stars are separated by average distances about 30 times larger than this view, which has a diameter of 11 000 AU. It is difficult to grasp the isolation of the stars. If the Sun were represented by a golf ball in Vancouver, the nearest star would be another golf ball in Calgary.

At this point, our view has expanded to a diameter of about 2 million AU. The Sun is at the centre, and we see a few of the nearest stars. These stars are so distant that it is not reasonable to give their distances in AU. Astronomers

astronomical unit (AU) Average distance from Earth to the Sun; 1.5×10^8 kilometres.

solar system The Sun and its planets, asteroids, comets, and so on.

planet A non-luminous body in orbit around a star, large enough to be spherical and to have cleared its orbital zone of other objects.

star A globe of gas held together by its own gravity and supported by the internal pressure of its hot gases, which generate energy by nuclear fusion.

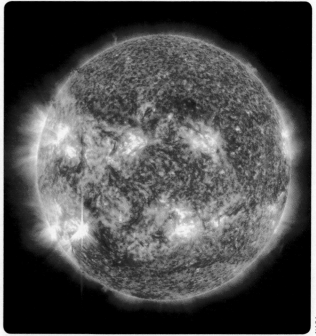

Figure 1.1 Our Star: The Sun

NASA

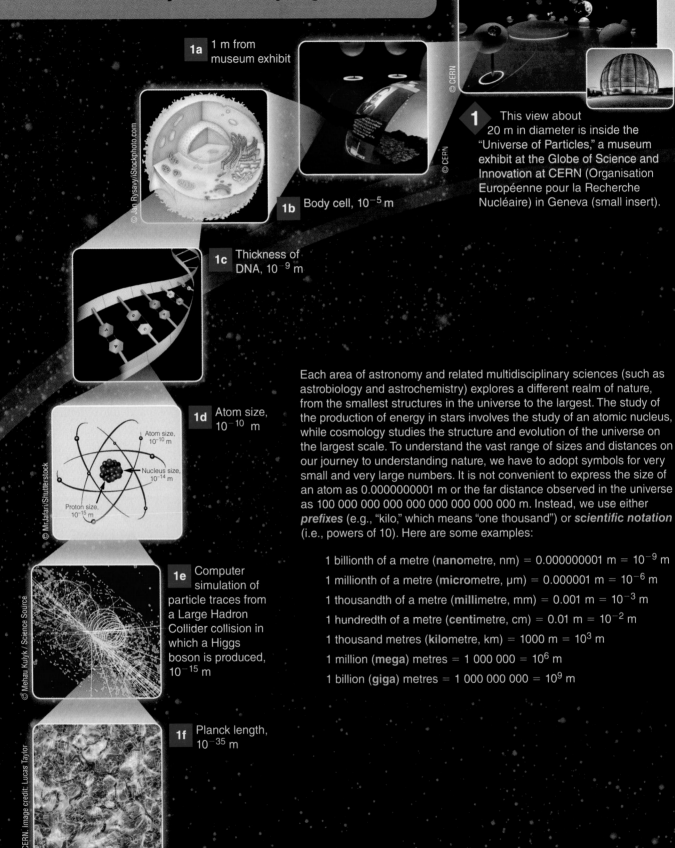

1a 1 m from museum exhibit

1b Body cell, 10^{-5} m

1 This view about 20 m in diameter is inside the "Universe of Particles," a museum exhibit at the Globe of Science and Innovation at CERN (Organisation Européenne pour la Recherche Nucléaire) in Geneva (small insert).

1c Thickness of DNA, 10^{-9} m

1d Atom size, 10^{-10} m

Atom size, 10^{-10} m
Nucleus size, 10^{-14} m
Proton size, 10^{-15} m

1e Computer simulation of particle traces from a Large Hadron Collider collision in which a Higgs boson is produced, 10^{-15} m

1f Planck length, 10^{-35} m

Each area of astronomy and related multidisciplinary sciences (such as astrobiology and astrochemistry) explores a different realm of nature, from the smallest structures in the universe to the largest. The study of the production of energy in stars involves the study of an atomic nucleus, while cosmology studies the structure and evolution of the universe on the largest scale. To understand the vast range of sizes and distances on our journey to understanding nature, we have to adopt symbols for very small and very large numbers. It is not convenient to express the size of an atom as 0.0000000001 m or the far distance observed in the universe as 100 000 000 000 000 000 000 000 000 m. Instead, we use either *prefixes* (e.g., "kilo," which means "one thousand") or *scientific notation* (i.e., powers of 10). Here are some examples:

1 billionth of a metre (**nano**metre, nm) = 0.000000001 m = 10^{-9} m

1 millionth of a metre (**micro**metre, μm) = 0.000001 m = 10^{-6} m

1 thousandth of a metre (**milli**metre, mm) = 0.001 m = 10^{-3} m

1 hundredth of a metre (**centi**metre, cm) = 0.01 m = 10^{-2} m

1 thousand metres (**kilo**metre, km) = 1000 m = 10^{3} m

1 million (**mega**) metres = 1 000 000 = 10^{6} m

1 billion (**giga**) metres = 1 000 000 000 = 10^{9} m

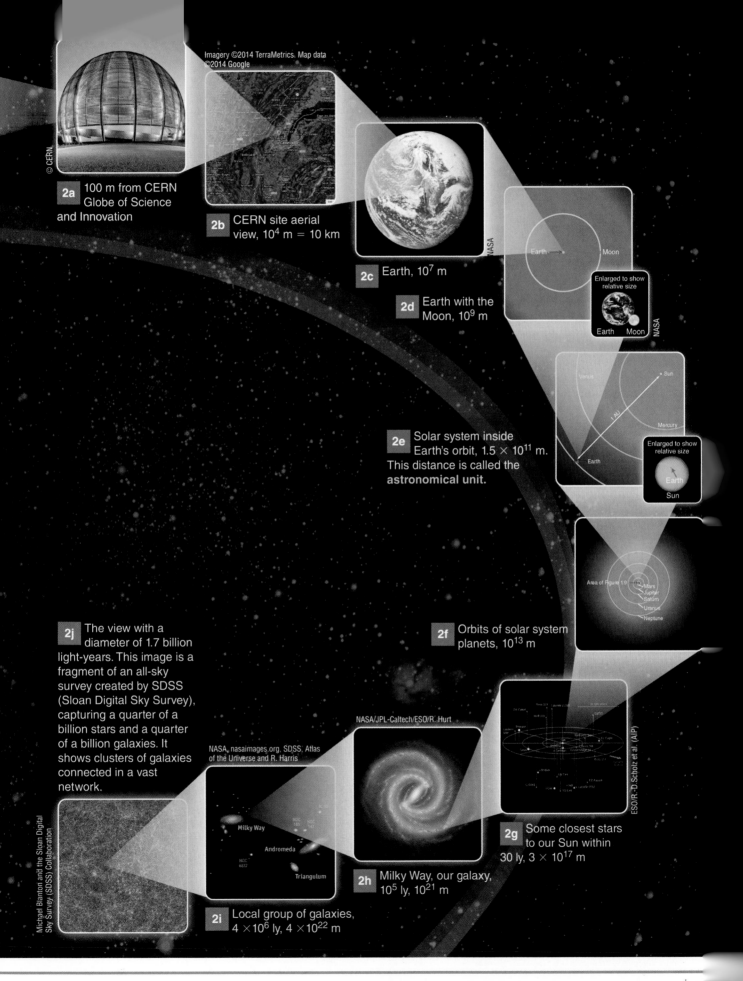

2a 100 m from CERN Globe of Science and Innovation

2b CERN site aerial view, 10^4 m = 10 km

2c Earth, 10^7 m

2d Earth with the Moon, 10^9 m

Enlarged to show relative size
Earth   Moon

2e Solar system inside Earth's orbit, 1.5×10^{11} m. This distance is called the **astronomical unit**.

Enlarged to show relative size
Earth   Sun

2f Orbits of solar system planets, 10^{13} m

2j The view with a diameter of 1.7 billion light-years. This image is a fragment of an all-sky survey created by SDSS (Sloan Digital Sky Survey), capturing a quarter of a billion stars and a quarter of a billion galaxies. It shows clusters of galaxies connected in a vast network.

2g Some closest stars to our Sun within 30 ly, 3×10^{17} m

NASA/JPL-Caltech/ESO/R. Hurt

NASA, nasaimages.org, SDSS, Atlas of the Universe and R. Harris

Milky Way

Andromeda

Triangulum

2h Milky Way, our galaxy, 10^5 ly, 10^{21} m

2i Local group of galaxies, 4×10^6 ly, 4×10^{22} m

have defined a new larger unit of distance, the light-year. One **light-year (ly)** is the distance that light travels in one year, roughly 10^{13} km, or 63 000 AU. In the diagram of the nearby stars in relation to the Sun, the diameter of our view is 30 ly (Figure 2g). The nearest star to the Sun, Proxima Centauri, is 4.2 ly from Earth. In other words, light from Proxima Centauri takes 4.2 years to reach Earth.

Although these stars are roughly the same size as the Sun, they are so far away that you cannot see them as anything but points of light. Even with the largest telescopes on Earth, you still see only points of light when you look at stars, and any planets that might circle those stars are much too small and faint to be visible. Of course, no one has ever journeyed thousands of light-years from Earth to look back and photograph the Sun's neighbourhood.

The space between the stars is filled with thin gas. Although those clouds of gas are thinner than the best vacuum produced in laboratories on Earth, it is those clouds that give birth to new stars. The Sun formed from such a cloud about 5 billion years ago.

Expanding our view by a factor of 3000, we see our galaxy (Figure 2h). A **galaxy** is a great cloud of stars, gas, and dust bound together by the combined gravity of all the matter. In the night sky, you see our galaxy from the inside as a great, cloudy band of stars ringing the sky as the **Milky Way**, and our galaxy is called the **Milky Way Galaxy**. Of course, no one has photographed our galaxy, but astronomers have evidence that the galaxy image in Figure 2h is similar to our own. Our Sun would be invisible in such a picture, but if we could see it, we would find it about two-thirds of the way from the centre to the edge. Our galaxy contains over 100 billion stars, and, like many others, has graceful **spiral arms** winding outward through the disk. You will discover in a later chapter that stars are born in great clouds of gas and dust as they pass through the spiral arms.

The visible disk of our galaxy is roughly 80 000 ly in diameter. Only a century ago, astronomers thought it was the entire universe—an island universe of stars in an otherwise empty vastness. Now we know that the Milky Way Galaxy is not unique; it is a typical galaxy in many respects, although larger than most. In fact, ours is only one of many billions of galaxies scattered throughout the universe.

CANADIANS IN ASTRONOMY
Canada's role in the global story of astronomy

Frederick Crouch courtesy of Barbara (McKellar) Bulman-Fleming.

Andrew McKellar

Andrew McKellar

What's the temperature of interstellar space? The first person to answer this question was Dr. Andrew McKellar in 1941. Born in Vancouver, British Columbia, Dr. McKellar worked at the Dominion Astrophysical Observatory in Victoria from 1935 until 1960, except for a brief interruption when he served in the Royal Canadian Navy during the Second World War. In 1940, he used molecular spectroscopy to study the interstellar medium and identified the presence of methane, a compound made of a carbon atom and a hydrogen atom, and cyanogen, made of a carbon atom and a nitrogen atom. He became the first person to demonstrate the existence of matter in interstellar space. Furthermore, he measured the temperature of the cyanogen molecules and thus estimated that the temperature of the interstellar space in which they existed was incredibly cold: roughly 2.4 degrees above absolute zero. Although Dr. McKellar did not know it at the time, he had measured the temperature of the cosmic microwave background (CMB), the radiation emitted roughly 13.8 billion years ago, just after the big bang occurred. Almost 25 years later, Arno Penzias and Robert Wilson detected this microwave radiation from all parts of the sky, corresponding to the temperature estimated by McKellar. Their discovery led to the widespread acceptance of the big bang theory by the worldwide astronomical community, and earned them a Nobel Prize in 1978, almost 20 years after the death of Dr. McKellar (the Nobel Prize cannot be awarded posthumously). In Dr. McKellar's honour, the 1.2-m telescope at the Dominion Astrophysical Observatory is named the McKellar telescope, and the McKellar crater on the Moon is also named after him.

Continuing our journey from the very small to the very large, we move away 40 times farther, and our galaxy appears as a tiny luminous speck surrounded by other specks in a region 4 million ly in diameter. Notice that our galaxy is part of a cluster of a few dozen galaxies called the Local Group (Figure 2i). Galaxies are commonly grouped together in clusters, and some of these galaxies have beautiful spiral patterns like our own galaxy, but others do not. In a later chapter you will investigate what produces these differences among the galaxies.

The image of a fragment of an all-sky survey created by SDSS (Sloan Digital Sky Survey) captures a quarter of a billion galaxies and represents a diameter of 1.7 billion light years (Figure 2j). It shows clusters of galaxies connected in a vast network. Clusters are grouped into **superclusters**—clusters of clusters—and the superclusters are linked to form long filaments and walls what outline voids that seem nearly empty of galaxies. These filaments and walls appear to be the largest structures in the universe.

If we expanded our view frame one more time, we would probably see a uniform fog of filaments and voids. As we puzzle over the origin of these structures, we are at the frontier of human knowledge. The sequence of figures ends here because it has reached the limits of possible observation of the universe. It is not possible to see any distance larger than 13.8 billion light-years. If the universe is 13.8 billion years old, the light from distances farther away than this would not have had the time to reach us. You will learn more about cosmology in Chapter 11.

> **supercluster** A cluster of galaxy clusters.

A problem in studying astronomy is keeping a proper sense of scale. Remember that each of the billions of galaxies contains billions of stars. Many of those stars probably have families of planets like our solar system, and on some of those billions of planets liquid-water oceans and protective atmospheres may have sheltered the spark of life. It is possible that some other planets are inhabited by intelligent creatures who share our curiosity, wonder at the scale of the cosmos, and are looking back at us when we gaze into the heavens.

How could anyone possibly know these secrets of nature? Science gives us a way to know how nature works (see **How Do We Know? 1.1** and **How Do We Know? 1.2**). As you explore the universe in the chapters that follow, notice not only *what* is known but also *how* it is known.

HOW DO WE KNOW? 1.1

The Scientific Method I

How do scientists learn about nature? You have probably heard of the *scientific method* as the process by which scientists form hypotheses and test them against evidence gathered by experiment and observation. Scientists use the scientific method all the time, and it is critically important, but they rarely think of it. It is such an ingrained way of thinking and understanding nature, so it is almost invisible to the people who use it most.

A hypothesis is a suggestion about how nature works, and the evidence is reality. If a hypothesis is compared to the evidence and confirmed, it must be tested further; if it is contradicted, it must be discarded or revised. In that way, ideas get tested and refined to better describe how nature works.

For example, Gregor Mendel (1822–1884) was an Austrian abbot who liked gardening. He formed a hypothesis that offspring usually inherit traits from their parents, not as a smooth blend as most scientists of the time believed, but as discrete units according to strict mathematical rules. Mendel cultivated and tested more than 28 000 pea plants, noting which produced smooth peas and which produced wrinkled peas and how that trait and others were inherited by successive generations. His studies confirmed his hypothesis and allowed the development of a series of laws of inheritance. Although the importance of his work was not recognized in his lifetime, Mendel is now called the father of modern genetics.

The scientific method is not a simple, mechanical way of grinding facts into understanding. It is actually a combination of many ways of analyzing information, finding relationships, and creating new ideas. A scientist needs insight and ingenuity to form and test a good hypothesis. Scientists use the scientific method almost automatically, forming, testing, revising, and discarding hypotheses sometimes minute-by-minute as they discuss new ideas. The so-called scientific method is a way of thinking and a way of knowing about nature. The **How Do We Know?** essays in this book will introduce you to some of the methods scientists use.

The Scientific Method II

How do scientists describe the laws of nature? Mathematics is a language that uses symbols to represent quantities that describe physical properties (mass, charge, energy, speed, etc.). The language of science precisely expresses complicated relationships among physical properties by using mathematical equations.

A simple example involves the well-known scientific equation, $F = ma$. In this equation, F is the force applied to an object, m is the mass of the object (amount of matter or stuff it contains), and a is its acceleration. We can translate the mathematical shorthand into a plain language sentence about the relationship between three quantities, force, mass, and acceleration: The more force you apply to an object, the more it accelerates. If you apply twice as much force the acceleration exactly doubles (assuming the mass remains the same). In mathematical terms we say that the force applied is directly proportional to the acceleration of the object of constant mass m. And the reverse applies

too. The acceleration of the object is directly proportional to the total force you can apply. You have experienced this relationship for yourself if you have ever tried to push an object like a cart. The harder you push (more force), the faster the cart goes (more acceleration). The equation $F = ma$ captures this idea in a precise and concise way. Not only does it express the relationship, it also allows us to precisely calculate "how much harder" and "how much faster."

Sometimes the relationship between physical quantities is an inverse proportionality. For example, consider the equation, $u = d/t$. Here, u is the speed of an object, d is the distance travelled, and t is the time taken to travel the distance d. In this equation, u and t are inversely proportional to each other—so the higher the speed of travel the shorter the time taken to travel a fixed distance d, and vice versa. And like the previous case, the relationship is precise: for example, if you double the speed, you cut your travel time exactly by half.

Although plain language sentences can be used to understand the laws of nature and the relationships between different quantities, as described above, the language of mathematics captures these relationships in the most accurate and concise way. If you understand the relationships encoded in a mathematical equation, you can grasp the science of astronomy without just memorizing mathematical formulae as a "recipe." In the main text of this book, most mathematical equations are described in plain language that describes the relationships between physical quantities. If you want to see the same relationships presented in the form of equations, check the Math Reference Cards at the back of the book. Try to understand the relationships expressed in the math equations after you have read the corresponding description in the text. Soon you will become fluent in this beautiful and elegant language of the universe.

1.2 The Cosmic Calendar: Concepts of Time

In the first part of this chapter you were taken on a journey through the universe from a spatial perspective to give you a sense of the immensity of the universe and how small our little corner of it really is. Equally important is that you gain an appreciation for the concept of time and how the average human lifetime, for instance, compares to the age of the universe. Our current understanding of the formation of the universe and its age leads us to believe that it has been about 13.8 billion years since the big bang, the instant the universe commenced and, perhaps, the beginning of time itself.

Let's imagine that the time our universe has existed is spread over a one-year calendar where each month is a little in excess of 1 billion years—we have, then,

a cosmic calendar (a concept devised by Carl Sagan, a well-known astronomer in the latter part of the 1900s). As shown in the timeline in Figure 1.2, the big bang occurred precisely at midnight on January 1; the Milky Way Galaxy starts to coalesce in late February or early March, which makes it one of the oldest galaxies (although there remains debate about the age of the galaxy, recent estimates place its age possibly as old as 13 billion years). Our solar system starts being built around mid-August, and by the end of September primitive life exists on Earth. However, it is not until mid-December on this cosmic calendar that complex living structures such as invertebrate life formed—and not until December 25 when dinosaurs roamed Earth. The end of the dinosaur era, which took place 65 million years ago, occurred yesterday, December 30, on the cosmic calendar.

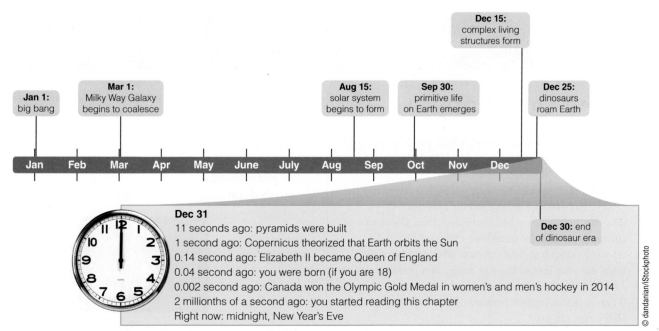

Figure 1.2 The Cosmic Year: A Timeline

The next day, December 31, is when all of recorded history occurred and even then not until much later in the day—within the last 30 seconds, in fact. The Egyptian pyramids were built about 11 seconds ago; Copernicus and others convinced humanity that Earth orbits the Sun about one second ago; Elizabeth II became Queen of England about 0.14 seconds ago; you were born about 0.04 seconds ago (assuming your age is 18); Canada won the 2014 Olympic Gold Medal in women's and men's hockey about 0.002 seconds ago; you started reading this chapter about 2-millionths of a second ago; and it is now exactly midnight on December 31—Happy New Year!

The Big Picture

Astronomy is important because it helps us understand what we are. We human beings live on the surface of planet Earth as it orbits the star we call the Sun. What are we? How did we and our planet and our star come to be here, and what does the future hold for us? Astronomy helps us answer those questions.

Our journey of discovery of the cosmos has led us to the amazing realization that we are intimately linked to the stars. Gravity and atoms work together to make stars, light the universe, generate energy, and create the chemical elements in our bodies. The atoms in our bodies were made deep inside stars, perhaps in a faraway galaxy. Stars died so that we could live! On the atomic level, we all have the same origins. Our similarities are far greater than our differences.

It's easy to be absorbed in our everyday lives and problems. But astronomy helps us appreciate humanity's place in the cosmos. We are part of a grand cycle of birth and death of stars. Although perhaps insignificant in space and time, life on Earth is a precious and fragile example of what the universe can produce over billions of years. Astronomy enriches our lives and gives us perspective on what it means to be here on Earth. Studying the stars and other planets enables us to be better caretakers of our own home: planet Earth.

The story of astronomy is a global story. Ancient civilizations all over the world observed the skies, and astronomy played a critical role in the development of art and culture, festivals and traditions. Our modern understanding of the universe is based on the discoveries of astronomers from around the world. Today, many nations, including Canada, work together on the International Space Station. Astronomy unites us in our journeys of self-knowledge and quests for the stars.

Review Questions

1. What is the largest dimension of which you have personal knowledge? Have you run a mile? Hiked 10 km? Run a marathon?
2. What is the difference between our solar system and our galaxy? Between our galaxy and the universe?
3. Why are light-years more convenient than kilometres or astronomical units for measuring certain distances?
4. Why is it difficult to detect planets orbiting other stars?
5. What does the size of the star image in a photograph tell you?
6. What is the difference between the Milky Way and the Milky Way Galaxy?
7. What are the largest known structures in the universe?
8. How does astronomy help answer the question, "What are we?"
9. **How Do We Know?** How does the scientific method give scientists a way to know about nature?

Discussion Questions

1. Do you think you have a duty to know the astronomy described in this chapter? Can you think of ways this knowledge helps you enjoy a richer life and be a better citizen?
2. How is a statement in a political speech different from a statement in a scientific discussion? Find examples in newspapers, magazines, and this book.

Learning to Look

1. In the image shown here the division between daylight and darkness is at the right on the globe of Earth. How do you know this is the sunset line and not the sunrise line?

NASA

2. Of the objects listed here, which would be contained inside the object shown in the photograph? Which would contain the object in the photo?
   - stars
   - planets
   - galaxy clusters
   - spiral arms

Bill Schoening/NOAO/AURA/NSF

3. In the photograph shown here, which stars are brightest, and which are faintest? How can you tell? Why can't you tell which stars in this photograph are biggest or which have planets?

NOAO/AURA/NSF

STUDY **TOOLS**

IN THE BOOK
- Tear out the Review Card for Chapter 1

ONLINE

Visit CENGAGENOW for ASTRO, 2Ce at www.nelson.com/student

- eBook
- Interactive Quizzing
- Animations
- Tutorials

Education has changed, your textbook should too.

4LTR P·R·E·S·S

www.nelson.com/student

2

User's Guide to the Sky: Patterns and Cycles

GUIDEPOST

The night sky is the rest of the universe seen from our planet. The previous chapter took you on a cosmic zoom out into the sky through deep space and deep time, setting the stage for the drama to come. In this chapter, your exploration will continue with a view of the sky from Earth with unaided eyes. You will discover that the turning of Earth on its axis and its orbital motion around the Sun produce corresponding motions in the sky. You will see how the Sun, Moon, and planets move against the background of stars. Some of those motions have direct influences on your life and produce dramatic sights. As you explore, you will find answers to four important questions:

- **How can you refer to stars by name, by constellation, and by brightness?**
- **How does the sky appear to move as Earth rotates and revolves?**
- **What causes the seasons?**
- **How does the motion of the Moon produce phases and eclipses?**

As you study the sky and its motions, you can begin to think of Earth as a planet moving through space. The next chapter tells the story of how humans first understood that Earth is a planet.

© 2014 by Fred Espenak. AstroPixels.com

Solar eclipses are dramatic. In June 2001 an automatic camera in southern Africa snapped pictures every five minutes as the afternoon Sun sank lower in the sky. From upper right to lower left, you can see the Moon crossing the disk of the Sun. A longer exposure was needed to record the total phase of the eclipse.

Space is for everybody. It's not just for a few people in science or math, or for a select group of astronauts. That's our new frontier out there, and it's everybody's business to know about space.

Christa McAuliffe,
Teacher and Challenger astronaut

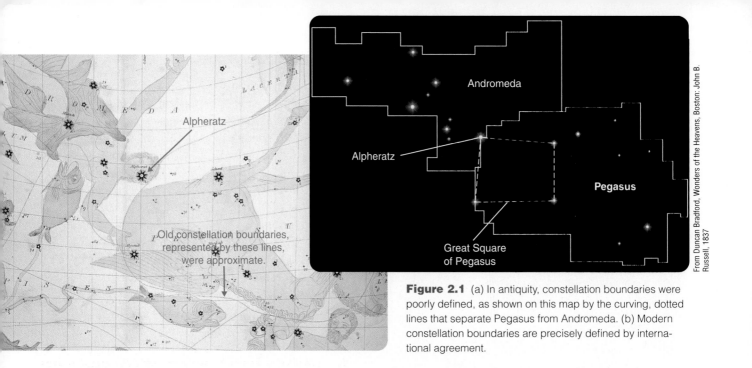

Figure 2.1 (a) In antiquity, constellation boundaries were poorly defined, as shown on this map by the curving, dotted lines that separate Pegasus from Andromeda. (b) Modern constellation boundaries are precisely defined by international agreement.

Image labels: Andromeda; Alpheratz; Old constellation boundaries, represented by these lines, were approximate.; Alpheratz; Pegasus; Great Square of Pegasus

From Duncan Bradford, Wonders of the Heavens, Boston: John B. Russell, 1837

2.1 The Stars

On a dark night far from city lights, you can see a few thousand stars in the sky. Your observations can be summarized by naming individual stars and groups of stars and by specifying their relative brightness.

Constellations

All around the world, ancient cultures celebrated heroes, gods, and mythical beasts by naming groups of stars called **constellations**. You should not be surprised that the star patterns do not look like the creatures they are named after any more than Victoria, British Columbia, looks like Queen Victoria.

The constellations named within western culture originated in ancient civilizations of Mesopotamia, Babylon, Egypt, and Greece beginning as much as 5000 years ago. Of those ancient constellations, 48 are still in use. In those former times, a constellation was simply a loose grouping of bright stars, and many of the fainter stars were not included in any constellation.

Regions of the southern sky not visible to ancient astronomers living at northern latitudes were not identified with any constellations. Constellation boundaries, when they were defined at all, were only approximate, so a star like Alpheratz could be

constellation One of the stellar patterns identified by name, usually of mythological gods, people, animals, or objects; also the region of the sky containing that star pattern.

asterism A named grouping of stars that is not one of the recognized constellations.

thought of both as part of Pegasus and as part of Andromeda (Figure 2.1).

In recent centuries astronomers have added 40 modern constellations to fill gaps, and in 1928 the International Astronomical Union (IAU) established a total of 88 official constellations with clearly defined permanent boundaries that together cover the entire sky. A constellation now represents not a group of stars but a section of the sky—a viewing direction—and any star within the region belongs only to that one constellation.

In addition to the 88 official constellations, the sky contains a number of less formally defined groupings called **asterisms**. The Big Dipper, for example, is an asterism you probably recognize as part of the constellation Ursa Major (the Great Bear). Another asterism is the Great Square of Pegasus, which includes three stars from Pegasus and the previously mentioned star Alpheratz, now considered to be part of Andromeda only.

Although constellations and asterisms are named as if they were real groupings, most are made up of stars that are not physically associated with one another. Some stars may be many times farther away than others in the same constellation and moving through space in different directions. The only thing they have in common is that they lie in approximately the same direction as viewed from Earth (see Figure 2.2).

The Names of the Stars

In addition to naming groups of stars, ancient astronomers named the brighter stars, and modern astronomers still use many of those names. The names of the

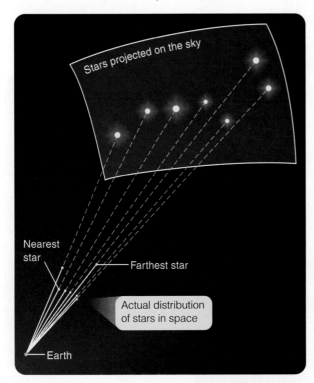

Figure 2.2 The stars you see in the Big Dipper are not at the same distance from Earth. You see the stars in a group in the sky because they lie in the same general direction as seen from Earth, not because they are all actually near each other. The sizes of the star dots in the star chart represent the apparent brightness of the stars.

constellations are in Latin or Greek, the languages of science in medieval and Renaissance Europe. Most individual star names derive from ancient Arabic, much altered over centuries. For example, the name of Betelgeuse, the bright red star in Orion, comes from the Arabic phrase *yad aljawza,* meaning "armpit of Jawza" (Orion). Aldebaran, the bright red eye of Taurus the bull, comes from the Arabic *al-dabar an,* meaning "the follower" (of Pleiades—an open cluster of stars in Taurus).

Another way to identify stars is to assign Greek letters to the bright stars in a constellation in approximate order of brightness. The brightest star is usually designated alpha (α), the second brightest beta (β), and so on. For many constellations, the letters follow the order of brightness, but some constellations, such as Orion, are exceptions (Figure 2.3). A Greek-letter star name also includes the possessive form of the constellation name; for example, the brightest star in the constellation Canis Major is alpha Canis Majoris. This name identifies the star and the constellation and gives a clue to the relative brightness of the star. Compare this with the ancient individual name for that star, Sirius, which tells you nothing about its location or brightness.

The Brightness of Stars

Astronomers measure the brightness of stars using the **magnitude scale**. The ancient astronomers divided the stars into six brightness groups. The brightest were called first-magnitude stars. The scale continued downward to sixth-magnitude stars, the faintest visible to the human eye. Thus, the *larger* the magnitude number, the *fainter* the star. This makes sense if you think of bright stars as first-class stars and the faintest stars visible as sixth-class stars.

The Greek astronomer Hipparchus (190–120 BCE) is believed to be the first to catalogue stars by their apparent brightness, which observers of the time perceived as related to size, hence the term *magnitude*. About 300 years later, around 140 CE, Claudius Ptolemy definitely used the magnitude system in his own catalogue. By the mid-nineteenth century astronomers had figured out that magnitudes had nothing to do with the angular sizes of stars because all stars were so far away as to appear as point sources of light. Rather, the brightness of a star was related to the intensity of the light produced by the star. Furthermore, using photometric measurements, it was determined that first-magnitude stars are about 100 times brighter than sixth-magnitude stars. This information made it possible to properly quantify the magnitude system using a logarithmic scale. (Refer to **Magnitudes** in the Math Reference Cards.) Star brightness expressed in this system is known as **apparent visual magnitude** (m_V), describing how the star looks to human eyes observing from Earth.

Brightness is quite subjective, depending on both the physiology of eyes and the psychology of perception. To be scientifically accurate you should refer to **flux**—a measure of the light energy from a star that hits one square metre in one second. With modern scientific instruments astronomers can measure the flux of starlight with high precision and then use the simple mathematical relationship that relates light flux to apparent visual magnitude. Instead of saying that the star known by the charming name Chort (Theta Leonis) is about third magnitude, you can say its magnitude is 3.34. Consequently, precise modern measurements of the brightness of stars are still connected to observations of apparent visual magnitude that go back to the time of Hipparchus.

Limitations of the apparent visual magnitude system have motivated astronomers to supplement this system in various ways: (1) Some stars are so

magnitude scale The astronomical brightness scale; the larger the number, the fainter the star.

apparent visual magnitude (m_V) A measure of the brightness of a star as seen by human eyes on Earth.

flux A measure of the flow of energy out of a surface, usually applied to light.

bright the magnitude scale must extend into negative numbers, as demonstrated in Figure 2.4. On this scale, Sirius, the brightest star in the sky, has a magnitude of –1.47. (2) With a telescope you can find stars much fainter than the limit for your unaided eyes, so the magnitude system has also been extended to numbers larger than sixth magnitude to include faint stars. (3) Although some stars emit large amounts of infrared or ultraviolet light, those types of radiation (discussed further in Chapters 4 and 5) are invisible to human eyes. The subscript "V" in m_V is a reminder that you are counting only light that is visible. Other magnitude systems have been invented to express the brightness of invisible light arriving at Earth from the stars. (4) An apparent magnitude tells only how bright the star is as seen from Earth but doesn't tell anything about a star's true power output because the star's distance is not included. You can describe the true power output of stars with another magnitude system that will be described in Chapter 6.

The brighter stars in a constellation are usually given Greek letters in order of decreasing brightness.

Orion

α Orionis is also known as Betelgeuse.

β Orionis is also known as Rigel.

In Orion β is brighter than α, and κ is brighter than η. Fainter stars do not have Greek letters or names, but if they are located inside the constellation boundaries, they are part of the constellation.

Photo by William Hartmann

Figure 2.3 Stars in a constellation can be identified by Greek letters. The spikes on the star images were produced by the optics of the camera.

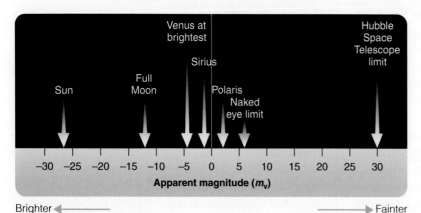

Venus at brightest

Sirius

Full Moon

Sun

Polaris

Naked eye limit

Hubble Space Telescope limit

−30 −25 −20 −15 −10 −5 0 5 10 15 20 25 30

Apparent magnitude (m_V)

Brighter ◄——————————————————————► Fainter

Figure 2.4 The scale of apparent visual magnitudes extends to negative numbers to represent the brightest objects and to positive numbers larger than 6 to represent objects fainter than the human eye can see.

2.2 The Sky and Its Motions

The sky above you seems to be a great blue dome in the daytime and a sparkling ceiling at night. Learning to understand the sky requires that you first recall the perspectives of people who observed the sky thousands of years ago.

The Celestial Sphere

Ancient astronomers believed the sky was a great sphere surrounding Earth with the stars stuck on the inside like thumbtacks in a ceiling. Modern astronomers know that the stars are scattered through space at different distances, but it is still convenient and useful in some contexts for you to think of the sky as a great sphere enclosing Earth, with all stars at one distance. The **celestial sphere** is an example

Scientific Models

Frameworks for thinking about nature. A scientific model is a carefully devised mental conception of how something works, a framework that helps scientists think about some aspect of nature. For example, astronomers use the celestial sphere as a way to think about the motions of the sky, Sun, Moon, and stars.

Some models are imprecise—the psychologist's model of how the human mind processes visual information into images, for instance. But other models are so specific that they can be expressed as a set of mathematical equations, such as those used to describe how gas falls into a black hole. You could use metal and plastic to build a celestial globe, but the importance of a model is its use as a mental conception more than its physical presence.

A model is not meant to be a statement of truth. The celestial sphere is not real; you know the stars are scattered through space at various distances. Nevertheless, you can imagine a celestial sphere and use it

to help you think about the sky. A scientific model does not have to be true to be useful. Chemists, for example, think about the atoms in molecules by visualizing them as spheres joined together by sticks. This model of a molecule is not really correct, but it is a helpful way to think about molecules; it gives chemists a framework within which to organize their ideas.

Because scientific models are not meant to be totally correct, you must always remember the assumptions on which they are based. If you begin to think a model is true, it can mislead you instead of helping you. The celestial sphere, for instance, can help you think about the sky, but you must remember that the universe is much larger and more complex than this ancient scientific model of the heavens.

© bilwissedition Ltd. & Co. KG / Alamy

---

of a **scientific model**, a common feature of scientific thought (see **How Do We Know? 2.1**). You can use the celestial sphere as a convenient model of the sky. You will learn about many scientific models in the chapters that follow.

As you study **Visualizing Astronomy 2.1, The Sky Around Us,** notice three important points:

1. The sky appears to rotate westward around Earth each day, but that is a consequence of the eastward rotation of Earth. This produces day and night.

2. What you can see of the sky depends on where you are on Earth. For example, Australians see many constellations and asterisms invisible from North America, but they never see the Big Dipper.

3. Astronomers measure distances across the sky as angles expressed in units of degrees and subdivisions of degrees called arc minutes and arc seconds.

> **scientific model** A concept that helps one think about some aspect of nature, but is not necessarily true.

Precession

In addition to the daily motion of the sky, Earth's rotation adds a second motion to the sky that can be detected only over centuries. More than 2000 years ago Hipparchus compared a few of his star positions with those made by other astronomers nearly two centuries before him and realized that the celestial poles and

1 The eastward rotation of Earth causes the Sun, Moon, and stars to move westward in the sky as if the celestial sphere were rotating westward around Earth. From any location on Earth you see only half of the celestial sphere, the half above the horizon. The **zenith** marks the top of the sky above your head, and the **nadir** marks the bottom of the sky directly under your feet. The drawing at right shows the view for an observer in North America. An observer in South America would have a dramatically different horizon, zenith, and nadir.

The apparent pivot points are the north celestial pole and the south celestial pole located directly above Earth's north and south poles. Halfway between the celestial poles lies the celestial equator. Earth's rotation defines the directions you use every day. The **north point** and **south point** are the points on the horizon closest to the celestial poles. The **east point** and the **west point** lie halfway between the north and south points. The celestial equator always meets the horizon at the east and west points.

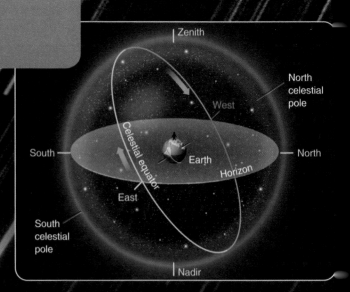

AURA/NOAO/NSF

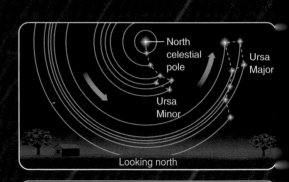

Looking north

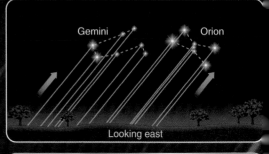

Looking east

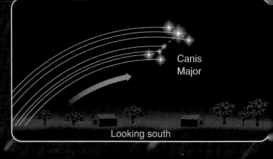

Looking south

1a This time exposure of about 30 minutes shows stars as streaks, called star trails, rising behind an observatory dome. The camera was facing northeast to take this photo. The motion you see in the sky depends on which direction you look, as shown at right. Looking north, you see the Favorite Star Polaris, the North Star, located near the north celestial pole. As the sky appears to rotate westward, Polaris hardly moves, but other stars circle the celestial pole. Looking south from a location in North America, you can see stars circling the south celestial pole, which is invisible below the southern horizon.

Astronomers measure distance across the sky as angles.

Angular distance

2 Astronomers might say, "The star is two degrees from the Moon." Of course, the stars are much farther away than the Moon, but when you think of the celestial sphere, you can measure distance *on the sky* as an angle. The angular distance between two objects is the angle between two lines extending from your eye to the two objects. Astronomers measure angles in degrees, arc minutes, 1/60th of a degree, and arc seconds, 1/60th of an arc minute. Using the term *arc* avoids confusion with minutes and seconds of time. The angular diameter of an object is the angular distance from one edge to the other. The Sun and Moon are each about half a degree in diameter, and the bowl of the Big Dipper is about 10° wide.

3 What you see in the sky depends on your latitude as shown at right. Imagine that you begin a journey in the ice and snow at Earth's North Pole with the north celestial pole directly overhead. As you walk southward, the celestial pole moves toward the horizon, and you can see farther into the southern sky. The angular distance from the horizon to the north celestial pole always equals your latitude (L)—the basis for celestial navigation. As you cross Earth's equator, the celestial equator would pass through your zenith, and the north celestial pole would sink below your northern horizon.

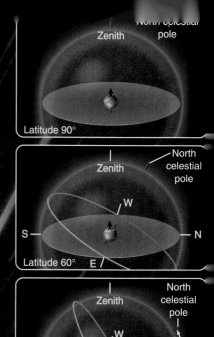

Latitude 90°

Zenith — North celestial pole

Latitude 60°

Zenith — North celestial pole — W — S — N — E

Latitude 30°

Zenith — North celestial pole — W — L — S — N — E

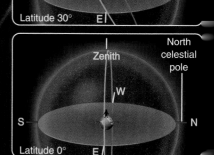

Latitude 0°

Zenith — North celestial pole — W — S — N — E

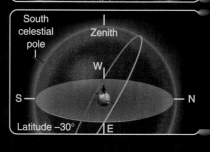

Latitude −30°

South celestial pole — Zenith — W — S — N — E

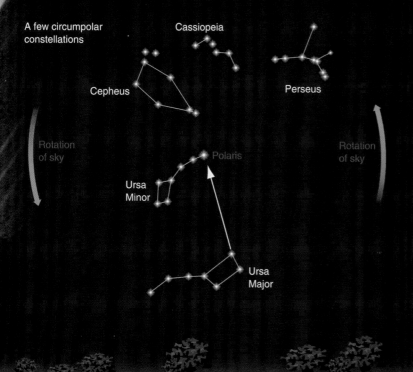

A few circumpolar constellations

Cassiopeia

Cepheus

Perseus

Rotation of sky

Polaris

Rotation of sky

Ursa Minor

Ursa Major

3a Circumpolar constellations are those that never rise or set. From mid-northern latitudes, as shown at left, you see a number of familiar constellations circling Polaris and never dipping below the horizon. As the sky rotates, the pointer stars at the front of the Big Dipper always point toward Polaris. Circumpolar constellations near the south celestial pole never rise as seen from mid-northern latitudes. From a high latitude, such as Norway, you would see more circumpolar constellations than viewing from Quito, Ecuador, located on the Earth's equator, where you would have no circumpolar constellations at all.

precession The slow change in orientation of Earth's axis of rotation. One cycle takes nearly 26 000 years.

rotation Motion around an axis passing through the rotating body.

revolution Orbital motion about a point located outside the orbiting body.

equator were slowly moving relative to the stars. Later astronomers understood that this apparent motion is caused by a special motion of Earth called **precession**.

If you have ever played with a toy top or gyroscope, you may recall that the axis of such a rapidly spinning object sweeps around relatively slowly in a circle. Look at Figure 2.5 and think about how the top moves. The weight of the top tends to make it tip, and this combines with its rapid rotation to make its axis sweep around slowly in precession motion.

Comparing Figure 2.5b to the motion of the top in Figure 2.5a, you can see that Earth spins like a giant top, but it does not spin upright relative to its orbit around the Sun. You can say either that Earth's axis is tipped 23.4 degrees from vertical or that Earth's equator is tipped 23.4 degrees relative to its orbit; the two statements are equivalent. Earth's large mass and rapid rotation keep its axis of rotation pointed toward a spot near the star Polaris (alpha Ursa Minoris), and its axis direction would not move if Earth were a perfect sphere. However, Earth has a slight bulge around its middle, and the gravity of the Sun and Moon both pull on this bulge, tending to twist Earth's axis upright relative to its orbit. The combination of these forces and Earth's rotation causes Earth's axis

to precess in a slow circular sweep, taking about 26 000 years for one cycle.

Because the celestial poles and equator are defined by Earth's rotational axis, precession moves these reference marks. Figure 2.5c shows the apparent path followed by the north celestial pole over thousands of years. You would notice no change at all from night to night or year to year, but precise measurements reveal their slow apparent motion. Over centuries, precession has dramatic effects. Egyptian records show that 4800 years ago the north celestial pole was near the star Thuban (alpha Draconis). The pole is now approaching Polaris and will be closest to it in about the year 2100. In another 12 000 years the pole will have moved to the apparent vicinity of the very bright star Vega (alpha Lyrae).

2.3 The Cycle of the Sun

The English language defines **rotation** as the turning of a body on its axis. **Revolution** means the motion of a body around a point outside the body. Earth rotates on its axis, and that produces day and night. Earth also revolves around the Sun, and that produces the yearly cycle.

The Annual Motion of the Sun

Even in the daytime the sky is actually filled with stars, but the glare of sunlight fills our atmosphere with scattered light, and you can see only the brilliant blue

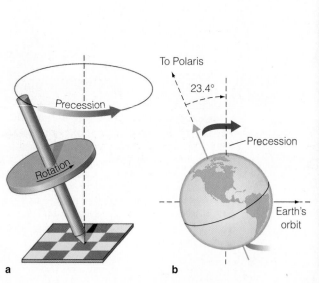

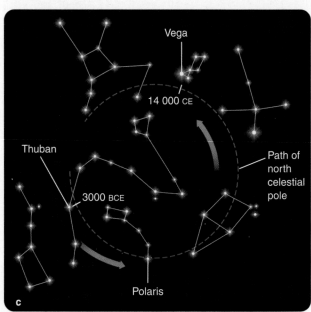

Figure 2.5 Precession. (a) A spinning top precesses in a slow circular motion around the perpendicular to the floor because its weight tends to make it fall over. (b) Earth precesses around the perpendicular to its orbit because the gravity of the Sun and Moon tend to twist it "upright." (c) Precession causes the north celestial pole to drift among the stars, completing a circle in 26 000 years.

sky. If the Sun were fainter and you could see the stars in the daytime, you would notice that the Sun appears to be moving slowly eastward relative to the background of the distant stars. This apparent motion is caused by the real orbital motion of Earth around the Sun. In January you would see the Sun in front of the constellation Sagittarius. By March you would see the Sun in front of Aquarius. Note that your angle of view in Figure 2.6 makes Earth's orbit seem very elliptical when it is really almost a perfect circle.

Through the year, the Sun moves eastward among the stars following a line called the **ecliptic**, the apparent path of the Sun among the stars. Recall the concept of the celestial sphere; if the sky were a great screen, the ecliptic would be the shadow cast by Earth's orbit. In other words, you can call the ecliptic the projection of Earth's orbit on the celestial sphere. Earth circles the Sun in 365.26 days, and consequently the Sun appears to go once around the sky in the same period. You don't notice this motion because you cannot see the stars in the daytime, but the apparent motion of the Sun caused by a real motion of Earth has an important consequence that you do notice— the seasons.

The Seasons

The seasons are caused by the revolution of Earth around the Sun, combined with a simple fact you

have already encountered: Earth's equator is tipped 23.4 degrees relative to its orbit. As you study **Visualizing Astronomy 2.2, The Cycle of the Seasons,** notice two important principles:

> **ecliptic** The apparent path of the Sun around the sky.

1. The seasons are *not* caused by variation in the distance between Earth and the Sun. Earth's orbit is nearly circular, so it is always about the same distance from the Sun.

2. The seasons *are* caused by changes in the amount of solar energy that Earth's northern and southern hemispheres receive at different times of the year, which results from the tip of Earth's equator and axis relative to its orbit.

Because the seasons are very important as a cycle of growth and harvest, cultures around the world have attached great significance to the ecliptic. It marks the centre line of the zodiac ("circle of animals"), and the motion of the Sun, Moon, and the five visible planets (Mercury, Venus, Mars, Jupiter, and Saturn) are the basis of the ancient superstition of astrology (see **How Do We Know? 2.2**). The signs of the zodiac are no longer important in astronomy. You can look for the planets along the ecliptic appearing as bright stars. Mars looks quite orange in colour. Venus and Mercury orbit inside Earth's

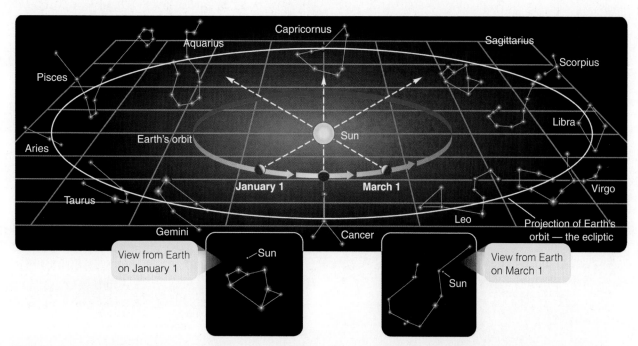

Figure 2.6 The motion of Earth around the Sun makes the Sun appear to move against the background of the stars. The circular orbit of Earth is thus projected on the sky as the ecliptic, the circular path of the Sun during the year as seen from Earth. If you could see the stars in the daytime, you would notice the Sun crossing in front of the distant constellations as Earth moves along its orbit.

1 You can use the celestial sphere to help you think about the seasons. The celestial equator is the projection of Earth's equator on the sky, and the ecliptic is the projection of Earth's orbit on the sky. Because Earth is tipped in its orbit, the ecliptic and equator are inclined to each other by 23.4° as shown at right. As the Sun moves eastward around the sky, it spends half the year in the southern half of the sky and half of the year in the northern half. That causes the seasons.

The Sun crosses the celestial equator going northward at the point called the **vernal equinox**. The Sun is at its farthest north at the point called the **summer solstice**. It crosses the celestial equator going southward at the **autumnal equinox** and reaches its most southern point at the **winter solstice**. These labels refer to seasons in the northern hemisphere.

1a The seasons are defined by the dates when the Sun crosses these four points, as shown in the table at the right. *Equinox* comes from the word for "equal"; the day of an equinox has equal amounts of daylight and darkness. *Solstice* comes from the words meaning "sun" and "stationary." *Vernal* comes from the word for "green." The "green" equinox marks the beginning of spring in the northern hemisphere.

Event	Date*	Season
Vernal equinox	March 20	Spring begins
Summer solstice	June 22	Summer begins
Autumnal equinox	September 22	Autumn begins
Winter solstice	December 22	Winter begins

* Northern hemisphere information, give or take a day due to leap year and other factors.

1b On the day of the summer solstice in late June, Earth's northern hemisphere is inclined toward the Sun, and sunlight shines almost straight down at northern latitudes. At southern latitudes, sunlight strikes the ground at an angle and spreads out. North America has warm weather, and South America has cool weather.

Earth's axis of rotation points toward Polaris, and, like a top, the spinning Earth holds its axis fixed as it orbits the Sun. On one side of the Sun, Earth's northern hemisphere leans toward the Sun; on the other side of its orbit, it leans away. However, the direction of the axis of rotation does not change.

Earth at summer solstice

Summer solstice light

1c Light striking the ground at a steep angle spreads out less than light striking the ground at a shallow angle. Light from the summer-solstice Sun strikes northern latitudes from nearly overhead and is concentrated.

Winter solstice light

Light from the winter solstice Sun strikes northern latitudes at a much steeper angle and spreads out. The same amount of energy is spread over a larger area, so the ground receives less energy from the winter Sun.

2 The two causes of the seasons are shown at right for someone in the northern hemisphere. First, the noon summer Sun is higher in the sky, and the noon winter Sun is lower, as shown by the longer winter shadows. Thus, winter sunlight is more spread out. Second, the summer Sun rises in the northeast and sets in the northwest, spending more than 12 hours in the sky. The winter Sun rises in the southeast and sets in the southwest, spending less than 12 hours in the sky. Both of these effects mean that northern latitudes receive more energy from the summer Sun, and summer days are warmer than winter days.

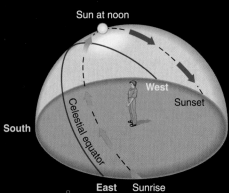

At summer solstice

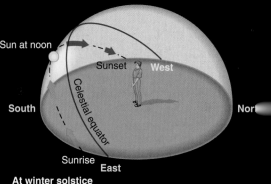

At winter solstice

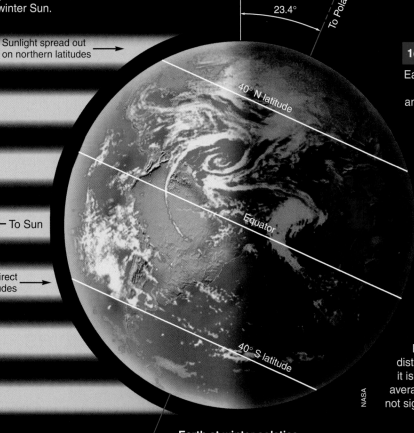

1d On the day of the winter solstice in late December, Earth's northern hemisphere is inclined away from the Sun and sunlight strikes the ground at an angle and spreads out. At southern latitudes, sunlight shines almost straight down and does not spread out. North America has cool weather and South America has warm weather.

Earth's orbit is only very slightly elliptical. On about January 3, Earth is at **perihelion**, its closest point to the Sun, when it is only 1.7 percent closer than average. On about July 5, Earth is at **aphelion**, its most distant point from the Sun, when it is only 1.7 percent farther than average. This small variation does not significantly affect the seasons.

Earth at winter solstice

Pseudoscience

What is the difference between a science and a pseudoscience? Astronomers have a low opinion of beliefs such as astrology, mostly because they are groundless but also because they *pretend* to be a science. They are *pseudosciences*, from the Greek *pseudo*, meaning false.

A pseudoscience is a set of beliefs that appear to be based on scientific ideas but that fail to obey the most basic rules of science. For example, some years ago a claim was made that pyramidal shapes focus cosmic forces on anything underneath and might have healing properties. Supposedly, a pyramid made of paper, plastic, or other materials would preserve fruit, sharpen razor blades, and do other miraculous things. Many books promoted the idea of the special power of pyramids, and this idea led to a popular fad.

A key characteristic of science is that its claims can be tested and verified. In this case, simple experiments showed that any shape, not just a pyramid, protects a piece of fruit from airborne spores and allows it to dry without rotting. Likewise, any shape allows oxidation to improve the cutting edge of a razor blade.

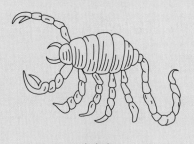

Because experimental evidence contradicted the claim and because supporters of the theory declined to abandon or revise their claims, you can recognize pyramid power as a pseudoscience. Disregard of contradictory evidence and alternate explanations is a sure sign of a pseudoscience.

Pseudoscientific claims can be self-fulfilling. For example, some believers slept under pyramidal tents to improve their rest. There is no logical mechanism by which such a tent could affect a sleeper, but because people wanted and expected the claim to be true, they reported that they slept more soundly. Vague claims based on personal testimony that cannot be tested are another sign of a pseudoscience.

Astrology is probably the best known pseudoscience. It has been tested over and over for centuries, and it doesn't work: There is probably no connection between the positions of the Sun, Moon, and planets and people's personalities, or events in their lives. Nevertheless, many people believe in astrology despite contradictory evidence. Many pseudosciences appeal to our need to understand and control the world around us. Some such claims involve medical cures, ranging from using magnetic bracelets and crystals to focus mystical power to astonishingly expensive, illegal, and dangerous treatments for cancer. Logic is a stranger to pseudoscience, but human fears and needs are not.

orbit, so they never get far from the Sun and are visible in the west after sunset or in the east before sunrise, as you can see in Figure 2.7. Venus can be very bright, but Mercury is difficult to see near the horizon. By tradition, any planet in the sunset sky is called an evening star, and any planet in the dawn sky is called a morning star. Perhaps the most beautiful is Venus, which can become as bright as magnitude –4.7. As Venus moves around its orbit, it can dominate the western sky each evening for many weeks, but eventually its orbit appears to carry it back toward the Sun as seen from Earth, and it is lost in the haze near the horizon. A few weeks later you can see Venus reappear in the dawn sky as a brilliant morning star. Months later it will switch back to being an evening star again.

2.4 The Cycles of the Moon

The Moon orbits eastward around Earth about once a month. Starting this evening, look for the Moon in the sky. If it is a cloudy night or if the Moon is in the wrong part of its orbit, you may not see it; but keep trying on successive

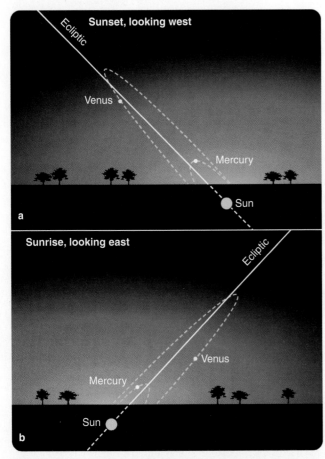

Figure 2.7 Mercury and Venus follow orbits that keep them near the Sun, and they are visible only soon after sunset or just before sunrise. Venus takes 584 days to move from morning sky to evening sky and back again, but Mercury zips around in only 116 days.

evenings, and within a week or two you will see the Moon. Then, watch for the Moon on following evenings, and you will see it move along its orbit around Earth and cycling through its phases as it has done for billions of years.

The Motion of the Moon

If you watch the Moon night after night, you will notice two things about its motion. First, you will see it moving relative to the background of stars; second, you will notice that the markings on its face don't change. These two observations can help you understand the motion of the Moon and the origin of the Moon's phases.

The Moon moves rapidly among the constellations. If you watch the Moon for just an hour, you can see it move eastward against the background of stars by slightly more than its own apparent diameter. Each night when you look at the Moon, you will see it is roughly half the width of a zodiac constellation (about 13 degrees) to the east of its location the night before. This movement is the result of the motion of the Moon along its orbit around Earth.

The Cycle of Moon Phases

The changing shape of the illuminated part of the Moon as it orbits Earth is one of the most easily observed phenomena in astronomy. You have surely seen the full Moon rising dramatically or a thin crescent moon hanging in the evening sky. Study **Visualizing Astronomy 2.3, The Phases of the Moon,** and notice three important points:

1. The Moon always keeps the same side facing Earth, and you never see the far side of the Moon. "The man in the Moon" (some cultures see "the rabbit in the Moon" instead) is produced by familiar features on the Moon's near side.

2. The changing shape of the Moon as it passes through its cycle of phases is produced by sunlight illuminating different parts of the side of the Moon you can see. You always see the same side of the Moon looking down on you, but the shifting shadows make the "man in the Moon" change moods as the Moon cycles through its phases (see also Figure 2.8).

3. The orbital period of the Moon around Earth is not the same as the length of a Moon phase cycle.

Figure 2.8 In this sequence of lunar phases, the Moon shrinks from a thin crescent, to full, and back to a thin crescent. You see the same face of the Moon, the same mountains, craters, and plains, but the changing direction of sunlight produces the lunar phases.

1 As the Moon orbits Earth, it rotates to keep the same side facing Earth, as shown at right. Consequently, you always see the same features on the Moon, and you never see the far side of the Moon. A mountain on the Moon that points at Earth will always point at Earth as the Moon revolves and rotates.

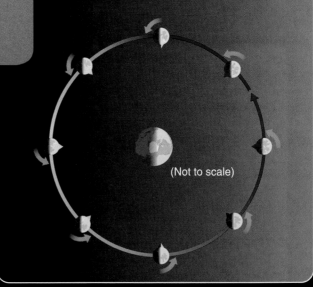

(Not to scale)

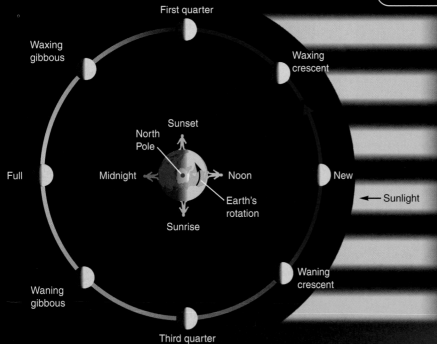

First quarter

Waxing gibbous

Waxing crescent

Sunset
North Pole
Midnight
Noon
Earth's rotation
Sunrise

Full

New

Waning crescent

← Sunlight

Waning gibbous

Third quarter

2 As seen at left, sunlight always illuminates half of the Moon. Because you see different amounts of this sunlit side, you see the Moon cycle through phases. At the phase called "new moon," sunlight illuminates the far side of the Moon, and the side you see is in darkness. At new moon you see no Moon at all. At full moon, the side you see is fully lit, and the far side is in darkness. How much you see depends on where the Moon is in its orbit.

Notice that there is no such thing as the "dark side of the Moon." All parts of the Moon experience day and night in a month-long cycle.

In the diagram at the left, you see that the new Moon is close to the Sun in the sky, and the full Moon is opposite the Sun. The time of day depends on the observer's location on Earth.

2a The first two weeks of the cycle of the Moon are shown below by its position at sunset on 14 successive evenings. As the Moon grows fatter from new to full, it is said to wax.

The first-quarter Moon is one week through its 4-week cycle.

Gibbous comes from the Latin word for humpbacked.

Waxing gibbous

Waxing crescent

The full Moon is two weeks through its 4-week cycle.

The full Moon rises at sunset

The new Moon is invisible near the Sun

THE SKY AT SUNSET

8
9
7
10
6
11
5
12
4
13
3
14
2
1

East

South

West

3 The Moon orbits eastward around Earth in 27.32 days. This is how long the Moon takes to circle the sky once and return to the same position among the stars.

A complete cycle of lunar phases takes 29.53 days.

Although you think of the lunar cycle as being about four weeks long, it is actually 1.53 days longer than four weeks. The calendar divides the year into 30-day periods called months (literally "moonths") in recognition of the 29.53-day synodic cycle of the Moon.

✳ To think about the changing phases of the Moon, imagine facing the southern sky, which is where people living in the northern hemisphere find the ecliptic. The Moon crosses from west to east, night by night, following the ecliptic.

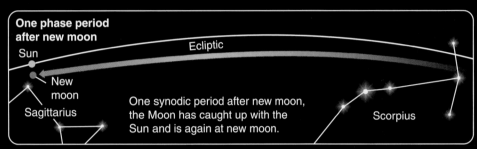

New moon

Ecliptic

Sun

New moon

Sagittarius

Scorpius

The Sun and Moon are near each other at new moon.

One orbital period after new moon

Ecliptic

Sun

Sagittarius

Moon

Scorpius

One sidereal period after new moon, the Moon has returned to the same place among the stars, but the Sun has moved on along the ecliptic.

One phase period after new moon

Ecliptic

Sun

New moon

Sagittarius

Scorpius

One synodic period after new moon, the Moon has caught up with the Sun and is again at new moon.

You can use the diagram on the opposite page to determine when the Moon rises and sets at different phases.

TIMES OF MOONRISE AND MOONSET

Phase	Moonrise	Moonset
New	Dawn	Sunset
First quarter	Noon	Midnight
Full	Sunset	Dawn
Third quarter	Midnight	Noon

2b The last two weeks of the cycle of the Moon are shown below by its position at sunrise on 14 successive mornings. As the Moon shrinks from full to new, it is said to wane.

The third-quarter Moon is 3 weeks through its 4-week cycle.

Waning crescent

Waning gibbous

The new Moon is invisible near the Sun

27 26 25 24 23 22 21 20 19 18 17 16 15 14

THE SKY AT SUNRISE

The full Moon sets at sunrise

East

South

West

CHAPTER 2 User's Guide to the Sky: Patterns and Cycles | **29**

2.5 Eclipses

Eclipses occur because of a seemingly complicated combination of apparent motions of the Sun and Moon, yet they are easy to predict once all the cycles are understood. Eclipses are also among the most spectacular of nature's sights you might witness.

Solar Eclipses

From Earth you can see a phenomenon that is not visible from most planets. The Sun is 400 times larger than our Moon and, on the average, 390 times farther away, so the Sun and Moon have nearly equal apparent diameters. (Refer to **The Small Angle Formula** in the Math Reference Cards.) Thus, the Moon is just about the right size to cover the bright disk of the Sun and cause a **solar eclipse**. In a solar eclipse, the Sun is hidden (eclipsed) and the Moon is "in the way."

A shadow consists of two parts, as you can see in Figure 2.9. The **umbra** is the region of total shadow. For example, if you were in the umbra of the Moon's shadow, you would see no portion of the Sun. The umbra of the Moon's shadow usually just barely reaches Earth's surface and covers a relatively small circular zone (Figure 2.9a). Standing in that umbral zone, you would be in total shadow, unable to see any part of the Sun's surface. That is called a total eclipse, as seen in Figure 2.9b. If you moved into the **penumbra**, however, you would be in partial shadow but could also see part of the Sun peeking around the edge of the Moon. This is called a partial eclipse. Of course, if you are outside the penumbra, you see no eclipse at all.

Because of the orbital motion of the Moon and the rotation of Earth, the Moon's shadow sweeps rapidly across Earth in a long, narrow path of totality. If you want to see a total solar eclipse, you must be in the path of totality. When the umbra of the Moon's shadow sweeps over you, you see one of the most dramatic sights in the sky—the totally eclipsed Sun (Figure 2.10).

The eclipse begins as the Moon slowly crosses in front of the Sun. It takes about an hour for the Moon to cover the solar disk, but as the last sliver of Sun disappears, darkness arrives in a few seconds. Automatic streetlights come on, drivers turn on their car's headlights, and birds go to roost. The sky usually becomes so dark you can even see the brighter stars. The darkness lasts only a few minutes because the umbra is never more than 270 km in diameter on the surface of Earth and sweeps across the landscape at over 1600 km/hr. On average, the period of totality lasts only two or three minutes and never more than 7.5 minutes. During totality you can see subtle features of the Sun's atmosphere, such as red flamelike projections that are visible only during these moments when the brilliant disk of the Sun is completely covered by the Moon. (The Sun's atmosphere is discussed in more detail in Chapter 5.) As soon as part of the Sun's disk reappears, the fainter features vanish in the glare, and the period of totality is over. The Moon moves on in its orbit, and in an hour the Sun is completely visible again.

Sometimes when the Moon crosses in front of the Sun it is too small to fully cover the Sun; in this case, you see an **annular eclipse**. That is a solar eclipse in

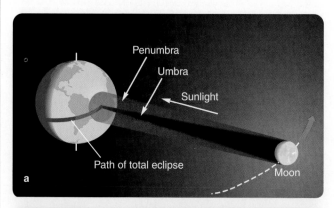

Figure 2.9 (a) The umbral shadow of the Moon sweeps over a narrow strip of Earth during a solar eclipse. (b) From a location inside the umbral shadow, you would see the Moon cover the bright surface of the Sun in a total solar eclipse. Note faint features of the Sun's atmosphere around the edge of the Moon's disk.

---

solar eclipse The event that occurs when the Moon passes directly between Earth and the Sun, blocking our view of the Sun.

umbra The region of a shadow that is totally shaded.

penumbra The portion of a shadow that is only partially shaded.

annular eclipse A solar eclipse in which the solar photosphere appears around the edge of the Moon in a bright ring, or annulus. Features of the solar atmosphere cannot be seen during an annular eclipse.

Figure 2.10 Solar Eclipse. The Moon moving from the right just begins to cross in front of the Sun. The disk of the Moon gradually covers the disk of the Sun. Sunlight begins to dim as more of the Sun's disk is covered. During totality, faint features of the atmosphere are often visible. A longer-exposure photograph during totality shows the extended solar atmosphere.

which an annulus (meaning "ring") of the Sun's disk is visible around the disk of the Moon. The eclipse never becomes total; it never quite gets dark, and you can't see the faint features of the solar atmosphere. Annular eclipses occur because the Moon follows a slightly elliptical orbit around Earth. If the Moon is in the farther part of its orbit during totality, its apparent diameter will be less than the apparent diameter of the Sun and you will see an annular eclipse. Furthermore, Earth's orbit is slightly elliptical, so the Earth-to-Sun distance varies slightly, and so does the apparent diameter of the solar disk, contributing to the effect of the Moon's varying apparent size.

If you plan to observe a solar eclipse, remember that the Sun is bright enough to burn your eyes and cause permanent damage if you look at it directly. This is true whether there is an eclipse or not. Solar eclipses can be misleading, tempting you to look at the Sun in spite of its brilliance and risking your eyesight.

During the few minutes of totality, the brilliant disk of the Sun is hidden, and it is safe to look at the eclipse, but the partial eclipse phases and annular eclipses can be dangerous. See Figure 2.11 for a safe way to observe the partially eclipsed Sun. Table 2.1 provides information that helps you determine

Table 2.1 | Total and Annular Eclipses of the Sun, 2015 through 2022*

Date	Total/Annular (T/A)	Time of Mid-Eclipse** (GMT)	Maximum Length of Total or Annular Phase (Min:Sec)	Region of Visibility
2015 March 20	T	09:47	2:47	North Atlantic, Arctic
2016 March 9	T	01:58	4:09	Indonesia, Pacific
2016 September 1	A	09:08	3:06	Atlantic, Africa, Indian Ocean
2017 February 26	A	14:55	0:44	South Pacific, South America, Africa
2017 August 21	T	18:27	2:40	Pacific, USA, Atlantic
2019 July 2	T	19:24	4:33	Pacific, South America
2019 December 26	A	05:19	3:39	Southeast Asia, Pacific
2020 June 21	A	06:41	0:38	Africa, Asia
2020 December 14	T	16:15	2:10	Southern South America
2021 June 10	A	10:43	3:51	North America, Europe, Asia
2021 December 4	T	07:35	1:54	Antarctica, South America

*The next solar eclipse visible from anywhere in Canada will occur on June 10, 2021 and then only in northern Ontario; the next solar eclipse visible from the United States will occur on August 21, 2017. There will be no total or annular solar eclipses in 2018 or 2022.
**Times are Greenwich Mean Time. Subtract 5 hours for Eastern Standard Time, 6 hours for Central Standard Time, 7 hours for Mountain Standard Time, and 8 hours for Pacific Standard Time. For Daylight Savings Time, add 1 hour to Standard Time.
Source: http://eclipse.gsfc.nasa.gov/SEdecade/SEdecade2011.html

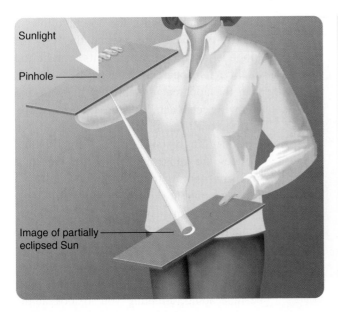

Sunlight

Pinhole

Image of partially
eclipsed Sun

Figure 2.11 A safe way to view the partial phases of a solar eclipse. Use a pinhole in a card to project an image of the Sun on a second card. The greater the distance between the cards, the larger (and fainter) the image will be.

when some upcoming solar eclipses will be visible from your location.

Lunar Eclipses

Occasionally, you can see the Moon darken and turn copper-red in a **lunar eclipse**. A lunar eclipse occurs at full moon when the Moon moves through the shadow of Earth. Because the Moon shines only by reflected sunlight, you see the Moon gradually darken as it enters the shadow. If you were on the Moon and in the umbra of Earth's shadow, you would see no portion of the Sun. If you moved into the penumbra, however, you would be in partial shadow and would see part of the Sun peeking around the edge of Earth, so the sunlight would be dimmed but not extinguished. In a lunar eclipse, the Moon is hidden in Earth's shadow, and Earth is "in the way" of the sunlight.

If the orbit of the Moon carries it through the umbra of Earth's shadow, you see a total lunar eclipse, as demonstrated in Figure 2.12a. As you watch the Moon in the sky, it first moves into the penumbra and dims slightly; the deeper it moves into the penumbra, the more it dims. In about an hour, the Moon reaches the umbra, and you see the umbral shadow darken part of the Moon. It takes about an hour for the Moon to enter the umbra completely and become totally eclipsed. The period of total eclipse may last as long as 1 hour 45 minutes, though the timing of the eclipse depends on where the Moon crosses the shadow.

When the Moon is totally eclipsed, it does not disappear completely. Although it receives no direct sunlight, the Moon in the umbra does receive some sunlight refracted (bent) through Earth's atmosphere. If you were on the Moon during totality, you would not see any part of the Sun because it would be entirely hidden behind Earth. However, you would be able to see Earth's atmosphere

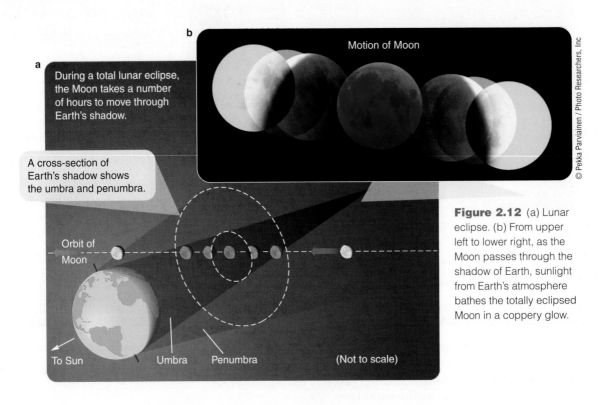

b Motion of Moon

© Pekka Parviainen / Photo Researchers, Inc

a During a total lunar eclipse, the Moon takes a number of hours to move through Earth's shadow.

A cross-section of Earth's shadow shows the umbra and penumbra.

Orbit of Moon

To Sun   Umbra   Penumbra   (Not to scale)

Figure 2.12 (a) Lunar eclipse. (b) From upper left to lower right, as the Moon passes through the shadow of Earth, sunlight from Earth's atmosphere bathes the totally eclipsed Moon in a coppery glow.

New Moon
Earth
Full Moon

Figure 2.13 Umbral shadows of Earth and the Moon. Because of the tilt of the Moon's orbit relative to the ecliptic, it is easy for the shadows to miss their mark at full moon and at new moon and fail to produce eclipses. (The diameters of Earth and the Moon are exaggerated by a factor of 2 for clarity.)

illuminated from behind by the Sun. The red glow from this ring—consisting of all Earth's simultaneous sunsets and sunrises—illuminates the Moon during totality and makes it glow coppery red, as shown in Figure 2.12b.

If the Moon passes a bit too far north or south of the centre of Earth's shadow, it may only partially enter the umbra, and you see a partial lunar eclipse. The part of the Moon that remains outside the umbra in the penumbra receives some direct sunlight, and the glare is usually great enough to prevent us from seeing the faint coppery glow of the part of the Moon in the umbra.

Lunar eclipses always occur at full moon, but not at every full moon. The Moon's orbit is tipped about 5 degrees to the ecliptic, so most full moons cross the sky north or south of Earth's shadow, and there is no lunar eclipse that month (see Figure 2.13). For the same reason, solar eclipses always occur at new moon but not at every new moon. The orientation of the Moon's orbit in space varies slowly, and as a result, solar and lunar eclipses repeat in a pattern called the **Saros cycle**, lasting 18 years and $11\frac{1}{3}$ days. Ancient peoples who understood the Saros cycle could predict eclipses without understanding what the Sun and Moon really were.

Although there are usually no more than one or two lunar eclipses each year, it is not difficult to see one. You need only be on the dark side of Earth when the Moon passes through Earth's shadow. That is, the eclipse must occur between sunset and sunrise at your location to be visible. Table 2.2 provides information for you to determine when some upcoming lunar eclipses will be visible.

Table 2.2 Total and Partial Eclipses of the Moon, 2013–2022*

Date	Time of Mid-Eclipse (GMT)**	Length of Totality (Hr:Min)	Length of Eclipse (Hr:Min)
2015 April 4	12:01	0:05	3:29
2015 September 28	02:48	1:12	3:20
2017 August 7	18:22	Partial	1:55
2018 January 31	13:31	1:16	3:23
2018 July 27	20:23	1:43	3:55
2019 January 21	05:13	1:02	3:17
2019 July 16	21:32	Partial	2:58
2021 May 26	11:20	0:15	3:07
2021 November 19	09:04	Partial	3:28
2022 May 16	04:13	1:25	3:27
2022 November 8	11:00	1:25	3:40

*There are no total or partial lunar eclipses during 2016 or 2020.
**Times are Greenwich Mean Time. Subtract 5 hours for Eastern Standard Time, 6 hours for Central Standard Time, 7 hours for Mountain Standard Time, and 8 hours for Pacific Standard Time. For Daylight Savings Time (mid-March through early November), add 1 hour to Standard Time. Lunar eclipses that occur between sunset and sunrise in your time zone will be visible, and those at midnight will be best placed.
Source: http://eclipse.gsfc.nasa.gov/SEdecade/SEdecade2011.html

2.6 Stellar Coordinates

Picture Earth hanging at the centre of the celestial sphere. Imagine Earth's latitude and longitude lines expanding outward and printing themselves onto the celestial sphere. This provides a coordinate grid on the sky that tells the position of any star, just as latitude and longitude tell the position of any point on Earth. In the sky, "latitude" is called **declination** and "longitude" is called **right ascension**.

Declination (dec) is expressed in degrees, arc minutes, and arc seconds, north (+) or south (−) of the **celestial**

Saros cycle An 18-year, 11⅓-day period, after which the pattern of lunar and solar eclipses repeats.

declination The angular distance of an object on the celestial sphere measured north (+) or south (−) from the celestial equator.

right ascension The angular east-west distance of an object on the celestial sphere measured from the vernal equinox, and measured in hours, minutes, and seconds, rather than angular degrees.

celestial equator The imaginary line around the sky directly above Earth's equator.

solar day The average time between successive crossings of the Sun on the local meridian (24 hours).

sidereal day The time between successive crossings of any star on the local meridian (23 hours, 56 minutes, 4.09 seconds).

synodic month The time for a complete cycle of lunar phases (about 29.5 days).

sidereal month The time for the Moon to orbit Earth once relative to any star (about 27.3 days).

sidereal year The time for Earth to complete one full orbit around the Sun relative to any star.

tropical year (solar year) The time between successive spring (or autumnal) equinoxes.

apparent solar time Time measured by the location of the Sun in the local sky such that noon occurs when the Sun crosses the meridian.

equator (just as latitudinal positions are described). Capella, the brightest star in the constellation Auriga, has a declination of +46° 0″ and is, therefore, about halfway between the celestial equator (dec = 0°) and the north celestial pole (dec = +90°).

Right ascension (RA) is expressed not in degrees but in hours (h), minutes (m), and seconds (s) of time, from 0 to 24 hours. Astronomers set up this arrangement long ago because Earth completes one turn in 24 hours, so the celestial sphere appears to take 24 hours to complete one turn around Earth. The zero of right ascension is, by convention, the longitudinal line that runs through the spring equinox. The RA for Capella is 5 hours 17 minutes east of the spring equinox; thinking about RA in angular degree terms results in Capella being about 80° east of the spring equinox. The celestial coordinates of stars remain constant over many years because they are so far away. On the other hand, the Sun, being much closer, moves along the ecliptic throughout the year, travelling through the complete 24-hour RA zones over the calendar year.

2.7 Timekeeping

Even to the casual observer, it is clear that the length of our day is related to Earth's rotational period; the number of days in a month must be associated with the lunar phase period, and the length of a year corresponds to the period of Earth's orbit around the Sun. By now you can see that astronomy is much more precise than vague correspondences.

Timekeeping by Day

Our local meridian is the imaginary line that ends at the north and south celestial poles and cuts through our zenith. The average length of time between successive passes of the Sun across the local meridian is called a **solar day**; this time varies slightly throughout a year, which is why we use

the word *average*. Another way of determining the length of a day is to measure the time it takes for any star to make successive passes across the local meridian, which we call a **sidereal day** (pronounced sy-deer-ial). A sidereal day is about 23 hours 56 minutes—shorter than a solar day by about 4 minutes. This difference of four minutes is because during a solar day, Earth has travelled along its orbit around the Sun and needs a little more time to rotate before the Sun crosses the meridian. A simple mathematical calculation shows that Earth moves about 1° per day around its orbit.

Timekeeping by Month

Timekeeping involving months comes from the lunar phase's cycle, which is about 29.5 solar days, corresponding roughly to the average length of a month, known as a **synodic month**. Synodic comes from the Latin word *synod*, meaning "meeting"—the meeting of the Sun and the Moon at each new moon phase. If, however, we use the stars to measure the length of the lunar cycle, a **sidereal month**, the time turns out to be 27.3 days, which is shorter than a synodic month for the same reason a sidereal day is shorter than a solar day.

Timekeeping by Year

The length of a year is clearly related to the time required for Earth to complete one full orbit around the Sun, about 365.25 days. Again, there are two slightly different timeframes. A **sidereal year** is the time taken for a complete orbit relative to the stars, whereas the time between successive spring (or autumnal) equinoxes is called a **tropical year (solar year)**. It should come as no surprise that these two years differ. A sidereal year is longer than a tropical year by about 20 minutes, and the difference is due to the precession of Earth's rotation. If the sidereal year were employed as a calendar, this 20-minute difference would result in seasons slowly shifting throughout the year, although this pattern would take 26 000 years to repeat.

What Time Is It?

After considering various options for timekeeping, what method do you think we actually use? The answer is that we use an aspect of solar time—sort of! The **apparent solar time** is determined by the Sun's position in the sky relative to our local meridian. When the Sun is right on the meridian it is noon; before the Sun gets to the meridian we say that it is *ante meridian* (*ante* meaning "before"), hence a.m. (or am). After noon, when the Sun has passed the meridian, we say that it is *post meridian* (*post* meaning "after"), hence p.m. (or pm). However, each solar day differs from 24 hours by a slight amount because Earth's orbit is not perfectly circular and because of Earth's 23.4° tilt. The average solar day is the more important concept and the one used to

Figure 2.14 Sir Sanford Fleming

keep track of time. Using apparent solar time would mean adjusting clocks each day, an unnecessary complication. Clearly, apparent solar time varies with longitude (because of Earth's spin on its axis), and so everybody's apparent solar time is different, unless they happen to be at precisely the same longitude. To alleviate this problem, the Canadian Sandford Fleming (Figure 2.14), proposed a system of dividing Earth into 24 different time zones so that within each time zone the time would be exactly the same. Such a system was adopted universally by the late 1800s.

Calendars

The tropical year (equinox to equinox) is about 365.25 days. If we choose 365 days for one year (the Egyptian concept), the seasons drift through the year by one day in every four years—not a great concept! Julius Caesar introduced the idea that every four years an extra day was to be added to account for this discrepancy: the "leap year." This, the so-called Julian calendar, represented a definite improvement. However, life is rarely this simple. The tropical year is not exactly 365.25 days but rather about 11 minutes short of this value, resulting in the spring equinox moving backwards through the calendar by 11 minutes each year, or about 14.5 hours per 80-year lifetime, or about 12 days every 1600 years. So, in 1582, Pope Gregory XIII introduced a slight variation in the calendar, which became known as the Gregorian calendar and is the one we use today. It first set the spring equinox to March 21 and then adjusted the leap

year schedule such that each century year would be skipped as a leap year unless it was divisible by 400 (so, the year 2000 would be a leap year, but not 1900, or 2100). This adjustment made the calendar good for thousands of years into the future, and it is now used globally.

2.8 Night Sky Tours

Many students take a university astronomy course to learn about the night sky, hoping to identify various star patterns. In this section, you will find a few "tours" of the night sky visible to Canadian viewers and that cover an entire year of observing. Fortunately, you will not need a telescope—although a decent pair of binoculars may enhance your viewing experience. Instead, you need a location with little or no light pollution, an outdoor easy chair on which to lay to force your eyes upward (a blanket might be required depending on the weather), and your eyes!

This section contains typical star charts, identical to the ones found at the back of your textbook. These charts show the evening sky as viewed from the northern hemisphere at a latitude typical of southern Canada or central Europe. Hold the chart so that the words *southern horizon* are at the bottom, and be sure you are facing south. The night sky will then appear above and behind you as you move up the page. The items indicated on the star chart to the left (eastern horizon) will appear above you and to the left, and so on. If you wish to begin by facing north, turn the star chart upside down and follow the same procedure.

You will notice two arced lines stretching across the chart. The yellow one, marked *equator*, is the celestial equator, an imaginary circle around the celestial sphere, and is merely an extension of Earth's equator. The orange arc marked *ecliptic* is the line described earlier in this chapter that represents the path followed by the Sun across the sky once each year. (The 12 signs of the zodiac, under one of which you were born, are found all along the ecliptic—but that's astrology!)

Now that you have a better understanding of star charts you are ready to take your first "tour" of the night sky, where you will see what the sky looks like over a three-or four-month period. This is possible because the sky does not change much from one night to the next, although over several months the stars visibly shift across the sky as Earth orbits around the Sun.

Our first night sky tour involves the winter sky, where we note some of the more important features of the following constellations: Orion (the Hunter) and his two dogs, Canis Major (the Great Dog), and Canis Minor (the Little Dog), Taurus (the Bull), Gemini (the Twins), and Auriga (the Charioteer) (see Figure 2.15). Orion is one of the most recognized constellations; in Canada, it appears low in the southern sky. Perhaps its most identifiable feature is the belt star formation that appears as a straight line of stars. Actually, these stars are at vastly different distances from us: from left to right they are Alnitak (826 ly), Alnilam (1359 ly), and Mintaka (919 ly). To the upper left is Betelgeuse, the fist star, which is a reddish variable star and 429 ly away; to the lower right is Rigel, the foot star, which is much larger and brighter than our Sun and about 777 ly from us. Just below Orion's belt is M42, a Messier object known as the Orion nebula. This is a collection of stars (some dying and some forming) and dust in our own galaxy—a spectacular telescopic sight, but visible to the naked eye only on a clear night from an area with no light pollution. In the late 1700s a comet hunter, Charles Messier, compiled a list of about 100 non-comet objects, mostly nebulae and star clusters, which became known as Messier objects and were labelled M1, M2, and so on. Today the list includes 110 such objects, and many astronomers endeavour to view the entire list over their lifetime. The belt stars in Orion point downward to Sirius, the Dog Star—the brightest star in the sky and one of the closest at 8.6 ly. Sirius is called the Dog Star because it is the main star in another well-known constellation,

Canis Major (the Great Dog). Canis Major is one of two heavenly hounds that follow Orion around the night sky. The other is Canis Minor (the Little Dog), found northeast of the Great Dog. Going in the other direction along Orion's belt, toward the zenith, we arrive at another bright star, Aldebaran, often considered the bull's eye in the constellation Taurus (the Bull). Two star clusters in Taurus are worth noting. The Hyades cluster appears to form the head of Taurus, and the more famous Pleiades (or Seven Sisters) is just northwest of Aldebaran. The horns of Taurus point toward the constellation Gemini (the Twins). The heads of the twins are identified by two equally bright stars, Castor and Pollux: Castor being slightly higher in the sky. To the astute observer, Pollux is somewhat orange in colour, while Castor is clearly white. Finally, we get to Auriga (the Charioteer), above Gemini. The brightest feature of Auriga is the star Capella—a well-known star, often used as a guide by navigators. Near Capella is a triangle of fairly bright stars known as the Kids; Auriga is supposed to have a whip or reins in his right hand (our left) and a family of little goats in his other arm. We could mention many more details about each of these constellations, but that is beyond the scope

Figure 2.15

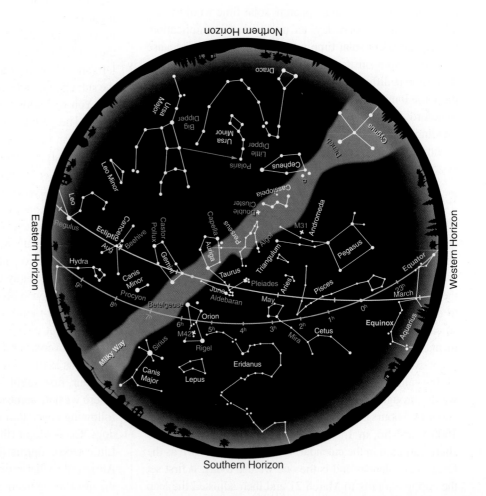

Northern Hemisphere Sky

November–December–January

November	midnight
December	10 p.m.
January	8 p.m.

Times are Standard Time; for Daylight Savings Time, add 1 hour.

Months along the ecliptic show the location of the Sun during the year.

Numbers along the celestial equator show right ascension.

of this little tour of the Canadian winter sky. There also is a lot of mythology intertwined with the history of these constellations—but that's another university course!

Our second night sky tour takes us through the northern summer sky, where the constellations reviewed include Leo (the Lion), Virgo (the Virgin), Ursa Major (the Great Bear) and Ursa Minor (the Little Bear), and finally Boötes (the Herdsman). Perhaps the most well-recognized northern image is the Big Dipper, which is part of Ursa Major. Interestingly, the Big Dipper by itself is not a constellation, but because it is close to the North Star (Polaris), it is visible throughout Canada all year (see Figure 2.16). Polaris is the brightest star in Ursa Minor, and you can find it by following the line defined by the two outer cup stars of the Big Dipper to the north. Actually, despite its reputation, Polaris is not an overly bright star, being about the 50th brightest star in the entire sky and, for a novice, not all that easy to find. Similarly, Ursa Minor is not always easily visible and requires patience and a current star chart to ensure discovery. Above Ursa Major and slightly to the west is Leo. Leo has several interesting features, not the least of which is a grouping of stars forming its head that is often referred to as the Sickle (because it is shaped like

one). Such a named grouping of stars within a constellation is called an *asterism;* the Big Dipper is an asterism. The brightest star in Leo is its foot star, Regulus, which is very close to the ecliptic plane. Farther along the ecliptic plane to the east is Virgo (the Virgin), yet another of the zodiacal constellations, often depicted as a reclining human form. The brightest star in Virgo is Spica, the 15th brightest star, a double star that is 11 times as massive as our Sun. The name Spica has Latin origins meaning "ear of wheat," and is so named because the Sun comes close to Spica in the fall (harvest time), and some say the ancients saw Virgo holding a shaft of wheat, the ripe heads represented by this bright star. Higher in the sky (above Virgo) is Arcturus, the 4th brightest star, and the main star in Boötes. Arcturus, quite orange in hue, has already started to die and is fusing helium into carbon in its core (see Chapter 8). Boötes is known as the Herdsman because he is seen to be keeping the celestial animals in order as he "chases" them around the sky. Arcturus, from the Greek for "bear watcher," keeps an eye on Ursa Major, Leo, and Lynx (not discussed here) as he follows them around the pole. Light from Arcturus was used to open the 1933 World's Fair in Chicago; the star was chosen because light had left it at

Figure 2.16

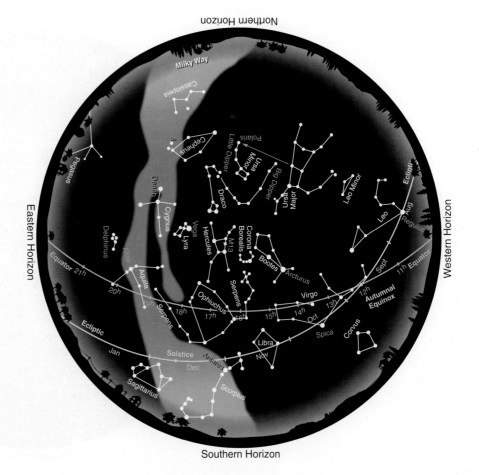

Northern Hemisphere Sky

May–June–July

May	midnight
June	10 p.m.
July	8 p.m.

Times are Standard Time; for Daylight Savings Time, add 1 hour.

Months along the ecliptic show the location of the Sun during the year.

Numbers along the celestial equator show right ascension.

Helen Sawyer Hogg

Helen Sawyer Hogg may have been Canada's most popular astronomer. For more than 30 years, she wrote a hugely popular column for the *Toronto Star*, called "With the Stars." In it, she described major celestial events, included tips for observing the night sky, and discussed important astronomical discoveries. As an undergraduate student in 1925, Helen Sawyer Hogg witnessed a total eclipse of the Sun, which inspired her to become an astronomer. She recalled that "the glory of the spectacle seems to have tied me to astronomy for life, despite my horribly cold feet as we stood almost knee deep in the snow." After graduating, she performed her doctoral studies at Harvard Observatory, but because Harvard did not at the time confer degrees in science to women, she officially obtained her PhD from Radcliffe College in 1931. She then moved to Victoria, British Columbia, where her husband had accepted a position at the Dominion Astrophysical Observatory. She was not offered a position, so acting as her husband's voluntary assistant, Dr. Sawyer Hogg began studying variable stars in globular clusters. She continued her work as a faculty member at the University of Toronto and became a leading world authority on globular clusters. She discovered hundreds of new variable stars and developed new techniques for distance measurements. Catalogues based on her observations are still widely used today. Dr. Sawyer Hogg won numerous awards and honours, and in 1976 she was made a Companion of the Order of Canada. The asteroid Sawyer Hogg is named after her.

Figure 2.17

Northern Hemisphere Sky

August–September–October

August	midnight
September	10 p.m.
October	8 p.m.

Times are Standard Time; for Daylight Savings Time, add 1 hour.

Months along the ecliptic show the location of the Sun during the year.

Numbers along the celestial equator show right ascension.

about the same time the fair was previously held in Chicago in 1893.

Our final tour begins along the swath of the Milky Way, which, during the fall and early Canadian winter, cuts across the sky from east to west. On a clear, moonless night away from light pollution, you can see a visibly white ribbon of billions of stars (first observed as such by Galileo more than 400 years ago using his newly constructed telescope) (see Figure 2.17). Peering into this ribbon of stars means you are looking into our galaxy from the vantage point of our solar system, about 28 000 ly from the Milky Way's centre. Our first stop is Cassiopeia (the Queen), almost directly overhead within the Milky Way band and whose brightest five stars form a distinct W. Being fairly close to Polaris, Cassiopeia is visible throughout the year to Canadian observers. Beside Cassiopeia is Cepheus (the King), a much dimmer constellation. Its fourth brightest star, δ Cephei, was determined to be a variable star in the late 1700s and is the star after which all Cepheid variable stars are named. On the other side of Cassiopeia is Andromeda (the Chained Princess), which is home to the famed Andromeda Galaxy (M31), our closest neighbouring galaxy (2.5 million ly away). In mythology Cassiopeia and Cepheus were the parents of Andromeda. The brightest star in Andromeda, Alpheratz, is the corner of the asterism the Great Square

Figure 2.18 Albireo

of Pegasus. Pegasus (the Winged Horse) is clearly right next to Andromeda; its Great Square makes up the body of the horse and is a great autumn landmark. Rounding out this overhead autumn tour, toward the western horizon but still in the Milky Way ribbon, is Cygnus (the Swan), whose brightest star, Deneb (at the back end of the swan), is one apex of the famous summer asterism the Summer Triangle. The swan's beak is denoted by Albireo, a lovely double star—one distinctly blue and one gold—that is nicely visible in even a small telescope (Figure 2.18).

The **Big Picture**

What Are We? Along for the Ride

We humans are planet walkers. We live on the surface of a whirling planet, and on clear, dark nights we can look outward into space for billions of light-years.

Most of the stars we see are actually not very far way. They are only hundreds, not billions, of light-years from Earth. The vast majority of the stars in the universe are too distant and consequently too faint to see with the unaided eye. For centuries, human cultures have labelled the visible stars with names and divided them into constellations. The constellation Hercules looked down on Plato and Aristotle just as it now looks down on you.

Nearly all of the energy Earth receives comes from the Sun, and as Earth spins on its axis and revolves around its orbit, the changing balance of sunlight produces the changing seasons. Winter and summer seasons have cycled for longer than there have been humans on Earth, and when you watch autumn leaves turn golden, you are part of one of the great astronomical cycles of our planet.

Through it all, the Moon orbits Earth, and cultures through history have made it their timepiece. Your calendar is divided into months, recognizing the cycle of the Moon; your months are divided into four weeks, recognizing the fourfold cycle of the moon's phases.

Busy as you are, take a moment to look up and enjoy the cycles of the sky. They will remind you that you are a planet walker.

Review and Discussion Questions

Review Questions

1. What is the difference between an asterism and a constellation? Give some examples.
2. How does the Greek-letter designation of a star give you a clue to its brightness?
3. How did the magnitude system originate in a classification of stars by brightness?
4. What does the word *apparent* mean in "apparent visual magnitude"?
5. In what ways is the celestial sphere a scientific model?
6. If Earth did not rotate, could you define the celestial poles and celestial equator?
7. Where would you go on Earth to place a celestial pole at your zenith?
8. Why does the number of circumpolar constellations depend on the latitude of the observer?
9. If Earth did not rotate, could you still define the ecliptic? Why or why not?
10. Why are the seasons reversed in the southern hemisphere relative to the northern hemisphere?
11. Do the phases of the Moon look the same from every place on Earth, or is the Moon full at different times as seen from different locations?
12. What phase would Earth be in if you were on the Moon when it was full? At first quarter? At waning crescent? Some other phase?
13. Why isn't there an eclipse at every new moon and at every full moon?
14. Why is the Moon red during a total lunar eclipse?
15. **How Do We Know?** What are the main characteristics of a pseudoscience? Can you suggest other examples?

Discussion Questions

1. Most cultures have given names to constellations. Why do you suppose this was a common practice?
2. If you were lost at sea, you could find your approximate latitude by measuring the altitude of Polaris. However, because Polaris isn't exactly at the celestial pole, what else would you need to know to measure your latitude more accurately?
3. Do planets orbiting other stars have ecliptics? Could they have seasons?

Learning to Look

1. This stamp shows the constellation Orion. Explain why this looks odd to residents of the northern hemisphere.
2. The photo below shows the annular eclipse of May 30, 1984. How is it different from the total eclipse shown in Figure 2.10? Why do you suppose it is different?

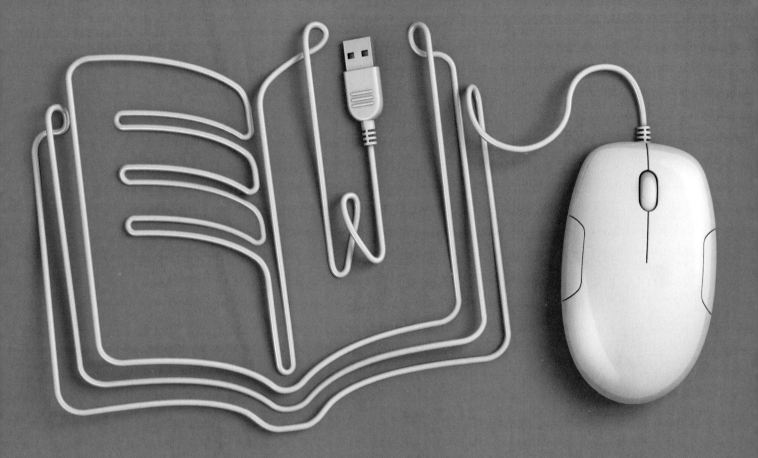

Your online study partner.

www.nelson.com/student

3

The Origin of Modern Astronomy

CHAPTER OUTLINE

GUIDEPOST

Have you ever looked up at the sky and marvelled at the multitude of tiny specks of light shining down on you? Have you tried to pick out patterns in the night sky? Have you stared at the full Moon or the sliver of a crescent moon on a dark night? Then you are following in the footsteps of our ancient ancestors who gazed up at the sky thousands of years ago and took the first steps along the long road that has led to our current knowledge of the universe. As you read on, you will learn how the science of astronomy grew out of careful observations and gradual development of the scientific method over thousands of years. You will find that every culture has engaged in and contributed to the development of astronomy, making it a truly global effort. And you will understand that ancient astronomy has shaped not only our scientific thinking but also our culture, art, language, religions, and traditions.

In this chapter you will find answers to four important questions:

- **What did early astronomers learn about the motion of stars and Earth's place in the universe?**
- **How did ancient astronomical theories get revised?**
- **Why was Galileo condemned by the Inquisition?**
- **How did the development of modern astronomy change the way people thought about nature and themselves?**

This chapter is not just about the history of astronomy. As astronomers struggled to understand Earth and the universe, they invented a new way of understanding nature—a way of thinking that is now called science.

© WIN-Initiative/Getty Images

If at first the idea is not absurd then there is no hope for it.
Albert Einstein,
Physicist and Nobel laureate

3.1 A Brief History of Ancient Astronomy

The origins of astronomy arose from the curiosity of our ancestors, who were excellent at observing and recording the world around them and recognizing patterns in what they observed. These skills were critical for their survival, but although they did not know it, careful observation and pattern recognition were also the first steps in what we now call the modern scientific method.

A marvellous example of ancient observations and recordkeeping can be found in Lascaux, France, where paleolithic cave paintings dating back to 15 000 BCE were discovered in 1940 (Figure 3.1). More than 900 images of animals show incredible attention to detail and anatomical precision. There are also numerous images of geometric figures. Some recent scientific studies indicate that the paintings may have been a star map or astronomical calendar, but there is no conclusive proof that this theory is correct. More convincing evidence of early astronomical observations has been found in Africa, where a carved bone that is 8500 years old shows pictographs of the crescent Moon. Ancient people of central Africa could predict seasons from the orientation of the horns of the crescent Moon each month (again, a result of careful observation

Figure 3.1 Paleolithic cave paintings in France from 15 000 BCE may be a star map or represent the zodiac, although this theory has not been conclusively proved.

and pattern recognition). This allowed them to determine when to plant seeds and grow their crops.

Archeological sites of ancient cultures of Egypt, British Isles, and Mesoamerica show the results of detailed observation and sophisticated knowledge of the night sky, including the cycles of the Sun, Moon, and planets (see Figure 3.2).

Around 2500 BCE the Egyptians used the first rising at dawn of the star Sirius to mark the beginning of a 365-day

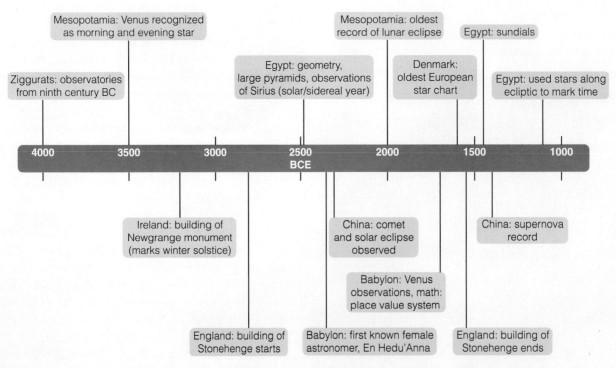

Figure 3.2 Timeline of Astronomy: 4000 BCE to 1000 BCE

calendar. Sirius, the brightest star in the sky, which they identified with the fertility goddess Isis, first appeared in the predawn sky each year just as the Nile began its life-giving floods. While the rising of the Nile varied year to year, Sirius appeared with perfect regularity. This regular cycle helped them predict planting season and prepare for the floods. The Egyptians were also the first to divide the night and day into 12 hours, but of varying lengths, based on the rising of certain bright stars during summer nights. Our modern 24 hour clock partially owes its origins to the Egyptians.

Other ancient cultures also used astronomical observations for timekeeping. The motions of both the Sun and the Moon played an important role in the marking of time, with the Sun used for predicting seasonal changes and the lunar phases defining monthly changes. A 4000-year-old stone circle in Scotland marks the rise and set of the Moon during a phenomenon called the lunar standstill, which occurs every 18.6 years due to the precession of the Moon's orbital plane. During this time, the most northerly and most southerly rising and setting of the Moon occur every month. It is amazing that the builders of the stone circles in Scotland as well as astronomers in other ancient civilizations appeared to have been aware of this long-term cycle, which required careful observations over many years. At the famous monument at Stonehenge, England, completed around 1550 BCE, giant boulders are roughly aligned with the seasonal motion of the Sun (Figure 3.3). The site may have served as an observatory as well as a sacred ceremonial ground. We cannot be sure of its purpose since there are no written records from

Figure 3.4 Early Astronomical Calendar. Dating from about 1000 BCE in Babylon, this early form of astronomical calendar shows the monthly pre-dawn rising of three stars.

that time. The Mayans also built massive ancient structures, such as the Templo Mayor, to mark seasonal events.

Some of the most careful observers and detailed record keepers were the Babylonians. In fact, the first female astronomer recorded in history was named in a Babylonian tablet from 2354 BCE (Figure 3.4). Her name was En Hedu'Anna, and her position was astronomer priestess of the Moon Goddess. Babylonian priests like her in Mesopotamia (modern Iraq) recorded the detailed motions of the visible planets on thousands of tablets more than 4000 years ago. In 763 BCE, a solar eclipse was also observed and recorded by the Babylonians. These ancient astronomers have left their mark on modern astronomy. Today, our constellations of the zodiac are based on patterns identified by the Babylonians.

In 1400 BCE an exciting event was observed and recorded in China—the sudden brightening and dimming of a "guest star." Although they did not know it at the time, the Chinese had made the earliest known record of a supernova explosion. The Chinese also recorded solar and lunar eclipses continuously from the fifth century BCE! In 1054 CE the Chinese recorded another powerful supernova explosion. This spectacular event may have also been depicted in a famous Anasazi rock painting found on the other side of the world, in New Mexico,

Figure 3.3 Stonehenge. Many ancient monuments such as the one in Stonehenge, England, may have been used to mark solar or lunar events.

CHAPTER 3 **The Origin of Modern Astronomy** |

Inuit Traditions

Living in bare landscape with very few landmarks, Inuit people used stars, the Sun, the Moon, snowdrifts, wind directions, and the behaviour of dogs for finding their way from place to place. Stars were reliable markers for orientation, including Betelgeuse, which the Inuit call Akuttujuuk, and Pleiades, which they call Sakiattiak. Stars were also reliable for predicting the weather: Sirius, or Singuuriq, changes the way it flickers with weather changes, allowing them to make a very precise forecast. Most Inuit societies kept time by the Moon; people used a 13-month lunar calendar whose names reflected natural events occurring in that month.

In the Far North of Canada, where the Sun never rises in deep winter, the Inuit devised ingenious methods based on the rising and setting of stars to mark time. For example, on the winter solstice, the Sun remains below the horizon, but scattered sunlight in the atmosphere is brightest around the star Aagjuk (the Inuit name for Altair). By noting when the Sun's twilight glow is centred on the bright star Altair, the Inuit could tell when the winter solstice occurred. This event was celebrated as it signalled the eventual return of the Sun. The Inuit name for Polaris is Nuuttuittuq, meaning "the one that never moves," a fitting name since Polaris lies almost along Earth's axis and hence does not rotate perceptibly to the naked eye in the night sky, unlike the other stars. The Inuit used Polaris and various bright star constellations to find their way across vast open stretches of snow-covered country, where other geographical markers are difficult to spot. Astronomy was used not only for time-keeping and navigation, but the stars, planets, and celestial phenomena such as the Northern Lights also played a central role in storytelling and Inuit mythology.

Twilight tree silhouettes and stars, with time-lapse photography showing star trails as the Earth orbits on its axis. The central star, Polaris/Nuuttuittuq, lies almost along the axis and does not perceptibly move. Photograph taken in Jasper National Park, Alberta.

© Corey Hochachka/Design Pics

USA (Figure 3.5). The supernova explosion was powerful enough to be brighter than Venus and visible during the day for 23 days. In recent times, modern telescopes have been used to capture stunning images of the Crab Nebula, which is the remnant of the supernova explosion of 1054 CE (see Figure 8.10).

The observed connection between the planting seasons and the position of celestial objects led to the development of religions centred on the Sun, the Moon, and other celestial objects personified as deities. Certain ceremonies were designed to please celestial beings, and prayers and rituals were performed to mark important seasonal changes. Many festivals and ceremonies still celebrated in various parts of the world have their roots

in ancient practices. Priests were important members of society due to their ability to predict celestial events, which was viewed as a connection to heavenly deities. The association of celestial objects with one or more gods led to the idea that these gods could affect individual human lives. This was the birth of astrology—the search for influences on human lives based on the positions of planets and stars in the sky. However, numerous scientific tests have shown that astrological predictions are no more accurate than can be expected from random chance.

As you can see, ancient civilizations were fascinated by the heavens and carefully studied the daily and seasonal motions of celestial objects. The days of the week were named for the Sun, the Moon, and the five planets visible

HOW DO WE KNOW? 3.1

Wayfinding: Astronomical Navigation

Thousands of years before the invention of modern navigational instruments, those who travelled vast distances, such as over expanses with very few landmarks, across Arctic snow, or across the Pacific Ocean, developed techniques of "wayfinding": that is, observing positions of stars and knowing their particular environment.

Indian and Pacific Ocean sailors created detailed star maps in their minds and elaborate ways of remembering them. The star compass was the basic mental construct for navigation. Hawaiian houses of the stars were places where stars came out of the ocean and went back into the ocean. To find their direction, travellers had to identify the stars and memorize where they rose and set. Constant observation of the sky and monitoring of changes in the Sun's position, ocean swells, types of waves, and bird paths, gave information about their position and direction. Polynesians and Micronesians who travelled thousands of kilometres across the open ocean used elaborate stick maps incorporating all the data.

© W. Robert Moore/National Geographic Society/Corbis

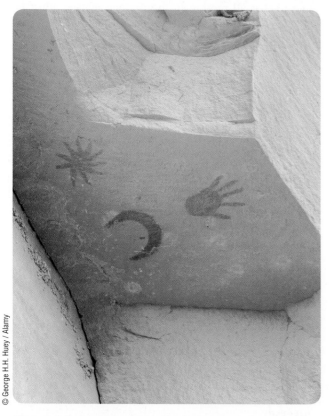

Figure 3.5 Anasazi rock painting that may be a depiction of the supernova of 1054 CE. The crescent Moon is shown relative to the supernova. The handprint signature may signify that the site is sacred.

© George H.H. Huey / Alamy

to the naked eye. Astronomical observations benefited and impacted ancient societies in many ways, including time-keeping, efficient agricultural practices, navigation, and the development of religious and ceremonial practices.

To this point, astronomy had involved making observations, recognizing patterns, and making predictions based on the patterns. Another crucial part of the scientific method—building and testing models and hypotheses—was developed in ancient Greece.

The Geocentric Model of the Universe

The ancient Greeks were interested in building models of nature based on reasoning and observation (Figure 3.6). Thales of Miletus, an influential scientist and mathematician, assumed that the world was understandable and attempted to create models to explain major events in the universe. It was said that he correctly predicted a solar eclipse, perhaps by using the ancient knowledge of the Babylonians. In 500 BCE, Pythagoras suggested that Earth is a sphere and not flat, as had been previously assumed. His model fit well with observations and the widely held belief that the sphere is an object of geometrical perfection. Based on this spherical model, Eratosthenes was able to calculate Earth's circumference by observing the position of the Sun at noon in two

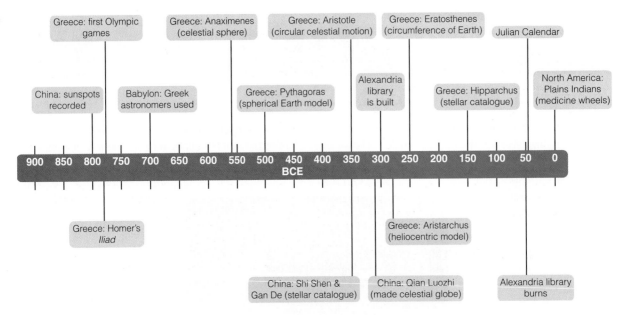

Figure 3.6 Timeline of Astronomy: 900 BCE to 0 CE

different cities on the first day of summer. Incredibly, his estimate was accurate to within a few percent of the currently known value.

The two great authorities of Greek astronomy were the brilliant philosopher Aristotle and Claudius Ptolemy (pronounced TAHL-eh-mee; the initial "P" is silent), a later follower of Aristotle's principles. Study **Visualizing Astronomy 3.1, The Ancient Universe,** and notice three important ideas:

1. Based on their observations, ancient Greek philosophers and astronomers believed that heavenly objects moved on circular paths at constant speed, with Earth motionless at the centre of the universe. This geocentric (Earth at the centre) model was championed by Aristotle. Although a few ancient writers mentioned the possibility that Earth might move, most of them did so in order to point out how that idea is "obviously" wrong.

2. As viewed by you from Earth, the planets seem to follow complicated paths in the sky, including episodes of "backward" (retrograde) motion that are difficult to explain in terms of motion on circular paths at constant speeds.

3. Finally, you can see how Ptolemy created an elaborate geometrical and mathematical model to explain details of the observed motions of the planets, while assuming Earth is motionless at the centre of the universe.

first principle Something that seems obviously true and needs no further examination.

Aristotle lived in Greece from 384 to 322 BCE (Figure 3.7). He believed as a **first principle** that the heavens were perfect. Because the sphere and circle were considered the only perfect geometrical figures, Aristotle also believed that all motion in the perfect heavens must be caused by the rotation of spheres carrying objects around in uniform circular motion. Aristotle's writings became so famous that he was known throughout the Middle Ages as "The Philosopher." He set about improving past models to develop an accurate mathematical description of planetary motion.

Claudius Ptolemy, a mathematician who lived roughly 500 years after Aristotle (Figure 3.8), believed in the basic ideas of Aristotle's universe but was interested in practical rather than philosophical questions. For Ptolemy, first principles took second place to accuracy. He set about making an accurate mathematical description of the motions of the planets. Ptolemy weakened the first principles of Aristotle by moving Earth a little off-centre in the model and inventing a way to slightly vary the planets' speeds. His model (published around 140 CE) was a better match to the observed motions and could handle the complicated retrograde motion of the planets. Aristotle's universe, as embodied in the mathematics of Ptolemy's model, dominated ancient astronomy for almost 1500 years (see **Visualizing Astronomy 3.1, The Ancient Universe**).

One of Aristotle's students was none other than the military leader Alexander the Great. Although he used military force to conquer much of the Middle

Figure 3.7 Aristotle, Copernicus, Brahe, and Kepler.

East all the way to India, he also promoted science and encouraged learning. He founded the city of Alexandria in Egypt, renowned for its great library that served as a major centre of knowledge for hundreds of years. One of the most famous library scholars was a female astronomer and mathematician named Hypatia, who was the director of the observatory in Alexandria. Hypatia, a well-respected scientist and teacher, wrote several books on algebra, geometry, and astronomy. She may have also corrected and extended past work by Ptolemy. She was eventually killed for religious and political reasons, and shortly afterward the library was destroyed. However, Greek knowledge was not lost; it was preserved in the Islamic world. Caliph Al-Ma'mun's House of Wisdom in Baghdad was a great centre of learning around 800 CE. Many ancient texts by scientists and mathematicians from India were also translated into Arabic during this time. Foremost among these was *Aryabhatiya*, by the Indian astronomer and mathematician Aryabhata. This text described a geocentric planetary model, but included the possibility of Earth spinning on its own axis.

Building on ancient texts from Greece, India, China, and Babylon, Arab scientists made many advances in mathematics and astronomy. The Greek geocentric models were expanded and corrected, and many new astronomical observations were made. The names of numerous stars today, such as Algol or Deneb, have their roots in this golden age of

1 For 2000 years, the minds of astronomers were shackled by a pair of ideas. The Greek philosopher Plato argued that the heavens were perfect. Because the only perfect geometrical shape is a sphere, which carries a point on its surface around in a circle, and because the only perfect motion is uniform motion, Plato concluded that all motion in the heavens must be made up of combinations of circles turning at uniform rates. This idea was called **uniform circular motion**.

Plato's student Aristotle argued that Earth was imperfect and lay at the centre of the universe. Such a model is known as a geocentric universe. His model contained 55 spheres turning at different rates and at different angles to carry the Moon, Mercury, Venus, the Sun, Mars, Jupiter, and Saturn across the sky.

Aristotle was known as the greatest philosopher in the ancient world, and for 2000 years his authority chained the minds of astronomers with uniform circular motion and geocentrism. See the model at right.

From *Cosmographi*
by Peter Apian (153

Seen by left eye

Seen by right eye

1a Ancient astronomers believed that Earth did not move because they saw no **parallax**, the apparent motion of an object because of the motion of the observer. To demonstrate parallax, close one eye and cover a distant object with your thumb held at arm's length. Switch eyes, and your thumb appears to shift position as shown at left. If Earth moves, ancient astronomers reasoned, you should see the sky from different locations at different times of the year, and you should see parallax distorting the shapes of the constellations. They saw no parallax, so they concluded Earth could not move. Actually, ancient astronomers did not observe the parallax of the stars because it is too small to see without a telescope.

2 Planetary motion was a big problem for ancient astronomers. In fact, the word *planet* comes from the Greek word for "wanderer," referring to the eastward motion of the planets against the background of the fixed stars. The planets did not, however, move at a constant rate, and they could occasionally stop and move westward for a few months before resuming their eastward motion. This backward motion is called **retrograde motion**.

Every 2.14 years, Mars passes through a retrograde loop. Two successive loops are shown here. Each loop occurs farther east along the ecliptic and has its own shape.

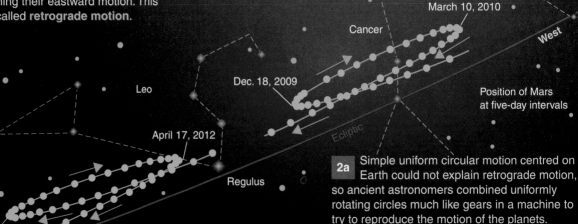

Gemini

March 10, 2010

Cancer

West

Dec. 18, 2009

Leo

Position of Mars
at five-day intervals

April 17, 2012

Ecliptic

2a Simple uniform circular motion centred on Earth could not explain retrograde motion, so ancient astronomers combined uniformly rotating circles much like gears in a machine to try to reproduce the motion of the planets.

Regulus

Jan. 24, 2012

East

3 Uniformly rotating circles were key elements of ancient astronomy. Claudius Ptolemy created a mathematical model of the Aristotelian universe in which the planet followed a small circle called the **epicycle** that slid around a larger circle called the deferent. By adjusting the size and rate of rotation of the circles, he could approximate the retrograde motion of a planet. See illustration at right.

To adjust the speed of the planet, Ptolemy supposed that Earth was slightly off centre and that the centre of the epicycle moved such that it appeared to move at a constant rate as seen from the point called the equant.

To further adjust his model, Ptolemy added small epicycles (not shown here) riding on top of larger epicycles, producing a highly complex model.

3a Ptolemy's great book *Mathematical Syntaxis* (c. 140 CE) contained the details of his model. Islamic astronomers preserved and studied the book through the Middle Ages, and they called it *Al Magisti* (*The Greatest*). When the book was found and translated from Arabic to Latin in the 12th century, it became known as *Almagest*.

3b The Ptolemaic model of the universe shown below was geocentric and based on uniform circular motion. Note that Mercury and Venus were treated differently from the rest of the planets. The centres of the epicycles of Mercury and Venus had to remain on the Earth–Sun line as the Sun circled Earth through the year.

Equants and smaller epicycles are not shown here. Some versions contained nearly 100 epicycles as generations of astronomers tried to fine-tune the model to better reproduce the motion of the planets.

Notice that this modern illustration shows rings around Saturn and sunlight illuminating the globes of the planets, features that could not be known before the invention of the telescope.

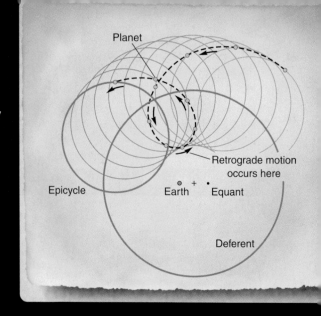

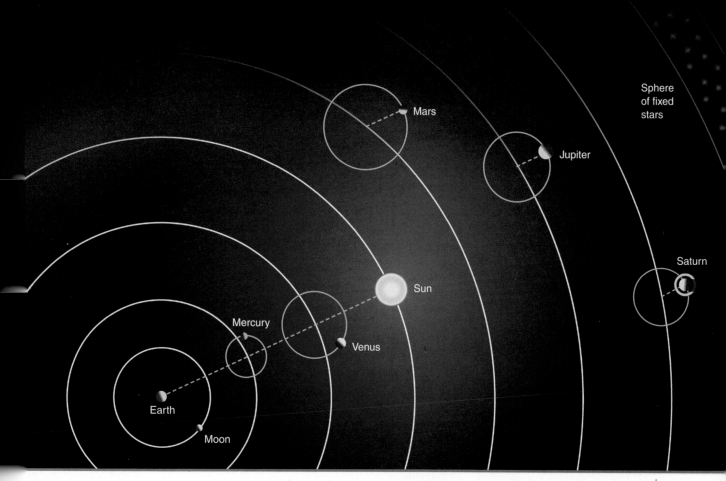

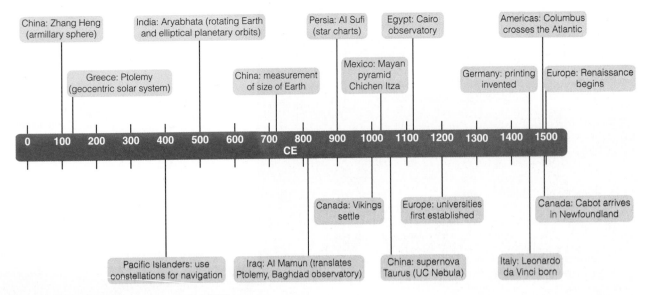

Timeline entries (top to bottom, left to right):

China: Zhang Heng (armillary sphere)

India: Aryabhata (rotating Earth and elliptical planetary orbits)

Persia: Al Sufi (star charts)

Egypt: Cairo observatory

Americas: Columbus crosses the Atlantic

Greece: Ptolemy (geocentric solar system)

China: measurement of size of Earth

Mexico: Mayan pyramid Chichen Itza

Germany: printing invented

Europe: Renaissance begins

0 100 200 300 400 500 600 700 800 900 1000 1100 1200 1300 1400 1500
CE

Canada: Vikings settle

Europe: universities first established

Canada: Cabot arrives in Newfoundland

Pacific Islanders: use constellations for navigation

Iraq: Al Mamun (translates Ptolemy, Baghdad observatory)

China: supernova Taurus (UC Nebula)

Italy: Leonardo da Vinci born

Figure 3.8 Timeline of Astronomy: 0 CE to 1500 CE

© Beaconstox / Alamy

Figure 3.9 This device is a modern recreation of an ancient Arabic Sun-and-Moon mechanical calendar by Abū Rayhān al-Bīrūnī (10th century CE).

astronomy. Although the Ptolemaic geocentric model was widely accepted, some philosophers—such as Abū Rayhān al-Bīrūnī—started thinking about arguments for a heliocentric model (Figure 3.9). It is likely that Arab astronomers were aware of the heliocentric model proposed by the Greek philosopher Aristarchus in 270 BCE. Meanwhile, in India, Nilakantha Somayaji developed a partially heliocentric model that included elliptical orbits and Earth's rotation. After the fall of Constantinople (Istanbul) in 1453, many scholars travelled to Europe, carrying with them knowledge that contributed to the birth of the Renaissance. The stage was set for a revolution in scientific thought.

geocentric universe A model of the universe with Earth at the centre, such as the Ptolemaic universe.

3.2 Nicolaus Copernicus

Nicolaus Copernicus (originally Mikolaj Kopernik) was born in 1473 in Poland (Figure 3.7). At the time of his birth—and throughout his life—astronomy was based on Ptolemy's model of Aristotle's universe. In spite of many revisions, the Ptolemaic model was still a poor predictor of planet positions, but because of the authority of Aristotle, it was the officially accepted model. Moreover, because in Aristotle's philosophy the most perfect region was in the heavens and the most imperfect region was at Earth's centre, the classical **geocentric universe** model matched the commonly held Christian view of the geometry of heaven and hell. Anyone who criticized Aristotle's model of the universe was thereby also challenging a belief in the locations of heaven and hell—risking at least criticism and perhaps a serious charge of heresy, with a possible death penalty.

The Heliocentric Model

Copernicus was associated with the Roman Catholic Church throughout his lifetime. Because of this connection to the Church and his fear of ridicule, he hesitated to publish his revolutionary ideas that challenged the Ptolemaic model and the geometry of heaven and hell.

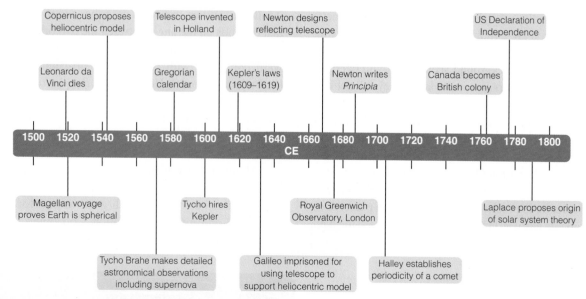

Figure 3.10 Timeline of Astronomy: 1500 CE to 1800 CE

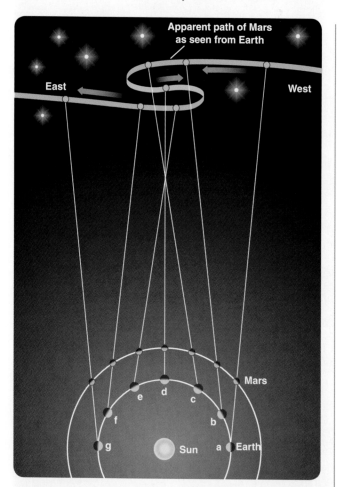

Figure 3.11 Explanation of apparent retrograde (backward) motion of planets in the heliocentric model. Earth and Mars are shown at equal intervals. Mars appears to slow its eastward motion as Earth overtakes Mars (a–c). As Earth passes Mars (d), Mars appears to move westward. As Earth draws ahead of Mars (e–g), Mars resumes its eastward motion against the background stars.

What were these revolutionary ideas? Copernicus believed that the Sun, not Earth, was the centre of the universe and that Earth rotated on its axis and revolved around the Sun. Copernicus apparently began doubting Ptolemy's geocentric model during his college days. A **heliocentric universe** model (sun-centred, from the Greek word for sun, *helios*) had been discussed occasionally before Copernicus's time, but Copernicus was the first person to produce a detailed model with substantial justifying arguments. Sometime before 1514, Copernicus wrote a short pamphlet summarizing his model and distributed it in handwritten form while he worked on his book.

De Revolutionibus

Copernicus's book *De Revolutionibus Orbium Coelestium* (*On the Revolutions of Celestial Spheres*) was essentially finished by about 1530. He hesitated to publish, although other astronomers, and even church officials concerned about reform of the calendar, knew about his work, sought his advice, and looked forward to the book's publication. In 1542 Copernicus finally sent the manuscript for *De Revolutionibus* off to be printed (Figure 3.10). He died in 1543 before the printing was completed.

The most important idea in the book was that the Sun was the centre of the universe. That single innovation had an impressive consequence—the retrograde motion of the planets was immediately explained in a straightforward way without the epicycles that Ptolemy used.

In Copernicus's model, Earth moves faster along its orbit than the planets that lie farther from the Sun (see Figure 3.11). Consequently,

> **heliocentric universe** A model of the universe with the Sun at the centre, such as the Copernican universe.

Earth periodically overtakes and passes these planets. Imagine that you are a runner on a track moving along an inside lane. Runners well ahead of you appear to be moving forward relative to background scenery. As you overtake and pass slower runners in outside lanes, they fall behind, seeming to move backward for a few moments relative to the scenery. The same thing happens as Earth passes a planet such as Mars. Although Mars moves steadily along its orbit, as seen from Earth, it seems to slow to a stop and move westward (retrograde) relative to the background stars as Earth passes it (Figure 3.11). Because the planets' orbits do not lie in precisely the same plane, a planet does not resume its eastward motion in precisely the same path

it followed earlier. Instead, it describes a loop with a shape that depends on the angle between the two orbital planes.

Copernicus's model was simple and straightforward compared with the multiple off-centre circles of the Ptolemaic model. However, *De Revolutionibus* failed to immediately disprove the geocentric model for one critical reason: the Copernican model could not predict the positions of the planets any more accurately than the Ptolemaic model could.

Although Copernicus proposed a revolutionary idea in making the solar system heliocentric, he was a classically trained astronomer with great respect for the old concept of uniform circular motion. Copernicus objected

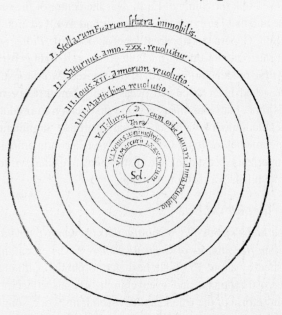

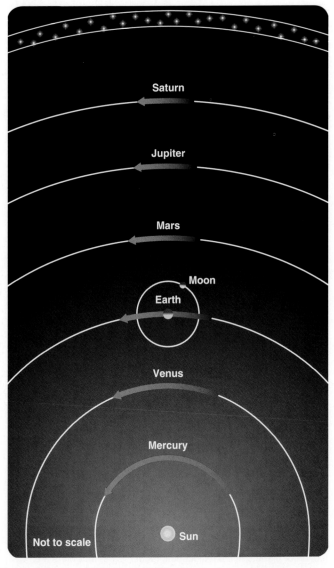

Figure 3.12 The Copernican universe, as reproduced in his book *De Revolutionibus*. (a) Earth and all the known planets revolve in separate circular orbits about the Sun (Sol) at the centre. The outermost sphere carries the immobile stars of the celestial sphere. Notice the orbit of the Moon around Earth (Terra). (b) The model is simple not only in the arrangement of the planets but also in their motions. Orbital velocities (blue arrows) decrease from that of Mercury, the fastest, to that of Saturn, the slowest. Note that Uranus, Neptune, and Pluto were not discovered before the invention of the telescope and are thus not included in this model.

to Ptolemy's schemes for moving Earth slightly off-centre and varying the speeds of planet motions. That seemed arbitrary and ugly to Copernicus, so he returned to a strong but incorrect belief in uniform circular motion. Therefore, even though his model put the Sun correctly at the centre of the solar system, it could not accurately predict the positions of the planets as seen from Earth. Copernicus even had to reintroduce small epicycles to match minor variations in the motions of the Sun, Moon, and planets. Astronomers today recognize those variations as due to the planets' real motions in elliptical orbits rather than the incorrect circular orbits that Copernicus had assumed.

You should notice the difference between the Copernican model and the Copernican hypothesis. The Copernican *model* is inaccurate. It includes uniform circular motion and thus does not precisely describe the motions of the planets. But the Copernican *hypothesis* that the solar system is heliocentric is correct—the planets do circle the Sun, not Earth. Why that hypothesis gradually won acceptance is a question historians still debate. There are probably a number of reasons, including the revolutionary spirit of the times, but the most important factor may be the simplicity of the idea. For one thing, placing the Sun at the centre of the universe produced a symmetry among the motions of the planets that is elegant, pleasing to the eye and mind (Figure 3.12). In the Ptolemaic model, Mercury and Venus had to be treated differently from the rest of the planets: Their epicycles had to remain centred on the Earth–Sun line. In Copernicus's model, all of the planets were treated the same. They all followed orbits that circled the Sun at the centre.

Although astronomers throughout Europe read and admired *De Revolutionibus* and found Copernicus's astronomical observations and mathematics to have great value, few astronomers believed, at first, that the Sun actually was the centre of the solar system and that Earth moved. How the Copernican hypothesis was gradually recognized as correct has been called the Copernican Revolution, because it was not just the adoption of a new idea but a total change in the way astronomers and the rest of humanity thought about the place of Earth.

The most important consequence of the Copernican hypothesis was not what it said about the Sun but what it said about Earth. By placing the Sun at the centre, Copernicus made Earth move along an orbit like the other planets. By making Earth a planet, Copernicus revolutionized humanity's view of its place in the universe and triggered a controversy that would eventually bring the astronomer Galileo Galilei before the Inquisition, a controversy over the nature of scientific and religious ideas that continues even today.

3.3 Tycho Brahe, Johannes Kepler, and Planetary Motion

As astronomers struggled to understand the place of Earth, they also faced the problem of planetary motion. How exactly do the planets move? That problem was solved by a nobleman who built a fabulous observatory and a poor commoner with a talent for mathematics.

Tycho Brahe

The Danish nobleman Tycho Brahe (pronounced Teekoe Bra) is remembered in part for wearing false noses to hide a duelling scar from his college days (Figure 3.7). He was reportedly very proud of his noble station, so his disfigurement probably did little to improve his lordly disposition.

In 1572, astronomers were startled to see a new star (now called Tycho's supernova) appear in the sky. Aristotle had argued that the heavens were perfect and therefore unchanging, so astronomers concluded that the new star had to be nearer than the Moon. Tycho could not detect the new star's parallax (see p. 50), meaning it had to be far beyond the Moon and this was a change in the supposedly unchanging starry sphere.

When Tycho wrote a book about his discovery, the king of Denmark honoured him with a generous income and the gift of an island, Hveen, where Tycho built a fabulous observatory. Tycho lived before the invention of the telescope, so his observatory was equipped with wonderful instruments for measuring the positions of the Sun, Moon, and planets using the naked eye and peering along sight lines. For 20 years, Tycho and his assistants measured the positions of the stars and planets.

After the death of the Danish king, Tycho Brahe moved to Prague where he became the Imperial Mathematician to the Holy Roman Emperor Rudolph II. Tycho hired a few assistants including a German school teacher named Johannes Kepler (Figure 3.7). Just before Tycho died in 1601, he asked Rudolph II to make Kepler Imperial Mathematician. The newcomer, Kepler, became Tycho's replacement (though at one-sixth Tycho's salary).

Johannes Kepler

No one could have been more different from Tycho Brahe than was Johannes Kepler. He was born in 1571, the oldest of six children in a poor family, and lived in what is now southwest Germany. His father, who fought as a mercenary soldier for whomever could afford his fees, eventually disappeared. Kepler's mother was apparently

Creating New Ways to See Nature: Scientific Revolutions

The Copernican Revolution is often cited as the perfect example of a scientific revolution. Over a few decades, astronomers abandoned a way of thinking about the universe that was almost 2000 years old and adopted a new **paradigm** (pronounced para-dyme), or set of scientific ideas and assumptions. The pre-Copernicus geocentric paradigm survived for many centuries, until a new generation of astronomers overthrew the old paradigm and established a new, heliocentric paradigm.

A scientific paradigm is powerful because it shapes perceptions by determining which questions are important and what evidence is significant. Therefore, it is often difficult to recognize how paradigms limit what you can understand. Though the geocentric paradigm contained problems that seem obvious to a modern mind, ancient astronomers lived and worked inside that paradigm and had difficulty seeing those problems. Overthrowing an existing

paradigm is not easy because you must learn to see nature in an entirely new way.

You can find examples of scientific revolutions in many fields. They have been difficult and controversial because they have involved the overthrow of accepted paradigms, but that is why scientific revolutions are exciting. They give you an entirely new insight into how nature works—a new way of seeing the world.

---

an unpleasant and unpopular woman. She was accused of witchcraft in her later years, and Kepler defended her (successfully) in a trial that dragged on for three years. Kepler himself had poor health, even as a child, so it is surprising that he did well in school, winning promotion to a Latin school and eventually a scholarship to the university at Tübingen, where he studied to become a Lutheran pastor.

While still a college student, Kepler had become a believer in the Copernican hypothesis. During his last year of study, Kepler accepted a teaching job in the town of Graz, in what is now Austria, which allowed him to continue his studies in mathematics and astronomy.

Life was unsettled for Kepler in Graz because of the persecution of Protestants in that region, so when Tycho Brahe invited him to Prague in 1600, Kepler went eagerly, ready to work with the famous astronomer. Tycho's sudden death in 1601 left Kepler in a position to use Tycho's extensive records of observations to analyze the motions of the planets.

Kepler began by studying the motion of Mars, trying to deduce from the observations how the planet actually moved. By 1606, he had solved the mystery: The orbit of Mars is an ellipse, not a circle. Thus, he abandoned

the ancient belief in the circular motion of the planets. But the mystery was even more complex. The planets do not move at uniform speeds along their elliptical orbits. Kepler recognized that they move faster when close to the Sun and slower when farther away, and so he abandoned both uniform motion and circular motion and thereby finally solved the problem of planetary motion. Later he discovered that the period of each planet's orbit is related to that orbit's radius. Kepler published his results in 1609 and 1619 in books called, respectively, *Astronomia Nova* (*New Astronomy*) and *Harmonice Mundi* (*The Harmony of the World*).

Kepler's Three Laws of Planetary Motion

Although Kepler dabbled in the philosophical arguments of the day, he was a mathematician, and his triumph was the solution of the problem of the motion of the planets. The key to his solution was the **ellipse**. An ellipse is a figure drawn around two points, called *foci*, in such a way that the distance from one focus to any point on the ellipse and back to the other focus equals a constant. This makes it easy to draw ellipses with two thumbtacks and a loop of string. Press the thumbtacks into a board, hook the string about the tacks, and place a pencil in the loop. As you can see in Figure 3.13a, if you keep the string taut as you move the pencil, you can trace out an ellipse.

The geometry of an ellipse is described by two simple numbers. The **semi-major axis, *a*,** is half of the longest

paradigm A commonly accepted set of scientific ideas and assumptions.

ellipse A closed curve around two points, called foci, such that the total distance from one focus to the curve and back to the other focus remains constant.

semi-major axis (*a*) Half of the longest diameter of an ellipse.

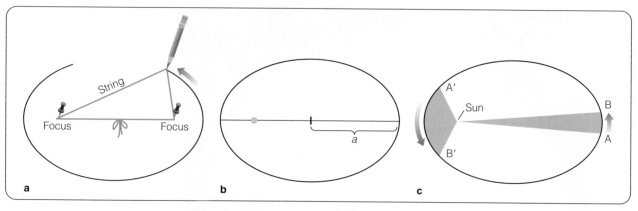

Figure 3.13 The geometry of elliptical orbits. (a) Drawing an ellipse with two tacks and a loop of string. (b) The semi-major axis, *a*, is half of the longest diameter. (c) Kepler's second law is demonstrated by a planet that moves from A to B in one month and from A′ to B′ in the same amount of time. The two blue segments have the same area. Hence the planet is travelling faster in its orbit from A′ to B′ than from A to B.

diameter (Figure 3.13b). The **eccentricity**, *e*, of an ellipse is half the distance between the foci divided by the semi-major axis. The eccentricity of an ellipse tells you about its shape: If *e* is nearly equal to one, the ellipse is very elongated; if *e* is close to zero, the ellipse is more circular. To draw a circle with the string and tacks shown in Figure 3.13a, you would move the two thumbtacks together, which shows that a circle is the same as an ellipse with eccentricity equal to zero. As you move the thumbtacks farther apart, the ellipse becomes flatter and the value of its eccentricity moves closer to 1.

Kepler used ellipses to describe the motion of the planets in three fundamental rules that have been tested and confirmed so many times that astronomers now refer to them as "natural laws." They are commonly called Kepler's laws of planetary motion; these are summarized in Table 3.1.

Kepler's first law states that the orbits of the planets around the Sun are ellipses with the Sun at one focus. Thanks to the precision of Tycho's observations and the sophistication of Kepler's mathematics, Kepler was able to recognize the elliptical shape of the orbits even though they are nearly circular. Of the planets known to Kepler, Mercury has the most elliptical orbit, which you can measure in Figure 3.14 but even it deviates only slightly from a circle.

Kepler's second law states that a line from the planet to the Sun sweeps over equal areas in equal intervals of time. This means that when the planet is closer to the Sun and the line connecting it to the Sun is shorter, the planet moves more rapidly to sweep over the same area that is swept over when the planet is farther from the Sun. For example in Figure 3.14, the planet would move from point *A* to point *B* in one month, sweeping over the area

Table 3.1	Kepler's Laws of Planetary Motion
I.	The orbits of the planets are ellipses with the Sun at one focus.
II.	A line from a planet to the Sun sweeps over equal areas in equal intervals of time.
III.	A planet's orbital period (expressed in years) squared is proportional to its average distance from the Sun (expressed in AU) cubed: $P_y^2 = a_{AU}^3$

shown. But when the planet is farther from the Sun, one month's motion would be shorter, from *A′* to *B′*. The time that a planet takes to travel around the Sun once is its orbital period, *P*, and its average distance from the Sun equals the semi-major axis of its orbit, *a*. Kepler's third law tells us that these two quantities, orbital period and semi-major axis, are related: Orbital period squared is proportional to the semi-major axis cubed. For example, Jupiter's average distance from the Sun (which equals the semi-major axis of its orbit) is 5.2 AU. The semi-major axis cubed would be about 140.6, so the period must be the square root of 140.6, roughly 11.8 years.

It is important to note that Kepler's three laws are **empirical**. That is, they describe a phenomenon based only on observations and without explaining why it occurs. Kepler derived them from Tycho's extensive observations without referring to any first principles, fundamental assumptions, or theory. In fact, Kepler never knew what held the planets in their orbits or why they continued to move around the Sun in the ways he discovered.

eccentricity (e) A number between 1 and 0 that describes the shape of an ellipse (how elongated it is); the distance from one focus to the centre of the ellipse divided by the semi-major axis.

empirical Description of a phenomenon based only on observations and without explaining why it occurs.

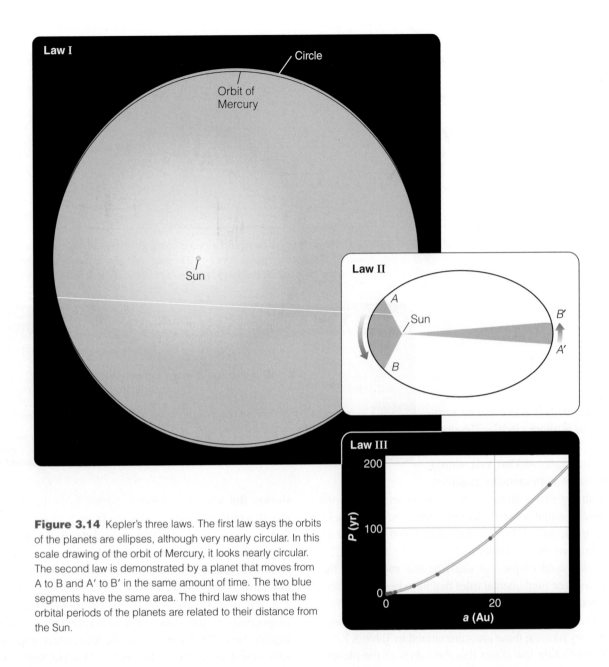

Figure 3.14 Kepler's three laws. The first law says the orbits of the planets are ellipses, although very nearly circular. In this scale drawing of the orbit of Mercury, it looks nearly circular. The second law is demonstrated by a planet that moves from A to B and A′ to B′ in the same amount of time. The two blue segments have the same area. The third law shows that the orbital periods of the planets are related to their distance from the Sun.

3.4 Galileo Galilei

Galileo Galilei was born in the Italian city of Pisa in 1564 and studied medicine at the university there. His true love, however, was mathematics, and he eventually became professor of mathematics at the university at Padua, where he remained for 18 years (Figure 3.15). During this time, Galileo seemed to have adopted the Copernican model, although he admitted in a 1597 letter to Kepler that he did not support that model publicly, fearing criticism.

Most people know two "facts" about Galileo, and both are wrong. Galileo did not invent the telescope, and he was not condemned by the Inquisition for believing that Earth moved around the Sun. As you learn about Galileo, you will discover that what was on trial were not just his opinions about the place of Earth but also the methods of science itself.

Telescopic Observations

It was the telescope that drove Galileo to publicly defend the heliocentric model. Galileo did not invent the

Figure 3.15 Galileo Galilei

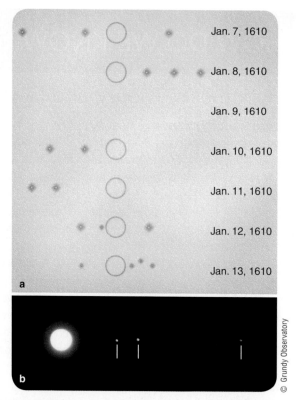

Jan. 7, 1610

Jan. 8, 1610

Jan. 9, 1610

Jan. 10, 1610

Jan. 11, 1610

Jan. 12, 1610

Jan. 13, 1610

a

b

Figure 3.16 (a) On the night of January 7, 1610, Galileo saw three small "stars" near the bright disk of Jupiter and sketched them in his notebook. On subsequent nights (except January 9, which was cloudy), he saw that the stars were actually four moons orbiting Jupiter. (b) This photograph, taken through a modern telescope, shows the overexposed disk of Jupiter and three of the four Galilean moons.

telescope. It was apparently invented around 1608 by lens makers in Holland. Galileo, hearing descriptions in the fall of 1609, was able to build working telescopes in his workshop. Galileo was also not the first person to look at the sky through a telescope, but he was the first person to observe the sky carefully and apply his observations to the main theoretical problem of the day—the place of Earth.

What Galileo saw through his telescopes was so amazing he rushed a small book into print, *Sidereus Nuncius* (*The Starry Messenger*). In that book he reported two major discoveries about the solar system. First, the Moon was not perfect. It had mountains and valleys on its surface, and Galileo used the shadows to calculate the height of the mountains. Aristotle's philosophy held that the Moon was perfect, but Galileo showed that it was not only imperfect but was even a world like Earth. Second, Galileo's telescope revealed four new "planets" circling Jupiter, planets that we know today as the Galilean moons of Jupiter, shown in Figure 3.16.

The moons of Jupiter supported the Copernican model over the Ptolemaic model. Critics of Copernicus had said Earth could not move because the Moon would be left behind; but Jupiter moved and kept its satellites. Galileo's discovery suggested that Earth, too, could move and keep its moon. Also, Aristotle's philosophy

included the belief that all heavenly motion was centred on Earth. Galileo showed that Jupiter's moons revolve around Jupiter, so there could be centres of motion other than Earth. Later, after the *Messenger* was published, Galileo noticed that Jupiter's innermost moon had the shortest orbital period and the moons further from Jupiter had proportionally longer periods. In this way, Jupiter's moons made up a harmonious system ruled by Jupiter, just as the planets in the Copernican universe were a harmonious system ruled by the Sun. This similarity didn't constitute proof, but Galileo saw it as an indication that the solar system could be Sun-centred and not Earth-centred.

In the years of further exploration with his telescope, Galileo made additional fundamental discoveries. When he observed Venus, Galileo saw that it was going through phases like those of the Moon. In the Ptolemaic model, Venus moves around an epicycle centred on a line between Earth and the Sun. If that were true, it

HOW DO WE KNOW? 3.3

Hypothesis, Theory, and Law: Levels of Confidence

A fact is a simple statement that everyone believes. It is innocent, unless found guilty. A hypothesis is a novel suggestion that no one wants to believe. It is guilty, until found effective.

Edward Teller

Even scientists misuse the words *hypothesis, theory,* and *law.* You must try to distinguish these terms from one another because they are key elements in science.

A **hypothesis** is a single assertion or conjecture that can be tested. It could be true or false. "All Canadians love maple syrup" is a hypothesis. To know whether it is true or false, you need to test it against reality by making observations or performing experiments. Copernicus asserted that the universe was heliocentric; his assertion was a hypothesis subject to testing.

In Scientific Models—in Chapter 2, **How Do We Know? 2.1**—you saw that a model is a description of some natural phenomenon; it can't be right or wrong. A model is not a conjecture of truth but merely a convenient way to think about a natural phenomenon. Consequently, a model such as the celestial sphere is not a hypothesis. Copernicus used his hypothesis to build a model, but they are not the same thing.

A **theory** is a system of rules and principles that can be applied to a wide variety of circumstances. A theory may have begun as one or more hypotheses, but it has been tested, expanded, and generalized. Many textbooks refer to the "Copernican theory," but some historians argue that it was not complete and had not been tested enough to be a theory. It is probably better to call it the Copernican hypothesis.

A **natural law** is a theory that has been refined, tested, and confirmed so often that scientists have great confidence in it. Laws are the most fundamental principles of scientific knowledge. Kepler's laws are good examples.

© Semen Barkovskiy/iStockphoto

Confidence is the key to understanding these terms. Scientists have more confidence in a theory than in a hypothesis and great confidence in a natural law. Nevertheless, scientists are not always consistent about these words. For example, Einstein's theory of relativity is much more accurate than Newton's laws of gravity and motion, but traditionally, scientists refer to "Einstein's theories" and "Newton's laws." Darwin's theory of evolution has been tested many times, and scientists have great confidence in it, but no one refers to Darwin's law. These distinctions are subtle and sometimes depend more on custom than on levels of confidence.

---

would always be seen as a crescent, like the model in Figure 3.17a. But Galileo saw Venus go through a complete set of phases, including full and gibbous, which proved that it did indeed revolve around the Sun (Figure 3.17b).

Sidereus Nuncius was popular and made Galileo famous. In 1611, Galileo visited Rome and was treated with great respect. He had friendly discussions with the powerful Cardinal Barberini, but because he was outspoken, forceful, and sometimes tactless he offended other important people who questioned his telescopic discoveries. Some critics said he was wrong, and others said he was lying. Some refused to look through a telescope lest it mislead them, and others looked and claimed to see nothing (hardly surprising given the awkwardness of those first telescopes). When Galileo visited Rome again in 1616, Cardinal Bellarmine interviewed him privately and ordered him to cease public debate about models of the universe, an order Galileo appears to have mostly followed.

The Inquisition banned books relevant to the Copernican hypothesis, although *De Revolutionibus* itself was only suspended pending revision because it was recognized as useful for its predictions of planet

hypothesis A conjecture, subject to further tests, that accounts for a set of facts.

theory A system of assumptions and principles applicable to a wide range of phenomena that has been repeatedly verified.

natural law A theory that has been so well confirmed that it is almost universally accepted as correct.

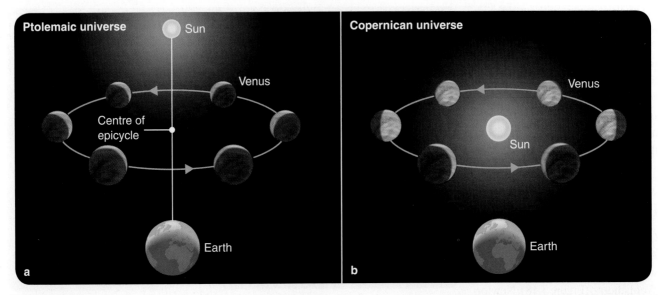

Figure 3.17 (a) If Venus moved in an epicycle centred on the Earth–Sun line, as required by the geocentric model, it would always appear as a crescent. (b) Galileo's telescope showed that Venus goes through a full set of phases, proving that it must orbit the Sun. Note that the Sun, Venus, and Earth lie in the same plane.

positions. Everyone who owned a copy of the book was required to cross out certain statements and add handwritten corrections stating that Earth's motion and the central location of the Sun were only theories and not facts.

Dialogo and Trial

In 1623, Galileo's friend Cardinal Barberini became pope, taking the name Urban VIII. Galileo went to Rome in an attempt to have the 1616 order to cease debate lifted. Although that attempt was unsuccessful, Galileo began to write a massive defence of Copernicus's model, completing it in 1629. After some delay, Galileo's book was approved by both the local censor in Florence and the head censor of the Vatican in Rome. It was printed in 1632.

Called *Dialogo Sopra i Due Massimi Sistemi del Mondo* (*Dialogue Concerning the Two Chief World Systems*), it confronts the ancient astronomy of Aristotle and Ptolemy with the Copernican model. Galileo wrote the book as a debate among three friends. Salviati is a swift-tongued defender of Copernicus; Sagredo is intelligent but largely uninformed; Simplicio is a dim-witted defender of Ptolemy. The book was a clear defence of Copernicus, and, either intentionally or unintentionally, Galileo exposed the pope's authority to ridicule. Urban VIII was fond of arguing that, as God was omnipotent, God could construct the universe in any form while making it appear to humans to have a different form, and

thus its true nature could not be deduced by mere observation. Galileo placed the pope's argument in the mouth of Simplicio. The pope took offence and ordered Galileo to face the Inquisition.

Galileo was interrogated by the Inquisition and possibly threatened with torture. The Inquisition condemned Galileo not primarily for heresy but for disobeying the orders given him in 1616. In 1633, at the age of 70, kneeling before the Inquisition, Galileo read a recantation admitting his errors. Legend has it that as he rose he whispered, *"E pur si muove"* ("Still it moves"), referring to Earth. Although he was sentenced to life imprisonment, he was actually confined at his villa for the next 10 years, perhaps through the intervention of the pope. He died there in 1642, 99 years after the death of Copernicus. Three hundred and fifty years later, in 1992, Pope John Paul II made a formal statement acknowledging the unjust condemnation of Galileo by the Roman Catholic Church.

3.5 Isaac Newton, Gravity, and Orbits

The problem of the place of Earth was resolved by the Copernican Revolution, but the problem of planetary motion was only partly solved by Kepler's laws. It was not known why the planets obeyed Kepler's laws. And how could the Earth move without leaving the Moon behind? For the last 10 years of his life, Galileo studied the nature of motion, especially the accelerated motion of falling bodies. Although he made some important progress, he was not able to relate his discoveries about motion to the heavens. That final step was taken by Isaac Newton.

Isaac Newton

Galileo died in January 1642. Almost a year later, Isaac Newton was born in the English village of Woolsthorpe (Figure 3.18). Newton was a quiet child from a farming family, but his work at school was so impressive that his uncle financed his education at Trinity College Cambridge, where he studied mathematics and physics. In 1665, plague swept through England, and the colleges were closed. During 1665 and 1666, Newton spent his time back home in Woolsthorpe, thinking and studying. It was during these years that he made most of his scientific discoveries. Among other things, he studied optics, developed three laws of motion, probed the nature of gravity, and invented calculus. The publication of his work in his book *Principia* in 1687 placed the fields of physics and astronomy on a new firm base.

It is beyond the scope of this book to analyze all of Newton's work, but his laws of motion and gravity had a huge impact on the future of astronomy. To understand his work, we must begin with a general framework for describing the motion of any object. Position and time specify where and when an object is. **Speed** is the rate at which an object moves (changes position). It is the total distance moved divided by the total time taken to move that distance. For example, if it took you two hours to travel 100 km, your speed was 50 km/h. Although we are used to thinking of speeds in km/h, in science the Standard International (SI) units are metres/second. **Velocity** specifies both speed and direction of travel of an object. For example, if car A moves 60 km east in 2 hours and car B moves 60 km south in 2 hours, they have

Figure 3.18 Sir Isaac Newton

© Jean-Leon Huens/National Geographic Creative

the same speed of 30 km/h, but their velocities are different because they are travelling in different directions. Velocity changes if (a) the speed changes, (b) the direction changes, or (c) both speed and direction change.

Acceleration is the rate of change of velocity with time: the change in velocity divided by the time taken for the change to occur. Since velocity changes if speed changes, speeding up is an example of acceleration, and slowing down is negative acceleration (in a direction opposing the direction of travel), that is, deceleration. On the other hand, velocity also changes if there is a change of direction, so turning is also an example of acceleration.

Newton realized that the motion of all objects is a result of the forces (pulls or pushes) acting on them. He was able to find three universal laws of motion that made it possible to predict exactly how a body would move if the forces acting on it were known (see Table 3.2). Newton's first law of motion states that an object remains at rest or at constant velocity unless a net force acts to change its speed or direction. For example, when your car is at rest or travelling at a constant speed and direction, the forces exerted by the wheels to drive you forward are balanced by the wind resistance and other forces in such a way that the net (total) force is zero. If you wanted to speed up or slow down or change direction, additional force must be applied by pushing on the accelerator or the brake, or by turning the wheel. The effect of this additional force is described by Newton's second law. If the mass (amount of matter) of the object does not change, the acceleration is proportional to the force exerted. Hence, if you want

speed The rate at which an object moves (changes position); the total distance moved divided by the total time taken to move that distance.

velocity Both the speed and direction of travel of an object.

acceleration The rate of change of velocity with time.

Table 3.2	Newton's Three Laws of Motion
I.	An object continues at rest or in uniform motion in a straight line unless acted upon by some force.
II.	An object's change of motion is proportional to the force acting on it, and is in the direction of the force.
III.	When one body exerts a force on a second body, the second body exerts an equal and opposite force back on the first body.

to double your acceleration the applied force must be doubled.

An example of acceleration that we are all familiar with is the acceleration due to gravity. All falling objects on Earth have a constant acceleration downward toward the centre of Earth. This acceleration was first pointed out by Galileo. The acceleration due to gravity, *g*, is 9.8 metres per second per second, more commonly written as 9.8 m/s². This means that if you drop any object, say an apple, from rest, its speed will increase by roughly 10 m/s with each second of falling, if one ignores air resistance. After the first second its speed will be roughly 10 m/s; after two seconds its speed will be 20 m/s, and so on until it crashes into the ground. Conversely, if you throw the apple into the air, there is still a constant acceleration of 9.8 m/s² downward. Hence, the speed of the apple will *decrease* by roughly 10 m/s every second until it comes to a standstill, at which point it will start falling back toward the ground with its speed increasing by 10 m/s every second.

The Universal Theory of Gravitation

When Newton thought carefully about motion, he realized that some force must pull the Moon toward Earth's centre. If there were no such force altering the Moon's motion, it would continue moving in a straight line and leave Earth forever. It can circle Earth only if Earth pulls on it. Newton's insight was to recognize that the force that holds the Moon in its orbit is the same force of gravity that makes apples and all other objects fall to the ground on Earth.

Newtonian gravitation is sometimes called universal mutual gravitation. Newton's third law points out that forces occur in pairs. If one body attracts another, the second body must also attract the first. Thus, gravitation is mutual. Furthermore, gravity is universal. That is, all objects with mass attract all other masses in the universe. The **mass** of an object is a measure of the amount of matter or "stuff" in the object, usually expressed in kilograms.

You may be used to thinking of "massive" objects as very large objects. However, in science massive objects are those that contain a lot of matter. They may or may not be large. For example, a two-centimetre ball of lead is more massive than a large balloon full of air. In everyday life, the terms mass and weight are used interchangeably. When you report your weight at the doctor's office as 60 kg you are actually reporting your mass. In science, mass is not the same as **weight**. Mass is an intrinsic property of an object and is the same no matter what forces are acting on an object. An object's weight is the force that gravity exerts on the object. An object in space far from Earth's gravitational force would have no weight, but it would contain the same amount of matter and would have the same mass that it has on Earth.

Newton found that the gravitational force of attraction between two objects is directly proportional to the product of the masses of the two objects. For example, doubling one of the masses would double the gravitational force, and doubling both masses would quadruple the force. Newton also realized that the distance between the objects is important. In other words, the gravitational force between two bodies depends not only on the masses of the bodies but also on the distance between them. He recognized that the force of gravity decreases as the square of the distance between the objects increases. Specifically, if the distance from, say, Earth to the Moon were doubled, the gravitational force between them would decrease by a factor of 2², or 4. If the distance were tripled, the force would decrease by a factor of 3², or 9. This relationship is known as the **inverse square relation**. Newton guessed that gravity works by an inverse square relation because he had already discovered that light behaves this way (discussed in detail in Chapter 6).

To summarize, Newton's universal law of gravitation states that the force of gravity attracting two objects to each other equals a constant times the product of their masses divided by the square of the distance between the objects. Gravity is universal: Your mass affects the planet Neptune and the galaxy M31, and every other object in

mass A measure of the amount of matter making up an object.

weight The force that gravity exerts on an object.

inverse square relation A rule that the strength of an effect (such as gravity) decreases in proportion as the distance squared increases.

the universe, and their masses affect you—although not much, because they are so far away and your mass is relatively very small. (Refer to **Laws of Motion and Gravitation** in the Math Reference Cards.)

Orbital Motion

Newton's laws of motion and gravitation make it possible for you to understand why and how the Moon orbits Earth and the planets orbit the Sun, and to discover why Kepler's laws work. To understand how an object can orbit another object, you need to see orbital motion as Newton did. Begin by studying **Visualizing Astronomy 3.2, Orbiting Earth,** and notice three important ideas:

1. An object orbiting Earth, and any orbiting object, is actually falling (being accelerated due to gravitational force) toward Earth's centre. An object in a stable orbit continuously misses Earth because of its horizontal velocity.

2. Objects orbiting each other actually revolve around their mutual centre of mass.

3. Notice the difference between closed orbits and open orbits. If you want to leave Earth never to return, you must give your spaceship a high enough velocity so it will follow an open orbit.

When the captain of a spaceship says to the pilot, "Put us into a circular orbit," the ship's computers must quickly calculate the velocity needed to achieve a circular orbit. That circular velocity depends only on the mass of the planet and the distance from the centre of the planet. Once the engines fire and the ship reaches circular velocity, the engines can shut down. The ship is in orbit and will fall around the planet forever, as long as it is above the atmosphere's friction. No further effort is needed to maintain orbit, in keeping with the laws Newton discovered. (Refer to **Circular Velocity** in the Math Reference Cards.)

Newton's laws of motion and his universal theory of gravitation enabled him to explain Kepler's laws of planetary motion. Kepler's first law—that the planets move in elliptical orbits—is a direct result of the inverse square law of gravitation. Newton proved that any object moving in a closed orbit according to the inverse square law must follow an elliptical path. Furthermore, just like the spaceship in stable orbit around Earth, the planets, the Moon, and all objects in the universe will remain on their respective paths forever unless an external force (such as a collision with another object) acts on them.

Newton's law of gravitation also explains Kepler's second law, which states that planets move faster when they are closer to the Sun in their orbits (see Table 3.1). To understand this, you must first understand that a measure of a planet's rotational motion is its angular momentum, which is proportional to its velocity and its distance from the Sun. As a result of Newton's laws, in the absence of additional rotational forces the total angular momentum of a planet is conserved (remains constant). When a planet's distance from the Sun increases, it moves slower to balance out the increased distance, and vice versa, to keep the angular momentum constant. The change in motion with distance from the Sun results in equal areas being swept out by the planet in equal amounts of time, as described in Kepler's second law (see Figure 3.13). You can observe the conservation of angular momentum for yourself by watching an ice skater spinning on the ice. She can increase or decrease how fast she rotates by pulling her arms in or spreading them out and in this way she increases or decreases her "distance" from her axis of rotation.

Newton was also able to combine his laws of motion with the law of gravitation to derive a relationship between a planet's orbital period and its average distance from the Sun, which was identical to Kepler's third law. You can now understand the power of Newton's work. He was able to explain all the patterns of planetary motion observed by Kepler by using very simple and universal rules. But this was not all. Gravity is also the key to understanding another critical phenomenon on Earth: ocean tides.

Tides: Gravity in Action

Newton understood that gravity is mutual—Earth attracts the Moon, and the Moon attracts Earth—and that means the Moon's gravity can explain the ocean tides. But Newton also realized that gravitation is universal, and that means there is much more to tides than simply Earth's oceans.

Tides are caused by small differences in gravitational force. As Earth and the Moon orbit around each other, they attract each other gravitationally. Because the side of Earth toward the Moon is a bit closer, the Moon pulls on it more strongly and that pulls up a bulge. Also, the Moon pulls on the near side of Earth a bit more than it pulls on Earth's far side and that produces a bulge on the far side (Figure 3.19). The oceans are deeper in these bulges, and as Earth rotates and carries you into a bulge,

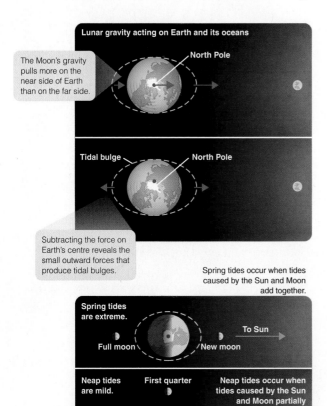

Lunar gravity acting on Earth and its oceans

North Pole

The Moon's gravity pulls more on the near side of Earth than on the far side.

Tidal bulge   North Pole

Subtracting the force on Earth's centre reveals the small outward forces that produce tidal bulges.

Spring tides occur when tides caused by the Sun and Moon add together.

Spring tides are extreme.

Full moon   New moon   To Sun

Neap tides are mild.   First quarter   Neap tides occur when tides caused by the Sun and Moon partially cancel out.

To Sun

Third quarter   Diagrams not to scale

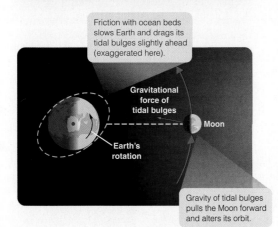

Friction with ocean beds slows Earth and drags its tidal bulges slightly ahead (exaggerated here).

Gravitational force of tidal bulges

Moon

Earth's rotation

Gravity of tidal bulges pulls the Moon forward and alters its orbit.

Figure 3.19 Tides are produced by small differences in the gravitational force exerted on different parts of an object. The side of Earth nearest the Moon feels a larger force than the side farthest away. Relative to Earth's centre, small forces are left over, and they cause the tides. Both the Moon and the Sun produce tides on Earth. Tides can alter both an object's rotation and orbital motion.

you see the tide creeping up the beach. Because there are two bulges, there are two high tides each day, although the exact pattern of tides at any given locality depends on details such as ocean currents, the shape of the shore, and so on.

The Sun also produces tides on Earth, although they are smaller than lunar tides. At new and full moons, the lunar and solar tides add together to produce extra high and extra low tides that are called **spring tides**. At first- and third-quarter moons, the solar tides cancel out part of the lunar tides so that high and low tides are not extreme (see Figure 3.19). These are called **neap tides**.

Whereas the oceans flow easily into tidal bulges, the nearly rigid bulk of Earth flexes into tidal bulges, and the plains and mountains rise and fall a few centimetres twice a day. Friction is gradually slowing Earth's rotation, and fossil evidence shows that Earth used to rotate faster. In the same way, Earth's gravity produces tidal bulges in the Moon, and, although the Moon used to rotate faster, friction has slowed it down, and it now keeps the same side facing Earth.

Tides can also affect orbits. The rotation of Earth drags the tidal bulges slightly ahead of the Moon, and the gravitation of the bulges of water pull the Moon forward in its orbit. This makes the Moon's orbit grow larger by about 4 cm a year, an effect that astronomers can measure by bouncing lasers off reflectors left on the Moon by the Apollo astronauts.

Newton's Universe

Newton's insights gave the world a new conception of nature. His laws of motion were *general* laws that described the motions of *all* bodies under the action of external forces. Just imagine: A few simple laws that can explain how your car accelerates, how the Canadian hockey team manoeuvres on ice, and even how the planets move! And furthermore, Newton's laws and the theory of gravitation allow us to break the bonds of Earth and the solar system and understand the motion of all objects in the universe. As you will see in later chapters, we can detect planets around other stars by observing the motion of the star as it gravitationally interacts with any planets orbiting it. We can calculate the mass of these new planets using the law of gravitation. Indeed, this has been used to calculate the mass of Earth and all other planets, and the Sun. We can even detect

spring tide Ocean tide of large range that occurs at full and new moon.

neap tide Ocean tide of small range occurring at first- and third-quarter moon.

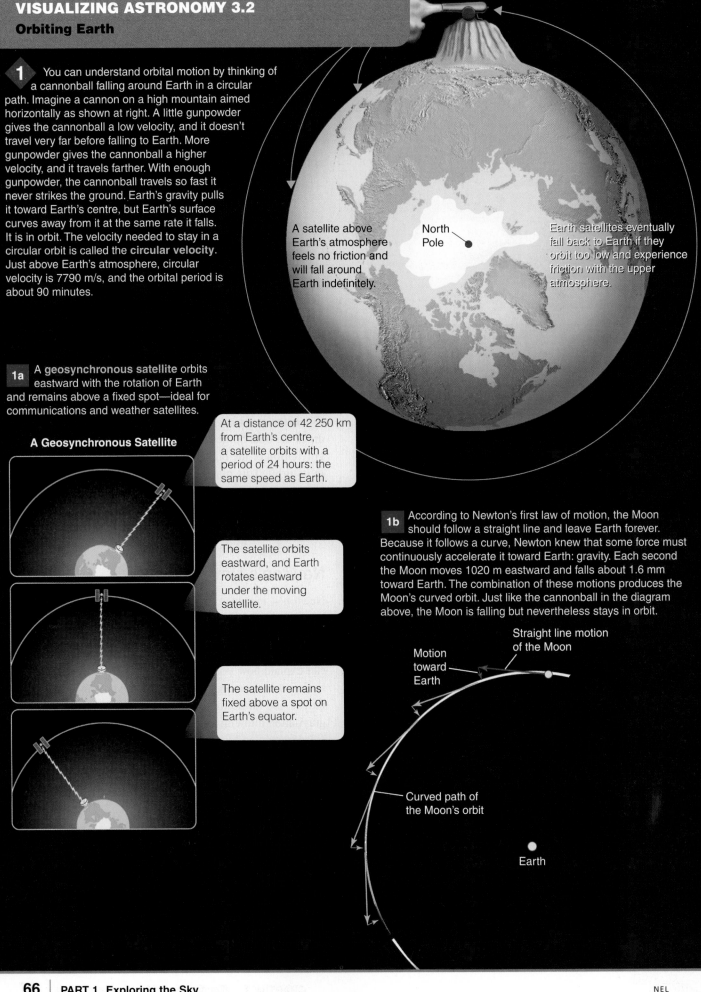

1 You can understand orbital motion by thinking of a cannonball falling around Earth in a circular path. Imagine a cannon on a high mountain aimed horizontally as shown at right. A little gunpowder gives the cannonball a low velocity, and it doesn't travel very far before falling to Earth. More gunpowder gives the cannonball a higher velocity, and it travels farther. With enough gunpowder, the cannonball travels so fast it never strikes the ground. Earth's gravity pulls it toward Earth's centre, but Earth's surface curves away from it at the same rate it falls. It is in orbit. The velocity needed to stay in a circular orbit is called the **circular velocity**. Just above Earth's atmosphere, circular velocity is 7790 m/s, and the orbital period is about 90 minutes.

A satellite above Earth's atmosphere feels no friction and will fall around Earth indefinitely.

North Pole

Earth satellites eventually fall back to Earth if they orbit too low and experience friction with the upper atmosphere.

1a A **geosynchronous satellite** orbits eastward with the rotation of Earth and remains above a fixed spot—ideal for communications and weather satellites.

A Geosynchronous Satellite

At a distance of 42 250 km from Earth's centre, a satellite orbits with a period of 24 hours: the same speed as Earth.

The satellite orbits eastward, and Earth rotates eastward under the moving satellite.

The satellite remains fixed above a spot on Earth's equator.

1b According to Newton's first law of motion, the Moon should follow a straight line and leave Earth forever. Because it follows a curve, Newton knew that some force must continuously accelerate it toward Earth: gravity. Each second the Moon moves 1020 m eastward and falls about 1.6 mm toward Earth. The combination of these motions produces the Moon's curved orbit. Just like the cannonball in the diagram above, the Moon is falling but nevertheless stays in orbit.

Motion toward Earth

Straight line motion of the Moon

Curved path of the Moon's orbit

Earth

n orbit around Earth feel weightless, but they are not "beyond
ity," to use a term from old science fiction movies. Like the Moon,
e accelerated toward Earth by Earth's gravity, but they travel fast
ir orbits that they continually "miss Earth." They are literally falling
ide or outside a spacecraft, astronauts feel weightless because
acecraft are falling at the same rate. Rather than saying they are
hould more accurately say they are in free fall.

cise you should not say that an object orbits Earth. Rather
jects orbit each other. Gravitation is mutual, and if Earth pulls
Moon pulls on Earth. The two bodies revolve around
ntre of mass, the balance point of the system.

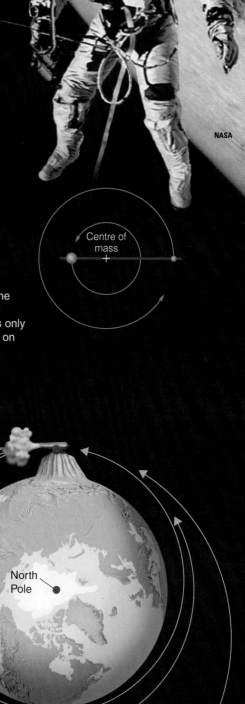

NASA

Centre of
mass

s of different mass balance at the centre of mass, which is located closer to the
sive object. As the two objects orbit each other, they revolve around their
f mass as shown at right. The centre of mass of the Earth–Moon system lies only
e centre of Earth, that is, inside Earth. As the Moon orbits the centre of mass on
wings around the centre of mass on the opposite side.

rbits return the orbiting object to its
t. The Moon and artificial satellites
ed orbits. Below, the cannonball
liptical or a circular closed
nball travels as fast as **escape velocity**,
ed to leave a body, it will enter an
en orbit does not return
Earth.

Hyberbola

A cannonball with a
velocity greater than
escape velocity will
follow a hyperbola and
escape from Earth.

Parabola

A cannonball
with escape
velocity will follow
a parabola and
escape.

North
Pole

Ellipse

Circle

Ellipse

epler's laws describing elliptical
nets around the Sun, an object
it around Earth has its lowest
s farthest from Earth (apogee),
elocity when it is closest to
Perigee must be above Earth's
iction will rob the satellite of
eventually fall back to Earth.

HOW DO WE KNOW? **3.4**

Testing a Theory by Prediction

When you read about any science, notice that scientific theories face in two directions. They look back into the past and explain previously observed phenomena. For example, Newton's laws of motion and gravity explained how the planets moved. But theories also face forward in that they enable you to make predictions about what you should find as you explore further. Newton's laws allowed astronomers to calculate the orbits of comets, predict their return, and eventually understand their origin.

Scientific predictions are important in two ways. First, if a theory leads to a prediction and scientists later discover the prediction was true, the theory is confirmed, and scientists gain confidence that it is a true description of nature. But predictions are important in science in a second way. Using an existing theory to make a prediction may lead you into an unexplored avenue of knowledge. For example, the first theories of genetics made predictions that confirmed the genetic theory of inheritance, but those predictions also created a new understanding of how living creatures evolve.

As you read about any scientific theory, think about both what it can explain and what it can predict.

black holes at the centre of galaxies by observing the motion of objects around it.

The story of the development of astronomy that you have just read is also the story of the development of the scientific method. Ancient astronomers began the process by carefully gathering and recording data. Gradually, models were developed that best fit the data and over time they were tested against observations and discarded if necessary. Good scientific theories are those that can make a broad range of predictions that can be confirmed against observations, and that can provide new insight into nature. Science and astronomy today progress through the careful application of this method of studying nature. As the Nobel Prize-winning physicist Sir William Lawrence Bragg said, "The important thing in science is not so much to obtain new facts as to discover new ways of thinking about them." Sometimes this requires a huge leap of imagination and a questioning of our most strongly held beliefs. The shift from the geocentric to the heliocentric viewpoint was a harsh lesson in humility for humanity. Earth became merely another planet orbiting the Sun. But this first revolution of thought started us on a fantastic journey of scientific discovery. The efforts of Newton and his predecessors, all the way back to our ancient ancestors, opened the door to our modern way of scientific thinking and our current understanding of the universe.

The **Big Picture**

Astronomy is one of the oldest and most universally practised sciences. Ancient civilizations all over the world observed the Sun, the Moon, and the stars for timekeeping, for agricultural planning, for religious and ceremonial purposes, and for navigation. Early models of the universe placed Earth in a special place, at rest in the centre of the universe. Based on observations and preliminary hypotheses of previous astronomers, Copernicus proposed a heliocentric model of the universe. Copernican Theory stimulated people to see Earth and humanity as part of an elegant and complex universe.

We are not in a special place ruled by mysterious planetary forces: Kepler showed that the planets move according to simple rules. Newton found laws that account for the fall of an apple, the ocean tides, and orbital motion. Earth, the Sun, and all of humanity are part of a universe whose motions can be described by a few fundamental laws of motion and gravity. And those simple rules open the universe to scientific study. Astronomy tells us that we are special because we can study the universe and eventually understand what we are.

Review and Discussion Questions

Review Questions

1. What did ancient astronomers observe, and how did it affect their society?
2. Why did Greek astronomers conclude that the heavens were made up of perfect spheres moving at constant speeds?
3. Why did early astronomers conclude that Earth had to be motionless?
4. How did the Ptolemaic model explain retrograde motion?
5. In what ways were the models of Ptolemy and Copernicus similar?
6. Why did the Copernican hypothesis win gradual acceptance?
7. Explain how Kepler's laws contradict uniform circular motion.
8. How do a hypothesis, a theory, and a law differ?
9. Review Galileo's telescopic discoveries and explain why they supported the Copernican model and contradicted the Ptolemaic model.
10. Explain why you might describe the orbital motion of the Moon with the statement, "The Moon is falling."
11. If you lived on Mars, which planets would describe retrograde loops? Which would always be seen near the Sun? Which would never be visible as crescent phases?
12. **How Do We Know?** How does a paradigm affect the questions you ask and the answers you find acceptable?
13. **How Do We Know?** How would you respond to someone who said, "Oh, that's only a theory."
14. **How Do We Know?** Why would it be appropriate to refer to evidence as the "reality checks" in science?

Discussion Questions

1. Science historian Thomas Kuhn has said that *De Revolutionibus* was a revolution-making book but not a revolutionary book. How was it classical and conservative?

Learning to Look

1. What three astronomical objects are represented on this excerpted image from a postage stamp? What are the two rings?

2. Why can the object shown below be bolted in place and used 24 hours a day without adjustment?

3. Why is it a bit misleading to say that this astronaut is weightless?

STUDY **TOOLS**

IN THE BOOK
- Tear out the Review Card for Chapter 3

ONLINE

Visit CENGAGENOW™ for ASTRO, 2Ce at www.nelson.com/student

- eBook
- Interactive Quizzing
- Animations
- Tutorials

4

Astronomical Telescopes and Instruments: Extending Humanity's Vision

GUIDEPOST

In earlier chapters, you looked at the sky the way ancient astronomers did, with the unaided eye, and had a glimpse through Galileo's telescope, which revealed wonderful things about the Moon, Jupiter, and Venus. Now you can study the telescopes, instruments, and techniques of the modern astronomer. Astronomy is almost entirely an observational science. Astronomers cannot visit distant galaxies and far-off worlds, so they must observe celestial objects using astronomical telescopes.

This chapter will help you answer the following questions:

- **What is light?**
- **How do telescopes work? What are their capabilities and limitations?**
- **How are observatories built, and how are good locations chosen for them?**
- **What kinds of instruments and techniques do astronomers use to record and analyze light?**
- **Why do astronomers sometimes use X-ray, ultraviolet, and infrared telescopes, and why must these types of telescopes operate in the upper atmosphere or in orbit?**

Light is a treasure that links us to the sky. An astronomer's quest is to gather as much light as possible from the Moon, the Sun, planets, stars, and galaxies in order to extract information about their natures. Telescopes, which gather and focus light for analysis, can help do that. Nearly all the interesting objects in the sky are very faint sources of light, so large

Everyone should have their mind blown once a day.
Neil DeGrasse Tyson,
Astrophysicist and science communicator

Long-exposure photograph showing star trails above the Canada-France-Hawaii telescope on the summit of Mauna Kea volcano, Big Island, Hawaii

telescopes like the one in Figure 4.1 are built to collect the greatest amount of light possible. This chapter's discussion of astronomical research concentrates on large telescopes and the special instruments and techniques used to analyze light. A normal telescope gathers visible light, but visible light is only one type of radiation arriving here from distant objects. Astronomers can extract information from other forms of radiation by using other types of telescopes. Radio telescopes, for example, give an entirely different view of the sky. Some of these specialized telescopes can be used from Earth's surface, but others must be placed high in Earth's atmosphere or even above it.

4.1 Radiation: Information from Space

Modern astronomers analyze light using sophisticated instruments and techniques to investigate the compositions, motions, internal processes, and evolution of celestial objects. To understand this, you need to learn about the nature of light.

Light as a Wave and as a Particle

Have you ever noticed the colours in a soap bubble? If so, you have seen one effect of light behaving as a wave. When that same light enters the light meter on a camera, it behaves as a particle. How light behaves depends on how you treat it—light has both wavelike and particle-like properties. Sound is another type of wave that you have already experienced. Sound waves are air pressure disturbances that travel through the air from a source to the ear. Sound requires a solid, liquid, or gas medium to carry it; so, for example, in space outside a spacecraft, there can be no

electromagnetic radiation Changing electric and magnetic fields that travel through space and transfer energy from one place to another; examples are light or radio waves.

wavelength The distance between successive peaks or troughs of a wave, usually represented by a lowercase Greek lambda, λ.

Figure 4.1 The northern Gemini telescope in Mauna Kea, Hawaii, stands over 19 m high when pointed straight up.

sound. In contrast, light is composed of a combination of electric and magnetic waves that can travel through empty space. Unlike sound, light waves do not require a medium and thus can travel through a vacuum.

Because light is made up of both electric and magnetic fields, it is referred to as **electromagnetic radiation**. Visible light is only one form of electromagnetic radiation. Electromagnetic radiation is a wave phenomenon—that is, it is associated with a periodically repeating disturbance (a wave) that carries energy. Imagine waves in water: If you disturb a pool of water, waves spread across the surface. Now imagine placing a ruler parallel to the travel direction of the wave. The distance between peaks is the **wavelength**. (Refer to **Wave Properties** in the Math Reference Cards.) The changing electric and magnetic fields of electromagnetic waves travel through space at about 300 000 kilometres per second. This is commonly referred to as the speed of light, but it is the speed of all electromagnetic radiation.

It may seem odd to use the word *radiation* when talking about light, but radiation really refers to anything that spreads outward from a source. Light radiates from a source, so you can correctly refer to light as a form of radiation.

The Electromagnetic Spectrum

The electromagnetic spectrum is simply the types of electromagnetic radiation arranged in order of increasing wavelength. Rainbows are spectra (plural) of visible light. The colours of visible light have different wavelengths: Red has the longest wavelength and violet the shortest, as shown in the visible spectrum at the top of Figure 4.2.

The average wavelength of visible light is about 0.0005 mm. Fifty light waves would fit end-to-end across the thickness of a sheet of paper. It is too awkward to measure such short distances in millimetres, so physicists and astronomers describe the wavelength of light using either the unit of the nanometre (nm), one-billionth of a metre (10^{-9} m), or the angstrom (Å), equal to 10^{-10} m or 0.1 nm.

The wavelength of visible light ranges between about 400 nm and 700 nm, or, equivalently, 4000 Å and 7000 Å. Infrared astronomers often refer to wavelengths using units of microns (10^{-6} m), while radio astronomers use millimetres, centimetres, or metres. Figure 4.2 shows how the visible spectrum makes up only a small part of the electromagnetic spectrum.

Beyond the red end of the visible range lies **infrared (IR)** radiation, with wavelengths ranging from 700 nm to about 1 mm. Your eyes are not sensitive to this radiation, but your skin can sense some of it as heat. A heat lamp is nothing more than a bulb that gives off large amounts of infrared radiation. English astronomer William Herschel discovered infrared radiation—and, thus, discovered that there is such a thing as invisible light (Figure 4.3).

infrared (IR) The portion of the electromagnetic spectrum with wavelengths longer than red light, ranging from 700 nm to about 1 mm, between visible light and radio waves.

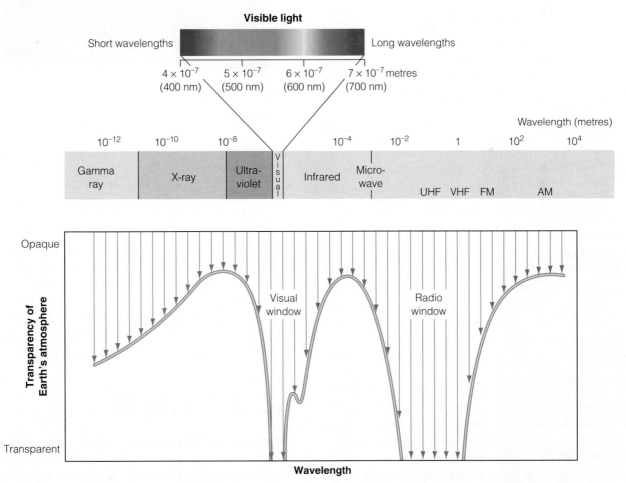

Figure 4.2 The spectrum of visible light, extending from red to violet, is only part of the electromagnetic spectrum. The lower panel shows that most radiation is absorbed in Earth's atmosphere, and only radiation with certain wavelengths, such as the visual and radio windows, can easily reach Earth's surface.

Radio waves have even longer wavelengths than IR radiation. The radio radiation used for AM radio transmissions has wavelengths of a few hundred metres, while FM, television, and also military, governmental, and amateur radio transmissions have wavelengths from a few tens of centimetres to a few tens of metres. Microwave transmissions, used for radar and long-distance telephone communications, have wavelengths from about 1 millimetre to a few centimetres.

Look at the electromagnetic spectrum in Figure 4.2 and notice that electromagnetic waves with wavelengths shorter than violet light are called **ultraviolet (UV)**. Electromagnetic waves with wavelengths shorter than UV light are called **X-rays**, and the shortest are **gamma rays**.

The distinction between these wavelength ranges is mostly arbitrary—they are simply convenient human-invented labels. For example, the longest-wavelength infrared radiation and the shortest-wavelength microwaves are the same. Similarly, very short-wavelength ultraviolet light can be considered X-rays. Nonetheless, it is all electromagnetic radiation, and you could say we are "making light" of it all, because all these types of radiation are the same phenomenon as light: Some types your eyes can see, and some types your eyes can't see.

Although light behaves as a wave, under certain conditions it also behaves as a particle. A particle of light is called a **photon**, and you can think of a photon as a bundle of electromagnetic waves. The amount of energy a photon carries depends on the wavelength of a light wave. (Refer to

ultraviolet (UV) The portion of the electromagnetic spectrum with wavelengths shorter than violet light, between visible light and X-rays.

X-rays Electromagnetic waves with wavelengths shorter than ultraviolet light.

gamma rays The shortest-wavelength electromagnetic waves.

photon A quantum of electromagnetic energy that carries an amount of energy that increases proportionally with its frequency, but decreases proportionally with its wavelength.

atmospheric window Wavelength region in which our atmosphere is transparent—at visual, radio, and some infrared wavelengths.

Wave Properties in the Math Reference Cards.) Shorter-wavelength photons carry more energy, and longer-wavelength photons carry less energy. A photon of visible light carries a small amount of energy, but an X-ray photon carries much more energy, and a radio photon carries much less.

Astronomers are interested in electromagnetic radiation because it carries almost all available clues to the nature of planets, stars, and other celestial objects. Earth's atmosphere is opaque to most electromagnetic radiation, as shown by the graph at the bottom of Figure 4.2. Gamma rays, X-rays, and

Figure 4.3 Depiction of Sir William Herschel, a German musician who lived in England in the 1800s. Herschel, interested in astronomy, made many advances in telescope mirrors and discovered that sunlight contained radiation that's detectable by thermometers but not by human eyes. He named that invisible light "infrared," meaning "below red." After discovering the planet Uranus, he became one of the leading English astronomers.

some radio waves are absorbed high in Earth's atmosphere, and a layer of ozone (O_3) at an altitude of about 30 km absorbs almost all UV radiation. Water vapour in the lower atmosphere absorbs long-wavelength IR radiation. Only visible light, some short-wavelength infrared radiation, and some radio waves reach Earth's surface through what are called **atmospheric windows**. To study the sky from Earth's surface, you must look out through one of these "windows" in the electromagnetic spectrum.

4.2 Telescopes

Astronomers build optical telescopes to gather light and focus it into sharp images. This requires careful optical and mechanical designs, and it leads astronomers to build very large telescopes. To understand that, you need to learn the terminology of telescopes, starting with the different types of telescopes and why some are better than others.

Two Kinds of Telescopes

Astronomical telescopes focus light into an image in one of two ways: either (1) a lens bends (refracts) the light as it passes through the glass and brings it to a focus to form an image, or (2) a mirror—a curved piece of glass with a reflective surface—forms an image by bouncing light. Figure 4.4 demonstrates the difference between the two configurations. Because there are two ways to focus light, there are two types of astronomical telescopes. **Refracting telescopes** use a lens to gather and focus the light, whereas **reflecting telescopes** use a mirror.

The main lens in a refracting telescope is called the **primary lens**, and the main mirror in a reflecting telescope is called the **primary mirror**. Both kinds of telescopes form a small, inverted image that is difficult to observe directly, so a lens called the **eyepiece** is used to magnify the image and make it convenient to view. The **focal length** is the distance from a lens or mirror to the image it forms of a distant light source such as a star. Creating the proper optical shape to produce a good focus

is an expensive process. The surfaces of lenses and mirrors must be shaped and polished to have no irregularities larger than the wavelength of light. Creating the optics for a large telescope can take months or years, involve huge precision machinery, and employ several expert optical engineers and scientists.

Refracting telescopes have serious disadvantages: They suffer from an optical distortion as a result of which you see a colour blur around every image; the glass in primary lenses must be pure and flawless because the light passes all the way through it; and the weight of the lens can be supported only around its outer edge. In contrast, light reflects from the front surface of a reflecting telescope's primary mirror but does not pass through it. Mirrors are less expensive to make than similarly sized lenses and the weight of telescope mirrors can be supported easily. For these reasons, every large astronomical telescope built since 1900 has been a reflecting telescope.

Optical telescopes gather visible light, but astronomers also build **radio telescopes** to gather radio radiation. Radio waves from celestial objects, such as visible light waves, penetrate Earth's atmosphere and reach the ground. You can see in Figure 4.5 how the dish reflector of a typical radio telescope focuses the radio waves so their intensity can be measured. Because radio wavelengths are so long, the disk reflector does not have to be as perfectly smooth as the mirror of a reflecting optical telescope.

refracting telescope A telescope that forms images by bending (refracting) light with a lens.

reflecting telescope A telescope that forms images by reflecting light with a mirror.

primary lens In a refracting telescope, the largest lens.

primary mirror In a reflecting telescope, the largest mirror.

eyepiece A short-focal-length lens used to enlarge the image in a telescope; the lens nearest the eye.

focal length The focal length of a lens or mirror is the distance from that lens or mirror to the point where it focuses parallel rays of light.

optical telescope Telescope that gathers visible light.

radio telescope Telescope that gathers radio radiation.

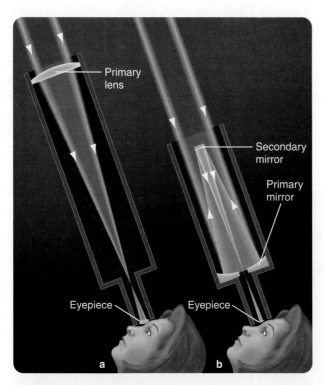

Figure 4.4 (a) A refracting telescope uses a primary lens to focus starlight into an image that is magnified by another lens called an eyepiece. The primary lens has a long focal length, and the eyepiece has a short focal length. (b) A reflecting telescope uses a primary mirror to focus the light by reflection. In this particular reflector design, called a Cassegrain telescope, a small secondary mirror reflects the starlight back down through a hole in the middle of the primary mirror to the eyepiece lens.

The Powers of a Telescope

Astronomers struggle to build large telescopes because a telescope can help human eyes in three important ways: light gathering, resolving, and magnifying power. These are called the three powers of a telescope. The two most important of these three powers depend on the diameter of the telescope. (Refer to **The Powers of a Telescope** in the Math Reference Cards).

Figure 4.5 In most radio telescopes, a dish reflector concentrates the radio signal on the antenna. The signal is then amplified and recorded. For all but the shortest radio waves, wire mesh is an adequate reflector.

Courtesy Seth Shostak/SETI Institute

Most celestial objects of interest to astronomers are faint, so you need a telescope that can gather large amounts of light to produce a bright image. **Light-gathering power** refers to the ability of a telescope to collect light. Catching light in a telescope is like catching rain in a bucket—the bigger the bucket, the more rain it catches. The light-gathering power is proportional to the *area* of the primary mirror, that is, proportional to the square of the primary's diameter. A telescope with a diameter of 2 m has four times the light-gathering power of a 1-m telescope. That is why astronomers use large telescopes and why telescopes are ranked by their diameters. One reason why radio astronomers build big radio dishes is to collect enough radio photons, which have low energies, and concentrate them for measurement.

The **resolving power** refers to the ability of the telescope to reveal fine detail. One consequence of the wavelike nature of light is that there is an inevitable small blurring, called a **diffraction fringe**, around every point of light in the image, and you cannot see any detail smaller than the fringe (Figure 4.6). Astronomers can't eliminate diffraction fringes, but the fringes are smaller in larger telescopes, and that means they have better resolving power and can reveal finer detail (see **How Do We Know? 4.1**). For example, a 2-m telescope has diffraction fringes half as large and therefore two times better resolving power than a 1-m telescope. The size of the diffraction fringes also depends on wavelength, and at the long wavelengths of radio waves, the fringes are large and the resolving power is poor. That's another reason radio telescopes need to be larger than optical telescopes.

One way to improve resolving power is to connect two or more telescopes in an **interferometer**, which has a resolving power equal to that of a telescope as large as the maximum separation between the individual telescopes (Figure 4.7a). The first interferometer was built with Canadian radio telescopes kilometres apart (Figure 4.7b).

light-gathering power The ability of a telescope to collect light; proportional to the area of the telescope's objective lens or mirror.

resolving power The ability of a telescope to reveal fine detail; depends on the diameter of the telescope objective.

diffraction fringe Blurred fringe surrounding any image, caused by the wave properties of light. Because of this, no image detail smaller than the fringe can be seen.

interferometer Separated telescopes combined to produce a virtual telescope with the resolution of a much larger-diameter telescope.

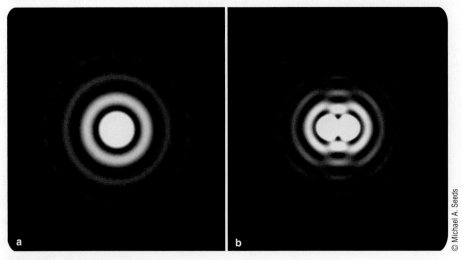

Figure 4.6 (a) Stars are so far away that their images are points, but the wavelike nature of light causes each star image to be surrounded with diffraction fringes, much magnified in this computer model. (b) Two stars close to each other have overlapping diffraction fringes and become difficult to detect separately.

© Michael A. Seeds

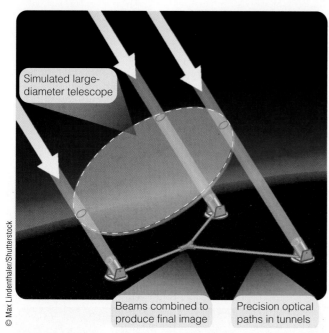

Simulated large-diameter telescope

Beams combined to produce final image

Precision optical paths in tunnels

© Max Lindenthaler/Shutterstock

Figure 4.7a In an astronomical interferometer, light collected by smaller telescopes can be combined to simulate a larger telescope with a resolution determined by the separation of the smaller telescopes. This technique was developed first for radio telescopes and is now being applied to infrared and optical telescopes.

Dominion

Algonquin

3074 kilometres

© age fotostock Spain, S.L./Alamy

Figure 4.7b The first successful long-distance interferometry experiment was conducted in 1967 in Canada, with the 25.6 m Dominion Radio Astrophysical Observatory telescope in Penticton, British Columbia (left), in conjunction with the 46 m telescope at the Algonquin Radio Observatory at Traverse Lake in Ontario (right) to simulate the resolution of a giant radio telescope measuring 3074 km, the physical distance between the two instruments.

Modern technology has allowed astronomers to connect optical telescopes to form interferometers with very high resolution.

Aside from diffraction fringes, two other factors—optical quality and atmospheric conditions—limit resolving power. A telescope must contain high-quality optics to achieve its full potential resolving power. Even a large telescope shows little detail if its optical surfaces have imperfections. In addition, when you look through a telescope, you look through kilometres of turbulence in Earth's atmosphere, which makes images dance and blur, a condition that astronomers call **seeing** (Figure 4.8). A related phenomenon is the twinkling of a star. The twinkles are caused by turbulence in Earth's atmosphere, and a star near the horizon, where you look through more air, twinkles more than a star overhead. On a night when the atmosphere is unsteady, the stars twinkle, the images are blurred, and the seeing is poor. Even with good seeing, the detail visible through a large telescope is limited, not just by its diffraction fringes but by the steadiness of the air through which the observer must look. A telescope performs best on a high mountaintop where the air is thin and steady, but even at good sites atmospheric turbulence spreads star images into blobs 0.5 to 1 arc seconds in diameter. That situation can be improved by a difficult and expensive technique called **adaptive optics**, in which rapid computer calculations adjust the telescope optics and partly compensate for seeing distortions (Figure 4.9).

This limitation on the amount of information in an image is related to the limitation on the accuracy of a measurement. All measurements have some built-in uncertainty, and scientists must learn to work within those limitations.

The third and, you may be surprised to learn, least important power of a telescope is **magnifying power**, the ability to make an image large. The magnifying power of a telescope equals the focal length of the primary mirror or lens divided by the focal length of the eyepiece. For example, a telescope with a primary mirror

seeing Atmospheric conditions on a given night. When the atmosphere is unsteady, producing blurred images, the seeing is said to be poor.

adaptive optics A computer-controlled optical system in an astronomical telescope used to partially correct for seeing.

magnifying power The ability of a telescope to make an image larger.

that has a focal length of 700 mm and an eyepiece with a focal length of 14 mm has a magnifying power of 50. Higher magnifying power does not necessarily show you more detail, because the amount of detail you can see in practice is limited by a combination of the seeing conditions and the telescope's resolving power and optical quality.

A telescope's primary function is to gather light and thus make faint things appear brighter, so the light-gathering power is the most important power and the diameter of

Figure 4.8 (a) The left half of this image of a galaxy is from a photograph recorded on a night of poor seeing. Small details are blurred. (b) The right half of this image is from a photo recorded on a night when the seeing was better—Earth's atmosphere above the telescope was steady. Much more detail is visible under good seeing conditions.

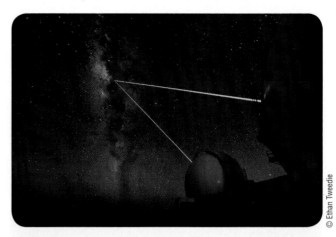

FIGURE 4.9a Laser beams (in the photo from Keck telescopes on Mauna Kea, Hawaii) create artificial stars in the night sky. The light of a star is analyzed by a computer that corrects the shape of the adaptive mirror for the atmosphere's blurring effects.

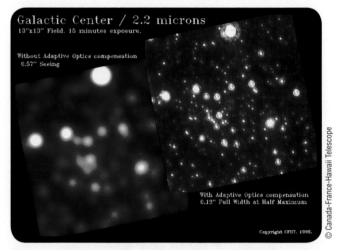

Figure 4.9b Canada-France-Hawaii telescope (CFHT), Mauna Kea, Hawaii, was one of the first in the world to use adaptive optics. This image shows the galactic centre region without (left) and with adaptive optics (right).

HOW DO WE KNOW? 4.1

Resolving Power and the Accuracy of a Measurement

Have you ever seen a movie in which the hero magnifies a newspaper photo and reads some tiny detail? It isn't really possible, because newspaper photos are made up of tiny dots of ink, and no detail smaller than a single dot is visible, no matter how much you magnify the photo. In fact, all images are made up of elements of some sort. In an image formed by a telescope, the size of the picture element is set by seeing or diffraction. It would be foolish to try to resolve (detect) any detail smaller than this limit.

This limitation is true of all measurements in science. A zoologist might specify that a snake was 43.28932 cm long, and a sociologist might say that 98.2491 percent of people oppose drunk driving, but a critic might question the accuracy of those measurements. The resolution of the techniques may not justify the accuracy implied.

Science is based on measurement, and whenever you take a measurement, you should ask yourself how accurate that measurement can be and what its limits are.

the telescope is its most important characteristic. Light-gathering power and resolving power are fundamental properties of a telescope that cannot be altered, whereas magnifying power can be changed simply by changing the eyepiece. (Refer to **The Powers of a Telescope** in the Math Reference Cards.)

4.3 Observatories on Earth: Optical and Radio

Most major observatories are located far from big cities and usually on high mountains. Optical astronomers avoid cities because light pollution, the brightening of the night sky by light scattered from artificial outdoor lighting, can make it impossible to see faint objects. In fact, many residents of cities are unfamiliar with the beauty of the night sky because they can see only the brightest stars. Radio astronomers face a problem of radio interference analogous to light pollution. Weak radio signals from the cosmos are easily drowned out by human radio interference—everything from automobiles with faulty ignition systems to poorly designed transmitters in communication. To avoid that, radio astronomers locate their telescopes as far from civilization as possible. Hidden deep in mountain valleys, they are able to listen to the sky protected from human-made radio noise.

As you learned previously, astronomers prefer to place optical telescopes on mountains because the air there is thin and more transparent, but, most importantly, they carefully select mountains where the airflow is usually not turbulent so the seeing is good. Building an observatory on top of a high mountain far from civilization is difficult and expensive, but the dark sky and good seeing make it worth the effort.

Study **Visualizing Astronomy 4.1, Modern Astronomical Telescopes**, and notice two important points:

1. Research telescopes must focus their light to positions at which cameras and other instruments can be placed.

2. Small telescopes can use other focal arrangements that would be inconvenient in larger telescopes.

Telescopes located on the surface of Earth, whether optical or radio, must move continuously to stay pointed at a celestial object as Earth turns on its axis. This is called **sidereal tracking** (*sidereal* refers to the stars).

> **sidereal tracking** The continuous movement of a telescope to keep it pointed at a star as Earth rotates.

CANADIANS IN ASTRONOMY
Canada's role in the global story of astronomy

Courtesy Wendy Freedman

Wendy Freedman

Wendy Freedman

In the early 20th century Edwin Hubble discovered the expansion of the universe, measuring distances to Cepheid variable stars (Figure 9.3) in other galaxies and giving the first estimate of the rate of expansion with what is known as the Hubble constant (Figure 10.4). In 1990, the Hubble Space Telescope was launched, aiming to measure more precisely the distances to the galaxies and the rate of expansion. The "Hubble Space Telescope Key Project on the Extragalactic Distance Scale" was led by Canadian astronomer Wendy Freedman. Freedman was already an accomplished professional. After receiving her Ph.D. from the University of Toronto in 1984, she became the first woman to join the Observatories of the Carnegie Institution for Science in Pasadena, California; 20 years later, she was named a director of the Carnegie Observatories. For her work on the measurement of the Hubble constant, Wendy Freedman was awarded the prestigious 2009 Gruber Cosmology Prize. She has received many honours for her studies of galactic evolution and the evolution of stellar populations, as well as for her leadership in bringing observational cosmology into the 21st century. During her work as co-leader of the Carnegie Supernova Project, research on the galactic distance scale and refinement of the estimate of cosmological expansion led her to identify better indicators of cosmological distances, that is, type Ia supernovae. She is currently chair of the board for the Giant Magellan Telescope Organization, a distinguished international consortium of leading universities and science institutions that is building a 25-m telescope at Carnegie's Las Campanas Observatory in Chile. With unprecedented resolving power—10 times greater than the Hubble Space Telescope—and adaptive optics to battle atmospheric disturbances, this 21st-century telescope will tackle the newest questions in cosmology.

1 Large astronomical telescopes must gather light and guide it to locations where it can be recorded with cameras or other instruments.

In larger telescopes, the light can be focused to a **prime focus** position high in the telescope tube, as shown at the right. Although it is a good place to image faint objects, the prime focus is inconvenient for large instruments. A **secondary mirror** can reflect the light through a hole in the primary mirror to a **Cassegrain focus**. This focal arrangement may be the most common form of astronomical telescope.

Secondary mirror

With the secondary mirror removed, the light converges at the prime focus. In large telescopes, astronomers can ride inside the prime-focus cage, although most observations are now made by instruments connected to computers in a separate control room.

The mirrors in astronomical telescopes must be ground and polished to precise shape to form the sharpest possible images. The mirrors must be carefully supported to prevent them from sagging under their own weight as the telescope moves around the sky, and many modern telescopes use computer-controlled thrusters to maintain the mirror shape.

The Cassegrain focus is convenient and has room for large instruments.

1a Smaller telescopes can use other focal arrangements. The Newtonian focus that Isaac Newton used in his first reflecting telescope is awkward for large telescopes, as shown at right, but is common for small telescopes.

Newtonian focus

Thin correcting lens

Schmidt–Cassegrain telescope

1b Many small telescopes such as the one at left use a Schmidt–Cassegrain focus. A thin correcting plate improves the image but is too slightly curved to introduce serious chromatic aberration.

1c Shown below, Canada-France-Hawaii telescope can be used at either the prime focus or the Cassegrain focus. Note the human figure at lower left.

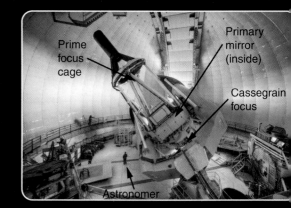

Prime focus cage

Primary mirror (inside)

Cassegrain focus

Astronomer

The days when astronomers worked beside their telescopes through long, dark, cold nights are nearly gone. The complexity and sophistication of telescopes require a battery of computers, and almost all research telescopes are run from warm control rooms.

High-speed computers have allowed astronomers to build new, giant telescopes with unique designs. The European Southern Observatory has built the Very Large Telescope (VLT) high in the remote Andes Mountains of northern Chile. The VLT actually consists of four telescopes, each with a computer-controlled mirror 8.2 m in diameter and only 17.5 cm thick (Figure 4.10a). The four telescopes can work singly or can combine their light to work as one large telescope. Italian and American astronomers have built the Large Binocular Telescope, which carries a pair of 8.4-m mirrors on a single mounting, Figure 4.10b. The Gran Telescopio Canarias, located atop a volcanic peak in the Canary Islands in Spain, carries a segmented mirror 10.4 m in diameter and holds, for the moment, the record as the largest single telescope in the world (Figure 4.10c). Other giant telescopes are being planned with innovative designs.

The largest fully steerable radio telescope in the world is at the National Radio Astronomy Observatory in West Virginia. The telescope has a reflecting surface 100 m in diameter made of 2004 computer-controlled panels that adjust to maintain the shape of the reflecting surface. The largest radio dish in the world is 300 m in diameter, and is built into a mountain valley in Arecibo, Puerto Rico. The antenna hangs on cables above the dish, and by moving the antenna, astronomers can point the telescope at any object that passes within 20 degrees of the zenith as Earth rotates (Figure 4.11a).

The Very Large Array (VLA) consists of 27 dishes spread in a Y-pattern across the New Mexico desert (Figure 4.11b). Operated as an interferometer, the

a

ESO/C.Madsen, H.Zodet

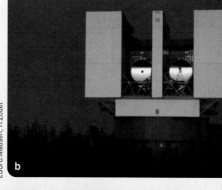

Large Binocular Telescope

b

Photo courtesy of John Hill and Large Binocular Telescope Observatory.

The mirrors in the VLT telescopes are each 8.2 m in diameter.

The mirror on the Gran Telescopio Canarias is composed out of 36 hexagonal mirrors.

© MAX ALEXANDER/SCIENCE PHOTO LIBRARY

c

Figure 4.10 (a) The four telescopes of the European Very Large Telescope (VLT) are housed in separate domes at Paranal Observatory in Chile. The mirrors in the VLT telescopes are each 8.2 m in diameter. (b) The Large Binocular Telescope (LBT) in Arizona carries two 8.4-m mirrors. The light gathered by the two mirrors can be analyzed separately or combined. The entire building rotates as the telescope moves. (c) The Gran Telescopio Canarias (GTC) on La Palma in the Canary Islands contains 36 hexagonal mirror segments in its 10.4-m primary mirror.

VLA has the resolving power of a radio telescope up to 36 km in diameter. Such arrays are very powerful, and radio astronomers are now planning the

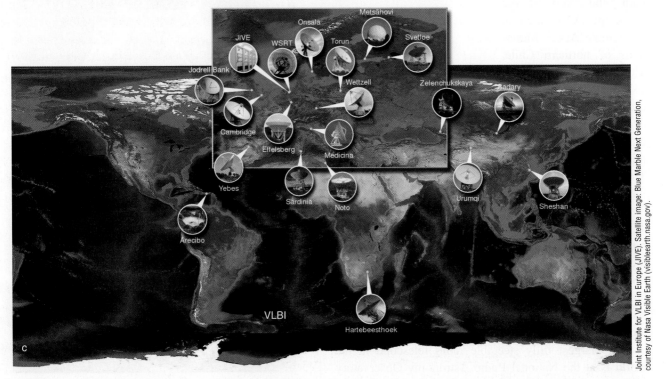

Figure 4.11 (a) The 305-m radio telescope in Arecibo, Puerto Rico, is nestled in a naturally bowl-shaped valley. The receiver platform is suspended over the dish. (b) The Very Large Array (VLA) radio telescope uses 27 radio dishes that can be moved to different positions along a Y-shaped set of tracks across the New Mexico desert. They are shown here in the most compact arrangement. The individual dishes are usually combined to make an interferometer capable of very-high-resolution radio maps of celestial objects. (c) The world network of Very Long Baseline Interferometry (VLBI).

Square Kilometre Array (SKA), which will consist of thousands of radio dishes in Australia and South Africa, spanning 6000 km and having a total collecting area of 1 square kilometre. Astronomers and engineers from more than 70 institutes in 20 countries are designing the SKA as a global telescope, with data processed in centres around the world. The interferometer will be 50 times more sensitive than any other telescope and will survey the sky 10 000 times faster. Atacama Desert in Chile is the site of another international radio interferometer

(Europe, North America, East Asia, and the Republic of Chile), Atacama Large Millimeter/Submillimeter Array (ALMA). ALMA is composed of 66 high-precision antennas located on the Chajnantor plateau, 5000 m above sea level in very dry air, which is needed for sensitive electronics.

The largest interferometers today operate through a technique called Very Long Baseline Interferometry (VLBI). VLBI uses multiple radio telescopes over very great distances. Figure 4.11c shows the telescopes of the European VLBI Network (EVN), which also includes telescopes in Puerto Rico, South Africa, Russia, and China. Other VLBI arrays include the Long Baseline Array (LBA) in Australia and the Very Long Baseline Array (VLBA) in the United States. VLBI started in 1967 in Canada, with the Dominion Radio Astrophysical Observatory and the Algonquin Radio Observatory experiment (Figure 4.7b).

4.4 Astronomical Instruments and Techniques

Just looking through a telescope doesn't tell you much. To learn about planets, stars, and galaxies, you must be able to analyze the light the telescope gathers. Special instruments attached to the telescope make that possible.

Imaging Systems and Photometers

The photographic plate was the first image-recording device used with telescopes. Brightness of objects imaged on a photographic plate can be measured with a lot of hard work, yielding only moderate precision. Astronomers also build **photometers**, sensitive light meters to measure the brightness of individual objects very precisely. Most modern astronomers use **charge-coupled devices (CCDs)** as both image-recording devices and photometers. A CCD is a specialized computer chip containing as many as a million or more microscopic light detectors arranged in an array about the size of a postage stamp. These array detectors can be used like a small photographic plate, but they have dramatic advantages over both photometers and photographic plates. CCDs can detect both bright and faint objects in a single exposure and are much more sensitive than a photographic plate. CCD images are digitized, or converted to numerical data, and can be read directly into a computer memory for later analysis. Although CCDs for astronomy are extremely sensitive and therefore expensive, less sophisticated CCDs are now used in commercial video and digital cameras. Infrared astronomers also use array detectors similar in operation to optical CCDs. At some other wavelengths, photometers are still used for measuring the brightness of celestial objects.

The digital data representing an image from a CCD or other array detector are easy to manipulate to bring out details that would not otherwise be visible. For example, astronomical images are sometimes reproduced as negatives, with the sky white and the stars dark. This makes the faint parts of the image easier to see (Figure 4.12). Astronomers also manipulate images to produce false-colour images in which the colours represent different levels of intensity and are not related to the true colours of the object. For example, because humans can't see radio waves, astronomers must convert them into something perceptible. One way is to measure the strength of the radio signal at various places in the sky and draw a map in which contours mark areas of uniform radio intensity. Compare such a map to Figure 4.13a, a seating diagram for a baseball stadium in which the contours mark areas in which the seats have the same price. Contour maps are very common in radio astronomy and are often reproduced using false colours (Figure 4.13b).

Spectrographs

To analyze light in detail, you need to spread the light out according to wavelength into a spectrum, a task performed by a **spectrograph**. You can understand how this works by reproducing an experiment performed by Isaac Newton in 1666. Boring a hole in his window shutter, Newton admitted a thin beam of sunlight into his darkened bedroom. When he placed a prism in the beam, the sunlight spread into a beautiful spectrum on the far wall. From this and similar experiments, Newton concluded that white light was made of a mixture of all the colours.

photometer Sensitive astronomical instrument that measures the brightness of individual objects very precisely.

charge-coupled device (CCD) An electronic device consisting of a large array of light-sensitive elements used to record very faint images.

spectrograph A device that separates light by wavelengths to produce a spectrum.

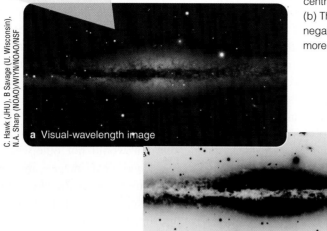

Galaxy NGC 891 in true color. It is edge-on and contains thick dust clouds.

Figure 4.12 (a) Astronomical images can be manipulated to bring out difficult-to-see details. The colour photo of this galaxy is dark, and the dust clouds in the galaxy's central plane do not show very well. (b) The observing team produced this negative image to show the dust clouds more clearly.

a Visual-wavelength image

C. Hawk (JHU), B Savage (U. Wisconsin), N.A. Sharp (NOAO)/WIYN/NOAO/NSF

b Visual-wavelength negative image

In this negative image of NGC 891, the sky is white and the stars are black.

C. Hawk (JHU), B Savage (U. Wisconsin), N.A. Sharp (NOAO)/WIYN/NOAO/NSF

Figure 4.13 (a) A contour map of a baseball stadium shows regions of similar admission prices. The most expensive seats are those behind home plate. (b) A false-colour radio map of Tycho's supernova remnant, the expanding shell of gas produced by the explosion of a star in 1572. The radio contour map has been colour-coded to show intensity.

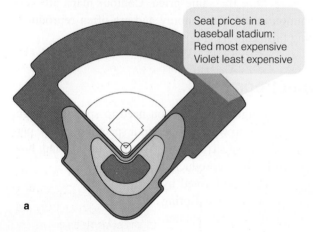

Seat prices in a baseball stadium:
Red most expensive
Violet least expensive

a

Radio energy map:
Red strongest
Violet weakest

b

NRAO/National Radio Astronomy Observatory

spectrum A range of electromagnetic radiation spread into its component wavelengths (colours)—for example, a rainbow; also the representation of a spectrum as a graph showing intensity of radiation as a function of wavelength or frequency.

Newton didn't think in terms of wavelength, but you can use that modern concept to see that the light passing through the prism is bent at an angle that depends on the wavelength (see Figure 4.14). Violet (short-wavelength) light bends most, and red (long-wavelength) light least.

Thus, the white light entering the prism is spread into what is called a **spectrum**. A typical prism spectrograph contains more than one prism to spread the spectrum wider, plus lenses to guide the light into the prism and to focus the light onto a photographic plate. Most modern spectrographs use a grating in place of a prism. A grating is a piece of glass with thousands of microscopic parallel lines scribed onto its surface. Different wavelengths of light reflect from the grating at slightly different angles, so white light is spread into a spectrum and can be recorded, often

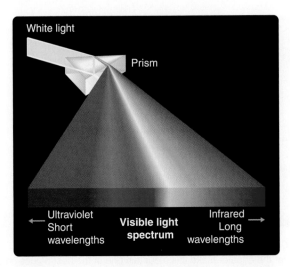

Figure 4.14 A prism bends light by an angle that depends on the wavelength of the light. Short wavelengths bend most and long wavelengths least. Thus, white light passing through a prism is spread into a spectrum.

White light

Prism

← Ultraviolet Short wavelengths

Visible light spectrum

Infrared Long wavelengths →

by a CCD camera. Recording the spectrum of a faint star or galaxy can require a long time exposure, so astronomers have developed multiobject spectrographs that can record the spectra of as many as 100 objects simultaneously. Multiobject spectrographs automated by computers have made large surveys of many thousands of stars or galaxies possible.

Because astronomers understand how light interacts with matter, a spectrum carries a tremendous amount of information, as you will see in more detail in Chapter 5. That makes a spectrograph the astronomer's most powerful instrument. Astronomers are likely to remark, "We don't know anything about an object until we get a spectrum," and that is only a slight exaggeration.

4.5 Airborne and Space Observatories

You have learned about the observations that ground-based telescopes can make through the two atmospheric windows in the visible and radio parts of the electromagnetic spectrum. Most of the rest of the electromagnetic spectrum—infrared, ultraviolet, X-ray, and gamma-ray radiation—never reaches Earth's surface. To observe at these wavelengths, telescopes must fly above the atmosphere in high-flying aircraft, rockets, balloons, and satellites. The only exceptions are observations that can be made in what are called the near-infrared and the near-ultraviolet, almost the same wavelengths as visible light.

The Ends of the Visual Spectrum

Astronomers can observe from the ground in the near-infrared just beyond the red end of the visible spectrum because some of this radiation leaks through the atmosphere in narrow, partially open, atmospheric windows ranging in wavelength from 1200 nm to about 30 000 nm. Infrared astronomers usually describe wavelengths in micrometres or microns (10^{-6} m), so they refer to this wavelength range as 1.2 to 30 microns. In this range, most of the radiation is absorbed by water vapour and carbon dioxide molecules in Earth's atmosphere, so it is an advantage to place telescopes on the highest mountains where the air is especially thin and dry. For example, a number of important infrared telescopes are located on the summit of Mauna Kea in Hawaii at an altitude of 4200 m (Figure 4.15a).

The far-infrared range, which includes wavelengths longer than 30 microns, can tell us about planets, comets, forming stars, and other cool objects, but these wavelengths are absorbed high in the atmosphere. To observe in the far-infrared, telescopes must venture to high altitudes. Remotely operated infrared telescopes suspended under balloons have reached altitudes as high as 41 km.

The Stratospheric Observatory for Infrared Astronomy (SOFIA), a Boeing 747SP aircraft that carries a 2.5-m telescope (Figure 4.15b), can get above more than 99 percent of the water vapour in Earth's atmosphere, allowing observations at infrared wavelengths otherwise accessible only from space telescopes.

A telescope that observes at far-infrared wavelengths must be cooled and kept cooled. Since heated objects emit infrared radiation, if a telescope becomes warm it will emit infrared radiation many times greater than that emitted by the distant object it is intended to observe. Imagine trying to look at a dim, moonlit scene through binoculars that are glowing brightly. In a telescope observing near-infrared radiation, only the detector, the element on which the infrared radiation is focused, must be cooled. To observe in the far-infrared, however, the entire telescope must be cooled.

At the short-wavelength end of the spectrum, astronomers can observe in the near-ultraviolet. Human eyes do not detect this radiation, but it can be recorded by photographic plates and CCDs. Wavelengths shorter than about 290 nm—the far-ultraviolet, X-ray, and gamma-ray ranges—are completely absorbed by the ozone layer extending from 20 km to about 40 km above Earth's surface. No mountain is that high, and no balloon or airplane can fly that high, so astronomers cannot observe far-UV, X-ray, and gamma-ray radiation without going into space.

Figure 4.15 (a) Optical, infrared, and submillimetre radio telescopes at 4200 m above sea level on Mauna Kea in Hawaii. The high altitude, low atmospheric moisture, lack of nearby large cities, and location near the equator make this mountain one of the best places on Earth to build an observatory. (b) SOFIA, the Stratospheric Observatory for Infrared Astronomy, a joint project of NASA and the German Aerospace Center (DLR), flies at altitudes up to 14 km, where it collect light at infrared wavelengths unobservable even from high mountaintops.

Telescopes in Space

Earth's atmosphere is transparent in two windows in the visible and radio parts of the electromagnetic spectrum. Most of the rest of the electromagnetic radiation—infrared, ultraviolet, X-ray, and gamma ray—never reaches Earth's surface; it is absorbed high in Earth's atmosphere. To observe at these wavelengths, telescopes must go above the atmosphere.

The Hubble Space Telescope, named after Edwin Hubble, the astronomer who discovered the expansion of the universe, is the most successful telescope ever to orbit Earth (Figure 4.16a). It was launched in 1990 and contains a 2.4-m mirror plus instruments that can observe at near-infrared, visual, and near-ultraviolet wave lengths. It is controlled from a research centre on Earth and observes continuously. Nevertheless, there is time to complete only a fraction of the projects proposed by astronomers from around the world.

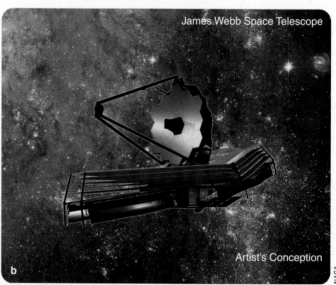

Figure 4.16 (a) The Hubble Space Telescope (HST) orbits Earth at an average of 570 km above the surface. In this image the telescope is viewing toward the upper left. (b) An artist's conception of the eventual successor to HST, the James Webb Space Telescope (JWST). JWST will be located in solar orbit 1.5 million km from Earth and will not have an enclosing tube; it will resemble a radio dish more than a conventional optical telescope. It will observe the universe from behind a multilayered sunscreen larger than a tennis court.

Most observations made by the Hubble Space Telescope are at visual wavelengths, so its greatest advantage in being above Earth's atmosphere is the lack of seeing distortion. It can see faint objects and detect fine detail by concentrating light into sharp objects.

The telescope is as big as a large bus and has been visited a number of times by the space shuttle so that astronauts could maintain its equipment and install new cameras and spectrographs. Astronomers hope that it will last until it is replaced by the James Webb Space Telescope, planned to launch in 2018 (Figure 4.16b). The Webb telescope's primary mirror will have a diameter of 6.6 m.

In 2009, NASA launched Kepler Mission, a space telescope designed to look for Earth-like planets around other stars, specifically for those that could be suitable for harbouring life, and made outstanding discoveries of hundreds of such systems. The Kepler telescope is in orbit around the Sun and observes galactic neighbourhoods in the Orion spiral arm; however, since the summer of 2013 its limited capabilities have changed the mission.

Telescopes that observe in the far-infrared must be protected from heat and must get above Earth's absorbing atmosphere. They have limited lifetimes because they must carry coolant to chill their optics. The most sophisticated of the infrared telescopes put in orbit, the Herschel Space Observatory was cooled to –269°C. Launched in 2009, it observes from behind a sunscreen. In fact, it could not observe from orbit around Earth because Earth is such a strong source of infrared radiation, so the telescope was sent to a position 1.5 million km from Earth in the direction away from the Sun. Named after William Herschel, the discoverer of infrared light, the Herschel telescope has made important discoveries concerning star and planet formation, distant galaxies, and more.

High-energy astrophysics refers to the use of X-ray and gamma-ray observations of the sky. Making such observations is difficult but can reveal the secrets of processes such as the collapse of massive stars and eruptions of supermassive black holes.

The largest X-ray telescope to date, the Chandra X-ray Observatory, was launched in 1999 and orbits a third of the way to the Moon. Chandra is named for the late Indian-American Nobel Laureate, Subrahmanyan Chandrasekhar, who was a pioneer in many branches of theoretical astronomy. Focusing X-rays is difficult because they penetrate most mirrors, so astronomers devised cylindrical mirrors in which the X-rays reflect from the polished inside of the cylinders and form images on special detectors. Chandra telescope has made important discoveries about everything from star formation to monster black holes in distant galaxies (Figure 4.17).

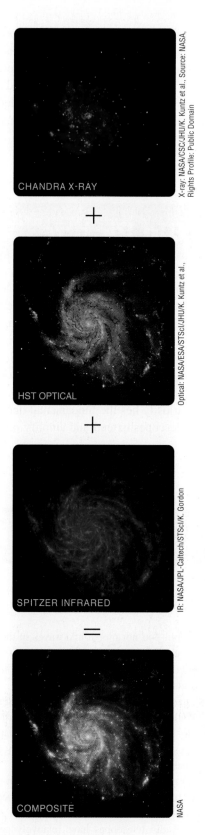

Figure 4.17 Images of the galaxy Messier 101 made by three space telescopes: the Chandra X-ray Observatory, the Hubble Space Telescope, and the Spitzer Space Telescope. Comparison and combination of these images yields abundant information about the life cycles of stars in a galaxy similar to our Milky Way Galaxy.

One of the first gamma-ray observatories was the Compton Gamma Ray Observatory, launched in 1991. It mapped the entire sky at gamma-ray wavelengths. The European INTEGRAL satellite was launched in 2002 and has been very productive in the study of violent eruptions of stars and black holes. The GLAST (Gamma-Ray Large Area Space Telescope), launched in 2008, is capable of mapping large areas of the sky to high sensitivity.

Modern astronomy has come to depend on observations that cover the entire electromagnetic spectrum. More orbiting space telescopes are planned that will be more versatile and more sensitive.

The Big Picture

Telescopes are creations of curiosity. You look through a telescope to see what the unaided eye cannot detect about the universe. The history of astronomy is the history of bigger and better telescopes gathering more and more light to search for fainter and more distant objects to try to satisfy human curiosity. Curiosity is a noble trait—the mark of an active, inquiring mind. At the limits of human curiosity lies the fundamental question, "What are we?" Telescopes extend and amplify our senses, but they also extend and amplify our curiosity about the universe around us. When people find out how something works, they say their curiosity is satisfied. Curiosity is an appetite-like hunger or thirst, but it is an appetite for understanding. And, like hunger, curiosity rises again and again, pushing the boundaries of human knowledge further and further. As astronomy expands our horizons and we learn how distant stars and galaxies work, we feel satisfied because we are learning about ourselves.

Review and Discussion Questions

Review Questions

1. Why would you not plot sound waves in the electromagnetic spectrum?
2. The Moon has no atmosphere at all. In what way could astronauts talk on the Moon?
3. If you had limited funds to build a large telescope, which type would you choose: a refractor or a reflector? Why?
4. Why do nocturnal animals usually have large pupils in their eyes? How is that related to the way astronomical telescopes work?
5. Why do optical astronomers often put their telescopes at the tops of mountains, while radio astronomers sometimes put their telescopes in deep valleys?
6. Why do radio telescopes have relatively poor resolving power?
7. The Moon has no atmosphere at all. What advantages would you have if you built an observatory on the lunar surface?
8. Why must telescopes observing at far-infrared wavelengths be cooled to low temperatures?
9. What purpose do the colours in a false-colour image or map serve?
10. Would the advancement in detector sensitivity enable us to receive X-rays and gamma rays from cosmic sources here on Earth's surface and thus eliminate the need for orbiting telescopes?
11. What might you detect with an X-ray telescope that you could not detect with an infrared telescope?
12. Why would radio astronomers build identical radio telescopes in many different places around the world?
13. **How Do We Know?** How is the resolution of an astronomical image related to the precision of a measurement?

Discussion Questions

1. Why does the wavelength response of the human eye match the visual window of Earth's atmosphere so well?
2. Most people like beautiful sunsets with brightly glowing clouds, bright moonlit nights, and twinkling stars. Astronomers don't. Why?

Problems

1. Compare the light-gathering power of one of the 10-m Keck telescopes with that of a 0.5-m telescope.
2. How does the resolving power of the 5-m telescope on Mount Palomar near San Diego compare with that of the 2.5-m Hubble Space Telescope? Why does HST generally still outperform the Palomar 5-m telescope?
3. If you build a telescope with a focal length of 1.3 m, what focal length does the eyepiece need to give a magnification of 100 times?

Learning to Look

1. The two images below show a star before and after an adaptive optics system attached to the telescope was switched on. What causes the distortion in the first image, and how do adaptive optics correct the image?

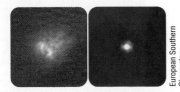

European Southern Observatory

2. The star images in the photo below are tiny disks, but the diameter of these disks is not related to the diameter of the stars. Explain why the telescope can't resolve the diameter of the stars. What does cause the apparent diameters of the stars?

NASA, ESA, and G. Meylan (Ecole Polytechnique Federale de Lausanne)

3. The X-ray image below shows the remains of an exploded star. Explain why images recorded by telescopes in space are often displayed in representational (false) colour rather than in the colours (wavelengths) received by the telescope.

NASA, CXC, PSU.S. Park

5

The Sun: The Closest Star

CHAPTER OUTLINE

GUIDEPOST

This chapter marks a change in the way you will look at nature. Up to this point, you have been considering what you can see with your eyes alone or aided by telescopes. In this chapter, you will begin to understand how astronomical observations can be linked with physics experiments and theory to unlock celestial secrets that lie beyond what can be seen directly.

The Sun, which is the main source of light and warmth in our solar system, has always been a natural subject of great human curiosity. In this chapter you will discover how careful analysis of sunlight, combined with an understanding of how matter and light interact, paints a detailed picture of the Sun's properties. Here you will find answers to four important questions:

- **How do atoms and light interact?**
- **What can you learn from spectra of celestial objects?**
- **What can you learn about the Sun by observing its surface and atmosphere?**
- **Why does the Sun go through cycles of activity?**

Although this chapter considers only the star at the centre of our solar system, understanding how astronomers study the Sun leads you onward and outward among the planets, stars, and galaxies that fill the universe, often using the rich information derived from their spectra.

© Science Source/Photo Researchers, Inc.

The sun, with all those planets revolving around it and dependent on it, can still ripen a bunch of grapes as if it had nothing else in the universe to do.

Galileo Galilei,
Scientist and Astronomer

We can see sunrises 16 times a day as we circle the Earth every 90 minutes!

Wang Yaping,
China's second female taikonaut (astronaut)

5.1 The Sun: Basic Characteristics

Earthbound humans knew almost nothing about the Sun until the early 19th century, when the German optician Joseph von Fraunhofer studied the solar spectrum and found that it is interrupted by some 600 dark lines, representing colours that are missing from the sunlight Earth receives. As scientists realized that these **spectral lines** were related to the presence of various types of atoms in the Sun's atmosphere, a window finally opened to real understanding of the Sun's nature. In this chapter, you will look through that window by considering the properties of sunlight and how atoms interact with light to make spectral lines. Once you understand that, you will know how astronomers have determined the chemical composition of the Sun, measured motions of gas on the Sun's surface and in its atmosphere, and detected magnetic fields that drive the Sun's cycle of activity.

In its general properties, the Sun is very simple. It is a great ball of hot gas held together by its own gravity. Deep inside the Sun's core, energy is produced by nuclear fusion, which is released in the form of radiation and heat. You will explore nuclear fusion in the Sun and other stars in more detail in Chapter 7. The tremendously hot gas inside the Sun has such a high pressure that it would explode were it not for its own confining gravity. The same gravity would make it collapse into a small, dense body were it not so hot inside. Like a soap bubble, the Sun is a simple structure balanced between opposing forces that, if unbalanced, would destroy it. These dramatic statements are also true for other stars, so you can study the Sun for insight into the rest of the stars in the universe.

Another reason to study the Sun is that life on Earth depends critically on the Sun. Very small changes in the Sun's luminosity can alter Earth's climate, and a larger change might make Earth uninhabitable. Nearly all of Earth's energy comes from the Sun—the energy in oil, gasoline, coal, and even wood is merely stored sunlight. Furthermore, the Sun's atmosphere of very thin gas extends beyond Earth's position, and changes in that atmosphere, such as eruptions or magnetic storms, can have a direct effect on Earth.

spectral line A bright or dark line in a spectrum at a specific wavelength produced by the absorption or emission of light by certain atoms.

transits of Venus Rare occasions when Venus can be seen as a tiny dot directly between Earth and the Sun.

Distance and Size

When you watch the Sun set in the west, you see a glowing disk that is 150 million kilometres from Earth and has a diameter 109 times that of Earth. How do you know this? Recall from Chapter 3 that, thanks to the work of Johannes Kepler in the 17th century, the relative sizes of the orbits of the planets were already known in astronomical units—one AU being equal to the average distance of the Sun from Earth. Recall from Chapter 3 that the true distance of a nearby object can be calculated from the size of the apparent shift in its position relative to the background as seen from two viewing positions (refer to **Visualizing Astronomy 3.1, The Ancient Earth**). That shift is called parallax. (Refer to **Parallax and Distance** in the Math Reference Cards).

If you and another astronomer on the opposite side of Earth agree to observe the position of a planet such as Venus at the same moment relative to more distant objects, you could measure that planet's parallax shift caused by you and your colleague's different observing locations. Then the distance of the planet in familiar "earthly" units can be calculated with some trigonometry. With further analysis, using a map of the solar system and Kepler's third law, you can find the real distance to the Sun. From the 17th century onward, astronomers made more and more accurate measurements of this type, especially on rare occasions called **transits of Venus**, when that planet can be seen as a tiny dot directly between Earth and the Sun, as shown in Figure 5.1, so the edge of the Sun's

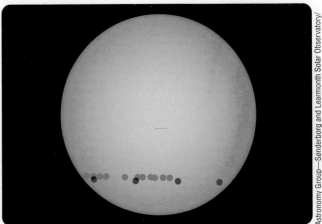

Astronomy Group—Sønderborg and Learmonth Solar Observatory/ ESO/Adapted from the GONG project and Amtsgymnasiet i Sønderborg

Figure 5.1 Comparison of Venus's path across the solar disk as observed from Australia (upper track) and Denmark (lower track). Measurement of the small parallax shift allows the distance to Venus to be calculated based on the known distance between the two observatories. Kepler's third law can then be used to find the distance to the Sun.

disk acts as a convenient position marker. The distance from Earth to the Sun, combined with the Sun's easily measured angular size, gives you the Sun's diameter in familiar units.

Mass and Density

Once you know the distance to the Sun, Newton's laws (Chapter 3) tell you what the Sun's mass needs to be to produce the necessary amount of gravitational force to keep Earth and the other planets in their orbits at their observed speeds. If you know the mass and diameter of the Sun, you can make an easy calculation of the Sun's **density** (mass per volume). Refer to the **Celestial Profiles** in Appendix C, and notice the Sun's mass, equivalent to 333 000 times the mass of Earth, and its average density, only a little bit denser than water. Although the Sun is very large and very massive, the low density and high temperature together tell you that it must be gas from its surface to its centre. When you look at the Sun you see only the outer layers—the surface and atmosphere—of this vast sphere of gas.

In the following sections of this chapter you will learn how, using the results of laboratory physics experiments on Earth, you can know facts as seemingly unknowable as the temperature and composition of the Sun: an object that has never been visited or touched by humans.

5.2 Properties of Blackbody Radiation

The Sun's surface glows for the same reason and by the same process that makes the coils in your toaster glow when they are hot. You probably have also noticed that your toaster's coils glow different colours as they heat up. If they are not too hot, the coils are deep red, but as they heat up they grow brighter and yellower. Yellow-hot is hotter than red-hot, but not as hot as white-hot. Different parts of the Sun's surface also glow slightly different colours depending on their temperatures. In order to understand the Sun's temperature, you must understand the structure and behaviour of the atoms that make up the Sun.

Atoms and Subatomic Particles

As you know, an **atom** has a massive, compact **nucleus** containing positively charged **protons**, usually accompanied

by electrically neutral **neutrons**. The nucleus is embedded in a large cloud of relatively low-mass, negatively charged **electrons**. These particles can also exist and move about unattached to an atom.

Charged particles, both protons and electrons, are surrounded by electric fields that they produce. Whenever you change the motion of a charged particle, the change in its electric field spreads outward at the speed of light as electromagnetic radiation. If you run a comb through your hair, you disturb electrons in both hair and comb, producing electric sparks and electromagnetic radiation, which you can sometimes hear as snaps and crackles if you are standing near a radio.

The Sun is hot, and there are plenty of electrons zipping around, colliding, changing directions and speeds, and thereby making electromagnetic radiation. Protons can also make electromagnetic radiation, but because electrons are less massive, usually it is electrons that do most of the moving around.

Temperature, Heat, and Blackbody Radiation

The particles inside any object—for example, atoms linked together to form **molecules**, individual atoms, or electrons inside atoms or wandering loose—are in constant motion, and in a hot object they are more agitated than in a cool object. You can refer to the total agitation as *thermal energy*. When you touch a hot object, you feel **heat** as that thermal energy flows into your fingers. **Temperature** is simply a number related to the average speed of the particles, the intensity of the particle motion.

Astronomers and physicists express temperatures of the Sun and other objects on the **Kelvin temperature scale**. Zero degrees

density Mass per volume.

atom The smallest unit of a chemical element, consisting of a nucleus containing protons and neutrons plus a surrounding cloud of electrons.

nucleus The central core of an atom containing protons and neutrons that carries a net positive charge.

proton A positively charged atomic particle contained in the nucleus of an atom. The nucleus of a hydrogen atom consists of a single proton.

neutron An atomic particle contained in the nucleus, with no charge and about the same mass as a proton.

electron Low-mass atomic particle carrying a negative charge.

molecule Two or more atoms bonded together.

heat Total energy stored in a material as agitation among its particles.

temperature A measure of the average agitation among the atoms and molecules of a material.

Kelvin temperature scale A temperature scale starting at absolute zero (−273°C). A one Kelvin change equals a one degree Celsius change.

Kelvin (written 0 K) is **absolute zero** (−273°C), the temperature at which an object contains no thermal energy that can be extracted. Water freezes at 273 K and boils at 373 K. The Kelvin temperature scale is useful in astronomy because it is based on absolute zero and, consequently, is related directly to the motion of the particles in an object.

Now you can understand why a hot object glows. The hotter an object is, the more motion there is among its particles. The agitated particles, including electrons, collide with each other, and when electrons are accelerated, part of the energy is carried away as electromagnetic radiation. The radiation emitted by an opaque object is called **blackbody radiation**, a name translated from a German term that refers to the way a perfectly opaque emitter and absorber of radiation would behave. At room temperature, such a perfect absorber would look black, but at higher temperatures it would visibly glow. In astronomy you will find the term *blackbody* actually refers to glowing objects.

absolute zero The theoretical lowest possible temperature at which a material contains no extractable heat energy. Zero on the Kelvin temperature scale.

blackbody radiation Radiation emitted by a hypothetical perfect radiator. The spectrum is continuous, and the wavelength of maximum emission depends on the blackbody's temperature.

wavelength of maximum intensity The wavelength at which a perfect radiator emits the maximum amount of energy; it depends only on the object's temperature.

Wien's law A law stating that the hotter a glowing object is, the shorter will be its wavelength of maximum intensity, inversely proportional to its temperature.

Stefan–Boltzmann law A law stating that hotter objects emit more energy than cooler objects of the same size, in proportion to the fourth power of temperature.

Blackbody radiation is quite common. In fact, it is the type of light emitted by an ordinary incandescent light bulb. Electricity flowing through the filament of the bulb heats it to a high temperature, and it glows. You can also recognize the light emitted by a toaster coil as blackbody radiation. Many objects in the sky, including the Sun, primarily emit blackbody radiation because they are mostly opaque.

Two simple laws describe how blackbody radiation works. A hot object radiates at all wavelengths, but there is a **wavelength of maximum intensity** at which it radiates the most energy. **Wien's law** says that the hotter an object is, the shorter is the wavelength of its maximum intensity. This makes sense because in a hotter object, the particles travel faster, collide more violently, and emit more energetic photons,

which have shorter wavelengths. This means that hot objects tend to emit radiation at shorter wavelengths and look bluer than cooler objects. Hot stars look bluer than cool stars.

The **Stefan–Boltzmann law** says that hotter objects emit more energy than cooler objects of the same size. That makes sense, too, because the hotter an object is, the more rapidly its particles move and the more violent and more frequent are the collisions that produce photons. In fact, very small changes in temperature lead to very large changes in the total energy emitted. In later chapters, you will use these two laws to understand stars and other objects.

Figure 5.2 shows plots of the intensity of radiation versus wavelength for three objects with different temperatures, illustrating both Wien's law and the Stefan–Boltzmann law. You can see how temperature determines the colour of a glowing blackbody. The hotter object has its strongest intensity at shorter wavelengths, so it emits more blue light than red and thus looks blue. The cooler object emits more red than blue light and consequently looks red. Also, the total area under each curve is proportional to the total energy emitted, so you can see that the hotter object emits more total energy than the cooler object.

Now you can understand why two famous stars, Betelgeuse and Rigel, have such different colours, which you saw in Chapter 2 in the section on naming stars. According to Wien's law, Betelgeuse is cooler than the Sun so it looks red, but Rigel is hotter than the Sun and looks blue. A star with the same temperature as the Sun will appear yellowish. Actually, the peak intensity of light from the Sun is for wavelengths corresponding to green light, but we see the Sun as yellowish because of the way our eyes detect the light. According to the Stefan–Boltzmann law, Rigel also produces more energy from each square metre of its photosphere than does the Sun, which in turn produces more energy from each square metre than does Betelgeuse.

Notice that cool objects may emit little visible radiation but are still producing blackbody radiation. For example, the human body has a temperature of 310 K and emits blackbody radiation mostly in the infrared part of the spectrum. Infrared security cameras can detect burglars by the radiation they emit, and mosquitoes can track you down in total darkness by homing in on your infrared radiation. You have a wavelength of maximum intensity in the infrared part of the spectrum. At your temperature you almost never emit photons with other than infrared

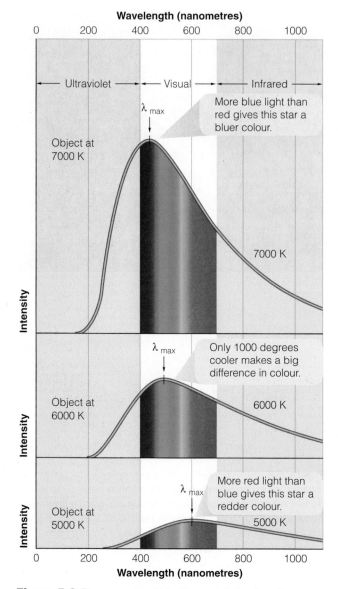

Figure 5.2 These graphs of blackbody radiation from three objects at different temperatures demonstrate that a hot object radiates more total energy (Stefan–Boltzmann law) and that the wavelength of maximum intensity is shorter for hotter objects (Wien's law). The hotter object here will look blue to your eyes, while the cooler object will look red.

The text labels within the figure read:

- Wavelength (nanometres)
- Ultraviolet | Visual | Infrared
- λ_{max}
- Object at 7000 K
- More blue light than red gives this star a bluer colour.
- 7000 K
- Object at 6000 K
- Only 1000 degrees cooler makes a big difference in colour.
- 6000 K
- Object at 5000 K
- More red light than blue gives this star a redder colour.
- 5000 K
- Intensity
- Wavelength (nanometres)

wavelengths. (Refer to **Blackbody Radiation** in the Math Reference Cards.)

5.3 The Sun's Surface

The Sun's disk looks like a mostly smooth layer of gas (Figure 5.3). Although the Sun seems to have a real surface, it is not solid. In fact, the Sun is gaseous from its outer atmosphere right down to its centre.

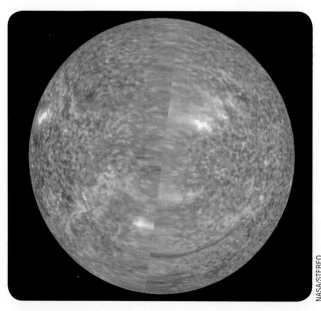

Figure 5.3 In 2011, NASA released the first-ever pictures of the Sun (front and back) taken by combining images from two probes positioned on opposite sides of the Sun. The small gap in the image existed because the probes were not yet separated by a full 180 degrees, but the gap has now been closed.

The Photosphere

The apparent surface of the Sun is called the **photosphere**. The photosphere is the layer in the Sun's atmosphere that is dense enough to emit plenty of light but not so dense that the light can't escape; so the photosphere is the source of most of the sunlight received by Earth. The photosphere is less than 500 km deep. If we built a scale model of the Sun using a bowling ball, the photosphere would be no thicker than a layer of tissue paper wrapped around the ball. If you measure the amount of light of each wavelength coming from the photosphere, plot a curve as in Figure 5.2, and then use Wien's law, you will find that the average temperature of the photosphere is about 5800 K.

Although the photosphere appears to be substantial, it is really a very-low-density gas, 3000 times less dense than the air you breathe. To find gases as dense as the air at Earth's surface, you would have to descend about 70 000 km below the photosphere, roughly 10 percent of the way to the Sun's centre. With fantastically efficient insulation, you could fly a spaceship right through the photosphere. The photosphere represents the depth where somebody outside the Sun would no longer be able to see the descending spaceship; conversely, onboard the ship, you would no longer be able to see the rest of the universe.

photosphere The bright visible surface of the Sun.

There are regions of the photosphere that appear darker than the rest. These are called **sunspots**. They produce less light than equal-sized pieces of the normal photosphere, and their colour is redder than the average, so from both the Wien and Stefan–Boltzmann laws you can conclude that sunspots are cooler than the photosphere. In fact, they are usually about 1000 to 1500 K cooler. Later in this chapter you will learn about the causes of sunspots and other solar dermatology problems.

Heat Flow in the Sun

At the temperature of 5800 K, every square millimetre of the Sun's photosphere must be radiating more energy than a 60-watt light bulb. Simple logic tells you that energy in the form of heat is flowing outward from the Sun's interior. With all that energy radiating into space, the Sun's surface would cool rapidly if energy did not flow up from inside to keep the surface hot.

As you learn more about the surface and atmosphere of the Sun, you will find many phenomena that are driven by this energy flow. Like a pot of boiling soup on a hot stove, the Sun is in constant activity as the heat comes up from below. In good photographs, the photosphere has a mottled appearance because it is made up of dark-edged regions called granules, and the visual pattern is called **granulation**, which you can see in Figure 5.4a. Each granule is about the size of Alberta and lasts for only 10 to 20 minutes before fading away. Faded granules are continuously replaced by new ones. The colour and amount of light from different portions of the granules show, by both Wien's law and the Stefan–Boltzmann law, that the centres of granules are a few hundred degrees hotter than their edges.

Astronomers recognize granulation as the surface effects of rising and falling currents of gas in and just below the photosphere (the Doppler effect that allows astronomers to measure speeds of these gas currents is discussed later in this chapter). The centres of granules are rising columns of hot gas, and the edges of the granules are cooler, sinking gas. The presence of granulation is clear evidence that energy is flowing upward through the photosphere by a process known as **convection**, which is demonstrated in Figure 5.4b.

Convection occurs when hot fluid rises and cool fluid sinks, as when, for example, a convection current of hot gas rises above a candle flame. You

sunspot Relatively cooler, dark spot on the Sun that contains intense magnetic fields.

granulation The fine structure of bright regions (grains) with dark edges covering the Sun's surface.

convection Circulation in a fluid driven by heat. Hot material rises and cool material sinks.

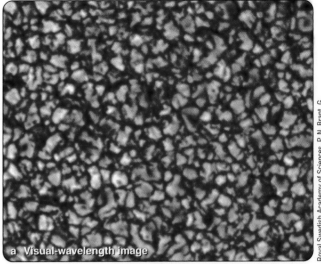

a Visual-wavelength image

Royal Swedish Academy of Sciences, P. N. Brant, G. Scharmer, G. W. Simpson, Swedish Vacuum Solar Telescope, La Palma

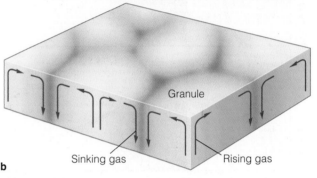

Granule

Sinking gas   Rising gas

b

Figure 5.4 (a) This ultra-high-resolution image of the photosphere shows granulation. The largest granules here are about the size of Alberta. (b) The granules are tops of rising convection currents just below the photosphere. Heat flows upward as rising currents of hot gas and downward as sinking currents of cool gas. The rising currents heat the solar surface in small regions seen from Earth as granules.

can watch liquid convection by adding a bit of cool non-dairy creamer to an unstirred cup of hot coffee. The cool creamer sinks, warms, expands, rises, cools, contracts, sinks again, and so on, creating small regions on the surface of the coffee that mark the tops of convection currents. Viewed from above, these regions look much like solar granules.

5.4 Light, Matter, and Motion

If light did not interact with matter, you would not be able to see these words. In fact, you would not exist, because, among other problems, photosynthesis would be impossible, and there would be no grass, wheat, bread, rice, or any other kind of food. The interaction of light and matter makes your life possible, and it also makes it possible for you to understand the universe.

Your study of light and matter begins here with a study of electrons that are within atoms. As you learned in the previous section, electrons and other charged particles produce light when they change speed or direction of their motion.

Electron Shells

The electrons are bound to the atom by the attraction between their negative charge and the positive charge of the nucleus. This attraction is known as the **Coulomb force**, after the French physicist Charles-Augustin de Coulomb (1736–1806). A positive **ion** is an atom with missing electrons, meaning fewer electrons than protons. For an atom to go through the **ionization** process, there needs to be a certain amount of energy to pull an electron completely away from the nucleus. This energy is the electron's **binding energy**, the energy that holds it to the atom.

The size of an electron's orbit is related to the energy that binds it to the atom. If an electron orbits close to the nucleus it is tightly bound, and a large amount of energy is needed to pull it away. Consequently, its binding energy is large. An electron orbiting farther from the nucleus is held more loosely, and less energy is needed to pull it away. That means it has less binding energy.

Nature permits atoms only certain amounts (quanta) of binding energy, and the laws that describe how atoms behave are called the laws of **quantum mechanics**. Much of this discussion of atoms is based on the laws of quantum mechanics.

Because atoms can have only certain amounts of binding energy, your model atom can have orbits of only certain sizes, called **permitted orbits**. These are like steps in a staircase: You can stand on the number-one step or the number-two step but not on the number-one-and-one-quarter step. The electron can occupy any permitted orbit, but not orbits in between.

The arrangement of permitted orbits depends primarily on the charge of the nucleus, which in turn depends on the number of protons. The number of protons in the nucleus is unique to each element. Consequently, as shown in the diagrams of hydrogen, helium, and boron in Figure 5.5, each kind of element has its own pattern of permitted orbits. Ionized forms of an element have orbital patterns

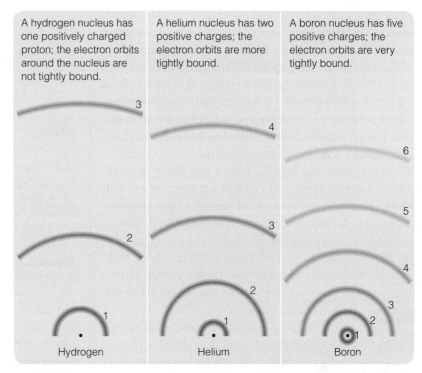

A hydrogen nucleus has one positively charged proton; the electron orbits around the nucleus are not tightly bound.

A helium nucleus has two positive charges; the electron orbits are more tightly bound.

A boron nucleus has five positive charges; the electron orbits are very tightly bound.

Figure 5.5 The electron in an atom may occupy only certain permitted orbits. Because different elements have different numbers of positively charged protons in their nuclei, the elements have different, unique patterns of permitted orbits. Figure shows only the innermost orbits, with the nucleus shown as a dot.

quite different from their un-ionized forms. The arrangement of permitted orbits differs for every kind of atom and ion. **Isotopes** are versions of a given element with different numbers of neutrons. Isotopes of an element have almost—but not quite—the same pattern of permitted electron orbits as each other because they have the same number of electrons but their nuclei have slightly different masses.

Excitation of Atoms

Each orbit in an atom represents a specific amount of binding energy, so physicists commonly refer to the orbits as **energy levels**. Using this terminology, you can say that

Coulomb force The electrostatic force of repulsion between like charges or attraction between opposite charges.

ion An atom that has lost or gained one or more electrons.

ionization The process in which atoms lose or gain electrons.

binding energy The energy needed to pull an electron away from its atom.

quantum mechanics The study of the behaviour of atoms and atomic particles.

permitted orbit One of the unique orbits that an electron may occupy in an atom.

isotopes Atoms that have the same number of protons but a different number of neutrons.

energy level One of the rungs of the ladder of allowed energy states an electron may occupy in an atom.

an electron in its smallest and most tightly bound orbit is in its lowest permitted energy level. You could move the electron from one energy level to another by supplying enough energy to make up the difference between the two energy levels. It would be like moving a flowerpot from a low shelf to a high shelf: The greater the distance between the shelves, the more energy you would need to raise the pot. The amount of energy needed to move the electron is the energy difference between the two energy levels.

If you move the electron from a low energy level to a higher energy level, you can call the atom an **excited atom**. That is, you have added energy to the atom by moving its electron. If the electron falls back to the lower energy level, that energy is released. An atom can become excited by collision. If two atoms collide, one or both may have electrons knocked into higher energy levels. This happens very commonly in hot gas, where the atoms move rapidly and collide often.

Another way an atom can get the energy that moves an electron to a higher energy level is to absorb a photon (packet) of electromagnetic radiation. Only a photon with exactly the right amount of energy corresponding to the energy difference between two levels can move the electron from one level to another. If the photon has too much or too little energy, the atom cannot absorb it, and the photon passes right by. Because the energy of a photon depends on its wavelength, only photons of certain wavelengths (certain colours) can be absorbed by a given kind of atom. The wavelength of a photon is inversely proportional to its energy. Thus, a photon with higher energy has a shorter wavelength than a photon with lower energy. (Refer to **Wave Properties** in the Math Reference Cards.)

Figure 5.6 shows the lowest four energy levels of the hydrogen atom along with three photons the atom could absorb. The longest-wavelength (reddest) photon has only enough energy to excite the electron from the first to the second energy level, but the shorter-wavelength (higher-energy, bluer) photons can excite the electron to higher levels. A photon with too much or

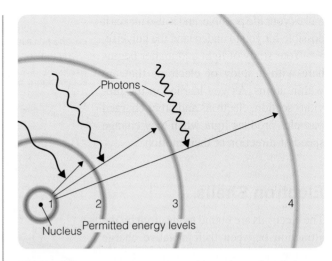

Figure 5.6 Allowed quantum leaps due to absorption of photons of differing wavelengths.

too little energy cannot be absorbed. Because the hydrogen atom has many more energy levels than shown in Figure 5.6, it can absorb photons of many different wavelengths.

Atoms, like humans, cannot exist in an excited state forever. The excited atom is unstable and must eventually (usually within a billionth to a millionth of a second) give up the energy it has absorbed and return its electron to a lower energy level. The lowest energy level an electron can occupy is called the **ground state**.

When the electron drops from a higher to a lower energy level, it moves from a loosely bound level to one more tightly bound. The atom then has a surplus of energy—the energy difference between the levels—that it can emit as a photon. Study the sequence of events in Figure 5.7 to see how an atom can absorb and emit photons. Jumps of electrons from one orbit to another are sometimes called **quantum leaps**. In popular expression, that term has come to mean a huge change, but now you see that it represents a very small change indeed. The quantum leap represents a change of electron motion, so electromagnetic radiation is either released or absorbed in the process.

excited atom An atom in which an electron has moved from a lower to a higher energy level.

ground state The lowest energy level an electron can occupy in an atom.

quantum leaps Jumps of electrons from one orbit or energy state to another.

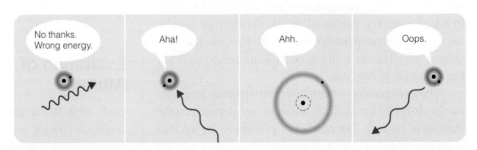

Figure 5.7 An atom can absorb a photon only if the photon has the correct amount of energy. The excited atom is unstable and within a fraction of a second returns to a lower energy level by reradiating a photon in a random direction.

Because each type of atom or ion has its unique set of energy levels, each type absorbs and emits photons with a unique set of wavelengths. As a result, you can identify the elements in a gas by studying the characteristic wavelengths (spectral lines) of light absorbed or emitted. It is important to note that the wavelengths (colours) emitted and absorbed by leaping electrons are determined not by the starting or ending energy level of the jump but by the difference between the levels (see **Visualizing Astronomy 5.1, Atomic Spectra**).

The process of excitation and emission is a common sight in urban areas at night. A neon sign glows when atoms of neon gas in the glass tube are excited by electricity flowing through the tube. As the electrons in the electric current flow through the gas, they collide with the neon atoms and excite them. And immediately after an atom is excited, its electron drops back to a lower energy level, emitting the surplus energy as a photon of a certain wavelength. The visible photons emitted by the most common electron jumps within excited neon atoms produce a reddish-orange glow. Street signs of other colours, erroneously called "neon," contain other gases or mixtures of gases instead of pure neon.

The Doppler Effect

The **Doppler effect** is an observed change in the wavelength of radiation caused by relative motion of a source and observer. Astronomers use it to measure the speed of blobs of gas in the Sun's atmosphere moving toward or away from Earth, as well as speeds of entire stars and galaxies.

When astronomers talk about the Doppler effect, they are talking about small shifts in the wavelength of electromagnetic radiation. The Doppler effect, however, can occur for waves of all types—sound waves, for example. You probably hear the Doppler effect in sound every day without realizing what it is. The pitch of a sound is determined by its wavelength. Sounds with long wavelengths have low pitches, and sounds with short wavelengths have higher pitches. You hear the Doppler effect every time a car or truck passes you and the pitch of its engine noise or emergency siren seems to drop. Its sound is shifted to shorter wavelengths and higher pitches while it is approaching and is shifted to longer wavelengths and lower pitches after it passes by.

Understanding the Doppler effect for sound lets you understand the similar Doppler effect for light. Imagine a light source emitting waves continuously as it approaches you. The light will appear to have a shorter wavelength, making it slightly bluer. This is called a **blueshift**. A light source moving away from you has a longer wavelength and is slightly redder. This is a **redshift**. Redshifted and blueshifted spectra produced by a moving light source are illustrated in Figure 5.8.

The terms *redshift* and *blueshift* are used to refer to any range of wavelengths. The light does not actually have to be red or blue, and the terms apply equally to wavelengths in the radio, X-ray, or gamma-ray parts of the spectrum. "Red" and "blue" refer

Doppler effect The observed change in the wavelength of radiation due to a source moving toward or away from the observer.

blueshift A Doppler shift toward shorter wavelengths caused by a source approaching the observer. The faster the source approaches, the larger the blueshift.

redshift A Doppler shift toward longer wavelengths caused by a source receding from the observer. The faster the source recedes, the larger the redshift.

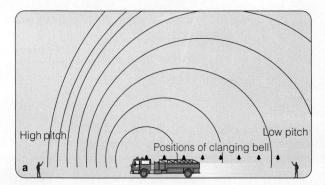
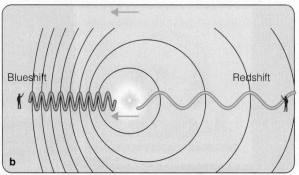

Figure 5.8 The Doppler effect. (a) The clanging bell on a moving fire truck produces sounds that move outward (black circles). An observer ahead of the truck hears the clangs closer together, while an observer behind the truck hears them farther apart. Similarly, the sound waves from a siren on an approaching truck will be received more often, and thus be heard with a higher pitch, than a stationary truck, and the siren will have a lower pitch if it is going away. (b) A moving source of light emits waves that move outward (black circles). An observer toward whom the light source is moving observes a shorter wavelength (a blueshift), and an observer for whom the light source is moving away observes a longer wavelength (a redshift).

1 To understand how to analyze a spectrum, begin with a simple incandescent light bulb. The hot filament emits blackbody radiation, which forms a **continuous spectrum**.

An **absorption spectrum** results when radiation passes through a cool gas. In this case you can imagine that the light bulb is surrounded by a cool cloud of gas. Atoms in the gas absorb photons of certain wavelengths, which are missing from the spectrum, and you see their positions as dark **absorption lines**. Such spectra are sometimes called **dark-line spectra**.

An **emission spectrum** is produced by photons emitted by an excited gas. You could see **emission lines** by turning your telescope aside so that photons from the bright bulb did not enter the telescope. The photons you would see would be those emitted by the excited atoms near the bulb. Such spectra are also called **bright-line spectra**.

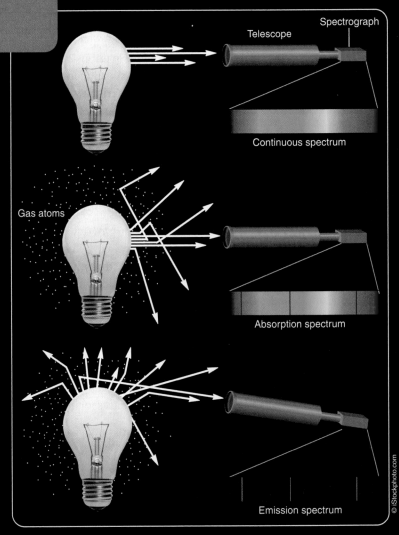

Spectrograph
Telescope

Continuous spectrum

Gas atoms

Absorption spectrum

Emission spectrum

© iStockphoto.com

1a The spectrum of a star is an absorption spectrum. The denser layers of the photosphere emit black-body radiation. Gases in the atmosphere of the star absorb their specific wavelengths and form dark absorption lines in the spectrum.

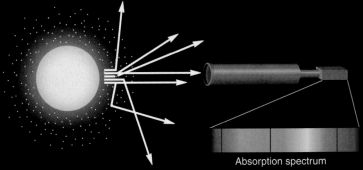

Absorption spectrum

GUSTAV ROBERT KIRCHHOFF
1824
1887
$\Sigma I_{i} = 0$
$\Sigma U_{i} = 0$
30
DEUTSCHE BUNDESPOST BERLIN

1b In 1859, long before scientists understood atoms and energy levels, the German scientist Gustav Kirchhoff formulated three rules, now known as **Kirchhoff's laws**, that describe the three types of spectra.

KIRCHHOFF'S LAWS

Law I: **The Continuous Spectrum**

A solid, liquid, or dense gas excited to emit light will radiate at all wavelengths and thus produce a continuous spectrum.

Law II: **The Emission Spectrum**

A low-density gas excited to emit light will do so at specific wavelengths and thus produce an emission spectrum.

Law III: **The Absorption Spectrum**

If light comprising a continuous spectrum passes through a cool, low-density gas, the result will be an absorption spectrum.

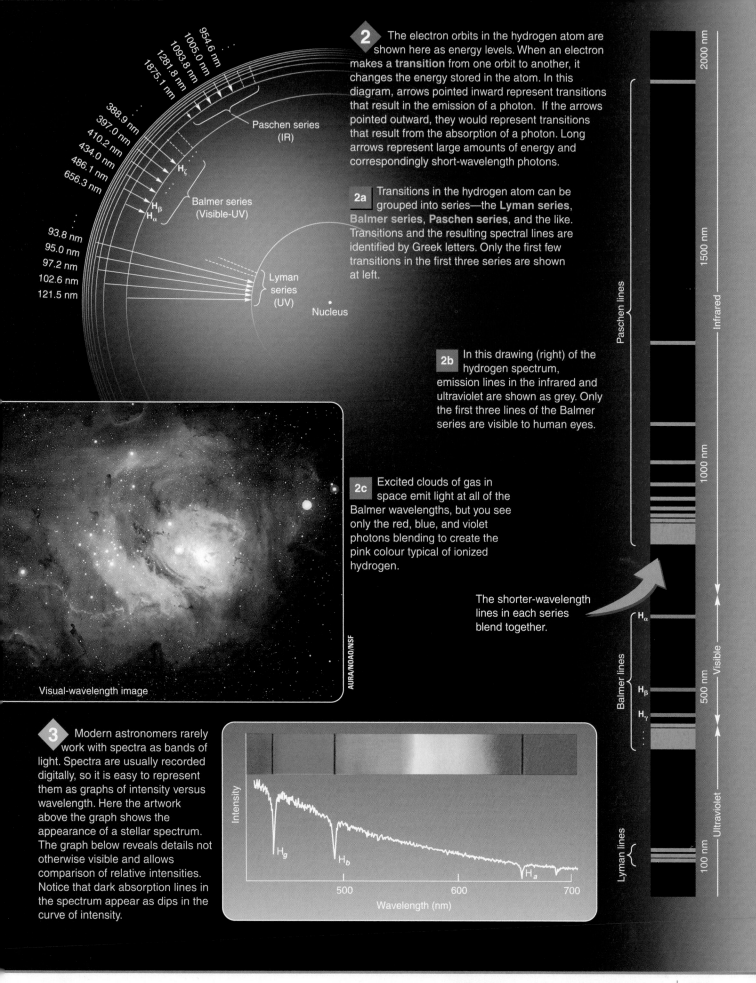

2 The electron orbits in the hydrogen atom are shown here as energy levels. When an electron makes a **transition** from one orbit to another, it changes the energy stored in the atom. In this diagram, arrows pointed inward represent transitions that result in the emission of a photon. If the arrows pointed outward, they would represent transitions that result from the absorption of a photon. Long arrows represent large amounts of energy and correspondingly short-wavelength photons.

2a Transitions in the hydrogen atom can be grouped into series—the **Lyman series**, **Balmer series**, **Paschen series**, and the like. Transitions and the resulting spectral lines are identified by Greek letters. Only the first few transitions in the first three series are shown at left.

2b In this drawing (right) of the hydrogen spectrum, emission lines in the infrared and ultraviolet are shown as grey. Only the first three lines of the Balmer series are visible to human eyes.

2c Excited clouds of gas in space emit light at all of the Balmer wavelengths, but you see only the red, blue, and violet photons blending to create the pink colour typical of ionized hydrogen.

The shorter-wavelength lines in each series blend together.

954.6 nm
1005.0 nm
1093.8 nm
1281.8 nm
1875.1 nm

Paschen series (IR)

388.9 nm
397.0 nm
410.2 nm
434.0 nm
486.1 nm
656.3 nm

H_ζ

Balmer series (Visible-UV)

H_β
H_α

93.8 nm
95.0 nm
97.2 nm
102.6 nm
121.5 nm

Lyman series (UV)

Nucleus

Visual-wavelength image

AURA/NOAO/NSF

3 Modern astronomers rarely work with spectra as bands of light. Spectra are usually recorded digitally, so it is easy to represent them as graphs of intensity versus wavelength. Here the artwork above the graph shows the appearance of a stellar spectrum. The graph below reveals details not otherwise visible and allows comparison of relative intensities. Notice that dark absorption lines in the spectrum appear as dips in the curve of intensity.

Intensity

H_g
H_b
H_a

500   600   700
Wavelength (nm)

Paschen lines

2000 nm
1500 nm
1000 nm
500 nm
100 nm

Infrared

Balmer lines

H_α
H_β
H_γ

Visible

Lyman lines

Ultraviolet

radial velocity (V_r) The component of an object's velocity that is directed directly away from or toward Earth.

to the relative direction of the shift, not to actual colour. Also, note that these shifts are much too small to change the colour of a star noticeably, but they are easily detected by changes in the positions of features in a star's spectrum, such as spectral lines (discussed in detail in the next section). The Doppler shift, blue or red, reveals the relative motion of wave source and observer. You measure the same Doppler shift if the light source is moving and you are stationary or if the light source is stationary and you are moving (see Figure 5.8).

The amount of change in wavelength depends on the speed of the source. A moving car has a smaller sound Doppler shift than a jet plane, and a slow-moving star has a smaller light Doppler shift than one that is moving at high velocity. You can measure the speed of a star toward or away from you by measuring the size of the Doppler shift of its spectral lines (Figure 5.9).

Note that the Doppler shift is sensitive only to the part of the velocity that's directed *directly* away from you or toward you; this is called the **radial velocity (V_r).** A star moving perpendicular to your line of sight, to the left for instance, would have no blueshift or redshift because its distance from Earth would not be decreasing or increasing. Police radar guns use the Doppler effect to measure the speeds of cars. The police park next to the highway and aim their "hair dryers" directly along the road because

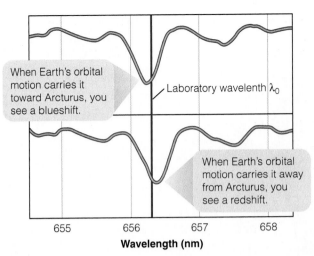

When Earth's orbital motion carries it toward Arcturus, you see a blueshift.

Laboratory wavelenth λ_0

When Earth's orbital motion carries it away from Arcturus, you see a redshift.

Figure 5.9 Balmer-alpha line in the spectrum of the star Arcturus.

they can measure only radial velocities, and they want to measure your full velocity along the highway. (Refer to **The Doppler Formula** in the Math Reference Cards.)

5.5 The Sun's Atmosphere

Science is a way of understanding nature, and the spectrum of the Sun tells you a great deal about such things as the Sun's temperature and the composition and motions

CANADIANS IN ASTRONOMY
Canada's role in the global story of astronomy

Gerhard Herzberg

Gerhard Herzberg

Nobel Prize–winning physicist Gerhard Herzberg recalled arriving in Saskatoon from Germany in 1935 with barely $2.50 in his pocket. Despite being a leading molecular physicist at the time, he was forced to leave Nazi Germany and decided to accept a position at the University of Saskatchewan. Over the next decade he continued his spectroscopic studies of atomic and molecular structure, writing several classic books on the subject. One of his early successes was the application of his methods to identify the molecule CH^+ in interstellar clouds. Dr. Herzberg subsequently worked at the University of Chicago's Yerkes Observatory for three years, fulfilling his past ambition of being an astronomer. There he developed novel methods to study planetary atmospheres and comets, which became standard techniques widely used around the world. When he returned to Canada in 1948, he joined the National Research Council (NRC) and helped make it a world leader in molecular spectroscopy. His research group made several important scientific discoveries including the detection of hydrogen in the atmospheres of planets and the presence of water in comets. Dr. Herzberg was awarded the Nobel Prize in Chemistry in 1971 for his contributions to molecular spectroscopy. Today, the Herzberg Canada Gold Medal is the highest honour for science and engineering in Canada, awarded annually in his memory by the Natural Sciences and Engineering Research Council (NSERC) of Canada.

of the gases in the solar photosphere and atmosphere. In later chapters you will use spectra to study stars, galaxies, and planets, but you can begin with spectra of the Sun.

Formation of Spectra

Spectra of the Sun and other stars are formed as light passes from their photospheres outward through their atmospheres. Study **Visualizing Astronomy 5.1, Atomic Spectra**, and notice three important properties of spectra:

1. There are three kinds of spectra described by three simple rules (Kirchhoff's laws). When you see one of these types of spectra, you can recognize the arrangement of matter that emitted the light. Dark (absorption) lines in the Sun's spectrum are caused by atoms in the Sun's (or Earth's) atmosphere between you and the Sun's photosphere. The photosphere itself produces a blackbody (continuous) spectrum.

2. Each type of atom has a unique absorption and emission spectrum. Hence, we can distinguish hydrogen from helium or other gases by observing the spectrum of the Sun. The wavelengths of the photons that are absorbed by a given type of atom are the same as the wavelengths of the photons emitted by that type of atom; both are determined by the electron energy levels in the atom. The emitted photons coming from a hot cloud of hydrogen gas have the same wavelengths as the photons absorbed by hydrogen atoms in the Sun's atmosphere. Although the hydrogen atom produces many spectral lines from the ultraviolet to the infrared, only three hydrogen lines are visible to human eyes.

3. Most modern astronomy books display spectra as graphs of intensity versus wavelength. Be sure you

see the connection between dark absorption lines and dips in the graphed spectrum.

The Sun's Chemical Composition

Identifying the elements in the Sun's atmosphere by identifying the lines in its spectrum is a relatively straightforward procedure (Figure 5.10a). For example, two dark absorption lines appear in the yellow region of the solar spectrum at the wavelengths 589.0 nm and 589.6 nm. The only atom that can produce this pair of lines is sodium, so the Sun must contain sodium. Over 90 elements in the Sun have been identified this way. The element helium was known in the Sun's spectrum first, before helium (from the Greek word *helios,* meaning "sun") was found on Earth.

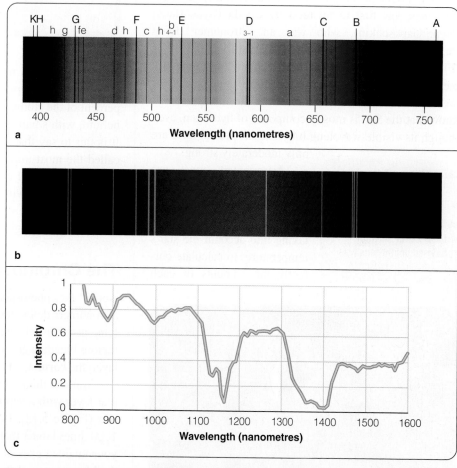

Figure 5.10 (a) The Sun's spectrum at visual wavelengths. The bright coloured background shows the continuous spectrum of blackbody emission from the Sun's photosphere. The dark spectral absorption lines represent precise colours (photons of exact energies) absorbed from the Sun's radiation by atoms in its atmosphere. (b) A model of the visual wavelength emission (bright-line) spectrum of NCG2392. Emission lines from ionized atoms of hydrogen (red), nitrogen (red) and oxygen (green), among others, are seen. (c) Near-infrared spectrum of the atmosphere and surface of Saturn's moon Titan measured by the Huygens probe at an altitude of 20 m using a light source on the bottom of the probe.

However, just because spectral lines that are characteristic of an element are missing, you cannot conclude that the element itself is absent. For example, although more than 90 percent of the atoms in the Sun are hydrogen, the hydrogen Balmer lines are weak in the Sun's spectrum (see **Visualizing Astronomy 5.1, Atomic Spectra**). The reason for this apparent paradox is that the Sun is too cool to produce strong Balmer lines. At the Sun's photosphere temperature, atoms do not usually collide violently enough to knock electrons in hydrogen atoms into the second energy level, which is the necessary starting place for Balmer line absorptions. Spectral lines of other varieties of atoms (for example, ionized calcium) are especially easy to observe in the Sun's spectrum because the Sun is the right temperature to excite those atoms to the energy levels that can produce visible spectral lines, even though those atoms are not very common in the Sun.

The effect of temperature on the visibility of spectral lines was first understood by Cecila Payne (later, Payne-Gaposchkin), who was an astronomer doing Ph.D. research work at Harvard Observatory in the 1920s (Figure 5.11). She used the new techniques of quantum mechanics to derive accurate chemical abundances for the Sun and other stars; so she was the first person to know that the Sun is mostly composed of hydrogen, even though its visible-wavelength hydrogen spectral lines are only moderately strong.

Astronomers must use the physics that describes the interaction of light and matter to analyze a star's spectrum, taking into account the star's temperature, to calculate correctly the amounts of each

chromosphere Bright gases just above the photosphere of the Sun.

corona The faint outer atmosphere of the Sun, composed of low-density, high-temperature gas.

Table 5.1	The Most Abundant Elements in the Sun	
Element	Percentage by Number of Atoms	Percentage by Mass
Hydrogen	91.0	70.9
Helium	8.9	27.4
Carbon	0.03	0.3
Nitrogen	0.008	0.1
Oxygen	0.07	0.8
Neon	0.01	0.2
Magnesium	0.003	0.06
Silicon	0.003	0.07
Sulphur	0.002	0.04
Iron	0.003	0.1

element present in the star. Such results show that nearly all stars have compositions similar to the Sun—about 90 percent of the atoms are hydrogen, and about 9 percent are helium, with small traces of heavier elements (Table 5.1). It is fair to say that Cecilia Payne, whose thesis has been called the most important doctoral work in the history of astronomy, figured out the true chemical composition of the universe. You will use her results in later chapters when you study the life stories of the stars, the history of our galaxy, and the origin of the universe.

The Chromosphere

Above the photosphere lies the **chromosphere**. Solar astronomers define the lower edge of the chromosphere as lying just above the visible surface of the Sun with its upper regions blending gradually with the atmosphere's outermost layer, the **corona**, which is described later in this chapter.

You can think of the chromosphere as being an irregular layer with a depth on average less than Earth's diameter (Figure 5.12). Because the chromosphere is roughly 1000 times fainter than the photosphere, you can see it with your unaided eyes only during a total solar eclipse when the Moon covers the brilliant photosphere. Then, the chromosphere flashes into view as a thin line of pink just above the photosphere. The word *chromosphere* comes from the Greek word *chroma*, meaning "colour." The pink colour is produced by combined light of three bright emission lines—the red, blue, and violet Balmer lines of hydrogen.

Astronomers know a great deal about the chromosphere from its spectrum. The chromosphere produces an

© Science Source

Figure 5.11 Dr. Cecilia Payne-Gaposchkin first showed that the Sun and other stars are mostly made of hydrogen. Her Ph.D. thesis has been called the most important in the history of astronomy.

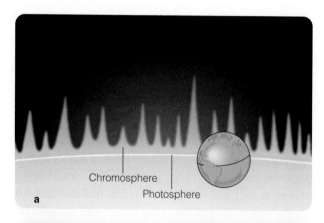

Chromosphere

Photosphere

a

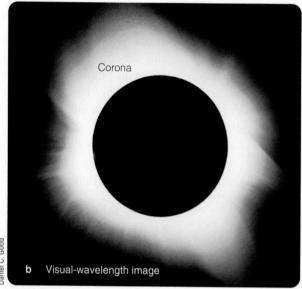

Corona

Daniel C. Good

b Visual-wavelength image

Figure 5.12 (a) A cross-section at the edge of the Sun shows the relative thickness of the photosphere and chromosphere. Earth is shown for scale. On this scale, the disk of the Sun would be more than 1.5 m in diameter. (b) The corona extends from the top of the chromosphere to a great distance above the photosphere. This photograph, made during a total solar eclipse, shows only the inner part of the corona.

emission spectrum, and Kirchhoff's second law tells you the chromosphere must be an excited, transparent, low-density gas viewed with a dark, cold background (see **Visualizing Astronomy 5.1, Atomic Spectra**). The density is about 100 million times less than that of the air you breathe.

Atoms in the lower chromosphere are ionized, and atoms in the higher layers of the chromosphere are even more highly ionized. That is, they have lost more electrons. From this, astronomers can find the temperature in different parts of the chromosphere. Just above the photosphere, the temperature falls to a minimum of about 4500 K and then rises to the extremely high temperatures of the corona.

Solar astronomers can take advantage of some of the physics of spectral line formation to study the chromosphere. A photon with a wavelength corresponding to one of the solar atmosphere's strong absorption lines is very unlikely to

escape from deeper layers and reach Earth since it is likely to be absorbed by the solar atmosphere. A **filtergram** is a photograph made using light in one of those dark absorption lines. Those photons can only come from high in the solar atmosphere. In this way, filtergrams reveal detail in the upper layers of the chromosphere. In a similar way, an image recorded in the far-ultraviolet or in the X-ray part of the spectrum reveals other structures in the hottest parts of the solar atmosphere.

Figure 5.13a shows a filtergram made at the wavelength of the H_α Balmer line. This image shows

filtergram A photograph (usually of the Sun) taken in the light of a specific region of the spectrum; for example, an H_α filtergram.

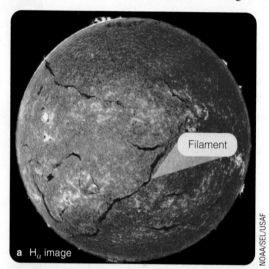

Filament

a H_α image

NOAA/SEL/USAF

Spicules

b H_α image

National Optical Astronomy Observatory/NOAO

Figure 5.13 H_α filtergrams reveal complex structures in the chromosphere, including (a) long, dark filaments and (b) spicules springing from the edges of supergranules that are larger than twice the diameter of Earth.

complex structure in the chromosphere, including long, dark **filaments** silhouetted against the brighter surface. **Spicules** are flamelike jets of gas extending upward into the chromosphere and lasting 5 to 15 minutes. Figure 5.13b shows how, at the limb of the Sun's disk, the spicules blend together and look like flames covering a burning prairie, but they are not flames at all. Spectra show that spicules are cooler gas from the lower chromosphere extending upward into hotter regions.

Spectroscopic analysis of the chromosphere shows that it is a low-density gas in constant motion, and its temperature increases rapidly with height. Just above the chromosphere lies even hotter gas.

The Corona

The outermost part of the Sun's atmosphere is called the *corona*, after the Greek word for "crown." The corona is so dim that it is not visible in Earth's daytime sky because of the glare of scattered light from the Sun's brilliant photosphere. During a total solar eclipse, however, when the Moon covers the photosphere, you can see the innermost parts of the corona, as shown in Figure 5.12b. Observations made with specialized telescopes called **coronagraphs** on Earth or in space can block the light of the photosphere and record the corona out beyond 20 solar radii,

almost 10 percent of the way to Earth. Such images reveal that sunspots are linked with features in the chromosphere and corona (Figure 5.14).

The spectrum of the corona can tell you a great deal about the coronal gases and simultaneously illustrate how astronomers analyze a spectrum. Some of the light from the corona produces a continuous spectrum that lacks absorption lines. Superimposed on the corona's continuous spectrum are emission lines of highly ionized gases. In the lower corona, the atoms are not as highly ionized as they are at higher altitudes, and this tells you that the temperature of the corona rises with altitude. Just above the chromosphere, the coronal temperature is about 500 000 K, but in the outer corona the temperature can be 2 000 000 K or more. Despite that very high temperature, the corona does not produce much light because its density is very low, only 10^6 atoms/cm³ or less. That is about one-trillionth the density of the air you breathe.

Astronomers have wondered for years how the corona and chromosphere can be so hot. Heat flows from hot regions to cool regions, never from cool to hot. So how can the heat from the photosphere, with a temperature of only 5800 K, flow out into the much hotter chromosphere and corona? Observations made by the SOHO satellite show a **magnetic carpet** of looped magnetic fields extending up through the photosphere. A magnetic field is a region in which a magnetic substance (such as iron, for example) will feel a magnetic force. If you sprinkle iron filings on a paper placed above a bar magnet, the iron filings align themselves along curved loops connecting the north and south poles. These loops show magnetic field lines running from the north pole to the south pole of the magnet. The lines map out the direction and strength of the magnetic force at each point. Remember that the gas of the chromosphere and corona has a very low density, so it can't resist movement in the magnetic fields. Turbulence below the photosphere seems to flick the magnetic loops back and forth and whip the gas about. That heats the gas. In this instance, energy appears

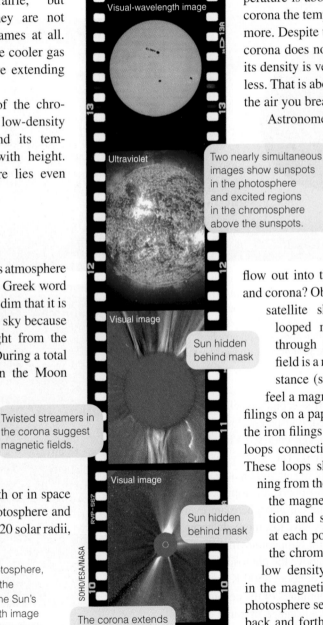

Visual-wavelength image

Ultraviolet

Visual image

Visual image

SOHO/ESA/NASA

Two nearly simultaneous images show sunspots in the photosphere and excited regions in the chromosphere above the sunspots.

Twisted streamers in the corona suggest magnetic fields.

Sun hidden behind mask

Sun hidden behind mask

The corona extends far from the disk.

Figure 5.14 Images of the photosphere, chromosphere, and corona show the relationship among the layers of the Sun's atmosphere. The visual wavelength image shows the Sun in white light, that is, as you would see it with your eyes.

to flow outward in the form of agitation of the magnetic fields. Solar magnetic phenomena will be discussed more thoroughly later in this chapter.

Not all of the Sun's magnetic field loops back toward the Sun; some of the field lines lead outward into space. Gas from the solar atmosphere follows along the magnetic fields that point outward and flows away from the Sun in a breeze called the **solar wind** that can be considered an extension of the corona. The low-density gases of the solar wind blow past Earth at 300 to 800 km/s with gusts as high as 1000 km/s.

Because of the solar wind, the Sun is slowly losing mass, but this is a minor loss for an object as massive as the Sun. The Sun loses about 10^7 tons per second, but that is only 10^{-14} of a solar mass per year. Later in life, the Sun, like many other stars, will lose mass rapidly. You will see in future chapters how this affects the evolution of stars.

Do other stars have chromospheres, coronae, and stellar winds like the Sun? Ultraviolet and X-ray observations suggest that the answer is yes. The spectra of many stars contain emission lines in the far-ultraviolet that could only have formed in the low-density, high-temperature gases of a chromosphere or corona. Also, many stars are sources of X-rays that appear to have been produced by the high-temperature gas in coronae. This observational evidence gives astronomers good reason to believe that the Sun, for all its complexity, is a typical star.

5.6 Solar Activity

The Sun is not quiet. It is home to slowly changing spots larger than Earth and rapid, vast eruptions that dwarf human imagination. All of these seemingly different forms of solar activity have one thing in common: magnetic fields.

Observing the Sun

Solar activity is often visible with even a small telescope, but you should be very careful about observing the Sun. It is not safe to look directly at the Sun, and it is even more dangerous to look at the Sun through any optical instrument such as a telescope, binoculars, or even the viewfinder of a camera. These concentrate sunlight and can cause severe injury. You can safely project an image of the Sun onto a screen, or you can use specially designed solar blocking filters.

In the early 17th century, Galileo observed the Sun and saw spots on its surface; day by day, he saw the spots moving across the Sun's disk. He correctly concluded that the Sun is a sphere and is rotating (Figure 5.15).

Sunspots

The dark sunspots that you see at visible wavelengths only hint at the complex processes that go on in the Sun's atmosphere. To explore those processes, you must turn to the analysis of images and spectra at a wide range of wavelengths. Study **Visualizing Astronomy 5.2, Sunspots and the Sunspot Cycle**, and notice five important points:

1. Sunspots are cool spots on the Sun's surface caused by strong magnetic fields.
2. Sunspots follow an 11-year cycle not only in the number of spots visible but also in their location on the Sun.
3. The Zeeman effect gives astronomers a way to measure the strength of magnetic fields on the Sun.
4. Characteristics of the sunspot cycle vary over centuries and appear to affect Earth's climate.
5. Finally, there is clear evidence that sunspots are part of a larger magnetic process that involves other layers of the Sun's atmosphere and parts of its interior.

The sunspot groups are merely the visible traces of magnetically active regions. But what causes this magnetic activity? The answer appears to be linked to the cyclical strengthening and weakening of the Sun's overall magnetic field.

Insight into the Sun's Interior

Almost no light emerges from below the photosphere, so you can't see into the solar interior. However, solar astronomers can use the vibrations in the Sun to explore its depths in a type of analysis called **helioseismology**. Random motions in the Sun constantly produce vibrations. Astronomers can detect these vibrations by observing Doppler shifts in the solar surface. These waves make the photosphere move up and down by small amounts—roughly plus or minus 15 km. This covers the surface of the Sun with a pattern of rising and falling regions that can be mapped, as in Figure 5.16.

In the Sun, a vibration with a period of 5 minutes is strongest, but other periods are observed ranging from 3 to 20 minutes. Just as geologists can study Earth's interior by analyzing vibrations from earthquakes, so solar astronomers can use

solar wind Rapidly moving atoms and ions that escape from the solar corona and blow outward through the solar system.

helioseismology The study of the interior of the Sun by the analysis of its modes of vibration.

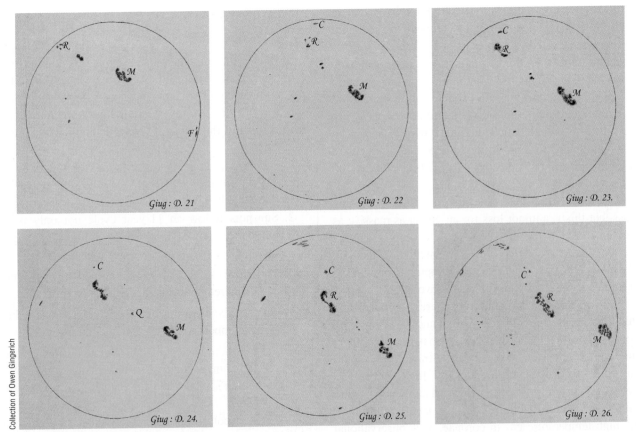

Figure 5.15 If you sketch the location and structure of sunspots on successive days, you will see the rotation of the Sun and gradual changes in the size and structure of sunspots, just as Galileo did in 1612.

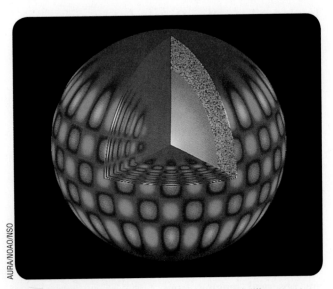

Figure 5.16 The Sun can vibrate in millions of different patterns or modes, and each mode corresponds to a different vibration wavelength that penetrates to a different level in the solar interior. By measuring Doppler shifts produced as the photosphere moves gently up and down, astronomers can map the inside of the Sun.

helioseismology to map the temperature, density, and rate of rotation in the Sun's invisible interior.

The Global Oscillation Network Group (GONG) is a worldwide network of observatories located in Australia, India, the United States, Chile, and the Canary Islands that makes continuous observations of "sunquakes"—the vibrations of the Sun. Large-scale collaborations of this type are increasingly common in current astronomy research efforts and are critical for our shared goal of understanding our Sun, our solar system, and our universe.

The Sun's Magnetic Cycle

Sunspots are magnetic phenomena, so the 11-year cycle of sunspots must be caused by cyclical changes in the Sun's magnetic field. To explore that idea, you can begin with the Sun's rotation.

The Sun does not rotate as a rigid body. It is a gas from its outermost layers down to its centre, and some parts of the Sun rotate faster than other parts. Figure 5.17

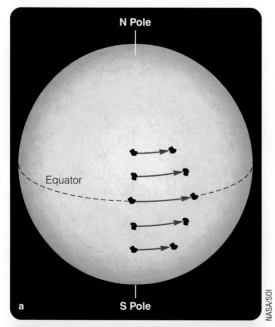

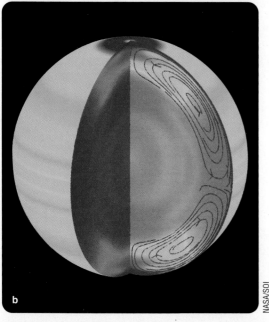

Figure 5.17 (a) In general, the photosphere of the Sun rotates faster at the equator than at higher latitudes. If you observed five sunspots in a row, they would not stay lined up as the Sun rotates. (b) Detailed analyses of the Sun's interior rotation from helioseismology reveal regions of slow rotation (blue) and rapid rotation (red). Such studies show that differential rotation occurs inside the Sun as well as on its surface.

demonstrates how the equatorial region of the photosphere rotates faster than do regions at higher latitudes. At the equator, the photosphere rotates once every 25 days, but at latitude 45° one rotation takes 28 days. Helioseismology can map the rotation throughout the interior (Figure 5.17b).

This phenomenon is called **differential rotation**, and it is clearly linked with the magnetic cycle.

The Sun's magnetic field appears to be powered by the energy flowing outward through the moving currents of gas. The gas is highly ionized, so it is a very good conductor of electricity. When an electrical conductor rotates rapidly and is stirred by convection, it can convert some of the energy flowing outward as convection into a magnetic field. This process is called the **dynamo effect**, and it is believed to operate also in the liquid metal of Earth's core to produce Earth's magnetic field. Helioseismology observations have found evidence that the Sun's magnetic field is generated by the dynamo effect at the bottom of the **convective zone** deep under the photosphere. The Sun's magnetic cycle is clearly related to how its magnetic field is created.

The magnetic behaviour of sunspots provides an insight into how the magnetic cycle works. Sunspots tend to occur in groups or pairs, and the magnetic field around the pair resembles that around a bar magnet with one end magnetic north and the other end magnetic south. At any one time, sunspot pairs south of the Sun's equator have reversed polarity compared to those north of the Sun's equator. Figure 5.18 illustrates this by showing sunspot pairs south of the Sun's equator with magnetic south poles leading and sunspots north of the Sun's equator with magnetic north poles leading. At the end of an 11-year sunspot cycle, the new spots appear with reversed magnetic polarity.

Babcock Model for Solar Activity

The Sun's magnetic cycle is not fully understood, but the **Babcock model** (named for its inventor) explains the magnetic cycle as a progressive tangling and then untangling of the solar magnetic field, demonstrated in Figure 5.19. Because the electrons in an ionized gas are free to move, the gas is a very good conductor of electricity, and any magnetic field in the gas is "frozen"

differential rotation The rotation of a body in which different parts of the body have different periods of rotation. This is true of the Sun, the Jovian planets, and the disk of the galaxy.

dynamo effect The process by which a rotating, convecting body of conducting matter, such as Earth's core, can generate a magnetic field.

convective zone The region inside a star where energy is carried outward as rising hot gas and sinking cool gas.

Babcock model A model of the Sun's magnetic cycle in which the differential rotation of the Sun winds up and tangles the solar magnetic field. This is thought to be responsible for the sunspot cycle.

1 The dark spots that appear on the Sun are only the visible traces of complex regions of activity. Observations over many years and at a range of wavelengths tell you that sunspots are clearly linked to the Sun's magnetic field. Spectra show that sunspots are cooler than the photosphere, with a temperature of about 4200 K. The photosphere has a temperature of about 5800 K. Because the total amount of energy radiated by a surface depends on its temperature raised to the fourth power, sunspots look dark in comparison. Actually, a sunspot emits quite a bit of radiation. If the Sun were removed and a only an average-size sunspot were left behind, it would be brighter than the full Moon.

A typical sunspot is about twice the size of Earth, but there is a wide range of sizes. They appear, last a few weeks to as long as 2 months, and then shrink away. Usually, sunspots occur in pairs or complex groups.

Earth to scale

NASA

Umbra

Sunspots are not shadows, but astronomers refer to the dark core of a sunspot as its umbra and the outer, lighter region as the penumbra.

Penumbra

Hinode JAXA/NASA

Visual wavelength image

Streamers above a sunspot suggest a magnetic field.

Hinode JAXA/NASA

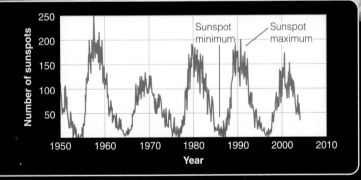

2 The number of spots visible on the Sun varies in a cycle with a period of 11 years. At maximum, there are often over 100 spots visible. At minimum, there are very few.

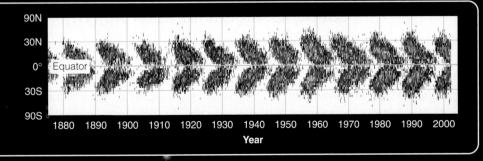

2a Early in the cycle, spots appear at high latitudes north and south of the Sun's equator. Later in the cycle, the spots appear closer to the Sun's equator. If you plot the latitude of sunspots versus time, the graph looks like butterfly wings, as shown in this **Maunder butterfly diagram**, named after E. Walter Maunder of Greenwich Observatory.

3 ▷ Astronomers can measure magnetic fields on the Sun using the **Zeeman effect** as shown below. When an atom is in a magnetic field, the electron orbits are altered, and the atom is able to absorb a number of different wavelength photons even though it was originally limited to a single wavelength. In the spectrum, you see single lines split into multiple components, with the separation between the components proportional to the strength of the magnetic field.

Sunspot groups

Magnetic fields around sunspot groups

Ultraviolet filtergram

Magnetic image

Simultaneous images

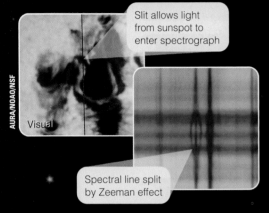

Slit allows light from sunspot to enter spectrograph

AURA/NOAO/NSF

Visual

Spectral line split by Zeeman effect

3a Images of the Sun above show that sunspots contain magnetic fields a few thousand times stronger than Earth's. The strong fields are believed to inhibit motion below the photosphere; consequently, convection is reduced below the suns and the surface there is cooler. Heat prevented from emerging through the sunspot deflected and emerges around the sunspot, which can be detected in ultraviolet an infrared images.

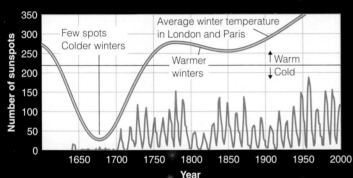

4 ▷ Historical records show that there were very few sunspot from about 1645 to 1715, a phenomenon known as the **Maunder minimum.** This coincides with a period called the "little ice age," a period of unusually cool weather in Europe and North America from about 1500 to about 1850, as shown in the graph left. Other such periods of cooler climate are known. The eviden suggests that there is a link between solar activity and the amou of solar energy Earth receives. This link has been confirmed by measurements made by spacecraft above Earth's atmosphere.

Magnetic fields can reveal themselves by their shape. For example, iron filings sprinkled over a bar magnet reveal an arched shape.

M. Seeds

The complexity of an active region becomes visible at short wavelengths.

Far-UV image

5 ▷ Observations at nonvisible wavelengths reveal that the chromosphere and corona above sunspots are violently disturbed in what astronomers call **active regions.** Spectrographic observations show that active regions contain powerful magnetic fields. Arched structures above an active region are evidence of gas trapped in magnetic fields.

Visual-wavelength image

Simultaneous images

Far-UV image

SOHO/EIT, ESA and NASA

CHAPTER 5   **The Sun: The Closest Star** |

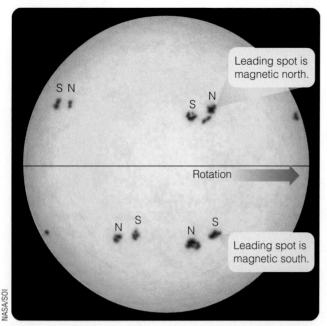

Figure 5.18 In sunspot groups, here simplified into pairs of major spots, the leading spot and the trailing spot have opposite magnetic polarity. Spot pairs in the southern hemisphere have reversed polarity from those in the northern hemisphere.

In the figure:
- Leading spot is magnetic north.
- Leading spot is magnetic south.
- Rotation

The Solar Magnetic Cycle

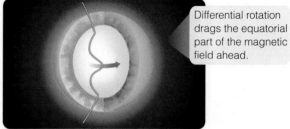

For simplicity, a single line of the solar magnetic field is shown.

Magnetic field line

Sun

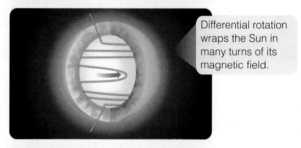

Differential rotation drags the equatorial part of the magnetic field ahead.

Differential rotation wraps the Sun in many turns of its magnetic field.

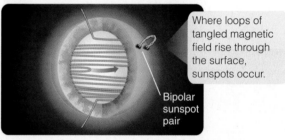

Where loops of tangled magnetic field rise through the surface, sunspots occur.

Bipolar sunspot pair

Figure 5.19 The Babcock model of the solar magnetic cycle explains the sunspot cycle as a consequence of the Sun's differential rotation gradually winding up the magnetic field near the base of the Sun's outer, convective layer.

(firmly embedded) in the gas. If the gas moves, the magnetic field must move with it. The Sun's magnetic field is frozen into its gases, and the differential rotation wraps this field around the Sun like a long string caught in a rotating wheel. Rising and sinking gas currents twist the field into ropelike tubes, which tend to float upward. Where these magnetic tubes burst through the Sun's surface, sunspot pairs occur.

The Babcock model explains the reversal of the Sun's magnetic field from cycle to cycle. As the magnetic field becomes tangled, adjacent regions of the Sun's surface are dominated by magnetic fields that point in different directions. After about 11 years of tangling, the field becomes so complex that adjacent regions of the surface are forced to change their magnetic field directions to align with neighbouring regions. The entire field quickly rearranges itself into a simpler pattern, and differential rotation begins winding it up to start a new cycle. The newly organized field is reversed, and the next sunspot cycle begins with magnetic north replaced by magnetic south. Consequently, the complete magnetic cycle is 22 years long, whereas the sunspot cycle is 11 years long.

This magnetic cycle seems to explain the Maunder butterfly diagram (see **Visualizing Astronomy 5.2, Sunspots and the Sunspot Cycle**). As a sunspot cycle begins, the twisted tubes of magnetic force first begin to float upward

and produce sunspot pairs at higher latitude. Later in the cycle, when the field is more tightly wound, the tubes of magnetic force arch up through the surface closer to the equator. As a result, the later sunspot pairs in a cycle appear closer to the equator.

Notice the power of a scientific model. The Babcock model may in fact be incorrect in some details, but it provides a framework on which to organize your thinking about all the complex solar activity. Even though the models of the sky you learned about in Chapter 2 and the models of atomic energy levels in this chapter are only partially correct, they serve as organizing themes to guide your explorations. Similarly, although the precise details of the solar magnetic cycle are not yet understood, the Babcock model gives you a general picture of the behaviour of the Sun's magnetic field.

If the Sun is truly a representative star, you might expect to find similar magnetic cycles on other stars, but they are too distant for spots to be directly visible. Some stars, however, vary in brightness over a period of days, in a way revealing that they are marked with dark spots believed to resemble sunspots. Other stars have features in their spectra that vary over periods of years, suggesting that they are subject to magnetic cycles much like the Sun's cycle. Once again, the evidence tells you that the Sun is a normal star.

Chromospheric and Coronal Activity

The solar magnetic fields extend high into the chromosphere and corona, where they produce beautiful and powerful phenomena. Study **Visualizing Astronomy 5.3, Magnetic Solar Phenomena**, and notice three important points:

1. All solar activity is magnetic. You do not experience such events on Earth because Earth's magnetic field is weak and Earth's atmosphere is not ionized, so it is free to move independent of the magnetic field. On the Sun, however, the "weather" is a magnetic phenomenon.

2. Tremendous energy can be stored in arches of magnetic fields. These are visible near the edge of the solar disk as prominences, and, seen from above, as filaments. When that stored energy is released, it can trigger powerful eruptions; and, although these eruptions occur far from Earth, they can affect Earth in dramatic ways, including auroral displays. Auroras, the eerie and pretty northern and southern lights, are produced when gases in Earth's upper atmosphere glow from energy delivered by the solar wind.

3. In some regions of the solar surface, the magnetic field does not loop back. High-energy gas from these regions flows outward and produces much of the solar wind.

Solar eruptions, although occurring millions of kilometres away, can eject enormous amounts of charged particles that can be severely disruptive to satellite

Figure 5.20 An e-CALLISTO spectrometer in Pune, India.

Christian Monstein

communications and to TV and cell phone signals on Earth. A radio solar telescope network run by the U.S. Air Force monitors such emissions but does not provide complete real-time coverage. Recently, a low-cost system of spectrometers called the e-CALLISTO network, originally designed by amateur astronomer Christian Monstein, has been set up at locations around the world, including Mongolia, Alaska, Egypt, Siberia, India, and Costa Rica (Figure 5.20). The network monitors the Sun 24 hours a day and can act as an early-warning system for disruptions caused by solar flares. "We wanted 24-hour coverage, but we also wanted to take radio astronomy to countries that could not afford it," said astrophysicist Arnold Benz, who worked with Monstein to distribute the CALLISTO instruments around the world.

You needed the entire range of physical principles presented in this chapter—parallax, Wien's law and the Stefan–Bolzmann law for blackbody radiation, atomic structure, Kirchhoff's laws for the formation of spectra, the Doppler effect, the Zeeman effect— to realize how the Sun's surface temperature and composition are known, and to understand solar activity cycles and their effects on Earth. In the next chapter you will learn how the Sun fits into the context of other stars.

1 Magnetic phenomena in the chromosphere and corona, like magnetic weather, result as constantly changing magnetic fields on the Sun trap ionized gas and produce beautiful arches and powerful outbursts. Some of this solar activity can affect Earth's magnetic field and atmosphere.

This ultraviolet image of the solar surface was made by the NASA TRACE spacecraft. It shows hot gas trapped in magnetic arches extending above active regions. At visual wavelengths, you would see sunspot groups in these active regions.

The gas in prominences may be 60 000 to 80 000 K, quite cold compared with the low-density gas in the corona, which may be as hot as a million Kelvin.

Trace/NASA

National Solar Observatory/AURA/NSF

H$_\alpha$ filtergram

1a A **prominence** is composed of ionized gas trapped in a magnetic arch rising up through the photosphere and chromosphere into the lower corona. Seen during total solar eclipses at the edge of the solar disk, prominences look pink because of the three Balmer emission lines. The image above shows the arch shape suggestive of magnetic fields. Seen from above against the Sun's bright surface, prominences form dark filaments.

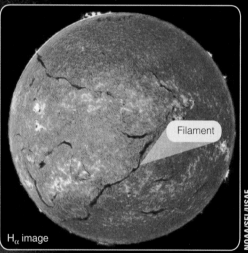

Filament

H$_\alpha$ image

NOAA/SEL/USAF

1b Quiescent prominences may hang in the lower corona for many days, whereas eruptive prominences burst upward in hours. The eruptive prominence below is many Earth diameters long.

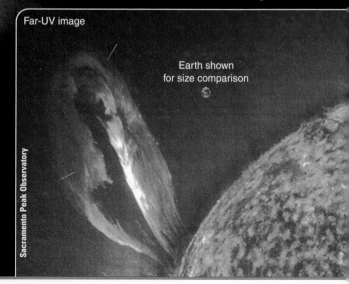

Far-UV image

Earth shown for size comparison

Sacramento Peak Observatory

2 Solar **flares** rise to maximum in minutes and decay in an hour. They occur in active regions where oppositely directed magnetic fields meet and cancel each other out in what astronomers call **reconnections**. Energy stored in the magnetic fields is released as short-wavelength photons and as high-energy protons and electrons. X-ray and ultraviolet photons reach Earth in eight minutes and increase ionization in our atmosphere, which can interfere with radio communications. Particles from flares reach Earth hours or days later as gusts in the solar wind, which can distort Earth's magnetic field and disrupt navigation systems. Solar flares can also cause surges in electrical power lines and damage to Earth satellites.

This multiwavelength image shows a sunspot interacting with a neighbouring magnetic field to produce a solar flare.

Hinode JAXA/NASA

2a At right, waves rush outward at 50 km/sec from the site of a solar flare 40 000 times stronger than the 1906 San Francisco earthquake. The biggest solar flares can be a billion times more powerful than a hydrogen bomb.

Helioseismology image

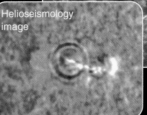

SOHO/MDI, ESA, and NASA

2b The solar wind, enhanced by eruptions on the Sun, interacts with Earth's magnetic field and can create electrical currents up to a million megawatts. Those currents flowing down into a ring around Earth's magnetic poles excite atoms in Earth's upper atmosphere to emit photons as shown below. Seen from Earth's surface, the gas produces glowing clouds and curtains of **aurora**.

Auroras occur about 130 km above Earth's surface.

© Ian Curtis

Coronal mass ejection

Ring of aurora around the north magnetic pole

NSSDC, Holzworth, and Meng

2c Magnetic reconnections can release enough energy to blow large amounts of ionized gas outward from the corona in **coronal mass ejections (CMEs)**. If a CME strikes Earth, it can produce especially violent disturbances in Earth's magnetic field.

3 Much of the solar wind comes from **coronal holes**, where the magnetic field does not loop back into the Sun. These open magnetic fields allow ionized gas in the corona to flow away as the solar wind. The dark area in this X-ray image at right is a coronal hole.

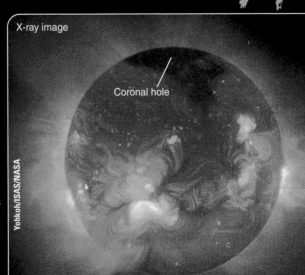

X-ray image

Coronal hole

Yohkoh/ISAS/NASA

Confirmation, Confidence, and Consolidation

Science is not always about upending paradigms and dramatically changing the way people view nature. Many experiments and observations are simply carried out to confirm hypotheses that have already been tested. The biologist knows that all worker bees in a hive are sisters, but a careful study of the DNA from different workers further confirms that hypothesis. By repeatedly confirming a hypothesis, scientists build confidence and extend its application. Much of the daily grind of science is confirmation.

Repeated confirmation of hypotheses increases confidence in those hypotheses. Confidence in well-tested scientific principles helps scientists avoid rushing to faulty judgments. For example, claims for perpetual motion machines occasionally crop up in the news, but the world's scientists don't instantly abandon the laws of energy and motion pending an analysis of the latest claim. Because the known laws of energy and motion have been well tested and no perpetual motion machine has ever been successful, scientists know which way to bet.

Confirmation and confidence enable scientists to broaden the application of hypotheses and link them to other phenomena through consolidation. Chemists may understand certain kinds of carbon molecules shaped like rings, but by repeated study they find a carbon molecule shaped like a hollow sphere. To consolidate their findings, they must show that the chemical bonding in the two molecules follows the same rules and that the molecules have certain properties in common.

The Babcock model of the solar magnetic cycle is an example of the scientific process in astronomy. Solar astronomers know that the model has shortcomings, but they work through confirmation and consolidation to better understand how the solar magnetic cycle works and how it is related to cycles in other stars.

The **Big Picture**

We live very close to a star and depend on it for survival. All of our food comes from sunlight that was captured by plants on land or by plankton in the oceans. We either eat those plants directly or eat the animals that feed on those plants. Whether you had salad, seafood, or a cheeseburger for supper last night, you dined on sunlight, thanks to photosynthesis. Almost all of the energy that powers human civilization comes from the Sun through photosynthesis in ancient plants that were buried and converted to coal, oil, and natural gas. New technology is making energy from plant products such as corn, soybeans, and sugar. It is all stored sunlight. Windmills generate electrical power, and the wind blows because of heat from the Sun. Photocells make electricity directly from sunlight.

Even our bodies have adapted to use sunlight to manufacture vitamin D.

Our planet is warmed by the Sun, and without that warmth the oceans would be ice and much of the atmosphere would be a coating of frost. Books often refer to the Sun as "our Sun" or "our star." It is ours in the sense that we live beside it and by its light and warmth, but we can hardly say it belongs to us. It is more correct to say that we belong to the Sun.

This chapter has helped you realize how little astronomers would know about the Sun were it not for analyses of its spectrum. Just a bit of spectroscopic ingenuity reveals that the brilliance of the Sun hides a complex atmosphere of hot gases, churned by powerful storms that affect our lives on Earth.

Review Questions

1. How was the distance to the Sun first determined?
2. How is the mass of the Sun determined?
3. Define density. How is the density of the Sun determined?
4. Why is the binding energy of an electron related to the size of its orbit?
5. Explain why ionized calcium can form absorption lines, but ionized hydrogen cannot.
6. Describe two ways an atom can gain energy and become what is called "excited," with one or more electrons moved to higher orbits.
7. Why do different atoms have different lines in their spectra?
8. Why do hot stars look bluer than cool stars?
9. What kind of spectrum does a neon sign produce?
10. If a nebula contains mostly hydrogen excited to emit photons, what kind of spectrum would you expect it to produce?
11. Why does the Doppler effect detect only radial velocity?
12. How are astronomers able to explore the layers of the Sun below the photosphere?
13. What evidence can you give that sunspots and prominences are magnetic?
14. How does the Babcock model explain the sunspot cycle?
15. How can solar flares affect Earth?

Discussion Questions

1. In what ways is the model of an atom a scientific model?
2. Explain why the presence of spectral lines of a given element in the solar spectrum tells you that element is present in the Sun, but the absence of the lines would not necessarily mean the element is absent from the Sun.
3. What observations would you make if you were ordered to set up a system that could warn astronauts in orbit of dangerous solar flares? (Such a warning system actually exists.)

Learning to Look

1. The glowing gas cloud shown in the next column contains mostly hydrogen excited to emit photons. What kind of spectrum would you expect this gas cloud to produce?

T. Rector, University of Alaska and WIYN, NURO/AURA/NSF

2. If the gas cloud in the image crosses in front of a star, and the gas cloud and star have different radial velocities, what would the combined spectrum of the gas cloud and the star look like?
3. The two images here show two solar phenomena. What are they, and how are they related? How do they differ?

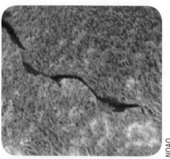

NOAO

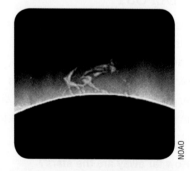

NOAO

6

The Family of Stars

GUIDEPOST

To discover the properties of stars, astronomers use telescopes and instruments such as photometers, cameras, and spectrographs in clever ways to learn the secrets hidden in starlight. The result is a family portrait of the stars. Knowing the distances to stars is the key to knowing most of their other properties, but measuring those distances is very difficult.

In this chapter you will find answers to five important questions about stars:

- **How far away are the stars?**
- **How much energy do stars emit?**
- **How do spectra of stars allow determination of their temperatures?**
- **How big are stars?**
- **How much mass do stars contain?**

With this chapter, you leave the Sun behind and begin your study of the billions of stars that dot the sky. In a sense, stars are the basic building blocks of the universe. If you hope to understand what the universe is, what our Sun is, what our Earth is, and what we are, you need to understand stars. Once you know how to find the basic properties of stars, you will be ready to trace the history of the stars from birth to death, a story that begins in the next chapter.

Shakespeare compared love to a star that can be seen easily and even used for guidance, but whose real nature is utterly unknown. He lived at

European Southern Observatory

The night is even more richly colored than the day. . . .
If only one pays attention to it, one sees that certain
stars are citron yellow, while others have a pink glow
or a green, blue and forget-me-not brilliance. And
without my expiating on this theme, it should be clear
that putting little white dots on a blue-black surface is
not enough.

Vincent van Gogh,
Painter

An image of the Jewel Box open star cluster, NGC 4755, located in the constellation Crux. Several blue supergiant stars and one red supergiant can be seen. The cluster is about 6400 light-years away. Characteristics of the stars in it provide evidence that the cluster is very young, only 16 million years old.

about the same time as Galileo and had no idea what stars actually are. By studying the history of the universe, the origin of Earth, and the nature of our human existence, you will learn something that people in Shakespeare's time did not know—the real nature of the stars. Unfortunately, it is quite difficult to find out what a star is like. When you look at a star, even through a telescope, you see only a point of light. Real understanding of stars requires careful analysis of starlight. This chapter concentrates on five goals: knowing how far away stars are, how much energy they emit, what their surface temperatures are, how big they are, and how much mass they contain. By the time you finish this chapter, you will know the family of stars well.

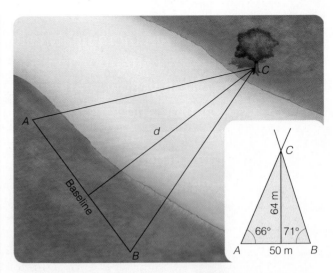

Figure 6.1 The distance across a river (d) can be determined by measuring the length of a baseline along with the angles at vertices A and B. A simple trigonometric calculation yields the value of d.

6.1 Star Distances

Distance is the most important and the most difficult measurement in astronomy, and astronomers have many different ways to find the distances to stars. Each way depends on a simple and direct geometrical method that is much like the method surveyors use to measure the distance across a river they cannot cross. You can begin by reviewing that method and then apply it to stars.

The Surveyor's Triangulation Method

To measure the distance across a river, a team of surveyors begins by driving two stakes into the ground. The distance between the stakes is called the *baseline*. The surveyors then choose a landmark on the opposite side of the river, a tree perhaps, thus establishing a large triangle marked by the two stakes and the tree, as in Figure 6.1. Using their instruments, the surveyors sight the tree from the two ends of the baseline and measure the two angles on their side of the river. Knowing two angles of this large triangle and the length of the baseline side between them, the surveyors can find the distance across the river by simple trigonometry. For example, if the baseline is 50 m and the angles are 66° and 71°, they can calculate that the distance from the baseline to the tree is 64 m.

stellar parallax (*p*) The small apparent shift in position of a nearby star relative to distant background objects due to Earth's orbital motion.

The Astronomer's Triangulation Method

To find the distance to a star, astronomers use a very long baseline, the size of Earth's orbit (see Figure 6.2). If you take a photograph of a nearby star and then wait six months, Earth will have moved halfway around its orbit. You can then take another photograph of the star from that slightly different location in space. When you examine the photographs, you will discover that the star is not in exactly the same place in the two photographs.

In Chapter 3 you learned that *parallax* is the term that refers to the common experience of an apparent shift in the position of a foreground object due to a change in the location of the observer's viewpoint. Your thumb, held at arm's length, appears to shift position against a distant background when you look first with one eye and then with the other. In that case, the baseline is the distance between your eyes, and the parallax is the angle through which your thumb appears to move when you switch eyes. The farther away you hold your thumb, the smaller the parallax. In Chapter 5 you learned that Venus shows a parallax when observed from different locations on Earth.

Because the stars are so distant, their parallaxes are very small angles, usually expressed in arc seconds. The quantity that astronomers call **stellar parallax (*p*)** is conventionally defined as half the total shift of the star (shown in Figure 6.2); in other words, the shift seen across a baseline of 1 AU rather than 2 AU. Astronomers measure the parallax, and surveyors measure the angles at the ends of the baseline, but both measurements tell the same thing—the shape and size of the triangle and therefore the

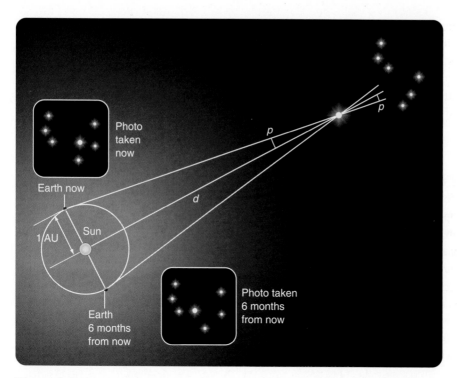

Figure 6.2 You can measure the parallax of a nearby star by photographing it from two points along Earth's orbit. For example, you might photograph it now and again in six months. Half of the star's total change in position from one photograph to the other is defined as its stellar parallax, *p*.

distance to the object in question. (Refer to **Parallax and Distance** in the Math Reference Cards.)

Measuring the parallax *p* is very difficult because it is such a small angle. The nearest star, Alpha Centauri, has a parallax of only 0.76 arc seconds, and more distant stars have even smaller parallaxes. To see how small these angles are, imagine a dime about three kilometres away from you. That dime covers an angle of about 1 arc second. Stellar parallaxes are so small that the first successful measurement of one did not happen until 1838, more than 200 years after the invention of the telescope.

The distances to the stars are so large that it is not convenient to use kilometres or astronomical units. For such large distances there are two main measurement units: light-years and parsecs. In this textbook we have chosen to use light-years because conceptually it is the simpler of the two options. A light-year (ly) is merely the distance light travels in one year. If we state the distance to the star Rigel in the constellation Orion is 772.5 ly, we mean that the light we are seeing today left Rigel 772.5 years ago. When you look at the sky at night you are actually looking back in time! Astronomers also measure distances to stars via parallax and therefore use the unit of distance called a **parsec (pc)**. The word *parsec* was created by combining *parallax* and arc *second*. One parsec equals the distance to an imaginary star that has a parallax of 1 arc second. A parsec is 206 265 AU,

which equals roughly 3.26 ly. In the following chapters we have tried to be consistent in our use of light-years as the unit of measurement; there may be a few instances when parsecs have been used as convenience and custom dictate.

The blurring caused by Earth's atmosphere makes star images appear to be about 1 arc second in diameter, and that makes it difficult to measure parallax. Even if you average together many observations made from Earth's surface, you cannot measure parallax with an uncertainty smaller than about 0.002 arc seconds. If you measure a parallax of 0.006 arc seconds from an observatory on the ground, your uncertainty will be about 30 percent. If you consider, as astronomers generally do, that 30 percent is the maximum acceptable level of uncertainty, then ground-based astronomers can't accurately measure parallaxes that are smaller than about 0.006 arc seconds. That parallax corresponds to a distance of about 550 ly.

In 1989, the European Space Agency launched the satellite *Hipparcos* to measure stellar parallaxes from above the blurring effects of Earth's atmosphere. That small space telescope observed for four years, and the data were used to produce two parallax catalogues in 1997. One catalogue contains 120 000 stars with parallaxes 20 times more accurate than ground-based measurements. The other catalogue contains over a million stars with parallaxes as accurate as ground-based parallaxes. Knowing accurate distances from the *Hipparcos* observations has given astronomers new insights into the nature of stars.

6.2 Apparent Brightness, Intrinsic Brightness, and Luminosity

Your eyes tell you that some stars look brighter than others, and in Chapter 2 you learned about the apparent magnitude scale that refers to stellar apparent brightness. However, the scale of apparent magnitudes tells you

parsec (pc) The distance to a hypothetical star whose parallax is 1 arc second.

only how bright stars appear to you on Earth. To know the true nature of a star you must know its **intrinsic brightness**, a measure of the amount of light the star produces. An intrinsically very bright star might appear faint if it is far away. Consequently, to know the intrinsic brightness of a star, you must take into account its distance.

Brightness and Distance

When you look at a bright light, your eyes respond to the visual-wavelength energy falling on your retinas, which tells you how bright the object appears. Brightness is related to the flux of energy entering your eye. Astronomers and physicists define **flux** as the energy in joules (J) per second falling on 1 square metre. Recall that a joule is about the amount of energy released when an apple falls from a table onto the floor. A flux of 1 joule per second is also known as 1 watt. The wattage of a light bulb tells you its *intrinsic* brightness. Compare that with the *apparent* brightness of a light bulb, which depends on its distance from you.

If you placed a screen 1 metre square near a light bulb, a certain amount of flux would fall on the screen. If you moved the screen twice as far from the bulb, the light that previously fell on the screen would be spread to cover an area four times larger, and the screen would receive only one-fourth as much light. If you tripled the distance to the screen, it would receive only one-ninth as much light. The flux you receive from a light source is inversely proportional to the square of the distance to the source. This is known as the inverse square relation (see Figure 6.3). You first encountered the inverse square relation in Chapter 3, where it was applied to the strength of gravity.

Now you can understand how the apparent brightness of a star depends on its distance. If astronomers know the apparent brightness of a star and its distance from Earth, they can use the inverse square law to correct for distance and find the intrinsic brightness of the star.

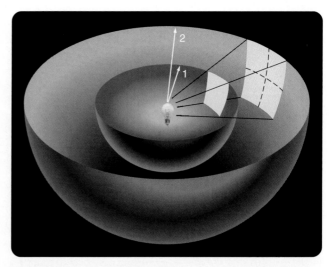

Figure 6.3 The inverse square relation. A light source is surrounded by imaginary spheres with radii of 1 unit and 2 units. The light falling on an area of 1 m² on the inner sphere spreads to illuminate an area of 4 m² on the outer sphere. Thus, the brightness of the light source is inversely proportional to the square of the distance.

If, however, you know the distance to a star, you can use the inverse square relation to calculate the brightness the star would have at some standard distance. Astronomers use 33 ly as the standard distance and refer to the intrinsic brightness of the star as its **absolute visual magnitude** (M_V), which is the apparent visual magnitude that star would have if it were 33 ly away. The subscript V tells you it is a visual magnitude, referring only to the wavelengths of light your eye can see. Other magnitude systems are based on other parts of the electromagnetic spectrum, such as infrared and ultraviolet radiation.

The Sun's absolute magnitude is easy to calculate because its distance and apparent magnitude are well known. The absolute visual magnitude of the Sun is about 4.8. In other words, if the Sun were only 33 ly from Earth (not a great distance in astronomy), it would have an apparent magnitude of 4.8 and look no brighter to your eye than the faintest star in the handle of the Little Dipper. (Refer to **Absolute Magnitude and Distance** in the Math Reference Cards.)

This path to find the distance to stars has led you to absolute magnitude, a measure of the intrinsic brightness of the stars.

Luminosity

The second goal for this chapter is to find out how much energy the stars emit. With the absolute magnitudes of the stars in hand, you can now compare stars using our Sun as a standard. The intrinsically brightest stars have

Absolute Visual Magnitude

If all the stars were the same distance away, you could compare one with another and decide which was intrinsically brighter or fainter. Of course, the stars are scattered at different distances, and you can't move them around to line them up for comparison.

absolute magnitudes of about –8. If such a star were 33 ly away from Earth, it would seem nearly as bright as the Moon. Such stars emit over 100 000 times more visible light than the Sun.

Absolute visual magnitude refers to visible light, but you want to know the total output including all types of radiation. Hot stars emit a great deal of ultraviolet radiation that you can't see, and cool stars emit plenty of infrared radiation. To add in the energy you can't see, astronomers make a mathematical correction that depends on the temperature of the star. With that correction, astronomers can find the total electromagnetic energy output of a star, which they refer to as its **luminosity** (*L*).

Astronomers know the luminosity of the Sun because they can send satellites above Earth's atmosphere and measure the amount of energy arriving from the Sun, adding up radiation of every wavelength, including the types blocked by the atmosphere. Of course, they also know the distance from Earth to the Sun very accurately, which is necessary to calculate luminosity. The luminosity of the Sun is about 4×10^{26} watts (joules per second).

You can express a star's luminosity in two ways. For example, you can say that the star Capella (Alpha Aurigae) is 100 times more luminous than the Sun. You can also express this in real energy units by multiplying by the luminosity of the Sun. The luminosity of Capella is 4×10^{28} watts.

When you look at the night sky, the stars look much the same, yet your study of distances and luminosities reveals an astonishing fact. Some stars are almost a million times more luminous than the Sun, and some are almost a million times less luminous. Clearly, the family of stars is filled with interesting characters.

6.3 Star Temperatures

The third goal for this chapter is to learn about the temperatures of stars. The surprising fact is that stellar spectral lines can be used as a sensitive star thermometer.

From the discussion of blackbody radiation in Chapter 5, you know that temperatures of stars can be estimated from their colour: red stars are cool, and blue stars are hot. The relative strengths of various spectral lines, however, give much greater accuracy in measuring star temperatures. Recall from Chapter 5 that, for stars, the term *surface* refers to the photosphere, which is the limit of our vision into the star from outside, but it is not an actual solid surface. Stars typically have surface temperatures of a few thousand or tens of thousands of degrees

Kelvin. As you will discover in Chapter 7, the centres of stars are much hotter than their surfaces—many millions of degrees hotter—but the spectra tell only about the outer layers from which the light you see departed.

As you learned in Chapter 5, hydrogen Balmer absorption lines are produced by hydrogen atoms with electrons initially in the second energy level. The strength of these spectral lines can be used to gauge the temperature of a star because scientists know the following details from lab experiments with gases and radiation, and also from theoretical calculations:

- If the surface of a star is as cool as the Sun or cooler, there are few violent collisions between atoms to excite the electrons, and most atoms will have their electrons in the ground (lowest) state. These atoms can't absorb photons in the Balmer series. As a result, you can expect to find weak hydrogen Balmer absorption lines in the spectra of very cool stars.

- In the surface layers of stars hotter than about 20 000 K, there are many violent collisions between atoms, exciting electrons to high energy levels or knocking the electrons completely out of most atoms, and so they become ionized. In this situation, few hydrogen atoms will have electrons in the second energy level to form Balmer absorption lines. As a result, you can also find weak hydrogen Balmer absorption lines in the spectra of very hot stars.

- At an intermediate temperature, roughly 10 000 K, the collisions have the correct amount of energy to excite large numbers of electrons into the second energy level. With many atoms excited to the second level, the gas absorbs Balmer-wavelength photons well and thus produces strong hydrogen Balmer lines.

The strength of the hydrogen Balmer lines therefore depends on the temperature of the star's surface layers. Both hot and cool stars have weak Balmer lines, but medium-temperature stars have strong Balmer lines.

Figure 6.4 shows the relationship between gas temperature and strength of spectral lines for hydrogen and other substances. Each type of atom or molecule produces spectral lines that are weak at high and low temperatures and strong at some intermediate temperature, although the temperature at which the lines reach maximum strength is different for each type of atom or molecule. Theoretical calculations of the type first made by Cecilia Payne (discussed

luminosity (*L*) The total amount of energy a star radiates per second at all wavelengths.

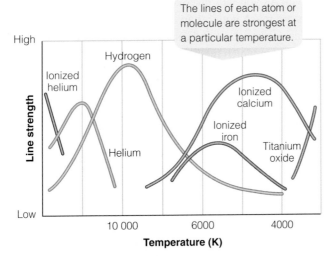

High

Line strength

Low

Ionized helium

Hydrogen

Helium

Ionized calcium

Ionized iron

Titanium oxide

The lines of each atom or molecule are strongest at a particular temperature.

10 000   6000   4000

Temperature (K)

Figure 6.4 The strength of spectral lines can tell you the temperature of a star. Using the lines of several atoms or molecules gives you the most accurate results.

in Chapter 5) can predict just how strong various spectral lines should be for stars of different temperatures. Astronomers can determine a star's temperature by comparing the strengths of its spectral lines with the predicted strengths.

From stellar spectra, astronomers have found that the hottest stars have surface temperatures above 40 000 K, and the coolest are about 2500 K. Compare these with the surface temperature of the Sun, which is about 5800 K.

Temperature Spectral Classification

You have seen that the strengths of spectral lines depend on the surface (photosphere) temperature of the star. From this you can predict that all stars of a given temperature should have similar spectra. Learning to recognize the pattern of spectral lines produced in the atmospheres of stars of different temperatures means there is no need

to do a full analysis every time each type of spectrum is encountered. Time can be saved by classifying stellar spectra rather than analyzing each spectrum individually. Astronomers classify stars by the lines and bands in their spectra, as shown in Table 6.1. For example, if a star has weak Balmer lines and lines of ionized helium, it must be classified as an O star.

The star classification system now used by astronomers was devised at Harvard University during the 1890s and 1990s. The origin of this classification system is an interesting one. The Harvard College Observatory was funded in the late 1800s through a private grant that the director, Edward Pickering, used to hire mostly women (graduates in physics or astronomy) to classify stellar spectra. One such "computer," as they were called, was Williamina Fleming, who classified more than 10 000 stars using the scheme for identifying the spectral lines of hydrogen. Later, another "computer," Annie Jump Cannon, extended Fleming's work and developed the system described on the previous picture, eventually classifying more than 400 000 stars! The spectra were first classified in groups labelled A through Q, but some groups were later dropped, merged with others, or reordered. The final classification includes seven main **spectral classes** or types that are still used today: O, B, A, F, G, K, M. This set of star types, called the **spectral sequence**, is important because it is a temperature sequence. The O stars are the hottest, and the temperature continues to decrease down to the M stars, the coolest. For further precision, astronomers divide each spectral class into 10 subclasses. For example, spectral class A consists of the subclasses A0, A1, A2 … A8, A9. Next come F0, F1, F2, and so on. These finer divisions define a star's temperature to a precision of about 5 percent. The Sun, for example, is not just a G star, but a G2 star, with a temperature of 5800 K.

spectral class A star's position in the temperature classification system O, B, A, F, G, K, M, based on the appearance of the star's spectrum.

spectral sequence The arrangement of spectral classes (O, B, A, F, G, K, M) ranging from hot to cool.

Table 6.1 | Spectral Classes

Spectral Class	Approximate Temperature (K)	Hydrogen Balmer Lines	Other Spectral Features	Unaided Eye Example
O	40 000	Weak	Ionized helium	Meissa (O8)
B	20 000	Medium	Neutral helium	Achernar (B3)
A	10 000	Strong	Ionized calcium weak	Sirius (A1)
F	7500	Medium	Ionized calcium weak	Canopus (F0)
G	5500	Weak	Ionized calcium medium	Sun (G2)
K	4500	Very weak	Ionized calcium strong	Arcturus (K2)
M	3000	Very weak	TiO strong	Betelgeuse (M2)

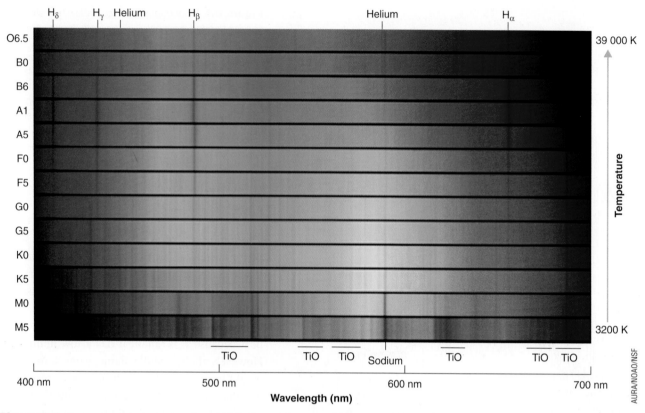

Figure 6.5 These spectra show stars from hot O stars at top to cool M stars at bottom. The hydrogen Balmer lines are strongest for about type A0, but the two closely spaced lines of sodium in the yellow are strongest for very cool stars. Helium lines appear only in the spectra of the hottest stars. Notice that the helium line visible in the top spectrum has nearly—but not exactly—the same wavelength as the sodium lines visible in cooler stars. Bands produced by the molecule titanium oxide are strong in the spectra of the coolest stars.

Generations of astronomy students have remembered the spectral sequence by using mnemonics such as "Oh, Be A Fine Girl/Guy, Kiss Me," or "Oh Boy, An F Grade Kills Me." You can make up your own phrase if you wish.

Figure 6.5 shows colour images of 13 stellar spectra ranging from the hottest at the top to the coolest at the bottom. Notice how spectral features change gradually from hot to cool stars. Although these spectra are attractive, astronomers rarely work with spectra as colour images. Rather, they display spectra as graphs of intensity versus wavelength, with dark absorption lines as dips in the graph in Figure 6.6. Such graphs show more detail than photographs. Notice also that the overall curves are similar to blackbody curves. The wavelength of maximum is in the infrared for the coolest stars and in the ultraviolet for the hottest stars. Compare Figures 6.5 and 6.6, and notice how the strength of spectral lines depends on temperature, as indicated in the previous discussion regarding Figure 6.4. It is fairly straightforward to determine a star's temperature from the details of its spectrum.

The study of spectral types is more than a century old, but astronomers continue to discover and define new types. The **L dwarfs**, found in 1998, are cooler and fainter than M stars. They are understood to be objects smaller than stars but larger than planets; they are called **brown dwarfs** and you will learn more about them in a later chapter. The spectra of M stars contain bands produced by metal oxides such as titanium oxide (TiO), but L dwarf spectra contain bands produced by molecules such as iron hydride (FeH). The **T dwarfs** are an even cooler and fainter type of brown dwarf than L dwarfs. Their spectra show absorption by methane (CH_4) and water vapour. In 2011, astronomers using infrared space telescopes, large ground-based telescopes, and highly sensitive infrared detectors discovered a class of objects with temperatures below 500 K that are labelled **Y dwarfs**.

brown dwarf A very cool, low-luminosity star whose mass is not sufficient to ignite nuclear fusion.

L dwarf, T dwarf Spectral classes of brown dwarf stars with lower surface temperatures and luminosities than M dwarfs.

Y dwarf A substellar object with temperature below 500 K, having inferred properties intermediate between brown dwarfs and Jovian planets.

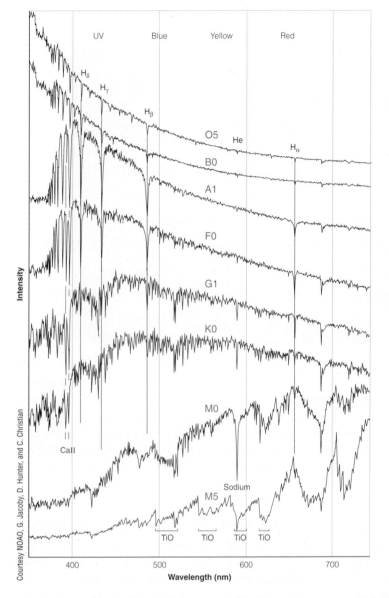

Figure 6.6 Modern digital spectra show how stellar spectra depend on spectral class. Here spectra are represented by graphs of intensity versus wavelength, and dark absorption lines appear as sharp dips in intensity. Hydrogen Balmer lines are strongest about A0, while lines caused by ionized calcium (Ca II) are strong in K stars. Bands produced by molecules such as TiO (titanium oxide) are strong in the coolest stars. Compare these spectra with Figures 6.4 and 6.5.

Luminosity, Temperature, and Diameter

The luminosity of a glowing object like a star is determined by its temperature (Stefan–Boltzmann law, Chapter 5) and its surface area. For example, you can eat dinner by candlelight because the candle flame has a small surface area, and, although it is very hot, it cannot radiate much heat because it is small; it has a low luminosity. However, if the candle flame were 4 m tall, it would have a very large surface area from which to radiate, and, although it might be the same temperature as a normal candle flame, its luminosity would drive you from the table.

In a similar way, a star's luminosity is proportional to its surface area. A hot star may not be very luminous if it has a small surface area, but it could be highly luminous if it were larger. Even a cool star could be luminous if it had a large surface area. You can use stellar luminosities to determine the diameters of stars if you can separate the effects of temperature and surface area. Thus, the luminosity of a star depends on two things: its size and its temperature. (Refer to **Luminosity, Radius, and Temperature** in the Math Reference Cards.)

The **Hertzsprung–Russell (H–R) diagram** is named after its originators, Ejnar Hertzsprung of the Netherlands and Henry Norris Russell of the United States, who independently thought of creating such a diagram. It is a graph that separates the effects of temperature and surface area on stellar luminosities and enables astronomers to sort the stars according to their diameters.

Before discussing the details of the H–R diagram, let's look at a similar diagram you might use to compare automobiles. You can plot a diagram such as Figure 6.7 to show horsepower versus mass for various makes of cars. In so doing, you will find that in general the more massive a car, the more horsepower it has. Most cars fall somewhere along the normal sequence of cars running

6.4 Star Sizes

The fourth goal for this chapter is to learn about the sizes of stars. Do they all have the same diameter as the Sun, or are some larger and some smaller? You certainly can't see their sizes through a telescope; the images of the stars are much too small for you to resolve their disks and measure their diameters. There is a way, however, to find out how big stars really are.

Hertzsprung–Russell (H–R) diagram A plot of the intrinsic brightness versus the surface temperature of stars. It separates the effects of temperature and surface area on stellar luminosity.

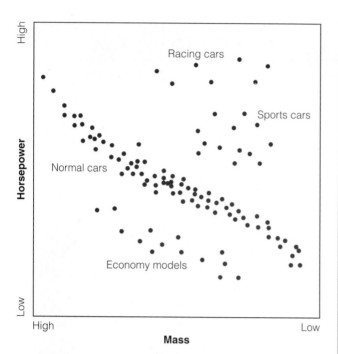

Figure 6.7 Analyzing automobiles by plotting horsepower versus mass reveals relationships among various models; most would be somewhere along the "main sequence" of normal cars.

from heavy, high-powered cars to light, low-powered models. You might call this the main sequence of cars. Some cars, however, have much more horsepower than normal for their mass—the sport or racing models—and the economy models have less power than normal for cars of the same mass. Just as this diagram helps you understand the different kinds of autos, so the H–R diagram can help you understand different kinds of stars.

An H–R diagram, seen in Figure 6.8, has luminosity on the vertical axis and temperature on the horizontal axis. A star is represented by a point on the graph that tells you its luminosity and temperature. Note that in astronomy the symbol $\odot$ refers to the Sun. Thus $L_\odot$ refers to the luminosity of the Sun, $T_\odot$ refers to the temperature of the Sun, and so on. The H–R diagram in Figure 6.8 also contains a scale of spectral types across the top. The spectral type of a star is determined by its temperature, so you can use either spectral type or temperature as the horizontal axis of an H–R diagram.

Astronomers use H–R diagrams so often that they usually skip the words "the point that represents the star." Rather, they will say that a star is located in a certain place in the diagram. Of course, they mean the point that represents the luminosity and temperature of the star, not the star itself. The location of a star in the H–R diagram has nothing to do with the location of the star in space. Furthermore, a star may move in the H–R diagram as it ages and its luminosity and temperature change, but such motion in the diagram has nothing to do with the star's motion in space.

In an H–R diagram, the location of a point representing a star tells you a great deal about the star. Points near the top of the diagram represent very luminous stars, and points near the bottom represent very-low-luminosity stars. Also, points near the right edge of the diagram represent very cool stars, and points near the left edge of the diagram represent very hot stars. Notice in Figure 6.8 how the artist has used colour to represent temperature. Cool stars are red, and hot stars are blue.

The **main sequence** is the region of the H–R diagram running from upper left to lower right. It includes roughly 90 percent of all normal stars, represented by a curved line with dots for stars plotted along it in Figure 6.8. As you might expect, the hot main-sequence stars are more luminous than the cool main-sequence stars. Look again at the classification diagram for cars in Figure 6.7. Vehicles not on the car main sequence have different kinds of engines than main-sequence cars. In Chapter 7 you will find that stars not on the main sequence have different nuclear reactions as their power sources than do main-sequence stars. In addition to temperature, size is important in determining the luminosity of a star. Notice in the H–R diagram that some cool stars lie above the main sequence. Although they are cool, they are luminous, and that must mean they are larger—have more surface area—than main-sequence stars of the same temperature. These are called **giant** stars, and they are roughly 10 to 100 times larger than the Sun. The **supergiant** stars at the top of the H–R diagram are as large as 1000 times the Sun's diameter. In contrast, **red dwarfs** at the lower end of the main sequence are not only cool but also small, giving them low luminosities.

At the bottom of the H–R diagram are the "economy models," stars that are very low in luminosity because they are very small. The **white dwarfs** lie in the lower left of the H–R diagram, and although some white dwarfs are among the hottest stars

main sequence The region of the H–R diagram running from upper left to lower right, which includes roughly 90 percent of all stars generating energy by nuclear fusion.

giant A large, cool, highly luminous star in the upper right of the H–R diagram, typically 10 to 100 times the diameter of the Sun.

supergiant An exceptionally luminous star whose diameter is 100 to 1000 times that of the Sun.

red dwarf A faint, cool, low-mass, main-sequence star.

white dwarf A dying star at the lower left of the H–R diagram that has collapsed to the size of Earth and is slowly cooling off.

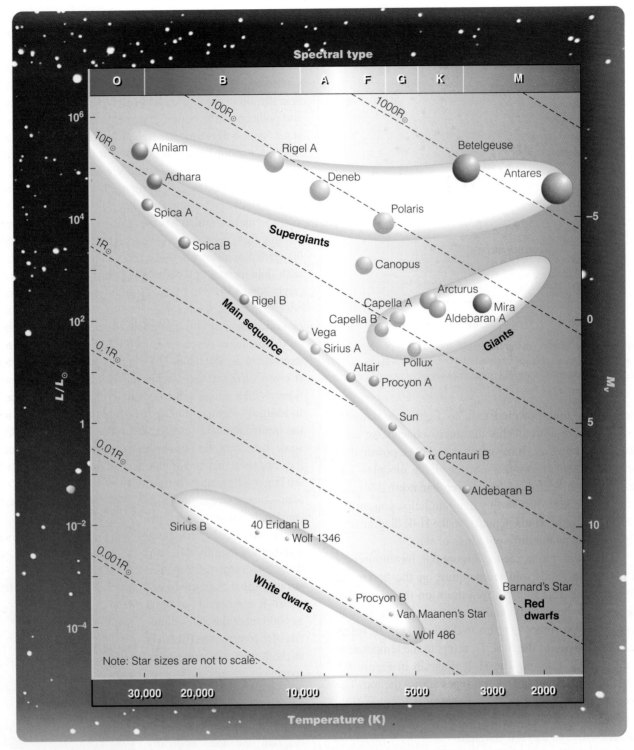

Figure 6.8 An H–R diagram showing the luminosity and temperature of many well-known stars. The dashed lines are lines of constant radius. The star sizes on this diagram are not to scale. (Individual stars that orbit each other are designated A and B, as in Spica A and Spica B.)

known, they are so small they have very little surface area from which to radiate, and that limits them to low luminosities.

A simple calculation can be made to draw precise lines of constant radius across the H–R diagram based on the luminosities and temperatures at each point as shown in Figure 6.8. For example, locate the line labelled 1 $R_\odot$ (1 solar radius) and notice that it passes through the point representing the Sun. Any star whose point is located along this line has a radius equal to the Sun's radius. Notice also that the lines of constant radius slope downward to the right, because cooler stars are always fainter than hotter stars of the same size, following the Stefan–Boltzmann law. These lines of constant radius show dramatically that the supergiants and giants are much larger than the Sun. In contrast, white dwarf stars fall near the line labelled 0.01 $R_\odot$. They all have about the same radius—approximately the size of Earth!

Notice the great range of sizes among stars. The largest stars are 100 000 times larger than the tiny white dwarfs. If the Sun were a tennis ball, the white dwarfs would be grains of sand, and the largest supergiant stars would be as big as football fields.

Luminosity Spectral Classification

A star's spectrum also contains clues as to whether it is a main-sequence star, a giant, or a supergiant. The larger a star is, the less dense its atmosphere is. The widths of spectral lines are partially determined by the density of the gas. If the atoms collide often in a dense gas, their energy levels become distorted, and the spectral lines are broadened. For example, in the spectrum of a main-sequence star, the hydrogen Balmer lines are broad because the star's atmosphere is dense and the hydrogen atoms collide often. In the spectrum of a giant star, the lines are narrower (Figure 6.9), because the giant star's atmosphere is less dense and the hydrogen atoms collide less often. In the spectrum of a supergiant star, the Balmer lines are very narrow.

The width of the spectral lines is clearly an indicator of how big a star is. As you learned earlier in this section, luminosity is dependent on both radius and temperature. So astronomers have further refined stellar classification by developing a **luminosity class** system that roughly designates the size of the star as well as its luminosity (see Table 6.2). Supergiants, for example, are very luminous because they are very large.

The luminosity classes are represented by the Roman numerals I through V, with supergiants further

Table 6.2 | Luminosity Classes

Class	Description	Example
Ia	Luminous supergiant	Rigel A
Ib	Regular supergiant	Polaris
II	Bright giant	Adhara
III	Giant	Capella
IV	Subgiant	Altair
V	Main sequence	Sun

subdivided into types Ia and Ib. For example, you can distinguish between a luminous supergiant (Ia) such as Rigel (Beta Orionis) and a regular supergiant (Ib) such as Polaris, the North Star (Alpha Ursa Minoris). The star Adhara (Epsilon Canis Majoris) is a luminous giant (II), Capella (Alpha Aurigae) is a giant (III), and Altair (Alpha Aquilae) is a subgiant (IV). The Sun is a main-sequence star (V). The luminosity class notation appears after the spectral type, as in G2V for the Sun. Sometimes an additional class is utilized for white dwarfs (wd or D).

The approximate positions of the supergiant, giant, and main-sequence luminosity classes are shown on the H–R diagram. Luminosity class doesn't really define stellar luminosities, sizes or temperatures very precisely. The H–R diagram in Figure 6.8 shows that supergiants (class I) have about the same luminosity but vary broadly in temperature and size. On the other hand, main-sequence stars (class V) have roughly the same size but vary greatly in both luminosity and temperature. Although luminosity classification is subtle and not very accurate, it is an important technique in modern astronomy because it provides clues to distance.

> **luminosity class** A category of stars of similar luminosity, determined by the widths of lines in their spectra.

Luminosity effects on the widths of spectral lines

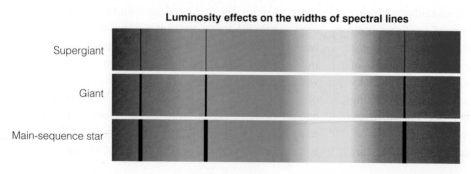

Supergiant

Giant

Main-sequence star

Figure 6.9 These schematic spectra show how the widths of spectral lines reveal a star's luminosity classification. Supergiants have very narrow spectral lines, and main-sequence stars have broad lines. Some spectral lines are more sensitive to this effect than others. Examining the details of a star's spectrum can determine its luminosity classification.

Most stars are too distant to have measurable parallaxes, but astronomers can find the distances to these stars if they can record the stars' spectra and determine their luminosity classes. From spectral type and luminosity class, astronomers can estimate the star's absolute magnitude, compare with its apparent magnitude, and compute its distance. Although this process finds distance and not true parallax, it is called **spectroscopic parallax**.

For example, Betelgeuse (Alpha Orionis) is classified M2 Ia, and its apparent magnitude averages about 0.4 (Betelgeuse is somewhat variable). You can plot this star in an H–R diagram such as Figure 6.8, where you would find that a temperature class of M2 and luminosity class of Ib (supergiant) corresponds to a luminosity of about 30 000 $L_\odot$. That information, combined with the star's apparent brightness, allows astronomers to estimate that Betelgeuse is about 640 ly from Earth (Refer to **Absolute Magnitude and Distance** in the Math Reference Cards.) The *Hipparcos* satellite finds the actual distance to be 427 ly, so the distance determined by the spectroscopic parallax technique is only approximate. Spectroscopic parallax does give a good first estimate of the distances of stars so far away that their parallax can't easily be measured.

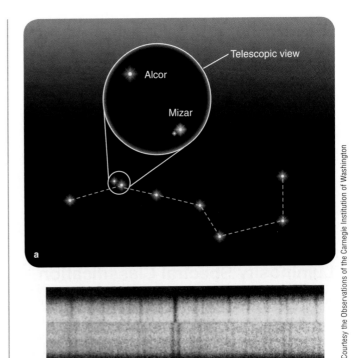

Courtesy the Observations of the Carnegie Institution of Washington

Figure 6.10 (a) At the bend of the handle of the Big Dipper lies a pair of stars, Mizar and Alcor. A telescope reveals that Mizar is a member of a visual binary system. (b) Spectra of these stars recorded at different times show that Mizar, its faint companion, and the nearby star Alcor are all spectroscopic binaries.

6.5 Star Masses: Binary Stars

The fifth goal for this chapter is to find out how much matter stars contain; that is, to know their masses. Do they all contain about the same mass as the Sun, or are some more massive than others?

Gravity is the key to determining mass. Matter produces a gravitational field. Astronomers can figure out how much matter a star contains if they watch an object such as another star move through the star's gravitational field.

spectroscopic parallax
The method of determining a star's distance by comparing its apparent magnitude with its absolute magnitude as estimated from its spectrum.

binary stars Pairs of stars that orbit around their common centre of mass.

Finding the masses of stars involves studying **binary stars**, pairs of stars that orbit each other. This may come as a surprise, but many of the familiar stars in the sky are pairs of stars orbiting each other (see Figure 6.10). Binary systems are common; more than half of all stars are members of binary star systems. Few, however, can be analyzed completely. Many are so far apart that their periods are much too long for practical mapping of their orbits. Others are so close together they are not visible as separate stars.

Binary Stars in General

The key to finding the mass of a binary star is an understanding of orbital motion (see Chapter 3). Each star in a binary system moves in its own orbit around the system's centre of mass: the balance point of the system (see **Visualizing Astronomy 3.2, Orbiting Earth**). If one star is more massive than its companion, the massive star is closer to the centre of mass and travels in a smaller orbit, while the lower-mass star whips around in a larger orbit (Figure 6.11). The ratio of the masses of the stars in the binary system portrayed in Figure 6.11 is M_A/M_B, which equals r_B/r_A, the inverse of the ratio of the radii of the orbits. For example, if one star in a binary system has an orbit twice as large as the other star's orbit, it must be half as massive. Getting the ratio of the masses is easy, but that doesn't tell you the individual masses of

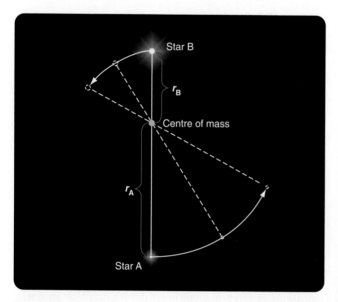

Figure 6.11 As stars in a binary star system revolve around each other, the line connecting them always passes through the centre of mass, and the more massive star is always closer to the centre of mass.

the stars, which is what you really want to know. That takes one more step.

To find the total mass of a binary star system, you must know the size of the orbits and the orbital period—the length of time the stars take to complete one orbit. The smaller the orbits are and the shorter the orbital period is, the stronger the stars' gravity must be to hold each other in orbit. From the sizes of the orbits and the orbital period, astronomers can use Kepler's third law (see Chapter 3) to figure out how much mass the stars contain in total. Combining that information with the ratio of the masses found from the relative sizes of the orbits reveals the individual masses of the stars. (Refer to **The Masses of Binary Stars** in the Math Reference Cards.)

Finding the mass of a binary star system is easier said than done. One difficulty is that the true sizes of the star orbits must be measured in units such as metres or Astronomical Units to find the masses of the stars in units such as kilograms or solar masses. Measuring the true sizes

HOW DO WE KNOW? 6.1

Chains of Inference

How do scientists measure something they can't detect? Sometimes scientists cannot directly observe the things they really want to study, so they must construct chains of inference that connect observable parameters to the unobservable quantities they want to know. You can't measure the mass of a star directly, so you must find a way to use what you can observe, orbital period and angular separation, to figure out step by step the parameters you need to calculate the mass.

Consider another example. Geologists can't measure the temperature and density of Earth's interior directly. There is no way to drill a hole to Earth's centre and lower a thermometer or recover a sample. However, the speed of vibrations from a distant earthquake

depends on the temperature and density of the rock they pass through. Geologists can't measure the speed of the vibrations deep inside Earth; but they can measure the delays in the arrival times at different locations on the surface, and that allows them to work their way back to the speed and, finally, the temperature and density.

Chains of inference can be non-mathematical. Biologists studying the migration of whales can't follow individual whales for years at a time, but they can observe them feeding and mating in different locations; take into consideration food sources, ocean currents, and water temperatures; and construct a chain of inference that leads back to the seasonal migration pattern for the whales.

This chapter contains a number of chains of inference. Almost all fields of science use chains of inference. When you can link the observable parameters step by step to the final conclusions, you gain a strong insight into the nature of science.

San Andreas fault: A chain of inference connects earthquakes to conditions inside Earth.

of the orbits in turn requires knowing the distance to the binary system. Therefore, the only stars whose masses astronomers know for certain are the ones in binary systems with orbits that have been determined, and their distances from Earth have been measured. Other complications are that the orbits of the two stars may be elliptical, and that the plane of their orbits can be tipped at an angle to your line of sight, which distorts the apparent shapes of the orbits. Astronomers must find ways to correct for these complications. Notice that finding the masses of binary stars requires a number of steps to get from what can be observed to what astronomers really want to know: the masses. Constructing such sequences of steps is an important part of science. (See **How Do We Know? 6.1.**)

Three Kinds of Binary Systems

Although there are many different kinds of binary stars, three types are especially important for determining stellar masses. Studying binary stars is also preparation for knowing how to find planets around stars other than our Sun, because a star with a planet orbiting around it is like a binary star system with one very small component. Each type of binary star system corresponds to a different technique for finding planets, as you will learn in Chapter 12.

In a **visual binary system**, the two stars are separately visible in the telescope and astronomers can watch the stars orbit each other over periods of years or decades, as the series of illustrations of Sirius A and B in Figure 6.12 demonstrates. From that, astronomers can find the orbital period and, if the distance of the system from Earth can be found, the size of the orbits. That is enough to find the masses of the stars.

Many visual binaries have such large orbits their orbital periods are hundreds or thousands of years, and astronomers have not yet seen them complete an entire orbit. Also, many binary stars orbit so close to each other they are not visible as separate stars. Such systems can't be analyzed as a visual binary.

If the stars in a binary system are close together, a telescopic view, limited by diffraction and atmospheric seeing, shows a single point of light. Only by looking at a spectrum, which is formed by light from both stars and contains spectral lines from both, can astronomers tell that there are two stars present, not one. Such a system is a **spectroscopic binary system**. Familiar examples of spectroscopic binary systems are the stars Mizar and Alcor in the handle of the Big Dipper (Figure 6.10b).

Figure 6.13 shows a pair of stars orbiting each other; the circular orbit appears elliptical because you see it nearly edge-on. If this were a true spectroscopic binary system, you would not see the separate stars. Nevertheless, the Doppler shift would tell you there were two stars orbiting each other. As the two stars move in their orbits,

A Visual Binary Star System

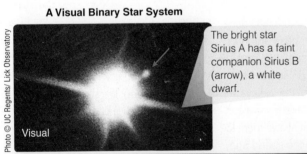

The bright star Sirius A has a faint companion Sirius B (arrow), a white dwarf.

Photo © UC Regents/ Lick Observatory

Visual

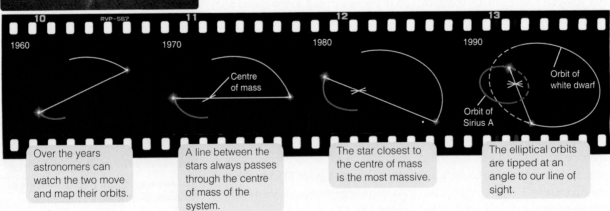

1960 1970 1980 1990

Centre of mass

Orbit of white dwarf

Orbit of Sirius A

Over the years astronomers can watch the two move and map their orbits.

A line between the stars always passes through the centre of mass of the system.

The star closest to the centre of mass is the most massive.

The elliptical orbits are tipped at an angle to our line of sight.

Figure 6.12 The orbital motion of Sirius A and Sirius B can reveal their individual masses.

A Spectroscopic Binary Star System

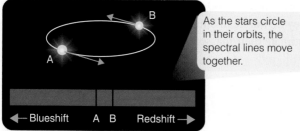

Stars orbiting each other produce spectral lines with Doppler shifts.

(first panel) Approaching — A — B — Receding
← Blueshift   A   B   Redshift →

As the stars circle in their orbits, the spectral lines move together.

(second panel) B, A
← Blueshift   A B   Redshift →

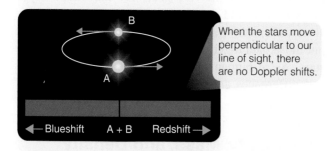

When the stars move perpendicular to our line of sight, there are no Doppler shifts.

(third panel) B, A
← Blueshift   A + B   Redshift →

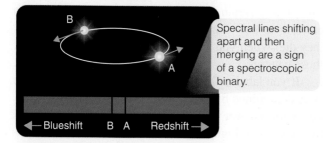

Spectral lines shifting apart and then merging are a sign of a spectroscopic binary.

(fourth panel) B, A
← Blueshift   B   A   Redshift →

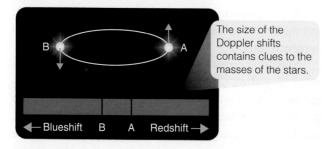

The size of the Doppler shifts contains clues to the masses of the stars.

(fifth panel) B, A
← Blueshift   B   A   Redshift →

Figure 6.13 From Earth, a spectroscopic binary looks like a single point of light, but the Doppler shifts in its spectrum reveal the orbital motion of the two stars. If the plane of their orbits is oriented very close to edge-on, the stars can pass in front of each other as they orbit and the system will be an eclipsing binary, as illustrated in Figure 6.14.

they alternately approach toward and recede from Earth, and their spectral lines are Doppler shifted alternately toward blue and then red wavelengths. Noticing pairs of spectral lines moving back and forth across each other would alert you that you were observing a spectroscopic binary.

Although spectroscopic binaries are very common, they are not as useful as visual binaries. Astronomers can find the orbital period easily, but they can't find the true size of the orbits because there is no way to find the angle at which the orbits are tipped. That means they can't find the true masses of a spectroscopic binary. All they can find is a lower limit to the masses.

If the plane of the orbits is nearly edge-on to Earth, the stars can cross in front of each other as seen from Earth. When one star moves in front of the other, it blocks some of the light, and the star is eclipsed. Such a system is called an **eclipsing binary system**.

Seen from Earth, the two stars are not visible separately. The system looks like a single point of light. But, when one star moves in front of the other star, part of the light is blocked, and the total brightness of the point of light decreases. Figure 6.14 shows a smaller star moving in an orbit around a larger star, first eclipsing the larger star and then being eclipsed as it moves behind. The resulting variation in the brightness of the system is shown as a graph of brightness versus time, a **light curve**.

The light curves of eclipsing binary systems contain plenty of information about the stars, but the curves can be difficult to analyze. Figure 6.14 shows an idealized example of such a system. Once the light curve of an eclipsing binary system has been accurately observed, astronomers can construct a chain of inference that leads to the masses of the two stars. They can find the orbital period easily and can get spectra showing the Doppler shifts of the two stars. They can find the orbital speed because they don't have to correct for the inclination of the orbits; you know the orbits are nearly edge-on, or there would not be eclipses. From that, astronomers can find the size of the orbits and the masses of the stars.

Earlier in this chapter you learned that luminosity and temperature can be used to determine the radii of stars, but eclipsing binary systems give a way to check those calculations by measuring the sizes of a few stars directly. The light curve shows how

eclipsing binary system A binary star system in which the stars cross in front of each other as seen from Earth.

light curve A graph of brightness versus time commonly used in analyzing variable stars and eclipsing binaries.

An Eclipsing Binary Star System

A small, hot star orbits a large, cool star, and you see their total light.

As the hot star crosses in front of the cool star, you see a decrease in brightness.

As the hot star uncovers the cool star, the brightness returns to normal.

When the hot star is eclipsed behind the cool star, the brightness drops.

The depths of the two eclipses depend on the relative surface temperatures of the stars.

Figure 6.14 From Earth, an eclipsing binary looks like a single point of light, but changes in brightness reveal that two stars are eclipsing each other. The light curve, shown here as magnitude versus time, combined with Doppler shift information from spectra, can reveal the size and mass of the individual stars.

mass–luminosity relation
The more massive a main-sequence star is, the more luminous it is.

long it takes for the stars to cross in front of each other, and multiplying these time intervals by the orbital speeds gives the diameters of the stars. There are complications due to the inclination and eccentricity of orbits, but often these effects can be taken into account, so observations of an eclipsing binary system can directly tell you not only the masses of its stars but also their diameters.

From the study of binary stars, astronomers have found that the masses of stars range from roughly 0.1 solar masses to nearly 100 solar masses. The most massive stars ever found in a binary system have masses of 83 and 82 solar masses. A few other stars are believed to be more massive, 100 solar masses to 150 solar masses, but they do not lie in binary systems, so astronomers can only estimate their masses.

6.6 Typical Stars

Having achieved the five goals for this chapter, you know how to find the distances, luminosities, temperatures, diameters, and masses of stars. Now you can put those data together to paint a family portrait of the stars. As in human family portraits, both similarities and differences are important clues to the history of the family.

Luminosity, Mass, and Density

The H–R diagram is filled with patterns that give you clues as to how stars are born, how they age, and how they die. When you add your data, you can see traces of those patterns.

If you label an H–R diagram with the masses of the stars determined by observations of binary star systems, you will discover the main-sequence stars are ordered by mass (see Figure 6.15). The most massive main-sequence stars are the hot stars. As you run your eye down the main sequence, you will find lower-mass stars, and the lowest-mass stars are the coolest, faintest, main-sequence stars.

Stars that do not lie on the main sequence are not in order according to mass. Some giants and supergiants are massive, while others are no more massive than the Sun. All white dwarfs have about the same mass, usually in the narrow range of 0.5 to about 1.0 solar masses.

Because of the systematic ordering of mass along the main sequence, these main-sequence stars obey a **mass–luminosity relation**: the more massive a star is, the more luminous it is (see Figure 6.16). In fact, the mass–luminosity relation can be expressed as follows: luminosity is proportional to mass to the 3.5 power. For example, a

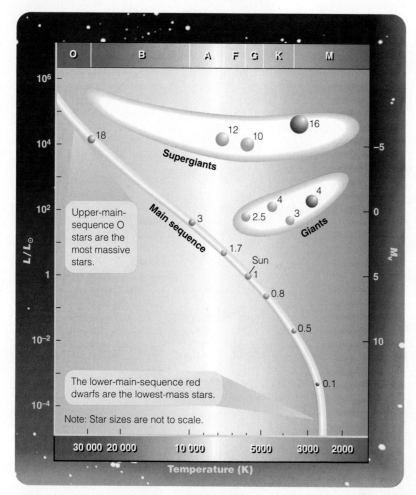

Figure 6.15 The masses of the plotted stars are labelled on this H–R diagram. Notice that the masses of main-sequence stars decrease from top to bottom, but the masses of giants and supergiants are not arranged in any ordered pattern.

star with a mass of 4.0 $M_{\odot}$ can be expected to have a luminosity of about $4^{3.5}$ or 128 $L_{\odot}$. Giants, supergiants, and white dwarfs do not follow the mass–luminosity relation. In the next chapters, the mass–luminosity relation of main-sequence stars will help you understand how these stars generate their energy. (Refer to **The Mass–Luminosity Relation** in the Math Reference Cards.)

Though mass alone does not reveal any pattern among giants, supergiants, and white dwarfs, density does. Once you know a star's mass and diameter, you can calculate its average density by dividing its mass by its volume. Stars are not uniform in density; they are most dense at their centres and least dense near their surface. The centre of the Sun, for instance, is about 150 times as dense as water (or about 7.5 times as dense as gold); its density near the photosphere is about 3400 times less dense than Earth's atmosphere at sea level. A star's average density is intermediate between its central and surface densities. The Sun's average density is approximately 1 gram per cubic centimetre—about the density of water.

Main-sequence stars have average densities similar to the Sun's density. As you learned earlier in the discussion about luminosity classification, giant stars are much larger in diameter than the main-sequence stars but not much larger in mass, so giants have low average densities, ranging from 0.1 to 0.01 g/cm³. The enormous supergiants have still lower densities, ranging from 0.001 to 0.000001 g/cm³. These densities are thinner than the air you breathe, and if you could insulate yourself from the heat, you could fly an airplane through these stars. Only near the centre would you be in any danger; astronomers calculate that the material there is very dense.

The white dwarfs have masses about equal to the Sun's mass, but in size are quite small: about the size of Earth. The matter is compressed to densities of 3 000 000 g/cm³ or more. A teaspoonful of this material would have a mass of about 15 000 kg, or about the mass of two adult elephants.

Density divides stars into three groups. Most stars are main-sequence stars with densities similar to the Sun's. Giants and supergiants are very-low-density stars, and white dwarfs are high-density stars. You will see in later chapters that these densities reflect different stages in the evolution of stars.

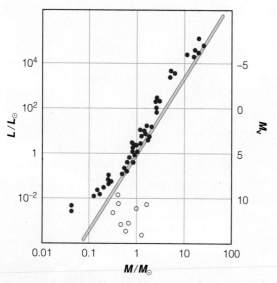

Figure 6.16 The mass–luminosity relation shows that the more massive a main-sequence star is, the more luminous it is. The open circles represent white dwarfs, which do not obey the relation.

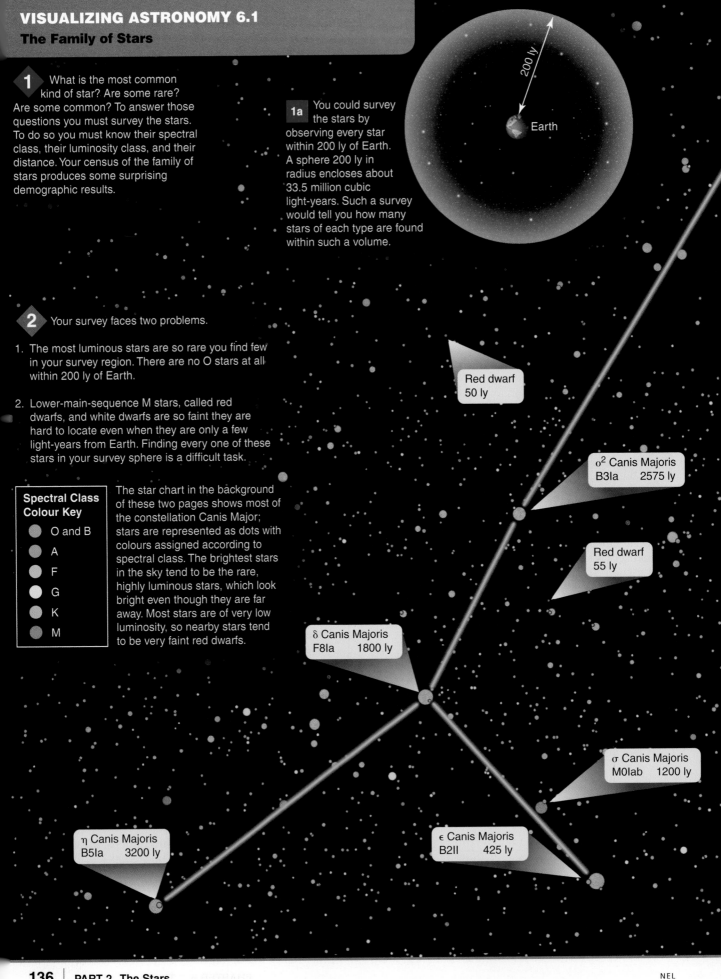

1 What is the most common kind of star? Are some rare? Are some common? To answer those questions you must survey the stars. To do so you must know their spectral class, their luminosity class, and their distance. Your census of the family of stars produces some surprising demographic results.

1a You could survey the stars by observing every star within 200 ly of Earth. A sphere 200 ly in radius encloses about 33.5 million cubic light-years. Such a survey would tell you how many stars of each type are found within such a volume.

200 ly

Earth

2 Your survey faces two problems.

1. The most luminous stars are so rare you find few in your survey region. There are no O stars at all within 200 ly of Earth.

2. Lower-main-sequence M stars, called red dwarfs, and white dwarfs are so faint they are hard to locate even when they are only a few light-years from Earth. Finding every one of these stars in your survey sphere is a difficult task.

Spectral Class Colour Key

- ○ O and B
- ○ A
- ○ F
- ○ G
- ○ K
- ○ M

The star chart in the background of these two pages shows most of the constellation Canis Major; stars are represented as dots with colours assigned according to spectral class. The brightest stars in the sky tend to be the rare, highly luminous stars, which look bright even though they are far away. Most stars are of very low luminosity, so nearby stars tend to be very faint red dwarfs.

Red dwarf
50 ly

o² Canis Majoris
B3Ia   2575 ly

Red dwarf
55 ly

δ Canis Majoris
F8Ia   1800 ly

σ Canis Majoris
M0Iab   1200 ly

η Canis Majoris
B5Ia   3200 ly

ε Canis Majoris
B2II   425 ly

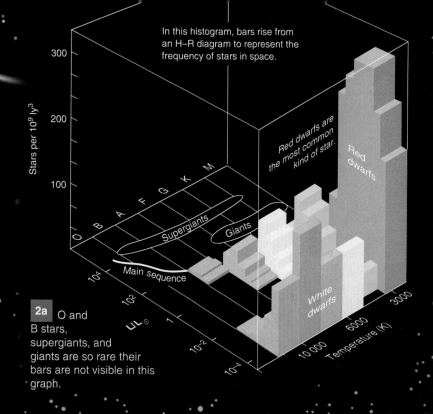

In this histogram, bars rise from an H–R diagram to represent the frequency of stars in space.

Red dwarfs are the most common kind of star.

2a O and B stars, supergiants, and giants are so rare their bars are not visible in this graph.

Sirius A (α Canis Majoris) is the brightest star in the sky. With a spectral type of A1V, it is not a very luminous star. It looks bright because it is only 8.6 ly away.

Sirius B is a white dwarf that orbits Sirius A. Although Sirius B is not very far away, it is much too faint to see with the unaided eye.

3 Luminous stars are rare but are easy to see. Most stars are very low luminosity. See the H–R diagrams at right.

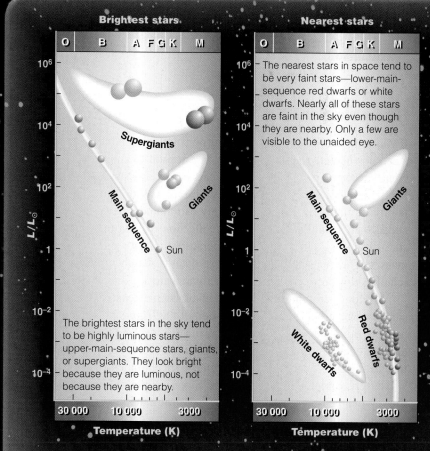

The brightest stars in the sky tend to be highly luminous stars—upper-main-sequence stars, giants, or supergiants. They look bright because they are luminous, not because they are nearby.

The nearest stars in space tend to be very faint stars—lower-main-sequence red dwarfs or white dwarfs. Nearly all of these stars are faint in the sky even though they are nearby. Only a few are visible to the unaided eye.

Although white dwarfs and red dwarfs are very common, not a single one is bright enough to be visible to the unaided eye.

Algonquin Radio Observatory at Algonquin Park, Ontario

© age fotostock Spain, S.L./Alamy

Arthur Edwin Covington

Arthur Covington, Canada's first radio astronomer, was a pioneer in microwave observations of our star—the Sun. He was the first to show that radio emissions from the Sun in the microwave region could be used as a measure of sunspot activity. This novel method of detecting sunspots is still used around the world today to study solar activity and its effects on radio communications.

Growing up in Saskatchewan and Vancouver, British Columbia, Covington showed an early interest in astronomy as well as in being an amateur radio operator. In 1942, he completed his doctoral degree in nuclear physics at University of California, Berkeley, and joined the National Research Council of Canada in Ottawa the same year, where he began developing new radar systems.

After World War II, Covington built a radio telescope out of surplus parts that operated in the microwave region around 10.7 cm. He noticed to his surprise that the Sun's microwave emissions did not simply follow the expected pattern of blackbody radiation, but instead were varying over time. He showed that this phenomenon was connected to sunspot activity, and his later studies contributed to the understanding of how sunspots are created.

Wanting to escape the interference of the growing "radio activity" of the Ottawa region in the late 1950s, Covington selected Algonquin Park (150 km northeast of Ottawa) as the site of a new radio telescope, the Algonquin Radio Observatory (ARO), becoming its director until his retirement in 1978. His research at the ARO provided evidence that major solar activity was preceded by microwave signals announcing, in effect, upcoming solar storms.

After Covington died in 2001, one of the buildings at the Herzberg Institute of Astrophysics in Penticton, BC, was named in his honour.

Surveying the Stars

If you want to know what the average person thinks about a certain subject, you take a survey. If you want to know what the average star is like, you can survey the stars. Such surveys reveal important relationships among the family of stars. Over the years, many astronomers have added their results to the growing collection of data on star distances, luminosities, temperatures, sizes, and masses. They can now analyze those data to search for relationships between these and other parameters.

Modern astronomers are deeply involved in extensive surveys. Remember the earlier mention of the *Hipparcos* satellite that surveyed the entire sky, measuring the parallax of over a million stars? Powerful computers to control instruments and analyze data make such immense surveys possible. For example, the Sloan Digital Sky Survey mapped a quarter of the sky, measuring the position and brightness of 100 million stars and galaxies. Also, the Two Micron All Sky Survey (2MASS) has mapped the entire sky at three near-infrared wavelengths. A number of other sky surveys are underway. Astronomers will mine these mountains of data for decades to come.

What could you learn about stars from a survey of the stars near the Sun? The evidence astronomers have is that the Sun is in a typical place in the universe. Therefore, such a survey could reveal general characteristics of the stars. Study **Visualizing Astronomy 6.1, The Family of Stars,** and notice three important points:

1. Taking a survey is difficult because you must be sure to get an honest sample. If you don't survey enough stars or if you miss some types of stars, your results could be biased.

2. M dwarfs and white dwarfs are so faint they are difficult to find even near Earth and may be undercounted in surveys.

3. Luminous stars, although they are rare, are easily visible even at great distances. Typical nearby stars have lower luminosity than our Sun.

The night sky is a beautiful carpet of stars. Some are giants and supergiants, and some are dwarfs. The family of stars is rich in its diversity. Pretend space is like a very clear ocean in which you are swimming. When you look at the night sky you are seeing mostly "whales," the rare very large and luminous stars, mostly far away. If instead you cast a net near your location, you would mostly catch "sardines," very-low-luminosity M dwarfs that make up most of the stellar population of the universe.

In this chapter you explored the basic properties of stars. Once you found the distance to the stars, you were able to find their luminosities. Knowing their luminosities and temperatures gives you their diameters. Studying binary stars gives you their masses. These are all rather mundane data. But you have now discovered a puzzling situation. The largest and most luminous stars are so rare you might joke that they hardly exist, and the average stars are such small low-mass things they are hard to see even if they are near Earth in space. Why does nature make stars in this peculiar way? To answer that question, you can explore the birth, life, and death of stars. That quest begins in the next chapter.

The Big Picture

We humans are medium creatures, and we experience medium things. You can see trees and flowers and small insects, but you cannot see the beauty of the microscopic world without ingenious instruments and special methods.

Similarly, you can sense the grandeur of a mountain range, but larger objects, such as stars, are too big for our medium senses. You have to use your ingenuity and imagination to experience the truth of such large objects. That is what science does for us. We live between the microscopic world and the astronomical world, and science enriches our lives by revealing the parts of the universe beyond our daily experience.

Experience is fun, but it is very limited. You may enjoy a flower by admiring its colour and shape and by smelling its fragrance. But the flower is more wonderful than your experience can reveal. To truly appreciate the flower you need to understand it: how complex it truly is, how it serves its plant, and how the plant came to create such a beautiful blossom.

Humans have a natural drive to understand as well as to experience. You have experienced the stars in the night sky, and now you are beginning to understand them as objects ranging from hot blue O stars to cool red M dwarfs. It is natural for you to wonder why these stars are so different. As you explore that story in the following chapters, you will discover that although you have medium senses, you can understand the stars.

Review and Discussion Questions

Review Questions

1. Why are Earth-based parallax measurements limited to the nearest stars?
2. Why was the *Hipparcos* satellite able to make more accurate parallax measurements than ground-based telescopes?
3. What do the words *absolute* and *visual* mean in the definition of absolute visual magnitude?
4. What does luminosity measure that is different from what absolute visual magnitude measures?
5. Why are Balmer lines strong in the spectra of medium-temperature stars and weak in the spectra of hot and cool stars?
6. Why are titanium oxide features visible in the spectra of only the coolest stars?

7. Explain the interrelationships among Table 6.1, Figure 6.4, Figure 6.5, Figure 6.6, and Figure 6.8.
8. Why does the luminosity of a star depend on both its radius and its temperature?
9. How can you be sure that giant stars really are larger than main-sequence stars?
10. What evidence shows that white dwarfs must be very small?
11. What observations would you make to classify a star according to its luminosity? Why does that method work?
12. Why does the orbital period of a binary star depend on its mass?
13. What observations would you make to study an eclipsing binary star, and what would those measurements tell you about the component stars?

14. Why don't astronomers know the inclination of a spectroscopic binary? How do they know the inclination of an eclipsing binary?

15. How do the masses of stars along the main sequence illustrate the mass–luminosity relation?

16. Why is it difficult to find out how common are the most luminous stars and the least luminous stars?

17. What is the most common type of star?

18. If you look only at the brightest stars in the night sky, what type of star are you likely to be observing? Why?

19. **How Do We Know?** What is the missing link in the chain of inference leading from observations of spectroscopic binaries to the masses of stars?

Discussion Questions

1. If someone asked you to compile a list of the nearest stars to the Sun based on your own observations, how would you select your sample, what measurements would you make, and how would you analyze the measurements to detect nearby stars?

2. Can you think of classification systems used to simplify what would otherwise be complex measurements? Consider foods, movies, cars, grades, and clothes.

3. The Sun is sometimes described as an average star. Is that true? What is the average star really like?

STUDY **TOOLS**

IN THE BOOK

- Tear out the Review Card for Chapter 6

ONLINE

Visit CENGAGENOW™ for ASTRO, 2Ce at www.nelson.com/student

- eBook
- Interactive Quizzing
- Animations
- Tutorials

The study habit that sets you apart.

www.nelson.com/student

7

The Structure and Formation of Stars

GUIDEPOST

In the previous chapter you discovered the wide range of differences within the family of stars. In this chapter you will combine observations and hypotheses to understand how nature makes stars, and learn the answers to five important questions:

- **How do astronomers study the gas and dust between the stars, called the interstellar medium?**
- **How do stars form from the interstellar medium?**
- **How do stars maintain their stability?**
- **How do stars generate energy?**
- **How do the luminosities and lifetimes of stars depend on their masses?**

Perhaps more important than these factual questions is the key question to ask in any scientific context: What's the evidence? Astronomers have evidence about how stars are born, how they remain stable, and how they generate energy. Testing hypotheses against evidence is the basic skill required of all scientists, and in the five chapters that follow you will have many opportunities to use this skill.

The stars are not eternal. When you look at the sky, you see hundreds of points of light. Each is an object like the Sun, held together by its gravity and generating tremendous energy in its core through nuclear reactions. The stars you see tonight are the same stars your parents, grandparents, and great-grandparents saw. Stars change hardly at all in a human lifetime, but they are not eternal. Stars are born, and stars die. This chapter begins that story. How can you know what the internal processes and life cycles of stars are when you

© NASA / Photo Researchers, Inc

Humans are natural-born scientists. When we're born, we want to know why the stars shine. We want to know why the sun rises.

Michio Kaku,
Physicist and popular science communicator

Nature has always had a trick of surprising us, and she will continue to surprise us. But she has never let us down yet.

Cecilia Payne-Gaposchkin,
Astronomer who first explained the composition of stars

Stars form in enormous clouds of gas and dust such as the spectacular "Pillars of Creation" in the Eagle

can't see inside them and humans don't live long enough to see them evolve? The answer lies in the methods of science. By constructing theories that describe how nature works and then testing those theories against evidence from observations, you can unravel some of nature's greatest secrets. In this chapter, you will see how the flow of energy from inside to the surfaces of the stars balances gravity, making the stars stable, and how nuclear reactions inside stars generate that energy. You will also see how gravity creates new stars from the thin dusty gas between the stars.

Table 7.1 | Four Laws of Stellar Structure

I. Conservation of mass	Total mass equals the sum of shell masses.
II. Conservation of energy	Total luminosity equals the sum of energy generated in all the layers in each shell.
III. Hydrostatic equilibrium	The weight on each layer is balanced by the pressure in that layer.
IV. Energy transport	Energy moves from hot to cool regions by conduction, radiation, or convection.

7.1 Stellar Structure

If there is a single idea in stellar astronomy that can be called crucial, it is the concept of balance. In this section you will discover that stars are simple, elegant power sources held together by their own gravity, balanced by the support of their internal heat and pressure.

Using the basic concept of balance, you can consider the structure of a star. What is meant here by structure is the variation in temperature, density, pressure, and so on between the surface of the star and its centre. It will be easier to think about stellar structure if you imagine that the star is divided into concentric shells like those in an onion. Knowing the four basic laws of stellar structure (Table 7.1) will also help you understand stars. With these laws you can consider the temperature, pressure, and density in each shell. These helpful shells exist only in the imagination; stars do not actually have such separable layers.

The Laws of Conservation of Mass and Energy

The first two laws of stellar structure have something in common—they are both what astronomers and physicists call *conservation* laws. Conservation laws say that certain things cannot be created out of nothing or vanish into nothing. Such conservation laws are powerful aids to help you understand how nature works.

The law of **conservation of mass** is a basic law of nature that can be applied to the structure of stars. It says

conservation of mass One of the basic laws of stellar structure: The total mass of the star must equal the sum of the shell masses.

conservation of energy One of the basic laws of stellar structure: The total luminosity must equal the sum of energy generated in all of the layers.

that the total mass of a star must equal the sum of the masses of its shells. This is like saying the weight of a cake must equal the sum of the weight of its layers.

The law of **conservation of energy** is another basic law of nature. It says that the amount of energy flowing out of the top of a layer in the star must be equal to the amount of energy coming in at the bottom, plus whatever energy is generated within the layer. That means that the energy leaving the surface of the star, its luminosity, must equal the sum of the energies generated in all the layers inside the star through fusion. This is like saying that all the new cars driving out of a factory must equal the sum of all the cars made on each of the production lines.

These two laws may seem so familiar or so obvious that they hardly need to be stated, but they are important clues to the structure of stars. The third law of stellar structure is a law about balance.

Hydrostatic Equilibrium

The weight of each layer of a star must be supported by the layer below. (The words *down* or *below* are conventionally used to refer to regions closer to the centre of a star.) Picture a pyramid of people in a circus stunt—the people in the top row do not have to hold up anybody else; the people in the next row down are holding up the people in the top row; and so on. In a star that is stable, the deeper layers must support the weight of all of the layers above. The inside of a star is made up of gas, so the weight pressing down on a layer must be balanced by gas pressure in that layer. If the pressure is too low the weight from above will compress and push down the layer; and if the pressure is too high the layer will expand and lift the layers above.

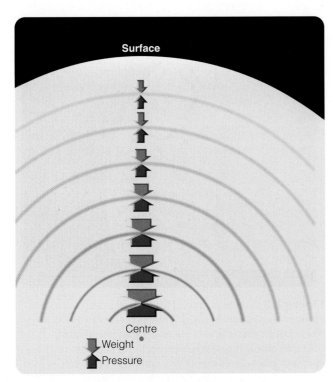

Figure 7.1 The principle of hydrostatic equilibrium says the pressure in each layer of a star must balance the weight of that layer. Consequently, as the weight increases from the surface of the star to its centre, the pressure must also increase.

This balance between weight and pressure is called **hydrostatic equilibrium**. *Hydro* (from the Greek word for water) tells you the material is a fluid, which by definition includes the gases of a star, and *static* tells you the fluid is stable, neither expanding nor contracting.

Figure 7.1 shows this hydrostatic balance in the imaginary layers of a star. The weight pressing down on each layer is shown by light-red arrows, which grow larger with increasing depth because the weight grows larger. The pressure in each layer is shown by dark-red arrows, which must grow larger with increasing depth to support the weight above.

The pressure in a gas depends on the temperature and density of the gas. Near the surface, there is little weight pressing down, so the pressure does not need to be high for stability. Deeper in the star, the pressure must be higher than at the surface, which means that the temperature and density of the gas must also be higher. Hydrostatic equilibrium tells you that stars must have high temperature, pressure, and density inside to support their own weight and be stable.

Although the law of hydrostatic equilibrium can tell you some things about the inner structure of stars, you need one more law to completely describe a star. You need to know how energy flows from the inside to the outside.

Energy Transport

Consider the fourth law shown in Table 7.1. The surface of a star radiates light and heat into space and would quickly cool if that energy were not replaced. Because the inside of the star is hotter than the surface, energy must flow outward to the surface, where it radiates away. This flow of energy through each shell determines its temperature which, as you saw previously, determines how much weight that shell can balance. To understand the structure of a star, you need to understand how energy moves from the centre to the surface.

The law of **energy transport** says that energy must flow from hot regions to cooler regions either by conduction, convection, or radiation. *Conduction* is the most familiar form of heat flow. If you hold the bowl of a spoon in a candle flame, the handle of the spoon grows warmer as heat, in the form of motion among the atoms of the spoon, is conducted from atom to atom up the handle (Figure 7.2). Conduction requires close contact between the atoms, so it is not an important cause of heat flow in normal stars because radiation or convection are much more efficient, even in their centres; it is only important in rare types of stars with extremely high densities.

The transport of energy by *radiation* is another familiar experience. Put your hand near a candle flame, and you can feel the heat. What you actually feel are infrared photons—packets of energy—radiated by the flame and absorbed by your hand. Radiation is the principal means of energy transport in the interiors of most stars. Photons are absorbed and re-emitted in random directions over and over as energy works its way from the hot interior toward the cooler surface.

The flow of energy by radiation depends on how difficult it is for photons to move through the gas. The **opacity** of the gas—its resistance to the flow of radiation— depends strongly on its temperature: A hot gas is more transparent than a cool gas. If the opacity is high, radiation cannot flow through the gas easily, and it backs up like water behind a dam. When enough heat builds up, the gas begins to churn as hot gas rises upward and cool gas sinks downward. This heat-driven

hydrostatic equilibrium One of the basic laws of stellar structure: The weight on each layer must be balanced by the pressure in that layer.

energy transport One of the basic laws of stellar structure: Energy must move from hot to cool regions by conduction, radiation, or convection.

opacity The resistance of a gas to the passage of radiation.

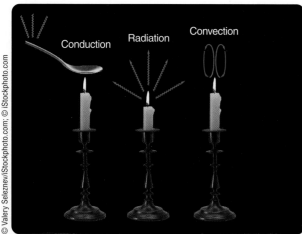

Figure 7.2 The three modes by which energy may be transported from the flame of a candle, as shown in this figure, are the three modes of energy transport within a star. Radiation and convection are much more important than conduction in the interiors of main-sequence stars.

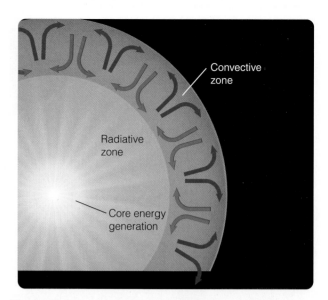

Figure 7.3 A cross-section of the Sun. Near the centre, nuclear fusion reactions sustain high temperatures. Energy flows through the radiative zone as photons are randomly deflected over and over by electrons. In the cooler, more opaque, outer layers the energy is carried by rising convection currents of hot gas (red arrows) and sinking currents of cooler gas (blue arrows).

circulation of a fluid is *convection*, the third way energy can move in a star. You are familiar with convection; the rising wisp of smoke above a candle flame is carried by convection. Energy is carried upward in these convection currents as both rising hot gas and also sinking cool gas. The cross-section of the Sun shown in Figure 7.3 indicates the location of the radiative and convective zones.

The four laws of stellar structure, when properly understood, tell you not only about the insides of stars but also about how stars are born, how they live, and how they die.

Stellar Models

The laws of stellar structure, described in general terms in the previous sections, can be written as mathematical equations. By solving those equations, astronomers can make a mathematical model of the inside of a star. To start constructing one of these models requires the type of information you learned in Chapter 6 about the external properties of a star: its diameter, luminosity, mass, surface temperature, atmospheric density, and composition.

If you want to build a model of a star, you could divide the star into, say, 100 concentric shells and then write down the four equations of stellar structure for each shell. You would then have 400 equations that would have 400 unknowns, namely, the temperature, density, mass, and energy flow in each shell. Solving 400 equations simultaneously is not easy, and the first such solutions, done by hand before the invention of electronic computers, took months of work. Now a properly programmed computer can solve the equations in a few seconds and print a table of numbers that represent the conditions in each shell of the star. Such a table is called a **stellar model**.

The table shown in Figure 7.4 is a model of the Sun. The bottom line, for radius equal to 0.00, represents the centre of the Sun, and the top line, for radius equal to 1.00, represents the surface. The other lines tell you the temperature and density in each shell, the mass inside each shell, and the fraction of the Sun's luminosity flowing outward through the shell. The bottom line tells you that the temperature at the centre of the Sun must be over 15 million Kelvin in order for the Sun to be stable. At such a high temperature, the gas is very transparent, and energy flows as radiation. Nearer the surface, the temperature is lower, the gas is more opaque, and energy moves by convection. This is confirmed by evidence of convection visible on the Sun's surface (see Chapter 5).

Stellar models also let you look into a star's past and future. In fact, you could use models as time machines

stellar model A table of numbers representing the conditions in various layers within a star.

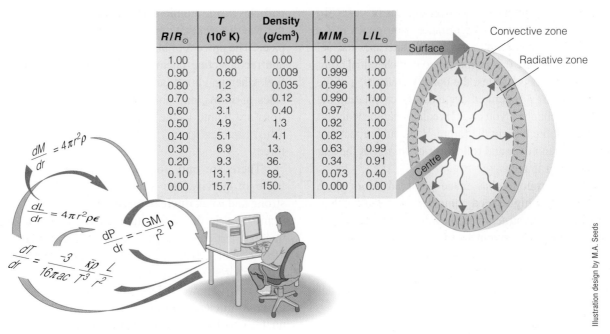

R/R_⊙	T (10^6 K)	Density (g/cm^3)	M/M_⊙	L/L_⊙
1.00	0.006	0.00	1.00	1.00
0.90	0.60	0.009	0.999	1.00
0.80	1.2	0.035	0.996	1.00
0.70	2.3	0.12	0.990	1.00
0.60	3.1	0.40	0.97	1.00
0.50	4.9	1.3	0.92	1.00
0.40	5.1	4.1	0.82	1.00
0.30	6.9	13.	0.63	0.99
0.20	9.3	36.	0.34	0.91
0.10	13.1	89.	0.073	0.40
0.00	15.7	150.	0.000	0.00

$$\frac{dM}{dr} = 4\pi r^2 \rho$$

$$\frac{dL}{dr} = 4\pi r^2 \rho \epsilon$$

$$\frac{dP}{dr} = -\frac{GM}{r^2}\rho$$

$$\frac{dT}{dr} = \frac{-3}{16\pi ac}\frac{\bar{\kappa}\rho}{T^3}\frac{L}{r^2}$$

Illustration design by M.A. Seeds

Figure 7.4 A stellar model is a table of numbers that represent conditions inside a star. Such tables can be computed using four laws of stellar structure, shown here in equation form, including the principle of hydrostatic equilibrium and the law of energy transport. The table in this figure describes the present-day Sun.

HOW DO WE KNOW? 7.1

Mathematical Models

One of the most powerful tools in science is the mathematical model, a group of equations carefully designed to describe the behaviour of the object that scientists want to study.

Many sciences use mathematical models. Medical scientists have created mathematical models of the nerves that control the heart, and physicists have made mathematical models of the inside of an atomic nucleus. Economists have mathematical models of certain aspects of systems such as the municipal bond market, and Earth scientists have mathematical models of Earth's atmosphere. In each case, the mathematical model allows scientists to study something that is difficult to study directly. The model can reveal regions scientists cannot observe, speed up a slow process, slow down a fast process, or allow scientists to perform experiments that would be impossible in reality. Astronomers, for example, can change the abundance of different chemical elements in a model star to see how its structure depends on its composition. Mathematical modelling is one of the most important research methods in astronomy, even though it often requires exceptionally large and fast computers.

As is true for any scientific model, a mathematical model is only as reliable as the assumptions that go into its creation. The celestial sphere (Chapter 2) is an adequate model of the sky for some purposes, but it doesn't work if you take it too literally. The same is true of mathematical models. You can think of a mathematical model as a numerical expression of one or more theories. Although such models can be very helpful, they are always based on theories and assumptions and so must be compared with the real world at every opportunity. As always in science, there is no substitute for a careful comparison with reality.

to follow the evolution of stars over billions of years. To look into a star's future, for instance, you could use a stellar model to determine how fast the star uses its fuel in each shell. As the fuel is consumed, the chemical composition of the gas changes, the opacity changes, and the amount of energy generated declines. By calculating the rate of these changes, you could predict what the star will look like at some time in the future. You could repeat that process over and over and follow the evolution of the star step-by-step as it ages.

Stellar astronomy has made great advances since the 1960s, when high-speed computers that could calculate models of the structure and evolution of stars began to be available. The summary of star formation later in this chapter is based on thousands of stellar models. You will continue to rely on theoretical models as you study main-sequence stars later in this chapter and the deaths of stars in the next chapter.

7.2 Nuclear Fusion in the Sun and Stars

Astronomers often use the wrong words to describe energy generation in the Sun and stars. Astronomers will say, "The star ignites hydrogen burning." You would normally use the word *ignite* to mean "catch on fire" and *burn* to mean "consume by fire." What goes on inside stars isn't really burning in the usual sense.

The Sun is a normal star, and it is powered by nuclear reactions that occur near its centre. Later in this section you will learn some of the evidence for this. The energy produced keeps a star's interior hot, and the gas is totally ionized. That is, the electrons are not attached to the atomic nuclei, and the gas is a soup of rapidly moving particles colliding with each other at high speed.

When astronomers discuss nuclear reactions inside stars, they refer to atomic nuclei, not to atoms. How exactly can the nucleus of an atom yield energy? The answer lies in the forces that hold the nuclei together.

nuclear forces The two forces of nature that only affect the particles in the nuclei of atoms.

nuclear fission Reactions that break the nuclei of atoms into fragments.

nuclear fusion Reactions that join the nuclei of atoms to form more massive nuclei.

Nuclear Binding Energy

The Sun generates its energy by breaking and reconnecting the bonds between the particles *inside* atomic nuclei. That is quite different from the way we generate energy by burning wood in a fireplace. The process of burning extracts energy by breaking and reconnecting chemical bonds between atoms in the fuel. Chemical bonds are formed by electrons on the outsides of atoms, and you saw in Chapter 5 that the electrons are bound to the atoms by electromagnetic force. Thus, chemical energy originates in the electromagnetic force.

There are only four known forces in nature: the force of gravity, the electromagnetic force, and the strong and weak **nuclear forces**. The weak nuclear force is involved in the radioactive decay of certain kinds of nuclear particles, and the strong force binds together atomic nuclei. Nuclear energy originates in the strong nuclear force.

Nuclear power plants on Earth generate energy through **nuclear fission** reactions that split uranium nuclei into less massive fragments. The Bruce Nuclear Generating Station on the shores of Lake Huron in southern Ontario is the largest such facility in North America and the second largest in the world (the Kashiwazaki-Kariwa nuclear power plant in Japan is the largest). A fissile uranium nucleus contains a total of 235 protons and neutrons, and it splits into a range of fragments containing roughly half as many particles. Because the fragments produced are more tightly bound than the uranium nuclei, energy is released during uranium fission, as demonstrated in Figure 7.5.

Stars generate energy through **nuclear fusion** reactions that combine light nuclei into heavier nuclei. The most common reaction, including that in the Sun, fuses hydrogen nuclei (single protons) into helium nuclei (two protons and two neutrons). Because the nuclei produced are more tightly bound than the original nuclei, energy is released. Notice in Figure 7.5 that both fusion and fission reactions move downward in the diagram, meaning they release the binding energy of nuclei and create more tightly bound nuclei.

Hydrogen Fusion

The Sun fuses four hydrogen nuclei to make one helium nucleus. Because one helium nucleus contains 0.7 percent less mass than four hydrogen nuclei, some mass vanishes in the process. In fact, that mass is converted to energy, and you could figure out how much energy by using Einstein's famous equation, $E = mc^2$. For example, converting 1 kg of matter completely into energy would produce an enormous amount of energy, 9×10^{16} joules, comparable to the amount of energy a big city such as

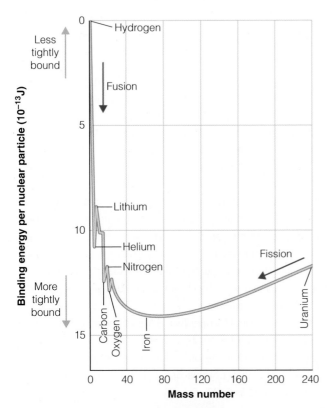

Figure 7.5 The red line in this graph shows the binding energy (the energy that holds an atomic nucleus together) for different types of atoms, which depends on atomic mass (the number of protons and neutrons in an atom's nucleus). Both fission and fusion nuclear reactions convert fuel nuclei to product nuclei, shown with arrows lower in the diagram, that have more tightly bound nuclei. Iron has the most tightly bound nucleus, so no nuclear reactions can begin with iron and release energy.

Calgary uses in a year. (Refer to **Hydrogen Fusion** in the Math Reference Cards.)

Making one helium nucleus releases a very small amount of energy, hardly enough to raise a housefly $\frac{1}{40}$ of a millimetre into the air. Only by concentrating many reactions in a small region can nature produce significant amounts of energy. The Sun has a voracious appetite and needs 10^{38} reactions per second, transforming 5 million tons of mass into energy every second, just to replace the energy pouring into space from its surface. That might sound as if the Sun is losing mass at a furious rate, but in its entire 10-billion-year lifetime, the Sun will convert less than 0.07 percent of its mass into energy.

Fusion reactions can occur only when the nuclei of two atoms get very close to each other. Because atomic nuclei carry positive charges, they repel each other with an electrostatic force called the Coulomb force. Physicists commonly refer to this repulsion between nuclei as the **Coulomb barrier**. To overcome this barrier, atomic nuclei must have violent collisions that are rare unless the gas is very hot, in which case the nuclei move at high speeds. (Recall that an object's temperature is just a measure of the average speed with which its particles move.) Although the core temperature of the Sun is not nearly high enough to allow protons to overcome the Coulomb barrier existing between them, it turns out that quantum effects (quantum tunnelling) are largely responsible for the fact that fusion takes place at all. A full discussion of this effect is beyond the scope of this textbook. Suffice it to say that quantum mechanics explains how fusion takes place in the cores of many main-sequence stars.

Nuclear reactions in the Sun take place only near the centre, where the gas is hot and dense. A high temperature ensures that collisions between nuclei are energetic enough to overcome the Coulomb barrier, and a high density ensures that there are enough collisions, and thus enough reactions, to produce enough energy to keep the Sun stable.

You can symbolize this process with a simple nuclear reaction:

$$4 \, {}^{1}\text{H} \rightarrow {}^{4}\text{He} + \text{energy}$$

In this equation, ${}^{1}\text{H}$ represents a proton, the nucleus of a hydrogen atom, and ${}^{4}\text{He}$ represents the nucleus of a helium atom. The superscripts indicate the total numbers of protons and neutrons in each nucleus.

The actual steps in the process are more complicated than this simple summary suggests. Instead of waiting for four hydrogen nuclei to collide simultaneously, which would be a highly unlikely event, the process can proceed by steps in a series of reactions called the proton–proton chain.

The **proton–proton chain** is a series of three nuclear reactions that builds a helium nucleus by adding protons one at a time. This process is efficient at temperatures above 10 000 000 K. The Sun, for example, generates its energy in this way. Recall from the previous section that models of the interior of the Sun based on its overall stability indicate the central temperature is about 15 000 000 K.

The three reactions in the proton–proton chain are:

$$\begin{aligned}
{}^{1}\text{H} + {}^{1}\text{H} &\rightarrow {}^{2}\text{H} + e^{+} + \nu \\
{}^{2}\text{H} + {}^{1}\text{H} &\rightarrow {}^{3}\text{He} + \gamma \\
{}^{3}\text{He} + {}^{3}\text{He} &\rightarrow {}^{4}\text{He} + {}^{1}\text{H} + {}^{1}\text{H}
\end{aligned}$$

Coulomb barrier The electrostatic force of repulsion between bodies of like charge, commonly applied to atomic particles.

proton–proton chain A series of three nuclear reactions that builds a helium atom by adding together protons; the main energy source in the Sun.

Jaymie Matthews

You have heard of the Hubble Space Telescope, but you may not know that the world's *smallest* space telescope is Canada's MOST (Microvariability and Oscillations of STars) telescope, affectionately called the Humble Space Telescope. The MOST project's principal investigator and mission scientist, Dr. Jaymie Matthews, and his team at the University of British Columbia use this suitcase-sized, low-cost telescope to study starquakes, that is, the vibrations of stars in our galaxy. Just as geologists can use seismic waves to study Earth's structure, stellar seismology—or asteroseismology—is the study of stars using the oscillations of the light waves emitted by the stars. Dr. Matthews describes it as listening to the music of the stars using an interstellar iPod: the MOST telescope. Despite its small size and limited budget, the telescope allows measurements at unprecedented levels of precision; it is the only existing device that can detect changes in the brightness of a star at the level of one part per million. Dr. Matthews and his team are analyzing the data from the MOST satellite to better understand the life of the Sun by comparing it to other stars, to estimate the age of the Universe, to study planets around other stars, and ultimately to search for Earth-like planets in the galaxy. Dr. Matthews is also involved in the steering committees of the international Gemini Twin 8-Metre Telescopes project and the Far-Ultraviolet Spectroscopic Explorer satellite. He is actively involved in astronomy outreach and education, and has appeared on a variety of TV shows to promote science. Dr. Matthews was awarded the Canadian Association of Physicists Education Medal in 2002, and was named an Officer of the Order of Canada in 2006.

In the first reaction, two hydrogen nuclei (two protons) combine, and one changes into a neutron, to result in a heavy hydrogen nucleus called **deuterium**, while emitting a particle called a **positron** (a positively charged electron, symbolized by e^+) and another called a **neutrino** (v). A positron is the antimatter counterpart of an electron. When an electron and a positron collide they annihilate each other and their mass gets converted completely into energy in the form of gamma rays—which is what happens to the positrons produced in the first reaction. In the second reaction, the heavy hydrogen nucleus absorbs another proton and, with the emission of a gamma ray (γ), becomes a lightweight helium nucleus (^{3}He). Finally, two light helium nuclei combine to form a normal helium nucleus and two hydrogen nuclei. Because the last reaction needs two ^{3}He nuclei, the first and second reactions must occur twice for each ^{4}He produced (see Figure 7.6). The net result of this chain reaction is the transformation of four hydrogen nuclei into one helium nucleus plus energy.

All main-sequence stars fuse hydrogen into helium to generate energy. The Sun and smaller stars fuse hydrogen by the proton–proton chain. Upper-main-sequence stars, more massive than the Sun, fuse hydrogen by a more efficient process called the **CNO (carbon–nitrogen–oxygen) cycle**. The CNO cycle begins with a carbon nucleus and transforms it first into a nitrogen nucleus, then into an oxygen nucleus, and then back to a carbon nucleus. The carbon is unchanged in the end, but along the way four hydrogen nuclei are fused to make a helium nucleus plus energy, just as in the proton–proton chain. A carbon nucleus has six times more positive electric charge than hydrogen, so the Coulomb barrier is higher than for combining two protons. Temperatures higher than 16 000 000 K are required to make the CNO cycle work: the centre of the Sun is not quite hot enough for this reaction. In stars more massive than about 1.1 solar masses, the cores are hot enough and the CNO cycle dominates over the slower proton–proton chain.

In both the proton–proton chain and the CNO cycle, energy appears in the form of gamma rays, positrons, and neutrinos. The gamma rays are photons that are absorbed by the surrounding gas before they can travel more than

deuterium An isotope of hydrogen in which the nucleus contains a proton and a neutron.

positron The antimatter equivalent of the electron; it has all the same properties as the electron except that its charge is positive instead of negative.

neutrino A neutral, nearly massless atomic particle that travels at or near the speed of light.

CNO (carbon–nitrogen–oxygen) cycle A series of nuclear reactions that use carbon as a catalyst to combine four hydrogen nuclei to make one helium nucleus plus energy; effective in stars more massive than the Sun.

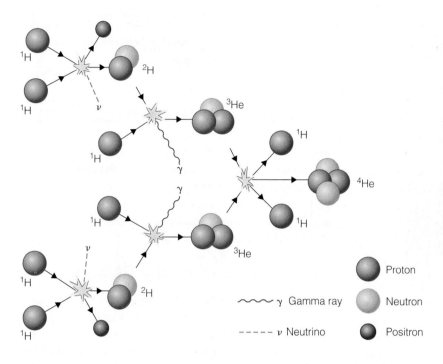

Figure 7.6 The proton–proton chain combines four protons (at far left) to produce one helium nucleus (at right). Energy is produced mostly as gamma rays and as positrons, which combine with electrons and convert their mass into more energy in the form of gamma rays. Neutrinos escape without helping to heat the gas.

your body every second. Even at night, neutrinos from the Sun rush through Earth as if it weren't there, up through your bed, through you, and onward into space. Certain particle reactions, however, can be triggered by a neutrino of the right energy.

Beginning in the 1960s, astrophysicists found several ways to detect solar neutrinos. Initial measurements, however, detected too few neutrinos—about one-third as many as predicted by models of the Sun's interior. This discrepancy is known as the *solar neutrino problem*.

The Sudbury Neutrino Observatory (SNO) was constructed in an active nickel mine in Sudbury, Ontario, by a Canadian-led international group of scientists beginning in 1990 (Figure 7.7). The neutrino detector is located in an underground rock cavern 22 m in diameter and 30 m high located two kilometres underground. It was fitted with a clear plastic sphere, 12 m in diameter, filled with 1000 tonnes of heavy water (D_2O), and surrounded by a shell of 9600 ultrasensitive phototubes immersed in ultrapure ordinary water. Neutrinos were detected by three types of reactions in the heavy water, each producing distinctive tiny emissions of photons. The detector was deep enough underground to filter out almost all cosmic rays that would produce interfering photons. The heavy water also enabled the detection of all three kinds of neutrinos, which physicists call "flavours."

The collection of data began in 1999, and about 15 events were recorded each day. Careful analysis of the data recorded over several years enabled SNO scientists to announce in May 2001 that there was strong evidence that about two-thirds of the neutrinos, which started out as so-called electron neutrinos in the Sun's core, changed to one of the other two flavours as they rushed through the Sun, across space to Earth, and to SNO's detector. Not only were the SNO's total neutrino numbers in excellent agreement with those predicted by solar theories—thereby solving the solar neutrino problem—but also the evidence for flavour change in neutrinos confirmed that solar neutrinos must have a tiny mass, a valuable by-product of the experiment. Although further lower-energy neutrino measurements are still continuing, SNO's strong confirmation of the basic correctness of models of the fusion processes in the Sun's core was a milestone accomplishment, and a good example of the interplay of theory and experiment in astrophysics.

a few centimetres. This heats the gas. The positrons produced in the first reaction combine with free electrons, and both particles vanish, converting their mass into more gamma rays. In this way, the positrons also help keep the centre of the star hot. The neutrinos, however, are particles that travel at nearly the speed of light and almost never interact with other particles. The average neutrino could pass unhindered through a lead wall more than one light-year thick. Consequently, the neutrinos do not help heat the gas but race out of the star, carrying away roughly 2 percent of the energy produced.

It is time to ask the critical question that lies at the heart of science: What is the evidence to support this theoretical explanation of how the Sun and other stars generate energy? The search for that evidence introduces you to one of the great triumphs of modern astronomy.

Neutrinos from the Sun's Core

Nuclear reactions in the Sun's core produce floods of neutrinos that rush out of the Sun and off into space. If you could detect these neutrinos you could probe the Sun's interior.

Because neutrinos almost never interact with atoms, neutrinos are extremely hard to detect. You never feel the flood of over 10^{12} solar neutrinos that flows through

Figure 7.7 The Sudbury Neutrino Observatory is a globe 12 m in diameter containing water rich in deuterium in place of ordinary hydrogen. Buried 2100 m deep in an Ontario mine, it can detect all three flavours of neutrinos, and it confirms that neutrinos change back and forth between the flavours.

The Pressure–Temperature Thermostat

Nuclear reactions in stars produce energy and heavy atoms under the supervision of a natural thermostat that keeps the reactions from erupting out of control. That thermostat is the relation between gas pressure and temperature.

In a star, the nuclear reactions generate just enough energy to balance the inward pull of gravity. Consider what would happen if the reactions began to produce too much energy. The star balances gravity by generating energy, so the extra energy flowing out of the star would force it to expand. The expansion would lower the central temperature and density and consequently slow the nuclear reactions until the star regained stability. Thus the star has a built-in regulator that keeps the nuclear reactions from occurring too rapidly.

The same thermostat keeps the reactions from dying down. Suppose the nuclear reactions began making too little energy. Then the star would contract slightly, increasing the central temperature and density, and resulting in an increase in the nuclear energy generation.

The overall stability of a star depends on the relation between gas pressure and temperature. If the material of the star has the property of normal gases—for which an increase or decrease in temperature produces a corresponding change in pressure—the nuclear reaction pressure–temperature thermostat can function properly and contribute to the stability of the star. In the next section you will see how this thermostat accounts for the relation between mass and luminosity for main-sequence stars.

7.3 Main-Sequence Stars

You can understand the deepest secrets of the stars by looking at the most obvious feature of the H–R diagram: the main sequence. Roughly 90 percent of all the stars that generate energy by nuclear fusion are main-sequence stars, and they obey a simple relationship that is the key to understanding the life and death of stars.

The Mass–Luminosity Relation

You learned in Chapter 6 that observations of the temperature and luminosity of stars show that main-sequence stars obey a simple rule: the more massive a star is, the more luminous it is. That rule is the key to understanding the stability of main-sequence stars. In fact, the mass–luminosity relation is predicted by the theories of stellar structure, giving astronomers direct observational confirmation of those theories.

To understand the mass–luminosity relation, you can consider both the law of hydrostatic equilibrium, which says that pressure balances weight, and the pressure–temperature thermostat, which regulates energy production. A star that is more massive than the Sun has more weight pressing down on its interior, so the interior must have a high pressure to balance that weight. That means the massive star's automatic pressure–temperature thermostat must keep the gas in its interior hot and the pressure high. A star less massive than the Sun has less weight on its interior. Therefore, it needs less internal pressure, and so its pressure–temperature thermostat is set lower. In other words, massive stars are more luminous because they must make more energy to support their larger weight. If they were not so luminous, they would not be stable.

Brown Dwarfs

The mass–luminosity relation also tells you why the main sequence has a lower end, a minimum mass. Objects with masses less than about 0.08 of the Sun's mass cannot raise their central temperature high enough to sustain hydrogen fusion. Called brown dwarfs, such objects are only about ten times the diameter of Earth—about the same size as Jupiter—and may still be warm from the processes of formation, but they do not generate energy by hydrogen fusion. They have contracted as much as they can and are slowly cooling off.

Brown dwarfs fall in the gap between low-mass M stars and massive planets like Jupiter. They would look dull orange or red to your eyes—which is why they are labelled "brown"—because they emit most of their energy in the infrared. The warmer brown dwarfs fall in spectral class L, the cooler ones in spectral class T, and the very cool ones in spectral class Y (see Chapter 6). Because they are so small and cool, brown dwarfs are very low-luminosity objects and thus difficult to find. Nevertheless, hundreds are known, and they may be as common as M stars.

The Life of a Main-Sequence Star

While a star is on the main sequence, it is stable, so you might think its life would be totally uneventful. But a main-sequence star balances its gravity by fusing hydrogen, and as the star gradually uses up its fuel, that balance must change. Consequently, even the stable main-sequence stars are changing as they consume their hydrogen fuel.

Recall that hydrogen fusion combines four nuclei into one. As a main-sequence star fuses its hydrogen, the total number of particles in its interior decreases. Each newly made helium nucleus can exert only the same pressure as a hydrogen nucleus. Because the gas has fewer nuclei, its total pressure is less. This condition unbalances the gravity–pressure stability, and gravity squeezes the core of the star more tightly. As the core contracts, its temperature increases, and the nuclear reactions run faster, releasing more energy. This additional energy flowing outward forces the outer layers to expand. Therefore, as a main-sequence star slowly turns hydrogen into helium in its core, the core contracts and heats up, and as the outer parts of the star become larger, the star becomes more luminous, and its surface cools down.

These gradual changes during the lifetime of main-sequence stars mean that the main sequence is not a sharp line across the H–R diagram, but rather a band. Stars begin their stable lives fusing hydrogen on the lower edge of this band, which is known as the **zero-age main sequence (ZAMS)**, but gradual changes in luminosity and surface temperature move the stars upward and slightly to the right, as shown in Figure 7.8. By the time they reach the upper edge of the main sequence, they have exhausted nearly all the hydrogen in their centres. If you precisely measure and plot the luminosity and temperature of main-sequence stars on the H–R diagram, you will find stars at various positions within the main-sequence band, indicating how much hydrogen has been converted to helium in their cores. Therefore, you can use the position of a star in the band, combined

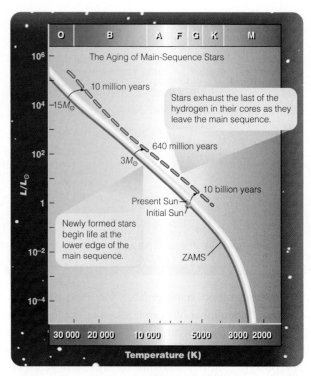

Figure 7.8 The aging of main-sequence stars. A newborn star reaches stability with properties that place it on the H–R diagram at the lower edge of the main-sequence band, along the line called the zero-age main sequence (ZAMS). As a star converts hydrogen in its core into helium, it moves slowly away from the ZAMS and across the main sequence, becoming slightly more luminous and cooler. Once a star consumes all the hydrogen in its core, it can no longer remain a stable main-sequence star. More massive stars age rapidly, but less massive stars use up the hydrogen in their cores more slowly and live longer main-sequence lives.

with stellar evolution models, as one way to estimate the star's age.

The Sun is a typical main-sequence star, and as it undergoes these gradual changes Earth will suffer. When the Sun began its main-sequence life about 5 billion years ago, it was only about 70 percent as luminous as it is now, and by the time it leaves the main sequence in about another 5 billion years, the Sun will have twice its present luminosity. Long before that, the rising luminosity of the Sun will raise Earth's average temperature, melt the polar caps, modify Earth's climate, and ultimately boil away and destroy Earth's oceans. Life on Earth will probably not survive these changes in the Sun, but humans have a billion years or more to prepare.

The average star spends 90 percent of its life on the main sequence. This explains why 90 percent of all true stars are main-sequence stars; you are most likely to see a

zero-age main sequence (ZAMS) The location in the H–R diagram where stars first reach stability as hydrogen-burning stars.

Table 7.2 | Main-Sequence Stars

Spectral Type	Mass (Sun = 1)	Luminosity (Sun = 1)	Approximate Years on Main Sequence
O5	40	400 000	1×10^6
B0	15	13 000	11×10^6
A0	3.5	80	440×10^6
F0	1.7	6.4	3×10^9
G0	1.1	1.4	8×10^9
K0	0.8	0.46	17×10^9
M0	0.5	0.08	56×10^9

star during that long, stable period while it is on the main sequence. The number of years a star spends on the main sequence depends on its mass (Table 7.2). Massive stars consume fuel rapidly and live short lives, but low-mass stars conserve their fuel and shine for billions of years. For example, a 25-solar-mass star will exhaust its hydrogen and die in only about 7 million years. The Sun has enough fuel to last about 10 billion years. The red dwarfs

interstellar medium (ISM)
The gas and dust distributed between the stars.

have little fuel, but they use it up very slowly and may be able to survive for 100 billion years or more. (Refer to **The Life Expectancies of Stars** in the Math Reference Cards.)

7.4 The Birth of Stars

The key to understanding star formation is the correlation between young stars, short-lived stars, and interstellar clouds of gas and dust. Where you find the youngest groups of stars, as well as stars with very short lifetimes, you also find large clouds of gas and dust illuminated by the hottest and brightest of the new stars (see Figure 7.9). This should lead you to suspect that stars form from such clouds.

The Interstellar Medium

A common misperception is to imagine that space is empty—a vacuum. In fact, if you glance at Orion's sword on a winter evening, you can see the Great Nebula in Orion, a glowing cloud of gas and dust. That cloud and others are prominent examples of the low-density gas and dust between the stars, which is called the **interstellar medium (ISM).**

About 75 percent of the mass of interstellar gas is hydrogen, and 25 percent is helium; there are also traces of carbon, nitrogen, oxygen, calcium, sodium,

Figure 7.9 Young stars are found in clouds of gas and dust from which they have been born. The nebula N44 is 170 000 ly from Earth in a nearby galaxy, and the Horsehead Nebula is only about 1500 ly distant in our own galaxy. Gas in both nebulae is excited to glow by hot, young stars. Interstellar dust is visible as dark, twisting clouds seen against the bright background gas.

and heavier atoms. Notice that this is very similar to the composition of the Sun (see Chapter 5) and other stars. Roughly 1 percent of the ISM's mass is made up of microscopic particles called **interstellar dust**. The dust particles are about the size of the particles in cigarette smoke. The dust seems to be made mostly of carbon and silicates (rocklike minerals) mixed with or coated with frozen water, plus some organic compounds.

This interstellar material is not uniformly distributed through space; it consists of a complex tangle of cool, dense clouds pushed and twisted by currents of hot, low-density gas. Although the cool clouds contain only 10 to 1000 atoms/cm³ (fewer than in any laboratory vacuum on Earth), astronomers refer to them as dense clouds, in contrast to the hot, low-density gas that fills the spaces between clouds. That thin gas contains only about 0.1 atom/cm³.

How do you know what the properties of the interstellar medium are? As you just learned, the ISM is in some cases easily visible as clouds of gas and dust, as in, for example, the Great Nebula in Orion. Astronomers call such a cloud a **nebula** from the Latin word for "cloud." Such nebulae (plural) give clear evidence of an interstellar medium. Study **Visualizing Astronomy 7.1, Three Kinds of Nebulae**, and notice three important points:

1. Very hot stars can excite clouds of gas and dust to emit light, and this reveals that these clouds contain mostly hydrogen gas at very low densities.

2. Where dusty clouds reflect the light of stars you see evidence that the dust in the clouds is made up of very small particles.

3. Some dense clouds of gas and dust are dark and therefore detectable only where they are silhouetted against background regions filled with stars or bright nebulae.

If a cloud is less dense the starlight may be able to penetrate it, and stars can be seen through the cloud; but the stars look dimmer because the dust in the cloud scatters some of the light. Because shorter wavelengths are scattered more easily than longer wavelengths, the redder photons are more likely to make it through the cloud, and the stars look redder than they should for their respective spectral types. This effect is called **interstellar reddening**, illustrated in Figure 7.10. The same

> **interstellar dust** Microscopic solid grains in the interstellar medium.
>
> **nebula** A relatively dense cloud of interstellar gas and dust.
>
> **interstellar reddening** The process in which dust scatters blue light out of starlight and makes the stars look redder.

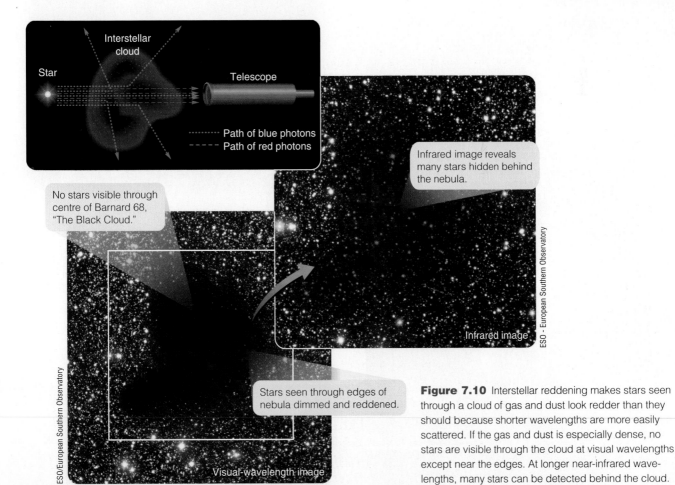

Figure 7.10 Interstellar reddening makes stars seen through a cloud of gas and dust look redder than they should because shorter wavelengths are more easily scattered. If the gas and dust is especially dense, no stars are visible through the cloud at visual wavelengths except near the edges. At longer near-infrared wavelengths, many stars can be detected behind the cloud.

1 Emission nebulae are produced when a hot star excites the gas near it to produce an emission spectrum. The star must be hotter than about B1 (25 000 K). Cooler stars do not emit enough ultraviolet radiation to ionize the gas. Emission nebulae have a distinctive pink colour produced by the blending of the red, blue, and violet Balmer lines. Emission nebulae are also called **HII regions**, following the custom of naming gas with a roman numeral to show its state of ionization. HI is neutral hydrogen, and HII is ionized.

In an HII region, the ionized nuclei and free electrons are mixed. When a nucleus captures an electron, the electron falls down through the atomic energy levels, emitting photons at specific wavelengths. Spectra indicate that the nebulae have compositions much like that of the Sun: mostly hydrogen. Emission nebulae have densities of 100 to 1000 atoms per cubic centimetre, better than the best vacuums produced in laboratories on Earth.

Visual-wavelength image

ESO/European Southern Observatory

2 A **reflection nebula** is produced when starlight scatters from a dusty nebula. Consequently, the spectrum of a reflection nebula is just the reflected absorption spectrum of starlight. Gas is surely present in a reflection nebula, but it is not excited to emit photons. See image below.

Reflection nebulae NGC 1973, 1975, and 1977 lie just north of the Orion Nebula. The pink tints are produced by ionized gases deep in the nebulae.

2a Reflection nebulae look blue for the same reason the sky looks blue. Short wavelengths scatter more easily than long wavelengths. See image below.

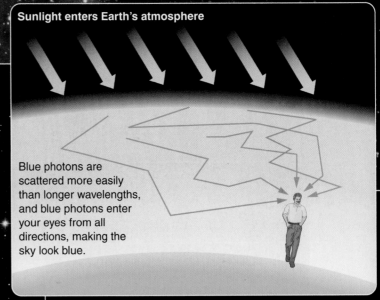

Sunlight enters Earth's atmosphere

Blue photons are scattered more easily than longer wavelengths, and blue photons enter your eyes from all directions, making the sky look blue.

Visual-wavelength image   Anglo-Australian Observatory/David Malin Images

2b The blue colour of reflection nebulae at left shows that the dust particles must be very small in order to preferentially scatter the blue photons. Interstellar dust grains must have diameters ranging from 0.01 mm down to 100 nm or so.

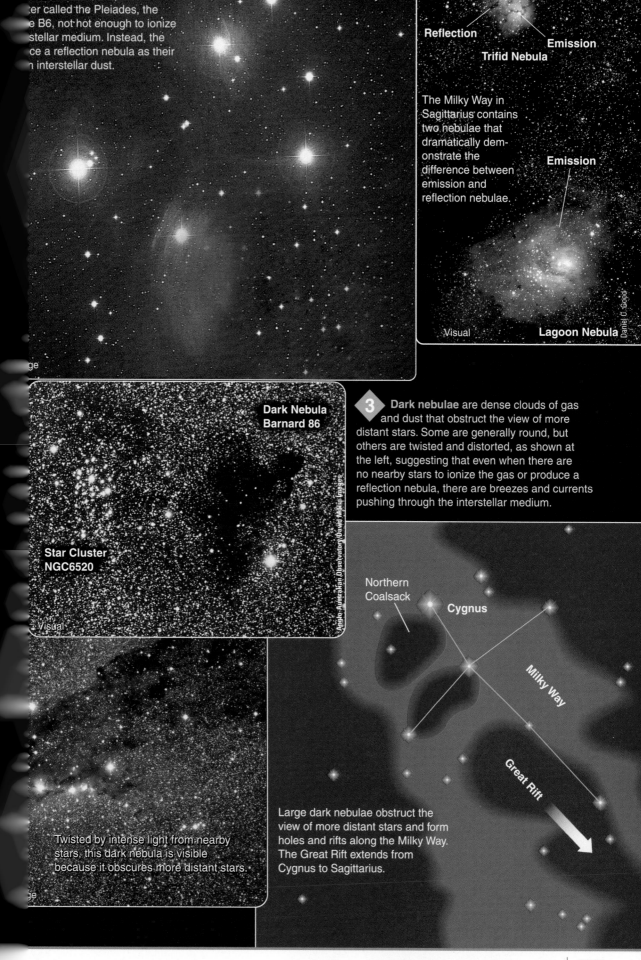

...ter called the Pleiades, the ... B6, not hot enough to ionize ...stellar medium. Instead, the ...ce a reflection nebula as their ... interstellar dust.

Reflection

Emission

Trifid Nebula

The Milky Way in Sagittarius contains two nebulae that dramatically demonstrate the difference between emission and reflection nebulae.

Emission

Visual

Lagoon Nebula

Daniel G. Good

Dark Nebula Barnard 86

Star Cluster NGC6520

Visual

Anglo-Australian Observatory/David Malin Images

3 **Dark nebulae** are dense clouds of gas and dust that obstruct the view of more distant stars. Some are generally round, but others are twisted and distorted, as shown at the left, suggesting that even when there are no nearby stars to ionize the gas or produce a reflection nebula, there are breezes and currents pushing through the interstellar medium.

Northern Coalsack

Cygnus

Milky Way

Great Rift

Twisted by intense light from nearby stars, this dark nebula is visible because it obscures more distant stars.

Large dark nebulae obstruct the view of more distant stars and form holes and rifts along the Milky Way. The Great Rift extends from Cygnus to Sagittarius.

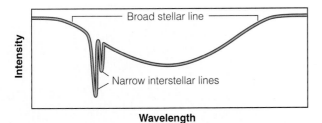

Figure 7.11 Interstellar absorption lines can be recognized easily because they are much nar-rower than spectral lines produced in stellar atmospheres. The multiple interstel-lar lines in this spectrum are produced by separate interstellar clouds with slightly different radial velocities and are seen superimposed on a broad stellar line.

physical process makes the setting Sun look red. The fact that distant stars are dimmed and reddened by intervening gas and dust is clear evidence of an interstellar medium.

Although you have been imagining the individual nebulae, the thin gas and dust of the interstellar medium also fills the spaces between the nebulae. You can see evidence of that because the gas forms interstellar absorp-tion lines in the spectra of distant stars, as shown in Figure 7.11. As starlight travels through the interstellar medium, gas atoms of elements such as calcium and sodium absorb photons of certain wavelengths, producing absorption lines. You can be sure those lines originate in the interstellar medium because they appear in the spectra of O and B stars: stars too hot to have visible calcium and sodium absorption lines in their own atmospheres. Also, the narrowness of the interstellar lines indicates they could not have been formed in the hot atmospheres of stars. The line widths indicate a very small range of

Doppler shifts, meaning the atoms are moving at speeds corresponding to temperatures of only 10 to 50 K.

Observations at nonvisible wavelengths provide valuable evidence about the interstellar medium. Infrared observations can directly detect dust in the interstellar medium. Although the dust grains are very small and very cold, there are huge numbers of grains in a cloud, and each grain emits infrared radiation at long wavelengths, as shown in Figure 7.12a. Furthermore, some molecules in the cold gas emit in the infrared, so infrared observa-tions can detect very cold clouds of gas. Also, infrared light penetrates ISM dust better than shorter-wavelength radiation, so astronomers can use infrared cameras to look into and through interstellar clouds that are opaque to visible light. X-ray observations can detect regions of very hot gas apparently produced by exploding stars, like those in the constellation Cygnus. Radio observations reveal the emissions of specific molecules in the inter-stellar medium—the equivalent of emission lines in vis-ible light. Such studies show that some of the atoms in space have linked together to form molecules.

There is no shortage of evidence concerning the interstellar medium. Clearly, space is not empty, and from the correlation between young stars and clouds of gas and dust, you can suspect that stars form from these clouds.

The Formation of Stars from the Interstellar Medium

To study the formation of stars, you can continue com-paring theory with evidence. The theory of gravity predicts

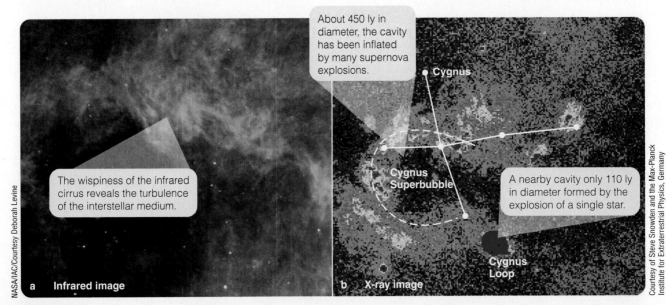

Figure 7.12 Infrared and X-ray observations reveal different parts of the interstellar medium. (a) This far-infrared image shows the infrared cirrus, wispy clouds of very cold dust and gas spread all across the sky. (b) The Cygnus Superbubble, detectable in X-rays, triggers star forma-tion where it pushes into the surrounding gas.

that the combined gravitational attraction of the atoms in a cloud of gas will shrink the cloud, pulling every atom toward the centre. That might lead you to expect that every cloud would eventually collapse and become a star; however, the thermal energy in the cloud resists collapse. Interstellar clouds are very cold; but, even at a temperature of only 10 K, the average hydrogen atom moves at about 0.33 km/s. That much thermal motion would make the cloud drift apart if gravity were too weak to hold it together.

Other factors can help a cloud resist its own gravity. Observations show that clouds are turbulent with currents of gas pushing through and colliding with each other. Also, magnetic fields in clouds may resist being squeezed. The thermal motion of the atoms, turbulence in a cloud, and magnetic fields resist gravity, and only the densest clouds are likely to contract.

The densest interstellar clouds contain from 10^3 to 10^5 atoms/cm^3 and have temperatures as low as 10 K. They include a few hundred thousand to a few million solar masses. In such dense clouds, hydrogen can exist as molecules (H_2) rather than as atoms. These densest parts of the ISM are called **molecular clouds**, and the largest are called giant molecular clouds. Although hydrogen molecules cannot be detected by radio telescopes, the clouds can be mapped by the emission lines of carbon monoxide molecules (CO) present in small amounts in the gas. By now you may have realized the main point: Stars can form inside molecular clouds when the densest parts of the clouds become unstable and contract under the influence of their own gravity.

Most clouds do not appear to be gravitationally unstable and do not contract to form stars on their own. However, a stable cloud colliding with a **shock wave** (the astronomical equivalent of a sonic boom) can be compressed and disrupted into fragments. Theoretical calculations show that some of these fragments can become dense enough to collapse under the influence of their own gravity and form stars (Figure 7.13).

Supernova explosions—exploding stars—produce shock waves that compress the interstellar medium, and recent observations show young stars forming at the edges of such shock waves. Another source of shock waves may be the birth of very hot stars. A massive star is so luminous and hot that it emits vast amounts of ultraviolet photons. When such a star is born, the sudden blast of light, especially ultraviolet radiation, can ionize and drive away nearby gas, forming a shock wave that could compress nearby clouds and trigger further star formation. Even the collision of two interstellar clouds can produce a shock wave and trigger star formation. Some of these processes are shown in Figure 7.14.

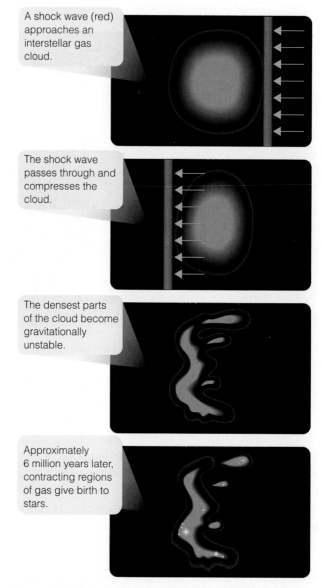

A shock wave (red) approaches an interstellar gas cloud.

The shock wave passes through and compresses the cloud.

The densest parts of the cloud become gravitationally unstable.

Approximately 6 million years later, contracting regions of gas give birth to stars.

Figure 7.13 Shock wave triggers star formation.

Although these are important sources of shock waves, the dominant trigger of star formation in our galaxy may be the spiral pattern itself. In Chapter 1 you learned that our galaxy contains spiral arms. As interstellar clouds encounter these spiral arms, the clouds become compressed, and star formation can be triggered (see Chapter 9).

Once begun, star formation can spread like a grass fire. Both high-mass and low-mass stars form together, but when the massive stars form, their intense radiation or eventual supernova explosions push back the surrounding gas and compress it. This compression

molecular cloud A dense interstellar gas cloud in which atoms are able to link together to form molecules such as H_2 and CO.

shock wave A sudden change in pressure that travels as an intense sound wave.

These massive stars were triggered into formation by compression from the formation of earlier stars out of the image to the left.

New stars are forming in these dense clouds because of compression from the stars to the left.

a Visual-wavelength image

NASA, and The Hubble Heritage Team AURA/STScI

Henize 206

Location of ancient supernova explosion

Arc of gas compressed by shock wave from supernova

Star formation triggered by compression

b Infrared image

NASA/JPL-CalTech/V. Gorjian and NOAO

Figure 7.14 (a) The blast of light and ultraviolet radiation from an earlier generation of massive stars has compressed neighbouring gas and triggered the formation of more stars. Those stars are now triggering the birth of a third generation. (b) The explosion of a supernova a few million years ago produced a shock wave that is triggering star formation where it slams into nearby clouds of gas and dust.

in turn can trigger the formation of more stars, some of which will be massive. Thus, a few massive stars can drive a continuing cycle of star formation in a giant molecular cloud.

A collapsing cloud of gas does not form a single star; because of instabilities, the cloud breaks into fragments, producing perhaps thousands of stars. A stable group of stars that formed and are held together by their combined gravity is called a **star cluster**. In contrast, a **stellar association** is a group of stars that formed together but are not gravitationally bound to one another. The stars in an association drift away from each other in a few million years. The youngest associations are rich in young stars, including O and B stars. O and B stars have lifetimes so short in astronomical terms (Table 7.2) that they must be located close to their birthplaces; so these stars serve as brilliant signposts pointing to regions of star formation.

star cluster A group of stars that formed together and orbit a common centre of mass.

stellar association A group of stars that formed together but are not gravitationally bound to one another.

protostar A collapsing cloud of gas and dust destined to become a star.

The Formation of Protostars

You might be wondering how the unimaginably cold gas of an interstellar cloud can heat up to form a star. The answer is gravity.

Once part of a cloud is triggered to collapse, gravity draws each atom toward the centre. At first the atoms fall unopposed; they hardly ever collide with each other. In this free-fall contraction, the atoms pick up speed as they fall until, by the time the gas becomes dense enough for the atoms to collide often, they are travelling very fast. Collisions convert the inward velocities of the atoms into random motions, and you remember that temperature is a measure of the random velocities of the atoms in a gas. Thus, the temperature of the gas goes up.

The initial collapse of the gas forms a dense core of gas, and as more gas falls in, a warm **protostar** develops, buried deep in the dusty gas cloud that continues to contract, although much more slowly than free-fall. A protostar is an object that will eventually become a star. Theory predicts that protostars are luminous red objects larger than main-sequence stars, with temperatures ranging from a few hundred to a few thousand degrees Kelvin.

Throughout its contraction, the protostar converts its gravitational potential energy into thermal energy. Half of this thermal energy radiates into space, but the remaining half raises the internal temperature. As the internal temperature climbs, the gas becomes ionized, changing into a mixture of positively charged atomic nuclei and free electrons. When the centre gets hot enough, nuclear reactions begin generating enough energy to replace the radiation leaving the surface of the star. The protostar then halts its contraction and becomes a stable, main-sequence star.

The time a protostar takes to contract from a cool interstellar gas cloud to a main-sequence star depends on its mass. The more massive the star, the stronger its gravity and the faster it contracts. The Sun took about 30 million years to reach the main sequence, but a 15-solar-mass star can contract in only 100 000 years. Conversely, a star of 0.2 solar mass takes 1 billion years to reach the main sequence.

Observations of Star Formation

By understanding what the interstellar medium is like and by understanding how the laws of physics work, astronomers have been able to work out the story of how stars must form. But you can't accept a scientific theory without testing it, and that means you must compare the theory with the evidence.

The protostar stage is predicted to be less than 0.1 percent of a star's total lifetime, so although that is a long time in human terms, you cannot expect to find many stars in the protostar stage. Furthermore, protostars form deep inside clouds of dusty gas that absorb any light the protostar might emit. Only when the protostar is hot enough to drive away its enveloping cloud of gas and dust does it become easy to observe at wavelengths your eye can see.

Although astronomers cannot easily observe protostars at visible wavelengths, protostars can be detected in the infrared. Protostars are cooler than stars and radiate as blackbodies predominantly at infrared wavelengths. The dust of the surrounding interstellar cloud absorbs light from the protostar and grows warm, and that warm dust radiates additional large amounts of infrared radiation. Infrared radiation also can penetrate the dust to reach us. Consequently, infrared observations reveal many bright sources of radiation that are protostars buried in interstellar clouds.

You can be sure that star formation is going on right now because astronomers find regions containing massive stars with lifetimes so short they must still be in their birthplaces. Small, very dense zones of gas and dust, called **Bok globules**, within larger nebulae probably represent the very first stages of star formation. Observations of jets coming from hidden protostars show that protostars are often surrounded by disks of gas and dust (see Figure 7.15). These jets appear to produce small flickering nebulae called **Herbig–Haro objects**. The same regions contain many stars with temperatures and luminosities that correspond to model predictions of the properties of very young stars. These include **T Tauri stars**, protostars with about the mass of the Sun, that show signs of active chromospheres—as you might expect from young rapidly rotating stars with strong magnetic dynamos (see Chapter 5). T Tauri stars are also often surrounded by thick disks of gas and dust that are very bright at infrared wavelengths.

These observations all confirm the theoretical models of contracting protostars. Although star formation still holds many puzzles, the general process seems clear. In at least some cases, interstellar

Bok globule Small, dark cloud only about 1 ly in diameter that contains 10 to 1000 solar masses of gas and dust, thought to be related to star formation.

Herbig–Haro object A small nebula that varies irregularly in brightness, evidently associated with star formation.

T Tauri star A young star surrounded by gas and dust, understood to be contracting toward the main sequence.

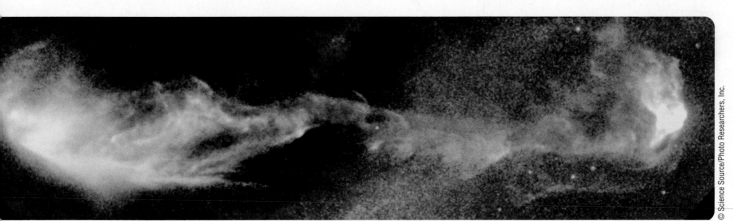

© Science Source/Photo Researchers, Inc.

Figure 7.15 Visible light image of the Herbig–Haro object HH 47, a jet of gas about half a light-year long. The wavy nature of the jet suggests that it is perturbed by a second body, perhaps a binary companion to the new star.

CHAPTER 7 The Structure and Formation of Stars |

The visible Orion Nebula shown below is a pocket of ionized gas on the near side of a vast, dusty molecular cloud that fills much of the southern part of the constellation Orion. The molecular cloud can be mapped by radio telescopes. To scale, the cloud would be many times larger than this page. As the stars of the Trapezium were born in the cloud, their radiation has ionized the gas and pushed it away. Where the expanding nebula pushes into the larger molecular cloud, it is compressing the gas (see diagram at right) and may be triggering the formation of the protostars that can be detected at infrared wavelengths within the molecular cloud.

Hundreds of stars lie within the nebula, but only the four brightest, those in the Trapezium, are easy to see with a small telescope. A fifth star, at the narrow end of the Trapezium, may be visible on nights of good seeing.

The cluster of stars in the nebula is less than 2 million years old. This must mean the nebula is similarly young.

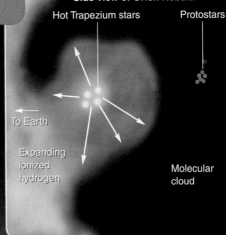

Side view of Orion Nebula

Hot Trapezium stars

Protostars

To Earth

Expanding ionized hydrogen

Molecular cloud

Trapezium

Visual-wavelength image

Credit: NASA, ESA, M. Robberto, STScI and the Hubble Space Telescope Orion Treasury Project Team

Infrared

The near-infrared image above reveals more than 50 low-mass, cool protostars.

Visual

Small dark clouds called **Bok globules**, named after astronomer Bart Bok, are found in and near star-forming regions. The one pictured above is part of nebula NGC 1999 near the Orion Nebula. Typically about 1 light-year in diameter, they contain from 10 to 1000 solar masses.

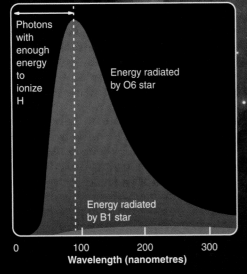

Photons with enough energy to ionize H

Energy radiated by O6 star

Energy radiated by B1 star

| 0 | 100 | 200 | 300 |

Wavelength (nanometres)

2 Of all the stars in the Orion Nebula, only one is hot enough to ionize the gas. Only photons with wavelengths shorter than 91.2 nm can ionize hydrogen. The second-hottest stars in the nebula are B1 stars, and they emit little of this ionizing radiation. The hottest star, however, is an O6 star 30 times the mass of the Sun. At a temperature of 40 000 K, it emits plenty of photons with wavelengths short enough to ionize hydrogen. Remove that one star, and the nebula would turn off its emission.

3 Below, a far-infrared image has been combined with an ultraviolet and visible image to reveal extensive nebulosity surrounding the visible Orion Nebula. Red and orange show the location of cold, carbon-rich gas molecules. Green areas outline hot, ionized gas around young stars. The infrared image reveals protostars buried in the gas cloud behind the visible nebula.

In this near-infrared image, known among some astronomers as the "Hand of God" image, fingers of gas rush away from the region of the infrared protostars.

Anglo-Australian Observatory / David Malin Images

NASA

Infrared

Dan Gezari, Dana Backman, and Mike Werner / NASA

Infrared image

BN

KL

The Becklin-Neugebauer object (BN) is a hot B star just reaching the main sequence. It is not detectable at visual wavelengths. The Kleinmann-Low Nebula (KL) is a cluster of cool young protostars also detectable only in the infrared.

NASA

The spectral types of the Trapezium stars are shown here. The gas looks green because of filters used to record the image.

Trapezium cluster

B3

B1

B1

O6

Visual-wavelength image

500 AU

Visual

4 As many as 85 percent of the stars in the Orion Nebula are surrounded by disks of gas and dust. One such disk is seen at the upper right of this Hubble Space Telescope image, magnified in inset. Radiation from the nearby hot Trapezium stars is evaporating gas from the disk and driving it away to form an elongated nebula.

Ultraviolet + visual + infrared image

NASA/JPL-Caltech/T. Megeath

NASA / JPL / Caltech

gas clouds are compressed by passing shock waves, and the clouds' gravity, acting unopposed, draws the matter inward to form protostars. Now you know how to make a star: Just find some way to compress more than 0.08 solar masses of interstellar material into a small enough region of space, and gravity will do the rest of the job.

The Orion Nebula

On a clear winter night, you can see with your unaided eye the Great Nebula of Orion as a fuzzy wisp in Orion's sword. With binoculars or a small telescope what you see is striking, and through a large telescope it is breathtaking. At the centre lie four brilliant blue-white stars known as the Trapezium, the brightest of a cluster of a few hundred stars. Surrounding the stars are the glowing filaments of a nebula more than 25 ly across. Like a great thundercloud illuminated from within, the churning currents of gas and dust suggest immense power. The significance of the Orion Nebula lies hidden, figuratively and literally, beyond the visible nebula. The region is ripe with star formation.

Evidence of Young Stars

You should not be surprised to find star formation in Orion. The constellation is a brilliant landmark in the winter sky because it is marked by hot blue stars. These stars are bright not because they are nearby but because they are tremendously luminous. These O and B stars cannot live more than a few million years, so you can conclude that they must have been born astronomically recently, near where they are seen now. Furthermore, the constellation contains large numbers of T Tauri stars, which are known to be young. Orion is rich with young stars.

The history of star formation in the constellation of Orion is written in its stars. The stars at Orion's west shoulder are about 12 million years old, whereas the stars of Orion's belt are about 8 million years old. The stars of the Trapezium at the centre of the Great Nebula are no older than 2 million years. Apparently, star formation began near the west shoulder, and the massive stars that formed there triggered the formation of the stars you see in Orion's belt. That star formation may have triggered the formation of the stars you see in the Great Nebula. Like a grass fire, star formation has swept across Orion from northwest to southeast.

Study **Visualizing Astronomy 7.2, Star Formation in the Orion Nebula**, and notice four points:

1. The nebula you see is only a small part of a vast, dusty molecular cloud. You see the nebula because the larger stars born within it have ionized the nearby gas and driven it outward, breaking out of the much larger molecular cloud.

2. A single very hot and short-lived O star is almost entirely responsible for ionizing the gas and making the nebula glow. This massive star has already become a main-sequence star, while its smaller siblings are still protostars.

3. Infrared observations reveal ongoing star formation deep in the molecular cloud behind the visible nebula.

4. Finally, notice that many stars visible in the Orion Nebula are surrounded by disks of gas and dust. Such disks do not last long and are clear evidence that the stars are very young.

Observations of stars in the Orion nebula show that some of the gas and dust in the cloud from which a star forms settles into a disk. Make special note of these disks, because planets may form in them. In Chapter 12 you will study how our solar system formed in the disk of gas and dust that encircled the young Sun.

The Big Picture

In the middle of winter, when light from the full Moon splashes across the blanket of snow outside your bedroom window, we are reminded that nature is a contrast between cold, crisp winter nights here on Earth and the furious, fiery plasma core of the stars that appear so innocently perched high in the sky. In this chapter you learned how stars form in the very cold interstellar medium where gravity, the weakest force, works unrelentingly, gathering molecular hydrogen in tight, dense balls with sufficiently high temperatures to make stars.

Our own star, the Sun, uses the proton–proton chain, the simplest of the fusion processes, to convert mass into the radiation energy on which life on Earth is so dependent. Our knowledge of stellar formation, structure, and function comes from a combination of mathematical models and interpretations of observations. But we didn't always understand the stars this way.

An ancient Aztec myth tells the story of the origin of the Moon and stars. The stars, known as the Four Hundred Southerners, and the Moon, the goddess Coyolxauhqui, plotted to murder their unborn brother, the great war god Huitzilopochtli. Hearing their plotting, he leapt from the womb fully armed, hacked Coyolxauhqui into pieces, and chased the stars away. You can see the Four Hundred Southerners scattered across the sky, and each month you can see the Moon chopped into pieces as it passes through its phases.

Stories like this helped make our universe and its origins more understandable to our ancestors. Science is a natural extension of our need to explain the world, and scientific theories have become more and more sophisticated as they have been repeatedly tested against reality. Present-day astronomers build theories for the same reason people used to tell myths. You can begin to appreciate how clever human beings are to have figured out so much about our galaxy, and indeed the universe, from the vantage point of this remote speck of rock we call home.

Review and Discussion Questions

Review Questions

1. Describe the principle of hydrostatic equilibrium as it relates to the internal structure of a star.
2. How does the CNO cycle differ from the proton–proton chain? How is it similar?
3. How does the pressure–temperature thermostat control the nuclear reactions inside stars?
4. Step-by-step, explain how energy flows from the centre of the Sun out into space.
5. Why is there a mass–luminosity relation?
6. Why is there a lower limit to the mass of a main-sequence star?
7. Why does a star's life expectancy depend on its mass?
8. Why do distant stars look redder than their spectral types suggest?
9. What evidence can you cite that the interstellar medium contains both gas and dust?
10. How is the blue colour of a reflection nebula related to the blue colour of the daytime sky?
11. Why are interstellar lines so narrow?
12. What factors resist the contraction of a cloud of interstellar matter?
13. How can a molecular cloud be triggered to form stars?
14. How does the contraction of a gas cloud increase its temperature?
15. What evidence is there that (a) star formation has occurred recently? (b) protostars really exist? (c) the Orion region is actively forming stars?
16. **How Do We Know?** How can mathematical models help you understand natural processes that occur in locations or with time scales that make them impossible to observe directly?

Discussion Questions

1. How does hydrostatic equilibrium relate to hot-air ballooning?
2. When you see distant streetlights through smog, they look dimmer and redder than they do normally. But when you see the same streetlights through fog or falling snow, they look dimmer, but not redder. Use your knowledge of the interstellar medium to discuss the relative sizes of the particles in smog, fog, and snowstorms compared to the wavelength of light.
3. If you could see a few stars through a dark nebula, how would you expect their spectra and colours to differ from similar stars just in front of the dark nebula?
4. Ancient astronomers, philosophers, and poets assumed that the stars were eternal and unchanging. Is there any observation they could have made or any line of reasoning that could have led them to conclude that stars don't live forever?

8

PART TWO

The Deaths of Stars

CHAPTER OUTLINE

GUIDEPOST

You are beginning to understand stars. The preceding chapter described how stars are born from clouds of gas and dust in the interstellar medium and how nuclear fusion maintains high temperatures and pressures inside stars, which keeps them from collapsing under the influence of their own gravity. Stars are the lighting system of the universe, but they can last only as long as their fuel supplies.

In this chapter you will learn what happens when a star runs out of fuel, what kind of "corpse" is left after its death, and how both of these conditions depend on its mass. You also will learn the surprising fact that star deaths are actually important to life on Earth because massive stars create the atomic elements of which you and everything on Earth are made. If stars didn't die, you would not exist.

Some of the matter that was once in stars becomes trapped in different types of remnants known as white dwarfs, neutron stars, and black holes. Other matter from dying stars escapes back into the interstellar medium and is incorporated into new stars and planets. The deaths of stars are part of a great cycle of stellar birth and death that includes the Sun, Earth, and you, and by understanding the deaths of stars, you can better understand your role in the evolution of the universe.

NASA/ESA/HEIC/Hubble Heritage Team

The black holes of nature are the most perfect macroscopic objects there are in the universe: the only elements in their construction are our concepts of space and time.

Subrahmanyan Chandrasekhar,
Astrophysicist and Nobel Laureate

We are made out of stardust. The iron in the hemoglobin molecules in the blood in your right hand came from a star that blew up 8 billion years ago. The iron in your left hand came from another star.

Jill Tarter,
Astronomer

Matter ejected repeatedly from the dying star at its centre has formed the nebula known as the Cat's Eye. Most of the atoms in our bodies were created by dying stars.

As you consider the fates of the stars, you will find answers to five important questions:

- **What happens to a star when it uses up the last of the hydrogen in its core?**
- **What is the evidence that stars really evolve?**
- **What happens if an evolving star is in a binary star system?**
- **How does theory predict the existence of neutron stars and black holes?**
- **What is the evidence that neutron stars and black holes really exist?**

This chapter ends the story of individual stars, but it does not end the story of stars. In the next chapter, you will begin exploring the giant communities in which stars live: the galaxies.

Gravity is patient—so patient it can kill stars. Astronomers occasionally see what seems to be a new star in the sky that grows brighter and then fades away after a few weeks or a year. You will discover that a **nova**, an apparently new star in the sky, is produced by an eruption around a stellar remnant, and that a **supernova**, a particularly luminous and long-lasting nova, is caused by the violent explosive death of a massive star. Modern astronomers find a few novae (plural of *nova*) each year, but supernovae (plural) are so rare that only one or two happen each century in our galaxy. In the previous chapter, you saw that stars resist their own gravity by generating energy through nuclear fusion. The energy keeps their interiors hot, and the resulting high pressure balances gravity and prevents the star from collapsing. Stars, however, have limited fuel. When they exhaust their fuel, gravity wins, and the stars die.

The mass of a star is critical in determining its fate. Massive stars use up their nuclear fuel at a furious rate and die after only a few million years. In contrast, the lowest-mass stars use their fuel sparingly and may be able to live hundreds of billions of years (see Table 7.2). Stars with different masses lead dramatically different lives and die in different ways.

nova From the Latin, meaning "new," a sudden and temporary brightening of a star, making it appear as a new star in the sky; evidently caused by an explosion of nuclear fuel on the surface of a white dwarf.

supernova A "new star" in the sky that is roughly 4000 times more luminous than a normal nova and longer lasting; evidently the result of an explosion of a star.

giant star Large, cool, highly luminous star in the upper right of the H–R diagram, typically 10 to 100 times the diameter of the Sun.

supergiant star Exceptionally luminous star whose diameter is 100 to 1000 times that of the Sun.

8.1 Giant Stars

A main-sequence star generates its energy by nuclear fusion reactions that combine hydrogen to make helium. A star remains on the main sequence for a time span equal to 90 percent of its total existence as an energy-generating star. When the hydrogen is exhausted, however, the star begins to evolve rapidly. It swells into a giant star and then begins to fuse helium into heavier elements. A star can remain in this giant stage for only about 10 percent of its total lifetime; then it must die. The giant-star stage is the first step in the death of a star.

Expansion into a Giant

The nuclear reactions in a main-sequence star's core produce helium. Helium can fuse into heavier elements only at temperatures higher than 100 000 000 K, and no main-sequence star has a core that hot, so helium accumulates at the star's centre like ashes in a fireplace. Initially, this helium ash has little effect on the star, but as hydrogen is exhausted and the stellar core becomes almost pure helium, the star's ability to generate nuclear energy is reduced. Because the energy generated at the centre is what opposes gravity and supports the star, the core begins to contract as soon as the energy generation starts to decline.

Although the core of helium ash cannot generate nuclear energy, it can grow hotter because it contracts and converts gravitational energy into thermal energy. The rising temperature heats the unprocessed hydrogen just outside the core—hydrogen that was never previously hot enough to fuse. When the temperature of the surrounding hydrogen becomes high enough, hydrogen fusion begins in a spherical layer, called a shell, surrounding the exhausted core of the star. Like a grass fire burning outward from an exhausted campfire, the hydrogen-fusion shell creeps outward, leaving helium ash behind and increasing the mass of the helium core.

Figure 8.1 illustrates how the flood of energy produced by the hydrogen-fusion shell pushes toward the surface, heating the outer layers of the star and forcing them to expand dramatically. Stars like the Sun become **giant stars** 10 to 100 times the present diameter of the Sun, and the most massive stars become **supergiant stars**, as much as 1000 times larger than the Sun.

The expansion of a star to giant or supergiant size cools the star's outer layers, and so the stars move toward the upper right in the H–R diagram. Look back at Figure 6.8 and notice that some of the most familiar stars, such as Aldebaran, Betelgeuse, and Polaris, are giants or supergiants.

Although the energy output of the hydrogen-fusion shell can force the envelope of the star to expand, it cannot

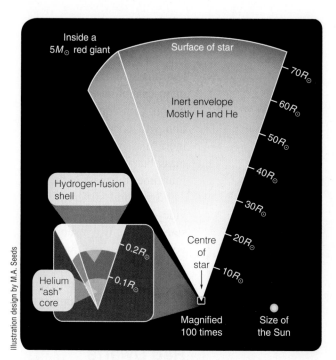

Figure 8.1 When a star runs out of hydrogen at its centre, the core contracts to a small size, becomes very hot, and begins nuclear fusion in a shell (blue). The outer layers of the star expand and cool. The red giant star shown here has an average density much lower than the air at Earth's surface. Here $M_\odot$ stands for the mass of the Sun, and $R_\odot$ stands for the radius of the Sun.

stop the contraction of the helium core. Because the core is not hot enough to fuse helium, gravity squeezes it to a relatively tiny size. If you represented a typical giant star as the size of a baseball stadium, its helium core would be only about the size of a baseball, yet it would contain about 10 percent of the star's mass.

Helium Fusion

As a star becomes a giant, fusing hydrogen in a shell, the inert core of helium ash contracts and grows hotter. When the core finally reaches a temperature of 100 000 000 K, helium nuclei can begin fusing to make carbon nuclei.

The ignition of helium in the core changes the structure of the star. The star now makes energy in two locations by two different processes, helium fusion in the core and hydrogen fusion in the surrounding shell. The energy flowing outward from the core halts the contraction of the core, and at the same time the star's envelope contracts and grows hotter. Consequently, the point that represents the star in the H–R diagram moves downward—corresponding to lower luminosities—and to the left—corresponding to higher surface temperatures—to a region above the main sequence called the **horizontal branch**. (See Figure 8.2 and **Visualizing Astronomy 8.1, Star Cluster**

H–R Diagrams.) Astronomers sometimes refer to stars with those characteristics as "yellow giants."

Helium fusion produces carbon and oxygen that accumulate in an inert core. Once again, the core contracts and heats up, and a helium-fusion shell ignites below the hydrogen-fusion shell. The star now makes energy in two fusion shells, so it quickly expands, and its surface cools once again. The point that represents the star in the H–R diagram moves back to the right, completing a loop to become a red giant again. The approximate rule is that if the core of a post–main-sequence star is "dead" (has no nuclear reactions), the star is a red giant, and if the core is "alive" (has fusion reactions), the star is a yellow giant.

Now you can understand why giant stars are relatively rare (see **Visualizing Astronomy 6.1, The Family of Stars**). A star spends about 90 percent of its lifetime on the main sequence and only 10 percent as a giant star. At any moment you look, only a fraction of the visible stars will be passing through the red and yellow giant stages.

What happens to a star after helium fusion depends on its mass, but in any event it cannot survive long. It must eventually collapse and end its career as a star. The remainder of this chapter will trace the details of this process of stellar death, but before you begin that story, you must ask the most important question in science: What is the evidence? What evidence shows that stars actually evolve as theory predicts? You can find the answers in observations of star clusters.

> **horizontal branch** The location in the H–R diagram of giant stars that are fusing helium.

Star Clusters: Evidence of Evolution

Astronomers look at star clusters and say, "Aha! Evidence to solve a mystery." The stars in a star cluster all formed at about the same time and from the same cloud of gas, so they must be about the same age and composition. Each star cluster freeze-frames and makes visible a moment in stellar evolution. The differences you see among stars in one cluster must arise from differences in their masses.

Study **Visualizing Astronomy 8.1, Star Cluster H–R Diagrams**, and notice three important points:

1. There are two kinds of star clusters, but they are similar in the way their stars evolve. You will learn more about these clusters in the next chapter.

2. You can estimate the age of a star cluster by observing the distribution of the points that represent its stars in the H–R diagram.

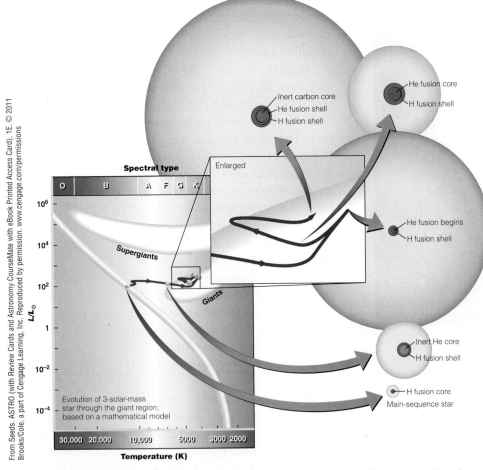

Figure 8.2 When a main-sequence star exhausts the hydrogen in its core, it evolves rapidly to the right in the H–R diagram as it expands to become a cool giant. It then follows a looping path (enlarged) as it fuses helium in its core and then fuses helium in a shell.

get very hot. This limits the nuclear fuels they can ignite. In Chapter 7 you saw that objects less massive than 0.08 solar mass cannot sustain hydrogen fusion. Consequently, this section will concentrate on stars more massive than 0.08 solar mass but no more than about four times the mass of the Sun.

Structural differences divide the lower-main-sequence stars into two subgroups: very-low-mass red dwarfs and medium-mass stars such as the Sun. The critical difference between the two groups is the extent of interior convection.

Red Dwarfs

Stars less massive than about 0.4 solar mass—the red dwarfs—differ from the more massive stars in two important ways. First, because they have very small masses, they have very little weight to support. Their pressure–temperature thermostats are set low, and they consume their hydrogen fuel very slowly. The discussion of the life expectancies of stars in Chapter 7 implies that red dwarfs have very long lives.

The red dwarfs have a second advantage because they are completely convective. That means they are stirred by circulating currents of hot gas rising from the interior and cool gas sinking inward, extending all the way from their cores to their surfaces. The interiors of these stars are mixed like a pot of soup that is constantly stirred as it cooks. Hydrogen is consumed and helium accumulates uniformly throughout the star, which means the star is not limited to using only the fuel in its core. It can use all of its hydrogen to prolong its life on the main sequence.

Because a red dwarf is mixed by convection, it won't develop an inert helium core surrounded by unprocessed hydrogen. Therefore, it never ignites a hydrogen shell and cannot become a giant star. Rather, nuclear fusion continues to convert hydrogen into helium, but the helium does not fuse into heavier elements because the star can never get hot enough. What astronomers know about stellar evolution indicates that these red dwarfs should use

3. Finally, a star cluster's H–R diagram shape is governed by the evolutionary path the stars take. By comparing clusters of different ages, you can visualize how stars evolve almost as if you were watching a film of a star cluster changing over billions of years.

Were it not for star clusters, astronomers would have little confidence in the theories of stellar evolution. Star clusters make that evolution visible and assure astronomers that they really do understand how stars are born, live, and die.

8.2 The Deaths of Low-Mass Stars

Contracting stars heat up by converting gravitational energy into thermal energy. Low-mass stars have little gravitational energy, so when they contract, they can't

up nearly all of their hydrogen and live very long lives on the lower main sequence. They could survive for a hundred billion years or more. Of course, astronomers can't test this part of their theories because the universe is only 13.8 billion years old (see Chapter 11), so not a single red dwarf has died of old age anywhere in the universe. Every red dwarf that has ever been born is still glowing today.

Medium-Mass Sunlike Stars

Stars like the Sun can ignite hydrogen and helium and become giants; however, if they contain fewer than 4 solar masses they cannot get hot enough to ignite carbon, the next fuel after helium. Note that this mass limit is uncertain, as are many of the masses quoted here. The evolution of stars is highly complex, and such parameters are difficult to specify.

There are two keys to the evolution of these Sunlike stars: the lack of complete mixing, and mass loss. The interiors of medium-mass stars are not completely mixed because, unlike the red dwarf stars, they are not completely convective. The helium ash accumulates in an inert helium core surrounded by unprocessed hydrogen. As described earlier, when this core contracts, the unprocessed hydrogen ignites in a shell and swells the star into a red giant. During red giant stages, stars tend to lose mass due to strong stellar winds. When the helium core finally ignites, the star becomes a yellow giant. The end of fusion for stars in the medium-mass range occurs when the core fills up with carbon–oxygen ash. This happens because they have masses too low to make their cores hot enough to ignite carbon fusion or oxygen fusion. The carbon–oxygen core is the dead end for these stars.

All of this discussion is based on theoretical models of stars and a general understanding of how stars evolve. Does it really happen? Astronomers need observational evidence to confirm this theoretical discussion, and the gas that is expelled from these giant stars gives visible evidence that Sunlike stars have gone through these stages of element-building and do indeed die in this way.

Planetary Nebulae

When a medium-mass star like the Sun becomes a distended giant, its atmosphere becomes cool and consequently more opaque. Light has to push against it to escape. At the same time, the fusion shells become thin and unstable, and they begin to flare, which pushes the atmosphere outward. An aging giant can expel its outer

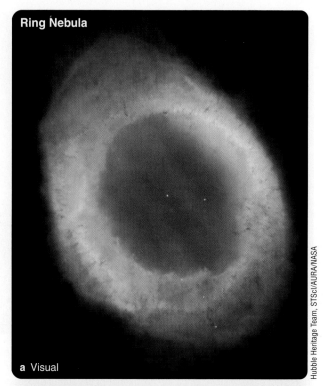

a Visual

Ring Nebula

Hubble Heritage Team, STScI/AURA/NASA

b Visual

M2-9

NASA

Figure 8.3 (a) The Ring Nebula in the constellation Lyra is visible even in small telescopes. Note the hot blue star at its centre and the radial texture in the gas that suggests outward motion. (b) Some planetary nebulae such as M2-9 are highly elongated, and it has been suggested that the Ring Nebula in (a) actually has a tubular shape, like M2-9, that happens to be pointed approximately toward Earth.

atmosphere in repeated surges to form one of the most beautiful objects in astronomy, a **planetary nebula**, so called because the first ones discovered looked like the greenish-blue disks of planets such as Uranus or Neptune. In fact, a planetary nebula has nothing to do with a planet. It is composed of ionized gases expelled by a dying star, like the nebulae shown in Figure 8.3.

You can understand what planetary nebulae are like by using simple observations and theoretical methods explained in Chapter 5, such as Kirchhoff's laws and the

planetary nebula An expanding shell of gas ejected from a medium-mass star during the latter stages of its evolution.

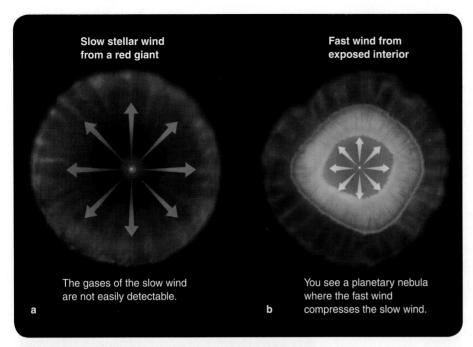

Slow stellar wind from a red giant

Fast wind from exposed interior

The gases of the slow wind are not easily detectable.

You see a planetary nebula where the fast wind compresses the slow wind.

a

b

Figure 8.4 The process that produces planetary nebulae involves two stellar winds. First, as an aging giant, the star gradually blows away its outer layers in a slow breeze of low-excitation gas that is not easily visible. Once the hot interior of the star is exposed, it ejects a high-speed wind that overtakes and compresses the gas of the slow wind—like a snowplow. The ultraviolet radiation from the hot remains of the central star excites the gases to glow like a giant neon sign.

Doppler effect. Although real nebulae are quite complex, the simple model shown in Figure 8.4 of a slow stellar wind followed by a fast wind explains their structures fairly well and provides a way to organize the observed phenomena. The complexities and asymmetries seen in planetary nebulae may be due to repeated expulsions of expanding shells and oppositely directed jets, much like the bipolar flows observed coming from protostars. Observations and stellar evolution models indicate the central star of a planetary nebula finally must contract and become a white dwarf.

White Dwarfs

As you have just learned, medium-mass stars die by ejecting gas into space and contracting into white dwarfs.

In Chapter 6 you surveyed the stars and learned that white dwarfs are the second most common kind of star (see **Visualizing Astronomy 6.1, The Family of Stars**). Only red dwarfs are more abundant. The billions of white dwarfs in our galaxy must be the remains of medium-mass stars.

degenerate matter Extremely high-density matter in which pressure no longer depends on temperature due to quantum mechanical effects.

compact object One of the three final states of stellar evolution, which generates no nuclear energy and is much smaller and denser than a normal star.

The first white dwarf discovered was the faint companion to the well-known star Sirius, the brightest star in the sky. Sirius is a visual binary star, the most luminous member of which is Sirius A. The white dwarf, Sirius B, is 10 000 times fainter than Sirius A. The orbital motions of the stars (Figure 6.12) reveal that the white dwarf's mass is 0.98 solar mass, and its blue-white colour tells you that its surface is hot, about 25 000 K. Although it is very hot, it has a very low luminosity, so it must have a small surface area. In fact, it is about the size of Earth. Dividing its mass by its volume reveals that it is very dense, about 2 million grams per cubic centimetre. On Earth, a teaspoonful of Sirius B material would weigh more than 11 tons. These basic observations and simple physics lead to the conclusion that white dwarfs are astonishingly dense.

A normal star is supported by energy flowing outward from its core, but a white dwarf cannot generate energy by nuclear fusion. It has exhausted its hydrogen and helium fuel and produced carbon and oxygen. As the star contracts into a white dwarf, it converts gravitational energy into thermal energy, and its interior becomes very hot, but it cannot get hot enough to fuse carbon into heavier elements.

The contraction of a white dwarf compresses the gases in its interior to such high densities that quantum mechanical laws become important and the electrons in the gas cannot get closer together. Such a gas is termed **degenerate matter**, and it takes on two properties that are important in understanding the structure and evolution of dying stars. A degenerate gas is millions of times harder to compress than solid steel, and the pressure in the gas no longer depends on the temperature. Unlike a normal star, which is supported by ordinary gas pressure, a white dwarf is supported against its own gravity by the resistance to compression of a degenerate gas.

Clearly, a white dwarf is not a true star. It generates no nuclear energy, is almost completely degenerate matter, and, except for a thin layer at its surface, contains no gas. Instead of calling a white dwarf a "star," you could call it a **compact object**. Later sections of this chapter discuss two other types of compact objects: neutron stars and black holes.

A white dwarf's future is bleak. As it radiates energy into space, its temperature gradually falls, but it cannot shrink any smaller because its degenerate electrons cannot get closer together. This degenerate matter is a very good thermal conductor, so heat flows to the surface and escapes into space, and the white dwarf gets fainter and cooler, moving downward and to the right in the H–R diagram. Because the white dwarf contains a tremendous amount of heat, it needs billions of years to radiate that heat through its small surface area. The coolest white dwarfs in our galaxy are about the temperature of the Sun.

Perhaps the most interesting thing astronomers have learned about white dwarfs has come from mathematical models. The equations predict that degenerate electron pressure cannot support an object with more than about 1.4 solar masses. A white dwarf with that mass would have such strong gravity that its radius would shrink to zero. This is called the **Chandrasekhar–Landau limit**, after the Indian astrophysicist Subrahmanyan Chandrasekhar and the Russian physicist Lev Davidovich Landau, who independently from each other calculated it. This seems to imply that a star more massive than 1.4 solar masses could not become a white dwarf unless it got rid of the extra mass in some way.

Can stars lose substantial amounts of mass? Observations provide clear evidence that young stars have strong stellar winds, and aging giants and supergiants also lose mass. This suggests that stars more massive than the Chandrasekhar–Landau limit can eventually end up as white dwarfs if they reduce their mass under the limit. Theoretical models show that stars that begin life with as many as 8 solar masses could lose mass fast enough to reduce their mass so low they can collapse to form white dwarfs with masses below 1.4 solar masses. With mass loss, a wide range of medium-mass stars can eventually die as white dwarfs.

The Fate of the Sun and the End of Earth

Astronomy is about you. Although this chapter has been discussing the deaths of medium-mass stars, it has also been discussing the future of Earth. The Sun is a medium-mass star and must eventually die by becoming a giant, possibly producing a planetary nebula, and collapsing into a white dwarf. That will spell the end of Earth.

Evolutionary models of the Sun suggest that it may survive for another 6 billion years or so. In about 5 billion years, it will exhaust the hydrogen in its core, begin burning hydrogen in a shell, and swell into a red giant star about 30 times its present radius. Later, helium fusion will

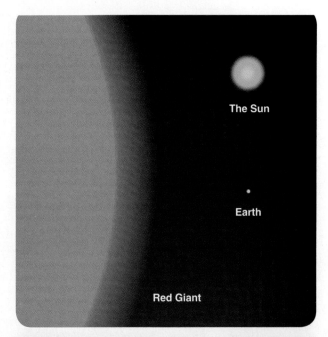

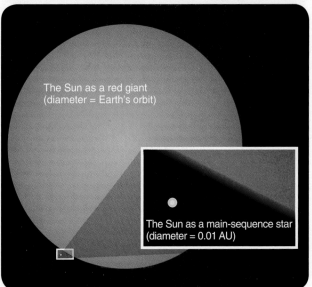

Figure 8.5 Relative sizes of the Sun now, the Sun as a red giant, and Earth as a reference for the Sun as an Earth-sized white dwarf at the end of its life.

ignite in the core, and the Sun will become a horizontal branch star. Once the helium fuel is exhausted in its core, helium fusion will begin in a shell, and the Sun will expand again. That second red giant version of the Sun will be about as large as the orbit of Earth (see Figure 8.5). Before that, the Sun's increasing luminosity will certainly evaporate Earth's oceans, drive away the atmosphere, and even vaporize much of Earth's crust.

Chandrasekhar–Landau limit The maximum mass of a white dwarf, about 1.4 solar masses. A white dwarf of greater mass cannot support itself and will collapse.

1 An **open cluster** is a collection of 10 to 1000 stars in a region about 80 ly in diameter. Some open clusters are quite small and some are large, but they all have an open, transparent appearance because the stars are not crowded together.

In a star cluster, each star follows its orbit around the centre of mass of the cluster.

Visual-wavelength image
AURA/NOAO/NSF

Open Cluster
The Jewel Box

1a A **globular cluster** can contain 10^5 to 10^6 stars in a region only 30 ly to 100 ly in diameter. The term *globular cluster* comes from the word *globe*, although globular cluster is pronounced like "glob of butter." These clusters are nearly spherical, and the stars are much closer together than the stars in an open cluster.

Astronomers can construct an H–R diagram for a star cluster by plotting a point to represent the luminosity and temperature of each star.

Globular Cluster
47 Tucanae

Anglo-Australian Observatory/David Malin Images

Visual-wavelength image

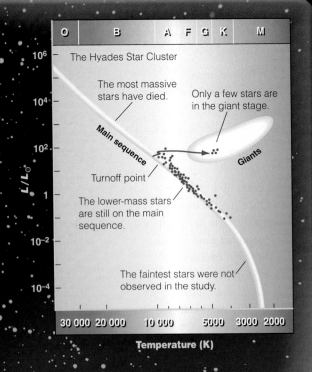

The Hyades Star Cluster

The most massive stars have died.

Only a few stars are in the giant stage.

Main sequence

Giants

Turnoff point

The lower-mass stars are still on the main sequence.

The faintest stars were not observed in the study.

$L/L_\odot$

Temperature (K)

2 The H–R diagram of a star cluster can make the evolution of stars visible. The key is to remember that all of the stars in the star cluster have the same age but differ in mass. The H–R diagram of a star cluster provides a snapshot of the evolutionary state of the stars at the time you happen to be alive. The diagram here shows the 650-million-year-old star cluster called the Hyades. The upper main sequence is missing because the more massive stars have died, and our snapshot catches a few medium-mass stars leaving the main sequence to become giants.

As a star cluster ages, its main sequence grows shorter like a candle burning down. You can judge the age of a star cluster by looking at the turnoff point, the point on the main sequence where stars evolve to the right to become giants. Stars at the **turnoff point** have lived out their lives and are about to die. Consequently, the life expectancy of the stars at the turnoff point equals the age of the cluster.

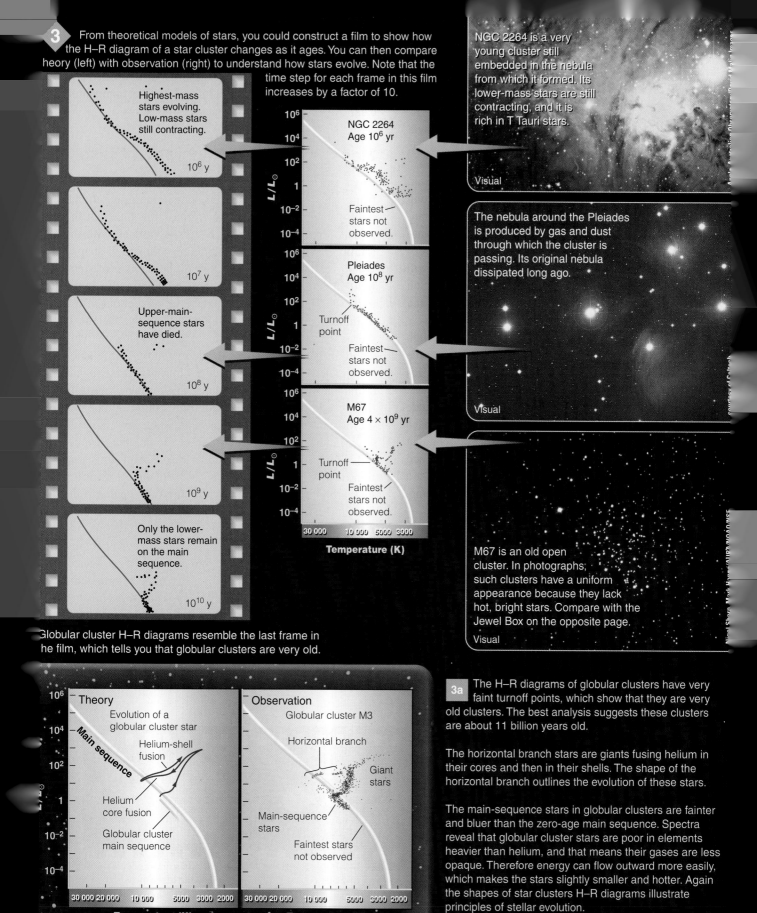

3 From theoretical models of stars, you could construct a film to show how the H–R diagram of a star cluster changes as it ages. You can then compare theory (left) with observation (right) to understand how stars evolve. Note that the time step for each frame in this film increases by a factor of 10.

Highest-mass stars evolving. Low-mass stars still contracting.

10^6 y

10^7 y

Upper-main-sequence stars have died.

10^8 y

10^9 y

Only the lower-mass stars remain on the main sequence.

10^{10} y

NGC 2264
Age 10^6 yr

Faintest stars not observed.

Pleiades
Age 10^8 yr

Turnoff point

Faintest stars not observed.

M67
Age 4×10^9 yr

Turnoff point

Faintest stars not observed.

$L/L_\odot$

Temperature (K)

NGC 2264 is a very young cluster still embedded in the nebula from which it formed. Its lower-mass stars are still contracting, and it is rich in T Tauri stars.

Visual

The nebula around the Pleiades is produced by gas and dust through which the cluster is passing. Its original nebula dissipated long ago.

Visual

M67 is an old open cluster. In photographs, such clusters have a uniform appearance because they lack hot, bright stars. Compare with the Jewel Box on the opposite page.

Visual

Globular cluster H–R diagrams resemble the last frame in the film, which tells you that globular clusters are very old.

Theory

Evolution of a globular cluster star

Main sequence

Helium-shell fusion

Helium core fusion

Globular cluster main sequence

Observation

Globular cluster M3

Horizontal branch

Giant stars

Main-sequence stars

Faintest stars not observed

Temperature (K)

3a The H–R diagrams of globular clusters have very faint turnoff points, which show that they are very old clusters. The best analysis suggests these clusters are about 11 billion years old.

The horizontal branch stars are giants fusing helium in their cores and then in their shells. The shape of the horizontal branch outlines the evolution of these stars.

The main-sequence stars in globular clusters are fainter and bluer than the zero-age main sequence. Spectra reveal that globular cluster stars are poor in elements heavier than helium, and that means their gases are less opaque. Therefore energy can flow outward more easily, which makes the stars slightly smaller and hotter. Again the shapes of star clusters H–R diagrams illustrate principles of stellar evolution.

Astronomers are still uncertain about some of the details, but computer models that include tidal effects predict that the expanding Sun eventually will engulf and destroy Mercury, Venus, and Earth.

While it is a giant star, the Sun will have a strong wind and lose a substantial fraction of its mass into space. The atoms that were once in Earth will be part of the expanding nebula around the Sun. Your atoms will be part of that nebula. If the white dwarf remnant Sun becomes hot enough, it will ionize the expelled gas and light it (and you) up as a planetary nebula.

Models of the Sun's evolution are not precise enough to predict whether its white dwarf remnant will become hot enough soon enough to light up its expelled gas and create a planetary nebula before that gas disperses. Whether the expelled gas lights up or not, it would include atoms that were once part of Earth. Theory suggests that a white dwarf might have a rigid core. Because carbon that is under high pressure and temperature crystallizes and becomes diamond, one might make the prediction that a white dwarf from a Sunlike star could become a stunning, Earth-sized degenerate diamond.

8.3 The Evolution of Binary Systems

Stars in binary systems can evolve independently of each other if they orbit at a large distance from each other. In this situation, one of the stars can swell into a giant and collapse without disturbing its companion. Other binary stars are as close to each other as 0.1 AU, and when one of those stars begins to swell into a giant, its companion can be disturbed in surprising ways.

Mass Transfer and Accretion Disks

Binary stars can sometimes interact by transferring mass from one star to the other. Of course, the gravitational field of each star holds its own mass together, but the gravitational fields of the two stars, combined with the rotation of the binary system, define a dumbbell-shaped volume called the **Roche lobes** around the pair of stars. Matter inside a star's Roche lobe is gravitationally bound to the star, but matter outside the lobe can be transferred to the other star or lost completely from the system. If the stars are close together the Roche lobes are relatively small and can interfere with the evolution of the stars. When an evolving star in a close binary system expands so far that it fills its Roche lobe, matter can flow from that star's lobe into the other lobe and onto the other star, as you can see in the series in Figure 8.6.

Matter flowing from one star to another cannot fall directly into the star. Rather, because of conservation of angular momentum, it must flow into a whirling disk around the star. **Angular momentum** refers to the tendency of a rotating object to continue rotating. All rotating objects possess some angular momentum, and in the absence of external forces, an object maintains (conserves) its total angular momentum. An ice dancer takes advantage of conservation of angular momentum by starting a spin slowly with arms extended and then drawing them in. As her mass becomes concentrated closer to her axis of rotation, she spins faster. The same effect causes the slowly circulating water in a bathtub to spin faster in a whirlpool as it approaches the drain.

The Evolution of a Binary System

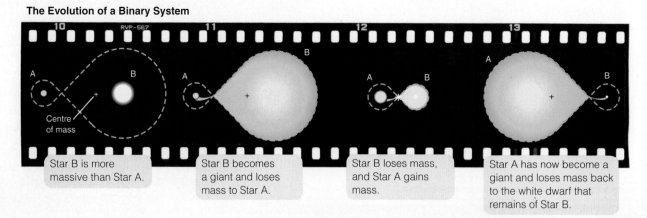

Star B is more massive than Star A.

Star B becomes a giant and loses mass to Star A.

Star B loses mass, and Star A gains mass.

Star A has now become a giant and loses mass back to the white dwarf that remains of Star B.

Figure 8.6 A pair of stars orbiting close to each other can exchange mass and modify their evolution.

Figure 8.7 Matter from an evolving red giant falls into a white dwarf and forms a whirling accretion disk. Friction and tidal forces can make the disk very hot. Such systems can lead to nova explosions on the surface of the white dwarf as shown in this artist's impression.

Mass transferred from one star to another in a binary star system must conserve its angular momentum. Thus, it must flow into a rapidly rotating whirlpool called an **accretion disk** around the second star (Figure 8.7). The gas in the disk grows hot due to friction and tidal forces (see Chapter 2) and eventually falls onto the second star. If that second star, the one receiving the matter lost from its companion, is a compact object like a white dwarf, the gas in the accretion disk can become very compressed. The gas temperature can exceed a million K, producing X-rays. In addition, the matter accumulating on the white dwarf can eventually cause a violent explosion called a nova.

Novae

At the beginning of this chapter you saw that the word *nova* refers to an apparently new star that appears in the sky for a while and then fades away. Modern astronomers know that a nova is not a new star but an old star flaring up. After a nova fades, astronomers can photograph the spectrum of the remaining faint point of light. Invariably, they find a normal star and a white dwarf in a close binary system. A nova is evidently an explosion involving a white dwarf.

Observational evidence can tell you how nova explosions occur. When the explosion begins, spectra show blueshifted absorption lines that indicate the gas is dense and coming toward you at a few thousand kilometres per second. After a few days, the spectral lines change to emission lines; this indicates the gas has thinned, but the blueshifts remain, showing that a cloud of debris has been ejected into space.

Nova explosions occur when mass transfers from a normal star into an accretion disk around a white dwarf (Figure 8.8). As the matter loses its angular momentum in the accretion disk, it settles inward onto the surface of the white dwarf and forms a layer of unused nuclear fuel—mostly hydrogen. As the layer deepens, it becomes denser and hotter until the hydrogen fuses in a sudden explosion that blows the surface off the white dwarf. Although the expanding cloud of debris contains less than 0.0001 solar mass, it is hot, and its expanding surface area makes it very luminous. Nova explosions can become 100 000 times more luminous than the Sun. As the debris cloud expands, cools, and thins over a period of weeks and months, the nova fades from view.

The explosion of its surface hardly disturbs the white dwarf and its companion star. Mass transfer quickly resumes, and a new layer of fuel begins to accumulate. How fast the fuel builds up depends on the rate of mass transfer. Accordingly, you can expect novae to repeat each time an explosive layer accumulates. Many novae take thousands of years to build an explosive layer, but some take only decades.

Type Ia Supernova: Thermonuclear or White Dwarf Supernova

A type Ia supernova (SnIa) is thought to occur when a white dwarf in a binary star system receives enough mass to exceed the Chandrasekhar–Landau limit and collapse. The core of the white dwarf contains carbon, an extremely combustible fuel. As the collapse begins, the temperature and density shoot up and the carbon–oxygen core begins to fuse in violent nuclear reactions. In a few seconds the carbon–oxygen interior is consumed, and the outermost layers are blasted away in a violent explosion. The white dwarf is entirely destroyed; no remnant is left behind. A supernova explosion generates temperatures high enough to trigger further fusion to heavy elements. The blast sends away an abundance of silicon, unburned carbon and oxygen, iron, and heavier elements, which become part of an interstellar cloud of gas enriched with elements that are crucial to life. As you will see later, a massive star supernova (type II) also produces fusion, but the majority of mass of a dying star is still left locked in the remnant. A type Ia supernova leaves no remnant; all the material is available for new stars to form their planetary systems and life forms. This is a perfect example of galactic recycling of material and the building blocks of life as we know it.

> **accretion disk** The rotating disk that forms in some situations as matter is drawn gravitationally toward a central body.

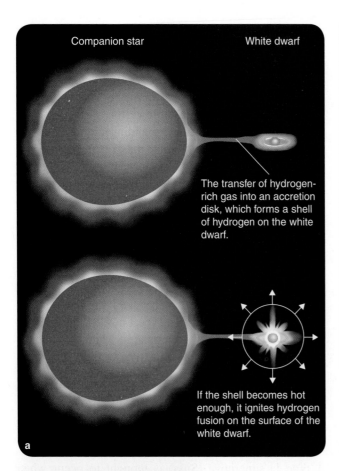

Figure 8.8 (a) Mass transfer from a dying star into an accretion disk around a white dwarf occasionally ignites hydrogen fusion on the surface of a white dwarf, increasing its luminosity and becoming visible. Historically, as this event appeared as a "new star" on the sky, it was called "nova." (b) Nova T Pyxidis erupts about every two decades. The shells of gas are visible through ground-based telescopes, but (c) the Hubble Space Telescope revealed much more detail. The shell consists of knots of excited gas, which presumably form when a new shell collides with the previously expelled shell.

A type Ia supernova is always the explosion of the same object, a 1.4-solar-mass white dwarf. Therefore, it always has very similar characteristics the same light curve (the solid blue line in Figure 8.12), and, most importantly, the same luminosity. Because of this property, it serves as a "standard candle" indicator of distances in the universe, as you will see in Chapter 10. According to the inverse square law, the farther away it is the dimmer it is (refer to Figure 6.3). We can find out the distance to an SnIa on the basis of its brightness.

Because their luminosity is immense, we can use these supernovae to trace large distances in the universe. You will also see in Chapter 11 their importance in regard to the expansion of the universe.

8.4 The Deaths of Massive Stars

Low- and medium-mass stars die relatively quietly as they exhaust their hydrogen and helium, and then some push away their surface layers to form planetary nebulae. In contrast, massive stars live spectacular lives and destroy themselves in violent explosions (see Figure 8.9).

Nuclear Fusion in Massive Stars

Stars on the upper main sequence have too much mass to die as white dwarfs, but their evolution begins much like that of their lower-mass cousins. They consume the hydrogen in their cores, ignite hydrogen shells, and become giants or, for the most massive stars, supergiants. Their cores contract and fuse helium first in the core and then in a shell, producing a carbon–oxygen core.

Unlike medium-mass stars, the massive stars finally can get hot enough to ignite carbon fusion at a temperature of about 1 billion Kelvin. Carbon fusion produces more oxygen plus neon. As soon as the carbon is exhausted in the core, the core contracts, and carbon ignites in a shell. This pattern of core ignition and shell ignition continues with a series of heavier nuclei as fusion fuel, and the star develops a layered structure with a hydrogen-fusion shell surrounding a helium-fusion shell surrounding a carbon-fusion shell surrounding, and so on (Figure 8.9). At higher temperatures than carbon fusion, nuclei of oxygen, neon, and magnesium fuse to make silicon and sulphur, and at even higher temperatures silicon can fuse to make iron.

The fusion of the nuclear fuels in this series goes faster and faster as the massive star evolves rapidly. The amount of energy released per fusion reaction decreases as the mass of the types of atoms involved

Figure 8.9 These massive stars contain 100 solar masses or more. The cores are composed of concentric layers of gases undergoing nuclear fusion. The iron core at the centre leads eventually to a star-destroying supernova explosion.

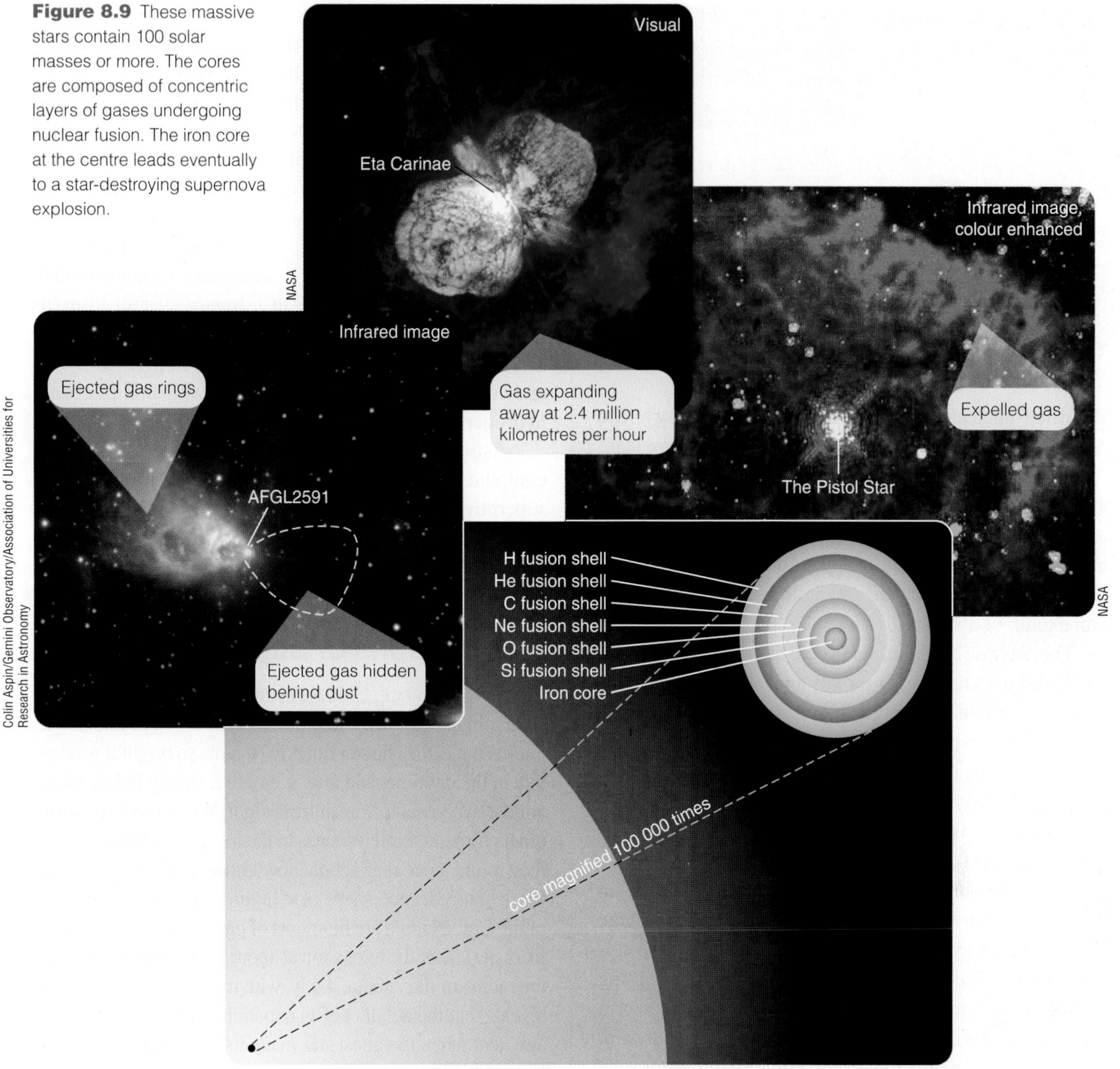

increases. To support its weight and remain stable, a star must fuse oxygen much faster than it fused hydrogen. Also, there are fewer nuclei in the core of the star by the time heavy nuclei begin to fuse. Four hydrogen nuclei make one helium nucleus, and three helium nuclei make one carbon; so there are 12 times fewer nuclei of carbon available for fusion than there were hydrogen nuclei. This means the heavy elements are used up, and fusion goes very quickly in massive stars (Table 8.1). Hydrogen fusion can last 7 million years in a 25-solar-mass star, but that same star fuses its oxygen in six months and its silicon in just one day.

Supernova Explosions of Massive Stars

Theoretical models of evolving stars combined with nuclear physics allow astronomers to describe what happens inside a massive star when the last nuclear fuels are exhausted. It begins with iron nuclei and ends in cosmic violence.

Silicon fusion produces iron, the most tightly bound of all atomic nuclei (refer to Figure 7.5). Nuclear fusion releases energy only when less tightly bound nuclei combine into a more tightly bound nucleus. Once the gas in the core of the star has been converted to iron, there are

Table 8.1	Heavy-Element Fusion in a 25-Solar-Mass Star	
Fuel	**Time**	**Percentage of Lifetime**
H	7 000 000 years	93.3
He	500 000 years	6.7
C	600 years	0.008
O	0.5 years	0.000007
Si	1 day	0.00000004

no further nuclear reactions that can release energy. The iron core is a dead end in the evolution of a massive star.

As a star develops an iron core, energy production begins to decline, and the core contracts. Nuclear reactions involving iron begin, but they remove energy from the core, causing it to contract even further. Once this process starts, the core of the star collapses inward in less than a tenth of a second.

The collapse of a giant star's core after iron fusion starts is calculated to happen so rapidly that the most powerful computers are unable to predict the details. Thus, models of supernova explosions contain many approximations. Nevertheless, the models predict exotic nuclear reactions in the collapsing core that should produce a flood of neutrinos (see Chapter 7). In fact, for a short time the core produces more energy per second than all the stars in all of the visible galaxies in the universe, and 99 percent of that energy is in the form of neutrinos. This flood of neutrinos carries large amounts of energy out of the core, allowing the core to collapse further. The models also predict that the collapsing core of the star must quickly become a neutron star or a black hole, while the envelope of the star is blasted outward.

To understand how the inward collapse of the core can produce an outward explosion, you can think about a traffic jam. The collapse of the innermost part of the degenerate core allows the rest of the core to fall inward, and this creates a tremendous traffic jam as all of the nuclei fall toward the centre. The position of the traffic jam, called a shock wave, begins to move outward as more in-falling material encounters the jam. The torrent of neutrinos, as well as the energy flowing out of the core in sudden, violent, convective turbulence, helps drive the shock wave outward. Within a few hours, the shock wave bursts outward through the surface of the star and blasts it apart.

The supernova seen from Earth is the brightening of the star as its envelope is blasted outward by the shock wave. As months pass, the cloud of gas expands, thins, and fades, but the manner in which it fades tells astronomers more about the death throes of the star. The rate at which the supernova's brightness decreases matches the rate at which radioactive nickel and cobalt decay, so the explosion must produce great abundances of those atoms. Because radioactive cobalt decays into iron, the destruction of iron in the core of the star is followed by the production of iron through nuclear reactions in the expanding outer layers.

The less common type Ib supernova is understood to occur when a massive star in a binary system loses its hydrogen-rich outer layers to its companion star. The remains of the massive star could develop an iron core and collapse, producing a supernova explosion that lacks hydrogen lines in its spectrum.

Astronomers working with the largest and fastest computers are using modern theory to try to understand supernova explosions. The companion to theory is observation, so the next section describes observational evidence that supports this story of supernova explosions.

Observations of Supernovae

In the year 1054 CE, Chinese astronomers saw a "guest star" appear in the constellation known in the Western tradition as Taurus the Bull. The star quickly became so bright it was visible in the daytime, and after a month it slowly faded, taking almost two years to vanish from sight. When modern astronomers turned their telescopes to the location of the guest star, they found a peculiar nebula now known as the Crab Nebula for its many-legged shape (see Figure 8.10). In fact, the legs of the Crab Nebula are filaments of gas that are moving away from the site of the explosion at about 1400 km/s. Comparing the radius of the nebula, 4.4 ly, with its velocity of expansion reveals that the nebula began expanding nine or 10 centuries ago, just when the guest star made its appearance. The Crab Nebula is clearly the remains of the supernova seen in 1054 CE. The next section describes the neutron star found at the centre of the Crab Nebula.

The blue glow of the Crab Nebula is produced by synchrotron radiation. This form of electromagnetic radiation, unlike blackbody radiation, is produced by rapidly moving electrons spiralling through magnetic fields and is common in the nebulae produced by supernovae. In the case of the Crab Nebula, the electrons travel so fast they emit visual wavelengths. In most such nebulae, the electrons move slower, and the synchrotron radiation is at radio wavelengths.

Supernovae are rare. Only a few have been seen with the naked eye in recorded history. Arab astronomers saw one in 1006 CE, and the Chinese and the Anasazi in North America saw one in 1054 CE. European astronomers

X-ray: NASA/CXC/SAO/F.Seward; Optical: NASA/ESA/ASU/J.Hester & A.Loll; Infrared: NASA/JPL-Caltech/ Univ. Minn./R.Gehrz

Filaments of gas rush away from the site of the supernova of 1054.

Jet

Neutron star

Glow produced by synchrotron radiation.

Figure 8.10 The Crab Nebula is located in the constellation Taurus the Bull, just where Chinese astronomers saw a brilliant guest star in the year 1054 CE. High-speed electrons produced by the central neutron star spiral through magnetic fields and produce the foggy glow of synchrotron radiation that fills the nebula. This visual+ infrared+X-ray image of the Crab Nebula reveals the neutron star, a disk of hot gas more than 1 ly across and a curving jet.

was critical in confirming the theoretical postulate of core collapse: at 2:35 a.m. EST on February 23, 1987, nearly four hours before the supernova was first seen, a blast of neutrinos swept through Earth. Neutrino detectors in Japan (Kamiokande II), the United States (IMB), and Russia (Baksan) recorded 19 neutrinos in less than 15 seconds. Since neutrinos are so difficult to detect, the 19 neutrinos that were actually detected indicated that some 10^{17} neutrinos must have passed through the detectors in those 15 seconds. Furthermore, the neutrinos were arriving from the direction of the supernova. Astronomers concluded that the burst of neutrinos was released when the iron core collapsed, and the supernova was first seen at visual wavelengths hours later when the shock wave blasted the star's surface into space.

Most supernovae are seen in distant galaxies, and careful observations allow astronomers to compare types, which can be done with charts like the one in Figure 8.12. Type Ia supernovae, caused by the collapse of white dwarfs, are more luminous at maximum brightness and decline rapidly at first and then more slowly. **Type II supernovae**, produced by the collapse of massive stars, are not as bright at maximum, and they decline in a more irregular way.

SN 1987A was a type II supernova, although its light curve is not typical (Figure 8.12). Models indicate that most type II supernovae are caused by the collapse of red supergiants, but SN 1987A was produced by the explosion of a hot, blue supergiant. Astronomers hypothesize that this star was once a red supergiant but later contracted and heated up slightly, becoming bluer before it exploded.

Although the supernova explosion fades to obscurity in a year or two, an expanding shell of gas marks the site of the explosion. The gas, originally expelled at 10 000 to 20 000 km/s, may carry away a fifth of the mass of the star. The collision of that expanding gas with the surrounding interstellar medium can sweep up even more gas and excite it to produce a **supernova remnant**, the nebulous remains of a supernova explosion. Figure 8.13 shows images of four supernova remnants; images made

observed two—one in 1572 CE (Tycho's supernova) and one in 1604 CE (Kepler's supernova). In addition, the guest stars of 185, 386, 393, and 1181 CE may have been supernovae.

In the centuries following the invention of the astronomical telescope in 1609, no supernova was bright enough to be visible to the naked eye. Then, in the early morning hours of February 24, 1987, astronomers around the world were startled by the naked-eye discovery of a supernova still growing brighter in the southern sky (Figure 8.11). The supernova known officially as SN 1987A is 170 000 ly away in the Large Magellanic Cloud, a small satellite galaxy to our own Milky Way Galaxy. This supernova, the first visual sighting in 383 years, has given astronomers a ringside seat for the most spectacular event in stellar evolution.

Canadian astronomer Ian Shelton and his Chilean colleague Oscar Duhalde, at Las Campanas Observatory high in the Andes Mountains in northern Chile, were the first to report the visual sighting. A third observer, Albert Jones in New Zealand, followed the supernova development in the first and most important hours. As soon as Shelton and Duhalde sent a telex, world telescopes in all wavelengths turned to observe the event. Another type of observation

type II supernova A supernova explosion caused by the collapse of a massive star.

supernova remnant The expanding shell of gas and dust marking the site of a supernova explosion.

Australian Astronomical Observatory/David Malin / Australian Astronomical Observatory/David MalinImages

Supernova 1987A

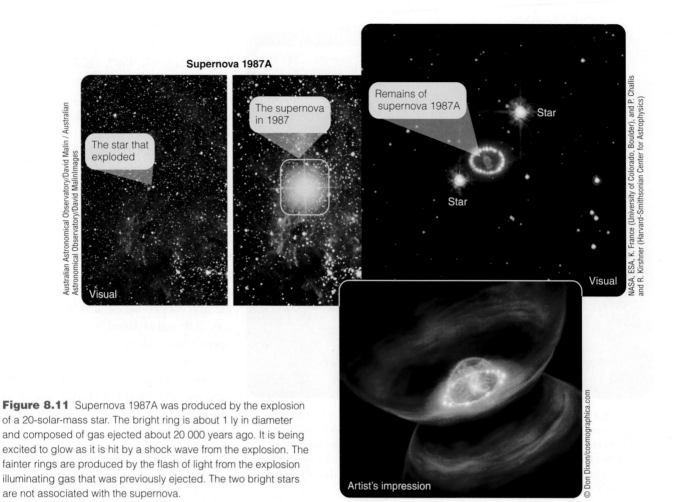

NASA, ESA, K. France (University of Colorado, Boulder), and P. Challis and R. Kirshner (Harvard-Smithsonian Center for Astrophysics)

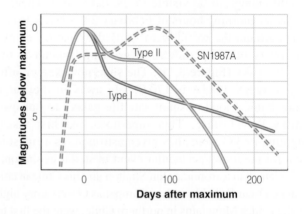

© Don Dixon/cosmographica.com

Figure 8.11 Supernova 1987A was produced by the explosion of a 20-solar-mass star. The bright ring is about 1 ly in diameter and composed of gas ejected about 20 000 years ago. It is being excited to glow as it is hit by a shock wave from the explosion. The fainter rings are produced by the flash of light from the explosion illuminating gas that was previously ejected. The two bright stars are not associated with the supernova.

at other than visible wavelengths are displayed in false colour (see Chapter 4).

Supernova remnants look quite delicate and do not survive very long—a few tens of thousands of years—before they gradually mix with the interstellar medium and vanish. The Crab Nebula is a young remnant, only about 950 years old and about 8.8 ly in diameter. Older remnants can be larger. Some supernova remnants are visible only at radio and X-ray wavelengths. They have become too tenuous to emit detectable light, but the collision of the expanding hot gas with the interstellar medium can generate radio and X-ray radiation. You learned in Chapter 7 that the compression of the interstellar medium by expanding supernova remnants can also trigger star formation.

Gravity always wins. However a star lives, theory predicts it must eventually die and leave behind one of three types of objects: a white dwarf, neutron star, or black hole. These compact objects are small monuments to the power of gravity. Almost all of the energy available has

type I supernova A supernova whose spectrum contains no hydrogen lines.

been squeezed out of compact objects, and you find them in their final, high-density states.

Figure 8.12 **Type I supernovae** decline in brightness rapidly at first and then more slowly, but type II supernovae pause for about 100 days before beginning a steep decline. Supernova 1987A was odd in that it did not rise directly to maximum brightness. These light curves have been adjusted to the same maximum brightness.

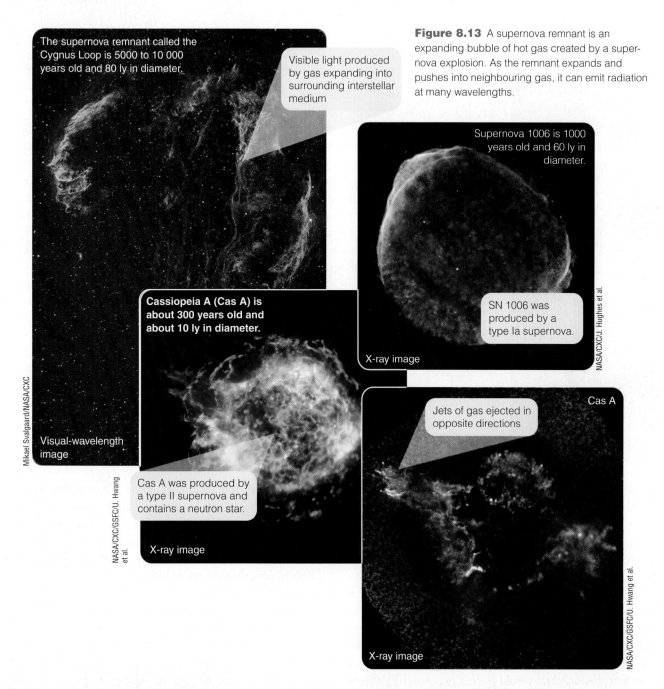

The supernova remnant called the Cygnus Loop is 5000 to 10 000 years old and 80 ly in diameter.

Visible light produced by gas expanding into surrounding interstellar medium

Cassiopeia A (Cas A) is about 300 years old and about 10 ly in diameter.

Cas A was produced by a type II supernova and contains a neutron star.

Visual-wavelength image

X-ray image

Mikael Svalgaard/NASA/CXC

NASA/CXC/GSFC/U. Hwang et al.

Supernova 1006 is 1000 years old and 60 ly in diameter.

SN 1006 was produced by a type Ia supernova.

X-ray image

NASA/CXC/J. Hughes et al.

Cas A

Jets of gas ejected in opposite directions

X-ray image

NASA/CXC/GSFC/U. Hwang et al.

Figure 8.13 A supernova remnant is an expanding bubble of hot gas created by a supernova explosion. As the remnant expands and pushes into neighbouring gas, it can emit radiation at many wavelengths.

8.5 Neutron Stars

A **neutron star** contains a little over 1 solar mass compressed to a radius of about 10 km. Its density is so high that the matter is stable only as a fluid of pure neutrons. These facts immediately raise two questions: How could any theory predict such a strange object? And how do we know they exist?

Theoretical Prediction of Neutron Stars

The subatomic particles called neutrons were discovered in a laboratory in 1932, and physicists quickly realized that because neutrons spin much like electrons, a gas of neutrons could become degenerate and therefore nearly incompressible. Just two years later, in 1934, two astronomers, Walter Baade and Fritz Zwicky, suggested that some of the most luminous novae in the historical record were not regular novae but were caused by the collapse and explosion of a massive star in a cataclysm they named a "super-nova." If the collapsing core is more massive than the Chandrasekhar–Landau limit of 1.4 solar masses, the weight would be too great to be supported by degenerate electron pressure, and the core could not become a

neutron star A small, highly dense star, with radius about 10 km, composed almost entirely of tightly packed neutrons.

CHAPTER 8 The Deaths of Stars |

Ian Keith Shelton

In 1987, Winnipeg-born Ian Keith Shelton discovered the first supernova visible to the naked eye since Johannes Kepler saw supernova SN 1604 almost 400 years earlier. After receiving his B.Sc. from the University of Manitoba in 1979, Shelton worked at the University of Toronto's Southern Observatory at Las Campanas, Chile. On February 24, 1987, while he was in Chile, Shelton noticed a bright light on a photograph of a nearby galaxy called the Large Magellanic Cloud. Thinking the photo was flawed, he walked outside to check the sky with the naked eye and confirmed his amazing discovery. It was light from a star born 11 million years ago that had exploded 166 000 years ago. Shelton and another observer Oscar Duhalde, also at Las Campas Observatory, reported the observation via telegram to the International Astronomical Union's Central Bureau for Astronomical Telegrams. They were credited with the discovery, together with Albert Jones who independently reported the event from New Zealand. The news of the discovery spread rapidly, and almost every telescope in the southern hemisphere was immediately turned toward this grand occurrence in the sky. Thanks to its early detection, this supernova designated SN 1987 A is the most well-observed supernova in history. Since its launch in 1990, the Hubble Space Telescope has regularly monitored the supernova remnant. Shelton became a graduate student at the University of Toronto in the fall of 1987. He received his M.Sc. in 1990 and Ph.D. in 1996. He has since worked as an astronomer at several observatories, including Japan's 8.3-metre Subaru Telescope in Hawaii, the 1.9-m David Dunlap Observatory in Toronto, Athabasca University north of Edmonton, and the 6.5-m MMT Observatory south of Tucson. The asteroid Shelton is named in his honour.

stable white dwarf. The collapse would force protons to combine with electrons and become neutrons. The envelope of the star would be blasted away in a supernova explosion, and the core of the star would be left behind as a small, tremendously dense sphere of neutrons that Zwicky called a "neutron star."

Mathematical models predict that a neutron star is only 10 or so kilometres in radius and has a density of about 10^{14} g/cm^3. That is roughly the density of atomic nuclei, and you can think of a neutron star as matter with all the empty space squeezed out of it. A sugar-cube-sized lump of this material would have a mass of 100 million tons, the mass of a small mountain.

Simple physics, the physics you have used in previous chapters to understand normal stars, predicts that neutron stars (1) spin rapidly, perhaps 100 to 1000 rotations per second; (2) are hot, with surface temperatures of millions of degrees K; and (3) have strong magnetic fields, up to a trillion times stronger than the Sun's or Earth's magnetic fields. For example, the collapse of a massive star's core would greatly increase its spin rate by conservation of angular momentum. Other processes during core collapse would likely create high temperature and strong magnetic fields. Despite their high temperature, neutron stars would be difficult to detect because of their tiny size.

What is the maximum mass for a stable neutron star? In other words, is there an upper limit to the mass of neutron stars: for example, the Chandrasekhar–Landau limit that defines the maximum mass of a white dwarf star? That is difficult to answer because physicists don't know enough about the properties of pure neutron material. It can't be made in a laboratory, and theoretical calculations in this case are very difficult. The most widely accepted results suggest that a neutron star can't be more massive than 2 to 3 solar masses. An object more massive than that can't be supported by degenerate neutron pressure, so it would collapse and presumably become a black hole.

What is the mass of stars that end their lives with supernova explosions that leave behind neutron star corpses? Theoretical calculations suggest that stars that begin life on the main sequence with 8 to about 15 solar masses end up as neutron stars. Stars more massive than about 15 solar masses are expected to form black holes when they die.

The Discovery of Pulsars

In November 1967, Jocelyn Bell, a graduate student at Cambridge University in England, found a peculiar pattern in the data from a radio telescope. Unlike other radio signals from celestial bodies, this was a series of regular pulses (see Figure 8.14). At first she and the leader of the project, Anthony Hewish, thought the signal was interference, but they found it day after day at the same celestial latitude and longitude. Clearly, it was cosmic in origin.

Another possibility, that it came from a distant civilization, led them to consider naming it LGM for Little Green Men. Within a few weeks, the team found three more objects in other parts of the sky pulsing with different periods. The objects were clearly natural, and the team dropped the name LGM in favour of **pulsar**—a "pulsing star." The pulsing radio source Bell had observed with her radio telescope was the first known pulsar. Hewish received the Nobel Prize in physics for this work, and Bell (now Bell Burnell) has been remarkably gracious about that.

As more pulsars were found, astronomers argued over their nature. The pulses, which typically last only about 0.001 second, gave astronomers an important clue. The pulse length places an upper limit on the size of the object producing the pulse. This is a very important principle in astronomy: An object cannot change its brightness significantly in an interval shorter than the time light takes to cross its diameter. If pulses from pulsars are no longer than 0.001 second, the objects cannot be larger than 0.001 light-second—or 300 km—in diameter, which is smaller than the diameter of white dwarfs, and this makes neutron stars the only reasonable explanation.

The missing link between pulsars and neutron stars was found in late 1968, when astronomers discovered a pulsar at the heart of the Crab Nebula (see Figure 8.10). The Crab Nebula is a supernova remnant, which agrees nicely with Zwicky and Baade's prediction that some supernovae should produce a neutron star. The short pulses and the discovery of the pulsar in the Crab Nebula are strong evidence that pulsars are neutron stars.

The modern model of a pulsar, which has been called the **lighthouse model**, is illustrated in Figure 8.15. In a

sense the name *pulsar* is inaccurate: A pulsar does not pulse (vibrate), rather it emits beams of radiation that sweep around the sky as the neutron star rotates, like a rotating lighthouse light. The mechanism that produces the beams involves extremely high energies and strong electric and magnetic fields and is not fully understood. There are pulsars with unimaginably strong magnetic fields—more than 1000 trillion times stronger than Earth's magnetic field—called *magnetars*. Around 2000 pulsars of all sorts are now known from various wavelengths of observation. Many more neutron stars are out there, undetected because their beams never point toward Earth. Someone else in the Milky Way (if anyone is out there) might see a neutron star beaming toward their stellar system, invisible to ours. For them, it would be a pulsar.

> **pulsar** A source of short, precisely timed radio bursts, understood to be spinning neutron stars.
>
> **lighthouse model** The explanation of a pulsar as a spinning neutron star sweeping beams of electromagnetic radiation around the sky.

The Evolution of Pulsars

Neutron stars are not simple objects, and modern astronomers need knowledge of frontier physics to understand them. Nevertheless, the life story of pulsars can be worked out to some extent. When a pulsar first forms, it may be spinning as many as 100 times a second. The energy it radiates into space ultimately comes from its energy of rotation, so as it blasts beams of radiation outward, its rotation slows. Judging from their pulse periods and rates at which they slow down, the average pulsar is apparently only a few million years old, and the oldest has an age of about 10 million years. Presumably, neutron stars older than that rotate too slowly to generate detectable radio beams. Supernova remnants last only about 50 000 years before they mix into the interstellar medium and disappear, so most pulsars have long outlived the remnants in which they were originally embedded.

You can expect that a young neutron star should emit especially strong beams of radiation powered by its rapid rotation. The Crab Nebula (Figure 8.10) provides an example of such a system. Only about 950 years old and spinning 30 times per second, the Crab pulsar is so powerful that astronomers can detect photons of radio, infrared, visible, X-ray, and gamma-ray wavelengths from it.

The explosion of supernova 1987A in February 1987 probably formed a neutron star. You can draw this conclusion because a burst of neutrinos was detected passing through Earth, and theory predicts that the collapse of a massive star's core into a ball of

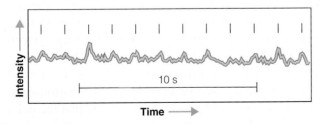

Figure 8.14 The 1967 detection of regularly spaced pulses in the output of a radio telescope led to the discovery of pulsars. This record of the radio signal from the first pulsar, CP1919, contains regularly spaced pulses (marked by ticks). The period is 1.33730119 seconds.

neutrons will produce such a burst of neutrinos. The neutron star initially would be hidden at the centre of the expanding shells of gas ejected into space by the supernova explosion, but as the gas continues to expand and become thinner, astronomers might eventually be able to detect it. As of this writing, no neutron star has been detected in the SN 1987A remnant, but astronomers continue to watch the site hoping to find the youngest pulsar known.

Binary Pulsars

One reason pulsars are so fascinating is the extreme conditions found in spinning neutron stars. To see even more extreme natural processes, you have only to look at the pulsars that are members of binary systems. These pulsars are of special interest because astronomers can learn more about the neutron star and about the behaviour of matter in unusual circumstances by studying them.

Binary pulsars can be sites of tremendous violence because of the strength of gravity at the surface of a neutron star. Matter falling onto a neutron star can release titanic amounts of energy. If you dropped a single marshmallow onto the surface of a neutron star from a distance of 1 AU, it would hit with an impact equivalent to a 3-megaton nuclear warhead. Even a small amount of matter flowing from a companion star to a neutron star can generate high temperatures and release X-rays and gamma rays.

For an example of such an active system, examine Hercules X-1 in Figure 8.16. It emits pulses of X-rays with a period of about 1.2 seconds, but every 1.7 days the pulses vanish for a few hours. Hercules X-1 seems to contain a 2-solar-mass star and a neutron star that orbit each other with a period of 1.7 days. Matter flowing from the normal star into an accretion disk around the neutron star reaches temperatures of millions of degrees and emits a powerful X-ray glow, some of which is in beams that sweep around with the rotating neutron star. Earth receives a pulse of X-rays every time a beam points this way. The X-rays shut off completely every 1.7 days when the neutron star is eclipsed behind the normal star. Hercules X-1 is an intricate system with many different high-energy processes going on simultaneously, and this quick analysis only serves to illustrate how complex and powerful such binary systems are during mass transfer.

A binary system in which both objects are neutron stars was discovered in 1974 when radio astronomers Joseph Taylor and Russell Hulse noticed that the pulse period of the pulsar PSR 1913+16 grew longer and then shorter in a cycle that takes 7.75 hours. Taylor and Hulse realized that must be the binary orbital period of the pulsar. They analyzed the system with the same

Neutron Star Rotation with Beams

The pulsing of a lighthouse is actually caused by the rotation of beams of light.

As in the case of Earth, the magnetic axis of a neutron star could be inclined to its rotational axis.

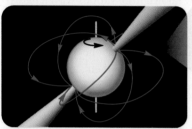

The rotation of the neutron star will sweep its beams around like beams from a lighthouse.

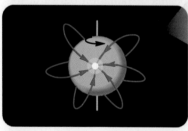

While a beam points roughly toward Earth, observers detect a pulse.

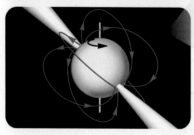

While neither beam is pointed toward Earth, observers detect no energy.

Figure 8.15 A neutron star contains a powerful magnetic field and spins very rapidly. The spinning magnetic field generates a tremendously powerful electric field, and the field causes the creation of electron-positron pairs that accelerate through the magnetic field, emit photons in the directions of their motion, and thereby produce powerful beams of electromagnetic radiation emerging from the neutron star's magnetic poles.

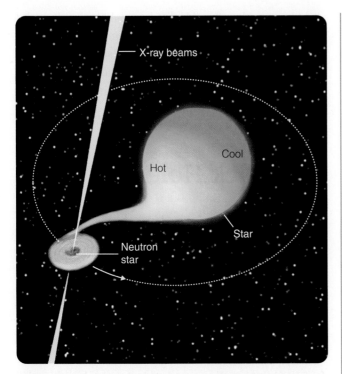

Figure 8.16 In Hercules X-1, matter flows from a star into an accretion disk around a neutron star producing X-rays, which heat the near side of the star to 20 000 K, compared with only 7000 K on the far side. X-rays turn off when the neutron star is eclipsed behind the star.

The Fastest Pulsars

This discussion of pulsars suggests that newborn pulsars should blink rapidly and old pulsars should blink slowly; however, a few that blink the fastest may be quite old. A number of **millisecond pulsars** have been found, so called because their pulse periods are almost as short as a millisecond (0.001 s). The energy stored in a neutron star rotating at this rate is equal to the total energy of a supernova explosion, and these pulsars generally have weak magnetic fields, consistent with advanced age. At first it seemed difficult to understand their rapid rotation. Astronomers hypothesized that an old neutron star could gain rotational energy from a companion star in a binary system. Some of the millisecond pulsars are caught in the act of receiving matter from companions in a fashion that should speed the pulsar's rotation to the observed high rates, so the hypothesis seems to be confirmed.

Scientists say, "show me," and in the case of neutron stars, the evidence seems very strong. Although you can never prove a scientific hypothesis or theory is absolutely true, the evidence for neutron stars is so strong that astronomers have great confidence that they really do exist. Other theories that describe how they emit beams of radiation and how they form and evolve are less certain, but continuing observations at many wavelengths are expanding the understanding of these last embers of massive stars. In fact, precise observations have turned up objects no one expected.

Pulsar Planets

Because a pulsar's period is so precise, astronomers can detect tiny variations by comparison with atomic clocks. When astronomers checked pulsar PSR 1257112, they found variations in the period of pulsation (Figure 8.17a) analogous to the variations caused by the orbital motion of the binary pulsar, but much smaller. When these variations were interpreted as Doppler shifts, it became evident that the pulsar was being orbited by at least two objects with planet-like masses of about four and three Earth masses. The gravitational tugs of the planets make the pulsar wobble around the centre of mass of the system

general theory of relativity Einstein's theory that describes gravity as due to curvature of space-time.

gravitational radiation Expanding waves in a gravitational field that transport energy through space at the speed of light, as predicted by general relativity.

millisecond pulsar A pulsar with a pulse period of only a few milliseconds.

techniques used to study spectroscopic binary stars (Chapter 6) to find that PSR 1913+16 consists of two neutron stars separated by a distance roughly equal to the radius of our Sun. The masses of the two neutron stars are each about 1.4 solar masses, in good agreement with models of neutron stars and how they are created.

A surprise was hidden in the motion of PSR 1913+16. This binary system was shown to be crucial for testing one of the most elusive predictions of the theory of gravity. In 1916, Einstein published his **general theory of relativity** that described gravity as a curvature of space-time (Figure 8.19). Einstein realized that any rapid change in a gravitational field should spread outward at the speed of light as **gravitational radiation**. Gravity waves themselves have not been detected yet, but Taylor and Hulse were able to show that the orbital period of the binary pulsar was slowly growing shorter because the stars were gradually spiralling toward each other at the rate expected if they radiate orbital energy away as gravitational radiation. Taylor and Hulse won the Nobel Prize in 1993 for their work with binary pulsars.

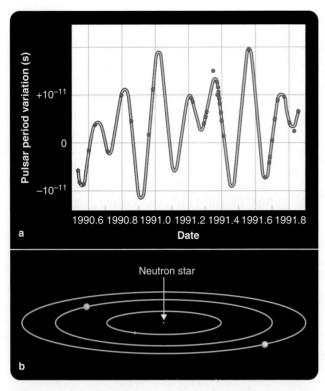

Figure 8.17 (a) The dots in this graph are observations showing that the period of pulsar PSR 1257 + 12 varies from its average value by a fraction of a billionth of a second. The blue line shows the variation that would be produced by planets orbiting the pulsar. (b) As the planets orbit the pulsar, they cause it to wobble by less than 800 km, a distance that is invisibly small in this diagram.

by about 800 km, and that produces the tiny changes in period that are observed (Figure 8.17b).

Astronomers greeted this discovery with both enthusiasm and skepticism. As usual, they looked for ways to test the hypothesis. Simple gravitational theory predicts that the planets should interact and slightly modify each other's orbit. When the data were analyzed that interaction was found, which further confirmed the hypothesis that the variations in the period of the pulsar are caused by planets. In fact, more observations and analyses have revealed the presence of a third planet of about twice the mass of Earth's moon, and possibly a fourth planet of only 3 percent the mass of Earth's moon. This illustrates the astonishing precision of studies based on pulsar timing.

Astronomers wonder how a neutron star can have planets. The inner three planets that orbit PSR 1257+12 are closer to the pulsar than Venus is to the Sun. Any planets that orbit a star would be lost or vaporized when the star exploded. Furthermore, a star about to explode as a supernova would be a large giant or a supergiant,

and planets only a few AU distant would be inside such a large star and could not survive. It seems more likely that these planets are the remains of a stellar companion that was devoured by the neutron star. In fact, PSR1257+12 is very fast (162 pulses per second), suggesting that it was spun up in a binary system.

8.6 Black Holes

You have studied white dwarfs and neutron stars, two of the three end states of dying stars. Now it's time to think about the third end state: black holes.

Although the physics of black holes is difficult to discuss without sophisticated mathematics, simple logic is sufficient to predict that they should exist. The problem is to use their predicted properties and attempt to confirm that they exist. What objects observed in the heavens could be real black holes? More difficult than the search for neutron stars, the quest for black holes has nevertheless met with success.

To begin, you can consider a simple question. How fast must an object travel to escape from the surface of a celestial body? The answer leads to black holes.

Escape Velocity

In Chapter 3 you learned that the escape velocity is the initial velocity an object needs to escape from a celestial body. Whether you are discussing a baseball leaving Earth or a photon leaving a collapsing star, the escape velocity depends on two things: the mass of the celestial body, and the distance from the centre of mass to the escapee's starting point. If the celestial body has a large mass, its gravity is strong, and it needs a high velocity to escape. But if its journey begins farther from the centre of mass it needs less velocity to escape. For example, to escape from Earth a spaceship has to leave Earth's surface at 11 km/s, but if spaceships could be launched from the top of a tower 1600 km high, the escape velocity would be only 10 km/s.

An object massive enough and/or small enough could have an escape velocity greater than the speed of light. Relativity says that nothing can travel faster than the speed of light, so even photons would not be able to escape. Such a small, massive object could never be seen because light could not leave it. This was first noted by British astronomer Reverend John Mitchell in 1783, long before Einstein and relativity.

HOW DO WE KNOW? 8.1

Theories and Proof

No scientific theory or hypothesis can be proved correct. You can test a hypothesis over and over by performing experiments or making observations, but you can never prove that the hypothesis is absolutely true. It is always possible that you have misunderstood the hypothesis or the evidence, and the next observation you make might disprove the hypothesis.

For example, you might propose the hypothesis that the Sun is mostly calcium and iron vapour because those elements are known to be abundant on Earth. You might test the hypothesis by looking at the calcium and iron lines in the solar spectrum, and the strength of the lines would suggest your hypothesis is right. Although your observation has confirmed your hypothesis, it has not proven the hypothesis is right. You might confirm the hypothesis many times in many ways before you realize that at the temperature of the Sun, iron and calcium atoms absorb photons

much more efficiently than hydrogen. Although the hydrogen lines are weak in the Sun's spectrum, a careful analysis shows that most of the atoms in the Sun are hydrogen, not iron or calcium.

The nature of scientific thinking can lead to two common misconceptions. Sometimes non-scientists will say, "You scientists just want to tear everything down—you don't believe in anything." Scientists test a hypothesis over and over to test its worth. If a hypothesis survives many tests, scientists begin to have confidence it is true, and the hypothesis "graduates" to being considered a theory.

The second common misconception arises when non-scientists say, "You scientists are never sure of anything." Again, the scientist knows that no hypothesis can be proved correct. That the Sun will rise tomorrow is very likely, and scientists have great confidence in that theory. But it is still only a

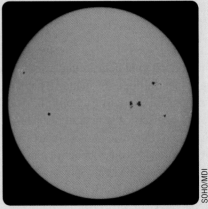

SOHO/MDI

Technically it is still a theory, but astronomers have great confidence that the Sun gets its power from nuclear fusion.

theory. People will say of an idea they dislike, "That is only a theory," as if a theory were simply a random guess. In fact, a theory is a hypothesis that has been well tested many times and so has become a model in which all scientists have great confidence. Yet you can never prove that any hypothesis or theory is absolutely true.

Schwarzschild Black Holes

If the core of a star collapses and contains more than about 3 solar masses, no force can stop the collapse. When the object reaches the size of a white dwarf, the collapse continues because degenerate electrons cannot support that much weight. Also, the collapse cannot stop when the object reaches the even smaller size of a neutron star; this is because degenerate neutrons cannot support that weight. No force remains to stop the object from collapsing to zero radius.

As an object collapses, its density and the strength of its surface gravity increase. If an object collapses to zero radius its density and gravity become infinite. Mathematicians call such a point a **singularity**, but in physical terms it is difficult to imagine an object of zero radius. Some theorists think that a singularity is impossible and that the laws of quantum physics must somehow

halt the collapse at some subatomic radius roughly 10^{20} times smaller than a proton. Astronomically, it seems to make little difference.

If the contracting core of a star becomes small enough, the escape velocity in a region around it is so large that no light can escape. You can receive no information about the object or about the region of space near it. Such a region is called a **black hole**. Note that the term *black hole* refers to a volume of space, not just the singularity at the region's centre. If the core of an exploding star collapsed to create a black hole, the expanding outer layers of the star could produce a supernova remnant, but the core would vanish without a trace.

singularity An object of zero radius and infinite density.

black hole A mass that has collapsed to such a small volume that its gravity prevents the escape of all radiation. Also, the volume of space from which radiation may not escape.

Albert Einstein's general theory of relativity treats space and time as a single entity: space-time. His equations showed that gravity could be described as a curvature of space-time, and almost immediately astronomer Karl Schwarzschild found a way to solve the equations to describe the gravitational field around a single, nonrotating, electrically neutral lump of matter. That solution contained the first general relativistic description of a black hole, and nonrotating, electrically neutral black holes are now known as Schwarzschild black holes. Interestingly, Einstein did not believe that the consequence of his own theory of gravity—black holes—made any physical sense, and he dismissed the possibility of black holes as physical objects. From the trenches of the First World War, Karl Schwarzschild sent Einstein a letter with his calculations showing that one of the consequences of the general theory of relativity is strange objects with such strong gravity that not even light could escape. (In a simpler form, this was also Mitchell's and Laplace's idea from the late 1700s based on Newton's physics). Einstein admired Schwarzschild's elegant calculations of his own theory, but never accepted the physical possibility of black holes. In recent decades, theorists such as Roy Kerr and Stephen Hawking have found ways to apply the sophisticated mathematical equations of the general theory of relativity and quantum mechanics to black holes that are rotating and have electrical charges. For the discussion in this chapter, these differences are minor, and you may proceed as if all black holes were Schwarzschild black holes.

Schwarzschild's solution shows that if matter is packed into a small enough volume, space-time curves back on itself. Objects can still follow paths that lead into the black hole, but no path leads out, so nothing can escape, not even light. Consequently, the inside of the black hole is totally beyond the view of an outside observer. The **event horizon** is the boundary between the isolated volume of space-time and the rest of the universe, and the radius of the event horizon is called the **Schwarzschild radius, R_S**—the radius within which an object must shrink to become a black hole (Figure 8.18). The event horizon is the sphere of no return for any object falling in later.

Although Schwarzschild's work is highly mathematical, his conclusions are quite simple. The size of a black hole, its Schwarzschild radius, is simply proportional to its mass. A 3-solar-mass black hole will have a Schwarzschild radius of about 9 km, a 10-solar-mass

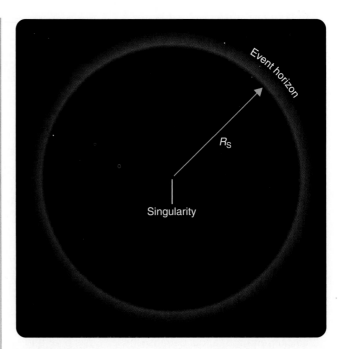

Figure 8.18 A black hole forms when an object collapses to a small size (perhaps to a singularity) and the escape velocity becomes so great light cannot escape. The boundary of the black hole is called the event horizon because any event that occurs inside is invisible to outside observers. The radius of the black hole R_S is the Schwarzschild radius.

black hole will have a Schwarzschild radius of 30 km, and so on. Note that even a very massive black hole would not be very large—just a few kilometres across.

It is a common misconception to think of black holes as giant vacuum cleaners that suck up everything in the universe. A black hole is just a gravitational field, and at a large distance its gravity is no greater than that of a normal object of similar mass. If the Sun were replaced by a 1-solar-mass black hole, the orbits of the planets would not change at all. The gravity of a black hole becomes extreme only when an object approaches close to it. Figure 8.19 illustrates this by representing gravitational fields as a curvature of the fabric of space-time. Physicists like to graph the strength of gravity around a black hole as curvature in a flat sheet. The graphs look like funnels in which the depth of the funnel indicates the strength of the gravitational field, but black holes themselves are not shaped like funnels; they are spheres or spheroids. Note that in Figure 8.19 the strength of the gravitational field around the black hole becomes extreme only if an object ventures too close.

This chapter has focused on black holes that could originate from the deaths of massive stars. In later chapters, you will encounter black holes located in the centres of galaxies whose masses might exceed a million solar masses.

Leaping into a Black Hole

Before you can search for real black holes, you must understand what theory predicts about the behaviour of a black hole. To explore that idea, imagine that you leap, feet first, into a Schwarzschild black hole.

If you were to leap a distance of an astronomical unit into a black hole of a few solar masses, the gravitational pull would not be very large, and you would fall slowly at first. Of course, the longer you fell and the closer you came to the centre, the faster you would travel. Your wristwatch would tell you that you fell for about two months before you reached the event horizon.

Your friends who stayed behind would see something different. They would see you falling more slowly as you came closer to the event horizon because, as described by general relativity, time slows down in curved space-time. This is known as **time dilation**. In fact, your friends would never actually see you cross the event horizon. To them you would fall more and more slowly until you seemed hardly to move. Generations later, your descendants could focus their telescopes on you and see you still inching closer to the event horizon. You, however, would have sensed no slowdown and would conclude that you had crossed the event horizon after about two months.

Another relativistic effect would make it difficult to see you with normal telescopes. As light travels out of a gravitational field, it loses energy, and its wavelength grows longer. This is known as the **gravitational redshift**. Although you would notice no effect as you fell toward the black hole, your friends would need to observe at longer and longer wavelengths in order to detect you.

While these relativistic effects seem merely peculiar, other effects would be quite unpleasant. Imagine again that you are falling feet first toward the event horizon of a black hole. You would feel your feet, which would be closer to the black hole, being pulled in more strongly than your head. This is a tidal force. At first it would be minor, but as you fell closer it would become very large. Another tidal force would compress you as your left side and your right side both fell toward the centre of the black hole. For any black hole with a

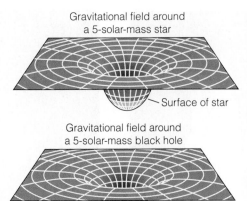

Gravitational field around a 5-solar-mass star

Surface of star

Gravitational field around a 5-solar-mass black hole

To the event horizon

Figure 8.19 If you fell into the gravitational field of a star, you would hit the star's surface before you fell very far. Because a black hole is so small, you could fall much deeper into its gravitational field and eventually cross the event horizon. At a distance, the two gravitational fields are the same.

mass like that of a star, the tidal forces would crush you laterally and stretch you longitudinally, long before you reached the event horizon (Figure 8.20). Needless to say, this would render you inoperative as a thoughtful observer.

You now know how to find a black hole: Look for a strong source of X-rays that may come from matter being compressed and stretched just before it disappears as it reaches the event horizon.

The Search for Black Holes

An isolated black hole is totally invisible because nothing can escape from the event horizon. But a black hole into which matter is flowing would be a source of X-rays. Of course, X-rays can't escape from *inside* the event horizon, but X-rays emitted by the heated matter flowing into the black hole can escape if the X-rays are emitted *before* the matter crosses the event horizon. An isolated black hole in space will not have much matter flowing into it, but a black hole in a binary system might receive a steady flow of matter transferred from its companion star. This suggests you can search for black holes by searching among X-ray binaries.

You have learned about X-ray binaries, such as Hercules X-1, which contain a neutron star and emit X-rays much as a binary containing a black hole should. You can tell the difference in two ways. If the compact object emits pulses, you know it is a neutron star. Otherwise, you can check the mass of the object. If the mass of the compact object is greater than about 3 solar masses, the object cannot be a neutron star, and you can conclude that it must be a black hole.

The first X-ray binary suspected of harbouring a black hole was Cygnus X-1 (see **Canadians in Astronomy** in

time dilation The slowing of moving clocks or clocks in strong gravitational fields.

gravitational redshift The lengthening of the wavelength of a photon as it escapes from a gravitational field.

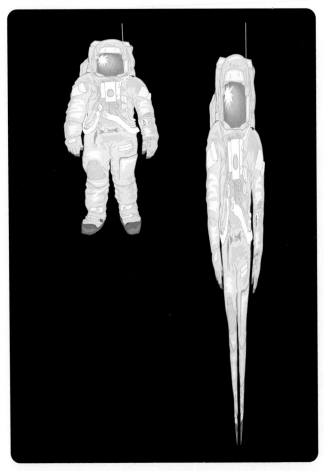

Figure 8.20 Leaping feet first into a black hole. A person of normal proportions (left) would be distorted by tidal forces (right) a long time before reaching the event horizon around a typical black hole of stellar mass. Tidal forces would stretch the body lengthwise while compressing it laterally. Astrophysicists call this effect "spaghettification."

Figure 8.21 The X-ray source Cygnus X-1 consists of a supergiant B star and a compact object orbiting each other. Gas from the supergiant's stellar wind flows into the hot accretion disk around the compact object, and astronomers detect X-rays from the disk.

Chapter 10). It contains a supergiant B0 star and a compact object orbiting each other with a period of 5.6 days. Matter flows from the B0 star as a strong stellar wind, and some of that matter enters a hot accretion disk around the compact object (Figure 8.21). The accretion disk is about five times larger in diameter than the orbit of Earth's moon, and the inner few hundred kilometres of the disk have a temperature of about 2 million Kelvin—hot enough to radiate X-rays. The compact object is invisible, but Doppler shifts in the spectrum reveal the motion of the B0 star around the centre of mass of the binary. From the geometry of the orbit, astronomers have calculated the mass of the compact object to be at least 3.8 solar masses, well above the maximum for a neutron star.

As X-ray telescopes have located more X-ray objects, the list of black hole candidates has grown to a few dozen. Some of these objects are shown in Table 8.2. Each candidate is a compact object surrounded by a hot accretion disk in a close X-ray binary system without regular pulsations. A few of the binary systems are easier to analyze than others, but it has become clear that some

of these objects are too massive to be neutron stars. Scientists cannot have absolute proof, but the evidence is now overwhelming: Black holes really do exist.

Another way to confirm that black holes are real is to search for evidence of their distinguishing characteristic—event horizons—and that search also has been successful. In one study, astronomers selected 12 X-ray binary systems, six of which seemed to contain neutron stars and six of which were expected to contain black holes. Using X-ray telescopes, the astronomers could see flares of energy as blobs of matter fell into the accretion disks and spiralled inward. In the six systems thought to contain neutron stars, the astronomers could also detect bursts of energy when the blobs of matter finally fell onto the surfaces of the neutron stars. In these six systems, however, the blobs of matter spiralled inward through the accretion disks and vanished without final bursts of energy. Evidently, those blobs of matter had approached the event horizons and become undetectable due

Table 8.2 | Seven Black Hole Binaries

Object	Star	Orbital Period	Mass of Black Hole
Cygnus X–1	BOI	5.6 days	10 $M_\odot$
LMC X–3	B3V	1.7 days	>8 $M_\odot$
A0620–00	KV	7.75 hours	11 ± 1.9 $M_\odot$
V404 Cygni	G-KV	6.47 days	12 ± 3 $M_\odot$
GRO J1655-40	F5V	2.61 days	6.9 ± 1 $M_\odot$
QZ Vul	KV	8 hours	10 ± 4 $M_\odot$
4U 1543–47	AV	1.123 days	2.7–7.5 $M_\odot$

to time dilation and gravitational redshift. This is dramatic evidence that event horizons are real.

Energy from Compact Objects: Jets

It is a common misconception to think that it is impossible to get any energy out of a black hole. A later chapter describes galaxies that radiate vast amounts of energy from massive black holes; in this section you will see how a compact object and an accretion disk can eject powerful jets and beams of energy.

Whether a compact object is a black hole or a neutron star, it has a strong gravitational field. Any matter flowing into that field is accelerated inward, and because it must conserve angular momentum, it flows into an accretion disk made so hot by friction that the inner regions can emit X-rays and gamma rays. Somehow the spinning accretion disk can emit powerful beams of gas and radiation along its axis of rotation. The process isn't well understood, but it seems to involve magnetic fields that get caught in the accretion disk and are twisted into tightly wound tubes that squirt gas and radiation out of the disk and confine it in narrow beams.

This process is similar to the bipolar outflows ejected by protostars (Chapter 7), but it is much more powerful. One example of this process is an X-ray binary called SS 433. Its optical spectrum shows sets of spectral lines that are Doppler-shifted by about one-fourth the speed of light, with one set shifted to the red and one set shifted to the blue. Apparently, SS 433 is a binary system in which a compact object (probably a black hole) pulls matter from its companion star and forms an extremely hot accretion disk. Jets of high-temperature gas blast away in beams aimed in opposite directions. SS 433 is a prototype that illustrates how the gravitational field around a compact object can produce powerful beams of radiation and matter.

Energy from Compact Objects: Gamma-Ray Bursts

During the 1960s the United States put a series of satellites in orbit to watch for bursts of gamma rays from Earth that would indicate nuclear weapons tests in violation of an international treaty. The experts were startled when the satellites detected about one **gamma-ray burst** coming from space per day. The Compton Gamma Ray Observatory launched in 1991 discovered that gamma-ray bursts were occurring all over the sky and not from any particular region. Starting in 1997, new satellites in orbit were able to detect gamma-ray bursts, determine their location in the sky, and immediately alert astronomers on the ground. When telescopes swivelled to image the locations of the bursts, they detected

fading glows that resembled supernovae. This has led to the conclusion that some relatively long gamma-ray bursts are produced by a kind of supernova explosion called a **hypernova** (Figure 8.22).

> **gamma-ray burst** A sudden, powerful burst of gamma rays.
>
> **hypernova** Produced when a very massive star collapses into a black hole; a possible source of gamma-ray bursts.

A Hypernova Explosion

The collapsing core of a massive star drives its energy along the axis of rotation because ...

... the rotation of the star slows the collapse of the equatorial regions.

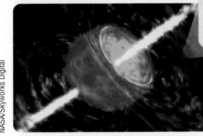

Within seconds, the remaining parts of the star fall in.

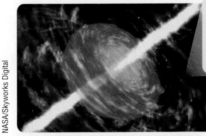

Beams of gas and radiation strike surrounding gas and generate beams of gamma rays.

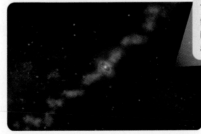

The gamma-ray burst fades in seconds, and a hot accretion disk is left around the black hole.

Figure 8.22 The collapse of the cores of extremely massive stars can produce hypernova explosions, which are thought to be the source of gamma-ray bursts longer than two seconds.

Theoretical calculations indicate that a star more massive than some threshold around 15 or 20 solar masses will collapse and become a black hole when its nuclear fuel is exhausted. Models show that the collapsing star would conserve angular momentum and spin very rapidly, and this would slow the collapse of the equatorial parts of the star. The poles of the star would fall in quickly, and that would focus the beams of intense radiation and ejected gas that was blasting out along the axis of rotation—resulting in a hypernova. If either of those beams happens to point in the right direction, Earth would receive a powerful gamma-ray burst. The evidence seems clear that at least some of the gamma-ray bursts are produced by hypernovae. Massive stars rarely explode as hypernovae in any one galaxy, but the gamma-ray bursts they produce are so powerful that astronomers can detect these explosions among a vast number of galaxies. Some gamma-ray bursts may be produced by the merger of two neutron stars or a neutron star and a black hole, and others by sudden shifts in the crusts of highly magnetized neutron stars.

Incidentally, if a gamma-ray burst occurred only 1000 ly from Earth, the gamma rays would shower Earth with radiation equivalent to a 10 000-megaton nuclear blast. (The largest bombs ever made were a few tens of megatons.) The gamma rays could create enough nitric oxide in the atmosphere to produce intense acid rain and destroy the ozone layer, exposing life on Earth to a deadly level of solar ultraviolet radiation. Gamma-ray bursts can occur relatively near Earth as often as every few 100 million years; these events could be one of the causes of the mass extinctions that show up in the fossil record.

The Big Picture

The life and death stories of stars are important because Earth depends on one star, the Sun. Perhaps even more important, the lives and deaths of previous generations of stars created the atomic elements of which Earth and you are made. If those stars hadn't lived and died, you would not exist. This chapter explored details of the life and death stories of stars and how the types of remains that stars produce depends on the mass of the individual star. Stars with masses like that of the Sun end as white dwarfs, but more massive stars leave behind the strangest beasts in the cosmic zoo: neutron stars and black holes. Some matter from dying stars escapes back into the interstellar medium and is incorporated into new stars and the planets that form with them. The death of stars is part of a great cycle of stellar birth and death that includes the Sun, Earth, and you, and by understanding the death of stars, you can better understand your role in the evolution of the universe.

Review and Discussion Questions

Review Questions

1. What happens to a star when it uses up the last of the hydrogen fuel in its core?
2. Why does helium fusion require a higher temperature than hydrogen fusion?
3. How will the Sun and stars smaller than the Sun die?
4. How can the contraction of an inert helium core trigger the ignition of a hydrogen-fusion shell?
5. Why does the expansion of a star's envelope make it cooler and more luminous?
6. How can star clusters confirm astronomers' theories of stellar evolution?
7. What causes an aging giant star to produce a planetary nebula?
8. Why can't a white dwarf have a mass greater than 1.4 solar masses?
9. How can a star of as much as 8 solar masses form a white dwarf when it dies?
10. What happens if an evolving star is in a binary star system?
11. How do massive stars die?
12. How can the inward collapse of the core of a massive star produce an outward explosion?
13. What is the difference between type I and type II supernovae?
14. What is the difference between a supernova explosion and a nova explosion?
15. What are neutron stars, and how do you know they really exist?

16. How are neutron stars and white dwarfs similar? How do they differ?
17. Why is there an upper limit to the mass of neutron stars?
18. If neutron stars are hot, why aren't they very luminous?
19. How does the lighthouse model explain pulsars?
20. What evidence can you cite that pulsars are neutron stars?
21. How can a neutron star in a binary system generate X-rays? How can a black hole emit X-rays?
22. What evidence can you cite that black holes really exist?
23. Discuss the possible causes of gamma-ray bursts.
24. **How Do We Know?** Why do scientists say that a hypothesis or theory is confirmed, but do not say it is proven?

Discussion Questions

1. Representational-colour radio images and time-exposure photographs of astronomical images show aspects of nature you can never see with unaided eyes. Can you think of common images in newspapers or on television that reveal phenomena you can't see?
2. In your opinion, has the link between pulsars and neutron stars been sufficiently tested to be called a theory, or should it be called a hypothesis? What about the existence of black holes?
3. Why wouldn't an accretion disk orbiting a giant star get as hot as an accretion disk orbiting a compact object?

Learning to Look

1. The star cluster in the photo at the right contains many hot, blue, luminous stars. Sketch its H–R diagram and discuss its probable age.

NASA, N. Walborn and J. Maíz-Apellániz (Space Telescope Science Institute, Baltimore, MD), R. Barbá (La Plata Observatory, La Plata, Argentina)

2. What processes caused a medium-mass star to produce the nebula at the right? The nebula is now about 0.1 ly in diameter and still expanding. What will happen to it?

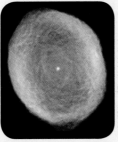

NASA/ESA and The Hubble Heritage Team/STScI/AURA

3. The image at right combines X-ray (blue), visible (green), and radio (red) images. Observations show the sphere is expanding at a high speed and is filled with very hot gas. What kind of object produced this nebula? Roughly how old do you think it must be?

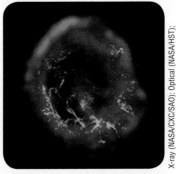

X-ray (NASA/CXC/SAO); Optical (NASA/HST); Radio (ACTA)

4. What is happening in the artist's impression at the right? How would you distinguish between a neutron star and a black hole in such a system?

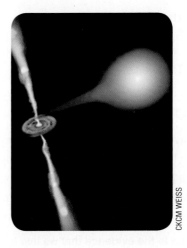

CKCM WEISS

9

The Milky Way Galaxy

CHAPTER OUTLINE

GUIDEPOST

You have traced the life stories of stars from their birth in clouds of gas and dust to their deaths as white dwarfs, neutron stars, or black holes. Now you are ready to step back and view stars in vast communities called galaxies. This chapter focuses on our home galaxy, the Milky Way, and addresses four important questions:

- **What is the evidence that we live in a galaxy?**
- **What is the evidence that our Milky Way is a spiral galaxy, and what are the spiral arms?**
- **How did the Milky Way Galaxy form and evolve?**
- **What lies at the centre of the Milky Way Galaxy?**

Discovering the Milky Way Galaxy by answering these questions will bring you one more step toward understanding the universe as a whole. In the chapters that follow, you will leave your home galaxy and voyage out among the billions of other galaxies that fill the depths of the universe.

The Stars Are Yours is the title of a popular astronomy book written by James S. Pickering in 1948. The point of the title is that the stars belong to everyone equally, and you can enjoy the stars as if you owned them. You live inside one of the largest of the star systems that fill the universe. Our Milky Way Galaxy is over 80 000 ly in diameter and contains over 100 billion stars. As you read this chapter, you will learn not only about your home galaxy but also how the stars of the galaxy have cooked up the atoms heavier than helium. You have already learned how the cores of massive stars make atoms heavier than helium and how supernovae

In less than a hundred years, we have found a new way to think of ourselves. From sitting at the center of the universe, we now find ourselves orbiting an average-sized sun, which is just one of millions of stars in our own Milky Way galaxy.

Stephen Hawking,
Physicist and author

The Milky Way over Ontario

blast those atoms back into space as well as other even heavier atoms made during the supernova explosion.

In this chapter you will see how the stars in the Milky Way Galaxy have, generation after generation, made the atoms now in your body.

9.1 The Discovery of the Galaxy

It seems odd to say astronomers discovered something that is all around you. However, until the early 20th century, no one knew what the Milky Way was.

It isn't obvious that you live in a galaxy. You are inside, and you see nearby stars scattered in all directions over the sky, whereas the more distant clouds of stars in the galaxy make a faint band of light circling the sky, as Figure 9.1 demonstrates. The ancient Greeks named that band *galaxias kuklos*, the "milky circle." The Romans changed the name to *via lactea*, "milky road" or "milky way." It was not until early in the 20th century that astronomers understood that humans live inside a great wheel of stars and that the universe is filled with other such star systems. Drawing on the Greek word for milk, astronomers called these star systems *galaxies*.

The Great Star System

Centuries before Galileo's definitive observational proof in 1610, philosophers and astronomers worldwide proposed that the Milky Way was a band of starlight. Greek philosophers Anaxagoras and Democritus, around 400 BCE, argued that the Milky Way consisted of myriad distant stars. The same description is found in the writings of Latin poet Manilius (1st century CE), Persian astronomer Abū-Rayhān al-Bīrūnī (11th century), Andalusian astronomer

Figure 9.1 The Milky Way looks quite different for observers at various latitudes. In the northern hemisphere, it looks fainter and smoother than in the southern hemisphere. Baltic cultures, the Finnish, and the Canadian Cree called it "the path of the birds." In Cree, the Milky Way is *Neepin Pinesisuk Meskinaw*, "the summer birds' path," which Niska, the celestial goose (known also as Cygnus, the "swan" constellation, seen in the centre as the large cross), and terrestrial birds followed when migrating. To the Vikings the Milky Way was a road to the gods ("Road to Valhalla") and to the Maya it was the way to the underworld. Going south, the Milky Way becomes richer; dark nebulae appear, breaking the structure into branches, like river systems. In Chinese, Japanese, Korean, Hindu, Australian (Yolngu), and Peruvian traditions, the Milky Way was regarded as the celestial counterpart of terrestrial rivers. To the Quechua of Peru, the Vilcanota River was a terrestrial reflection of a heavenly river, and the two rivers were exchanging water in a unique water system. !Kung people from the Kalahari in Botswana and Chumash from California saw the Milky Way straight overhead and considered it "the backbone of night."

© Thomas G. Matheson

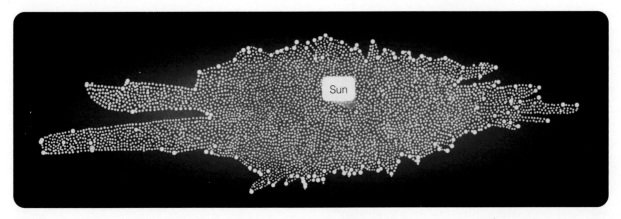

Figure 9.2 In 1785, William Herschel published this diagram showing the shape of the star system as if it could be viewed edge-on from outside.

Avempace (12th century), and famous Suni philosopher Ibn Qayyim Al-Jawziyya (14th century).

Galileo's telescope revealed that the glowing Milky Way is made up of stars, and later astronomers realized that the great cloud of stars in which the Sun is located, which they called the star system, must be wheel shaped. If the star system were spherical, for example, you would see stars scattered more or less uniformly in all directions over the sky. Only a wheel or disk shape would look, from the inside, like the Milky Way band encircling the sky.

The English astronomers Sir William Herschel (1738–1822) and his sister Caroline Herschel attempted to gauge the true shape of the star system by counting stars in 683 different directions in the sky. In directions where they saw more stars, they assumed the star system extended further into space. They concluded that the star system has a disk shape with some noticeable "holes" where stars were lacking around the edges. Figure 9.2 illustrates the diagram the Herschels published in 1785. Modern astronomers know that those apparent holes are caused by dense clouds of gas and dust that block the view of more distant stars. The Herschels counted similar numbers of stars in most directions around the Milky Way and concluded that the Sun and Earth are near the centre of the star system.

As the 20th century began, astronomers still believed that the Sun was located near the centre of a wheel-shaped star system that they estimated was about 15 000 ly in diameter. How humanity realized the truth about the size of the galaxy, Earth's location in it, and the galaxy's location in a much larger universe of other galaxies, is an adventure that begins with a woman studying stars that pulsate and leads to a man studying distant star clusters. The next section follows that story because it is an important historical moment in human history and because it illustrates how scientists build on the work of their predecessors; step-by-step they refine their ideas about the natural world.

The Size of the Milky Way

It is a common misconception of poets that the stars are eternal and unchanging, but astronomers have known for centuries that some stars change in brightness. Of course, novae and supernovae burst into view, grow brighter, and then fade, but many other variable stars actually pulsate like beating hearts. The period of pulsation is the time it takes a star to complete a cycle from bright to faint to bright again. You will learn next how the properties of some types of variable stars allowed astronomers to measure the size of the galaxy.

In 1912, Henrietta Leavitt (1868–1921) was studying a star cloud in the southern sky known as the Small Magellanic Cloud. On her photographic plates she found many variable stars, and she noticed that the brightest had the longest periods. Because all the variables were in the same cloud at nearly the same distance, she concluded that there was a relationship between the pulsation periods and intrinsic brightness—that is, the luminosity or true total power output—of those variable stars.

The stars Leavitt saw, **Cepheid variable stars**, are named after the first such star discovered, Delta Cephei. They are giant and supergiant stars with pulsation periods of 1 to 60 days and with properties that lie in a region of the H–R diagram known as the **instability strip** (Figure 9.3). As stars evolve, and the points that represent their temperatures and luminosities move in the H–R diagram, they can cross into the instability strip and start pulsating; they stop pulsating when they evolve out of the strip. Massive stars are larger and pulsate more slowly. Lower-mass

Cepheid variable stars Variable stars with pulsation periods of 1 to 60 days and whose period of variation is related to their luminosity.

instability strip The region of the H–R diagram in which stars are unstable to pulsation. A star evolving through this strip becomes a variable star.

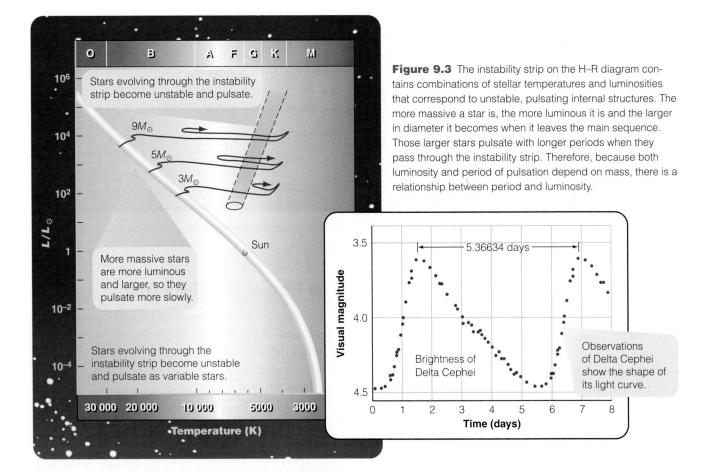

Figure 9.3 The instability strip on the H–R diagram contains combinations of stellar temperatures and luminosities that correspond to unstable, pulsating internal structures. The more massive a star is, the more luminous it is and the larger in diameter it becomes when it leaves the main sequence. Those larger stars pulsate with longer periods when they pass through the instability strip. Therefore, because both luminosity and period of pulsation depend on mass, there is a relationship between period and luminosity.

stars are less luminous and, being smaller, pulsate faster. This explains why, as first noticed by Leavitt, the long-period Cepheids are more luminous than the short-period Cepheids. That is now known as the **period–luminosity relation**, shown graphically in Figure 9.4. You may be interested to learn that the North Star, Polaris, is a Cepheid variable with a pulsation period of 4 days.

Star Clusters and the Centre of the Galaxy

A young astronomer named Harlow Shapley (1885–1972) began the discovery of the true nature of the Milky Way when he noticed that different kinds of star clusters have different distributions in the sky. In Chapter 8 you learned about two types of star clusters: open clusters and globular clusters. Open clusters are concentrated along the Milky Way. Globular clusters are widely scattered, but Shapley noticed that the globular clusters were more common toward the constellations Sagittarius and Scorpius (see Figure 9.5a).

Shapley assumed that the concentration of globular clusters is controlled by the combined gravitational field of all the stars in the galaxy. In that case, he realized he could study the size and extent of the galaxy by studying the globular clusters. To do that he needed to measure the distances to as many globular clusters as possible.

Globular clusters are much too far away to have measurable parallaxes, but they do contain variable stars. Shapley knew of Leavitt's work on these stars, which depended on their relative, rather than true, luminosities. Cepheids are rare, and there are none near enough to have measurable parallaxes, so their true luminosities were not then known. Shapley realized that he could calculate the distance to the globular clusters if he found the true luminosities of the Cepheid variable stars in the clusters.

Through a statistical process involving measurements of position shifts due to their motions along the celestial sphere, called **proper motions**, Shapley found the average distances of a few of the nearest Cepheids, and from that their average luminosities. That meant he could replace Leavitt's apparent magnitudes with absolute magnitudes on the period–luminosity diagram (Figure 9.4).

period–luminosity relation The relation between period of pulsation and intrinsic brightness among Cepheid variable stars.

proper motion The rate at which a star moves across the sky, measured in arc seconds per year.

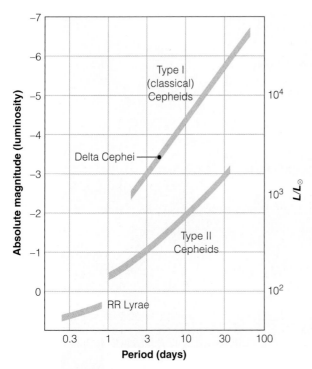

Figure 9.4 The period–luminosity diagram is a graph of the luminosity of variable stars versus their periods of pulsation. The diagram is used for distance calculations in which we compare apparent and absolute magnitudes. For that reason, it is most convenient to represent luminosity on the vertical axis with absolute magnitude. Modern astronomers know there are two types of Cepheids as well as other similar types of variable stars. This is something astronomers in the early 20th century could not recognize in their limited data, which caused some errors in the first determinations of the size of the Milky Way.

Astronomers say that Shapley **calibrated** the variable stars for distance (see **How Do We Know ? 9.1**).

Having calibrated the Cepheids, Shapley could find the distance to the globular star clusters. He identified the variable stars in the clusters and determined their apparent magnitudes from his photographs. Comparison of apparent and absolute magnitudes gave him the distance to the star cluster based on the inverse square law for light (see Chapter 6).

Finally, Shapley plotted the direction and distance to the globular clusters and saw that they form a great swarm that is not centred on the Sun. Instead, the centre of the galaxy's cloud of clusters lies many thousands of light-years in the direction of Sagittarius. By analogy, if you see a bunch of tall buildings, and they are all together in one direction away from you, you might conclude that downtown is over there, and you are in the suburbs. Evidently the centre of the star system is in Sagittarius and far away. The star system is much bigger than anyone had suspected (Figure 9.5b). You live not near the centre of a small star system but in the suburbs of a very big wheel of stars, a galaxy.

Why did astronomers before Shapley think humanity lived near the centre of a small star system? The answer: Space is filled with gas and dust that dims the view of distant stars. When you look toward the band of the Milky Way, you can see only the neighbourhood near the Sun. Most of the star system is hidden and, like a traveller in a fog, you seem to be at the centre of a small region. Shapley was able to see the globular clusters at greater distances because they lie outside the plane of the Milky Way and are not dimmed very much by the interstellar dust.

Building on Shapley's work, other astronomers began to suspect that some of the faint patches of light visible through telescopes were other galaxies like our own. In 1923, Edwin Hubble photographed individual stars in the Andromeda Galaxy, and in 1924, he identified Cepheids there, allowing its distance to be estimated. As a result, it became clear that our galaxy is just one in a universe filled with galaxies.

Components of the Galaxy

Our galaxy, like many others, contains two primary components: a disk and a sphere. Figure 9.6 shows these components and other features discussed in this section.

The **disk component** consists of all matter confined to the plane of rotation—that is, everything in the disk itself. This includes stars, open star clusters, and nearly all of the galaxy's gas and dust. As you will learn in more detail in the next section, the disk is the site of most of the star formation in the galaxy because it contains a lot of gas. Consequently, the disk is illuminated by recently formed brilliant, blue, massive stars and has an overall relatively blue colour.

The diameter of the disk and the position of the Sun are difficult to determine accurately. Interstellar dust blocks the view in the plane of the galaxy, so astronomers cannot see to the centre or to the edge easily, and the outer edge of the disk is not well defined. Most recent studies suggest the Sun is about 26 000 ly from the centre. The Sun and Earth seem to be about two-thirds of the way from the centre to the edge, so the diameter of our galaxy appears to be about 80 000 ly, but that isn't known to better than 10 percent precision. This is the diameter of the luminous part of our galaxy, the part you would see from a distance. You will learn later that strong evidence shows that our galaxy is much larger than that, but the outer parts are not luminous. It may surprise you to learn that

calibrate To make observations of reference objects, checks on instrument performance, calculations of unit conversions, and so on, needed to completely understand measurements of unknown quantities.

disk component All material confined to the plane of the galaxy.

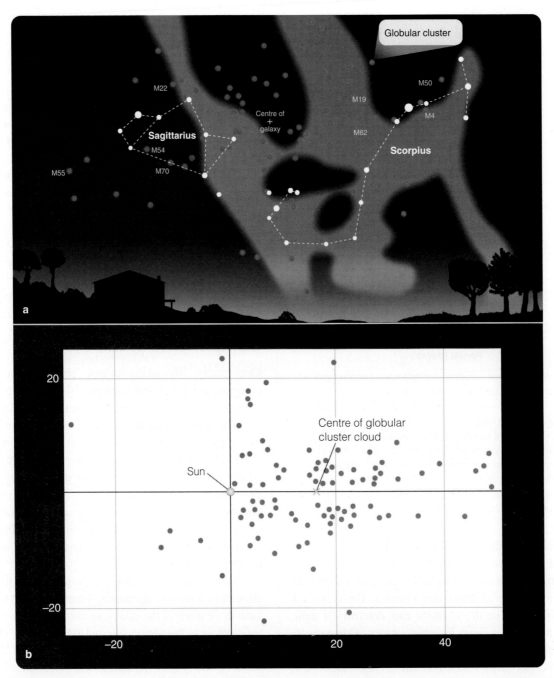

Figure 9.5 (a) Nearly half the catalogued globular clusters (red dots) are located in or near Sagittarius and Scorpius. A few of the brighter globular clusters (labelled with their catalogue designations) are visible with binoculars or small telescopes. Constellations are shown as they appear above the southern horizon on a summer night as seen from latitude 40° N in the northern hemisphere. (b) This is a "side view" of the Milky Way Galaxy's globular clusters. Shapley's study of the clusters and their distances shows that the globular clusters were not centred on the Sun, which is located at the origin of this graph, but rather they formed a great cloud centred far away in the direction of Sagittarius. Distances are given in thousands of parsecs and correspond to Shapley's original calibration that produced values more than two times larger than the modern calibration.

spiral arms Long spiral pattern of bright stars, star clusters, gas, and dust. Spiral arms extend from the centre to the edge of the disk of spiral galaxies.

the disk of spiral galaxies is very thin; in fact, the disk of the Milky Way spiral galaxy is merely 300 ly.

Observations made at other than visual wavelengths can help astronomers peer through the dust and gas. Infrared and radio photons have wavelengths long enough to be unaffected by the dust. Thus, a map of the sky at long infrared wavelengths reveals the disk of our galaxy (Figure 9.7).

The most striking features of the disk component are the **spiral arms**—long curves of bright stars, star clusters,

Figure 9.6 An artist's conception of the Milky Way Galaxy: seen face-on and edge-on. Note the position of the Sun and the distribution of globular clusters in the halo. Hot, blue stars light up the spiral arms. Only the inner halo is shown here. At this scale, the entire halo would be larger than a dinner plate. Also note that globular clusters are not to scale in this figure.

gas, and dust. Such spiral arms are easily visible in other galaxies, and you will see later how astronomers found that our own galaxy has a spiral pattern.

The second component of our galaxy is the **spherical component**, which includes all matter in our galaxy scattered in a roughly spherical distribution around the centre. This includes a large halo and the central bulge.

The **halo** is a spherical cloud of thinly scattered stars and globular star clusters. It contains only about 2 percent as many stars as the disk of the galaxy and has very little gas and dust. Consequently, with no raw material available, no new stars are forming in the halo. In fact, the halo stars are mostly old, cool giants or dim lower-main-sequence stars, plus, as revealed by recent careful studies, old white dwarfs that are difficult to detect. Astronomers can map the halo of our galaxy by studying the more easily detected giant stars.

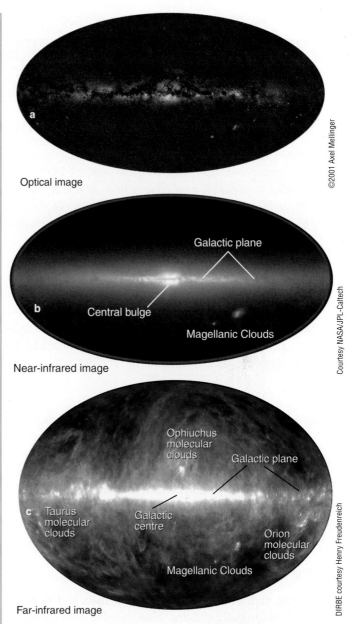

Figure 9.7 In these images, the entire sky has been projected onto ovals with the centre of the galaxy at the centre of each oval. The Milky Way extends from left to right. (a) In the human visible image, the gas and dust obscure the view of inner parts of the Milky Way, such as the central bulge. (b) In the near-infrared image, the central bulge is prominent, and dust clouds block the view along the Milky Way. (c) At far-infrared wavelengths, the dust emits significant blackbody radiation and glows brightly.

The **central bulge** is the dense cloud of stars that surrounds the centre of our galaxy. It has a radius of about 6500 ly and is a slightly

spherical component The part of the galaxy that includes all matter in a spherical distribution around its centre (the halo and central bulge).

halo The spherical region of a spiral galaxy, containing a thin scattering of stars, star clusters, and small amounts of gas.

central bulge The dense cloud of stars that surrounds the centre of our galaxy.

HOW DO WE KNOW? 9.1

The Calibration of One Parameter to Find Another

Astronomers often say that Shapley "calibrated" the Cepheids for the determination of distance, meaning that he did all the detailed background work so that the Cepheids could be used to find distances. Other astronomers could then use the Cepheids without repeating the calibration.

Calibration is actually very common in science. Chemists, for instance, have carefully calibrated the colours of certain compounds against acidity. They can quickly measure the acidity of a solution by dipping it into a slip of paper containing the indicator compound and looking at the colour. They don't have to repeat the careful calibration of the paper slips every time they measure acidity.

Engineers in steel mills have calibrated the colour of molten steel against its temperature. They can use a handheld device that measures the colour of the blackbody radiation from a ladle of molten steel and then looks up the temperature from a calibrated table. They don't have to repeat the calibration every time. Astronomers have made the same kind of colour–temperature calibration for stars.

As you read about any science, notice how calibrations are used to simplify common measurements. But notice, too, how important it is to get the calibration right. An error in calibration can throw off every measurement made with that calibration. Some of the biggest errors in science have been errors of calibration.

flattened spheroid. It is hard to observe because thick dust in the disk scatters and absorbs radiation of visible wavelengths, but observations at longer wavelengths can penetrate the dust. The bulge seems to contain little gas and dust, and there is not much star formation there. Most of the stars in the central bulge are old, cool stars like those in the halo.

The Mass of the Galaxy

The vast numbers of stars in the disk, halo, and central bulge lead to a basic question: How massive is the galaxy?

When you needed to find the masses of stars, you studied the orbital motions of the pairs of stars in binary systems. To find the mass of the galaxy, you must look at the orbital motions of the stars within the galaxy. Every star in the galaxy follows an orbit around the centre of mass of the galaxy. In the disk, the stars follow parallel circular orbits, and astronomers say the disk of the galaxy rotates. That rotation can allow an estimate of the mass of the galaxy. Consequently, any discussion of the mass of the galaxy is also a discussion of the rotation of the galaxy and the orbits of the stars within the galaxy.

Astronomers can find the orbits of stars by finding how they move. Of course, the Doppler effect reveals a star's radial velocity (see Chapter 5). In addition, if astronomers can measure the distance to a star and its proper motion, they can find the velocity of the star perpendicular

to the radial direction. Combining all of this information, astronomers can find the shape of the star's orbit.

As you can see in Figure 9.8, the orbital motions of the stars in the halo are strikingly different from those in the disk. In the halo, each star and globular cluster follows its own randomly tipped elliptical orbit. (To review globular clusters see **Visualizing Astronomy 8.1, Star Cluster**

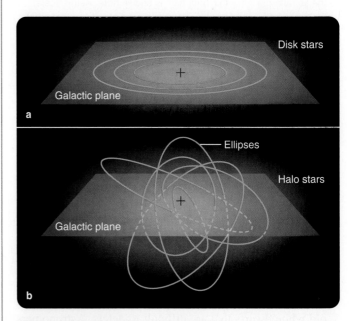

Figure 9.8 (a) Stars in the galactic disk have nearly circular orbits that lie in the plane of the galaxy. (b) Stars in the halo have randomly oriented, highly eccentric, elongated orbits.

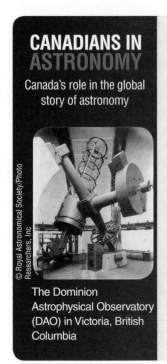
John Stanley Plaskett

John S. Plaskett, originally from Hickson, Ontario, worked as a mechanic in the physics department at the University of Toronto. At the age of 30 he decided to enter undergraduate studies. After graduating in 1899, he was hired at Ottawa's Dominion Observatory—first as a mechanic, then as an astronomer. Plaskett made great contributions to astronomy in many areas. He discovered a massive binary star, named after him as Plaskett's Star. His work on the radial velocities of galactic stars confirmed Oort's model of galactic rotation. In 1935, he published the first detailed analysis of the structure of the Milky Way Galaxy. Interested in engineering and astronomy, he improved the Dominion Observatory telescope, building a spectroscope for it. He lobbied the Canadian parliament for a 1.8-m telescope that was, under his supervision, built for the Dominion Astrophysical Observatory in Victoria, BC. When completed in 1918, this was the world's largest telescope. Still working, it is named the Plaskett Telescope. He was the director of the Dominion Astrophysical Observatory until 1935. In 1984, Minor Planet No 2905 was named Plaskett in honour of J. S. Plaskett and his son H. H. Plaskett, also an astronomer. The Royal Astronomical Society of Canada and the Canadian Astronomical Society have established the Plaskett Medal, which is awarded to the top graduate from a Canadian university who is judged to have submitted the most outstanding doctoral thesis in astronomy and astrophysics.

H–R Diagrams). These orbits carry the stars and clusters far out into the spherical halo where they move slowly, but when they fall back into the inner part of the galaxy, their velocities increase. Motions in the halo do not resemble a general rotation but are more like the random motions of a swarm of bees. In contrast, the stars in the disk of the galaxy move in the same direction in nearly circular orbits that lie in the plane of the galaxy. The Sun is a disk star and follows a nearly circular orbit around the galaxy that always remains within the disk.

You can use the orbital motion of the Sun to find the mass of the galaxy inside the Sun's orbit. By observing the radial velocity of distant galaxies in various directions around the sky, astronomers can tell that the Sun moves at about 240 km/s in the direction of Cygnus, carrying Earth and the other planets of our solar system along with it. Because its orbit is a circle with a radius of 6000 ly, you can divide the circumference of the orbit by the velocity and find that the Sun completes a single orbit in about 210 million years.

If you think of the Sun and the centre of mass of our galaxy as two objects orbiting each other, you now have enough information to determine the mass of the galaxy. The Milky Way Galaxy must have a mass of about 100 billion solar masses. This estimate is uncertain for a number of reasons. First, you don't know the radius of the Sun's orbit with great certainty. Astronomers estimate the radius as 26 000 ly, but they could be wrong by 10 percent or more, and the radius gets cubed in the calculation, which has a large effect. Second, this estimate of the mass includes only the mass inside the Sun's orbit. A uniform spread of mass outside the Sun's orbit will not affect its orbital motion. Thus, 100 billion solar masses is a lower limit for the mass of the galaxy. However, no one knows exactly how much to increase the estimate to include the rest of the mass in the galaxy that lies outside the Sun's orbit.

The measured motion of the stars shows that the disk does not rotate as a solid body. Each star follows its own orbit, and stars in some regions have shorter or longer orbital periods than the Sun. This is called differential rotation. (Recall from Chapter 5 the term *differential rotation* as it applied to the Sun.) The graph in Figure 9.9 provides an example of the orbital velocity of stars at various orbital radii in the galaxy; the graph is called a **rotation curve**. If all of the mass in the galaxy were concentrated at its centre, the orbital velocity would be high near the centre and decline away from the centre. This kind of motion has been called *Keplerian motion* because it follows Kepler's third law, and it applies to our solar system, where nearly all the mass is in the Sun.

You already know the galaxy's mass is not all concentrated at its centre, but if most of the mass were inside the orbit of the Sun, the orbital velocities should decline at greater distances. Many observations confirm, however, that velocities do not decline and may actually increase at greater distance; this observation shows that larger and larger orbits enclose more and more mass. Although it is difficult to

rotation curve A graph of orbital velocity versus radius in the disk of a galaxy.

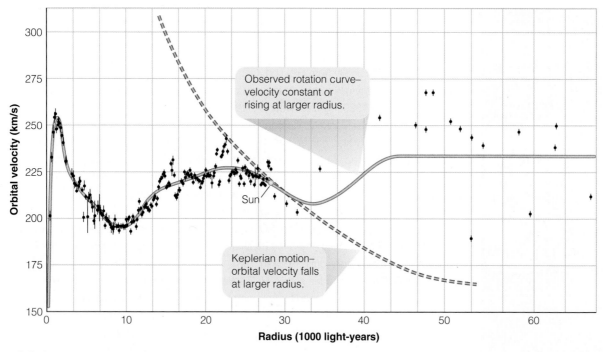

Figure 9.9 The rotation curve of our galaxy is plotted here as orbital speed versus radius. Data points show measurements made by radio telescopes. Observations outside the orbit of the Sun are much more uncertain, and the data points scatter widely. Orbital speeds do not decline outside the orbit of the Sun, as you would expect if most of the mass of the galaxy were concentrated toward the centre. Rather, the curve is approximately flat at great distances, suggesting that the galaxy contains significant mass outside the orbit of the Sun.

dark halo The low-density extension of the halo of our galaxy, believed to be composed of dark matter.

dark matter Nonluminous matter that is detected only by its gravitational influence.

determine a precise edge to the visible galaxy, it seems clear that large amounts of matter are located beyond what seems to be the limit of the galaxy's luminous matter.

The evidence is clear that extra mass lies in an extended halo sometimes called a **dark halo**. It may extend up to 10 times farther than the edge of the visible disk and could contain up to 2 trillion solar masses (see Figure 10.6). Some small fraction of this mass is made up of low-luminosity stars and white dwarfs, but most of the matter is not producing any light. Astronomers call it **dark matter** and conclude that it must be some as yet unknown form of matter. The following two chapters return to the question of dark matter, one of the fundamental problems of modern astronomy.

9.2 Spiral Arms and Star Formation

The most striking feature of galaxies like the Milky Way is the system of spiral arms that wind outward through the disk and contain swarms of hot, blue stars; clouds of dust

and gas; and young star clusters. These young objects hint that the spiral arms involve star formation. As you try to understand the spiral arms, you face two questions. First, how can you be sure our galaxy has spiral arms when Earth is embedded inside the galaxy and your view is obscured by gas and dust? Second, why doesn't the differential rotation of the galaxy destroy the arms? The answers to both questions involve star formation.

Tracing the Spiral Arms

Studies of other galaxies show that the spiral arms contain hot, blue stars, and so one way to study the spiral arms of our own galaxy is to locate these stars. Fortunately, this is not difficult, since O and B stars are often found in associations and are easy to detect across great distances because they are very luminous. Unfortunately, at these great distances their parallax is too small to measure, so their distances must be found by other means, usually by spectroscopic parallax (see Chapter 6).

O and B associations in the sky are not located randomly; rather they outline three spiral arms near the Sun, which have been named for the prominent constellations through which they pass (Figure 9.10). Objects used to map spiral arms are

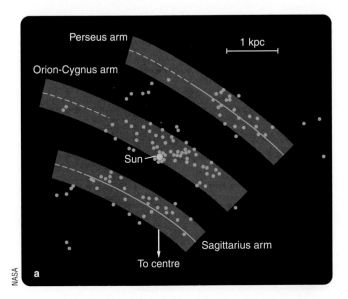

Figure 9.10 (a) Within the Milky Way Galaxy, gas and dust block your view of most of the galaxy's disk, but near the Sun, young O and B stars fall along bands that appear to be segments of spiral arms. (b) Many of the galaxies in the sky are disk shaped, and most of those galaxies have spiral arms. Images of other galaxies show that spiral arms are marked by hot, luminous stars that must be very young; this should make you suspect that spiral arms are related to star formation.

Enhanced visual image

Emission from hydrogen ionized by hot, young stars

Galaxy M51 contains two main spiral arms.

called **spiral tracers**. O and B associations are good spiral tracers because they are bright and easy to see at great distances. Other tracers include young open clusters, clouds of hydrogen ionized by hot stars (emission nebulae), and certain higher-mass variable stars.

Notice that all spiral tracers are young objects. O stars, for example, live for only a few million years. If their orbital velocity is about 200 km/s, they cannot have moved more than about 1600 ly since they formed. This is less than the width of a spiral arm. Because they don't live long enough to move away from the spiral arms, they must have formed there. The youth of spiral tracers provides an important clue about spiral arms. Somehow they are associated with star formation.

Radio telescopes can detect emission from clouds of cool, neutral hydrogen gas. In 1995, the Canadian Galactic Plane Survey started mapping gas and dust in the galactic disk. This project initiated a wide international collaboration. To date, large radio telescopes around the globe—in Argentina, Australia, Canada, China, Europe, India, Taiwan, and the United States—cover almost 90 percent of our Milky Way's gaseous dusty disk, revealing the complex structure of our "galactic ecosystem." Radio maps of the galaxy disk, combined with optical and infrared data, allow astronomers to deduce the spiral pattern of our galaxy. The segments near the Sun are part of a spiral pattern that continues throughout the disk. However, the maps show that the spiral arms are rather irregular and interrupted by branches, spurs, and gaps. The stars in Orion, for example, appear to be a detached segment of a spiral arm, a spur (Figure 9.10a). There are

significant sources of error in the mapping methods, but many of the irregularities along the arms seem real, and images of nearby spiral galaxies show similar features (Figure 9.10b). Studies comparing all the available data on our galaxy's spiral pattern with patterns seen in other galaxies do not necessarily agree, although the newest models suggest that the central bulge in our galaxy is elongated into a bar (Figure 9.11). In the next chapter you will learn that such bars are common in spiral galaxies.

Spiral tracers show that the arms contain young objects, and that suggests active star formation. The radio maps confirm this suspicion by showing that the material needed to make stars, hydrogen gas, is abundant in spiral arms.

Star Formation in Spiral Arms

Having mapped the spiral pattern, you can ask, "What are spiral arms?" You can be sure that they are not physically connected structures. Like a kite string caught on a spinning hubcap, such arms would be wound up and pulled apart by differential rotation within a few tens of millions of years. Yet spiral arms are common in disk-shaped galaxies and must be reasonably permanent features.

The most prominent theory about spiral arms is called the **density wave theory**, which proposes that

spiral tracer Object used to map the spiral arms—for example, O and B associations, open clusters, clouds of ionized hydrogen, and some types of variable stars.

density wave theory Theory proposed to account for spiral arms as compressions of the interstellar medium in the disk of the galaxy.

the arms are waves of compression that move around the galaxy triggering star formation. The density wave is a bit like a traffic jam behind a truck moving slowly along a highway. Seen from an airplane overhead, the jam seems a permanent, though slow-moving, feature. But individual cars overtake the jam from behind, slow down, move up through the jam, wait their turn, pass the truck, and resume speed along the highway. Similarly, clouds of gas overtake the spiral density wave, become compressed in the "traffic jam," and eventually move out in front of the arm, leaving the slower-moving density wave behind.

Of course, star formation will occur where the gas clouds are compressed. Stars pass through the spiral arms unaffected, like bullets passing through a wisp of fog, but large clouds of gas slam into the spiral density wave from behind and are suddenly compressed. The series of images in Figure 9.12 demonstrates how this movement occurs. In Chapter 7 you saw that sudden compression could trigger the formation of stars in a gas cloud. Thus, new stars should form along the spiral arms. The spiral arms are not wound up by differential rotation because they are patterns, not physically connected structures.

The brightest stars, the O and B stars, live such short lives that they never travel far from their birthplace and are found only along the arms. Their presence is what makes the spiral arms glow so brightly, due to both their own light and the emission from clouds of gas excited by UV radiation from the stars (Figure 9.13). Lower-mass stars such as the Sun live longer and have time to move out of the arms and continue their journey around the galaxy. The Sun may

have formed in a star cluster almost 5 billion years ago when a gas cloud smashed into a spiral arm. Since that time, the Sun has escaped from its birth cluster and made about 20 trips around the galaxy, passing through spiral arms many times.

The Spiral Density Wave

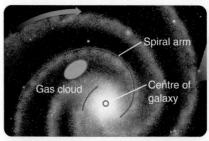

Orbiting gas clouds overtake the spiral arm from behind.

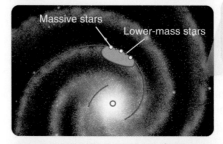

The compression of a gas cloud triggers star formation.

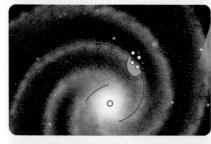

Massive stars are highly luminous and light up the spiral arm.

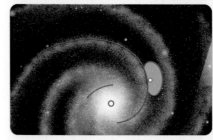

The most massive stars die quickly.

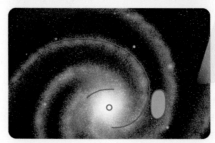

Low-mass stars live long lives but are not highly luminous.

Figure 9.11 This artist's impression of a two-armed model is based on observations with the Spitzer infrared space telescope, 2008. Notice the large central bar.

Figure 9.12 According to the spiral density wave theory, star formation occurs as gas clouds pass through spiral arms.

Visual-wavelength images

a   M100

b   NGC 300

Figure 9.13   (a) Some galaxies are dominated by two spiral arms, but even in these galaxies, minor spurs and branches are common. The spiral density wave can generate the two-armed, grand-design pattern, but self-sustained star formation may be responsible for the irregularities. (b) Many spiral galaxies do not appear to have two dominant spiral arms. Abundant spurs and branches nevertheless suggest that star formation is proceeding robustly in such galaxies. Observations indicate that our Milky Way Galaxy's spiral pattern is intermediate between these two examples.

The density wave theory is very successful in explaining general properties of spiral galaxies, but it has two problems. First, what stimulates the formation of the spiral pattern in the first place? Theorists calculate that minor fluctuations in the galaxy's disk shape or gravitational interactions with passing galaxies may be able to start a density wave. Second, the density wave theory does not account for the branches and spurs in the spiral arms of our own and other galaxies. The solution to this second problem may lie in a process that sustains star formation once it begins.

Star formation can control the shape of spiral patterns if the birth of stars in a cloud of gas can cause the birth of more new stars. Massive stars evolve so quickly that their lifetimes are only an instant in the history of a galaxy, and then they explode as supernovae. You learned in Chapter 7 that bursts of luminosity and jets from newborn stars and the expanding gases of supernova explosions can compress neighbouring clouds of gas and trigger more star formation. This process is known as **self-sustaining star formation.** The Orion complex, consisting of the Great Nebula in Orion and the protostars buried deep in the dark interstellar clouds behind the nebula seems to be a region of self-sustaining star formation (see **Visualizing Astronomy 7.2, Star Formation in the Orion Nebula**).

Astronomers have calculated models indicating that the differential rotation of the galaxy can drag the inner edge of a star-forming region ahead and let the outer edge lag behind to produce a cloud of star formation shaped like a segment of a spiral arm. Self-sustaining star formation in combination with differential rotation may produce the branches and spurs so prominent in some galaxies (Figure 9.13b), including our own, but only the spiral density wave can generate the beautiful two-armed grand spiral patterns.

9.3 The Origin and History of the Milky Way

Just as paleontologists reconstruct the history of life on Earth from the fossil record, astronomers try to reconstruct our galaxy's past from the fossil it left behind as it formed and evolved. That fossil is the spherical component of the galaxy. The stars in the halo formed when the galaxy was young. The chemical composition and the distribution of these stars can provide clues to how our galaxy formed.

The Age of the Milky Way

To begin, you can easily answer the question of how old our galaxy is because you already know how to find the age of star clusters. But that easy answer is hard to interpret because there are uncertainties.

self-sustaining star formation The process by which the birth of stars compresses the surrounding gas clouds and triggers the formation of more stars.

The oldest open clusters have ages of about 9 to 10 billion years (see **Visualizing Astronomy 8.1, Star Cluster H–R Diagrams**). These ages, determined by analyzing the turnoff point in the cluster H–R diagram, are somewhat uncertain. Nevertheless, from open clusters you can get a rough age for the disk of our galaxy of at least 9 billion years.

Globular clusters have faint turnoff points in their H–R diagrams and are clearly old, but finding their ages accurately is difficult. Clusters differ slightly in chemical composition, which must be accounted for in calculating the stellar models from which ages are determined. Also, to find the age of a cluster, astronomers must know the distance to the cluster. Precise parallaxes from the Hipparcos satellite have allowed astronomers to increase the precision of the Cepheid variable stars' calibration, and careful studies with the newest large telescopes have refined the cluster H–R diagrams. Globular cluster ages seem to average about 11 billion years, with the oldest being a bit over 13 billion years old. The halo of our galaxy therefore seems to be at least 13 billion years old, older than the disk.

Stellar Populations

In the 1940s, astronomers realized there were two types of stars in the galaxy. They were most accustomed to studying the first type, the stars located in the disk, such as stars near the Sun. These they called **population I stars**. The stars of the second type, called **population II stars**, are usually found in the halo, in globular clusters, or in the central bulge. In other words, the two stellar populations are associated with the disk and spherical components of the galaxy, respectively.

The stars of the two populations fuse nuclear fuels and evolve in nearly identical ways. They differ only in their abundance of atoms heavier than helium, atoms that astronomers refer to collectively as **metals**. (Note that this is definitely not the way the word *metal* is commonly used by non-astronomers.) Population I stars are relatively metal rich, containing 2 to 3 percent metals. Population II stars are metal poor, containing only about 0.1 percent metals or less. The metal content of a star defines its population.

population I star Stars rich in atoms heavier than helium, nearly always relatively young stars found in the disk of the galaxy.

population II star Stars poor in atoms heavier than helium, nearly always relatively old stars found in the halo, globular clusters, or the central bulge.

metal In astronomical usage, all atoms heavier than helium.

Table 9.1 | Stellar Populations

	Population I		Population II	
	Extreme	**Intermediate**	**Intermediate**	**Extreme**
Location	Spiral arms	Disk	Central bulge	Halo
Metals (%)	3	1.6	0.8	Less than 0.8
Shape of orbit	Circular	Slightly elliptical	Moderately elliptical	Highly elliptical
Average age (yr)	0.2 billion and younger	0.2–10 billion	2–10 billion	10–13 billion

Population I stars, sometimes called *disk population stars*, have circular orbits in the plane of the galaxy and are relatively young stars that formed within the last few billion years. The Sun is a population I star. Population II stars belong to the spherical component of the galaxy and are sometimes called *halo population stars*. These stars have randomly tipped orbits with a wide range of shapes. A few follow circular orbits, but most follow elliptical orbits. The population II stars are all lower-mass main-sequence stars or giants. They are old stars. The metal-poor globular clusters are part of the halo population. Since the discovery of stellar populations, astronomers have realized that there is a gradation between populations, as illustrated in Table 9.1.

Why do the disk and halo stars have different metal abundances? The two types of stars must have formed at different stages in the life of the galaxy, specifically, at times when the chemical composition of the galaxy differed. This is a clue to the history of our galaxy, but to use this clue, you must understand the cycle of element building.

The Element-Building Cycle

The atoms of which you are made were created in a process that spanned a number of generations of stars. The process that built the chemical elements over the history of our galaxy led to the possibility of Earth and life on Earth.

You saw in Chapter 8 how elements heavier than helium but lighter than iron are built up by nuclear reactions inside evolving stars. More massive atoms are made only by short-lived nuclear reactions that occur during a supernova explosion. This explains why lower-mass atoms like carbon, nitrogen, and oxygen are more common and why more massive atoms—such as gold, silver, platinum, and uranium—are so rare and, often, valuable. Figure 9.14a shows the abundance of the chemical elements, but notice that the graph has an exponential scale. To get a feeling for the true abundance of the elements, you should draw this graph using a linear scale as in

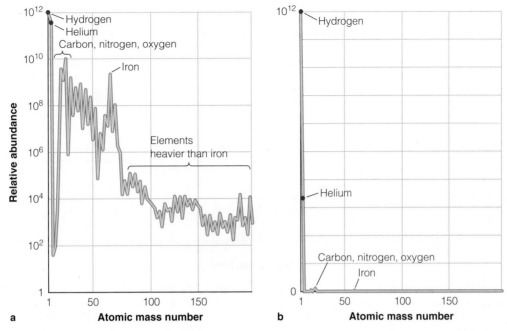

Figure 9.14 The abundance of the elements in the universe. (a) When the elements are plotted on an exponential scale, you see that elements heavier than iron are about a million times less common than iron and that all elements heavier than helium (referred to by astronomers as metals) are quite rare. (b) The same data plotted on a linear scale provide a more realistic impression of how rare the metals are. Carbon, nitrogen, and oxygen make small peaks near atomic mass 15, and iron is just visible in the graph.

Figure 9.14b. With that scale you see how rare the elements heavier than helium really are.

Most of the matter in stars is hydrogen and helium. Other elements, including carbon, nitrogen, oxygen, and the rest of what astronomers call metals, were cooked up inside stars. When the galaxy first formed, there should have been no metals because stars had not yet manufactured any. Judging from the composition of stars in the oldest clusters, the gas from which the galaxy originally condensed must have contained about 90 percent hydrogen atoms and 10 percent helium atoms. The hydrogen and helium came from the big bang that began the universe, which you will study in Chapter 11.

The first stars to form from this gas were metal poor, and now, 13 billion years later, their spectra still show few metal lines. Of course, they may have manufactured many atoms heavier than helium in their cores, but because the stars' interiors are not mixed, those heavy atoms stay trapped at the centres of the stars where they were produced and do not affect the spectra (Figure 9.15). The population II stars in the halo are the survivors of an earlier generation of stars that formed in the galaxy.

Most of the first stars evolved and died, and various types of star death throes, including supernovae, enriched the interstellar gas with metals. Succeeding generations of stars formed from gas clouds that were more enriched, and each generation added to the enrichment with its death. By the time the Sun formed, roughly 5 billion years ago, the element-building process had added about 1.6 percent metals. Since then, the metal abundance has increased further, and stars forming at the present time incorporate 2 to 3 percent metals and become extreme population I stars. Consequently, metal abundance varies between populations because heavy atoms were produced in successive generations of stars as the galaxy aged.

The oxygen atoms you are breathing, the carbon atoms in your flesh, and the calcium atoms in your bones were all created in the interiors of red and yellow giant stars hot enough to sustain fusion reactions beyond helium. The gold and silver atoms in your jewellery and dental fillings, and the iodine atoms in your thyroid gland were all created in a few moments during supernova explosions, because those are the only places in the universe hot enough to make these types of atoms. This idea is perhaps the most significant one to take away from an introductory astronomy course and textbook—you, and everything on Earth, are made of stardust.

The History of the Milky Way Galaxy

The lack of metals in the spherical component of the galaxy tells you it is very old, a fossil left behind by the galaxy when it was young and drastically different from its present disk shape. The study of element-building and stellar populations leads to the fundamental question, "How did our galaxy form?"

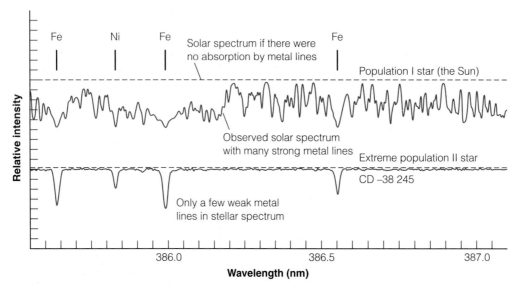

Figure 9.15 The difference between spectra of population I stars and population II stars is dramatic. A graph of such spectra reveals overlapping absorption lines of metals completely blanketing the population I spectrum. The lower spectrum is that of an extremely metal-poor star with only a few weak metal lines of iron (Fe) and nickel (Ni). This population II star contains about 10,000 times less metal than the Sun.

In the 1950s, astronomers began to develop a hypothesis, sometimes called the **monolithic collapse model**, or "top-down" hypothesis, to explain the formation of our galaxy. Recent observations are forcing a major re-evaluation and revision of that traditional hypothesis.

The traditional hypothesis says that the galaxy formed from a single large cloud of turbulent gas over 13 billion years ago. Stars and star clusters that formed from this material went into randomly shaped and randomly tipped orbits. These first stars were metal poor because no stars had existed earlier to enrich the gas with metals. In this way, the initial contraction of a large, turbulent gas cloud produced the spherical component of the galaxy.

The second stage of this hypothesis accounts for the disk component. The turbulent motions would eventually have cancelled out, leaving the cloud with uniform rotation. A rotating, low-density cloud of gas cannot remain spherical. A star is spherical because its high internal pressure balances its gravity, but in a low-density cloud, the pressure cannot support the weight. Like a blob of pizza dough spun in the air, such a cloud must flatten into a disk (Figure 9.16).

This contraction into a disk took billions of years, with the metal abundance gradually increasing as generations of stars were born from the gradually flattening gas cloud. The stars and globular clusters that formed first in the halo would not have been affected by the motions of the gas and would have been left behind

monolithic collapse model An early hypothesis that says that the galaxy formed from the collapse of a single large cloud of turbulent gas over 13 billion years ago.

by the cloud as it collapsed and flattened. Later generations of stars formed in flatter distributions. The gas distribution in the galaxy now is so flat that the youngest stars are confined in a thin disk only about 300 ly thick. These stars are metal rich and have nearly circular orbits.

This monolithic collapse hypothesis accounts for many of the Milky Way's properties. Advances in technology, however, have improved astronomical observation and, beginning in the 1980s, contradictions between theory and observation arose. For example, not all globular clusters have the same age, but, surprisingly, some of the younger clusters seem to be in the outer halo. In contrast, the monolithic collapse hypothesis says that the halo formed first and predicts that the clusters within it should either have a uniform age or the most distant ones should be slightly older. Another problem is that the oldest stars are observed to be metal poor but not completely metal free. There must have been at least a few massive stars to create these metals during a generation before the formation of the oldest stars now seen in the halo.

Can the original hypothesis be modified to explain these observations? Perhaps the galaxy began with the contraction of a gas cloud to form the central bulge, and the halo later accumulated from gas clouds that had been slightly enriched in metals by an early generation of massive stars. That first generation of stars would have formed from almost pure hydrogen and helium gas, which mathematical models indicate would form only stars with very high masses. Those stars would have lived very short lives, made metals, and died in supernova explosions; none would be left today. This would explain the metals in the oldest stars surviving today.

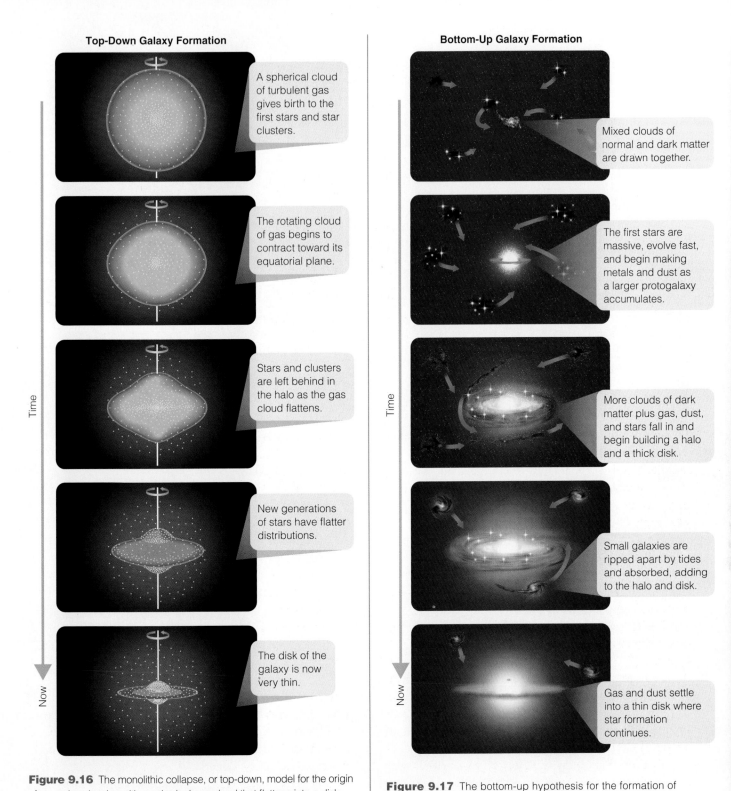

Top-Down Galaxy Formation

A spherical cloud of turbulent gas gives birth to the first stars and star clusters.

The rotating cloud of gas begins to contract toward its equatorial plane.

Stars and clusters are left behind in the halo as the gas cloud flattens.

New generations of stars have flatter distributions.

The disk of the galaxy is now very thin.

Time

Now

Bottom-Up Galaxy Formation

Mixed clouds of normal and dark matter are drawn together.

The first stars are massive, evolve fast, and begin making metals and dust as a larger protogalaxy accumulates.

More clouds of dark matter plus gas, dust, and stars fall in and begin building a halo and a thick disk.

Small galaxies are ripped apart by tides and absorbed, adding to the halo and disk.

Gas and dust settle into a thin disk where star formation continues.

Time

Now

Figure 9.16 The monolithic collapse, or top-down, model for the origin of our galaxy begins with a spherical gas cloud that flattens into a disk.

There is also evidence that entire small galaxies were captured by the growing Milky Way, and that fresh gas was added to the disk in several episodes over the life of the galaxy; it did not form during a single gravitational collapse. An alternative bottom-up hypothesis proposes that our galaxy was assembled from smaller objects (Figure 9.17).

Figure 9.17 The bottom-up hypothesis for the formation of the Milky Way Galaxy proposes that smaller star systems accumulated to form larger ones. To see how this could have built our galaxy, start with the first frame, only a few hundred million years after the beginning of the universe: small clouds of matter begin accumulating and stars begin forming in them. In the second frame, the central object has grown larger, and in the third frame, the galactic halo and disk are forming. By the last frame, representing today, the disk of the galaxy has become very thin.

1 There is so much interstellar dust in the plane of the Milky Way that you cannot observe the nucleus of our galaxy at visual wavelengths. The image below is a radio image of the innermost 1000 ly. Many of the features are supernova remnants (labelled SNR), and a few are star formation clouds. Peculiar features such as threads, the Arc, and the Snake may be gas trapped in magnetic fields. At the centre of the image lies Sagittarius A*, the location of the nucleus of our galaxy.

Arc

Radio image

The radio map above shows Sgr A and the Arc filaments: 150 ly across. The image was made with the VLA radio telescope. The contents of the white box are shown on the opposite page.

Sgr D HII

Sgr D SNR

SNR 0.9 + 0.1

Sgr B2

Apparent angular size of the Moon for comparison

Sgr B1

New SNR 0.3 + 0.0

Threads

The Cane

Arc

Background galaxy

Sgr A

Threads

2 The image below shows the central region of the Milky Way Galaxy, combining data from three space telescopes. The exact center of the galaxy is located within the bright white region near the right edge of the frame. The full image width is about half the angular diameter of the full Moon (compare with radio map above; note that the horizontal axis here is the diagonal axis above).

Radio image

Sgr C

The Pelican

Coherent structure?

Snake

Sgr E

Courtesy NASA/JPL-Caltech

Infrared image

SNR 359.1 – 00.5

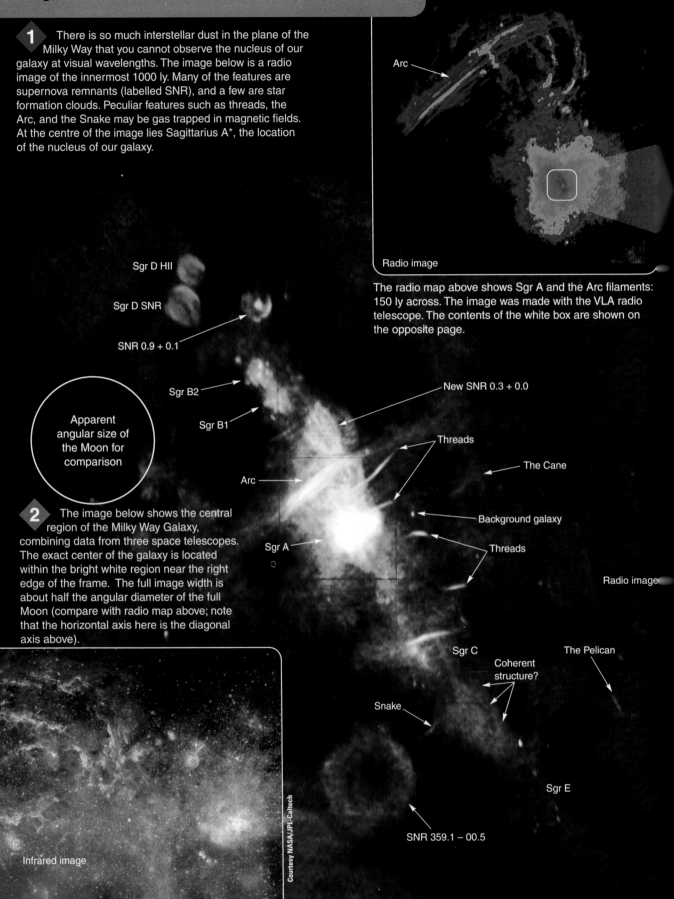

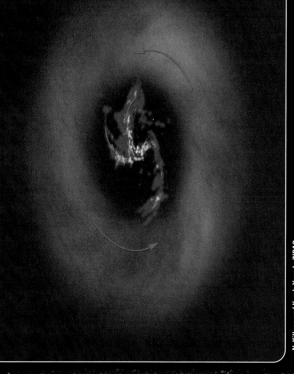

1a This high-resolution radio image of Sgr A (within the white box in the small-scale map on the opposite page) reveals a spiral swirl of gas around an intense radio source known as SgrA*. About 10 ly across, this spiral lies in a low-density cavity inside a larger disk of neutral gas. The arms of the spiral are thought to be streams of matter flowing into SgrA* from the inner edge of the larger disk (drawing at right).

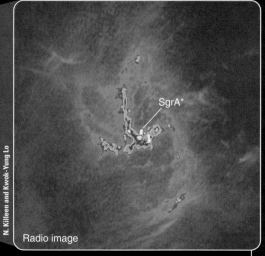

SgrA*

Radio image

N. Killeen and Kwok-Yung Lo

N. Killeen and Kwok-Yung Lo/NRAO

Evidence of a Black Hole in the Nucleus of Our Galaxy

3 Since the middle 1990s, astronomers have been able to use large infrared telescopes and active optics to follow the motions of stars orbiting around SgrA*. A few of those orbits are shown here. The size and period of the orbit allows astronomers to calculate the mass of SgrA* using Kepler's third law. The orbital period of the star SO-2, for example, is 15.2 years, and the semi-major axis of its orbit is 950 AU. The combined motions of the observed stars suggest that SgrA* has a mass of 4 million solar masses.

The Chandra X-ray Observatory has imaged SgrA* and detected over 2000 other X-ray sources in the area.

Infrared image

European Southern Observatory

At its closest, SO-2 comes within 17 light-hours of SgrA*. Alternative theories that SgrA* is a cluster of stars, of neutron stars, or of stellar black holes are eliminated. Only a single black hole could contain so much mass in so small a region.

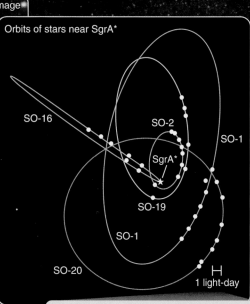

Orbits of stars near SgrA*

SO-16

SO-2

SO-1

SgrA*

SO-19

SO-1

SO-20

1 light-day

For comparison, the diameter of the planetary region of our solar system, defined by Neptune's orbit, is half a light-day.

NASA/CXC/MIT/F.K. Baganoff et al.

3a A black hole with a mass of 4 million solar masses would have an event horizon with a size on the scale of this diagram smaller than the period at the end of this sentence. A slow dribble of only 0.0002 solar mass of gas per year flowing into the black hole could produce the observed energy. A sudden increase, such as when a star falls in, could produce a violent eruption.

The evidence of a massive black hole at the centre of our galaxy seems conclusive. It is much too massive to be the remains of a dead star, however, and astronomers conclude that it probably formed as the galaxy first took shape.

Sagittarius A* The powerful radio source located at the core of the Milky Way Galaxy.

If our galaxy absorbed a few small but partially evolved galaxies, some of the globular clusters in the halo may be hitchhikers that originally belonged to the captured galaxies. This could explain the range of globular cluster ages and compositions. The next chapter explains that such galaxy mergers do occur.

The problem of the formation of our galaxy is frustrating because the explanations are incomplete. The older monolithic collapse hypothesis has proven inadequate to explain all of the observations, and you see astronomers attempting to refine the observations and devise new theories. The metal abundances and ages of the stars in our galaxy seem to be important clues, but metal abundance and age do not tell the whole story. In the next section you will learn that the nucleus of our galaxy, like many other galaxies, contains a mysterious and massive object capable of powerful outbursts that could have profoundly influenced galactic evolution.

9.4 The Nucleus

The most mysterious region of our galaxy is its very centre, the nucleus. At visual wavelengths, this region is totally hidden by gas and dust that dim the light by 30 magnitudes (Figure 9.18). If a trillion (10^{12}) photons of light left the centre of the galaxy on a journey to Earth, only one would make it through the gas and dust. The longer-wavelength infrared photons are scattered much less often: One in every ten makes it to Earth. Consequently, visual-wavelength observations reveal nothing about the nucleus, but it can be observed at longer wavelengths, such as in the infrared and radio parts of the spectrum.

Observations of the Galactic Nucleus

Harlow Shapley's study of globular clusters placed the centre of our galaxy in Sagittarius, and the first radio maps of the sky showed a powerful radio source located in Sagittarius. The first infrared map of the central bulge made by Eric Becklin in 1968 showed the location of intense radiation where the stars are most crowded together, which identified the gravitational centre of the galaxy. Later high-resolution radio maps of that stellar centre revealed a complex collection of radio sources, and one of those sources—**Sagittarius A*** (abbreviated SgrA* and pronounced "sadge A-star")—was at the expected location of the galactic core.

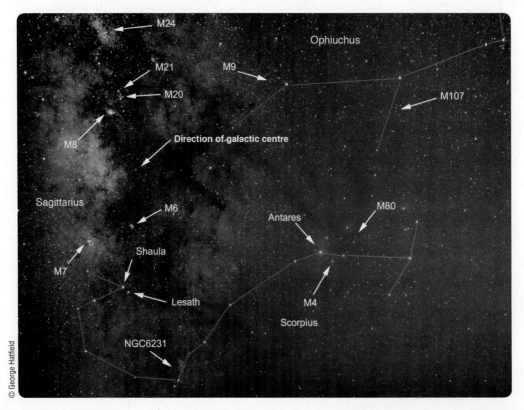

Figure 9.18 Looking toward Sagittarius, we cannot see anything that suggests this is the centre of the galaxy. Gas and dust block our view.

Observations show that SgrA* is only a few astronomical units in diameter but is a powerful source of radio energy. The tremendous amount of infrared radiation coming from the central area appears to be produced by crowded stars and by dust warmed by those stars. But the question was, what could be as relatively tiny as SgrA* and produce so much radio energy?

Study **Visualizing Astronomy 9.1, Sagittarius A***, and notice three important points:

1. Observations at radio wavelengths reveal complex structures near SgrA* that are caused by magnetic fields and by rapid star formation. Supernova remnants show that massive stars have formed there recently and died explosively.

2. The centre is very crowded. Tremendous numbers of stars plus radiation from SgrA* heat the dust, producing strong infrared emission.

3. There is evidence that SgrA* is a supermassive black hole into which gas is flowing.

From 1992 until 2008, German astronomers continuously followed 28 stars in the vicinity of the galactic centre using the European Southern Observatory at La Silla, Chile (see the graph in **Visualizing Astronomy 9.1, Sagittarius A***). UCLA Milky Way Center Group did a similar observation, with 17 stars, using the Keck telescope on Mauna Kea, Hawaii. Orbital characteristics confirmed that a supermassive black hole could be responsible for very high velocities of stars.

Astronomers continue to test the hypothesis that the centre of our galaxy contains a supermassive black hole. Such an object is sufficient to explain the observations, but is it necessary? Is there some other way to explain what is observed? For example, astronomers have suggested that gas flowing toward the centre of the galaxy could trigger tremendous bursts of star formation. Such hypotheses have been considered and tested against the evidence, but none appears to be adequate to explain all the observations. So far, the only hypothesis that seems adequate is that our galaxy's nucleus is home to a supermassive black hole.

Meanwhile, observations are allowing astronomers to improve their models. For instance, SgrA* is not as bright in X-rays as it should be if it had a hot accretion disk with matter constantly flowing into the black hole. Observations of X-ray and infrared flares lasting only a few hours suggest that mountain-size blobs of matter may occasionally fall into the black hole and be heated and ripped apart by tidal forces (see Chapter 8). The black hole may be mostly dormant and lack a fully developed hot accretion disk because the rate of matter flow into it is relatively low at the present time.

Such a supermassive black hole could not be the remains of a single dead star. It contains much too much mass. It probably formed when the galaxy first formed over 13 billion years ago. In the next chapter you will learn that supermassive black holes are commonly found in the centres of galaxies.

The **Big Picture**

Hang on tight. The Sun, with Earth in its clutches, is ripping along at high velocity as it orbits the centre of the Milky Way Galaxy, our "parent" galaxy. Except for hydrogen atoms, which have survived unchanged since the universe began, you and Earth are made of metals, atoms heavier than helium. All of these atoms were cooked up by stars during their life—or death—throughout the history of our galaxy. Each generation of stars has produced elements heavier than helium and spread them into the interstellar medium. The abundance of metals has grown slowly in the galaxy. About 4.6 billion years ago a cloud of gas enriched by heavy atoms slammed into a spiral arm and produced the Sun, Earth, and you.

Review and Discussion Questions

Review Questions

1. How do you know you live in a galaxy?
2. How do you know ours is a spiral galaxy, and what are the spiral arms?
3. How did our galaxy form and evolve?
4. What lies at the very centre of our galaxy?
5. Why didn't astronomers before Shapley realize how large the galaxy is?
6. What is the evidence that our galaxy contains a large amount of dark matter?
7. Contrast the motion of the disk stars and that of the halo stars. Why do their orbits differ?
8. Why are all spiral tracers young?
9. Why couldn't spiral arms be physically connected structures? What would happen to them?
10. Why does self-sustaining star formation produce clouds of stars that look like segments of spiral arms?
11. Why are metals less abundant in older stars than in younger stars?
12. What evidence contradicts the monolithic collapse hypothesis for the origin of our galaxy?
13. Describe the kinds of observations you would make to study the galactic nucleus.
14. Why must astronomers use infrared telescopes to observe the motions of stars around SgrA*?
15. What evidence can you cite that the nucleus of the galaxy contains a supermassive black hole?

Discussion Questions

1. How would the information in this chapter differ if interstellar dust did not block starlight?
2. Why doesn't the Milky Way circle the sky along the celestial equator or the ecliptic?

Learning to Look

1. Why does the galaxy shown below have so much dust in its disk? How big do you suppose the halo of that galaxy really is?

NASA/Hubble Heritage Team/STScI/AURA

2. Why are the spiral arms in the galaxy below blue? What colour would the halo be if it were bright enough to see in this photo?

NASA/Hubble Heritage Team and A. Riess, STScI

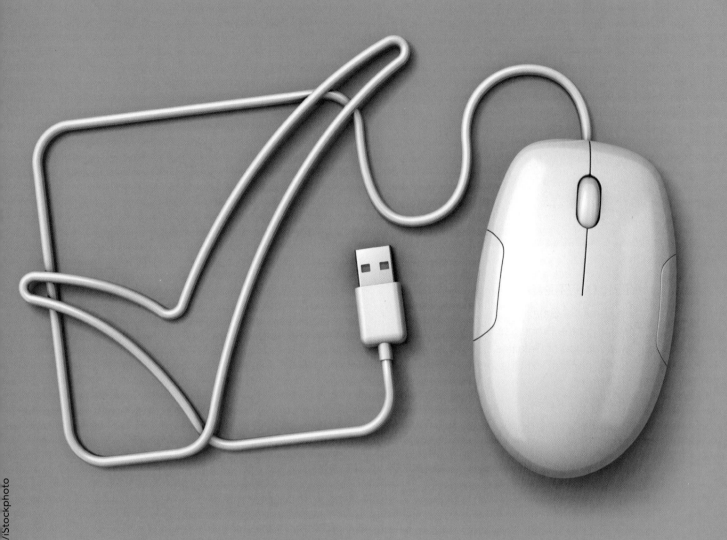

Your online study partner.

www.nelson.com/student

10

Galaxies

CHAPTER OUTLINE

GUIDEPOST

The Milky Way Galaxy is only one of the many billions of galaxies visible in the sky. In this chapter you will learn about different kinds of galaxies and their complex histories and violent eruptions, and you will find answers to four important questions:

- **How do astronomers know what galaxies are like?**
- **Do other galaxies contain dark matter and supermassive black holes, as does our own galaxy?**
- **Why are there different kinds of galaxies?**
- **Why do some galaxies produce tremendous eruptions?**

Less than a century ago, astronomers did not understand that galaxies exist. Nineteenth-century telescopes revealed faint nebulae scattered among the stars, some with spiral shapes. Astronomers argued about the nature of these nebulae, but it was not until the 1920s that astronomers understood that many of those nebulae are other galaxies much like our own, and it was not until recent decades that astronomical telescopes could reveal the variety, intricacy, and beauty of the galaxies. In this chapter, you will learn current theories about the formation and evolution of galaxies and discover that the amount of gas and dust in a galaxy is a critical clue. You will also discover that interactions between galaxies can dramatically influence their structure and evolution.

A number of theories about the evolution of galaxies are conflicting and open for debate, not finalized. However, the basis of building a theory of evolution of galaxies is basic data gathering. You can classify the different

The most exciting phrase to hear in science, the one that heralds the most discoveries, is not "Eureka!", but "That's funny..."

Isaac Asimov,
Scientist and best-selling author

Every object in this image is a galaxy.

kinds of galaxies and discover their fundamental properties: diameter, luminosity, and mass. After you know the typical properties of galaxies, you can start to theorize about their origin and evolution.

This chapter also covers some of the most energetic events in the universe, in particular, that the energy pouring out of the nuclei of certain galaxies is enormously greater than explosions of supernovae.

10.1 The Family of Galaxies

Astronomers classify galaxies according to various properties. Creating a system of classification is fundamental technique in science (see **How Do We Know? 10.1**). Classification according to their shape was developed in the 1920s by Edwin Hubble (after whom the Hubble Space Telescope is named).

Study **Visualizing Astronomy 10.1, Galaxy Classification**, and notice the following important points:

1. There are galaxies with no disk, no spiral arms, and almost no gas, dust, or new stars forming. Those are elliptical galaxies. They range in size and mass from small dwarfs to huge giants.

2. Disk-shaped galaxies usually have spiral arms—that are either less or more prominent—and generally large amounts of gas and dust and ongoing stellar formation.

3. Some galaxies have an irregular shape, with gas, dust, and star-forming nebulae; they include the Milky Way's neighbours, the **Large Magellanic Cloud** and the **Small Magellanic Cloud**.

4. Different kinds of galaxies have different colours, depending mostly on howmuch star formation is happening in them. Spirals and irregulars usually contain plenty of young stars, including massive, hot, luminous O and B stars. They produce most of the light and give spirals and irregulars a distinct blue tint. In contrast, elliptical galaxies usually have few young stars. The most luminous stars in the elliptical galaxies are red giants, which give those galaxies a red tint.

Large Magellanic Cloud The larger of two irregular galaxies visible in the southern sky passing near the Milky Way Galaxy.

Small Magellanic Cloud The smaller of two irregular galaxies visible in the southern sky passing near the Milky Way Galaxy.

You might also wonder what proportion of the galaxies are elliptical, spiral, and irregular, but that is a difficult question to answer. In some catalogues of galaxies about 70 percent are spiral, but that is the result of what scientists call a selection effect (see **How Do We Know? 10.2**). Spiral galaxies contain hot, bright stars and are consequently very luminous and easy to see (Figure 10.1). From careful studies, astronomers conclude that ellipticals are more common than spirals, and irregulars make up about 25 percent of all galaxies. Among spiral galaxies, about two-thirds are barred spirals.

How many galaxies are there? A research effort called GOODS (Great Observatories Origins Deep Survey) has used the Hubble Space Telescope, the Chandra X-ray Observatory, the Spitzer Space Telescope, and the XMM-Newton X-ray Telescope, as well as the largest ground-based telescopes, to study two selected areas in the northern and southern skies. The GOODS images reveal tremendous numbers of galaxies; for example, see this chapter's opening image. There are good reasons to believe that the two regions of the sky chosen for study are typical, so evidently the entire sky is carpeted with galaxies. The result of the GOODS research is an estimate that at least 100 billion galaxies would be visible if today's telescopes were used for an all-sky census.

M83 12 million ly

Dust clouds glow red in this infrared image.

Infrared image

ESO 510-G13 150 million ly

Dusty disk of galaxy warped by interaction with another galaxy

New stars forming in dust clouds.

Visual-wavelength image

ESO/Hubble Heritage Team/AURA/STScI/NASA

Figure 10.1 A century ago, photos of galaxies looked like spiral clouds of haze. Modern images of these relatively nearby galaxies reveal dramatically beautiful objects filled with newborn stars and clouds of gas and dust.

HOW DO WE KNOW? 10.1

Classification in Science

What does classification tell a scientist? Classification is one of the most basic and most powerful scientific tools. Establishing a system of classification is often the first step in studying a new aspect of nature, and it can produce unexpected insights.

Charles Darwin sailed around the world from 1831 to 1836 with a scientific expedition aboard the ship HMS *Beagle*. Everywhere he went, he studied the living things he saw and tried to classify them. For example, he classified different types of finches he saw on the Galapagos Islands based on the shapes of their beaks. He found that those that fed on seeds with hard shells had thick, powerful beaks, whereas those that picked insects out of deep crevices had long, thin beaks. His classifications of these and other animals led him to think about how natural selection shapes creatures to survive in their environment, which led him to understand how living things evolve.

Years after Darwin's work, paleontologists classified dinosaurs into two orders, lizard-hipped and bird-hipped dinosaurs. This classification, based on the shapes of dinosaur hip joints, helped the scientists understand patterns of evolution of dinosaurs. It also led to the conclusion that modern birds, including the finches that Darwin saw on the Galapagos, evolved from dinosaurs.

Astronomers use classifications of galaxies, stars, moons, and many other objects to help them see patterns, trace relationships, and generally make sense of the astronomical world. Whenever you encounter a scientific discussion, look for the classifications on which it is based. Classifications are the orderly framework on which much of science is built.

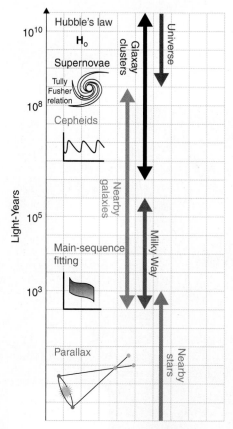

Figure 10.2 Cosmological distance ladder. Different methods are used to measure distances in the universe. Methods higher in the diagram rely on calibrations based on methods lower in the diagram.

10.2 Measuring the Properties of Galaxies

Looking beyond the edge of the Milky Way Galaxy, astronomers find many billions of galaxies. What are the properties of these star systems? What are the diameters, luminosities, and masses of galaxies? Just as you did in studying stellar characteristics (Chapter 6), the first step in studying galaxies is to find out how far away they are. Once you know a galaxy's distance, its size and luminosity are relatively easy to find. Later in this section you will see that finding the masses of galaxies is more difficult, but the results are intriguing.

Distance Ladder

Astronomers use calibration to build a distance scale reaching from the nearest stars to the most distant visible galaxies (see **How Do We Know? 9.1**). Astronomers often refer to this distance scale as the **distance ladder** because each step depends on the steps below it (Figure 10.2). The extragalactic distance scale rests on determining luminosities of stars, which is based on measuring stellar parallax (see Chapter 6).

> **distance ladder** The calibration used to build a distance scale extending from the size of Earth to the most distant visible galaxies.

1 **I. *Morphological classification:***

Elliptical galaxies are round or elliptical, contain no visible gas and dust, and have few or no bright stars. They are classified with a numerical index ranging from 0 to 7; E0s are round, and E7s are highly elliptical. The index is calculated from the largest and smallest diameter of the galaxy used in the following formula and rounded to the nearest integer.

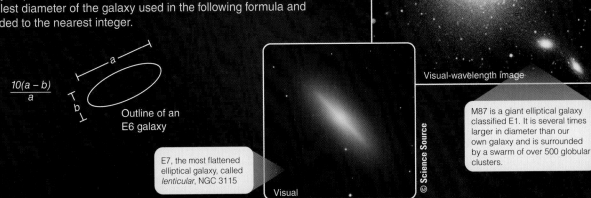

$$\frac{10(a-b)}{a}$$

Outline of an E6 galaxy

Visual-wavelength image

E7, the most flattened elliptical galaxy, called *lenticular*, NGC 3115

Visual

AURA/NOAO/NSF

© Science Source

M87 is a giant elliptical galaxy classified E1. It is several times larger in diameter than our own galaxy and is surrounded by a swarm of over 500 globular clusters.

2 **Spiral galaxies** contain a disk and spiral arms. Their halo stars are not visible, but presumably all spiral galaxies have halos. Spirals contain gas and dust and hot, bright O and B stars. The presence of short-lived O and B stars alerts us that star formation is occurring in these galaxies.

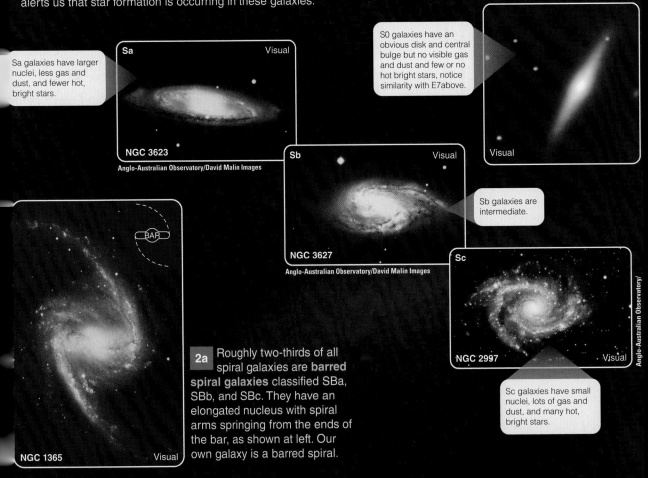

Sa galaxies have larger nuclei, less gas and dust, and fewer hot, bright stars.

Sa   Visual

NGC 3623

Anglo-Australian Observatory/David Malin Images

S0 galaxies have an obvious disk and central bulge but no visible gas and dust and few or no hot bright stars, notice similarity with E7above.

Visual

Sb   Visual

NGC 3627

Anglo-Australian Observatory/David Malin Images

Sb galaxies are intermediate.

Sc

NGC 2997   Visual

Anglo-Australian Observatory/

BAR

NGC 1365   Visual

2a Roughly two-thirds of all spiral galaxies are **barred spiral galaxies** classified SBa, SBb, and SBc. They have an elongated nucleus with spiral arms springing from the ends of the bar, as shown at left. Our own galaxy is a barred spiral.

Sc galaxies have small nuclei, lots of gas and dust, and many hot, bright stars.

3 Irregular galaxies (classified Irr) are a chaotic mix of gas, dust, and stars with no obvious central bulge or spiral arms. The Large and Small Magellanic Clouds are visible to the unaided eye as hazy patches in the southern hemisphere sky. Telescopic images show that they are irregular galaxies that are interacting gravitationally with our own much larger galaxy. Star formation is dramatic in the Magellanic Clouds. The bright pink regions are emission nebulae excited by newborn O and B stars. The brightest nebula in the Large Magellanic Cloud is called the Tarantula nebula.

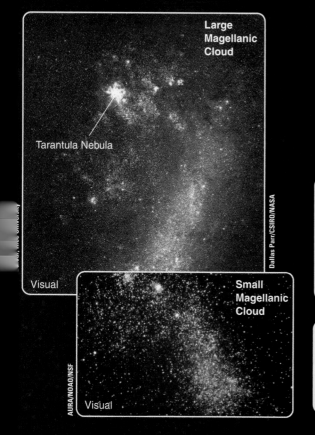

Large Magellanic Cloud

Tarantula Nebula

Visual

Dallas Parr/CSIRO/NASA

Small Magellanic Cloud

AURA/NOAO/NSF

Visual

Combined radio and visible-light image: The Milky Way is the light blue band in the centre of the image. The brown clumps are interstellar dust clouds in our galaxy. The Magellanic Clouds, satellite galaxies of the Milky Way, are the white regions at the bottom right, with the gaseous stream, tidal tail, shown in pink.

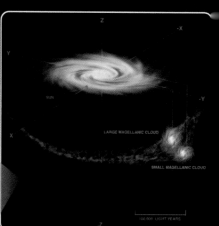

Milky Way and its neighbours, the two irregular galaxies, Small Magellanic Cloud and Large Magellanic Cloud. In this artistic conception, we see the tidal tails of the two galaxies, created by the gravitational tug of the Milky Way.

4 **II. _Quantitative galaxy classification:_**

Similar to H–R diagram for stars is a colour-luminosity plot of galaxies. Most galaxies fall into two groups, blue cloud and red sequence. Blue cloud contains mostly spiral and irregular galaxies with an ongoing star formation, hence the blue colour. The red sequence consists primarily of elliptical galaxies, with no star formation, therefore majority of stars are red in colour.

Graph of galaxy luminosity and colour. The brightest colour represents the number of galaxies with the corresponding colour and luminosity.

H–R diagram for stars, luminosity and colour classification. Refer to Chapter 6, Figure 6.28.

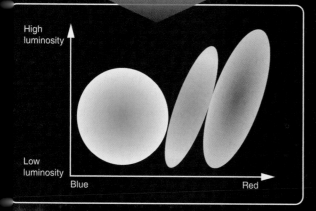

High luminosity

Low luminosity

Blue   Red

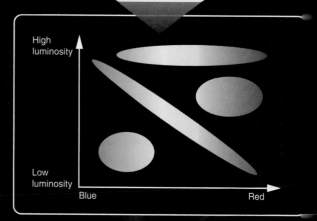

High luminosity

Low luminosity

Blue   Red

Selection Effects in Science

Many different kinds of science depend on selecting objects to study. Scientists studying insects in the rainforest, for example, must choose which ones to catch. They can't catch every insect they see, so they might decide on some way to select the ones they do catch. If they are not careful, a selection effect could bias their data and lead them to incorrect conclusions without their ever knowing it. The reason selection effects are dangerous in science is that they can have powerful influences without always being obvious. Scientists can avoid selection effects only by carefully designing a research project.

For example, suppose you decide to measure the speed of cars on a highway. There are too many cars to measure every one, so you reduce the workload and measure the speed of only red cars.

It is quite possible that this selection criterion will mislead you because people who buy red cars may be more likely to be younger and drive faster. Should you measure only brown cars? No, because you might suspect that only older, more sedate people would buy a brown car. Should you measure the speed of any car in front of a truck? Perhaps you should pick any car following a truck? Again, you may be selecting cars that are travelling a bit faster or a bit slower than normal. Only by very carefully designing your experiment can you be certain that the cars you measure are travelling at speeds truly representative of the entire population of cars.

Astronomers face the danger of selection effects quite often. Very luminous stars are easier to see at great distances than faint stars. Spiral galaxies are brighter, bluer, and more noticeable than elliptical galaxies. What astronomers see through a telescope depends on what they notice, and that is powerfully influenced by selection effects.

Scientists engaged in observation must spend considerable time designing their experiments. They must be careful to observe an unbiased sample if they expect to make logical deductions from their results. The scientists in the rainforest, for example, should not catch and study only the red insects. Often, the most brightly coloured insects are poisonous (or at least taste bad) to predators. Catching only brightly coloured insects could produce a highly biased sample of the insect population. Scientists must plan their work with great care and avoid any possible selection effects.

Astronomers use the stellar parallax method to determine distances to the nearest stars for which parallax angle can be observed for now: that is, distances up to 1500 light-years. For distances farther than that but within the Milky Way Galaxy, astronomers use the method called main-sequence fitting to determine the distances to clusters of stars by placing the cluster on H–R diagram. Knowing the stars' luminosity and measuring their apparent brightness allows us to determine the distance to the cluster.

The distances to galaxies are so large that it is not convenient to express them in light-years or even parsecs. Instead, astronomers use the unit megaparsec (Mpc), or 1 million pc. One Mpc equals 3.26 million ly, or approximately 3×10^{19} km.

standard candle Object of known brightness that astronomers use to find distance—for example, Cepheid variable stars and supernovae.

Tully-Fisher relationship The linear relation between luminosity and the rotational rate of spiral galaxies used to determine the distance to spiral galaxies as standard candles.

To find the distance to a galaxy, astronomers must search among its stars, nebulae, and star clusters for familiar objects whose luminosity they know. Such objects are called **standard candles**. If you can find a standard candle in a galaxy, you can judge its distance.

Cepheid variable stars are reliable standard candles because their period is related to their luminosity (refer to Figure 9.4). If you know the period of a star's variation, you can use the period–luminosity diagram to learn its absolute magnitude. Then, by comparing its absolute and apparent magnitudes, you can find its distance. Figure 10.3 shows a galaxy in which the Hubble Space Telescope detected Cepheids. Even with the Hubble Space Telescope, Cepheids are not detectable much beyond 100 million ly, so astronomers must search for other methods and less common but brighter distance indicators, and calibrate them using nearby galaxies containing detectable Cepheids. Tully and Fisher discovered the relationship between luminosity and the rotational rate of spiral galaxies: called the **Tully-Fisher relationship**.

Visual-wavelength image

April 23
May 4
May 9
May 16
May 20
May 31

J. Trauger, JPL; Courtesy of The Observatories of the Carnegie Institution of Washington.

Figure 10.3 The vast majority of spiral galaxies are too distant for Earth-based telescopes to detect Cepheid variable stars. The Hubble Space Telescope, however, can locate Cepheids in some of these galaxies (for example, in the bright spiral galaxy M100). From a series of images taken on different dates, astronomers can locate Cepheids (see inset), determine the period of pulsation, and measure the average apparent brightness. They can then deduce the distance to the galaxy, which is 52 million ly for M100.

supernovae are much brighter than Cepheids, they can be seen in galaxies at great distances. The drawback is that supernovae are rare, and during your lifetime none may occur in a galaxy you are studying. You will see in Chapter 11 how these distance indicators have reshaped our understanding of the history of the universe.

Telescopes as Time Machines

The most distant visible galaxies are a little over 10 billion ly away. At such distances you can see an effect like time travel. When you look at a galaxy that is millions of light-years away, you do not see it as it is now but as it was millions of years ago when its light began the journey toward Earth. When you look at a distant galaxy, you look into the past by an amount called the **look-back time**, a time in years equal to the distance to the galaxy in light-years.

The look-back time to nearby objects is usually not significant. To the Moon it is only 1.3 seconds, to the Sun eight minutes, and to the nearest star about four years. The Andromeda Galaxy has a look-back time of about 2 million years, but that is a mere blink of the eye in the lifetime of a galaxy. When astronomers look at more distant galaxies, the look-back time becomes an appreciable part of the age of the universe. In Chapter 11 you will see evidence that the universe began about 13.8 billion years ago. When astronomers observe the most distant visible galaxies, they are looking back over 10 billion years to a time when the universe may have been significantly different.

The Hubble Law

Although astronomers find it difficult to measure the distance to a galaxy precisely, they often estimate such distances using a simple relationship. Early in the 20th century, astronomers noticed that the lines in galaxy spectra are generally

We can determine a galaxy's rotation rate from the Doppler shift of its spectral lines and thereby judge its luminosity. The same applies for any other standard candle; we can measure the brightness and calculate the distance to the galaxy.

When a supernova explodes in a distant galaxy, astronomers rush to observe it. Studies show that type Ia supernovae, those caused by the collapse of a white dwarf, all reach about the same luminosity at maximum (which makes them more like "standard bombs" than standard candles). By searching for Cepheids and other distance indicators in nearby galaxies where type Ia supernovae have occurred, astronomers have been able to calibrate these supernovae. As a result, when type Ia supernovae are seen in more distant galaxies, astronomers can measure the apparent brightness at maximum and then compare that information with the known luminosity of these supernovae to find their distances. Because type Ia

look-back time The amount by which you look into the past when you look at a distant galaxy; a time that equals the distance to the galaxy in light-years.

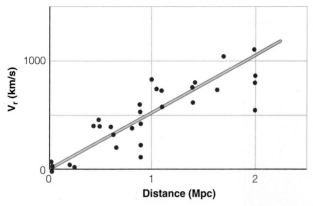

Figure 10.4 Edwin Hubble's first diagram of the apparent velocities of recession and distances of galaxies did not probe very deeply into space. Although Hubble's distance scale (horizontal axis) was later recalibrated, the diagram did show that the galaxies are receding at speeds proportional to their distances.

shifted toward longer wavelengths, that is, redshifted (Chapter 5). These redshifts imply that the galaxies are receding from Earth.

In 1929, the American astronomer Edwin Hubble published a graph that plotted the apparent velocity of recession versus distance for a number of galaxies. The points in the graph fell along a straight line (Figure 10.4). This relation between apparent velocity of recession and distance is known as the **Hubble law**, and the slope of the line is known as the **Hubble constant**, symbolized by H_0.

The Hubble law is important in astronomy for two reasons: to estimate the distance to galaxies, and as evidence that the universe is expanding. The distance to a galaxy can be found by dividing its apparent velocity of recession by the Hubble constant. (Refer to **The Hubble Law** in the Math Reference Cards.) This is a very useful calculation because it is usually possible to obtain a spectrum of a galaxy and measure its redshift even if it is too far away to have observable standard candles. Obviously, knowing the precise value of the Hubble constant is important.

Edwin Hubble's original measurement of H_0 was too large because of errors in his measurements of the distances to galaxies. Subsequently, astronomers have struggled to measure this important constant. The most precise measurements of the Hubble constant, made using NASA's infrared Spitzer Space Telescope yield a value for H_0 of about 23 km/s for every million light-years, or 74.3 km/s/Mpc with an uncertainty of about 3 percent. This means that a galaxy at a distance of 1 million light-years from the Milky Way is receding from us at a rate of 23 km/s, a galaxy 2 million light-years away is receding at 46 km/s, and so on.

Note that the redshifts of galaxies are not really Doppler shifts, even though astronomers often express the redshifts in kilometres per second as if they were true velocities. Although there are more sophisticated ways of understanding these redshifts, modern astronomers interpret redshifts of galaxies as caused by the expansion of the universe, and the Hubble law allows them to estimate the distance to a galaxy from its redshift.

Galaxy Diameters and Luminosities

The distance to a galaxy is the key to finding its diameter and its luminosity. With even a modest telescope and a CCD camera (see Chapter 4, page 83), you could photograph a galaxy and measure its angular diameter. If you know the distance to the galaxy you can find its linear diameter. Also, if you measure the apparent brightness of the galaxy you can use the distance to find its luminosity, as you learned regarding stars in Chapter 6.

The results of such observations show that galaxies differ dramatically in size and luminosity. Irregular galaxies tend to be small, 1 to 25 percent the diameter of our galaxy, and of low luminosity. Although they are common, they are easy to overlook. The Milky Way Galaxy is large and luminous compared with most spiral galaxies, though astronomers know of a few spiral galaxies that are even larger and more luminous. Elliptical galaxies cover a wide range of diameters and luminosities. The largest, called giant ellipticals, are five or more times the diameter of the Milky Way Galaxy, but many so-called dwarf elliptical galaxies are only 1 percent the diameter of our galaxy.

Clearly, the diameter and luminosity of a galaxy do not determine its type. Some small galaxies are irregular, and some are elliptical. Some large galaxies are spiral, and some are elliptical. Other factors must influence the evolution of galaxies.

Galaxy Masses

Although the mass of a galaxy is difficult to determine, it is an important quantity. It tells you how much matter the galaxy contains, which provides clues to the galaxy's origin and evolution.

The most precise method for measuring the mass of a disk galaxy is called the **rotation curve method** (Figure 10.5). To use this method you need to know (1) the true sizes of the orbits of stars or gas clouds within

Hubble law The linear relation between the distances to galaxies and the apparent velocity of recession.

Hubble constant A measure of the rate of expansion of the universe; the average value of the apparent velocity of recession divided by distance, about 70 km/s/Mpc.

rotation curve method A method of determining a galaxy's mass by observing the orbital velocity and orbital radius of stars in the galaxy.

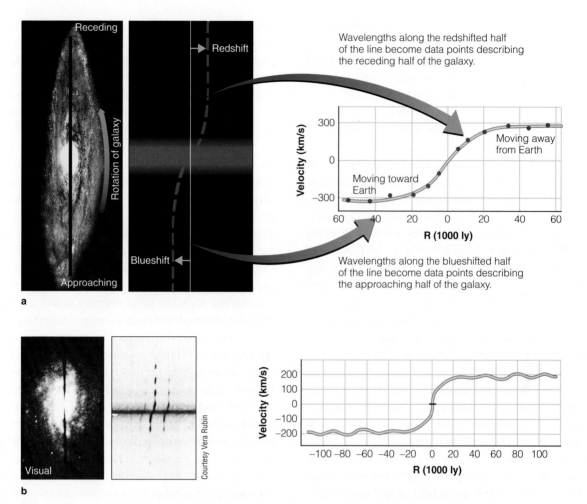

Figure 10.5 (a) In the artwork in the upper half of this diagram, the astronomer has placed the image of the galaxy over a narrow slit so that light from the galaxy can enter the spectrograph and produce a spectrum. A very short segment of the spectrum shows an emission line redshifted on the receding side of the rotating galaxy and blueshifted on the approaching side. Converting these Doppler shifts into velocities, the astronomer can plot the galaxy's rotation curve (right). (b) Real data are shown in the bottom half of this diagram. Galaxy NGC 2998 is shown over the spectrograph slit, and the segment of the spectrum includes three emission lines.

a galaxy, which requires knowing the distance of that galaxy; and (2) the orbital speeds of the stars or gas clouds, measured from the Doppler shifts of their spectral lines. That is enough information to use Kepler's third law and find the mass of the part of the galaxy contained within the star orbits with measured sizes and speeds (Chapter 9). The rotation curve method works only for disk galaxies near enough to be well resolved. More distant galaxies appear so small that astronomers cannot measure the radial velocity at different points across the galaxy and must use other, less precise, methods to estimate masses. Masses of elliptical galaxies are estimated on the basis of the motion of stars, stellar clusters, and gas clouds.

The masses of galaxies cover a wide range. The smallest contain about 10^{-6} as much mass as the Milky Way, and the largest contain as much as 50 times more mass than the Milky Way. The most common galaxies in the universe are small elliptical galaxies. However, if they are massive, elliptical galaxies are the most massive galaxies of all, and gravitationally dominate in the centres of clusters.

Dark Matter in Galaxies

Given the size and luminosity of a galaxy, astronomers can make a rough guess as to the amount of matter it should contain. Astronomers know how much light stars produce, and they know about how much matter there is between the stars, so it should be possible to estimate very roughly the mass of a galaxy from its luminosity. When astronomers measure the masses of galaxies from gravitational effects, they often find that the measured masses are much larger than expected from the luminosities of the galaxies. You discovered this effect in the previous chapter when you studied the rotation curve of our own galaxy and concluded that it must contain large amounts of dark matter, especially in its outer regions (refer to Figure 9.9).

In the 1930s, Swiss astronomer Fritz Zwicky noticed that in the Coma cluster, the galaxies move so fast that their visible mass would not be sufficient to keep the cluster together. There had to be additional gravity from some invisible matter. Forty years later, analysis of the rotational curves of galaxies indicated the same thing. The outer parts of galaxies were rotating too fast to be held by gravity of only luminous matter, which we can see and measure. So there had to be another component of matter that does not show itself through emitting electromagnetic radiation; we call it the dark matter. Australian astronomer Kenneth Freeman measured this paradox by examining galaxy NGC 300, and he was one of the first astronomers to recognize the role and importance of dark matter in spiral galaxies. Estonian astronomer Jaan Einasto conducted the same measurement for our Local Group of galaxies. Soon after, American astronomer Vera Rubin, Canadian Jim Peebles, and many others around the world, confirmed the same findings in other galaxies and clusters: see section Dark Matter in Clusters of Galaxies later in this chapter. Measured masses of galaxies amount to 10 to 100 times more mass than you can see (Figure 10.6).

Dark matter is difficult to detect, and it is even harder to explain. Some astronomers have suggested that dark matter consists of low-luminosity white dwarfs and brown dwarfs scattered through the halos of galaxies. Searches for white dwarfs and brown dwarfs in the halo of our galaxy have found a few, but not enough to make up most of the dark matter. The dark matter can't be hidden in vast numbers of black holes and neutron stars, because astronomers don't see the X-rays these objects would emit. The evidence indicates there is 10 to 100 times more dark matter than visible matter in galaxies, and if there were that many black holes they would produce X-rays that would be easy to detect.

Because observations imply that the dark matter can't be composed of familiar objects or material, astronomers are forced to conclude that the dark matter is made up of unexpected forms of matter. Until recently neutrinos were thought to be massless, but studies now suggest they have a very small mass. Thus, they can be part of the dark matter, but their masses are too low to make up all of the dark matter. There must be some other undiscovered form of matter in the universe that is detectable only by its gravitational field. One of the most likely candidates for dark matter are WIMPs (weakly interacting massive particles). These subatomic particles are not made up of ordinary matter, otherwise we would be able to detect them in some electromagnetic wave range. They are weakly interacting, so they can pass through ordinary matter without any effects. They have a mass and must interact with visible matter gravitationally. The problem becomes even more obvious in clusters of galaxies.

Dark matter remains one of the fundamental unresolved problems of modern astronomy. Observations of galaxies and clusters of galaxies reveal that 90 to 95 percent of the matter in the universe is invisible matter and energy. The universe you see—the kind of matter that you and the stars are made of—has been compared to the foam on an invisible ocean. This problem of dark matter will be picked up again in Chapter 11 with a discussion of how dark matter affects the nature of the universe, its past, and its future.

Supermassive Black Holes in Galaxies

Doppler shift measurements show that the stars near the centres of many galaxies are orbiting very rapidly. To hold stars in such small, short-period orbits, the centres of those galaxies must contain masses of a million to a few billion solar masses, yet no object is visible. The evidence seems to require that the nuclei of many galaxies contain supermassive black holes. Recall from Chapter 9 that the Milky Way Galaxy contains a supermassive black hole at its centre, which is typical of galaxies. However, it is a common misconception that the orbits of stars throughout a galaxy are controlled by the central black hole. The masses of those black holes, large as they may seem, are negligible compared with a galaxy's mass. The 4.3-million-solar-mass black hole at the centre of the Milky Way Galaxy contains only a thousandth of 1 percent of the total mass of the galaxy.

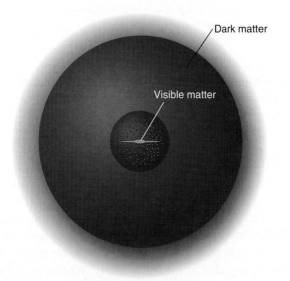

Figure 10.6 Rotation curves of spiral galaxies show that only 10 percent of mass is in the form of visible (regular) matter. Ninety percent is something invisible and does not interact, or only very weakly interacts, with regular matter; it is called the *dark matter*. Visible matter seems to be embedded in a massive halo of dark matter.

Charles Thomas Bolton

Tom Bolton never expected to discover a black hole. As a postdoctoral researcher at the University of Toronto in 1971, he was observing binary stars at the David Dunlap observatory in Ontario. He focused on a binary pair in which a blue giant is orbiting its partner, a strong source of X-rays, at unexpectedly high speeds. At first Bolton thought the X-ray source, Cygnus X-1, was a neutron star, but when a colleague suggested that it might be a black hole, his first reaction was disbelief. As he gathered further data, he realized that Cygnus X-1 was too massive to be a neutron star, and could only be a black hole. Matter from the blue star was being pulled into an accretion disk around the black hole, and the inner parts of the disk became hot enough to produce the X-rays observed by Bolton. Meanwhile, two English astronomers published their studies of the same binary pair, but their results were not conclusive. Bolton decided to publish his data and staked his scientific reputation on his claim that Cygnus X-1 was a black hole. The astronomical community was skeptical of this work by a relatively unknown astronomer, and it took another year before it was widely accepted that Bolton had made the first-ever discovery of a black hole. His publication in the journal *Nature* is considered one of the most important astronomy papers ever written. Bolton describes that incredible summer of 1971 as the most exciting time of his career.

10.3 The Evolution of Galaxies

Your goal in this chapter is to understand the process of building a theory to explain the evolution of galaxies. The test of any scientific understanding is whether you can put all the evidence and theory together to tell the history of the objects studied. Can you describe the origin and evolution of the galaxies? Just a few decades ago, it would have been impossible, but the evidence from space telescopes and new-generation telescopes on Earth combined with advances in computer modelling and theory allow astronomers to outline the story of the galaxies.

In Chapter 9, you learned about two models of galaxy formation that can possibly describe the origin of the Milky Way Galaxy: the monolithic collapse model (Figure 9.16) and the bottom-up galaxy formation model (Figure 9.17). Presumably, other spiral galaxies formed in a similar way. But why did some galaxies become spiral, some elliptical, and others irregular? Clues to that mystery lie in the images of the farthest objects, from the early universe.

The Hubble Space Telescope image shows young galaxies or galactic building blocks, each containing dust, gas, and a few billion stars (Figure 10.7). These young objects could be the ancient building blocks of today's galaxies because they are close enough in space to eventually collide or merge with each other. Each building block is larger than a normal star cluster, but smaller than a present-day galaxy

1	2	3	4	5
4.00	4.88	4.90	5.42	5.76

Galaxy Building Blocks in the Hubble Ultra Deep Field
Hubble Space Telescope • ACS/WFC

NASA, ESA, and N. Pirzkal (STScI/ESA)   STScI-PRC07-31

NASA, ESA, and N.Pirzkal (STScI/ESA)

Figure 10.7 Hubble Ultra Deep Field. A few objects have been identified as the faintest, most compact galaxies ever observed in the distant universe. They are so far away that we see them as they looked less than 1 billion years after the big bang.

(as seen in bottom row, with their distances expressed in redshift value; refer to **The Doppler Formula** and **The Hubble Law** in Math Reference Cards.). Some young objects look disrupted, which is an indication that they may be interacting and merging with neighbouring galaxies to form a larger structure: a full-size galaxy. This is a strong support for bottom-up galaxy formation model. Depending on the density of matter in a protogalaxy, and the interaction between matter and dark matter, galaxies merged out of building blocks into spiral or elliptical galaxies.

The following sections describe the further evolution of the galaxies through galaxy groupings into clusters and galaxy collisions or mergers.

Clusters of Galaxies

The distribution of galaxies is not entirely random. Galaxies tend to occur in clusters, ranging from a few galaxies to thousands. Deep photographs made with the largest telescopes reveal clusters of galaxies scattered out to the limits of visibility. This clustering of the galaxies can help you understand their evolution.

For this discussion, you can sort clusters of galaxies into two groups, rich and poor. **Rich galaxy clusters** contain over a thousand galaxies, mostly elliptical, crowded into a spherical volume about 10 million light-years in diameter. The Coma cluster (located 300 million ly from Earth in the direction of the constellation Coma Berenices) is an example of a rich cluster, seen in Figure 10.8. It contains at least 1000 galaxies, mostly E and S0 types (for types of galaxies, refer to **Visualizing Astronomy 10.1, Galaxy Classification**).

Close to its centre are a giant elliptical galaxy and a large S0 galaxy. Rich clusters often contain one or more giant elliptical galaxies at their centres.

Poor galaxy clusters contain fewer than 1000 galaxies and are irregularly shaped and less crowded toward the centre. Our own **Local Group**, which contains the Milky Way, is a good example of a poor cluster (Figure 10.9). It contains a few dozen members scattered irregularly through a volume slightly more than 3 million ly in diameter. Of the brighter galaxies, 14 are elliptical, three are spiral, and four are irregular.

rich galaxy cluster A cluster containing 1000 or more galaxies, usually mostly ellipticals, scattered over a volume only a few Mpc in diameter.

poor galaxy cluster An irregularly shaped cluster that contains fewer than 1000 galaxies, many of which are spiral, and no giant ellipticals.

Local Group The small cluster of a few dozen galaxies that contains the Milky Way Galaxy.

gravitational lensing The curving of light by a large mass when the light passes between the source and the observer. Multiple images of the source can be seen.

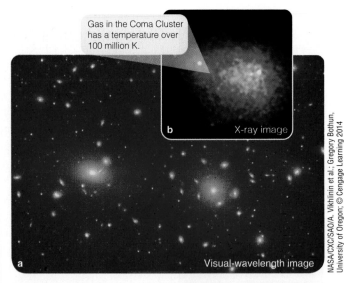

Gas in the Coma Cluster has a temperature over 100 million K.

b   X-ray image

a   Visual-wavelength image

NASA/CXC/SAO/A. Vikhlinin et al.; Gregory Bothun, University of Oregon; © Cengage Learning 2014

Figure 10.8 (a) The Coma cluster of galaxies contains at least 1000 galaxies and is expecially rich in E and S0 galaxies. Two giant galaxies lie near its centre. The only central arena of the cluster is shown in this image. If the cluster were visible in the sky, it would span eight times the diameter of the full Moon. (b) In false colours, this X-ray image of the Coma cluster shows it filled and surrounded by hot gas. Note that the two brightest galaxies are visible in the X-ray image.

Classifying galaxy clusters into rich and poor clusters reveals a fascinating and suggestive clue to the evolution of galaxies. In general, rich clusters tend to contain 80 to 90 percent E and S0 galaxies, and few spirals. Poor clusters contain a larger percentage of spirals; among isolated galaxies—those not in clusters—80 to 90 percent are spirals. This suggests that a galaxy's environment is important in determining its structure, and this has led astronomers to suspect that one of the secrets to galaxy evolution lies in the collisions between galaxies.

Dark Matter in Clusters of Galaxies

Masses of clusters of galaxies show even larger discrepancies between visible mass (in all wavelengths) and gravitational mass, which is mass inferred from gravity effects. Estimates of gravitational mass can be done in several ways. The most direct ones are (1) observing galaxies orbiting the massive central elliptical galaxies, and (2) gravitational lensing. Galaxies move like bees around a hive, and from their orbits and velocities we can calculate the mass of a cluster. Gravitational lensing, on the other hand, is the effect a cluster has on light from objects in the background.

Gravitational lensing was first mentioned by Isaac Newton when he postulated that light was composed of particles and that they should be attracted via gravity to

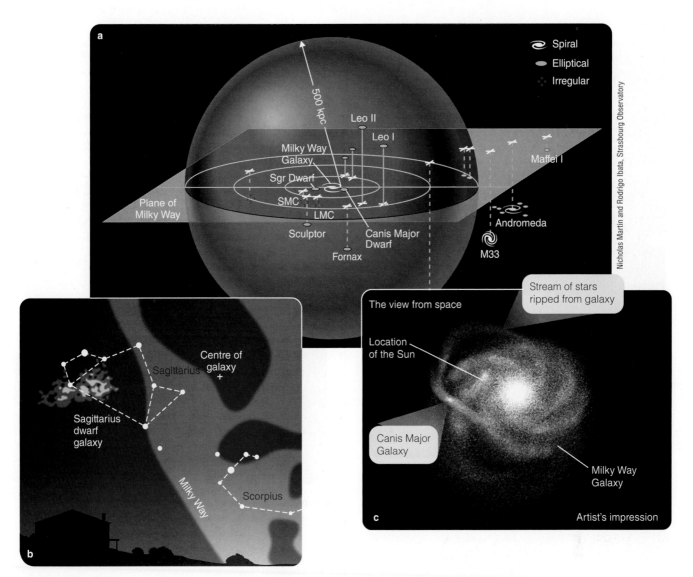

Figure 10.9 (a) The Local Group. Our galaxy is located at the centre of this diagram. The vertical lines giving distances from the plane of the Milky Way are solid above the plane and dashed below. (b) The Sagittarius Dwarf Galaxy (Sgr Dwarf) lies on the other side of our galaxy. If you could see it in the sky, it would be 17 times larger than the full Moon. (c) The Canis Major Dwarf Galaxy, shown in this simulation, is even closer to the Milky Way Galaxy. It is the remains of a small galaxy that is being pulled apart by our galaxy and is hidden behind the stars of the constellation Canis Major.

large masses. Einstein, 200 years after, proposed a theory of gravity called *general relativity*. The origin of gravity, according to general relativity, is the curving of space-time in the presence of a mass, so that all other masses follow the curvature when they move (see Figure 8.19). Light is also subject to curving. Light from a star, for example, would pass by a mass between the observer and the source (called lens), curve in the gravity field, and continue in the deflected direction. The observer would see a "mirage" some distance away from the real star (Figure 10.10a). In perfect alignment of object, lens, and observer in a straight line, the observer should see an infinite number of images—a ring around the lens. Indeed, this alignment, called Einstein's ring, has been observed (Figure 10.10b).

Einstein needed some experimental support when he proposed this strange idea in 1913 (see his original letter with the gravitational lens drawing in Figure 10.11). The perfect alignment for such observation was a solar eclipse. The Sun, a large mass, would deflect starlight; above all, the stars would be visible in that moment. All that needed to be done was to observe known stars in the moment of total eclipse and measure the deflection. However, you cannot observe a solar eclipse where you live unless your location is due for one. Right after Einstein's proposal in 1913, expeditions were planned. A few were unsuccessful—for example,

Gravitational lensing

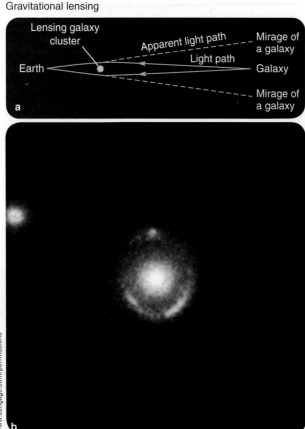

Figure 10.10 Schematic drawing of the deflection of starlight by the Sun's gravity. (a) The observer sees two images (mirages) of the real object. (b) Einstein's ring gravitational lens: SDSS J073728.45 + 321618.5.

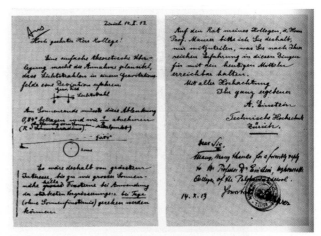

Figure 10.11 Einstein's original drawing of a gravitational lens from 1913.

Figure 10.12 Massive cluster of galaxies exhibits strong gravitational lensing.

German astronomer Erwin Finlay-Freundlich went to Russia in August 1914 to observe an eclipse, but World War I was declared and he was arrested. The first expedition that was able to show light deflection, was by British astronomer Sir Arthur Eddington, to Africa; however, the results were not very accurate. The expeditions in 50s and radio observations in the 60s obtained measurements that were in agreement with theoretical prediction.

Clusters of galaxies often have arcs around them, as in the case of Abel 2281 (Figure 10.12). Those are smeared images of an object—for example, a galaxy that lies behind the lensing cluster. These are extreme cases of lensing, and they imply that masses of lenses are enormous. We can calculate, on the basis of images, the orientation of observer–lens–object, as well as the mass of the lens. With this method, masses of clusters of galaxies are found to be incredibly larger than all luminous mass together, in all wavelengths observed and summed up.

Colliding Galaxies

Astronomers are finding more and more evidence that galaxies collide, interact, and merge. In fact, collisions among galaxies may dominate their evolution.

Do not be surprised that galaxies collide with each other. The average separation between galaxies is only about 20 times their diameter, so galaxies should bump into each other fairly often, astronomically speaking. In comparison, stars almost never collide because the typical separation between stars is about 10^7 times their diameter. A collision between two stars is about as likely as a collision between two gnats flitting about in a baseball stadium.

When two galaxies collide, they can pass through each other without stars colliding because the stars are so far apart relative to their sizes. Gas clouds and magnetic fields do collide, but the biggest effects may be tidal. Even when two galaxies just pass near each other, tides

Galaxy interactions can stimulate the formation of spiral arms

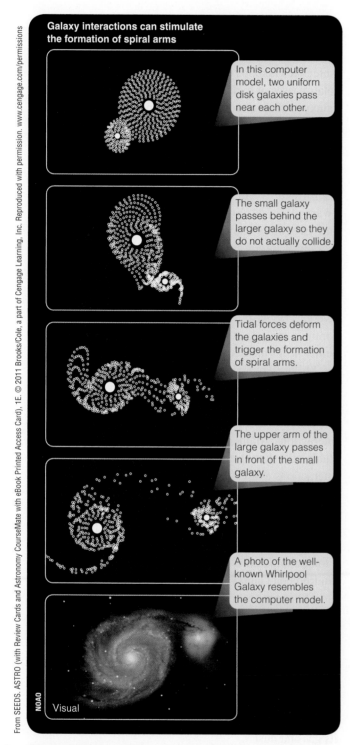

In this computer model, two uniform disk galaxies pass near each other.

The small galaxy passes behind the larger galaxy so they do not actually collide.

Tidal forces deform the galaxies and trigger the formation of spiral arms.

The upper arm of the large galaxy passes in front of the small galaxy.

A photo of the well-known Whirlpool Galaxy resembles the computer model.

Visual

NOAO

Figure 10.13 Computer simulation of galaxy interaction.

can cause dramatic effects, such as long streamers called **tidal tails** (Figure 10.13).

In some cases, two galaxies can merge and form a single galaxy, with intense star formation triggered by the collision, like the Cartwheel Galaxy (Figure 10.14).

When a galaxy swings past a massive object such as another galaxy, tides are severe. Stars near the massive

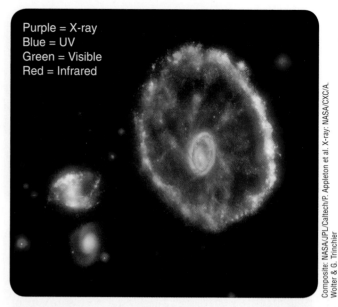

Purple = X-ray
Blue = UV
Green = Visible
Red = Infrared

Composite: NASA/JPL/Caltech/P. Appleton et al. X-ray: NASA/CXC/A. Wolter & G. Trinchier

Figure 10.14 The Cartwheel Galaxy was once a normal galaxy but is now a **ring galaxy**. One of its smaller companions has plunged through it at a high speed almost perpendicular at the galaxy's disk. That has triggered a wave of star formation, and the more massive stars have exploded, leaving behind black holes and neutron stars. Some of those are in X-ray binaries, and that makes the outer ring bright in X-rays.

object try to move in smaller, faster orbits, while stars farther from the massive object follow larger, slower orbits. Such tides can distort a galaxy or even rip it apart, as seen in the Mice galaxies (Figure 10.15).

Computer simulation of a similar scenario (Figure 10.16), derived from NASA Hubble Space Telescope measurements of the motion of Andromeda Galaxy, now 2.5 million light-years away, shows the collision course with the Milky Way Galaxy due to the mutual pull of gravity between the two galaxies and the invisible dark matter that surrounds them both. The galaxies will collide in 4 billion years, and it will take an additional 2 billion years after the encounter for the interacting galaxies to completely merge under the tug of gravity and reshape into a single elliptical galaxy, similar to the kind commonly seen in the local universe. The galaxies will go through each other, and stars inside each galaxy are so far apart that they will not collide with other stars during the encounter. However, the stars will be thrown into different orbits around the new galactic centre. Simulations show that our solar system will probably be tossed much farther from the galactic core than it is today.

tidal tail A long streamer of stars, gas, and dust torn from a galaxy during its close interaction with another passing galaxy.

ring galaxy A galaxy that resembles a ring around a bright nucleus, resulting from a head-on collision between two galaxies.

The Mice • Interacting Galaxies NGC 4676
Hubble Space Telescope • Advanced Camera for Surveys

NASA, H. Ford (JHU), G. Illingworth (UCSC/LO), M. Clampin (STScI), G. Hartig (STScI) and the ACS Science Team • STScI-PRC02-11d

Computer model of the Mice

Figure 10.15 The Mice galaxies are pulling each other apart. They have likely already passed through each other and will probably collide again and again until they coalesce.

The Milky Way Galaxy is currently snacking on the two Magellanic Clouds that orbit around it. Its tides are also pulling apart two other small satellite galaxies, the Sagittarius Galaxy and Canis Major Dwarf Galaxy, producing great streamers of stars wrapped around the Milky Way (see Figure 10.9 and **Visualizing Astronomy 10.1, Galaxy Classification**). Almost certainly, our galaxy has dined on other small galaxies in the past.

Newest observations of interacting galaxy clusters show a large presence of dark matter. Abell 520 was formed when two clusters of galaxies merged due to collision. The optical images in Figure 10.17 show, in orange, galaxies (NASA's Hubble Space Telescope) and starlight from galaxies (Canada-France-Hawaii Telescope). Green regions show hot gas from the collision (NASA's Chandra X-ray Observatory). Gravitational lensing observed by the Hubble Wide Field Planetary Camera 2, reveals that most of the mass of the cluster is dominated by dark matter, shown in blue.

The largest elliptical galaxies appear to be the product of galaxy mergers, which triggered star formation that used up the gas and dust. In fact, astronomers see a high level of star formation in many galaxies (Figure 10.18). These **starburst galaxies** are

starburst galaxy A galaxy undergoing a rapid burst of star formation.

very luminous in the infrared because a collision has triggered a burst of star formation that is heating the dust. The warm dust reradiates the energy in the infrared. The Antennae Galaxies (Figure 10.19) contain over 15 billion solar masses of hydrogen gas and will become a starburst galaxy as their ongoing merger continues to trigger rapid star formation.

A few collisions and mergers could leave a galaxy with no gas and dust from which to make new stars. Astronomers now suspect that some large ellipticals are formed by the merger of two or more galaxies. The dwarf ellipticals (too small to be formed by mergers) and irregulars may be fragments left over from the merger of larger galaxies.

In contrast, spirals seem never to have suffered major collisions. Their thin disks are delicate and would be destroyed by tidal forces in a collision with a massive galaxy. Also, they retain plenty of gas and dust and continue making stars. Our Milky Way Galaxy has evidently never merged with another large galaxy. However, the Milky Way Galaxy along with its large spiral neighbour the Andromeda Galaxy seem to have cannibalized smaller galaxies.

Barred spiral galaxies also may be the product of tidal interactions. Mathematical models show that bars are not stable and should eventually dissipate. It may take tidal interactions with other galaxies to regenerate the bars. Because well over half of all spiral galaxies have bars, you can suspect that these tidal interactions are common. The Milky Way Galaxy is probably a barred spiral (refer to Figure 9.11); its interaction with its two Magellanic Cloud companions or the more distant but very massive Andromeda Galaxy could be the cause.

Other processes can alter galaxies. The S0 galaxies, which have disks and bulges like a spiral galaxy, but no spiral arms, may have lost much of their gas and dust while moving through the gas trapped in the dense clusters to which they belong. For example, X-ray observations show that the Coma cluster contains thin, hot gas between the galaxies (Figure 10.8). A galaxy moving through that gas would encounter a tremendous wind that could strip away its gas and dust.

Observations with the largest and most sophisticated telescopes take astronomers back to the age of galaxy formation. At great distances the look-back time is so large that they see the universe as it was soon after the galaxies began to form. There were more spirals then and fewer ellipticals. The observations show that galaxies were closer together then; about 33 percent of all distant galaxies are in close pairs, but only 7 percent of nearby (in other words, present-day) galaxies are in pairs. The

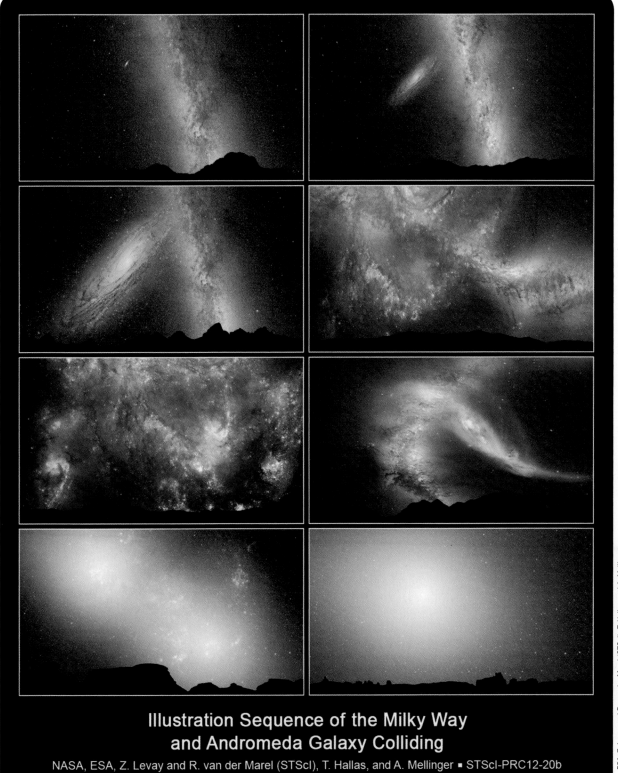

Illustration Sequence of the Milky Way
and Andromeda Galaxy Colliding

NASA, ESA, Z. Levay and R. van der Marel (STScI), T. Hallas, and A. Mellinger ▪ STScI-PRC12-20b

Figure 10.16 Collision of Milky Way and Andromeda galaxies in 4 billion years, represented as seen from Earth.

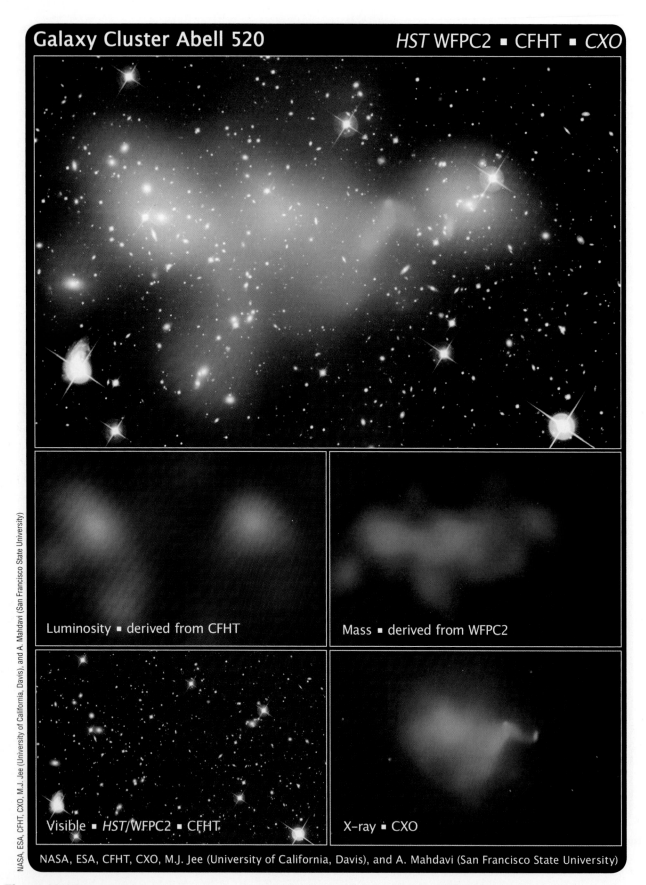

Galaxy Cluster Abell 520

HST WFPC2 ▪ CFHT ▪ *CXO*

Luminosity ▪ derived from CFHT

Mass ▪ derived from WFPC2

Visible ▪ *HST*/WFPC2 ▪ CFHT

X-ray ▪ CXO

NASA, ESA, CFHT, CXO, M.J. Jee (University of California, Davis), and A. Mahdavi (San Francisco State University)

Figure 10.17 Dark matter in merging galaxy cluster Abell 520. This composite image shows the distribution of dark matter, galaxies, and hot gas in the core of the merging galaxy cluster Abell 520, formed from a violent collision of massive galaxy clusters.

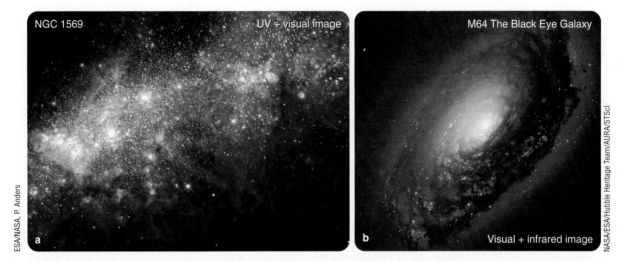

Figure 10.18 Rapid star formation. (a) NGC 1569 is a starburst galaxy filled with clouds of young stars and supernovae. At least some starbursts are triggered by interactions between galaxies. (b) The inner parts of M64, known as the Black Eye Galaxy, are filled with dust produced by rapid star formation. Radio Doppler shift observations show that the inner part of the galaxy rotates backward compared to the outer part of the galaxy, a product of a merger. Star formation is stimulated where the counter-rotating parts of the galaxy collide.

observational evidence clearly supports the hypothesis that galaxies have evolved by merger.

The evolution of galaxies is not a simple process. A good theory helps you understand how nature works, and astronomers are just beginning to understand the exciting and complex story of the galaxies. Nevertheless, it is already clear that galaxy evolution has some resemblance to a pie-throwing contest and is just about as neat.

10.4 Active Galaxies and Quasars

Many galaxies have powerful energy sources in their nuclei that in some cases produce powerful jets and other outbursts. These are called **active galaxies**. By looking far away and back in time, astronomers have discovered that the origin of active galaxy energy sources and outbursts is closely related to the formation and history of galaxies.

The first type of active galaxy was discovered in the 1950. These were named **radio galaxies** because they are sources of unusually strong radio waves. By the 1970s, astronomers had put space telescopes in orbit and

The Antennae

Brad Whitmore, STScI/ NASA

Ground-based
visual image

Hubble Space Telescope
visual image

Figure 10.19 Hubble Space Telescope galaxy images of NGC 4038 and 4039, known as the Antennae Galaxies, reveal that the two galaxies are blazing with star formation. Roughly a thousand massive star clusters have been born. Spectra show that these galaxies are 10 to 20 times richer in elements such as magnesium and silicon than the Milky Way Galaxy. Such metals are produced by massive stars and spread by supernova explosions.

active galaxy A galaxy whose centre emits large amounts of excess energy, often in the form of radio emissions. Active galaxies have massive black holes in their centres into which matter is flowing.

radio galaxy A galaxy that is a strong source of radio signals.

discovered that radio galaxies are generally bright at many other wavelengths. The flood of energy pouring out of active galaxies originates almost entirely in their nuclei, which are referred to as **active galactic nuclei (AGN)**.

Seyfert Galaxies

In 1943, astronomer Carl K. Seyfert conducted a study of spiral galaxies in which he noted that about 2 percent of spirals have small, highly luminous nuclei in their bulges (see Figure 10.20). Today, these **Seyfert galaxies** are recognized by the peculiar spectra of these luminous nuclei that contain broad emission lines of highly ionized atoms. Emission lines come from low-density gas; the presence of ionized atoms is evidence that the gas is very hot; broad spectral lines indicate large Doppler shifts produced by high gas velocities. The velocities of gas clouds at the centres of Seyfert galaxies are roughly 10 000 km/s, about 30 times greater than velocities at the centre of normal galaxies. Something violent is happening in the cores of Seyfert galaxies.

Astronomers later discovered that the brilliant nuclei of Seyfert galaxies change brightness rapidly, in only a few hours or minutes, especially at X-ray wavelengths. As you saw in Chapter 8, an astronomical body cannot change its brightness significantly in a time shorter than the time it takes light to cross its diameter. If a Seyfert nucleus can change in a few minutes, then it cannot be larger in diameter than a few light-minutes. For comparison, the distance from Earth to the Sun is 8 light-minutes.

Figure 10.20 Seyfert galaxies are spiral galaxies with small, highly luminous nuclei. Some interact with nearby companions and appear distorted with tidal tails and bridges.

Yet, despite their small size, the brightest Seyfert nuclei emit a hundred times more energy than the entire Milky Way Galaxy. Something in the centres of these galaxies not much bigger than Earth's orbit produces a galaxy's worth of energy.

Seyfert nuclei are three times more common in interacting pairs of galaxies than in isolated galaxies (see **How Do We Know? 10.3**). Also, about 25 percent of Seyfert galaxies have peculiar shapes, suggesting tidal interactions with other galaxies. This statistical evidence hints that Seyfert galaxies may have been triggered into activity by collisions or interactions with companions. Some Seyferts are observed to be expelling matter in oppositely directed jets, a geometry you have seen on smaller scales when matter flows into neutron stars and black holes and forms an accretion disk plus jets.

The accumulated evidence leads modern astronomers to conclude that the core of a Seyfert galaxy contains a supermassive black hole, with a mass as high as a billion solar masses, plus a correspondingly large accretion disk. Gas in the centres of Seyfert galaxies is travelling so fast it would escape from a normal galaxy, and only large central masses could exert enough gravity to hold the gas inside the nuclei. Encounters with other galaxies could throw matter toward the black hole, and lots of energy can be liberated by matter flowing through an accretion disk into a black hole. As you learned in Chapter 9, the Milky Way Galaxy contains a massive central black hole, but one that seems to be on a starvation diet and is therefore relatively inactive.

Double-Lobed Radio Sources

Beginning in the 1950s, radio astronomers found that some sources of radio energy in the sky consist of pairs of radio-bright regions. When optical telescopes studied the locations of these **double-lobed radio sources**, they revealed galaxies located between the two lobes. The geometry suggests that radio lobes are inflated by jets of excited gas emerging in two directions from the central galaxy. Statistical evidence indicates that jets and radio lobes, like Seyfert nuclei, are associated with interacting galaxies. The AGN jets seem to be related to matter falling into a central black hole via an accretion disk, although the details of this process are not understood.

The violence of these active galaxies is so great it can influence entire clusters of galaxies. The Perseus galaxy cluster contains thousands of galaxies and is one of the largest objects in the universe. One of its galaxies, NGC 1275, is among the largest galaxies

Statistical Evidence

How can statistics be useful if they can't be specific? Some scientific evidence is statistical. Observations suggest, for example, that Seyfert galaxies are more likely to be interacting with a nearby companion than a normal galaxy is. This is statistical evidence, so you can't be certain that any specific Seyfert galaxy will have a companion. How can scientists use statistical evidence to learn about nature when statistics contain built-in uncertainty?

Meteorologists use statistics to determine how frequently hurricanes of a certain size are likely to occur. Small storms happen every year, but big storms may happen on average only every ten years. Hundred-year hurricanes are much more powerful but occur much less frequently: on average only once in a hundred years.

Those meteorological statistics can help you make informed decisions—as long as you understand the powers and limitations of statistics. Would you buy a house protected from a river by a levee that was not designed to withstand a hundred-year storm? In any one year, the chance of your house being destroyed would be only 1 in 100. You know the storm will hit eventually, but you don't know when. If you buy the house, a storm might destroy the levee the next year, but you might own the house for your whole life and never see a hundred-year storm. The statistics can't tell you anything about a specific year.

Before you buy that house, there is an important question you should ask the meteorologists: "How much data do you have on storms?" If they have only ten years of data they don't really know much about hundred-year storms. If they have three centuries of data their statistical data are significant.

Sometimes people dismiss important warnings by saying, "Oh, that's only statistics." Scientists can use statistical evidence if it passes two tests. It cannot be used to draw conclusions about specific cases, and it must be based on large enough data samples so the statistics are significant. With these restrictions, statistical evidence can be a powerful scientific tool.

Statistics can tell you that a bad storm will eventually hit, but it can't tell you when.

---

known. It is pumping out jets of high-energy particles, heating the gas in the galaxy cluster, and inflating low-density bubbles that distort the huge gas cloud (Figure 10.21). The hot gas observed in galaxy clusters is heated to multimillion-degree temperatures as galaxy after galaxy goes through eruptive stages that can last for hundreds of millions of years. NGC 1275 is erupting now, and it is so powerful and has heated the surrounding gas to such high temperatures that the gas can no longer fall in and the galaxy has probably limited its own growth.

Quasars

The largest telescopes detect multitudes of faint points of light with peculiar emission spectra, these are objects called **quasars** (also known as *quasi-stellar objects*, or *QSOs*). Although astronomers now recognize quasars as extreme examples of AGN as well as some of the most distant visible objects in the universe, they were a mystery when they were first identified.

In the early 1960s, photographs of the location of some radio sources that resembled radio galaxies revealed only single starlike points of light. The first of these objects identified was 3C 48, and later the source 3C 273 was found. They were obviously not normal radio galaxies. Even the most distant photographable galaxies look fuzzy, but these objects looked like stars. Their spectra, however, were totally unlike stellar spectra, so the objects were called quasi-stellar objects.

For a few years, the spectra of quasars were a mystery. A few unidentifiable emission lines were superimposed on a continuous spectrum. In 1963, astronomer Maarten Schmidt calculated that if hydrogen Balmer lines were redshifted by $z = 0.158$ (meaning each line's change in wavelength divided by its lab wavelength equals 0.158 see The Doppler Formula and The Hubble Law in math reference Cards), they would fit the observed lines in 3C 273's spectrum (Figure 10.22). Other quasar spectra quickly yielded to this type of analysis, revealing even larger redshifts.

quasar Small, powerful source of energy in the active core of a very distant galaxy.

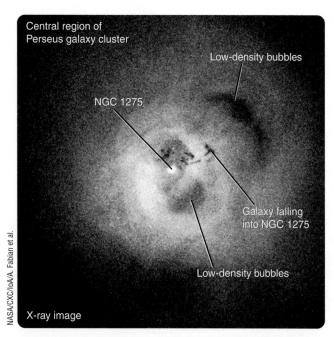

Central region of Perseus galaxy cluster

Low-density bubbles

NGC 1275

Galaxy falling into NGC 1275

Low-density bubbles

X-ray image

NASA/CXC/IoA/A. Fabian et al.

Figure 10.21 NGC 1275 in the Perseus galaxy cluster is spewing out jets and streamers of high-energy particles that are inflating low-density cavities in the hot gas within the cluster. The entire galaxy cluster is roughly 50 times larger in diameter than this image.

To understand the significance of these large redshifts and the large velocities of recession they imply, recall the Hubble law from earlier in this chapter, which states that galaxies have apparent velocities of recession proportional to their distances. (Refer to **The Hubble Law** in the Math Reference Cards.) The large redshifts of the quasars imply that they must be at great distances, some farther away than any known galaxy. Many quasars are evidently so far away that galaxies at those distances are very difficult to detect, yet the quasars are easily photographed. This leads to the conclusion that quasars must be ultraluminous, 10 to 1000 times the luminosity of a large galaxy.

Soon after quasars were discovered, astronomers detected fluctuations in their brightness over time scales of hours or minutes. The rapid fluctuations in quasars showed that they are small objects like AGN, only a few light-minutes or light-hours in diameter. Evidence, such as that seen in Figure 10.23, has accumulated that quasars are the most luminous AGN and are located in very distant galaxies. For example, some quasars, such as AGN, are at the centres of double radio lobes plus jets.

Perhaps you have a skeptical question about quasar distances at this point; that is, how can you be sure quasars really are that far away? Astronomers faced with explaining how a small object could produce so much energy have asked themselves the same question. In the early 1980s, astronomers were able to photograph faint nebulosity surrounding some quasars, which was called quasar fuzz. The spectra of quasar fuzz looked like the spectra of normal but very distant galaxies with the same redshift as the central quasar. In other cases, quasar light shines through the outskirts of a distant galaxy, and the quasar spectrum has extra absorption lines from gas at the redshift of the galaxy, smaller than the quasar's redshift. This means the quasar is farther away than the galaxy containing the gas that absorbed some of the quasar's light on its way to Earth. Both of these observations confirm that galaxy and quasar redshifts indicate distances in a mutually consistent way.

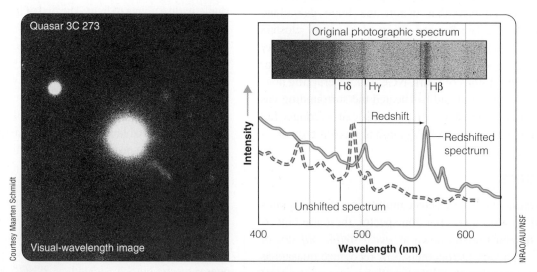

Quasar 3C 273

Courtesy Maarten Schmidt

Visual-wavelength image

Original photographic spectrum

Hδ Hγ Hβ

Redshift

Redshifted spectrum

Unshifted spectrum

Intensity

400   500   600

Wavelength (nm)

NRAO/AUI/NSF

Figure 10.22 This image of 3C 273 (left) shows the bright quasar at the centre surrounded by faint fuzz. Note the jet protruding to lower right. The spectrum of 3C 273 (right, top) contains three hydrogen Balmer lines redshifted by 15.8 percent. The drawing shows the unshifted positions of the spectrum.

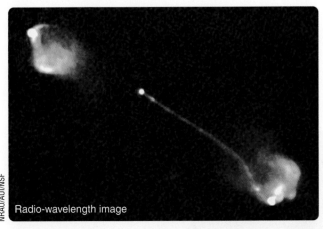

Figure 10.23 This radio image of quasar 3C 175 reveals the quasar is ejecting a jet, and it is flanked by radio lobes. Presumably you see only one jet because it is directed approximately toward Earth, and the other jet is invisible because it is directed away from Earth. The presence of jets and radio lobes indicates that quasars are the active cores of distant galaxies.

The Search for a Unified Model

Astronomers studying galaxies are now developing a **unified model** of AGN and quasars. A monster black hole is the centrepiece (Figure 10.24).

Even a supermassive black hole is quite small compared with a galaxy. A 10-million-solar-mass black hole would be only one-fifth the diameter of Earth's orbit. This means that matter in an accretion disk can get very close to the black hole, orbit very fast, and grow very hot. Theoretical calculations indicate that the disk immediately around the black hole is "puffed up," thick enough to hide the central black hole from some viewing angles. The hot inner disk seems to be the source of the jets often seen coming out of active galaxy cores, but astronomers don't yet understand the process by which these jets are generated. Mathematical models indicate that the outer part of the disk is a fat, relatively cold torus (doughnut shape) of dusty gas.

According to the unified model depicted in Figure 10.24, when you view the core of an AGN or QSO what you see depends on how its accretion disk is tipped with respect to your line of sight.

1. If you view the accretion disk from the edge, you cannot see the central zone at all because the thick dusty torus blocks your view. Instead, you see radiation emitted by gas lying above and below the central disk, which is therefore relatively cool and moving relatively slowly, with small Doppler shifts. Thus, you see narrower spectral lines coming from what is called the narrow-line region.

2. If the accretion disk is tipped slightly, you may be able to see some of the intensely hot gas in the central cavity. This is called the broad-line region because the gas is hot and also orbiting at high velocities. The resulting high Doppler shifts spread out the spectral lines.

3. If you look directly into the central cavity around the black hole—down the dragon's throat, so to speak—you see the jet emerging perpendicular to the accretion disk and coming straight at you. Model calculations indicate this would result in a very luminous and highly variable source with few or no emission lines. This is the appearance of AGN known as **blazars**.

Astronomers are now using this unified model to sort out the different kinds of active galaxies and quasars so they can understand how they are related. For example, about 1 percent of quasars are strong radio sources, and the radio radiation may come from synchrotron radiation (see Chapter 8) produced in the high-energy gas and magnetic fields in the jets. Another example: Using infrared cameras to see through dust, astronomers observed the core of the double-lobed radio galaxy Cygnus A and found an object much like a quasar. Astronomers have begun to refer to such hidden objects as "buried quasars."

The unified model is far from complete. The detailed structure of accretion disks is poorly understood, as is the process by which the disks produce jets. Furthermore, the spiral Seyfert galaxies are clearly different from the giant elliptical galaxies that have double radio lobes. Unification does not explain all of the differences among active galaxies. Rather, it is a model that provides some clues to what is happening in AGN and quasars.

The Origin of Supermassive Black Holes

If you are wondering where these supermassive black holes in the nuclei of galaxies came from, that question is linked to a second question: What makes a supermassive black hole erupt? Answering these two questions will help you understand how galaxies form.

Evidence is accumulating that most galaxies

unified model An attempt to explain the different types of active galactic nuclei using a single model viewed from different directions.

blazar A type of active galaxy nucleus that is especially variable and has few or no spectral emission lines.

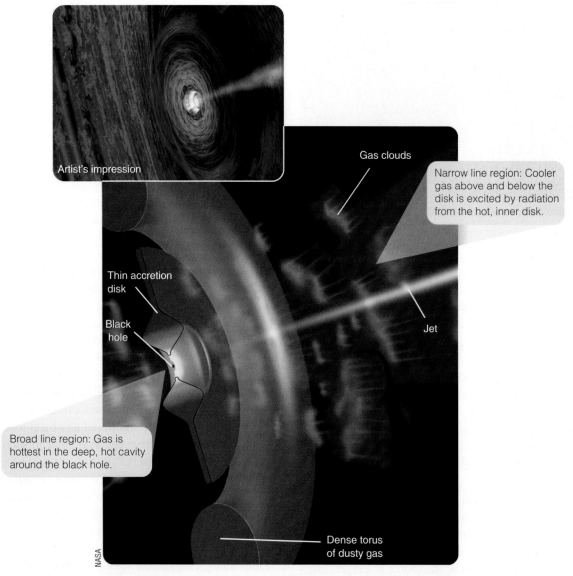

Figure 10.24 The features visible in the spectrum of an AGN depend on the angle at which it is viewed. The unified model, shown in cross-section, suggests that matter flowing inward passes first through a large, opaque torus; then into a thinner, hotter disk; and finally into a small, hot cavity around the black hole. Telescopes viewing such a disk edge-on would see only narrow spectral lines from cooler gas, but a telescope looking into the central cavity would see broad spectral lines formed by the hot gas. This diagram is not to scale. The central cavity may be only 0.03 ly in radius, while the outer torus may be 3000 ly in radius.

contain a supermassive black hole at their centre (Figure 10.25). Even our Milky Way Galaxy and the nearby Andromeda Galaxy contain central black holes. Only a few percent of galaxies, however, have obviously active galactic nuclei. That must mean that most of the supermassive black holes are dormant. Presumably they are not being fed large amounts of matter. A slow trickle of matter flowing into the supermassive black hole at the centre of our galaxy could explain the relatively mild activity seen there. It would take a larger meal to trigger an eruption such as those seen in active galactic nuclei.

What could trigger a supermassive black hole to erupt? The answer—tides—is something you studied in Chapter 3. As you have learned, tides twist interacting galaxies and rip matter away into tidal tails. Active galaxies are often distorted. They have evidently been twisted by tidal forces as they interacted or merged with another galaxy. Mathematical models show that those interactions can also throw stars plus clouds of interstellar gas and dust inward toward the galaxies' centres. A sudden flood of matter flowing into a supermassive black hole would trigger it into eruption. Figure 10.26 shows how a passing star would be shredded and partially consumed by a supermassive hole. A steady diet of inflowing gas, dust, and an occasional star would keep the supermassive black hole in an AGN active.

A few dozen supermassive black holes have measured masses, and their masses are correlated with the masses of the host galaxies' central bulges. In each case, the mass of the black hole is about 0.5 percent the mass of the surrounding central bulge. Apparently, as a galaxy forms its central bulge, a certain fraction of the mass sinks to the centre, where it forms a supermassive black hole. All of that matter flowing together to form the black hole would release a tremendous amount of energy and trigger a violent eruption. Long ago, when galaxies were actively forming, the birth of the central bulges must have triggered many AGN. Later episodes of AGN activity could be triggered by interactions or mergers with other galaxies.

NGC 4261

Visual (white) radio (orange)

Figure 10.25 The elliptical galaxy NGC 4261 is ejecting jets and inflating radio lobes. High-resolution images show that the core contains a small, bright nucleus orbited by a spinning disk. The orbital velocity and size of the disk confirm that the central object is a supermassive black hole.

Perpendicular to the axis of the jets leading into radio lobes, this disk encloses 1.2 billion solar masses.

800 ly

Visual-wavelength image

L. Ferrarese (John Hopkins University) and Nasa; Walter Jaffe/Leiden Observatory, Holland Ford/JHU/STScl

Quasars through Time

In the next chapter, you will see evidence that the universe began 13.8 billion years ago. Some quasars are over 10 billion light-years away, and because of their large look-back times they appear as they were when the universe was only 10 percent of its present age. Evidently, quasars are embedded in distant galaxies. Some of the closest quasars are located in the centres of elliptical galaxies. Perhaps we can assume that distant quasars seen when the universe was just 4 billion years old, are located in the ancestors of elliptical galaxies. The Hubble Space Telescope observation of quasars reveals the existence of early galaxies that are bluer than nearby elliptical galaxies. This could imply that we are seeing elliptical galaxies in formation. The first clouds of gas that formed galaxies would have also made supermassive black holes at the centres of those galaxies' central bulges. The abundance of matter flooding into those early black holes could have triggered outbursts that are seen as quasars.

Note that galaxies were closer together when the universe was young and had not expanded very much.

Because they were closer together, the forming galaxies collided more often, and these collisions between galaxies could throw matter into central supermassive black holes and trigger eruptions. Quasars are often located in host galaxies that are distorted as if they were interacting with other galaxies (Figure 10.27).

Quasars are most common with redshifts a little over 2 and less common with redshifts above 2.7. The largest quasar redshifts are over 6, but such high-redshift quasars are quite rare. Evidently, if you looked at quasars with redshifts a bit over 2, you would be looking back to an age when galaxies were actively forming, colliding, and merging. In that era, quasars were about 1000 times more common than they are now. Even so, only a fraction of galaxies had quasars erupting in their cores at any one time. If you look back to higher redshifts, you would see fewer quasars because you would be looking back to an age when the universe was so young it had not yet begun to form many galaxies and quasars.

Then where are all the dead quasars? There is no way to get rid of supermassive black holes. Astronomers have discovered that nearly all galaxies contain supermassive black holes, and those black holes may have suffered quasar eruptions when the universe was younger, galaxies were closer together, and infalling gas and dust were more plentiful. Quasar eruptions

Star Falling into a Black Hole

A star, perhaps disturbed by an encounter with another star, drifts toward a supermassive black hole.

As the near side of the star tries to orbit faster than the far side, the star is torn apart by tidal forces.

Most of the mass of the star is flung away from the black hole …

… but roughly 1 percent falls into the black hole as an accretion disk forms.

ESA and Stefanie Komossa (Max Planck Institute for Extraterrestrial Physics)

Figure 10.26 This artist's conception represents the cause of an X-ray flare in the galaxy RX J1242-11 that was detected by X-ray telescopes in orbit around Earth. Equalling the energy of a supernova explosion, the flare was evidently caused when a star wandered too close to the 100-million-solar-mass black hole at the centre of the galaxy. When tidal forces ripped the star apart, some of the mass fell into the black hole, and the rest was flung away. That sudden meal for the black hole was enough to trigger an outburst.

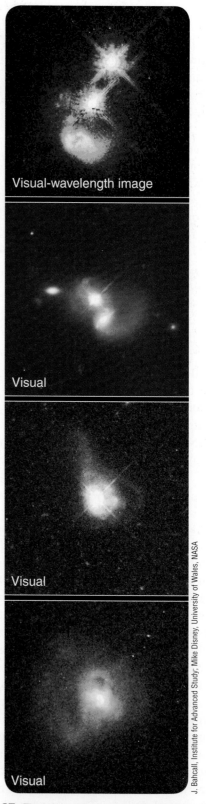

Visual-wavelength image

Visual

Visual

Visual

J. Bahcall, Institute for Advanced Study; Mike Disney, University of Wales, NASA

Figure 10.27 The bright object at the centre of each of these images is a quasar. Fainter objects near and around the quasars are galaxies distorted by collisions. Compare the ring-shaped galaxy in the first image below with the ring galaxy shown in Figure 10.14, and compare the tail in the third image with the Antennae Galaxies shown in Figure 10.19.

became less common as galaxies became more stable and as the abundance of gas and dust in the centres of galaxies was exhausted. The Milky Way Galaxy is a good example. It could have been a quasar long ago, but today its supermassive black hole is resting. Dormant black holes at the centres of galaxies today can be reawakened to become AGN by galaxy collisions and interactions.

The Big Picture

You are riding a small planet orbiting a humdrum star that is just one of at least 100 billion in the Milky Way Galaxy. You have just learned that there are at least 100 billion galaxies visible with existing telescopes, and that each of these galaxies contains roughly 100 billion stars. Humans fight wars over politics, religion, and economics; we do our work, play our games, and wash our laundry. It's all important stuff, but next time you are frantically rushing to a meeting, glance up at the sky.

When you look at galaxies, you are looking across voids deeper than human imagination. You can express such distances with numbers, but the distance is truly beyond human comprehension. Some people say astronomy makes them feel humble, but before you agree, consider how you can feel small without feeling humble. We humans live out our little lives on our little planet, but we are figuring out some of the biggest mysteries of the universe. We are exploring deep space and deep time and coming to understand what galaxies are and how they evolve. Most of all, we are beginning to understand what we are. That's something to be proud of.

Review and Discussion Questions

Review Questions

1. What types of galaxies exist?
2. How do astronomers measure the distances to galaxies, and how does that allow the sizes, luminosities, and masses of galaxies to be determined?
3. Why are there different kinds of galaxies, and how do galaxies evolve?
4. What is the energy source for active galaxies, what can trigger the activity, and what does that reveal about the history of galaxies?
5. How do long-exposure photos of two selected areas of the sky reveal that galaxies are very common?
6. What is the difference between an Sa and an Sb galaxy? Between an S0 and an Sa galaxy? Between an Sb and an SBb galaxy? Between an E7 and an S0 galaxy?
7. Explain how the rotation curve method of finding a galaxy's mass is similar to the method used to find the masses of binary stars.
8. Explain how the Hubble law allows you to estimate the distances to galaxies.
9. How can collisions affect the shapes of galaxies?
10. What evidence can you cite that galactic cannibalism really happens?
11. What evidence suggests that Seyfert galaxies have suffered recent interactions with other galaxies?
12. What evidence shows that quasars are ultraluminous but must be small?
13. What evidence is there that quasars occur in distant galaxies?
14. **How Do We Know?** Classification helped Darwin understand how creatures evolve. Has classification helped you understand how galaxies evolve?
15. **How Do We Know?** How would you respond to someone who said, "Oh, that's only statistics"?

Discussion Questions

1. From what you know about star formation and the evolution of galaxies, do you think irregular galaxies should be bright or faint in the infrared relative to visible wavelengths? Why or why not? What about starburst galaxies? What about elliptical galaxies?

2. Do you think that our galaxy is currently an active galaxy? Do you think it ever was in the past? Could it have hosted a quasar when it was young?

Learning to Look

1. In the image at right you see two interacting galaxies; one is nearly face-on and the other is nearly edge-on. Discuss the shapes of these galaxies and describe what is happening.

WIN/NOAO/NSF

2. The image at right combines visual (blue) with radio (red) to show the galaxy radio astronomers call Fornax A.

Explain the features of this image. Is it significant that the object is a distorted elliptical galaxy in a cluster?

NRAO/AUI

STUDY **TOOLS**

IN THE BOOK
- Tear out the Review Card for Chapter 10

ONLINE

Visit CENGAGENOW™ for ASTRO, 2Ce at www.nelson.com/student

- eBook
- Interactive Quizzing
- Animations
- Tutorials

Learning like never before.

4LTR P·R·E·S·S

www.nelson.com/student

11

Cosmology in the 21st Century

CHAPTER OUTLINE

GUIDEPOST

Beginning with Chapter 1, you have been on an outward journey through the universe. At this point, you have reached the limit of your travels in space and time and can contemplate the universe as a whole. The ideas in this chapter are among the biggest and most difficult in all of science. Can you imagine a limitless universe, or the first instant of time?

As you explore this chapter, you will find answers to three important questions:

- **Does the universe have a centre and an edge?**
- **What is the evidence that the universe began with a big bang?**
- **How has the universe evolved, and what will be its fate?**

When you finish studying this chapter, you will have a modern insight into the nature of the universe, as well as where you are and what you are.

Look at your thumb. The matter in your thumb was present in the fiery beginning of the universe. **Cosmology**, the study of the universe as a whole, can tell you where your body's matter comes from, and it can tell you where that matter is going. Cosmology is a mind-bending, weird subject, and you can enjoy it for its strange ideas. It is fun to think about space stretching like a rubber sheet, invisible energy pushing the universe to expand faster and faster, and the origin of vast walls of galaxy clusters. Notice that this is better than speculation—it is all supported by evidence. Cosmology, however strange it may seem, is a serious and logical attempt to understand how the universe works, and it leads to wonderful insights into how we came to be a part of it.

cosmology The study of the nature, origin, and evolution of the universe.

Mankind has made giant steps forward. However, what we know is really very, very little compared to what we still have to know.

Fabiola Gianotti,
Physicist and leader of the ATLAS
experiment that discovered the Higgs boson

The big bang. Conceptual computer artwork of the origin and evolution of the universe. The term *big bang* describes the initial expansion of all matter in the universe from an infinitely compact state 13.8 billion years ago. The initial conditions are not known, but less than a second after the beginning, temperatures were trillions of degrees Celsius, and the primordial universe was much smaller than an atom. It has been expanding and cooling ever since.

11.1 Introduction to the Universe

Many people have an impression of the universe as a vast sphere filled with stars and galaxies. Your vision may be similar to the composite image shown in Figure 11.1. However, as you begin exploring the universe, you need to become aware of your assumptions so they do not mislead you. The first step is to deal with an expectation so obvious that most people, for the sake of a quiet life, don't even think about it.

The Edge–Centre Problem

In your daily life, you are accustomed to boundaries. Rooms have walls, athletic fields have boundary lines, countries have borders, and oceans have shores. It is natural to think of the universe as having an edge, but that idea can't be right.

If the universe had an edge, imagine going to the edge. What would you find there: A wall? A great empty space? Nothing? Even a child can ask, if there is an edge to space, what's beyond it? A true edge would have to be more than just an end of the

Olbers's paradox The conflict between theory and evidence regarding the darkness of the night sky.

distribution of matter, it would have to be an end of space itself; but then, what would happen if you tried to reach past or move past that edge?

Modern observations indicate that the universe could be infinite and have no edge. Note that you find the centres of things—galaxies, globular clusters, oceans, pizzas—by referring to their edges. If the universe has no edge, it cannot have a centre.

It is a common misconception to imagine that the universe has a centre, but, as you have just learned, that is impossible. As you study cosmology, you need to take care to avoid thinking that there is a centre of the universe.

The Necessity of a Beginning

The simple observation that the night sky is dark is an important one. This is because reasonable assumptions about the universe can lead us to conclude that the night sky would actually glow blindingly bright! This conflict between observation and theory is called **Olbers's paradox**, after Heinrich Olbers, an Austrian physician and astronomer who publicized the problem in 1826; in fact, *problem* or *question* would be more accurate words than *paradox*. Olbers was not the first to pose the question, but it is named after him because modern cosmologists were not aware of the earlier discussions. After revising your assumptions about the

R. Williams, STScI HDF-South Team, NASA

Visual + infrared image

Figure 11.1 In this image of a typical spot on the sky, bright objects with spikes caused by diffraction in the telescope are nearby stars. All other objects are galaxies, ranging from the nearby face-on spiral at upper right to the most distant galaxies visible only in the infrared, shown as red in this composite image.

Figure 11.2 Olbers's paradox. If the universe is infinite and filled with stars any line from Earth should eventually reach the surface of a star. This assumption predicts that the night sky should glow as brightly as the surface of the average star.

x

Figure 11.3 Every direction you look in a forest eventually reaches a tree trunk, and you cannot see out of the forest.

universe, you will be able to answer Olbers's question and understand why the night sky is dark.

The point Olbers made seems simple. Suppose you assume that the universe is infinite and filled with stars. (The clumping of stars into galaxies can be shown mathematically to make no difference.) If you look in any direction, your line of sight must eventually reach the surface of a star (see Figure 11.2). Now think about trying to see out of a forest. When you are deep in a forest, every line of sight ends on a tree trunk, and you cannot see out of the forest (Figure 11.3). By analogy, every line of sight from Earth out into space should eventually end on the surface of a star, so the entire sky should be as bright as the surface of an average star—like suns crowded "shoulder to shoulder," covering the sky from horizon to horizon. It should not get dark at night.

Today, cosmologists believe they understand why the sky is dark. Olbers's paradox makes an incorrect prediction because it is based on a hidden assumption. The universe may be infinite in size, but it is not eternal—that is, not infinitely old. That answer to Olbers's question was suggested by Edgar Allan Poe in 1848. He proposed that the night sky is dark because the universe is not infinitely old but instead began at some time in the past. The more distant stars are so far away that light from

them has not yet reached Earth. That is, if you look far enough, the look-back time is greater than the age of the universe. The night sky is dark because the universe had a beginning.

This is a powerful idea because it clearly illustrates the difference between the universe and the observable universe. The universe is everything that exists, but the **observable universe** is the part that you can see. As you have learned, astronomers now know the universe is 13.8 billion years old. Because of that, the observable universe is limited by a light travel time of 13.8 billion years. Do not confuse the observable universe, which is finite, with the universe as a whole, which could be infinite.

Cosmic Expansion

In 1929, Edwin P. Hubble published his discovery that the sizes of galaxy redshifts are proportional to galaxy distances (refer to Figure 10.4). Nearby galaxies have small redshifts, but more distant galaxies have larger redshifts. These redshifts imply that the galaxies are receding from each other. Figure 11.4 shows spectra of galaxies in clusters

> **observable universe** The part of the universe that you can see from your location in space and in time.

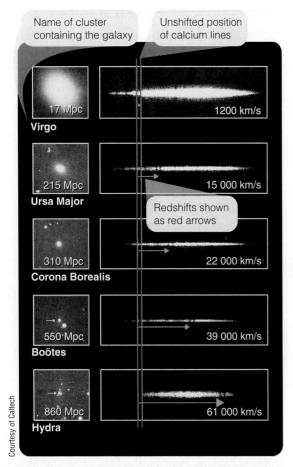

Name of cluster containing the galaxy

Unshifted position of calcium lines

17 Mpc · 1200 km/s
Virgo

215 Mpc · 15 000 km/s
Ursa Major

Redshifts shown as red arrows

310 Mpc · 22 000 km/s
Corona Borealis

550 Mpc · 39 000 km/s
Boötes

860 Mpc · 61 000 km/s
Hydra

Figure 11.4 These galaxy spectra extend from the near-ultraviolet at left to the blue part of the visible spectrum at right. The two dark absorption lines of once-ionized calcium are prominent in the near-ultraviolet. The redshifts in galaxy spectra are expressed here as apparent velocities of recession. Note that the apparent velocity of recession is proportional to distance.

at various distances. The Virgo cluster is relatively nearby, and its redshift is small. The Hydra cluster is very distant, and its redshift is so large that the two dark lines formed by ionized calcium are shifted from near-ultraviolet wavelengths well into the visible part of the spectrum.

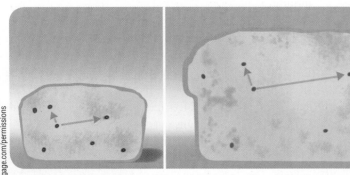

Figure 11.5 An illustration of the raisin bread analogy for the expansion of the universe. As the dough rises, raisins are pushed apart with velocities proportional to distance.

The expansion of the universe does not imply that Earth is at the centre. To see why, think about raisin bread. As the dough rises, it pushes the raisins away from each other uniformly at speeds that are proportional to their distances from each other (see Figure 11.5). Two raisins that were originally close are pushed apart slowly, but two raisins that were far apart, having more dough between them, are pushed apart faster. If bacterial astronomers lived on a raisin in your raisin bread, they could observe the redshifts of the other raisins and derive a bacterial Hubble law. They would conclude that their universe was expanding uniformly. It does not matter which raisin the bacterial astronomers lived on, they would get the same Hubble law; no raisin has a special viewpoint. Similarly, astronomers in any galaxy will see the same law of expansion—no galaxy has a special viewpoint.

When you think about that loaf of bread, you see the edge of the loaf, and you can identify a centre to the loaf of bread. The raisin bread analogy for the expanding universe no longer works when you consider the crust—the edge—of the bread. Remember that the universe cannot have an edge or a centre, so there can be no centre to the expansion.

11.2 The Big Bang Theory

The expansion of the universe led astronomers to conclude that the universe must have begun with an event of astounding cosmic intensity.

Necessity of the Big Bang

Imagine that you have a video of the expanding universe, and you run it backward. You would see the galaxies moving toward each other. There is no centre to the expansion of the universe, so you would not see galaxies approaching a single spot. Rather, you would see the space between galaxies disappearing, distances between all galaxies decreasing without the galaxies themselves moving, and eventually galaxies beginning to merge. If you ran your video far enough back, you would see the matter and energy of the universe compressed into a high-density, high-temperature state. You can conclude that the expanding universe began with expansion from that condition of extremely high

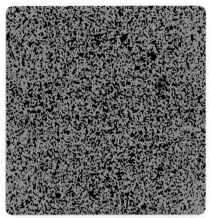

a A region of the universe during the big bang

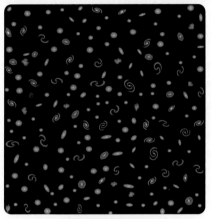

b A region of the universe now

c The present universe as it appears from our galaxy. In every direction, we see nearby, recently formed galaxies. As we look farther away in every direction, we see light that comes from the early stages of the universe (yellow arrows). The outermost pink ring depicts the earliest stages of the universe. Light from this period just after the big bang reaches us today as infrared and radio energy.

Figure 11.6 This diagram shows schematically the expansion of a small part of the universe. Although the universe is now filled with galaxies, the look-back time distorts what you see. Nearby you can see galaxies, but at greater distances, the look-back time reveals the universe at earlier stages. At very great distances, the big bang is detectable as infrared and radio energy arriving from all directions from the hot gas that filled the universe soon after the big bang.

density and temperature, which modern astronomers call the **big bang**.

How long ago did the universe begin? You can estimate the age of the universe with a simple calculation. If you must drive to a city 100 km away and you can travel 50 km/hr, divide distance by speed of travel to learn the travel time: in this example, two hours. To find the age of the universe, divide the distance between galaxies by the speed with which they are separating, and find out how much time was required for them to have reached their present separation. You will fine-tune your estimate later in this chapter, but for the moment you can conclude that basic observations of the recession of the galaxies require that the universe began with a big bang approximately 14 billion years ago. That estimated span is called the **Hubble time**. (Refer to **The Age of the Universe** in the Math Reference Cards.)

Your instinct is to think of the big bang as a historical event, like John Cabot's arrival in what is now Newfoundland: something that happened long ago and can no longer be observed. But the look-back time makes it possible to observe the big bang directly. The look-back time to nearby galaxies is only a few million years, but the look-back time to more distant galaxies is a large fraction of the age of the universe (see Chapter 10). If you looked between and beyond the distant galaxies, back to the time of the big bang, you should be able to detect the hot gas that filled the universe long ago.

Again, do not think of an edge or a centre when you think of the big bang. It is a very common misconception that the big bang was an explosion and that the galaxies are flying away from a centre. Although your imagination may try to visualize the big bang as a localized event, you must keep firmly in mind that the big bang did not occur at a single place; rather it filled the entire volume of the universe. We cannot point to any particular place and say, "The big bang occurred over there." At the time of the big bang, all the galaxies, stars, and atoms in the observable universe were confined to a very small volume. That hot, dense state—the big bang—occurred everywhere, and that includes right where you are now. The matter of which you are made was part of the big bang, so you are inside the remains of that event, and the universe continues to expand around you. In whatever direction astronomers look, at great distances they can see back to the age when the universe was filled with dense, hot gas (Figure 11.6).

big bang The high-density, high-temperature state from which the expanding universe of galaxies began.

Hubble time The age of the universe, equivalent to 1 divided by the Hubble constant. The Hubble time is the age of the universe based on its expansion at a constant rate since the big bang.

Evidence for the Big Bang: The Cosmic Microwave Background

The radiation that comes from great distance has a tremendous redshift. The most distant visible objects are faint galaxies and quasars, with redshifts of about 8; this means their light arrives at Earth with wavelengths nine times longer than when it started the journey. In contrast, the radiation from the hot gas of the big bang is calculated to have a redshift of about 1100. That means the light emitted by the big bang gases arrives at Earth as far-infrared radiation and short-wavelength radio waves. You can't see this radiation with your eyes, but it should be detectable with infrared and radio telescopes. Amazingly, the big bang can still be detected by the radiation it emitted.

In the mid-1960s two Bell Laboratories physicists, Arno Penzias and Robert Wilson, were measuring weak radio signals from space (Figure 11.7) when they discovered a peculiar radio noise coming from all directions. At first they attributed this to signal errors caused by droppings from pigeons living in the telescope, but the noise persisted even after the birds were removed. Physicists George Gamow and Ralph Alpher had predicted in the 1940s that the big bang would have emitted blackbody

cosmic microwave background (CMB) Radiation from the hot matter of the universe soon after the big bang. The large redshift makes it appear to come from a blackbody with a temperature of 2.7 K.

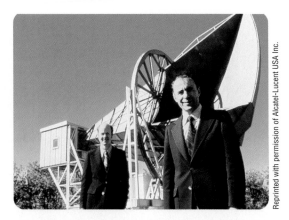

Figure 11.7 In 1965, Arno Penzias (right) and Robert Wilson first detected the background radiation left over from the big bang; they used the horn antenna behind them in this photograph.

radiation that should now be in the far-infrared and radio parts of the spectrum. In the early 1960s, Physicist Robert Dicke and his team at Princeton University began building a receiver to detect that radiation. When Penzias and Wilson learned about this earlier work, they realized with the help of Dicke, Peebles, Roll, and Wilkinson that the radio noise—now called the **cosmic microwave background (CMB)**—is actually radiation from the big bang. They received the 1978 Nobel Prize in physics for their discovery. You can observe the evidence for the big bang yourself on any analog television. When your TV is not tuned to a particular station, the antennas pick up

CANADIANS IN ASTRONOMY
Canada's role in the global story of astronomy

Jim Peebles

Jim Peebles

Phillip James E. Peebles was inspired to study physics as an undergraduate student thanks to four exceptional professors at the University of Manitoba. After graduating in 1958, he moved to Princeton University, where he met his graduate supervisor and mentor Robert Dicke, who sparked his interest in theoretical physics and cosmology. Together, they played a major role in confirming the existence of the cosmic microwave background radiation (CMB), the afterglow of the big bang. The existence and temperature of this background radiation in the universe had been debated since the 1940s. In 1964, when Arno Penzias and Robert Wilson found a source of excess noise in their radio receiver at Bell Laboratories, Peebles and Dicke, together with Peter Roll and David Wilkinson, correctly interpreted this noise to be the CMB. Peebles also correctly calculated the amount of helium in the universe as a result of the big bang. He has made many other important contributions to a variety of topics in cosmology, including the origin of galaxies, large-scale structures in the universe, and the nature of dark matter and dark energy. His book *Physical Cosmology* helped define and guide future studies in cosmology. He is the recipient of numerous awards during his distinguished career, including the prestigious Eddington Medal, the Heineman Prize, and the A. C. Morrison Award, and he was the co-recipient of the first Gruber Cosmology Prize. The Peebles asteroid is named in his honour.

background radio signals, which you can observe as static or snow on your TV screen. About 1 percent of this comes from the CMB radiation left over from the ancient event we now call the big bang.

The detection of the background radiation was tremendously exciting, but astronomers wanted confirmation. Critical observations in the far-infrared were needed to check whether the CMB really has the predicted blackbody spectrum, but they could not be made from the ground. It was not until January 1990 that satellite measurements confirmed that the CMB is blackbody radiation with an apparent temperature of 2.725 +/– 0.002 K, which agrees well with theoretical predictions (Figure 11.8).

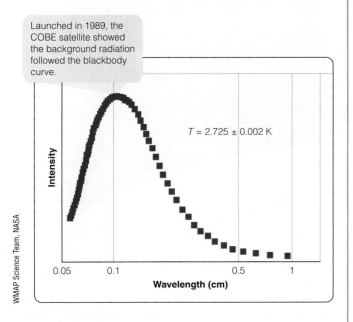

Launched in 1989, the COBE satellite showed the background radiation followed the blackbody curve.

$T = 2.725 \pm 0.002$ K

Intensity

Wavelength (cm)

0.05　　0.1　　　　　　0.5　　1

WMAP Science Team, NASA

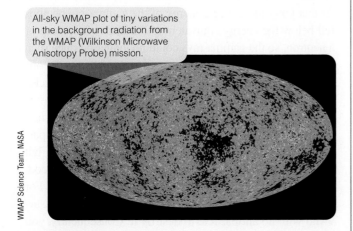

All-sky WMAP plot of tiny variations in the background radiation from the WMAP (Wilkinson Microwave Anisotropy Probe) mission.

WMAP Science Team, NASA

Figure 11.8 When the CMB was first detected in 1965, technology did not allow measurements at many wavelengths. Not until infrared detectors could be put in orbit was it conclusively shown that the background radiation, as predicted by theory, follows a blackbody curve very precisely.

It may seem strange that the hot gas of the big bang appears to have a temperature 2.7 degrees above absolute zero, but recall the tremendous redshift. Observers on Earth see light that has a redshift of about 1100: that is, the wavelengths of the photons are about 1100 times longer than when they were emitted. The gas clouds that emitted the photons had a temperature of about 3000 K, and they emitted blackbody radiation with a λ_{max} of about 1000 nm. (See further information on Wien's law in Chapter 5 and in **Blackbody Radiation** in the Math Reference Cards.) The expansion of the universe has redshifted the wavelengths about 1100 times longer, so λ_{max} is now about 1 million nm (1 mm). That is why the hot gas of the big bang seems to be 1100 times cooler now, about 2.7 K.

Particles and Nucleosynthesis: The First Seconds and Minutes

Simple observation of the darkness of the night sky and the redshifts of the galaxies tells us that the universe must have had a beginning. Furthermore, the CMB is clear evidence that conditions at the beginning were hot and dense. Theorists combine these observations with knowledge from physics about how atoms and subatomic particles behave to work out the story of how the big bang occurred. You can follow the story of evolution of the universe—particularly the important eras of evolution immediately after the big bang—in Figure 11.9.

Cosmologists cannot begin their history of the big bang at time zero, because no one understands the behaviour of matter and energy under such extreme conditions, but they can come amazingly close. One of the largest experimental devices, the Large Hadron Collider (LHC), is capable of generating energies large enough to recreate the conditions at the instant after the big bang (see **Visualizing Astronomy 11.1, The Large Hadron Collider**). If you could visit the universe when it was only one 10-millionth of a second old, you would find it filled with high-energy photons having a blackbody temperature well over 1 trillion (10^{12}) K and a density (using Einstein's equation $E = mc^2$ to calculate the mass equivalent to a certain amount of energy) greater than 5×10^{13} g/cm^3, nearly the density of an atomic nucleus.

If photons have enough energy, two photons can combine and convert their energy into a pair of particles: a particle of normal matter and a particle of

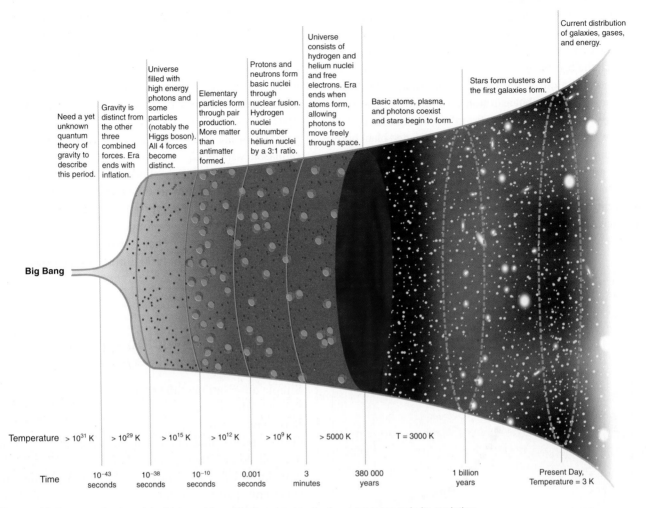

Figure 11.9 A visualization of the history of the universe, showing the important stages in its evolution.

antimatter. Particles of antimatter, or "antiparticles," have the same mass as the corresponding particles of regular matter, but have opposite charge. For example, a positron, which is the antiparticle corresponding to the electron, has the same mass as an electron but one unit of positive charge. And when an antimatter particle meets its matching particle of normal matter, the two particles annihilate each other and convert their mass back into energy in the form of two gamma rays. In the early universe, photons had enough energy to produce proton–antiproton pairs or neutron–antineutron pairs. When these particles collided with their antiparticles, they converted their mass back into photons. Thus, the early universe was filled with a dynamic soup of energy flickering from photons into particles and back again.

antimatter Matter composed of antiparticles, which, upon colliding with a matching particle of normal matter, annihilates, converting the mass of both particles into energy. In comparison to corresponding particles of normal matter, antiparticles have the same mass but opposite charge.

While all this went on, the expansion of the universe cooled the radiation. By the time the universe was 0.0001 second old, its blackbody temperature had fallen to 10^{12} K. At that point the average energy of the gamma-ray photons fell below the energy equivalent to the mass of a proton or a neutron, so the gamma rays could no longer produce such heavy particles, and the creation of protons and neutrons stopped. Those particles combined with their antiparticles and quickly converted most of the mass into photons.

You might guess from this that all of the protons and neutrons would have been annihilated with their antiparticles, and the universe should now consist of nothing but photons. However, for reasons that are poorly understood, a small excess of normal particles apparently existed. For every billion protons annihilated by antiprotons, one survived with no antiparticle to destroy it. Consequently, you live in a world of normal matter, and antimatter is very rare.

Although the gamma rays did not have enough energy to produce protons and neutrons after the universe fell below 10^{12} K, electron–positron pairs, having lower mass, could still be produced. That continued until the universe was about four seconds old, at which time the expansion had cooled the gamma rays to the point where they could no longer create even electron–positron pairs. Most of the electrons and positrons combined to form photons, and only one in a billion electrons survived. The protons, neutrons, and electrons of which our universe is made were produced during the first four seconds of its history.

This soup of hot gas and radiation continued to cool. By the time the universe was about two minutes old, protons and neutrons could link to form deuterium, the nucleus of a heavy hydrogen atom, and not be broken apart again. By the end of the next minute, further reactions began converting deuterium into helium, but almost no heavier atoms could be built because there are no stable nuclei with atomic weights of 5 or 8 (in units of the hydrogen atom); these heavier atoms fall apart as soon as they are created. Cosmic element building during the big bang had to proceed rapidly, step by step, like someone hopping up a flight of stairs. The lack of stable nuclei at atomic weights of 5 and 8 meant there were missing steps in the stairway, and the step-by-step reactions had great difficulty jumping over these gaps. Astronomers can calculate that the big bang produced a tiny amount of lithium (atomic weight 7), but no elements heavier than that.

By the time the universe was three minutes old, it had become so cool that most nuclear reactions had stopped, and by the time it was 30 minutes old the nuclear reactions had ended completely. At that time about 25 percent of the mass was in the form of helium nuclei, and the rest was in the form of hydrogen nuclei (protons). That is the abundance of hydrogen and helium observed today in the oldest stars. This evidence provided further confirmation of our model of the big bang. The cosmic abundance of hydrogen and helium was essentially fixed during the first minutes of the universe. The hydrogen nuclei in water molecules in your body have survived unchanged since they formed during the first moments of the big bang. Heavier elements were built by nucleosynthesis inside later generations of stars (see Chapters 8 and 9).

Recombination and Reionization: The First Thousands and Millions of Years

At first the universe was so hot that the gas was totally ionized, and the electrons were not attached to nuclei. Free electrons interact with photons so easily that a photon could not travel very far before it encountered an electron and was deflected (Figure 11.10a). The radiation and matter interacted continuously with each other and cooled together as the universe expanded.

As the young universe expanded, it went through three important changes. First, when the universe reached

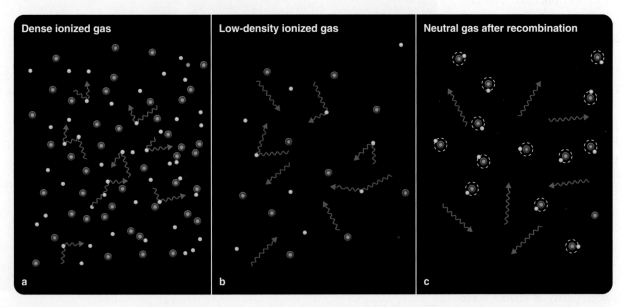

Figure 11.10 Photons easily scatter (bounce) off electrons (blue), but hardly at all from the much more massive protons (red). (a) When the universe was very dense and ionized, photons could not travel very far before they scattered off an electron. This means the gas was opaque. (b) As the universe expanded, the electrons spread further apart, and the photons could travel farther; this made the gas more transparent. (c) After the era of recombination, most electrons were locked to protons to form neutral atoms, and the universe became almost completely transparent.

recombination The stage, within 400 000 years of the big bang, when neutral hydrogen formed and the gas became transparent to radiation.

dark age The period of time after the glow of the big bang faded into the infrared and before the birth of the first stars, during which the universe expanded in darkness.

reionization The stage in the early history of the universe when ultraviolet photons from the first stars ionized the gas that filled space.

an age of roughly 50 000 years, the density of the energy present in the form of photons became less than the density of the gas. Before that time, matter could not clump together because the intense sea of photons smoothed the gas out. Once the density of the radiation fell below that of matter, the matter could begin to draw together under the influence of gravity and form the clouds that eventually became galaxy clusters and galaxies.

The expansion of the universe spread the particles of the ionized gas farther and farther apart. As the universe reached the age of about 400 000 years, the second important change began. As the density decreased and the falling temperature of the universe reached 3000 K, protons could capture and hold free electrons to form neutral hydrogen. This process is called **recombination**, but *combination* would be more accurate because this was the first time this process occurred. As the free electrons were gobbled up into atoms, they could no longer deflect photons. The photons could travel easily through the gas, so the gas became transparent (Figure 11.10c), and the photons retained the blackbody temperature of 3000 K, which the gas and photons together had at the time of recombination. Those photons are what are observed today as the CMB, with a large redshift that makes their temperature now about 2.7 K.

Recombination left the gas of the big bang neutral, hot, dense, and transparent. At first the universe was filled with the glow of the hot gas, which would have been partly at visible wavelengths. As the universe expanded and cooled, the glow faded, and the universe entered what cosmologists call the **dark age**, a

period lasting hundreds of millions of years until the formation of the first stars. During the dark age, the universe expanded in darkness.

The dark age ended as the first stars began to form. The gas from which those first stars formed contained almost no metals and was consequently quite transparent. Mathematical models show that the first stars formed from this metal-poor gas would have been very massive, very luminous, and very short-lived. That first burst of star formation produced enough ultraviolet light to begin ionizing the gas, and today's astronomers, looking back to the most distant visible quasars and galaxies, can see traces of that **reionization** of the universe (Figure 11.11). Reionization marks the end of the dark ages and the beginning of the age of stars and galaxies that continues today.

Look carefully at Figure 11.12: it summarizes the story of the big bang, from the formation of helium in the first three minutes through energy–matter equality, recombination, and reionization of the gas. It may seem amazing that mere humans trapped on Earth can draw such a diagram, but remember that it is based on evidence and on the best understanding of how matter and energy interact.

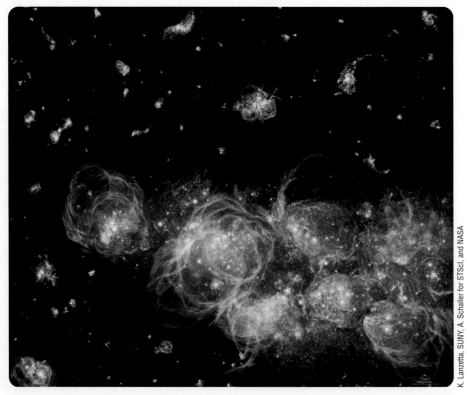

Figure 11.11 In this artist's conception of reionization, the first stars produce floods of ultraviolet photons that ionized the gas in expanding bubbles. Such a storm of star formation ended an age when the universe had expanded in darkness. Spectra of the most distant quasars reveal that those first galaxies were surrounded by neutral gas that had not yet been fully ionized. Thus, the look-back time allows modern astronomers to observe the age of reionization.

K. Lanzetta, SUNY, A. Schaller for STScI, and NASA

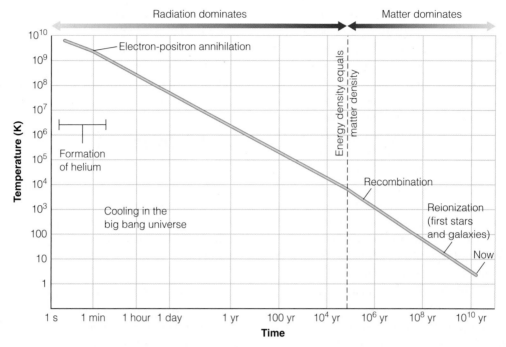

Figure 11.12 During the first few minutes of the big bang, some hydrogen fused to produce helium, but the universe quickly became too cool for such fusion reactions to occur. The rate of cooling increased as matter began to dominate over radiation. Recombination freed the radiation from the influence of the gas, and the birth of the first stars caused reionization. Note how the exponential scale in time stretches early history and compresses recent history.

11.3 Space and Time, Matter and Energy

How can the big bang have happened everywhere? To solve the puzzle, you must put what seem to be reasonable expectations on hold and look carefully at how space and time behave on cosmic scales.

Looking at the Universe

The universe looks about the same whichever way you look. That is called **isotropy**. Of course, there are local differences. If you look toward a galaxy cluster you see more galaxies, but that is only a local variation. On the average, you see similar numbers of galaxies in every direction. Furthermore, the background radiation is also almost perfectly uniform across the sky. The universe is observed to be highly isotropic, almost exactly the same in all directions when viewed from our position.

The universe also seems to be homogenous; **homogeneity** is the property of being the same everywhere. Of course there are local variations. Some regions contain more galaxies and some fewer. Also, as the universe evolves, at large look-back times you see galaxies at an earlier stage. When we account for these well-understood variations, the universe seems to be, on average, the same everywhere. This is harder to check because we can't actually go to the locations of distant galaxies and check in detail that things are about the same there as here, but all astronomical observations indicate this is so.

Isotropy and homogeneity together lead to the **cosmological principle**. According to the cosmological principle, any observer in any galaxy sees that the universe has the same general properties, after accounting for relatively minor local and evolutionary variations. This principle implies that there are no special places in the universe. What you see from the Milky Way Galaxy is typical of what all intelligent creatures see from their respective home galaxies. Furthermore, the cosmological principle is another way of saying that the universe has no centre or edge. Such locations would be special places, and the cosmological principle means there are no special places.

The Cosmic Redshift

Distance is the separation between two points in space; time is the separation between two moments.

isotropy The observation that, in its general properties, the universe looks the same in every direction.

homogeneity The observation that, on the large scale, matter is uniformly spread through the universe.

cosmological principle The assumption that any observer in any galaxy sees the same general features of the universe.

Einstein's theories of special relativity and general relativity (published respectively in 1905 and 1916) describe how space and time are related and can be considered together as the fabric of the universe: space-time. You can think of space-time as the canvas on which the universe is painted. Einstein's theories predict that the canvas of space-time can potentially expand (or contract); amazingly, this has been confirmed by observations.

The stretching of space-time explains one of the most important observations in cosmology: cosmological redshifts. Modern astronomers understand that, except for small local motions within clusters of galaxies, the galaxies are basically at rest and have kept approximately the same "address" in space since the big bang. The distances between them increase as space-time expands. Furthermore, as space-time expands, it stretches photons travelling through space to longer wavelengths (see Figure 11.13). Photons from distant galaxies spend more time travelling through space and are stretched more than photons from nearby galaxies. That is why redshift depends on distance. Note that objects held together by gravity or electromagnetic forces—such as the Milky Way, Earth, and you—do not expand as the universe expands.

Astronomers often express redshifts as if they were radial velocities, but the redshifts of the galaxies are not Doppler shifts. That is why this book is careful to refer to a galaxy's *apparent* velocity of recession. All a cosmological redshift tells you directly is how much the universe has expanded since the light began its journey to Earth. The formula to calculate the distance a photon has travelled, given its redshift, is complicated, and not all the parameters have been measured precisely. Nevertheless, Hubble's law does apply, and redshifts can be used to estimate the distances to galaxies.

Model Universes

Almost immediately after Einstein published his theory, theorists were able to solve the highly sophisticated mathematics to compute simplified descriptions of the behaviour of space-time and matter. Those "model universes" dominated cosmology throughout the 20th century.

The equations allowed three general possibilities. Space-time might be curved in ways that are called an **open universe** or a **closed universe**, or space-time might have no overall curvature at all, a situation that is called a **flat universe**. Most people find the curved space-time models difficult to imagine. Fortunately, modern observations have shown that the flat universe model is almost certainly correct, so you don't have to wrap your brain around the curved models. Note that *flat* does not mean two dimensional. Rather, it means that the familiar rules of geometry you learned in elementary and high school, for instance that the circumference of a circle is 2π times its radius and that the interior angles of a triangle add up to 180 degrees, are true on the largest scales. Different rules of geometry would apply on large scales if the universe were curved.

A main criterion separating the three models is the average density of the universe, which, according to general relativity, determines the overall curvature of space-time. If the average density of matter and energy in the

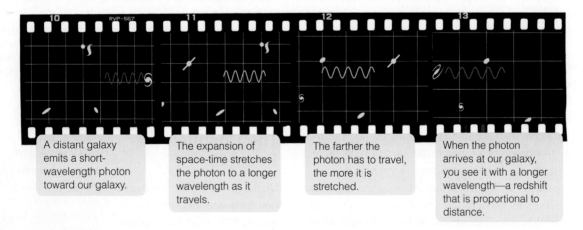

A distant galaxy emits a short-wavelength photon toward our galaxy.

The expansion of space-time stretches the photon to a longer wavelength as it travels.

The farther the photon has to travel, the more it is stretched.

When the photon arrives at our galaxy, you see it with a longer wavelength—a redshift that is proportional to distance.

Figure 11.13 As the universe (space-time) expands, the light waves become stretched to longer wavelengths.

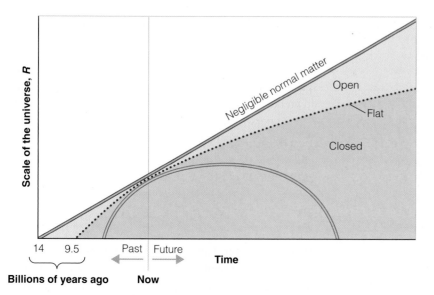

Figure 11.14 Illustrations of some simple universe models that depend only on the effect of gravity. Under that assumption, open universe models expand without end, and the corresponding curves fall in the region shaded orange. Closed models expand and then contract again (the red curve is one example). A flat universe (dotted line) marks the boundary between open and closed universe models. The relationship between the estimated age and actual age of the universe depends on the geometry of space-time. The age of the universe for each model is shown on the graph as the horizontal distance from "Now" back to the time when the universe scale factor R equalled 0.

universe equals what is called the **critical density**, calculated to be about 1×10^{-29} g/cm³ (depending on the exact value of Hubble constant), space-time is flat. If the average density is more than the critical density, the universe must be closed; if it is less, the universe must be open.

The expansions versus time of the three different models are compared in Figure 11.14. The parameter R on the vertical axis is a measure of the extent to which the universe has expanded. You could think of it, essentially, as the average distance between galaxies. In this figure you can see that closed universes may expand and then contract, and open universes may expand forever. Notice also that each of the three curves intersects the horizontal axis at a different point. The distance between the present and this intersection point gives the age of the universe. Therefore, you need to know whether the universe is open, flat, or closed to estimate the age of the universe. The Hubble time, discussed earlier in this chapter as a rough estimate of the age of the universe, is actually the age the universe would be if it were totally open; this means it would have to contain almost no matter at all.

Dark Matter in Cosmology

Later in this chapter you will see how observational evidence indicates that the universe is probably flat.

For now, you must solve a different problem. If the universe is flat, its average density must equal the critical density, yet when astronomers added up the matter they could detect, they found only a few percent of the critical density. They wondered if the dark matter made up the rest.

In Chapters 9 and 10, you learned that our galaxy, other galaxies, and galaxy clusters have much stronger gravitational fields than expected based on the amount of visible matter. Even when you add in the nonluminous gas and dust that you expect to find, their gravitational fields are stronger than expected. Galaxies must contain dark matter—in fact, much more dark matter than normal matter (refer to Figures 9.9 and 10.6).

The protons and neutrons that make up normal matter, including Earth and you, belong to a family of subatomic particles called *baryons*. Modern evidence based on what can be determined about the products of nuclear reactions in the first few minutes after the big bang shows that the dark matter is not baryonic. If there were lots of baryons present during those early moments, they would have (1) collided with and destroyed deuterium nuclei and (2) collided with some of the helium to make lithium.

Figure 11.15 shows that the observed amount of deuterium sets a lower limit on the density of the universe, and the observed abundance of lithium-7 sets an upper limit. Those limits indicate that the baryons you and Earth and the stars are made of cannot add up to more than 4 percent of the critical density. Yet observations show that galaxies and galaxy clusters contain as much as 30 percent of the critical density in the form of dark matter. Only a small amount of the matter in the universe can be baryonic, so the dark matter must be **nonbaryonic matter**.

The true nature of dark matter remains one of the mysteries of astronomy. The most successful models of galaxy formation require that the dark matter be made up of **cold dark matter**, meaning

critical density The average density of matter and energy in the universe needed to make its curvature flat.

nonbaryonic matter Proposed dark matter made up of particles other than protons and neutrons (baryons).

cold dark matter Dark matter that is made of slow-moving particles.

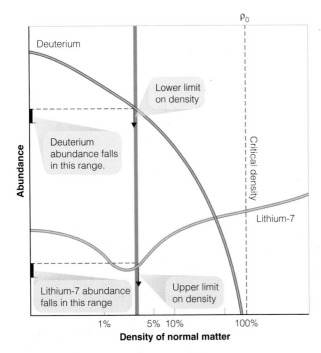

Figure 11.15 This diagram compares observation with theory. Theory predicts how much deuterium and lithium-7 you would observe for different densities of normal matter (red and blue curves). The observed density of deuterium falls in a narrow range shown at upper left and sets a lower limit on the possible density of normal matter. The observed density of lithium-7 sets an upper limit. This means the true density of normal matter must fall in a narrow range represented by the green column. Certainly, the density of normal matter is much less than the critical density.

the particles move slowly and can clump into structures with sizes that explain the galaxies and galaxy clusters you see today. There are several experiments around the world focusing on trying to detect dark matter. These include underground labs in Boulby, UK; Minnesota, USA; and Sudbury, Canada (SNOLAB).

Although the evidence is very strong that dark matter exists, it is not abundant enough by itself to make the universe flat. Dark matter appears to constitute no more than about 30 percent of the critical density. As you will see later in this chapter, there is more to the universe than meets the eye and more even than dark matter.

flatness problem The peculiar circumstance that the early universe must have contained almost exactly the right amount of matter to make space-time flat.

horizon problem The circumstance that the primordial background radiation seems much more isotropic than can be explained by the standard big bang theory.

inflationary big bang A version of the big bang theory, derived from grand unified theories of particle physics, that includes a rapid expansion when the universe was very young.

11.4 Modern Cosmology

If you are a little dizzy from the weirdness of expanding space-time and dark matter, make sure you are sitting down before you read further. As the 21st century began, astronomers made a discovery that startled all cosmologists: the expansion of the universe is actually accelerating. To get a running start on these new discoveries, you'll have to go back a couple of decades.

Inflation

By 1980, the big bang model was widely accepted, but it faced two problems that led to the development of an improved theory—a big bang model with an important addition.

One of the problems is called the **flatness problem**. The curvature of space-time seems to be near the transition between an open and a closed universe. That is, the universe seems approximately flat. It seems peculiar that the actual density of the universe is anywhere near the critical density that would make it flat. To be so near critical density now, the density of the universe during its first moments must have been very close, within 1 part in 10^{49}, of the critical density. So the flatness problem is, *Why was the universe so close to exactly flat, with no space-time curvature, at the time of the big bang?*

The second problem with the original big bang theory is called the **horizon problem**. When astronomers correct for the motion of Earth, they find that the CMB is very isotropic, the same in all directions to a precision of better than 1 part in 1000. However, background radiation coming from two points in the sky separated by more than an angle of one degree is from two parts of the big bang that were far enough apart that they should not have been connected at any previous time. That is, when the CMB photons were released, the universe was not old enough for energy to have travelled at the speed of light from one of those regions to the other—the regions should always have been beyond each other's "horizon" and could not have exchanged heat to make their temperatures equal. So the horizon problem is, *How did every part of the observable universe get to be so nearly the same temperature by the time of recombination?*

The key to these two problems and to other problems with the simple big bang model may lie with a modified model called the **inflationary big bang** that predicts there was a sudden extra expansion when the universe was very young, even more extreme than that predicted by the original big bang model. According to the inflationary universe model, the universe expanded and cooled until about

10^{-36} seconds after the big bang. Then the universe became cool enough that the forces of nature (see Chapter 7), which at earlier extremely high temperatures would have behaved identically, began to differ from each other. Physicists calculate this would have released tremendous amounts of energy and suddenly inflated the universe by a factor of 10^{50} or larger. Inflation ended 10^{-32} seconds after the big bang. As a result, the part of the universe that is now visible from Earth, the entire observable universe, expanded rapidly from 35 orders of magnitude smaller than a proton to roughly a metre across, and then continued a slower expansion to its present state. Figure 11.16 illustrates the history of the universe and its expansion process—inflation, followed by slowing of the expansion rate, followed by an increased rate of expansion.

Sudden inflation can solve both the flatness problem and the horizon problem. The inflation of the universe would have forced whatever curvature it had toward zero, just as inflating a balloon makes a small spot on its surface flatter. You now live in a universe that has almost perfectly flat space-time geometry because of that sudden inflation long ago. In addition, because the observable part of the universe was no larger in volume than an atom before inflation, it was small enough to have equalized its temperature by then. Now you live in a universe that has the same CMB temperature in all directions.

The inflationary theory predicts that the universe is almost perfectly flat. Observations, however, give evidence that the masses scientists know about (baryonic matter plus dark matter) add up only to about 30 percent of the amount needed to make space-time flat. Can there be more to the universe than baryonic matter and dark matter? What could be weirder than dark matter? Read on.

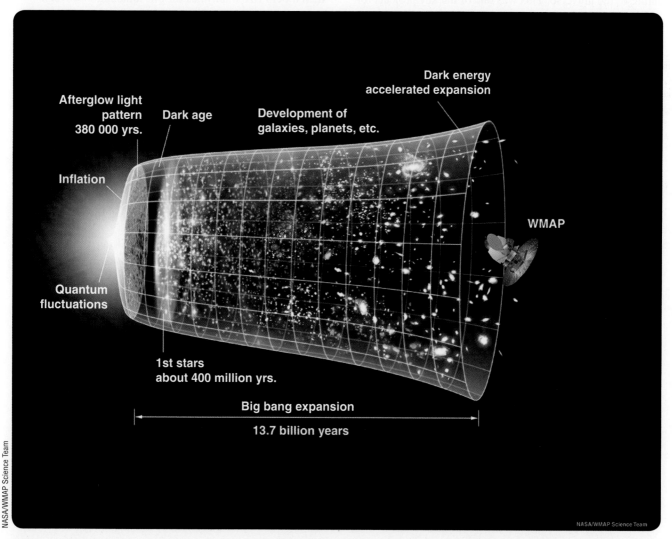

Figure 11.16 A schematic of the expansion of the universe from the big bang to present day. Less than a moment after the big bang, a period of rapid expansion—known as inflation—occurred, followed by a long period of slowing expansion over billions of years, due to the gravitational pull of the matter in the universe. Recent measurements indicate that a repulsive force termed dark energy overcame the pull of gravity about 6 billion years ago and resulted in an increasing expansion rate. (The current estimate for the age of the universe is 13.8 billion years.)

The Acceleration of the Universe

Both common sense and mathematical models suggest that as the galaxies recede from each other the expansion should be slowed by gravity trying to pull the galaxies toward each other. How much the expansion is slowed should depend on the amount of matter in the universe. If the density of matter is less than the critical density, the expansion should be slowed only slightly, and the universe should expand forever. If the density of matter in the universe is greater than the critical density, the expansion should be slowing down dramatically, and the universe should eventually begin contracting.

For decades, astronomers struggled to measure the distance to very distant galaxies directly, compare distances with redshifts, and thereby detect the slowing of the expansion. The rate of slowing would in turn reveal the true curvature of the universe. This was one of the key projects for the Hubble Space Telescope. Two international teams of scientists used the Hubble telescope as well as telescopes in Hawaii, Chile, and Australia to study the expansion of the universe. They calibrated type Ia supernovae as standard candles by locating such supernovae that occur in nearby galaxies whose distances were known from Cepheid variables and other reliable distance indicators (see Chapter 10). Once they determined the peak luminosity of type Ia supernovae, they could use that information to find the distances of much more distant galaxies.

Both teams announced their results in 1998. They agreed that the expansion of the universe is not slowing down. Contrary to expectations, it is speeding up! In other words, the expansion of the universe is accelerating (Figure 11.17). In 2011, the leaders of the two teams—Saul Perlmutter, Brian Schmidt, and Adam Riess—were awarded the Nobel Prize in physics for this amazing discovery.

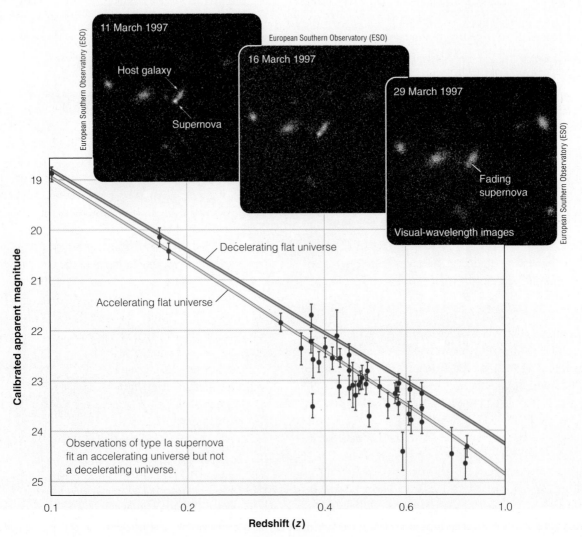

Figure 11.17 From the way supernovae fade over time, astronomers can identify those that are type Ia. Once calibrated, those supernovae can be compared with their redshifts, revealing that distant type Ia supernovae are about 25 percent fainter than expected. That must mean they are farther away than expected, given their redshifts. This is strong evidence that the expansion of the universe is accelerating.

The announcement that the expansion of the universe is accelerating was totally unexpected, and astronomers immediately began testing it. The most likely problem was thought to be that the calibration of the supernovae by the original teams might be incorrect. However, that type of problem has been ruled out by measurements of more recently discovered supernovae at very great distances. Other possible problems have been checked and appear to have been eliminated. The universe really does seem to be expanding faster and faster.

Dark Energy and Acceleration

If the expansion of the universe is accelerating, there must be a force of repulsion in the universe, and astronomers are struggling to understand what it could be. One possibility leads back to Albert Einstein.

When Einstein published his theory of general relativity in 1916, he noticed that his equations describing space-time implied that the universe should contract because of the gravitational attraction of galaxies for each other. In 1916, astronomers did not yet know that the universe was expanding, so Einstein thought he needed to balance the attractive force of gravity by adding a constant to his equations called the **cosmological constant**, representing a force of repulsion that would make the universe hold still. Thirteen years later, in 1929, Edwin Hubble announced that the universe was expanding, and Einstein said that introducing the cosmological constant was his biggest blunder. Modern astronomers aren't so sure.

One explanation for the acceleration of the universe is that there is a cosmological constant after all, representing a real force that drives a continuing acceleration in the expansion of the universe. The cosmological constant, as its name implies, would be constant in strength over time. Another possibility is a type of energy that is not constant in strength over time. Astronomers have begun referring to this type of energy as **quintessence**. In either case, the observed acceleration is evidence that some form of energy, either a cosmological constant or quintessence, is spread throughout space. Astronomers refer to this as **dark energy**, energy that drives the acceleration of the universe but does not contribute to starlight or the CMB. Understanding the nature of dark energy is one of the most important and interesting scientific challenges today.

Recall that acceleration and dark energy were first discovered when astronomers found that supernovae a few billion light-years away were slightly *fainter* than expected. Since then even more distant supernovae have

been determined to be a bit *brighter* than expected, meaning they are not as far away as the redshifts of their galaxies would seemingly indicate. This means that sometime about 6 billion years ago the universe shifted gears from deceleration to acceleration. The careful calibration of type Ia supernovae allows astronomers to observe this change from deceleration to acceleration. This discovery has the important consequence of increasing previous estimates of the age of the universe by several billion years.

Dark energy can also help you understand the lack of curvature of space-time. The theory of inflation makes the specific prediction that the universe is flat. Dark energy seems to fit with that prediction. As mentioned earlier in this chapter, energy and matter are equivalent, so dark energy is equivalent to mass spread through space. Baryonic matter plus dark matter makes up about a third of the critical density, and dark energy appears to make up two-thirds. That is, when you include dark energy, the total mass-plus-energy density of the universe equals the critical density, making the universe flat.

The Fate of the Universe

For many years, cosmologists enjoyed saying: "Geometry is destiny." Thinking about models of open, closed, and flat universes, they concluded that the density of a model universe determines its geometry, and its geometry determines its fate. In other words, they were sure that an open universe must expand forever, and a closed universe must eventually begin contracting. That is true, however, only if the universe is ruled by gravity. If the power of dark energy dominates gravity, then geometry is not destiny, and even a closed universe might expand forever.

The ultimate fate of the universe depends on the nature of dark energy. If dark energy is described by the cosmological constant, the force driving acceleration does not change with time, and our flat universe will expand forever. The galaxies will get farther and farther apart, use up their gas and dust making stars, and the stars will ultimately all die, until each galaxy is isolated, burnt out, dark, and alone. If, however, dark energy is described by quintessence, its strength could increase with time, and the universe expansion may accelerate faster and faster as space pulls the galaxies away

cosmological constant A constant in Einstein's equations of space and time that represents a force of repulsion.

quintessence A possible form of dark energy that can change in strength as the universe ages.

dark energy The energy believed to drive the acceleration of the expanding universe.

from each other and eventually pulls the galaxies apart, then pulls the stars apart, and finally rips individual atoms apart. This has been called the **big rip**. Don't worry. Even if a big rip is in the future, nothing will be happening for at least 30 billion years.

There will probably be no big rip. Researchers in France and Canada used images of distant supernovae from the Canada-France-Hawaii Telescope in Hawaii to show that dark energy is described by Einstein's cosmological constant to within 10 percent. Furthermore, important observations made by the Chandra X-ray Observatory have been used to measure the amount of hot gas and dark matter in 25 galaxy clusters. These observations are important for two reasons. First, the redshifts and distance of these galaxies confirm that the universe expansion initially slowed down, but then shifted gears about 6 billion years ago

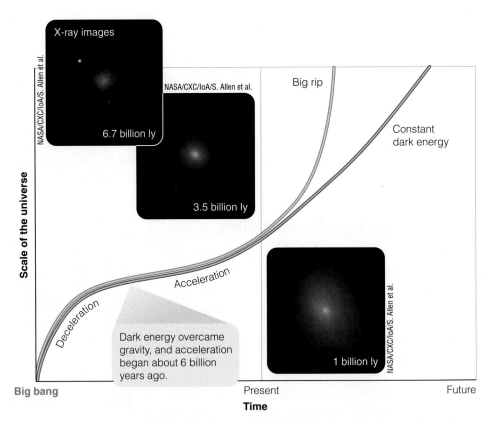

Figure 11.18 X-ray observations of hot gas in galaxy clusters confirm that in its early history the universe was decelerating because gravity was stronger than the dark energy. As expansion weakened the influence of gravity, dark energy began to produce acceleration. The evidence is not conclusive, but it most directly supports the cosmological constant and weighs against quintessence, which means the universe may not face a big rip. This diagram is only schematic, and the two curves are drawn separated for clarity; at the present time the two curves have not diverged from each other.

and is now accelerating. The results are also important because they are almost good enough to rule out quintessence. If dark energy is described by the cosmological constant and not by quintessence, then there will be no big rip (Figure 11.18). Notice that this method does not depend on type Ia supernovae at all, so it provides an independent confirmation that acceleration is real. When a theory is confirmed by observations of many different types, scientists have much more confidence that it is a true description of nature.

The Origin of Structure

On the largest scales, the universe is isotropic, meaning it looks the same in all directions. On smaller scales, there are irregularities. Galaxies are grouped in clusters ranging from a few galaxies to thousands, and those clusters appear to be grouped into superclusters. The Local Supercluster in which we live is a roughly disk-shaped swarm of galaxy clusters 160 to 245 million light-years in diameter. By measuring the redshifts and positions of thousands of galaxies in great slices across the sky, astronomers have been able to create maps revealing that the superclusters are not scattered at random. They are distributed in long, narrow filaments and thin walls that outline great voids nearly empty of galaxies (see Figure 11.19). These aggregations and gaps are referred to as **large-scale structure**.

This large-scale structure is a problem because the cosmic microwave background radiation is uniform, and that means the gas of the big bang must have been extremely uniform at the time of recombination. Yet the look-back time to the farthest known galaxy clusters, galaxies, and quasars is about 95 percent of the way back to the big bang. How did the uniform gas at the time of recombination coagulate so quickly to form galaxy clusters, galaxies, and supermassive black holes in the centres of galaxies so early in the history of the universe? The answer appears to lie in the characteristics of dark matter.

big rip The fate of the universe if dark energy increases with time, and galaxies, stars, and even atoms are eventually ripped apart by the accelerating expansion of the universe.

large-scale structure The distribution of clusters and superclusters of galaxies in filaments and walls enclosing voids.

Figure 11.19 Nearly 70 000 galaxies are plotted in this double slice of the universe. The nearest galaxies are shown in red and the more distant in green and blue. The Sloan Great Wall is almost 1.4 billion light-years long and is the largest known structure in the universe.

Approx. 3 billion ly

Sloan Great Wall

Earth

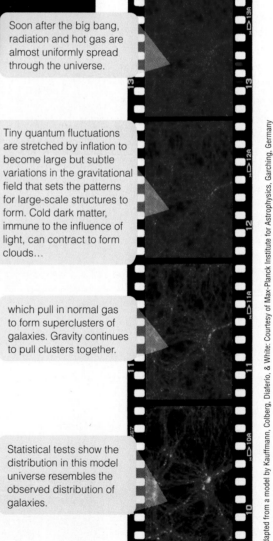

Soon after the big bang, radiation and hot gas are almost uniformly spread through the universe.

Tiny quantum fluctuations are stretched by inflation to become large but subtle variations in the gravitational field that sets the patterns for large-scale structures to form. Cold dark matter, immune to the influence of light, can contract to form clouds...

which pull in normal gas to form superclusters of galaxies. Gravity continues to pull clusters together.

Statistical tests show the distribution in this model universe resembles the observed distribution of galaxies.

Baryonic matter is so rare in the universe that it did not have enough gravity to pull itself together quickly after the big bang. As you learned earlier, astronomers propose that dark matter is nonbaryonic and therefore immune to the smoothing effect of the intense radiation that prevented normal matter from contracting. Dark matter was able to collapse into clouds and then pull in the normal matter to begin the formation of galaxies, clusters, and superclusters. Mathematical models, such as shown in Figure 11.20, attempt to describe this process, and cold dark matter does seem capable of jump-starting the formation of structure.

But what started the clumping of the dark matter? Theorists say that space is filled with tiny, random quantum mechanical fluctuations smaller than the smallest atomic particles. At the moment of inflation, those tiny fluctuations would have been stretched to become very large, but very subtle, variations in gravitational fields, which could have later led to the formation of clusters, filaments, and walls. The structure you see in Figure 11.19 may be the ghostly traces of quantum fluctuations in the infant universe.

CMB Irregularities and the Curvature of Space-Time

Observations of tiny irregularities in the background radiation can also reveal details about inflation and

Figure 11.20 Mathematical model of the growth of structure in the universe.

VISUALIZING ASTRONOMY 11.1
The Large Hadron Collider

By the time you finish reading this book, it could be that it will need to be re-written, chapter by chapter. The reason is the Large Hadron Collider (LHC), the largest experiment in history, designed to explore the most fundamental questions about the universe. If you want to understand cosmology, the origins of the universe, and the nature of matter, you must turn to particle physics. One of the largest experimental devices for such research today, the LHC is a particle accelerator and smasher. It produces high-energy collisions of beams of hadrons (fundamental particles composed of quarks; for example, protons), accelerated to 99.9999991 percent of the speed of light, to generate energies large enough to recreate the conditions at the instant after the big bang. In order to achieve acceleration to such speeds and energies, powerful magnets are used, cooled to a few degrees above absolute zero (−273°C). The paths of the particle beams also have to be extremely long. This is currently the longest accelerator in the world, with a circular tunnel measuring 27 km in circumference. It is located 100 m under the ground at the border between Switzerland and France. With such high speeds, each proton crosses the French-Swiss border 40 000 times every second!

ATLAS Experiment © 2011 CERN

1 CERN's LHC area, under which the accelerator's tunnel runs, is shown here—near Geneva and Lac Leman, with the French Alps and Mont Blanc in the background.

© CERN Geneva

2 Coexisting worlds: seemingly quiet everyday life, undisturbed by simulations of the big bang and black holes only 100 m below. Concerns were raised by the media and the public regarding experiments generating black holes and the large energies achieved in the accelerator. However, the sizes of potentially generated black holes would be such that they would evaporate almost instantaneously via the radiation postulated by Stephen Hawking. Several reports were published on the safety of LHC experiments, and all ruled out any doomsday scenario. The events created in the LHC experiments occur in nature without any hazard to life. High-energy cosmic rays colliding with the Earth generate far more energy than those reached in the LHC. For example, each collision of a pair of protons in the LHC releases an amount of energy comparable to that of a few colliding mosquitoes.

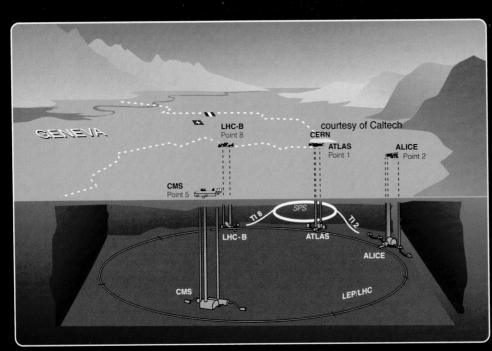

© CERN Geneva

courtesy of Caltech

3 This diagram shows the locations of the four main experiments (ALICE, ATLAS, CMS, and LHCb) between 50 m and 150 m underground.

All of the collisions are observed in six detectors.

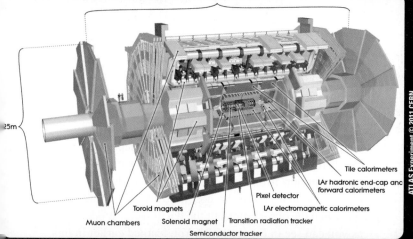

25m

Tile calorimeters

LAr hadronic end-cap and forward calorimeters

Pixel detector

LAr electromagnetic calorimeters

Toroid magnets

Solenoid magnet

Transition radiation tracker

Muon chambers

Semiconductor tracker

ATLAS Experiment © 2011 CERN

4 ATLAS detector. ATLAS is one of the largest collaborative efforts ever attempted in the physical sciences, involving physicists from 38 countries and 174 universities and laboratories. ATLAS is about 45 metres long, more than 25 metres high, about half as big as the Notre Dame Cathedral in Paris, and weighs about 7000 tons—about the same as the Eiffel Tower, or a hundred empty 747 jets.

LHC is a large international collaboration, run by CERN—Conseil Européen pour la Recherche Nucléaire (European Organisation for Nuclear Research). Around 10 000 scientists around the world are involved in this project. Canada contributed to the LHC by making parts o one of the detectors, ATLAS.

5 ATLAS detector with graphic simulation of big bang experiment superimposed on the real photograph of the detector. Crashing together in the centre of ATLAS, the particles produce conditions of the early universe and will help shed light on the basic forces that have shaped our universe, the origin of mass, extra dimensions of space, microscopic black holes, and evidence for dark matter candidates in the universe.

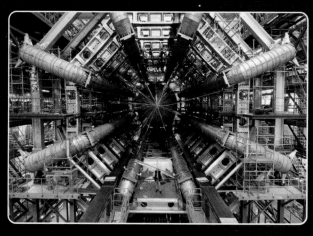

In 2012, the discovery of the Higgs boson was announced at CERN. This was a monumental discovery—the end result of a 40-year search for this elusive particle. The Higgs particle was the last missing piece of what scientists call the Standard Model, which describes all the fundamental particles and the interactions between them. This discovery explains why particles have mass; therefore, the Higgs boson is critical for a complete picture of the Standard Model. The 2013 Nobel Prize in physics was awarded to Peter Higgs and Francois Englert, who predicted the existence of this particle in 1964. Further experiments and analysis will be performed over the coming years to verify the discovery and better understand the nature of the Higgs boson. Science progresses through careful testing, healthy skepticism, and exciting new discoveries.

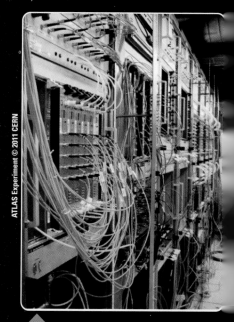

ATLAS Experiment © 2011 CERN

6 Storing data from numerous experiments poses a large problem in every branch of science today. Data from ATLAS fill up one CD every second (it records only a fraction of the data—those that may show signs of new physics). A worldwide grid of 100 000 computers is set up for analysis. It is no surprise or coincidence that the World Wide Web was first created at CERN in 1989.

© 2005 CERN

7 This sculpture of the dancing Shiva at CERN symbolizes the cosmic dance of creation and destruction. Ancient Indian cosmological models were the only ones that discussed time scales for the universe in terms of billions of years. The universe was thought to have been created and destroyed in a recurring cycle that occurred over many billions of years—an ancient precursor to our big bang and big crunch theories today.

acceleration. In fact, the inflationary theory of the universe makes very specific predictions about the sizes of the irregularities an observer on Earth should see in the CMB. The Wilkinson Microwave Anisotropy Probe (WMAP), a space infrared telescope, has made extensive observations of the type required to test those predictions (see Figure 11.8). More recently, the European Space Agency's Planck space telescope has made the most accurate observations of the cosmic microwave background to date.

The background radiation is highly isotropic; it looks almost exactly the same in all directions. However, when the average intensity is subtracted from each spot on the sky, small irregularities are evident. That is, some spots on the sky look a tiny bit hotter and brighter than other spots. In 1992, data from the Cosmic Background Explorer (COBE) space mission showed evidence of this anisotropy, and in 2006, George Smoot and John Mather won the Nobel Prize for their work on the COBE analysis.

Cosmologists can analyze those irregularities in the intensity of the CMB by using sophisticated mathematics to measure how often spots of different sizes occur. The analysis confirms that spots about 1 degree in diameter

are the most common, but spots of other sizes occur as well. A graph such as Figure 11.21 can be plotted to show the irregularities of various sizes and how common these are.

Theory predicts that most of the irregularities in the hot gas of the big bang should be about 1 degree in diameter if the universe is flat. If the universe were open, the most common irregularities would be smaller. The size of the irregularities in the cosmic background radiation show that the observations fit the flat universe model well, as you can see in Figure 11.21. You learned earlier in this chapter that a flat universe is most easily explained by inflation. Not only is the theory of inflation supported, an exciting result itself, but these data show that the universe is flat, which indirectly confirms the existence of dark energy and the acceleration of the universe.

The results from the WMAP and Planck observations make a complicated curve in Figure 11.21, and details of the wiggles tell cosmologists a great deal about the universe. The curve shows that the universe is flat, accelerating, and will expand forever. The age of the universe derived from the data is 13.8 billion years. Furthermore, the smaller peaks in the curve reveal that the universe contains 4.9 percent baryonic (normal) matter, 26.8 percent dark matter, and 68.3 percent dark energy. The Hubble constant is calculated to be 67.3 km/s/Mpc. The inflationary theory is confirmed, and the data support the cosmological constant version of dark energy, although quintessence is not quite ruled out. The dark matter needs to be "cold" (meaning, in this context, slow-moving) in order for it to clump together rapidly enough after the big bang to make the first galaxies, quasars, and galaxy clusters.

Please reread the preceding paragraph. What it says is truly amazing. WMAP and other studies of the cosmic microwave background radiation and the distribution of galaxies have revolutionized cosmology. At last, astronomers have accurate observations against which to test theories. The basic constants are known to a precision of a few percent.

On reviewing these results, one cosmologist announced, "Cosmology is solved!" But that might be premature. The latest data from the Planck mission shows anomalies in the large scale structure of the cosmic microwave background that cannot be explained by our current models of cosmology. Scientists also don't understand dark matter or the dark energy that drives the acceleration, so over 95 percent of the universe is not understood. Hearing this, another astronomer suggested that a better phrase is "Cosmology is in crisis!" Certainly there are further mysteries to be explored, but cosmologists are growing more confident that they can describe the origin and evolution of the universe.

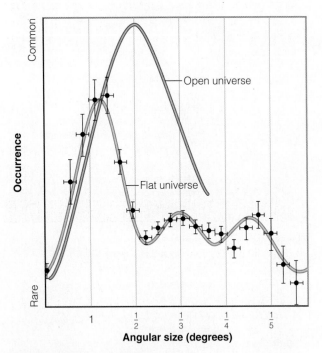

Figure 11.21 This graph shows how commonly the irregularities of different sizes occur in the cosmic microwave background radiation. Irregularities of about 1 degree in diameter are most common. Models of the universe that are open or closed are ruled out. The data fit a flat model of the universe very well. Crosses on data points show the uncertainty in the measurements.

The **Big Picture**

You have traced the origin of the universe, the creation of the chemical elements, the birth of galaxies, and the births and deaths of stars. You now have a perspective that few humans share, and you have tried to tackle some of the biggest and most difficult ideas in science.

As you review the history and structure of the universe, it is wise to recognize the mysteries that remain; but note that they are mysteries that may be solved and not mysteries that are unknowable. Only a century ago, humanity didn't know there were other galaxies, or that the universe was expanding, or that stars generate energy by nuclear fusion. Human curiosity has solved many of the mysteries of cosmology and will solve more during your lifetime.

Review and **Discussion Questions**

Review Questions

1. How does the darkness of the night sky tell you something important about the universe?
2. Why can't the universe have a centre?
3. What evidence shows that the universe is expanding? What evidence shows that it began with a big bang?
4. Why couldn't atomic nuclei exist when the age of the universe was less than two minutes?
5. Why are measurements of the present density of the universe important?
6. How does the inflationary universe theory resolve the flatness problem? How does it resolve the horizon problem?
7. If the Hubble constant were really 100 instead of 67.3 km/s/Mpc, much of what astronomers understand about the evolution of stars and star clusters would have to be wrong. Explain why. (*Hint*: What would the age of the universe be?)
8. What is the evidence that the universe was very uniform during its first 400 000 years?
9. What evidence can you cite that the expansion of the universe is accelerating?
10. What evidence can you cite that the universe is flat?

Discussion Questions

1. Do you think Copernicus would have accepted the cosmological principle? Why or why not?
2. If you reject any model of the universe that has an edge in space because you can't comprehend such a thing, shouldn't you also reject any model of the universe that has a beginning? Isn't a beginning like an "edge" in time, or is there a difference?

Learning to Look

1. The image at the right shows irregularities in the background radiation. Why isn't the background radiation perfectly uniform? What does the size of these irregularities tell you?

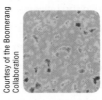

Courtesy of the Boomerang Collaboration

12

The Origin of the Solar System

CHAPTER OUTLINE

GUIDEPOST

In this vast universe, our local neighbourhood consists of our Sun and the planets, moons, asteroids, and comets of our solar system. The solar system is our home in the universe. Because humans are an intelligent species, we have the ability and the responsibility to wonder what we are. Our kind has inhabited this solar system for several million years, but only within the past hundred years have we begun to understand what a solar system is. To understand our place in the universe, we will explore the origins of the solar system and find answers to four important questions:

- **What are the observed properties of the solar system as a whole?**
- **How did the solar system form?**
- **How do planets form?**
- **What do astronomers know about other planetary systems?**

One reason to learn about the origin of the solar system is that we live here, but there is another reason. In the next two chapters you will explore each of the planets in more detail. By studying the origin of the solar system before studying individual planets, you will have a framework for understanding these fascinating worlds as well as for studying other planetary systems in the universe.

When you look at the stars and the galaxy, you feel that you are not just from any particular piece of land, but from the solar system.

Kalpana Chawla, NASA astronaut

NEL

12.1 The Great Chain of Origins

You are linked through a great chain of origins that leads back in time to the first instant when the universe began 13.8 billion years ago. The gradual discovery of the links in that chain is one of the most exciting adventures of the human intellect. In earlier chapters, you studied some of that story: the origin of the universe in the big bang, the formation of galaxies, the origin of stars, and the production of the chemical elements. Here you will explore further and consider the origin of planets.

The History of the Atoms in Your Body

By the time the universe was a few minutes old, the protons, neutrons, and electrons in your body had come into existence (see Chapter 11). You are made of very old matter.

Although those particles formed quickly, they were not linked together to form the atoms that are common today. Most of the matter was hydrogen, and about 25 percent of the mass was helium. Very few of the heavier atoms were made in the big bang. Although your body does not contain helium, it does contain many of those ancient hydrogen atoms unchanged since the universe began.

Within a few hundred million years after the big bang, matter began to collect to form galaxies containing billions of stars. You have learned how nuclear reactions inside stars combine low-mass atoms such as hydrogen to make heavier atoms. Generations of stars cooked the original particles, fusing them into atoms such as carbon, nitrogen, and oxygen (see Chapters 8 and 9). Those are common atoms in your body. Even the calcium atoms in your bones were assembled inside stars.

Most of the iron in your body was produced by carbon fusion in type Ia supernovae and by the decay of radioactive atoms in the expanding matter ejected by type II supernovae. Some atoms heavier than iron (for example, iodine), critical in the functioning of your thyroid gland, were created by rapid nuclear reactions that can occur only during supernova explosions (see Chapter 8). Elements uncommon enough to be expensive, such as the gold, silver, and platinum in jewellery, were also produced during the violent deaths of rare massive stars.

Our galaxy contains at least 100 billion stars, including the Sun. It formed from a cloud of gas and dust about 5 billion years ago, and the atoms in your body were part of that cloud. How the Sun took shape, how the cloud gave birth to the planets, how the atoms in your body found their way onto Earth and into you is the story of this chapter. As you explore the origin of the solar system, keep in mind the great chain of origins that created the atoms. As the geologist Preston Cloud remarked, "Stars have died that we might live."

The Origin of the Solar System

Astronomers have a theory for the origin of our solar system that is consistent both with observations of the solar system and with observations of star formation, and now they are refining the details.

The **solar nebula theory** proposes that planets form in rotating disks of gas and dust around young stars (Figure 12.1). These young stars form at the centre of a rotating cloud of gas and dust that starts to contract due to gravity. Collisions between particles in the rotating cloud tend to flatten the cloud into a disk shape. In addition, as the cloud shrinks it spins faster due to the conservation of angular momentum. Most of the material in the spinning disk forms a star in the centre, while the remaining material forms the planets and other bodies such as asteroids and comets. There is now clear evidence that disks of gas and dust are common around young stars. This idea is so comprehensive and explains so many observations that it can be considered to have "graduated" from being just a hypothesis to being properly called a theory. Bipolar flows from protostars (see Chapter 7) were the first evidence of such disks, but modern techniques, like those used by the Hubble telescope in Figure 12.2, can image the disks directly. Our own planetary system formed in such a disk-shaped cloud around the Sun. When the Sun became luminous enough, the remaining gas and dust were blown away into space by the solar wind (a stream of charged particles from the Sun), leaving the planets orbiting the Sun.

According to the solar nebula theory, Earth and the other planets of our solar system formed billions of years ago as the Sun condensed from the interstellar medium. This theory predicts that most stars should have planets because planet formation is a natural part of star formation, and therefore planets should be very common in the universe, probably more common than stars.

solar nebula theory A theory of formation of the solar system consistent with our current observations that describes how a rotating cloud of gas and dust gravitationally collapsed and flattened into a disk around the Sun forming at the centre, from which the planets were formed.

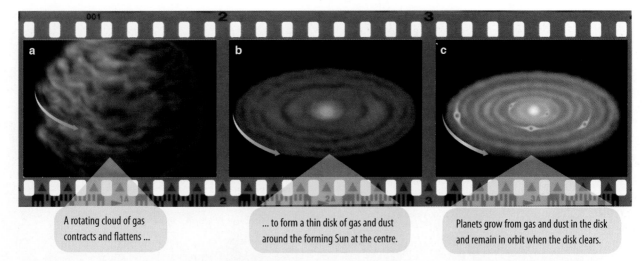

Figure 12.1 The solar nebula theory. (a) A rotating cloud of gas contracts and flattens. (b) The cloud of gas forms a thin disk of gas and dust around the Sun forming at the centre. (c) Planets grow from gas and dust in the disk and remain in orbit due to the Sun's gravity.

A rotating cloud of gas contracts and flattens ...

... to form a thin disk of gas and dust around the forming Sun at the centre.

Planets grow from gas and dust in the disk and remain in orbit when the disk clears.

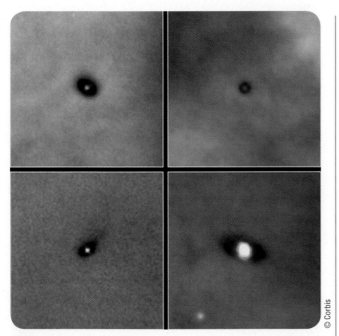

© Corbis

Figure 12.2 Dust and gas disks around young stars are evident in these Hubble telescope images of the Orion Nebula.

12.2 A Survey of the Planets

To explore consequences of the solar nebula theory, astronomers search the present solar system for evidence of its past. The next two sections provide a survey of the solar system and a list of its most significant characteristics, which are potential clues to how it formed.

Begin with the most general view of the solar system. It is, in fact, almost entirely empty space (refer to **Visualizing Astronomy 1.1**, **The Scale of the Very Small and Very Large: Powers of 10**). Imagine that you reduce the solar system until Earth is the size of a small grain of table salt, about 0.3 mm in diameter. The Sun is the size of a small plum 4 m from Earth. Jupiter is an apple seed 20 m from the Sun. Neptune, at the edge of the solar system, is a large grain of sand located 120 m from the central plum. You can see that planets are tiny specks of matter scattered around the Sun; they are the last significant remains of the solar nebula.

Revolution and Rotation

The planets revolve around the Sun in orbits that lie close to a common plane (Figure 12.3). Recall from Chapter 2 that the words *revolve* and *rotate* refer to different motions; a planet revolves around the Sun but rotates on its axis. Mercury, the closest planet to the Sun, has an orbit around the Sun that is tipped 7.0° to Earth's orbit. The rest of the planets' orbital planes are inclined by no more than 3.4°. The solar system is basically "flat" and disk shaped.

The rotation of the Sun and planets on their axes also seems related to the same overall direction of motion. The Sun rotates with its equator inclined only 7.2° to Earth's orbit, and most of the other planets' equators are tipped less than 30°. However, the rotations of Venus and Uranus are peculiar. Venus rotates backward compared to the other planets, and Uranus rotates on its "side" (with its equator almost perpendicular to its orbit). Later in this chapter you will learn a hypothesis about how these planet may have acquired their peculiar rotations.

Apparently, the preferred direction of motion in the solar system—counter-clockwise as seen from the

Figure 12.3 All the planets in our solar system orbit in the same direction; all their orbits lie roughly in one plane. Comets, however, have orbits that are often inclined out of the plane of the planetary orbits. These are all clues to how the solar system formed. The planets shown here are roughly 2000 times larger than their true diameters relative to the size of their orbits.

north—is related to the rotation of the disk of material that became the planets. All the planets revolve around the Sun in that direction, and with the exception of Venus and Uranus, they rotate on their axes in that same direction. Furthermore, nearly all the moons in the solar system, including Earth's moon, orbit around their planets in that direction. With only a few exceptions, most of which astronomers think they understand, revolution and rotation in the solar system both follow a common theme.

Two Kinds of Planets

Perhaps the most striking clue to the origin of the solar system comes from the obvious division of the planets into two categories: the small Earth-like worlds and the giant Jupiter-like worlds. The difference is so dramatic that you are led to say, "Aha, this must mean something!" Study **Visualizing Astronomy 12.1, Terrestrial and Jovian Planets,** and notice three important points:

1. The two kinds of planets are distinguished by their location. The four inner (Terrestrial) planets are quite different from the four outer (Jovian) planets.

2. Almost every solid surface in the solar system is covered with craters.

3. The two groups of planets are also distinguished by properties such as composition, rings, and moons. Any theory of the origin of planets needs to explain these properties.

The division of the planets into two families is a clue to how our solar system formed.

asteroid Small, rocky world. Most orbit between Mars and Jupiter in the asteroid belt.

However, the present properties of individual planets do not tell you everything you need to know about their origins. The planets have all evolved since they formed. For further clues you can look at smaller objects that have remained largely unchanged since the birth of the solar system.

12.3 Space Debris: Asteroids, Comets, and Meteoroids

The Sun and planets are not the only remains of the solar nebula. The solar system is littered with three kinds of space debris: asteroids, comets, and meteoroids. Although these objects represent a tiny fraction of the mass of the system, they are a rich source of information about the origin of the planets.

Asteroids

The **asteroids**, sometimes called minor planets, are small rocky worlds, most but not all of which orbit the Sun in a belt between the orbits of Mars and Jupiter. More than 100 000 asteroids have orbits that are charted, of which at least 2000 follow orbits that bring them into the inner solar system where they can occasionally collide with a planet; in fact, Earth has been struck many times in its history. Some asteroids share Jupiter's orbit, and others have been found beyond the orbit of Saturn.

About 200 asteroids are more than 100 km in diameter, and tens of thousands are estimated to be more than

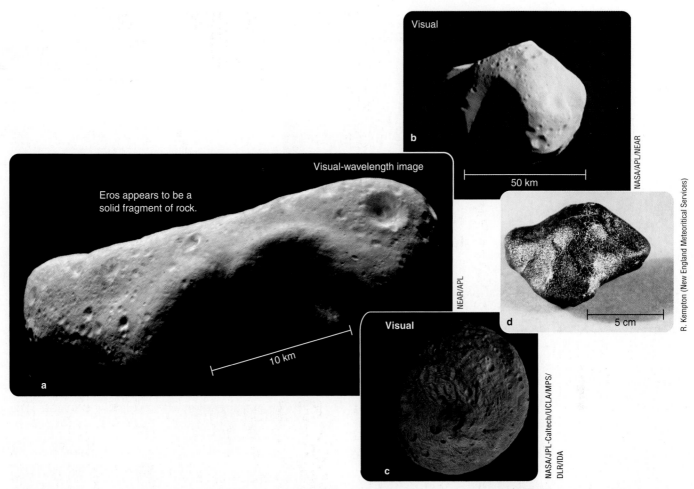

Figure 12.4 (a) The *Near Earth Asteroid Rendezvous* (*NEAR*) spacecraft visited the asteroid Eros in 2000 and found it heavily cratered by collisions and covered by a layer of crushed rock and dust. (b) The asteroid Mathilde, photographed by the *NEAR* spacecraft during a flyby, has a very low density, similar to other known asteroids that may be rubble piles with large empty spaces between solid fragments. (c) The large asteroid Vesta has a spectrum resembling solidified lava. Vesta seems to have had internal heat and volcanic activity in its past, perhaps due to decay of radioactive minerals. This image of the asteroid Vesta, taken from a distance of 2700 km (1700 mi) by NASA's *Dawn* spacecraft, shows Vesta's south polar region, which is dominated by the Rheasilvia impact basin. (d) One class of meteorites that is spectroscopically identical to Vesta is made of basalt, a volcanic rock.

10 km in diameter. There are probably a million or more that are larger than 1 km and billions that are smaller. Because even the largest are only a few hundred kilometres in diameter, Earth-based telescopes can detect no details on their surfaces, and even the Hubble Space Telescope can image only the largest features.

Photographs returned by robotic spacecraft and space telescopes show that asteroids are generally irregular in shape and battered by impact cratering (Figure 12.4). In fact, some asteroids appear to be piles of broken fragments clumped together by gravity, and a few asteroids are known to be double objects or to have small moons in orbit around them. These are understood by astronomers to be evidence of multiple collisions among the asteroids. A few larger asteroids show signs of volcanic activity on their surfaces that may have happened when those asteroids were young.

Astronomers recognize the asteroids as debris left over during planet formation at a distance of about 3 AU from the Sun. A good theory should be able to explain why a planet didn't form there but instead left behind a belt of construction material.

Comets

In contrast to the rocky asteroids, the brightest **comets** are impressively beautiful objects (see Figure 12.5). Most comets are faint, however, and difficult to locate even at their brightest. A comet may take months to sweep through the inner solar system, during which time it

> **comet** One of the small, icy bodies that orbit the Sun and produce tails of gas and dust when they approach the Sun.

CHAPTER 12   **The Origin of the Solar System**

1 The distinction between the Terrestrial planets and the Jovian planets is dramatic. The inner four planets, Mercury, Venus, Earth, and Mars, are **Terrestrial planets**, meaning they are small, dense, rocky worlds. The outer four planets, Jupiter, Saturn, Uranus, and Neptune, are **Jovian planets**, meaning they are large, low-density worlds with thick atmospheres and liquid or ice interiors.

The planets and the Sun to scale. Saturn's rings would just reach from Earth to the Moon.

1a Of the Terrestrial planets, Earth is most massive, but the Jovian planets are much more massive. Jupiter is over 300 Earth masses, and Saturn is nearly 100 Earth masses. Uranus and Neptune are 15 and 17 Earth masses.

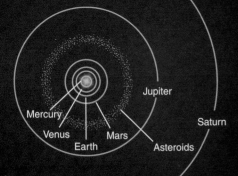

Planetary orbits to scale. The Terrestrial planets lie quite close to the Sun, whereas the Jovian planets are spread far from the Sun.

Mercury is only 40 percent larger than Earth's moon, and its weak gravity cannot retain a permanent atmosphere. Like the Moon, it is covered with craters from meteorite impacts.

NASA/Johns Hopkins University Applied Physics Laboratory/Carnegie Institution of Washington

Earth's moon

© UC Regents/Lick Observatory

2 Craters are common on all of the surfaces in the solar system that are strong enough to retain them. Earth has about 150 impact craters, but many more have been erased by erosion. Besides the planets, the asteroids and nearly all of the moons in the solar system are scarred by craters. Ranging from microscopic to hundreds of kilometres in diameter, these craters have been produced over the ages by meteorite impacts. When astronomers see a rocky or icy surface that contains few craters, they know that the surface is young.

difficult to study from Earth. The *Mariner 10* and *MESSENGER* spacecraft flew past Mercury in 1974 and 2008–9, respectively, and were able to take detailed close-up photos of the planet's surface. *MESSENGER* has been in orbit around Mercury since 2011.

These five worlds are shown in proper relative size.

Moon

Earth

NASA

The surface of Venus is no visible through its cloudy atmosphere, but radar maps reveal a dry world of craters and volcanoes

Venus (radar image)

3 The Terrestrial planets have densities like that of rock or metal. The Jovian planets all have low densities, and Saturn's density is only 70 percent the density of water. It would float in a big-enough bathtub.

The atmospheres of the Jovian planets are turbulent, and some are marked by great storms such as the Great Red Spot on Jupiter, but the atmospheres are not deep. If Jupiter were shrunk to a few centimetres in diameter, its atmosphere would be no deeper than the fuzz on a badly worn tennis ball.

Mars

Mars has a thin atmosphere and little water. Craters and volcanoes are common on its desert surface.

These Jovian worlds are shown in proper relative size.

3a The interiors of the Jovian planets contain small cores of heavy elements such as metals, surrounded by a liquid. Jupiter and Saturn contain hydrogen forced into a liquid state by the high pressure. Less massive Uranus and Neptune contain heavy-element cores surrounded by partially solid water mixed with heavy material such as rocks and methane ices.

Venus at visual wavelengths

NASA

Jupiter

Great Red Spot

The Terrestrial planets are drawn here to the same scale as the Jovian planets.

The Jovian planets have extensive systems of satellites. For example, Jupiter is orbited by four large moons, discovered by Galileo in 1610, and dozens of smaller moons discovered up to the present day.

Saturn's rings seen through a small telescope.

Neptune

Uranus

Saturn

NASA

3b All four Jovian planets have ring systems. Saturn's rings are made of ice particles. The rings of Jupiter, Uranus, and Neptune are made of dark rocky particles. Terrestrial planets have no rings.

CHAPTER 12 The Origin of the Solar System |

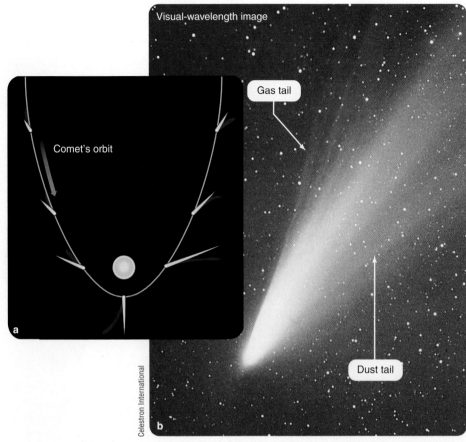

Visual-wavelength image

Comet's orbit

a

Gas tail

Dust tail

Celestron International

b

Figure 12.5 (a) A comet in a long, elliptical orbit becomes visible when the Sun's heat vaporizes its ices and pushes the gas and dust away in separate tails. (b) A comet may remain visible in the evening or morning sky for weeks as it moves through the inner solar system. Comet West was in the sky during March 1976.

appears as a glowing head with an extended tail of gas and dust.

The beautiful tail of a comet can be longer than an AU, but it is produced by an icy nucleus (sometimes described as a dirty snowball) only a few tens of kilometres in diameter. The nucleus remains frozen and inactive while the comet is far from the Sun. As the nucleus moves along its elliptical orbit into the inner solar system, the Sun's heat begins to vaporize the ices, releasing gas and dust. The pressure of sunlight and the solar wind pushes the gas and dust away, forming a long tail. The gas and dust respond differently to the forces acting on them, so they sometimes separate into two separate sub-tails (Figure 12.5a). The solar wind pushes the gas tail to point directly away from the Sun, whereas the motion of the nucleus along

volatile Easily evaporated.

Kuiper belt The collection of icy planetesimals orbiting in a region from just beyond Neptune out to 50 AU or more.

Oort cloud The hypothetical source of comets, a swarm of icy bodies understood to lie in a spherical shell extending to 100 000 AU from the Sun.

its orbit and the pressure of sunlight cause the dust tail to point approximately away from the Sun (Figure 12.5b).

Comet nuclei contain ices of water and other **volatile** (easily vaporized) compounds, such as carbon dioxide, carbon monoxide, methane, and ammonia. These ices are the kinds of compounds that should have condensed from the outer solar nebula, and that makes astronomers think that comets are ancient samples of the gases and dust from which the outer planets formed.

Five spacecraft flew past the nucleus of Comet Halley when it passed through the inner solar system in 1985 and 1986. Since then spacecraft have visited the nuclei of several other comets. Images show that comet nuclei are irregular in shape and very dark, with jets of gas and dust spewing from active regions on the nuclei (Figure 12.6). In general, these nuclei are darker than a lump of coal, which suggests their composition is similar to certain dark, water- and carbon-rich meteorites.

Since 1992, astronomers have discovered roughly a thousand small, dark, icy bodies orbiting in the outer fringes of the solar system beyond Neptune. This collection of objects is called the **Kuiper belt**, after the Dutch-American astronomer Gerard Kuiper (pronounced coy-per), who predicted their existence in the 1950s. Some Kuiper belt objects are quite large. Eris is in fact larger than Pluto. Other large bodies include Sedna and Orcus. You will learn more about Pluto and its connection to the Kuiper belt in Chapter 13. There are probably 100 million bodies larger than 1 km in the Kuiper belt, and any successful theory should explain how they came to be where they are. Astronomers have evidence that some comets—those that move in the plane of the solar system with relatively short orbital periods—come from the Kuiper belt.

The longer-period comets do not always orbit in the plane of the solar system, but can approach the Sun from random directions. They are believed to originate from the **Oort cloud**, a roughly spherical cloud of comets that

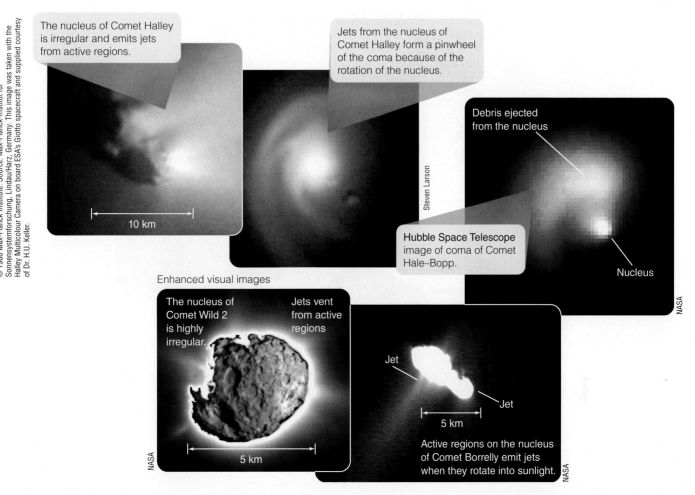

The nucleus of Comet Halley is irregular and emits jets from active regions.

Jets from the nucleus of Comet Halley form a pinwheel of the coma because of the rotation of the nucleus.

Steven Larson

10 km

Debris ejected from the nucleus

Hubble Space Telescope image of coma of Comet Hale–Bopp.

Nucleus

NASA

Enhanced visual images

The nucleus of Comet Wild 2 is highly irregular.

Jets vent from active regions

NASA

5 km

Jet

Jet

5 km

Active regions on the nucleus of Comet Borrelly emit jets when they rotate into sunlight.

NASA

Figure 12.6 Visual-wavelength images made by spacecraft and by the Hubble Space Telescope show how the nucleus of a comet produces jets of gases from regions where sunlight vaporizes ices.

is believed to lie much farther away at a distance of almost 1 light-year from the Sun. The Oort cloud is named after the Dutch astronomer Jan Oort who first suggested its existence in 1950. Several trillion objects larger than 1 km in size are estimated to lie in the Oort cloud. The edge of the Oort cloud forms the outer boundary of our solar system. You will understand how the solar nebula theory can explain these two different sources of comets.

There have been numerous unmanned spacecraft launched to study asteroids and comets. The *International Cometary Explorer* (ICE) spacecraft, jointly operated by NASA and the European Space Agency (ESA), performed the first flyby of a comet when it flew through the tail of comet Giacobini-Zinner in 1978. Halley's Comet, which can be seen from Earth every 75 years, was the subject of a flyby mission by Japan's *Sakigake* spacecraft in 1985. NASA's *Galileo* performed the first asteroid flyby in 1985 and also discovered the first asteroid moon, Dactyl. It was not until 2000 that the spacecraft *NEAR Shoemaker*

performed the first asteroid landing by touching down on the asteroid Eros. In 1999, the spacecraft *Stardust* collected samples from the coma of the comet Wild 2, and the sample capsules successfully returned to Earth. The Japanese *Hayabusa* asteroid lander became the first to return samples from an asteroid in 2003. *Deep Impact* was launched in 2005 to send an impactor to collide with a comet in order to study the interior of the comet. The mission showed that the comet was less icy and more dusty than expected. The probe *Dawn* was launched in 2007 to study the massive asteroids Vesta and Ceres. It orbited Vesta in 2011 before continuing toward Ceres. The data from *Dawn* will give scientists insights into the origins of the solar system. The European Space Agency is planning a similar impactor mission to an asteroid to study whether this could be used to redirect an asteroid that may be on course to collide with Earth. As space agencies around the world continue their efforts to explore our solar system, you may one day hear about human beings landing on an asteroid or a comet.

Figure 12.7 (a) Iron meteorites are very heavy for their size and have a dark, irregular surface. (b) A stony-iron meteorite cut and polished reveals a mixture of iron and rock. (c) Stony meteorites tend to have a fusion crust caused by melting in Earth's atmosphere. (d) Chondrules are small, glassy spheres found in chondrites.

Meteoroids, Meteors, Meteorites

Unlike the stately comets, **meteors** flash across the sky in momentary streaks of light. They are commonly called "shooting stars," but they are not stars. They are small bits of rock and metal falling into Earth's atmosphere and bursting into incandescent vapour about 80 km above the ground due to friction with the air. This vapour condenses to form dust, which settles slowly to the ground, adding about 40 000 tons per year to Earth's mass.

Technically, the word *meteor* refers to the streak of light in the sky. In space, before its fiery plunge, the object is called a **meteoroid**. Most meteoroids are the size of dust, grains of sand, or tiny pebbles. Almost all the meteors you see in the sky are produced by meteoroids that weigh less than 1 gram. Only rarely is a meteoroid massive and strong enough to survive its plunge and reach Earth's surface. Such a rock is called a **meteorite**.

Meteorites can be divided into three broad categories. *Iron* meteorites are solid chunks of iron and nickel. *Stony* meteorites are silicate masses that resemble Earth rocks. *Stony-iron* meteorites are mixtures of iron and stone. These types of meteorites are illustrated in Figure 12.7.

One type of stony meteorite is called **carbonaceous chondrite**. These meteorites generally contain abundant volatile compounds, including significant amounts of carbon and water, and may have similar composition to comet nuclei. Heating would have modified and driven off these fragile compounds, so carbonaceous chondrites must not have been heated ever since they formed. Astronomers conclude that carbonaceous chondrites, unlike the planets, have not changed since they formed, so they give direct information about the early solar system.

meteor A small bit of matter heated by friction to incandescent vapour as it falls into Earth's atmosphere.

meteoroid A meteor in space before it enters Earth's atmosphere.

meteorite A meteor that survives its passage through the atmosphere and strikes the ground.

carbonaceous chondrite Stony meteorite that contains small, glassy spheres—called chondrules—and volatiles. These chondrites may be the least-altered remains of the solar nebula still present in the solar system.

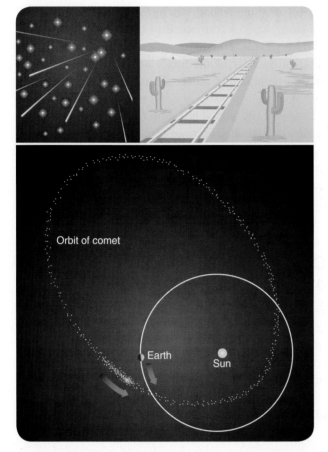

Figure 12.8 Meteors in a meteor shower enter Earth's atmosphere along parallel paths, but, much like lines on a road, perspective makes them appear to diverge from a radiant point in the sky. Meteors in a shower are debris left behind as a comet's icy nucleus vaporizes. The rocky and metallic bits of matter spread along the comet's orbit. If Earth passes through such material, you can see a meteor shower.

You can see evidence of the origin of meteors by watching a **meteor shower**, a display of meteors that are clearly related by a common origin and one of the most pleasant observations in astronomy. For example, the Perseid meteor shower occurs each year in August, and during the height of the shower you might see as many as 40 meteors per hour. The Perseid shower is so named because all its meteors appear to come from a point in the constellation Perseus. Meteor showers are seen when Earth passes near the orbit of a comet (Figure 12.8). The Eta Aquariids meteor shower, best viewed from the southern hemisphere, is caused by Earth passing through dust released by Halley's Comet. The meteors in meteor showers must be produced by dust and debris released from the icy head of the comet. In contrast, the orbits of some meteorites have been calculated to lead back into the asteroid belt.

An important reason to mention meteorites here is for one specific clue they give concerning the solar nebula: Meteorites can reveal the age of the solar system.

12.4 The Story of Planet Formation

The challenge for modern planetary astronomers is to compare the characteristics of the solar system with the solar nebula theory and tell the story of how the planets formed.

The Age of the Solar System

According to the solar nebula theory, the planets should be about the same age as the Sun. The most accurate way to find the age of a rocky body is to bring a sample into the laboratory and determine its age by analyzing the radioactive elements it contains.

When a rock solidifies, the process of cooling causes it to incorporate known proportions of the chemical elements. A few of these elements are radioactive and decay into other elements, called daughter elements or isotopes. The **half-life** of a radioactive element is the time it takes for half of the radioactive atoms to decay into the daughter elements. For example, potassium-40 decays with a half-life of 1.3 billion years into daughter isotopes calcium-40 and argon-40. Another example, uranium-238 decays with a half-life of 4.5 billion years into lead-206 and other isotopes. As time passes, the abundance of a radioactive element in a rock gradually decreases, and the abundances of the daughter elements gradually increase (Figure 12.9). You can estimate the original abundances of the elements in the rock from rules of chemistry and observations of rock properties in general. Thus, measuring the present abundances of the parent and daughter elements allows you to find the age of the rock. This works best if you have several radioactive element "clocks" that can be used as independent checks on each other.

To determine a radioactive age, you need a sample in the laboratory, and the only celestial bodies from which scientists have samples are Earth, the Moon, Mars, and meteorites. Tiny zircon crystals discovered in Australia have been dated to 4.4 billion years old. The oldest known rock on the planet was found in the Northwest Territories of Canada. It is 4 billion years old. The surface of Earth is active, and the crust is continually destroyed and

meteor shower A display of meteors that appear to come from one point in the sky; understood to be cometary debris.

half-life The time required for half of the radioactive atoms in a sample to decay.

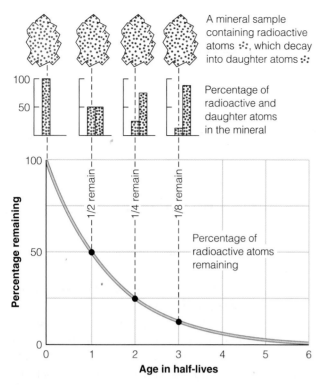

Figure 12.9 The radioactive atoms in a mineral sample (red) decay into daughter atoms (blue). Half the radioactive atoms are left after one half-life, a fourth after two half-lives, an eighth after three half-lives, and so on.

reformed from material welling up from beneath the crust (see Chapter 13). Consequently, the age of these oldest rocks tells us only that Earth is *at least* 4.4 billion years old.

Unlike Earth's surface, the Moon's surface is not being recycled by constant geologic activity, so you can guess that more of it might have survived unaltered since early in the history of the solar system. The oldest rocks brought back from the Moon by the Apollo astronauts are 4.48 billion years old. That means the Moon must be at least 4.48 billion years old. Although no one has yet been to Mars, over a dozen meteorites found on Earth have been identified by their chemical composition as having come from Mars. The oldest has an age of approximately 4.5 billion years. Mars must be at least that old.

The most important source for determining the age of the solar system is meteorites (Figure 12.10). Recall that the composition of carbonaceous chondrite meteorites indicates that they have not been heated much or otherwise altered since they formed. They have a range of ages with a consistent and precise upper limit of 4.56 billion years This number, often rounded to 4.6 billion years, is widely accepted as the age of

the solar system. That is in agreement with the age of the Sun, which is estimated to be 5 billion years plus or minus 1.5 billion years: an estimate based on mathematical models of the Sun's interior (see Chapter 7) that are completely independent of meteorite radioactive ages.

Apparently, all the bodies of the solar system formed at about the same time some 4.6 billion years ago. This is the final item on your list of characteristic properties of the solar system (Table 12.1). Each of these characteristics needs to be explained by a good theory of the formation of the solar system.

Chemical Composition of the Solar Nebula

Everything astronomers know about the solar system and star formation suggests that the solar nebula was a fragment of an interstellar gas cloud. Such a cloud would have been mostly hydrogen, with some helium and minor traces of the heavier elements.

This is precisely what you see in the composition of the Sun (refer to Table 5.1). Analysis of the solar

University Relations–University of Alberta

Figure 12.10 On the morning of January 18, 2000, a huge fireball was observed over northwestern Canada as a 1.3-ton meteorite slammed into Tagish Lake, British Columbia. Within days, several fragments of the rock were recovered in an uncontaminated state, making these the most pristine rocks from the solar system ever recovered. The Tagish Lake meteorite is one of the most primitive types of meteorites and is thought to have remained more or less unchanged since the solar system first formed. Primitive organic molecules have been discovered in the fragments, and extraterrestrial ice may have been preserved in some of the frozen rocks. This gives scientists a unique opportunity to study conditions in the early solar system and the origins of life on Earth.

Table 12.1	Characteristic Properties of the Solar System
1.	Disk shape of the solar system Orbits in nearly the same plane Common direction of revolution and rotation
2.	Two planetary types Terrestrial—inner planets—small, high density Jovian—outer planets—large, low density
3.	Planetary rings and large satellite systems around the Jovian planets, not around the Terrestrial planets
4.	Space debris—asteroids, comets, and meteors Two types of composition—rocky and icy Two types of orbits—inner solar system and outer solar system
5.	Common age of about 4.6 billion years for Earth, the Moon, Mars, meteorites, and the Sun

spectrum shows that the Sun is mostly hydrogen, with a quarter of its mass being helium and only about 2 percent being heavier elements. Although solar nuclear reactions fuse some hydrogen into helium, this happens in the Sun's core and does not affect its surface composition. This means the composition of the Sun's atmosphere revealed in its spectrum is essentially the composition of the solar nebula gases from which it formed.

The same solar nebula composition is reflected in the chemical compositions of the planets. The composition of Jupiter and the other Jovian planets resembles the composition of the Sun. Furthermore, if low-density gases escaped from a blob of Sun-stuff, the remaining heavier elements would resemble the composition of Earth, the other Terrestrial planets, and meteorites.

Condensation of Solids

The key to understanding the process that converted the nebular gas into solid matter is the observed variation in density among solar system objects. Recall that the four inner planets are high-density Terrestrial bodies, and the outer, Jupiter-like planets are low-density, giant planets. This division is due to the different ways gases condensed into solids in the inner and outer regions of the solar nebula.

HOW DO WE KNOW? 12.1

Reconstructing the Past from Evidence and Hypothesis

Scientists often solve problems in which they must reconstruct the past. Some of these reconstructions are obvious, such as an archaeologist excavating the ruins of a burial tomb, but others are less obvious. In each case, success requires the interplay of hypotheses and evidence to recreate a past that no longer exists.

Astronomers reconstruct the past when they use evidence gathered from meteorites to study the origin of the solar system, but a biologist studying a centipede is also reconstructing the past. Although their focus might at first seem to be anatomy, the biologist must reconstruct the ancient environment that gave rise to the centipedes.

The astronomer's problem is not just to understand what the planets are like but to understand how they got that way. That means planetary astronomers must look at the evidence they can see today and reconstruct a history of the solar system, a past that is quite different from the present. If you had a time machine like Dr. Who, it would be a fantastic adventure to go back and watch the planets form. Even without time machines, scientists can use the grand interplay of evidence and theory—the distinguishing characteristic of science—to journey back billions of years and reconstruct a past that no longer exists.

© Cezza / Alamy

Even among the four Terrestrial planets, you will find a pattern of slight differences in density. The **uncompressed densities**—the densities the planets would have if their gravity did not compress them, or put another way, the densities of their original construction material—can be calculated from the actual densities and masses of each planet. In general, the closer a planet is to the Sun, the higher is its uncompressed density.

This density variation is understood to have originated when the solar system first formed solid grains. The kind of matter that condensed in a particular region would depend on the temperature of the gas there. In the inner regions, the temperature seems to have been 1500 K or so. The only materials that can form grains at this temperature are compounds with high melting points, such as metal oxides and pure metals, which are very dense, corresponding to the composition of Mercury. Farther out in the nebula it was cooler, and silicates (rocky material) could condense. These are less dense than metal oxides and metals, corresponding more to the compositions of Venus, Earth, and Mars. Somewhere farther from the Sun there was a boundary called the **ice line** beyond which the water vapour could freeze to form ice. Not much farther out, compounds such as methane and ammonia could condense to form other ices. Water vapour, methane, and ammonia were abundant in the solar nebula, so beyond the ice line, the nebula was filled with a blizzard of ice particles, and those ices have low densities, as have the Jovian planets.

Table 12.2 | The Condensation Sequence

Temperature (K)	Condensate	Object (Estimated Temperature of Formation, K)
1500	Metal oxides	Mercury (1400)
1300	Metallic iron and nickel	
1200	Silicates	
1000	Feldspars	Venus (900)
680	Troilite (FeS)	Earth (600)
		Mars (450)
175	H_2O ice	Jovian (175)
150	Ammonia–water ice	
120	Methane–water ice	
65	Argon–neon ice	Pluto (65)

The sequence in which different materials condensed from the gas at different distances from the Sun is called the **condensation sequence** (Table 12.2). This is really a hypothesis that says the planets that formed at different distances from the Sun would have accumulated from different kinds of materials. The original chemical composition of the solar nebula should have been roughly the same throughout the nebula. The important factor was temperature. The inner nebula was hot, and only metals and rock could condense there; the outer nebula was cold, and so lots of ices as well as metals and rock could form. The ice line seems to have been between Mars and Jupiter, and it separates the formation of the dense Terrestrial planets from that of the lower-density Jovian planets.

Formation of Planetesimals

In the development of a planet, three groups of processes operate to collect solid bits of matter—rock, metal, or ices—into larger bodies called **planetesimals**, which eventually build the planets. The study of planet-building is the study of these three groups of processes: condensation, accretion, and gravitational collapse.

According to the solar nebula theory, planetary development in the solar nebula began with the growth of dust grains. These specks of matter, whatever their composition, grew from microscopic size first by condensation, then by accretion.

A particle grows by **condensation** when it adds matter one atom or molecule at a time from a surrounding gas. Snowflakes, for example, grow by condensation in Earth's atmosphere. In the solar nebula, dust grains were continuously bombarded by atoms of gas, some of which stuck to the grains.

The second process is **accretion**, the sticking together of solid particles. You may have seen accretion

uncompressed density The density a planet would have if its gravity did not compress it.

ice line A boundary beyond which water vapour could freeze to form ice.

condensation sequence The sequence in which different materials condense from the solar nebula, depending on their distance from the Sun.

planetesimal One of the small bodies that formed from the solar nebula and eventually grew into a protoplanet.

condensation The growth of a particle by addition of material from the surrounding gas, atom by atom.

accretion The sticking together of solid particles to produce a larger particle.

in action if you walked through a snowstorm with big, fluffy flakes. If you caught one of those flakes on your mitten and looked closely, you could see that each of them was made up of many tiny, individual flakes that had collided as they fell and accreted to form larger particles. Model calculations indicate that in the solar nebula the dust grains were, on the average, no more than a few centimetres apart, so they collided frequently and accreted into larger particles.

There is no clear distinction between a very large grain and a very small planetesimal. An object can be considered a planetesimal when its diameter approaches a kilometre or so: the size of a typical small asteroid or comet.

Objects in the solar nebula larger than a centimetre were subject to processes that tended to concentrate them. For example, collisions with the surrounding gas and with each other would have caused growing planetesimals to settle into a thin disk, with an estimated thickness of about 0.01 AU in the central plane of the rotating nebula. This concentration of material would have made further planetary growth more rapid. Computer models show that the rotating disk of particles should have been gravitationally unstable and would have been disturbed by spiral density waves much like those found in spiral galaxies. This would have further concentrated the planetesimals and helped them coalesce into objects up to about 100 km in diameter.

Through these processes the nebula became filled with trillions of solid particles ranging in size from pebbles to small planets. As the largest began to exceed 100 km in diameter, new processes began to alter them, and a new stage in planet-building began: the formation of protoplanets.

Growth of Protoplanets

With the coalescing of planetesimals, **protoplanets** eventually formed—the massive objects destined to become planets. As these larger bodies grew, new processes began making them grow faster and altered their physical structure.

If planetesimals collided at orbital velocities, it is unlikely that they would have stuck together. The average orbital velocity in the solar system is about 10 km/s. Head-on collisions at this velocity would have vaporized the material. However, the planetesimals were all moving in the same direction in the nebular plane and didn't collide head-on. Instead, they merely "rubbed shoulders," so to speak, at low relative velocities. Such gentle collisions would have been more likely to combine them than to shatter them.

The largest planetesimals would grow the fastest because they had the strongest gravitational field and could more easily attract additional material. Computer models indicate that these planetesimals grew quickly to protoplanetary dimensions, sweeping up more and more material.

Protoplanets had to begin growing by accumulating solid material because they did not have enough gravity to capture and hold large amounts of gas. In the warm solar nebula, the atoms and molecules of gas were travelling at velocities much larger than the escape velocities of modest-size protoplanets. Because of that, in their early development, the protoplanets could grow only by attracting solid bits of rock, metal, and ice. Once a protoplanet approached a mass of 15 Earth masses or so, it could begin to grow by **gravitational collapse**, the rapid accumulation from the nebula of large amounts of infalling gas.

In its simplest form, the theory of Terrestrial protoplanet growth supposes that all the planetesimals in each orbital zone had about the same chemical composition. The planetesimals accumulated gradually to form a planet-size ball of material that was of homogeneous composition throughout. As the planet formed, heat accumulated in its interior both from the impacts of infalling planetesimals and from the decay of short-lived radioactive elements. This heat eventually melted the planet and allowed it to differentiate. **Differentiation** is the separation of material according to density. When the planet melted, the heavy metals such as iron and nickel settled to the core, while the lighter silicates floated to the surface to form a low-density crust. Figure 12.11 depicts the story of planet formation, including the accretion of planetesimals followed by differentiation.

This process depends on the presence of short-lived radioactive elements whose rapid decay would have released enough heat to melt the interior of planets. Astronomers know such radioactive elements were present because the oldest meteorites contain daughter isotope magnesium-26 that is produced by the decay of aluminum-26 with a half-life of only 0.74 million years. The aluminum-26 and similar short-lived radioactive elements are gone now, but they must have been

protoplanet Massive object, destined to become a planet, resulting from the coalescence of planetesimals in the solar nebula.

gravitational collapse The process by which a forming body such as a planet gravitationally captures gas rapidly from the surrounding nebula.

differentiation The separation of planetary material inside a planet according to density.

outgassing The release of gases from a planet's interior.

produced in a supernova explosion that occurred no more than a few million years before the formation of the solar nebula. In fact, many astronomers suspect that this supernova explosion compressed nearby gas and triggered the formation of stars, one of which became the Sun. Our solar system may exist because of a supernova explosion that occurred about 4.6 billion years ago.

If planets formed and were later melted by radioactive decay, gases released from the planet's interior would have formed an atmosphere. The creation of a planetary atmosphere from a planet's interior is called **outgassing**. Models of the formation of Earth indicate that the local planetesimals would not have included much water, so some astronomers now think that Earth's water and some of its present atmosphere accumulated late in the formation of the planets, as Earth swept up volatile-rich planetesimals that were forming in the cooling solar nebula. Such icy planetesimals may have formed in the outer parts of the solar nebula and been scattered by encounters with the Jovian planets, creating a solar system-wide bombardment of comets.

According to the solar nebula theory, the Jovian planets began growing by the same processes that built the Terrestrial planets, but the outer solar nebula contained not only solid bits of metals and silicates, but also abundant ices. The Jovian planets grew rapidly and quickly became massive enough to grow by gravitational collapse, drawing in large amounts of gas from the solar nebula. Ices could not condense as solids at the locations of the Terrestrial planets, so those planets developed slowly and never became massive enough to grow by gravitational collapse.

The Jovian planets must have grown to their present size in less than about 10 million years, which is when astronomers calculate that the Sun became hot and luminous enough for the solar wind to blow away the gas remaining in the solar nebula. The Terrestrial planets grew from solids, not from the gas, so they could have continued to grow by accretion from the solid debris left behind when the gas was blown away. Model calculations indicate the process of planet formation was almost completely finished by the time the solar system was about 30 million years old.

Bombardment of the Planets

Astronomers have good reason to believe that comets and asteroids can hit planets. Meteorites hit Earth every

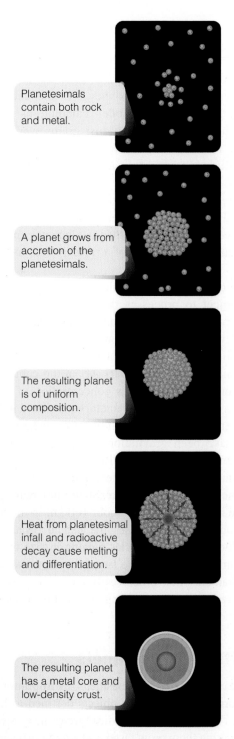

Planetesimals contain both rock and metal.

A planet grows from accretion of the planetesimals.

The resulting planet is of uniform composition.

Heat from planetesimal infall and radioactive decay cause melting and differentiation.

The resulting planet has a metal core and low-density crust.

Figure 12.11 This simple model of accretion assumes planets formed from planetesimals that were of uniform composition, containing both metals and rocky material, and the planets later differentiated, meaning they melted and separated into layers by density and composition.

day, and occasionally a large one can form a crater (Figure 12.12). Earth is marked by about 150 known meteorite craters. In a sense, this bombardment represents the slow continuation of the accretion of the

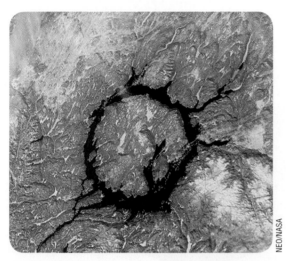

Figure 12.12 The Manicouagan crater in Quebec is one of the largest known impact craters on Earth, with a diameter of about 65 km. It is believed to have been created by an asteroid impact over 200 million years ago. The heat and pressure of the impact caused rings similar to the ripples of a stone dropped in water. An annular (ring-shaped) lake is visible in this photo taken from the space shuttle.

planets. Earth's moon, Mercury, Venus, Mars, and most of the moons in the solar system are covered with craters. A few of these craters have been formed recently by the steady rain of meteorites that falls on all planets in the solar system. However, most of the craters appear to have been formed more than 4 billion years ago in what is called the **heavy bombardment**; at that time much of the remaining solid debris in the solar nebula was swept up by the planets. In Chapter 13 you will learn that the heavy bombardment may have had more than one episode.

Sixty-five million years ago, at the end of the Cretaceous period, over 75 percent of the species on Earth, including the dinosaurs, went extinct. Scientists have found a thin layer of clay (called the K-Pg or K-T boundary) all over the world that was laid down at that time, and it is rich in the element iridium—common in meteorites but rare in Earth's crust. This suggests that a large impact altered Earth's climate and caused the worldwide extinction. Mathematical models predict that a major impact ejected huge amounts of pulverized rock high above the atmosphere. As this material fell back, Earth's atmosphere turned into a glowing oven of red-hot meteorites streaming through the air, and the heat triggered massive forest fires around the world. Soot from such fires has been found in the final Cretaceous clay layers. Once the firestorms cooled, the remaining dust in the atmosphere blocked sunlight and produced deep darkness for a year or more, killing off most plant life. Other effects, such as acid rain and enormous tsunamis (tidal waves), are also predicted by these models.

Planetary geologist Adriana Ocampo and her colleagues have located a crater at least 180 km in diameter centred near the village of Chicxulub (pronounced cheek-shoe-lube) in the northern Yucatán region of Mexico (Figure 12.13). Although the crater is completely covered by sediments, mineral samples show that it contains shocked quartz typical of impact sites and that it is the right age. The impact of an object 10 to 14 km in diameter formed the crater about 65 million years ago, just when the dinosaurs and many other species died out. Most Earth scientists now consider this to be the scar of the impact that ended the Cretaceous period.

Earthlings watched in awe during six days in the summer of 1994 as 20 or more fragments from the head of Comet Shoemaker–Levy 9 slammed into Jupiter and produced impacts equalling the detonation of millions of megatons of TNT. Each impact created a fireball of hot gases and left behind dark smudges that remained visible for months afterward (Figure 12.14). Another such impact produced a single scar observed in 2009. Carolyn and Eugene Shoemaker, David Levy, and Philippe Bendjoya were co-discoverers of Comet Shoemaker–Levy 9. American astronomer Carolyn Shoemaker holds the record for being the most successful comet hunter alive; remarkably, she accomplished this after she took up astronomy at age 51. Canadian amateur astronomer David Levy is the first person to have discovered comets using visual, photographic, and electronic methods.

Major impacts occur less often on Earth because Earth is smaller than the Jovian planets, but such impacts are inevitable. We are sitting ducks. All of humanity is spread out over Earth's surface and exposed to anything that falls out of the sky. Meteorites, asteroids, and comets bombard Earth, producing impacts that vary from dust settling on rooftops to blasts capable of destroying all life. As we know from the impact that led to the extinction of the dinosaurs, it would take an object of only a few kilometres in diameter to create a mass extinction event. Such an impact would have 10 million times more energy than the bomb that was dropped on Hiroshima. In this case, the scientific evidence is conclusive and highly unwelcome. But statistically, you are quite safe. The chance that a major impact will

heavy bombardment The intense cratering that occurred sometime during the first 0.5 billion years in the history of the solar system.

Figure 12.13 The giant impact scar buried in Earth's crust near the village of Chicxulub in the Yucatán region of Mexico was formed about 65 million years ago by the impact of a large comet or asteroid. The gravity map above shows the extent of the crater hidden below limestone that was deposited long after the impact.

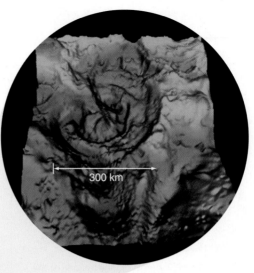

300 km

United States

Mexico

Chicxulub crater

Yucatán

Virgil L. Sharpton, University of Alaska, Fairbanks

occur during your lifetime is so small that it is hard to estimate. However, the consequences of such an impact are so severe that humanity should be preparing. One way to prepare is to find the **NEOs (near-Earth objects)** that could hit this planet, map their orbits in detail, and identify any that are dangerous. Spaceguard programs around the world focus on surveying the skies to discover NEOs. These programs include Near-Earth Asteroid Tracking (NEAT); Catalina Sky Survey, the most prolific NEO discovery program; the Japan Spaceguard Association; Europe's Asiago DLR Asteroid Survey; and the Beijing Schmidt CCD Asteroid Program. You can help too, by joining the growing global network of amateur astronomers who are watching the skies from their backyards and helping to guard our planet.

NEO (near-Earth object) A small solar system body (asteroid or comet) with an orbit near enough to Earth that it poses some threat of eventual collision.

evolutionary theory An explanation of a phenomenon involving slow, steady processes.

catastrophic theory An explanation of a phenomenon involving special, sudden, perhaps violent, events.

Explaining the Characteristics of the Solar System

Now you have learned enough to put all the pieces of the puzzle together and explain the distinguishing characteristics of the solar system as outlined in Table 12.1.

The first fact in Table 12.1 is that the Sun and planets revolve and rotate in the same direction. This happens because they formed from the same rotating gas cloud. Also, the orbits of the planets lie in the same plane because the rotating solar nebula collapsed into a disk, and the planets formed in that disk.

According to the solar nebula theory, continuing evolutionary processes gradually build the planets. Scientists call this type of explanation an **evolutionary theory**. In contrast, a **catastrophic theory** invokes special, sudden, even violent, events. For example, the peculiarities of rotation of Uranus, which rotates on its side, and Venus, which rotates backward, could have been caused by an off-centre impact of a massive planetesimal on each planet while they were forming—an explanation of the catastrophic type. Similarly, Earth's unusually large moon could be a result of a giant impact that stripped debris from Earth, which accreted to form the Moon. On the other hand, computer models suggest that the Sun can produce tides in the thick atmosphere of Venus, which eventually could have resulted in the reversal of that planet's rotation—an explanation of the evolutionary type.

The second point in Table 12.1 refers to the division of the planets into Terrestrial and Jovian worlds, which can be explained by the condensation sequence.

Impacts were visible from the *Galileo* spacecraft.

Visual

NASA

Impact site just out of sight as seen from Earth

At visual wavelengths, impact sites were dark smudges that lasted for many days.

Fragments of comet falling toward Jupiter

Visual image composite

NASA

Larger than Earth

Visual

NASA

Impact L occurred out of sight beyond Jupiter's horizon.

Mike Skrutskie

Minutes after impact, the rising fireball was visible above the horizon.

Mike Skrutskie

Only 9 minutes after impact L, the fireball was brilliant in the infrared.

Infrared images

Mike Skrutskie

Impact sites remained bright in the infrared as the rotation of Jupiter carried them into sight from Earth.

Infrared

© Richard Wainscoat

Figure 12.14 The impact of Comet Shoemaker–Levy 9 with Jupiter was the first collision between two objects in our solar system that was directly observed from Earth.

The Terrestrial planets formed in the inner part of the solar nebula, where the temperature was high, and only compounds such as metals and silicates could condense to form solid particles. That produced the small, dense Terrestrial planets. In contrast, the Jovian planets formed in the outer solar nebula, where the lower temperature allowed the gas to form large amounts of ices, perhaps three times more ices than silicates. That allowed the Jovian planets to grow rapidly and become massive, low-density worlds. Also, the massive planets Jupiter and Saturn eventually grew even larger by drawing in gas directly from the solar nebula. The Terrestrial planets could not do this because they never became massive enough.

The **heat of formation** (the energy released by infalling matter) was tremendous for these massive planets. Jupiter must have grown hot enough to glow with a luminosity of about 1 percent that of the present Sun. However, because it never got hot enough to start nuclear fusion as a star would, it never generated its own energy. Jupiter is still hot inside. In fact, both Jupiter and Saturn radiate more heat than they absorb from the Sun, so they are evidently still cooling.

Mathematical models show Jupiter grew into such a massive planet that it was able to gravitationally disturb the motion

heat of formation In planetology, the heat released by infalling matter during the formation of a planetary body.

CHAPTER 12 **The Origin of the Solar System** |

of nearby planetesimals. The bodies that might have formed a planet between Mars and Jupiter were broken up, thrown into the Sun, or ejected from the solar system due to the gravitational influence of massive Jupiter. The asteroids seen today are the last remains of those rocky planetesimals.

The comets, in contrast, are evidently the last of the icy planetesimals. Some may have formed in the outer solar nebula beyond Neptune, but many probably formed among the Jovian planets, where ices could condense easily. Mathematical models show that the massive Jovian planets could have ejected some of these icy planetesimals into the far outer solar system, into the region of the Oort cloud, from which come comets that have very long periods and orbits that are highly inclined to the plane of the solar system (Figure 12.15).

The icy Kuiper belt objects, including Pluto, appear to be ancient planetesimals that formed in the outer solar system but were never incorporated into a planet. They orbit slowly far from the light and warmth of the Sun and, except for occasional collisions, have not changed much since the solar system was young. You will learn more about Pluto's origins and differences from the other outer planets in Chapter 14.

The third point in Table 12.1 notes that all four Jovian worlds have ring systems and numerous moons. To understand this, consider the large mass of these worlds and their remote location in the solar system. A large mass makes it easier for a planet to hold on to orbiting ring particles, and, being farther from the Sun, the ring particles are not as easily swept away by the pressure of sunlight and the solar wind. So it is not surprising that the Terrestrial planets, low-mass worlds located near the Sun, have no planetary rings. As the

Figure 12.15 Comet SWAN, discovered in 2006, emerged from the Oort cloud and passed through the inner solar system.

Jovian planets formed, spinning, flattening, and heating formed disks of material around them. Condensation and accretion occurred in these mini solar systems, leading to the formation of numerous large moons. For example, Jupiter has over a dozen moons. In contrast, Earth is the only Terrestrial planet to have an unusually large moon. You will learn more about Earth's moon and the Jovian moons in Chapters 13 and 14.

The fourth point in Table 12.1 refers to the common ages of solar system bodies. The solar nebula theory has no difficulty explaining that characteristic because it predicts that the planets formed at the same time as the Sun, and they should all have roughly the same age.

12.5 Planets Orbiting Other Stars

Are there planets orbiting other stars? Yes, that is now certain. Are there planets like Earth? The evidence so far makes that seem likely.

Planet-Forming Disks around Other Stars

You have learned that dense disks of gas and dust surround stars that are forming. For example, at least 50 percent of the stars in the Orion Nebula are encircled by dense disks of gas and dust that have more than enough mass to make planetary systems like our own. The Orion star-forming region is only a few million years old, so it seems unlikely that planets have finished forming there yet. Nevertheless, the important point for astronomers is that disks of gas and dust that could become planetary systems are a common feature of star formation.

Debris Disks

In addition to these planet-forming disks around young stars, infrared astronomers have found cold, low-density dust disks around older stars such as Vega and Beta Pictoris. Although much younger than the Sun, these stars are on the main sequence and have completed their formation, so they are clearly in a later stage than the newborn stars in Orion. These low-density disks generally have even lower-density inner zones where planets may have formed (see Figure 12.16). Such tenuous dust

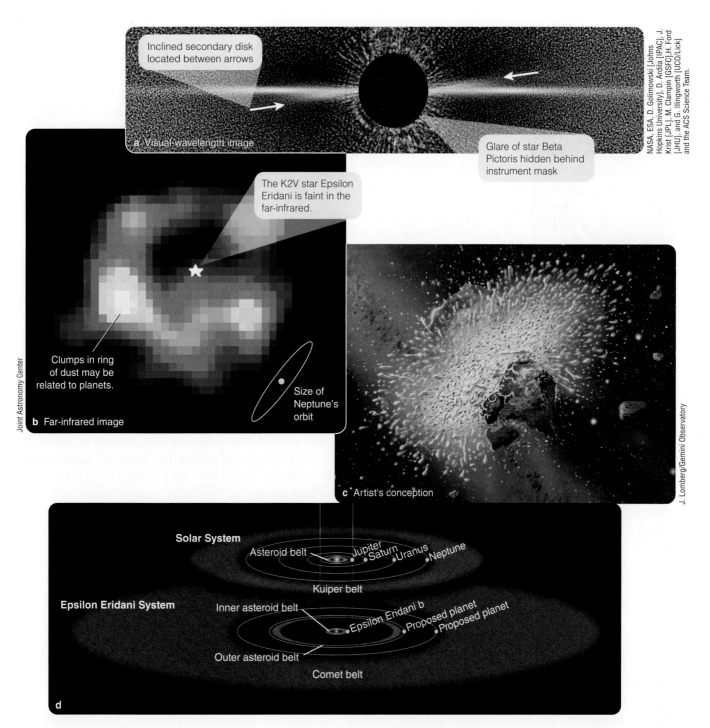

Figure 12.16 Dust disks around other stars. (a) Hiding the bright star behind a mask reveals a dust disk around Beta Pictoris. A second fainter disk may mark the orbital plane of a massive planet. (b) At far infrared wavelengths, dust disks can be brighter than the star. (c) Asteroid collisions are rare but produce lots of dust, which is blown away quickly. The presence of such dust is evidence of planetesimals. (d) Star Epsilon Eridani has dust disks comparable to those in our solar system. In both cases, planets control the extent of the dust. Dust in debris belts around older main-sequence stars indicates ongoing collisions of remnant planetesimals such as asteroids and comets. Such activity in our solar system is ultimately driven by the gravitational influence of planets. The locations of debris belt edges may be defined by adjacent orbits of planets. The inferred architecture of the Epsilon Eridani planetary system is shown in comparison with our solar system.

Ray Jayawardhana

Growing up in Sri Lanka, Ray Jayawardhana was inspired to explore space when his father told him about humans landing on the Moon. In 1985, when Halley's Comet was visible, he joined an amateur astronomy club in Sri Lanka. He learned English just to be able to read astronomy books. After obtaining an undergraduate degree at Yale and a Ph.D. at Harvard, he became interested in star formation and the diversity of planetary systems. Now he works as a professor of astronomy and astrophysics at the University of Toronto and is Canada Research Chair in Observational Astrophysics. He is one of many Canadian scientists who are playing an important role in the search for extrasolar planets. His studies of extrasolar planetary systems led to the discovery of planemos—mini-planetary systems orbiting objects much smaller than our Sun. In 2008, he and his collaborators took infrared images of a planet orbiting a sunlike star. Jayawardhana has won numerous professional awards, and has been named among Canada's Top 40 Under 40. He is an award-winning writer whose articles have been published in *The Economist, Scientific American, New Scientist, Astronomy*, and *Sky & Telescope*. He is also a popular speaker, a frequent commentator for the media, and creator of innovative outreach programs such as CoolCosmos, featuring 3000 ads in Toronto's subway cars, streetcars, and buses to celebrate the International Year of Astronomy.

disks are sometimes called **debris disks** because they are understood to consist of dusty debris released during collisions among small bodies such as comets, asteroids, and Kuiper belt objects. Our own solar system contains such dust, and astronomers have evidence that the Sun has an extensive debris disk of cold dust extending far beyond the orbits of the planets. Many of the debris disks have details of structure and shape that are probably caused by the gravity of planets orbiting within or at the edges of the debris.

Notice the difference between the two kinds of disks that astronomers have found. The low-density dust disks such as the one around Beta Pictoris are produced by dust from collisions among remnant planetesimals, such as comets, asteroids, and Kuiper belt objects. Such disks are evidence that planetary systems have already formed. In contrast, the dense disks of gas and dust, such as those seen around the stars in Orion, are sites where planets could be forming right now.

debris disk A disk of dust around some stars, found by infrared observations. The dust is debris from collisions among asteroids, comets, and Kuiper belt objects.

extrasolar planet A planet orbiting a star other than the Sun.

Extrasolar Planets

A planet orbiting another star is called an **extrasolar planet** or exoplanet. Such a planet would be quite faint and difficult to detect so close to the glare of its star. But there are ways to find these planets. To see how, all you have to do is imagine walking a dog.

Recall that Earth and its Moon orbit around their common centre of mass, and two stars in a binary system orbit around their centre of mass. When a planet orbits a star, the star moves very slightly as it orbits the centre of mass of the planet–star system. Think of someone walking a poorly trained dog on a leash; the dog runs around pulling on the leash, and even if it were an invisible dog, you could plot its path by watching how its owner was jerked back and forth. Astronomers can detect a planet orbiting another star by watching how the star moves as the planet tugs on it.

In 1988, Canadian astronomers Bruce Campbell, G. A. H. Walker, and S. Yang discovered the first extrasolar planet orbiting a binary star system, but their discovery was not confirmed until 2002. The first planet orbiting a sunlike star was discovered in 1995 by Swiss astrophysicist Michel Mayor and his Ph.D. student Didier Queloz. It orbits the star 51 Pegasi. As the planet circles the star, the star wobbles slightly, and this very small motion of the star is detectable as Doppler shifts in the star's spectrum, as shown in Figure 12.17a. This technique is the same as the one used to study

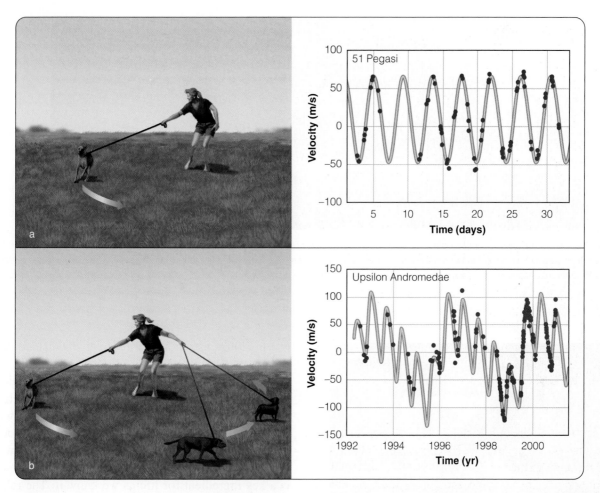

Figure 12.17 (a) Just as someone walking a lively dog is tugged around, the star 51 Pegasi is tugged around by the planet that orbits it every 4.2 days. The wobble is detectable in precision observations of its Doppler shift. (b) Someone walking three dogs is pulled about in a more complicated pattern, and you can see something similar in the Doppler shifts of Upsilon Andromedae, which is orbited by at least three planets.

spectroscopic binary stars (see Chapter 6, Figure 6.13). From the motion of the star and estimates of the star's mass, astronomers can deduce that the planet has half the mass of Jupiter and orbits only 0.05 AU from the star. Half the mass of Jupiter amounts to 160 Earth masses, so this is a large planet, larger than Saturn. Note also that it orbits very close to its star.

Astronomers were not surprised by the announcement that a planet orbited 51 Pegasi; for years they had assumed that many stars had planets. Nevertheless, they greeted the discovery with typical skepticism. That skepticism led to careful tests of the data and further observations that confirmed the discovery. In fact, hundreds of planets are now being discovered in this way, including at least three planets orbiting the star Upsilon Andromedae (Figure 12.17b). Just as a large dog on a short leash would tug at the walker more strongly, large planets orbiting close to a star would cause a greater wobble in the star's orbit, and that would be easier to detect. This is why most of the earliest planets to be discovered were "Hot Jupiters": very massive planets orbiting close to their stars.

Another way to search for planets is to look for changes in the brightness of the star when the orbiting planet crosses in front of or behind the star. The decrease in light is very small, but it is detectable. This is the same transit technique used to study eclipsing binary stars (see Chapter 6, Figure 6.14). This technique is used by France's *COROT* spacecraft, the first space mission to be dedicated to finding extrasolar planets. *Kepler*, NASA's first planet-finding mission, launched in 2008, has also been tremendously successful in identifying and confirming new planets around other stars using the transit detection technique.

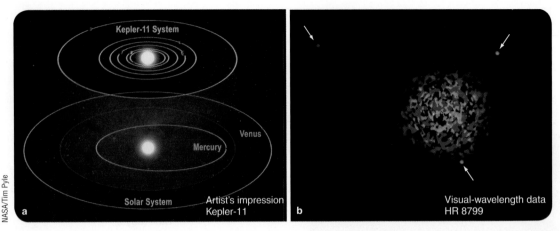

Figure 12.18 (a) Artist's conception comparing the Kepler-11 planetary system with our solar system. Observations indicate that the six planets so far discovered around Kepler-11 orbit their star in approximately the same plane, like the planets in our solar system. (b) Images of three planets at apparent distances of 25, 40, and 70 AU from the star HR 8799.

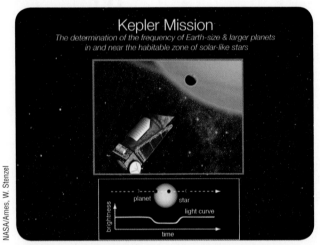

Figure 12.19 NASA's *Kepler* satellite detects planets by measuring small changes in the brightness of a star when an orbiting planet transits in front of it.

Actually getting an image of a planet orbiting another star is about as easy as photographing a bug crawling on the bulb of a searchlight many kilometres away. Planets are small and dim and get lost in the glare of the stars they orbit. Nevertheless, in 2008 an international team led by Christian Marois of Canada's Herzberg Institute of Astrophysics and members from the United States and United Kingdom managed to image planets around two A-type stars using the Gemini and Keck telescopes on the ground and the Hubble Space Telescope (see Figure 12.18).

In 2007, astronomers discovered what could be low-mass, Earth-like planets in the habitable zone around a red dwarf star named Gliese 581, which is located a mere 20.3 light-years away. The habitable or "Goldilocks" zone is the distance from a star at which the temperature would be not too warm and not too cold, but just right for water to exist in liquid form on a planet with enough atmospheric pressure. Liquid water is a key ingredient for life as we know it. The relative closeness of Gliese 581 means that, in future, astronomers could be able to directly detect the atmosphere of the planet. NASA's *Kepler* has revealed several planetary systems with significantly smaller planets than the previously discovered hot, Jupiter-like ones (Figure 12.19). The main aim of the *Kepler* mission is to find Earth-like planets in habitable zones around other stars. For the first time in the history of our search for the worlds that resemble our own, we have the technical capability to see small rocky planets. Spectral analyses of trails of smaller planets show traces of silicates (building blocks of rocks), ice, and water. The Spitzer infrared telescope, which prior to the *Kepler* mission discovered numerous large, hot, Jupiter-like planets around their stars, is being used to confirm the *Kepler* telescope findings. In 2007, the Spitzer telescope detected water on an exoplanet, and in 2008, the Hubble telescope found the first evidence of organic molecules on an extrasolar planet.

As of 2014, over 1800 exoplanets have been identified. Some planets orbiting brown dwarfs have been discovered.

Over 470 of the known planets exist in multiplanetary systems. You can find out more about extrasolar planetary discoveries from *The Extrasolar Planets Encyclopaedia*. For example, you can learn about some unusual arrangements of planets that have been discovered, such as two planets sharing an orbit; the planets are arranged in the exact angular distance that theoretically allows for such an arrangement. Seeing such variety of possibilities allows us to explore and test many hypotheses about our own solar system's origin and formation.

In December 2011, the first Earth-sized planet was confirmed to be orbiting in the habitable zone around a star called Kepler-22 in the Cygnus constellation. Of all the confirmed extrasolar planets, 22 planets have been identified as of 2014, as potentially habitable worlds capable of supporting life (Figure 12.20). Most are larger in size than Earth, but this may be because larger worlds are easier to detect. Scientists estimate that there may be several billion planets the size of Earth in the Milky Way Galaxy. As the technology and accuracy of planet-finding missions improve, we may soon find Earth-size, potentially habitable planets and get closer to answering the question: are we alone?

HOW DO WE KNOW? 12.2

Scientists: Nature's Detectives

"Scientists are just a bunch of skeptics who don't believe in anything." That is a common misconception among people who don't understand the methods and goals of science. Scientists are skeptical not because they want to disprove everything but because they want to be sure that a new description of nature is correct before it is accepted.

Skeptical scientists question every aspect of a new discovery. They may wonder if another scientist's instruments were properly calibrated or if the scientist's mathematical models are correct. Other scientists will want to repeat the work themselves using their own instruments to see if they can obtain the same results. Observations are tested, discoveries are confirmed, and only an idea that survives many of these tests begins to be accepted as a scientific idea.

Scientists are prepared for this kind of treatment at the hands of other scientists. In fact, they expect it. Among scientists it is not bad manners to say, "Really, how do you know that?" or "Why do you think that?" or "Show me the evidence!" And it is not just new or surprising claims that are subject to such scrutiny. Astronomers had long expected to discover planets orbiting other stars. But when a planet was finally discovered circling 51 Pegasi, astronomers were skeptical—not because they thought the observations were flawed but because that is how science works.

Some people use the phrase "telling a story" to describe someone who is telling a fib. But the stories that scientists tell are exactly the opposite; perhaps you could call them antifibs, because they are as true as scientists can make them. Skepticism eliminates stories with logical errors, flawed observations, or misunderstood evidence and eventually leaves only the stories that best describe nature.

Just as a good detective must examine all the evidence, question everyone, and develop a theory that best fits the facts of the case, a good scientist also must "question everything," examine all the scientific evidence, and develop a scientific theory that best fits all the data. Even a single violation of a scientific theory is sufficient to invalidate the theory. Imagine what would happen if a single apple were to defy the theory of gravity and begin to float! Scientists could not ignore such an event. The exception does not prove the rule. Such new observations would lead to further studies and theories that took these new results into account. Hence, science progresses through conscientious skepticism.

© The Kobal Collection at Art Resource, NY

Figure 12.20 The relative sizes of various planetary candidates detected by the *Kepler* planet-finding mission.

Within the figure:

Current Potentially Habitable Exoplanets
Ranked by Distance from Earth in Light Years (ly)

PHL
MAPPING THE HABITABLE UNIVERSE

ARTISTIC REPRESENTATIONS

[12 ly] Tau Ceti e*
[13 ly] Kapteyn b
[16 ly] Gliese 832 c
[17 ly] Gliese 682 c*
[24 ly] Gliese 667C c

[24 ly] Gliese 667C e
[24 ly] Gliese 667C f
[38 ly] Gliese 180 b*
[38 ly] Gliese 180 c*
[41 ly] Gliese 422 b*

[42 ly] HD 40307 g
[49 ly] Gliese 163 c
[490 ly] Kepler-186 f
[620 ly] Kepler-22 b
[1060 ly] Kepler-61 b

[1170 ly] Kepler-174 d
[1200 ly] Kepler-62 e
[1200 ly] Kepler-62 f
[1550 ly] Kepler-298 d
[1690 ly] Kepler-296 f

[1740 ly] Kepler-283 c

Earth
Mars
Jupiter
Neptune

Closest Star [4.2 ly]
Radial Velocity Detected Planets
Kepler Planets

SUN   10 ly   100 ly   1,000 ly   10,000 ly

*planet candidates

CREDIT: PHL @ UPR Arecibo (phl.upr.edu) August 4, 2014

Planetary Habitability Laboratory University of Puerto Rico at Arecibo

The **Big Picture**

The matter you are made of came from the big bang, and it has been cooked into a wide range of atoms inside stars. Now you can see how those atoms came to be part of Earth. Your atoms were in the cloud of gas that formed the Sun 4.6 billion years ago, and nearly all of that matter contracted to form the Sun, but a small amount left behind in a disk formed planets. In the process, your atoms became part of Earth.

Are there other planet-walkers like you in the universe? Now you know that planets are common, and you can reasonably suppose that there are more planets in the universe than there are stars, suggesting there may indeed be planet-walkers living on other worlds.

Review and **Discussion Questions**

Review Questions

1. What produced the helium now present in the Sun's atmosphere? In Jupiter's atmosphere? In the Sun's core?
2. What are the observed properties of the solar system that must be explained by the theory of its origin?
3. What is the evidence that the solar system formed about 4.6 billion years ago?
4. According to the solar nebula theory, why is Earth's orbit nearly in the plane of the Sun's equator?
5. Why does the solar nebula theory predict that planetary systems are common?
6. How do planets form?
7. What is the difference between condensation and accretion?
8. What does the term *differentiated* mean when applied to a planet? Would you expect to find that planets are usually differentiated? Why?

9. What are asteroids and comets, what are their connections to meteors and meteorites, and what clues do they give about the origin of the solar system?

10. What processes cleared the nebula away and ended planet-forming

11. Why is almost every solid surface in our solar system scarred by craters?

12. Why would the formation of Jovian planets be difficult to understand if gas and dust disks around forming stars had short lifetimes in astronomical terms?

13. How does the solar nebula theory explain the dramatic density difference between the Terrestrial and Jovian planets?

14. By what methods have the extrasolar planets been discovered?

Discussion Questions

1. If you visited some other planetary system while the planets were forming, would you expect to see the condensation sequence at work, or was that most likely unique to our solar system? How do the properties of the extrasolar planets discovered so far affect your answer?

2. In your opinion, do most planetary systems have asteroid belts? Would all planetary systems show evidence of an age of heavy bombardment?

3. Do you think the government should spend money to find NEOs (near-Earth objects)? How serious is the risk?

Learning to Look

1. What do you see in this image of the nucleus of Comet Borrelly that tells you how comets produce their tails?

NASA

2. What do you see in the image below that indicates this planet formed far from the Sun?

NASA/JPL/Space Science Institute

3. Why do astronomers conclude that the surface of Mercury, shown below, is old? When did the majority of those craters form?

NASA

PART FOUR

13

Comparative Planetology of the Terrestrial Planets

CHAPTER OUTLINE

GUIDEPOST

In 1600, the monk Giordano Bruno was burned at the stake in Rome. One of his many offences was teaching that Earth was a planet that rotates on its axis and revolves around the Sun. You know that Earth is a planet, but what is a planet? In this chapter and the next, you will study the planets of our solar system. Here you start with the planets that, like Earth, are made of rock and metal, and you will find answers to four important questions:

- **Why are some planets cratered, airless worlds while others have atmospheres and weather?**
- **How does size and distance from the Sun influence the evolution of planets?**
- **How does the history of the Moon illuminate the history of Earth and the other planets?**
- **How does evidence tell planetary scientists that Venus and Mars were once more Earth-like?**

You can learn about the unearthly worlds of our solar system by using **comparative planetology**, the study of planets by comparison and contrast. As you study these planets, you will learn more about our own world. Understanding the terrible heat of Venus and the frigid deserts of Mars will tell you more about our own beautiful planet. In the next chapter, you will meet even stranger worlds in the outer solar system, but they too will help you see Earth in new light.

comparative planetology
Understanding planets by searching for and analyzing contrasts and similarities among them.

© Craig Cozart/Thinkstock

Once you've been in space, you appreciate how small and fragile the Earth is.

Valentina Tereshkova,
Cosmonaut, first woman in space

13.1 A Travel Guide to the Terrestrial Planets

In this chapter you will visit five worlds: Earth, Earth's moon, Mercury, Venus, and Mars. This preliminary section is your guide to important features and comparisons.

The Scale of the Solar System

You can begin with the most general view of the solar system, which is almost entirely empty space (refer to **Visualizing Astronomy 1.1, The Scale of the Very Small and Very Large: Powers of 10**). Imagine reducing the scale of the solar system until the Sun is the size of cherry, about 33 mm in diameter. The Earth is located 4 m away, and is the size of a grain of salt (0.3 mm). The Moon, about 25 percent Earth's size, is orbiting it at a radius of about 1 cm. Jupiter, the largest planet, is an apple seed 18 m from the Sun. Neptune, at the edge of the planetary zone, is a grape seed (1.2 mm across) and more than 110 m from the central cherry. Your model solar system would be larger than two football fields, and you would need a powerful microscope to detect the asteroids orbiting between Mars and Jupiter. The planets are tiny specks of matter scattered around the Sun.

Revolution and Rotation

The planets revolve around the Sun in orbits that lie close to a common plane. Recall from Chapter 2 that *revolve* and *rotate* refer to different types of motion; a planet revolves around the Sun, but it rotates on its axis. The orbit of Mercury, the closest planet to the Sun, is tipped 7.0° to Earth's orbit. Remember that Earth's orbit defines the ecliptic plane, the reference plane for all other planetary orbits. The rest of the planets' orbital planes are inclined by no more than 3.4°. The solar system is basically flat and disk-shaped.

The rotation of the Sun and planets on their axes also seems related to the rotation of the disk. The Sun rotates with its equator inclined only 7.2° to Earth's orbit, and most of the other planets' equators are tipped less than 30°. The rotations of Venus and Uranus are peculiar; Venus rotates backward compared with the other planets, and Uranus rotates on its side with its equator almost perpendicular to its orbit.

mantle The layer of dense rock and metal oxides that lies between the molten core and Earth's surface, or a similar layer in another planet.

The preferred direction of motion in the solar system is counter-clockwise as seen from the north. All the planets revolve around the Sun in that direction, and all the planets also rotate on their axes in that direction—except Venus and Uranus. Furthermore, nearly all the moons in the solar system, including Earth's moon, orbit around their respective planets in that same direction.

Two Kinds of Planets

Perhaps the most striking clue to the origin of the solar system comes from the obvious division of the planets into two groups, the small Earth-like worlds and the giant Jupiter-like worlds. The difference is so dramatic that we are inclined to say, "Aha, this must mean something!" In Chapter 12, this division into two groups of planets was an important clue for explaining how the Sun and the solar system formed 4.6 billion years ago.

The four inner planets—Mercury, Venus, Earth, and Mars—are small, dense worlds composed of rock and iron. They are called Terrestrial planets because they resemble the rock and metal composition of Earth (*Terra* in Latin). The four outer planets—Jupiter, Saturn, Uranus, and Neptune—are large, low-density worlds rich in hydrogen, water, and other low-density materials. They are known as Jovian planets because they are Jupiter-like (*Jove* in Latin). You could not stand on any of these planets as you can on any of the Terrestrial planets. You will study the Jovian worlds in the next chapter.

To begin your study of the five Terrestrial worlds—the Moon and the four inner planets—compare their features as shown in Figure 13.1. First notice their diameter. The Moon is small, and Mercury is not much bigger. Earth and Venus are large and similar in size, and Mars is a medium-sized world. You will discover that size is a key factor in determining a world's attributes; small worlds tend to be internally cold and geologically dead, but larger worlds can be geologically active.

Core, Mantle, and Crust

Notice that these Terrestrial worlds are made up of rock and metal. All of them are differentiated, with rocky, low-density crusts, high-density metal cores, and **mantles** composed of dense rock between the cores and crusts.

As you learned in Chapter 12, when the planets formed, their surfaces were subjected to heavy bombardment by leftover planetesimals and fragments; the cratering rate then was as much as 10 000 times what it is at present. There are many craters on the Terrestrial worlds, especially on Mercury and the Moon. Notice that heavily

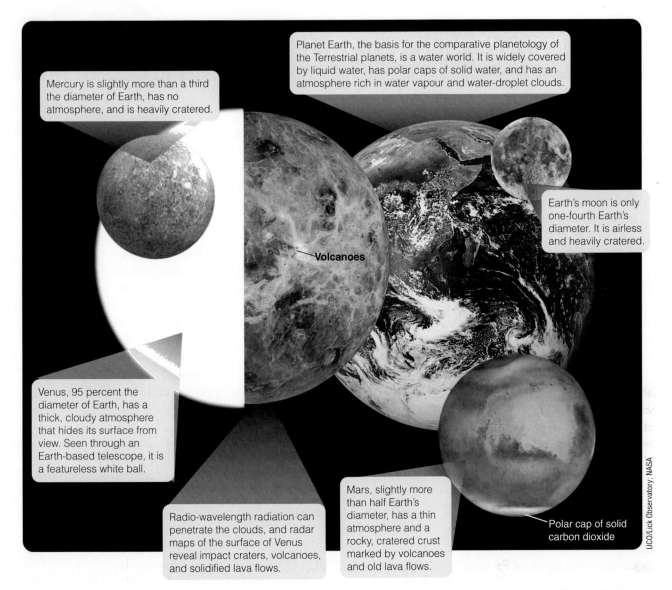

Mercury is slightly more than a third the diameter of Earth, has no atmosphere, and is heavily cratered.

Planet Earth, the basis for the comparative planetology of the Terrestrial planets, is a water world. It is widely covered by liquid water, has polar caps of solid water, and has an atmosphere rich in water vapour and water-droplet clouds.

Earth's moon is only one-fourth Earth's diameter. It is airless and heavily cratered.

Volcanoes

Venus, 95 percent the diameter of Earth, has a thick, cloudy atmosphere that hides its surface from view. Seen through an Earth-based telescope, it is a featureless white ball.

Radio-wavelength radiation can penetrate the clouds, and radar maps of the surface of Venus reveal impact craters, volcanoes, and solidified lava flows.

Mars, slightly more than half Earth's diameter, has a thin atmosphere and a rocky, cratered crust marked by volcanoes and old lava flows.

Polar cap of solid carbon dioxide

UCO/Lick Observatory; NASA

Figure 13.1 Planets in comparison. Earth and Venus are similar in size, but their atmospheres and surfaces are very different. The Moon and Mercury are much smaller, and Mars is intermediate in size.

cratered surfaces are old. For example, where a lava flow covered up some cratered landscape to make a new surface after the end of the heavy bombardment, few craters could later be formed on that surface because most of the debris in the solar system was gone. When you see a smooth plain on a planet, you can assume that surface is younger than the cratered areas.

One important way to study a planet is by following its energy (see **How Do We Know? 13.1**). The heat in the interior of a planet may be what remained after the formation of the planet, or it may be heat generated by radioactive decay, but it must flow outward toward the cooler surface where it is radiated into space. In flowing outward, the heat can cause convection currents in the mantle, magnetic fields, plate motions, quakes, faults,

volcanism, mountain-building, and more. Heat flowing upward through the cooler crust makes a large world like Earth geologically active. In contrast, the Moon and Mercury, both small worlds, cooled fast, so they have little heat flowing outward now and are relatively inactive.

Atmospheres

When you look at airless Mercury and the Moon in Figure 13.1, you can see their craters and plains and mountains, but the surface of Venus is completely hidden by a cloudy atmosphere much thicker than Earth's. Mars, the medium-sized Terrestrial planet, has a relatively thin atmosphere.

You might ponder two questions. First, why do some worlds have atmospheres while others do not?

Understanding Planets: Follow the Energy

What causes change? One of the best ways to think about a scientific problem is to follow the energy. According to the principle of cause and effect, every effect must have a cause, and every cause must involve energy. Energy moves from regions of high concentration to regions of low concentration and, in doing so, produces changes. For example, coal burns to make steam in a power plant, and the steam passes through a turbine and then escapes into the air. In flowing from the burning coal to the atmosphere, the heat spins the turbine and makes electricity.

Scientists commonly use energy as a key to understanding nature. A biologist might ask where certain birds get the energy to fly thousands of miles, and a geologist might ask where the energy comes from to power a volcano. Energy is everywhere, and when it moves, whether it is in birds or molten magma, it causes change. Energy is the "cause" in "cause and effect."

The flow of energy from the inside of a star to its surface helps you know how the Sun and other stars work. The outward flow of energy supports

Heat flowing out of Earth's interior generates geological activity such as that at Yellowstone National Park.

the star against its own weight, drives convection currents that produce magnetic fields, and causes surface activity such as spots, prominences,

and flares. You can understand stars by knowing how energy flows from their interiors to their surfaces and into space.

Scientists think of a planet by following the energy. The heat in the interior of a planet may be left over from the formation of the planet, or it may be heat generated by radioactive decay, but it must flow outward toward the cooler surface, where it is radiated into space. In flowing outward, the heat can cause convection currents in the mantle, magnetic fields, plate motions, quakes, faults, volcanism, mountain building, and more.

When you think about any world, be it a small asteroid or a giant planet, think of its interior as a source of heat that flows through the planet's surface into space. When you follow that energy flow, you can understand a great deal about the world. A planetary astronomer once said, "The most interesting thing about any planet is how its heat gets out."

You will discover that both size and temperature are important. The second question is more complex. Where did these atmospheres come from? To answer that question, you need to study the geological history of these worlds.

13.2 Earth: The Active Planet

Earth is the basis for your comparative study of the Terrestrial planets, so pretend to visit it as if you don't live here. It is an active planet with a molten interior and heat flowing outward that powers volcanism and earthquakes,

and it has an active crust. Almost 75 percent of Earth's surface is covered by liquid water, and the atmosphere contains a significant amount of oxygen.

Earth's Interior

From what you know of the formation of Earth (see Chapter 12), you can expect it to have differentiated, but what does the evidence reveal about Earth's interior?

Earth's mass divided by its volume gives its average density, about 5.5 g/cm^3, but the density of Earth's rocky crust is only about half that. Clearly, a large part of Earth's interior must be made of material denser than rock.

Each time an earthquake occurs, seismic waves travel through the interior and register on seismographs all over the world. Analysis of these waves shows that Earth's interior is divided into a metallic core, a dense rocky mantle, and a thin, low-density crust.

The core has a density of 14 g/cm³, denser than lead; mathematical models indicate it is composed of iron and nickel at a temperature of roughly 6000 K. The core of Earth is as hot as the gaseous surface of the Sun, but high pressure keeps the metal a solid near the middle of the core and a liquid in its outer parts.

Earth's magnetism gives further clues about the core. The presence of a magnetic field is evidence that part of Earth's core must be a liquid metal. Convection currents stir the molten liquid, and because it is a very good conductor of electricity and is rotating as Earth rotates, it generates a magnetic field through the dynamo effect—a different version of the process that creates the Sun's magnetic field (see Chapter 5).

Earth's mantle is a deep layer of dense rock that lies between the molten core and the solid crust. Models indicate the mantle material has the properties of a solid but is capable of flowing slowly, like asphalt used in paving roads, which shatters if struck with a sledgehammer but bends slightly under the weight of a truck. Just below Earth's crust, where the pressure is less than at greater depths, the mantle flows most easily.

The Earth's rocky crust is made up of low-density rocks. The crust is thickest under the continents, up to 60 km thick, and thinnest under the oceans, where it is only about 10 km thick.

Earth's Active Crust

Earth's crust is composed of lower-density rock that floats on the mantle. The image of rock floating may seem odd, but recall that the rock of the mantle is denser than crust rocks. Also, just below the crust, the mantle rock tends to be more fluid, so sections of low-density crust do indeed float on the mantle like great lily pads floating on a pond.

The motion of the crust and the erosive action of water make Earth's crust highly active and changeable. Study **Visualizing Astronomy 13.1, The Active Earth**, and notice three important points:

1. The motion of crustal plates produces much of the geological activity on Earth. Earthquakes, volcanism, and mountain building are linked to motions in the crust and the location of plate boundaries. While thinking about volcanoes, you can correct a common misconception. The molten rock that emerges from volcanoes comes from pockets of melted rock in the upper mantle and lower crust, not from the molten core.

2. The continents on Earth's surface have moved and changed over periods of hundreds of millions of years. A hundred million years is only 0.1 billion years, 1/45 of the age of Earth, so sections of Earth's crust are in geologically rapid motion.

3. Notice that most of the geological features you know—the Rocky Mountains, the Great Lakes, and even the outline of the continents—are recent products of Earth's active surface.

The Earth's surface is constantly renewed, and small crystals called zircons are the oldest known Earth material. They are from Western Australia and are 4.4 billion years old. Most of the crust is much younger than that. The mountains and valleys you see around you are probably no more than a few tens or hundreds of millions of years old.

Earth's Atmosphere

When you think about Earth's atmosphere, consider three questions: How did it form? How has it evolved? How are humans changing it? Answering these questions will help you understand other planets as well as our own.

Our planet's first atmosphere, its **primary atmosphere**, was once thought to contain gases captured from the solar nebula, such as hydrogen and methane. Modern studies, however, indicate that the planets were hot when they formed, so gases such as carbon dioxide, nitrogen, and water vapour were cooked out of—outgassed from—the rock and metal (see Chapter 12). In addition, the final stages of planet building may have seen Earth and the other planets accreting planetesimals rich in volatile materials, such as water, ammonia, and carbon dioxide. Thus, the primary atmosphere must have been rich in carbon dioxide, nitrogen, and water vapour. The atmosphere you breathe today is a **secondary atmosphere**, produced later in Earth's history.

Soon after Earth formed, it began to cool; once it cooled enough, oceans began to form, and carbon dioxide began to dissolve in the water. Carbon dioxide is highly soluble in water, which explains the easy manufacture of carbonated beverages. As the oceans removed carbon dioxide from the atmosphere, the carbon dioxide reacted with dissolved compounds in the ocean water to form silicon dioxide, limestone, and other mineral sediments. Consequently, the oceans transferred carbon dioxide from the atmosphere to the seafloor and left the air richer in other gases, especially nitrogen.

primary atmosphere A planet's first atmosphere.

secondary atmosphere A planet's atmosphere that replaces the primary atmosphere—for example, due to outgassing, the impact of volatile-bearing planetesimals, or biological activity.

Our world is an astonishingly active planet. Not only is it rich in water and therefore subject to rapid erosion, s crust is divided into moving sections called plates. re plates spread apart, lava wells up to form new crust; e plates push against each other, they crumple the crust m mountains. Where one plate slides over another, you olcanism. This process is called **plate tectonics**, ring to the Greek word for "builder." (An architect is lly an arch builder.)

ical view anet Earth

Mountains are common on Earth, but they erode away rapidly because of the abundant water.

Photo by William K. Hartmann

©Janet Seeds

A rift valley forms where cont plates begin to pull apa Red Sea has formed Africa has be pull awa the A pen

Mid-ocean rise

Red Sea

Mid-ocean rise

National Geophysical Data Center

1a Evi of tectonics first found i ocean floors, plates spread apa magma rises to form mid-ocean rises made of rock called basalt, a rock typica solidified lava. Radioactive dating shows that the basalt is younger near the mid-ocean rise. Also, the ocean floor ca less sediment near the mid-ocean rise. As Earth's magne field reverses back and forth, it is recorded in the magnet fields frozen into the basalt. This produces a magnetic pa in the basalt that that the seafloor spreading away f the mid-ocean ris

A subduction zone is a deep trench where one slides under another. ng releases low-density ma that rises to form anoes such as those g the northwest coast of America, including Mt. elens.

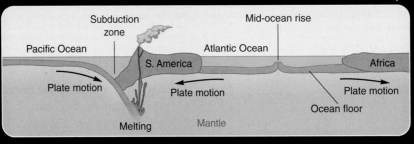

Subduction zone

Mid-ocean rise

Pacific Ocean

Atlantic Ocean

S. America

Africa

Plate motion

Plate motion

Plate motion

Ocean floor

Melting

Mantle

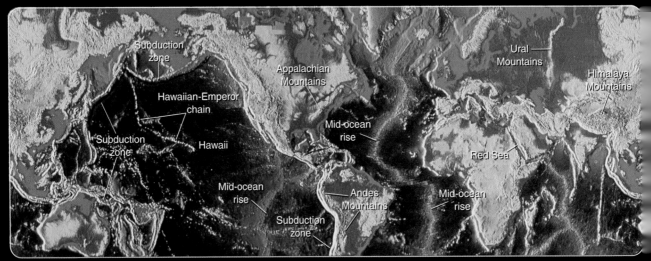

Subduction zone

Ural Mountains

Appalachian Mountains

Himalaya Mountains

Hawaiian-Emperor chain

Mid-ocean rise

Subduction zone

Hawaii

Red Sea

Mid-ocean rise

Andes Mountains

Mid-ocean rise

Subduction zone

Hot spots caused by rising magma in the mantle can poke through a plate and cause volcanism such as that in Hawaii. As the Pacific plate has moved northwestward, the hot has punched through to form a chain of volcanic islands, now mostly worn below sea level. ed mountain ranges can form where plates push against each other. For example, the Ural ntains lie between Europe and Asia, and the Himalaya Mountains are formed by India ing north into Asia. The Appalachian Mountains are the remains of a mountain range ed up when North America collided with Africa.

1d The floor of the Pacific Ocean is sliding into subduction zones in many places around its perimeter. This pushes up mountains such as the Andes and triggers earthquakes and active volcanism all around the Pacific in what is called the Ring of Fire. In places such as southern California, the plates slide past each other, causing frequent earthquakes.

National Geophysical Data Center

Hawaii

Yellow lines on this globe mark plate boundaries. Red dots mark earthquakes since 1980. Earthquakes within the plate, such as those at Hawaii, are related to volcanism over hot spots in the mantle.

Continental Drift

About 300 million years ago, Earth's continents came together to form one continent.

Pangaea

200 million years ago

Pangaea broke into a northern and a southern continent.

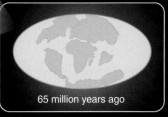

Laurasia

Gondwanalan

135 million years ago

Notice India moving north toward Asia.

65 million years ago

The continents are still drifting on the highly plastic upper mantle.

Today

2 The floor of the Atlantic Ocean is not being subducted. It is locked to the continents and is pushing North and South America away from Europe and Africa at about 3 cm per year, a motion called continental drift. Radio astronomers can measure this motion by timing pulsars from both European and North American radio telescopes. Roughly 200 million years ago, North and South America were joined to Europe and Africa. Evidence of that lies in similar fossils and similar rocks and minerals found in the matching parts.

M. Seeds

Formation of Earth

Heavy bombardment

?

Oldest fossil life

Formation of Grand Canyon

Age of dinosaurs

Breakup of Pangaea

First animals emerge on land

4.6   4   3   2   1   Now

Billions of years ago

3 Plate tectonics pushes up mountain ranges and causes bulges in the crust, and water erosion wears the rock away. The Colorado River began cutting the Grand Canyon only about 10 million years ago when the Colorado plateau warped upward under the pressure of moving plates. That sounds like a long time ago, but it is only 0.01 billion years. A kilometre and a half down, at the bottom of the canyon, lie rocks 0.57 billion years old, the roots of an earlier mountain range that stood as high as the Himalayas. It was pushed up, worn away to nothing, and covered with sediment long ago. Many of the geological features we know on Earth have been produced by very recent events.

That removal of carbon dioxide is critical to Earth because an atmosphere rich in carbon dioxide can trap heat by a process called the **greenhouse effect**. When visible-wavelength sunlight shines through the glass roof of a greenhouse, it heats the interior. Infrared radiation from the warm interior can't get out through the glass, heat is trapped in the greenhouse, and the temperature climbs until the glass itself grows warm enough to radiate heat away as fast as sunlight enters (see Figure 13.2a). This is also called the "parked car effect," for obvious reasons.

Like the glass roof of a greenhouse, a planet's atmosphere can allow sunlight to enter and warm the surface. Note the similarity between the flow of light into the greenhouse in Figure 13.3a and into the atmosphere in Figure 13.2b. Carbon dioxide and other greenhouse gases such as water vapour and methane are opaque to infrared radiation, so an atmosphere containing enough of these greenhouse gases can trap heat and raise the temperature of a planet's surface.

It is a common misconception that the greenhouse effect is always bad. Without the greenhouse effect, Earth would be colder by at least 30°C, with a planetwide average temperature far below freezing. The problem is that human civilization is adding greenhouse gases to those that were already in the atmosphere. For 4 billion years, Earth's oceans and plant life have been absorbing carbon dioxide and burying it in the form of carbonates such as limestone and in carbon-rich deposits of coal, oil, and natural gas. In the last century or so, human civilization has begun digging up those fuels, burning them for energy, and releasing the carbon back into the atmosphere as carbon dioxide (Figure 13.3c). This process is steadily increasing the carbon dioxide concentration in the atmosphere and warming Earth's climate in what is called **global warming**. Evidence based on the proportions of carbon isotopes and oxygen in the atmosphere shows that most of the added CO_2 is the result of burning fossil fuels. There is now overwhelming evidence that humans are responsible for the increase in atmospheric greenhouse gases. The UN Intergovernmental Panel on Climate Change (IPCC) stated in its September 2013 report that "there is 95 percent certainty that humans have caused most of the warming of the planet's surface that has occurred since the 1950s." Over the past century, the average surface temperature has risen by almost 1°C.

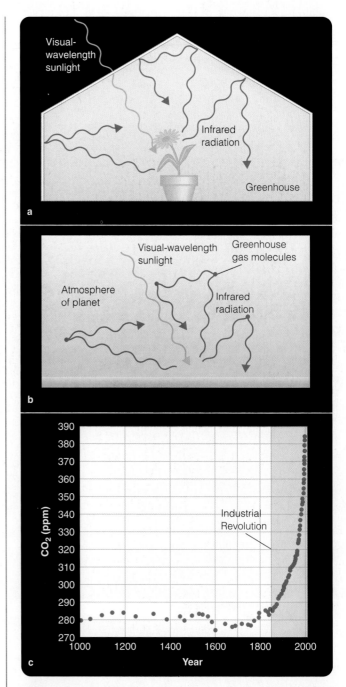

Figure 13.2 The greenhouse effect. (a) Visual-wavelength sunlight can enter a greenhouse and heat its contents, but the longer-wavelength infrared radiation cannot get out. (b) The same process can heat a planet's surface if its atmosphere contains greenhouse gases such as CO_2. (c) The concentration of CO_2 in Earth's atmosphere as measured in Antarctic ice cores remained roughly constant for thousands of years until the beginning of the Industrial Revolution around the year 1800. Since then it has increased by more than 30 percent. (Note that the bottom of the vertical scale is not at zero.)

Global warming is a critical issue not just because it affects agriculture. It changes climate patterns by warming some areas and cooling other areas. In addition, the warming is melting permanently frozen ice in the polar caps, causing sea levels to rise. A rise of just a metre will flood major land areas. When you study Venus, you will see a planet dominated by a runaway greenhouse effect.

Oxygen in Earth's Atmosphere

When Earth was young, its atmosphere had no free oxygen. Oxygen is very reactive and quickly forms oxides in the soil, so the activity of plant life is needed to keep a steady supply of oxygen in the atmosphere. Photosynthesis makes energy for the plant by absorbing carbon dioxide and releasing free oxygen. About 2 to 2.5 billion years ago plants began to produce oxygen faster than chemical reactions could remove it from the atmosphere. Atmospheric oxygen then increased rapidly.

Because there is oxygen (O_2) in the atmosphere now, there is also a layer of ozone (O_3) at altitudes of 15 to 30 km. Many people hold the common misconception that ozone is bad because they hear it mentioned as part of smog. Breathing ozone is bad for you, but we need the ozone layer in the upper atmosphere to protect us from harmful UV photons. Certain compounds called chlorofluorocarbons (CFCs) used in refrigeration and industry can destroy ozone when they leak into the atmosphere.

Since the late 1970s, the ozone concentration has been falling, and the intensity of harmful UV radiation at Earth's surface has been increasing year by year. Note that ozone depletion is an additional Earth environmental issue that is separate from global warming. While this poses an immediate problem for public health, it is also of interest astronomically. When you study Mars, you will see the effects of an atmosphere without ozone.

A Short Geological History of Earth

As Earth formed in the inner solar nebula, it passed through three stages that also describe the histories of the other Terrestrial planets to varying extents. When astronomers try to tell the story of each planet in our solar system, they pull together all the known facts and hypotheses and try to make them into a logical history of how the planet got to be the way it is. Of course, these stories are incomplete because scientists don't yet understand all the factors affecting the history of the planets.

The first stage of planetary evolution is *differentiation*, the separation of each planet's material into layers according to density. Some of that differentiation may have occurred very early as the heat released by infalling matter melted the growing Earth. Some of the differentiation, however, may have occurred later as radioactive decay released more heat and further melted Earth, allowing the denser metals to sink to the core.

CP PHOTO/Bill Becker

Roberta Bondar

Roberta Bondar

In January 1992, Dr. Roberta Bondar made history. When she launched from Earth in the space shuttle Discovery, she became Canada's first woman in space and the world's first neurologist-astronaut. As a young girl she had envied birds for being able to fly and had dreamed of being an astronaut. Her interest in science was encouraged by her parents, who built her a laboratory in their basement. This fuelled her passion for science, and after obtaining undergraduate and master's degrees in zoology and pathology, she obtained a Ph.D. in neuroscience at the University of Toronto and an M.D. from McMaster University, thus becoming both a scientist and a doctor by age 31. She then added "astronaut" to her list of occupations when in 1983 she was selected to be part of the first Canadian Astronaut Program and became the payload specialist for the first International Microgravity Laboratory Mission. During her mission in space in 1992, she conducted experiments for 14 countries. After returning to Earth, she headed an international research team at NASA that investigated the effects of exposure to space on the human body. Dr. Bondar is also an accomplished photographer and a passionate advocate for environmental education and protection. The Roberta Bondar Foundation educates people about the environment by combining photography and science. Dr. Bondar has been awarded the NASA Space Medal and the Order of Canada, and has been inducted into the Hall of Fame of the International Women's Forum.

The second stage, *cratering and giant basin formation*, could not begin until a solid surface formed. The heavy bombardment in the early solar system cratered Earth just as it did the other Terrestrial planets. Some of the largest craters, called basins, were likely big enough to break through to the upper mantle where rocks are partly molten. The molten rock would have welled up through cracks to fill some of the basins and craters. On planets with liquid water, the basins may also have been the first oceans. As the debris of planet formation cleared away, the rate of impacts and crater formation fell to its present low rate.

The third stage, *slow surface evolution*, has continued for at least the past 3.5 billion years. Earth's surface is constantly changing as sections of crust slide over and past each other, push up mountains, and shift continents. In addition, moving air and water erode the surface and wear away geological features. Almost all traces of the earlier stages of differentiation and cratering have been destroyed by the active crust and erosion. Life apparently started on Earth around the beginning of the slow surface evolution stage, and the secondary atmosphere began to replace the primary atmosphere. That may be unique to Earth and may not have happened on the other Terrestrial planets.

Terrestrial planets pass through these stages, but differences in masses, temperature, and composition emphasize some stages over others and produce surprisingly different worlds.

13.3 The Moon

We know the Moon is too small to have retained any atmosphere, so strolling on the surface requires a spacesuit similar to that used by the lunar astronauts. As well, plans for such exploration need to take into account the fact that the temperature difference from sunshine to shade is extreme. Review the Moon's data in the **Celestial Profiles** in Appendix C.

Lunar Geology

There are two kinds of terrain on the Moon. The dark grey areas visible from Earth are the smooth lunar lowland, which astronomers have named **maria** (plural of *mare*, pronounced mah-ray), drawing on the Latin word for "seas." The lighter-coloured regions are the mountainous lunar highlands. The Moon looks quite bright in the night sky seen from Earth. In fact, the **albedo** of the near side of the Moon is only 0.12, meaning it reflects only 12 percent of the light that hits it. The Moon looks bright only in contrast to the night sky. In reality, it is a dark grey world.

Wherever you go on the Moon, you will find craters. The highlands are marked heavily by craters, but the smooth lowlands contain fewer craters. The craters on the Moon were formed by impacts, as evidenced by their distinguishing characteristics such as shape and the material (**ejecta**) they have spread across the Moon's surface. Craters range in size from giant basins hundreds of kilometres across to microscopic pits found in Moon rocks. Most of the craters on the Moon are old. A comparison of the ages of Moon rocks collected from both the heavily cratered highlands and also the somewhat younger, less heavily cratered maria clearly shows that the craters were formed long ago when the solar system was young.

Twelve American astronauts from *Apollo* missions visited both the Moon's maria and the highlands in six expeditions between 1969 and 1972 (Figure 13.3). Most of the rocks they found in both the highlands and the maria were typical of hardened lava. The maria are actually ancient basalt lava flows. In contrast, the highlands are composed of low-density rock: for example **anorthosite**—a light-coloured rock that contributes to the brightness of the highlands' compared to the darkness of the maria—would have been among the first material to solidify and float to the top of molten rock. Many rocks found on the Moon are **breccias**, made up of fragments of broken rock cemented together under pressure. The breccias show how extensively the Moon's surface has been shattered by meteorites, as does the surface layer of powdery dust kicked up by the astronaut's boots.

The Origin of Earth's Moon

Over the last two centuries, astronomers developed three hypotheses for the origin of Earth's moon. The *fission hypothesis* proposed that the Moon broke from a rapidly spinning proto-Earth. The *condensation hypothesis* suggested that Earth and its Moon condensed from the same cloud of matter in the solar nebula. The *capture hypothesis* suggested that the Moon formed elsewhere in the solar nebula and was later captured by Earth. Each of these earlier ideas had problems and failed to survive when all the evidence was compared.

maria Lunar lowlands filled by successive flows of dark lava; from the Latin for *sea*.

albedo The ratio of the amount of light reflected from an object to the amount of light received by the object. Albedo equals 0 for perfectly black and 1 for perfectly white.

ejecta Pulverized rock scattered by meteorite impacts on a planetary surface.

anorthosite Aluminium- and calcium-rich silicate rock found in the lunar highlands.

breccia Rock composed of fragments of older rocks bonded together.

Figure 13.3 Rocks from the Moon show that the Moon's surface formed in a molten state, that it was heavily fractured by cratering when it was young, and that it is now affected mainly by micrometeorite erosion.

Rocks exposed on the lunar surface become pitted by micrometeorites.

Vesicular basalt contains bubbles frozen into the rock when it was molten.

A breccia is formed by rock fragments bonded together by heat and pressure.

In the 1970s, a new hypothesis was proposed that combined some aspects of the three previous hypotheses. The **large-impact hypothesis** proposes that the Moon formed when a planetesimal, estimated to have been at least as large as Mars, smashed into the proto-Earth. Model calculations indicate that this collision would have ejected a disk of debris into orbit around Earth and that would have quickly formed the Moon (Figure 13.4).

This hypothesis explains a number of phenomena. If the collision had occurred off-centre, it would have spun the Earth–Moon system rapidly, and this would explain its present high angular momentum. If the proto-Earth and its impactor both had already differentiated, the ejected material would have been mostly iron-poor mantle and crust, and this would explain the Moon's low density and iron-poor composition. Furthermore, the material would have lost many of its volatile components while it was in space, so the Moon would have formed lacking those materials. Such an impact would have melted the proto-Earth, and the material falling together to form the Moon would have been heated hot enough to melt. This

fits the evidence that the highland anorthosite in the Moon's oldest rocks formed by differentiation of large quantities of molten material. The large-impact hypothesis passes tests of comparison with the known evidence and is now considered likely to be correct.

The History of Earth's Moon

The history of Earth's moon since its formation is dominated by a single fact—the Moon is small, only one-quarter the diameter of Earth. The escape velocity is low, so it has been unable to hold any atmosphere, and it cooled rapidly as its internal heat flowed outward into space.

The *Apollo* Moon rocks are the source of information about the timing of events during the Moon's history. For example, they show that the Moon must have formed in a mostly molten state. Planetary geologists now refer to the exterior of the

large-impact hypothesis
Hypothesis that the Moon formed from debris ejected during a collision between Earth and a large planetesimal.

newborn Moon as a **magma ocean**. Denser materials sank toward the centre, and low-density minerals floated to the top to form a low-density crust. In this way the Moon partly differentiated. The radioactive ages of the Moon rocks show that the surface solidified about 4.4 billion years ago.

The second stage, cratering and basin formation, began as soon as the crust solidified, and the older highlands show that cratering was intense for approximately 0.5 billion years—during the heavy bombardment at the end of the solar system's period of planet-building. The Moon's crust was shattered, and the largest impacts formed giant **multiringed basins** hundreds of kilometres in diameter (Figure 13.5). Some evidence indicates that roughly 4 billion years ago there was a sudden, temporary increase in the cratering rate. Astronomers refer to this as the **late heavy bombardment** and hypothesize that it could have been caused by the final accretion and migration of Uranus and Neptune (see Chapter 12) scattering remnant planetesimals across the solar system to collide with the Moon and planets. About 3.8 billion years ago the cratering rate fell rapidly to the current low rate.

The tremendous impacts that formed the lunar basins cracked the crust as deep as 10 kilometres and led to flooding by lava. Though Earth's moon cooled rapidly after its formation, radioactive decay heated the subsurface material, and part of it melted, producing lava that followed the cracks up into the giant basins (Figure 13.5a). Studies of rocks brought back from the Moon by *Apollo* astronauts show that the basins were flooded by successive lava flows of dark basalts from roughly 4 to 2 billion years ago, forming the maria. The Moon's crust is thinner on the side toward Earth, perhaps due to tidal effects. Consequently, while lava flooded the basins on the Earth-facing side, it was unable to rise through the thicker crust to flood the lowlands on the far side.

The third stage, slow surface evolution, was limited both because the Moon cooled rapidly and because it lacks water. Flooding on Earth included water, but the Moon has never had an atmosphere and thus has never had liquid water. With no air and no water, erosion is limited to the constant bombardment of **micrometeorites** and rare, larger impacts.

magma ocean The exterior of the newborn Moon, a shell of molten rock hundreds of kilometres deep.

multiringed basin Large impact feature (crater) containing two or more concentric rims formed by fracturing of the planetary crust.

late heavy bombardment The sudden, temporary increase in the cratering rate in our solar system that occurred about 4 billion years ago.

micrometeorite Meteorite of microscopic size.

The Large-Impact Hypothesis

A protoplanet nearly the size of Earth differentiates to form an iron core.

Another body that has also formed an iron core strikes the larger body and merges, trapping most of the iron inside.

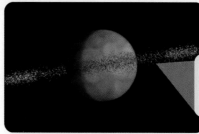

Iron-poor rock from the mantles of the two bodies forms a ring of debris.

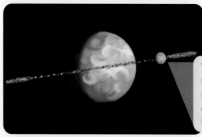

Volatiles are lost to space as the particles in the ring begin to accrete into larger bodies.

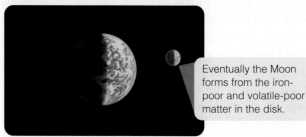

Eventually the Moon forms from the iron-poor and volatile-poor matter in the disk.

Figure 13.4 The large-impact hypothesis. The large-impact hypothesis holds that when the solar system was about 50 million years old, a massive collision produced the Moon in its orbit inclined to the Earth's equator.

Indeed, a few meteorites found on Earth have been identified as Moon rocks ejected from the Moon by impacts within the last few million years. As the Moon lost its internal heat, volcanism died down, and the Moon became geologically

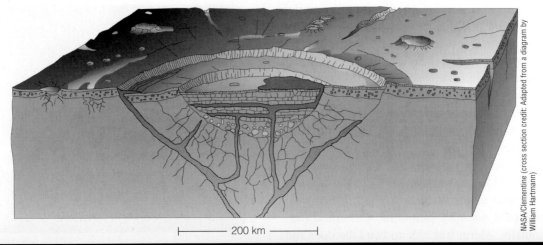

NASA/Clementine (cross section credit: Adapted from a diagram by William Hartmann)

a ├─── 200 km ───┤

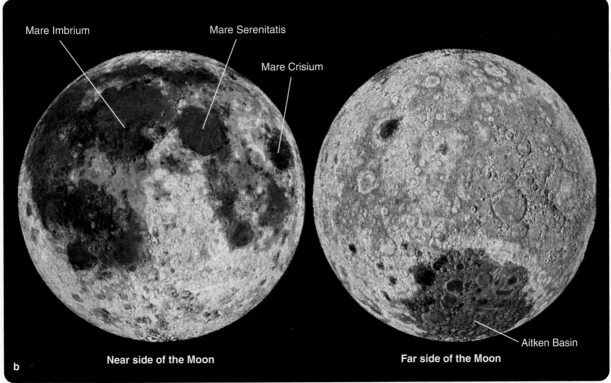

Mare Imbrium Mare Serenitatis

Mare Crisium

Aitken Basin

b **Near side of the Moon** **Far side of the Moon**

NASA

Figure 13.5 Much of the near side of the Moon is marked by great, generally circular lava plains called maria. The crust on the far side is thicker, and there was much less flooding. Even the huge Aitken Basin near the lunar south pole contains little lava flooding. In these maps colour marks elevation, with red the highest regions and purple the lowest.

dead. Its crust never divided into moving plates—there are no folded mountain ranges—and the Moon is now a "one-plate" planet.

Human Spaceflight: One Small Step

The greatest journey that human beings ever set out on took place in July 1969, when the first astronauts travelled to the Moon and back. Between 1969 and 1972, NASA's *Apollo* program, which involved scientists from around the world, including Canada, landed 12 humans on the

Moon. *Apollo 11*, launched on July 16, 1969, successfully landed Edwin (Buzz) Aldrin and Neil Armstrong on the lunar surface on July 10, 1969.

The mission, although extremely inspirational, was a dangerous one that almost ended in tragedy. The first stage involved being hurled toward the Moon by enormous Saturn V rockets. These rockets, designed by German-born scientist Wernher von Braun, were the most powerful rockets ever built and held millions of litres of highly explosive fuel. A single stray spark could have caused a disastrous explosion.

The most complicated stage after launch was the landing process on the Moon. The lunar lander's computer system was the most sophisticated at that time but had the computing power of today's basic calculator, and was overloaded during landing with two minutes of fuel left in the descent engine's tank. At this stage, the computer's landing target was a rocky area, but Armstrong managed to manually land the craft in a crater with only about 15 seconds of fuel left.

After the eventful landing, the crew was unable to sleep and decided to venture out onto the Moon's surface. This proved problematic as well because the hatch door would not open due to the pressure difference. Eventually, Aldrin was able to bend the door and equalize the pressure, allowing the astronauts to take their first historic steps on the lunar surface. The crew proceeded to collect soil samples and conduct the first-ever experiments on the Moon.

The final problem was one that could have left the crew stranded on the Moon forever: a circuit breaker essential to the functioning of the lander's engine broke off. The crew had no spare parts, so Aldrin used a pen to push the circuit breaker in and get the engine started.

Finally, the astronauts were able to rendezvous with the orbiter, and they made the long trip home to Earth. Their story of courage and innovation in the face of disaster remains an inspiration for humanity's future expeditions to space.

13.4 Mercury

Like Earth's moon, Mercury is small and nearly airless. Being the closest planet to the Sun, it is visible either at dawn near the eastern horizon or at dusk near the western horizon. It has a moderately high eccentric orbit, whose orbital plane is the highest of all the modern planets at 7°. Mercury's orbital period is 88 days, but its rotation is relatively slow, resulting in a solar day that is 176 Earth days long. Mercury cooled too quickly to develop plate tectonics, so it is a cratered, dead world. Consult **Celestial Profiles** in Appendix C for more data on Mercury.

Spacecraft at Mercury

Mercury orbits close to the Sun and is difficult to observe from Earth. It was little known until

NASA

Figure 13.6 The first spacecraft to visit Mercury, *Mariner 10.*

1974–1975, when the *Mariner 10* spacecraft flew past Mercury three times and revealed a planet with a heavily cratered surface, much like that of Earth's moon (see Figure 13.6). More recently, a spacecraft called *MESSENGER* made three flybys of Mercury in 2008 and 2009, taking impressive high-resolution images and measurements of the parts of the planet not covered by *Mariner 10's* cameras. *MESSENGER* went into orbit around Mercury in March 2011 and began an extended, close-up study. Analysis shows that large areas were once flooded by lava and then cratered. The largest impact feature on Mercury is the Caloris Basin, a multiringed area 1500 km in diameter (Figure 13.7).

Mercury is quite dense, and models indicate that it must have a large metallic core. In fact, the metallic core occupies about 70 percent of the radius of the planet. Mercury is essentially a metal planet with a thin rock mantle. *Mariner 10* photos reveal long curving ridges up to 3 km high and 500 km long (see Figure 13.6). The ridges even cut through craters, which indicates they formed after most of the heavy bombardment. Planetary scientists understand these ridges as evidence that long ago Mercury shrank as it cooled and its crust wrinkled to form the curving ridges. Since *MESSENGER* has gone into orbit, three major discoveries have been made that have put early theories of Mercury's formation into doubt: (a) the planet's global magnetic field, although only 1 percent as strong as Earth's, is strangely misaligned with Mercury's rotational axis, which is offset from its north pole by almost 500 km; (b) Mercury's surface composition contains much more magnesium, sodium, and sulphur and far less aluminum and iron than either Earth

The impact that formed the multiringed basin Caloris pushed up mountain ranges as high as 3 km.

The surface of Mercury is heavily cratered.

a Visual-wavelength images

Discovery Rupes, a long curved ridge called a lobate scarp, cuts through craters that must have formed first.

Courtesy of Lowell Observatory/NASA/JHU/APL; © Cengage Learning

Figure 13.7 (a) Mercury is an airless, cratered world. (b) The Caloris multiringed basin was half in shadow and half in sunlight when the *Mariner 10* spacecraft flew past the planet. (c) Lobate scarps are distributed all around Mercury. (d) The origin of the spider formation photographed by *MESSENGER* is a puzzle.

or the Moon; and (c) there is strong evidence for water ice existing deep in the permanently shadowed craters around both north and south poles.

A History of Mercury

Like Earth's moon, Mercury is small, and that fact has determined much of its history. Not only is Mercury too small to retain an atmosphere but also it has lost much of its internal heat; therefore, it is not geologically active.

Early in its formation, Mercury differentiated to form a metallic core and a rocky mantle. The presence of a magnetic field is evidence of a large metallic core. Astronomers thought for decades that Mercury has a lot of iron because it formed near the Sun where rock is less stable, but detailed calculations show that Mercury contains even more iron than expected. Drawing on the large-impact hypothesis for the origin of Earth's moon, scientists proposed that Mercury suffered a major impact that shattered and drove away much of the rocky mantle. However, data from *MESSENGER* indicate that the crust contains significant volatiles that would not have survived a giant impact. So a giant impact may not, after all, explain Mercury's large metal core.

In the second stage of planet formation, cratering battered the crust, and lava flows welled up to fill the lowlands, just as they did on the Moon. As the small world lost internal heat, its large metal core contracted, and its crust compressed and broke to form the long ridges, much as the peel of a drying apple wrinkles.

Lacking an atmosphere to erode it, Mercury has changed little since the last lava hardened, and it is now a "one-plate" planet like Earth's moon.

13.5 Venus

You might expect Venus to be much like Earth. Its diameter is 95 percent that of Earth's, its average density is similar, and it is only 30 percent closer to the Sun. However, because of a **runaway greenhouse effect** on Venus, its surface is perpetually hidden below thick clouds. Only in the last few decades have planetary scientists discovered that Venus is a hot desert world of volcanoes, lava flows, and impact craters that lie at the bottom of a deep, hot atmosphere that is 90 times more dense than Earth's—no spacesuit would allow you to visit this planet's surface. Although its orbit is almost circular, interestingly, Venus rotates backward, a fact discovered within the last 60 years. Its slow retrograde rotation results in a solar day that is 116.75 Earth days long—with, of course, the Sun rising in the west and setting in the east. Consult **Celestial Profiles** in Appendix C for a more detailed comparison of Earth's and Venus's data.

The Atmosphere of Venus

In composition, temperature, and density, the atmosphere of Venus is more Hades than Heaven. The air is unbreathable, very hot, and very dense. How do planetary scientists know this? Because space probes have descended into the atmosphere and in some cases landed on the surface.

In composition, the atmosphere of Venus is roughly 96 percent carbon dioxide. The rest is mostly nitrogen, with some argon, sulphur dioxide, and small amounts of sulphuric acid, hydrochloric acid, and hydrofluoric acid. There is only a tiny amount of water vapour. On the whole, the composition is deadly and most certainly smells bad.

runaway greenhouse effect
A greenhouse effect so dramatic that it amplifies itself, becoming stronger with time.

Spectra show that the impenetrable clouds that hide the surface are made up of droplets of sulphuric acid and microscopic crystals of sulphur.

This unbreathable atmosphere is 90 times denser than Earth's. We breathe air that is 1000 times less dense than water, but on Venus the air is only 10 times less dense than water. If you could survive the unpleasant composition and intense heat, you could strap wings on your arms and fly.

The surface temperature on Venus is hot enough to melt lead, which is understandable because the thick atmosphere creates a severe greenhouse effect. Sunlight filters down through the clouds and warms the surface, but infrared radiation cannot escape because the atmosphere is opaque to infrared. It is the overwhelming abundance of carbon dioxide that makes the greenhouse effect on Venus much more severe than on Earth.

The Surface of Venus

Although the thick clouds and atmosphere on Venus are opaque to visible and infrared light, they are transparent to radio waves. Orbiting spacecraft have mapped Venus by radar, revealing details as small as 100 m in diameter (Figure 13.8).

Radar maps of Venus are reproduced using arbitrary colours. For example, lowlands are represented in blue on some maps. However, this is somewhat misleading because there are no oceans on Venus. For other maps the scientists have chosen to give Venus an overall orange tint because sunlight filtering down through the clouds bathes the landscape in a perpetual sunset glow. Some radar maps are coloured grey, the natural colour of the rocks.

Radar maps show that Venus is similar to Earth in one way, but strangely different in other ways. Nearly 75 percent of Earth is covered by low-lying basaltic sea floors, and 85 percent of Venus is covered by basaltic lowlands. On Venus the lowlands are not seafloors, and the remaining highlands are not the well-defined continents you see on Earth. Whereas Earth is dominated by plate tectonics, something different is happening on Venus.

The highland area Ishtar Terra, named for the Babylonian goddess of love, is about the size of Australia (Figure 13.8). At its eastern edge, the mountain called Maxwell Montes thrusts up 12 km (Everest, the tallest mountain on Earth, is 8.8 km high). The mountains bounding Ishtar Terra, including Maxwell, resemble folded mountain ranges, which suggests that some horizontal motion in the crust as well as volcanism has helped form the highlands.

Many features on Venus testify to its volcanic history. Long, narrow lava channels meander for thousands of kilometres. Radar maps reveal many smaller volcanoes, faults, and sunken regions produced when magma below the surface drained away. Other volcanic features include

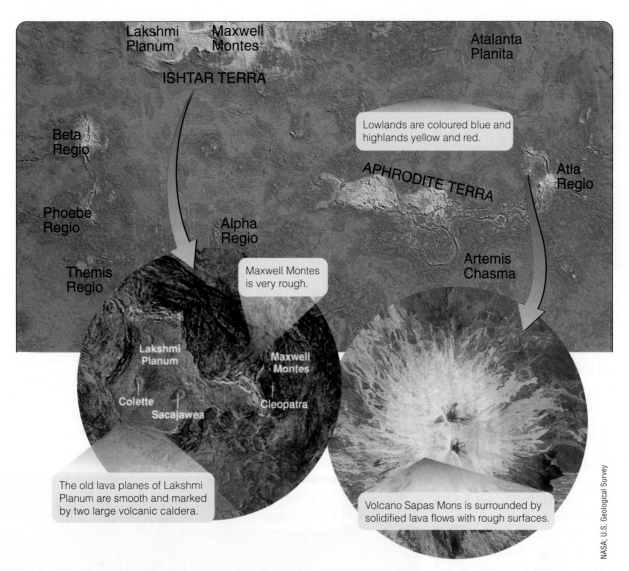

Lakshmi Planum | Maxwell Montes | Atalanta Planita

ISHTAR TERRA

Beta Regio

Lowlands are coloured blue and highlands yellow and red.

APHRODITE TERRA

Atla Regio

Phoebe Regio

Alpha Regio

Maxwell Montes is very rough.

Artemis Chasma

Themis Regio

Lakshmi Planum

Maxwell Montes

Colette

Sacajawea

Cleopatra

NASA; U.S. Geological Survey

The old lava planes of Lakshmi Planum are smooth and marked by two large volcanic caldera.

Volcano Sapas Mons is surrounded by solidified lava flows with rough surfaces.

Figure 13.8 Notice how three radar maps show different things. The main radar map, made by the Magellan robot probe, shows elevation over most of the surface of Venus, omitting the polar areas. The detailed map of Maxwell Montes and Lakshmi Planum are coloured according to roughness, with orange the roughest terrain. The map of volcano Sapas Mons also shows roughness but is given an orange colour to mimic the colour of sunlight reaching the surface through the thick atmosphere.

the **coronae**: circular bulges up to 2100 km in diameter bordered by fractures, volcanoes, and lava flows (Figure 13.9). These appear to be produced by rising convection currents of molten magma that push up under the crust. When the magma withdraws, the crust sinks back, and the circular fractures mark the edge of the original upwelling.

Radar images also show that Venus is marked by numerous craters. Meteorites big enough to make craters larger than 3 km in diameter have no trouble penetrating the thick atmosphere of Venus, but have formed only about 10 percent as many craters there as on the maria of Earth's moon. The number of craters shows that the crust of Venus is younger than the lunar maria but older than most of Earth's active surface. The average age of

the surface of Venus is estimated to be roughly half a billion years old. Clearly, geological processes cannot be renewing the surface as rapidly as they do on Earth.

Both Russian and American robot probes landed successfully on the surface of Venus in the 1970s and 80s and managed to survive the heat and pressure for a few minutes or hours, transmitting data to Earth. Some of those spacecraft analyzed the rock and snapped a few photographs (Figure 13.10). The surface rocks on Venus are dark grey basalts, much like those in Earth's ocean floors. This evidence confirms that volcanism is important.

coronae On Venus, the large, round geological faults in the crust caused by the intrusion of magma below the crust.

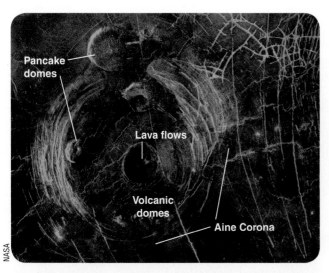

Figure 13.9 Radar map of surface features on Venus. Aine Corona, about 200 km in diameter, is marked by faults, lava flows, small volcanic domes, and pancake domes of solidified lava.

The History of Venus

To tell the story of Venus, you must draw together all the evidence and find hypotheses to explain two things: the thick carbon dioxide atmosphere and the peculiar geology.

Calculations show that Venus and Earth have outgassed about the same amount of carbon dioxide, but Earth's oceans have dissolved most of that and converted it to sediments such as limestone. If all of the carbon in Earth's sediments and crust were dug up and converted back to carbon dioxide, our atmosphere would be about as dense as the air on Venus, and with similar composition. This suggests that the main difference between Earth and Venus is the lack of water on Venus.

Venus may have had oceans when it was young and much more Earth-like than at present, but, being closer to the Sun than Earth, it was warmer, and the carbon dioxide in the atmosphere created a greenhouse effect that made the planet even warmer. That process could have dried up any oceans that did exist and prevented Venus from purging its atmosphere of carbon dioxide. In fact, evidence from the composition of Venus's atmosphere indicates that an ocean's worth of water might have been vapourized and lost

due to dissociation by ultraviolet light from the Sun. This dissociation of water removed the two hydrogen atoms from the oxygen atom, allowing the lighter hydrogen to escape into space, while the slower moving and more massive oxygen atom combined with other atoms. As carbon dioxide continued to be outgassed, the greenhouse effect grew even more severe. Thus, planetary scientists conclude that Venus was trapped in a runaway greenhouse effect.

The intense heat at the surface may have affected the geology of Venus by making the crust drier and more flexible, so it was unable to break into moving plates as on Earth. There is no sign of plate tectonics on Venus, but there is evidence that convection currents below the crust are deforming the crust to make coronae, push up mountains such as Maxwell, and create some folded mountains like those around Ishtar Terra by minor horizontal crust motions.

As you learned earlier, the small number of craters on the surface of Venus hints that the entire crust has been replaced within the last one-half billion years or so. This may have occurred in a planetwide overturning as the old crust broke up and sank and lava flows created a new crust. Comparisons between Earth and Venus may eventually reveal more about how our own world's volcanism and tectonics work.

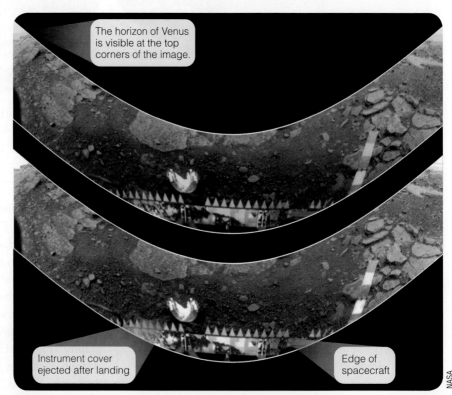

Figure 13.10 The Soviet *Venera 13* lander touched down on Venus in 1982 and carried a camera that swiveled from side to side to photograph the surface. The orange glow in the image is produced by the thick atmosphere; when that glow is corrected digitally, you can see that the rocks are dark grey. Isotopic analysis suggests they are basalts.

13.6 Mars

If you ever want to visit another world, Mars may be your best choice. You will need a heated, pressurized spacesuit, but Mars is not as inhospitable as the Moon. It is also more interesting, including the weather, complex geology, craters, volcanoes, and signs that water once flowed over its surface. Mars is about 50 percent farther from the Sun than Earth but its rotational period is very similar to that of Earth, with a solar day of 24.66 hours. As well, its rotational axis is tilted at 25.2° to its orbit; this is similar to that of Earth (23.4°), so there are distinct seasons on Mars. See **Celestial Profiles** in Appendix C for further details on the properties of Mars.

The Atmosphere of Mars

The Martian air contains 95 percent carbon dioxide, 3 percent nitrogen, and 2 percent argon. That is similar to the composition of air on Venus, but the Martian atmosphere is very thin, less than 1 percent as dense as Earth's atmosphere and 1/10 000 as dense as that of Venus.

There is very little water in the Martian atmosphere. Liquid water cannot survive on the surface of Mars because the air pressure is too low: any liquid water would immediately boil away. The polar caps appear to be composed of frozen water ice coated with frozen carbon dioxide (dry ice). Whatever water is present on Mars is frozen either within the polar caps or as **permafrost** in the soil.

Although the present atmosphere of Mars is very thin, there is evidence that the climate once permitted liquid water to flow over the surface, so Mars must have once had a thicker atmosphere. As a Terrestrial planet, it should have outgassed significant amounts of carbon dioxide, nitrogen, and water vapour, but because it was small it could not hold on to its atmosphere. The escape velocity on Mars is only 5 km/s, less than half of Earth's, so it was easier for rapidly moving gas molecules to escape into space. Furthermore, if Mars had been colder, the gas molecules in its atmosphere would have travelled more slowly and not escaped as easily.

Another process reduced Mars's atmosphere: the lack of an ozone layer to screen out UV radiation. Sunbathing on Mars would be a fatal mistake. Solar UV photons can break atmospheric molecules into smaller fragments. Water, for example, can be broken by UV into hydrogen and oxygen. The hydrogen then escapes into space, and the oxygen easily combines chemically with rocks and soil to form oxides. Iron oxide (rust) in the soil gives Mars its reddish landscape (Figure 13.11). Mars may have had a substantial atmosphere when it was young, but it gradually lost much of that, both by direct escape and by UV destruction. As a result, with a thin atmosphere that does not provide much greenhouse warming nor permit liquid water to persist on the surface, Mars is now a cold, dry world.

permafrost Permanently frozen soil.

Figure 13.11 This image taken by the Mast Camera on the *Curiosity* rover highlights the interesting geology of Mount Sharp, a mountain inside Gale Crater where the rover landed. Prior to the rover's landing, observations from orbiting satellites indicate that the lower reaches of the mountain are rock layers containing water-bearing minerals.

Exploring the Surface of Mars

Data recorded by orbiting satellites show that the southern hemisphere of Mars is a heavily cratered highland region up to 4 billion years old. The northern hemisphere is mostly a much younger lowland plain with few craters (see Figure 13.12).

Volcanism is dramatically evident in the Tharsis region of Mars, a highland region of volcanoes and lava flows bulging 10 km above the surrounding surface. A similar uplifted volcanic plain, the Elysium region, is more heavily cratered and eroded and appears to be older than the Tharsis bulge. The lack of impact craters on the slopes of some volcanoes in both Tharsis and Elysium suggests that there has been volcanic activity within the past few hundred million years, and maybe even more recently.

All the volcanoes on Mars are **shield volcanoes**: very broad mountains with gentle slopes that on Earth are produced by hot spots penetrating upward through the crust. Shield volcanoes are not related to plate tectonics; in fact, the large shield volcanoes on Mars, the largest of which is Olympus Mons, provide evidence that plate tectonics has not been significant on that planet. Olympus Mons is 700 km in diameter at its base and rises 25 km high. In comparison, the largest volcano on Earth, also a shield volcano, is Mauna Loa in Hawaii, rising only 10 km

shield volcano Wide, low-profile volcanic cone produced by highly liquid lava.

above its base on the seafloor (Figure 13.13a). On Earth, volcanoes like those that formed the Hawaiian Islands occur over rising currents of hot material in the mantle. Because the crust plate moves horizontally, a chain of volcanoes is formed instead of a single large feature (Figure 13.13b). A lack of plate motion on Mars has allowed rising currents of magma to heat the crust repeatedly in the same places and build Olympus Mons as well as other very large volcanic shields, especially in the Tharsis region (Figure 13.12).

When the crust of a planet is strained, it may break, producing faults and rift valleys. Near the Tharsis region is a great valley, Valles Marineris, named after the *Mariner 9* spacecraft that first photographed it (see Figure 13.12). The valley is a block of crust that has dropped downward along parallel faults. Erosion and landslides have further modified the valley into a great canyon. It is four times deeper, nearly 10 times wider, and over 10 times longer than the Grand Canyon. To put this into perspective, Valles Marineris is about as long as the distance from Calgary to Halifax and twice as wide as Vancouver Island in many spots. The number of craters in the valley indicates that it is 1 to 2 billion years old, placing its origin sometime before the end of the most active volcanism in the Tharsis region.

Searching for Water on Mars

To tell the story of Mars, you must first consider a difficult issue—water. How much water has Mars had, how much

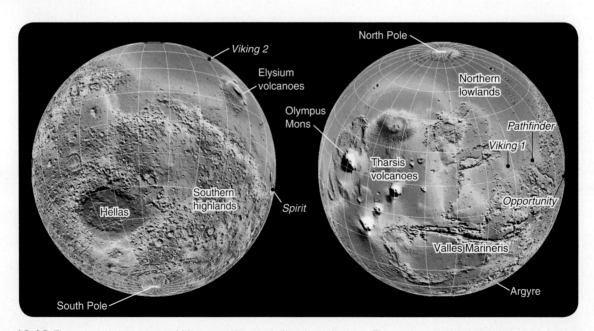

Figure 13.12 These hemisphere maps of Mars are colour coded to show elevation. The northern lowlands lie about 4 km below the southern highlands. Volcanoes are very high (white), and the giant impact basins, Hellas and Argyre, are low. Note the depth of the great canyon Valles Marineris.

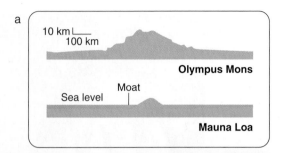

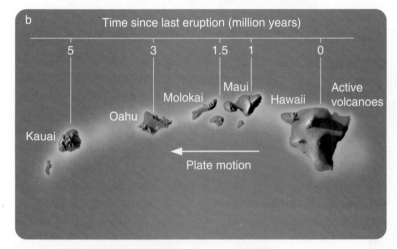

Figure 13.13 (a) Olympus Mons on Mars is much larger than Mauna Loa, the largest mountain on Earth. Mauna Loa is so heavy that it has sunk into Earth's crust, producing an undersea moat, but Olympus Mons has not, suggesting Mars's crust is much stronger than Earth's. (b) Volcanoes such as Mauna Loa do not grow very large on Earth because the crust plates move horizontally and carry older volcanoes away from hot spots.

has been lost, and how much remains? As you learned earlier, liquid water cannot exist on the surface of Mars now because of its low atmospheric pressure and low temperature. Observations from orbiting spacecraft, however, have revealed landforms that suggest the effects of flowing water on Mars, and rovers on the surface have turned up positive proof of surface water.

In 1976, the two *Viking* spacecraft reached orbit around Mars and photographed its surface. Those photos revealed two kinds of water-related features. **Outflow channels** appear to have been cut by massive floods carrying as much as 10 000 times the water flowing down the St. Lawrence River. In a matter of hours or days, such floods swept away geological features and left scarred land such as that shown in the following images made by *Viking* orbiters and the *Mars Global Surveyor*. In contrast, **valley networks** look like meandering riverbeds with sandbars, deltas, and tributaries typical of streams that flowed for extended periods of time (Figure 13.14). The number of craters on top of these features reveals that they are quite old.

Spacecraft in orbit around Mars have used remote instruments to detect large amounts of water frozen in the soil. A radar study has found frozen water extending at least a kilometre beneath both polar caps. Images made from orbit also show regions of jumbled terrain and gullies leading down slopes, suggesting water has flowed onto the surface from underground sources, perhaps melting of subsurface ice. The terrain at the edges of the northern lowlands has been compared to shorelines, and some scientists suspect that the northern lowlands were filled with an ocean roughly 3 billion years ago. Look again at Figure 13.12, where the lowlands have been colour-coded blue, and notice the major outflow channels leading from highlands into lowlands, like rivers flowing into an ocean.

Rovers named *Spirit* and *Opportunity* landed in January 2004 and carried sophisticated instruments to explore the rocky surface (Figure 13.15). Both rovers landed in areas suspected of having had water on their surfaces, and both made exciting discoveries. Using close-up cameras, the rovers found small spherical concretions of the mineral hematite (dubbed "blueberries") that must have formed in water. In other places, they found layers of sediments with ripple marks and crossed layers showing deposits that must have formed in moving water. You can see both of these features in Figure 13.16. Chemical analysis revealed minerals in the soil, such as sulphates, that are left behind when standing water evaporates.

In 2008, the space probe *Phoenix* landed in the north polar region of Mars and used its robotic arm to uncover water ice frozen in the Martian soil. Detailed chemical analyses of soil samples were completed confirming the presence of water and minerals necessary for any life that might exist there.

Finally, in August 2012, NASA's Mars Science Laboratory mission successfully landed the largest rover to date, *Curiosity*, in the Gale Crater, a site near the Martian equator. This huge 150-km-wide crater is highlighted by Aeolis Mons, a mountain that rises to 5.5 km at its peak. This landing site was chosen because it appeared to harbor many signs that water was present sometime in its history. Early in its wanderings *Curiosity* found clear evidence of a watery past by finding rounded rocks that must have been shaped by tumbling in rapid waterways. Other evidence points to a wetter and warmer past in this part of the Martian landscape.

outflow channel Geological features on Mars and Earth caused by flows of vast amounts of water released suddenly.

valley network A system of dry drainage channels on Mars that resembles the beds of rivers and tributary streams on Earth.

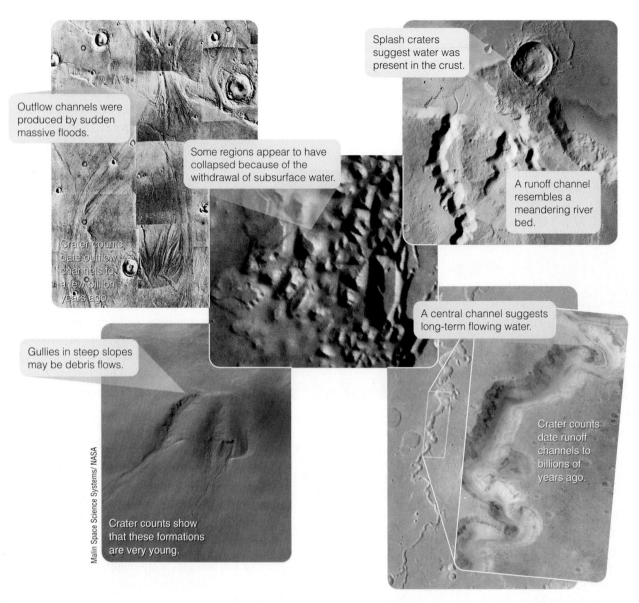

Figure 13.14 These visual-wavelength images made by the *Viking* orbiters and *Mars Global Surveyor* show some of the features that suggest liquid water on Mars. Outflow channels and runoff channels are old, but some gullies may be quite recent.

Figure 13.15 Mars is a red desert planet, as shown in this true-colour photograph by the rover *Opportunity*. The rock outcrop is a metre-high crater wall. Dust suspended in the atmosphere colours the sky red-orange. Data from orbiters, landers, and rovers show that billions of years ago Mars was less of a desert and had water on its surface.

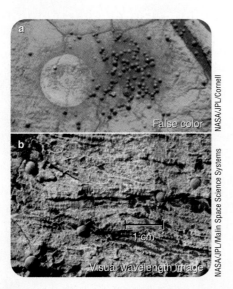

Figure 13.16 (a) Rover *Opportunity* photographed hematite concretions ("blueberries") weathered from rock. The round mark is a spot cleaned by the rover. The spheres appear to have grown as minerals collected around small crystals in the presence of water. Similar concretions are found on Earth. (b) The layers in this rock were deposited as sand and silt in rapidly flowing water. From the way the layers curve and cross each other, geologists can estimate that the water was at least 10 centimeters deep. A few "blueberries" are also visible in this image.

By now there is no doubt that water once existed in large quantities on Mars. Will we find proof that life originated and perhaps even flourished for a time in Mars's past? This important question will probably result in continuing exploration of the red planet.

A History of Mars

Did Mars ever have plate tectonics? Where did the water go? These fundamental questions challenge you to assemble the evidence and hypotheses for Mars and tell the story of its evolution. (See **How Do We Know? 13.2**.)

The history of Mars, like that of Venus, has been dominated by volcanism, but the differences are striking. Read **Visualizing Astronomy 13.2, When Good Planets Go Bad**, and notice four important points:

1. The difference between Venus and Earth is not in the amount of CO_2 they have outgassed but in the amount they have removed from their atmospheres. Being warmer and consequently having less liquid water on its surface sealed Venus's fate in having runaway greenhouse effect.

HOW DO WE KNOW? 13.2

The Present Is the Key to the Past

How can we know what happened long ago if there weren't any witnesses? Geologists are fond of saying, "The present is the key to the past." By that they mean that you can learn about the history of Earth by looking at the present condition of Earth's surface. The position and composition of various rock layers in the Grand Canyon, for example, tell you that the western United States was once at the floor of an ocean. This principle of geology is still relevant for understanding the history of other planets such as Venus and Mars.

In the late 1700s, naturalists first recognized that the present gave them clues to the history of Earth. At the time, that was astonishing because most people assumed that Earth had no history. That is, they assumed either that Earth had been created in its present

state as described in the Old Testament or that Earth was eternal. In either case, people commonly assumed that the hills and mountains they saw around them had always existed, more or less, as they were. By the 1700s, naturalists began to see evidence that the hills and mountains were not eternal but were the result of past processes and were slowly changing. That gave rise to the idea that Earth had a history.

As those naturalists made the first attempts to thoughtfully and logically explain the nature of Earth by looking at the evidence, they were inventing modern geology as a way of understanding Earth. What Copernicus, Kepler, and Newton did for the heavens in the 1500s and 1600s, the first geologists did for Earth beginning in the 1700s. Of course, the invention

of geology as the study of Earth led directly to the modern attempts to understand the geology of other worlds.

Geologists and astronomers share a common goal: to reconstruct the past from the evidence. Whether you study Earth, Venus, or Mars, you are looking at the present evidence and trying to reconstruct the past history of the planet by drawing on observations and logic to test each step in the story. How did Venus get to be covered with lava, and how did Mars lose its atmosphere? The final goal of planetary astronomy is to draw together all the available evidence (the present) to tell the story (the past) of how the planet got to be the way it is. Those first geologists in the 1700s would be fascinated by the stories planetary astronomers tell today.

Venus: Runaway Greenhouse

Venus and Mars haven't really gone wrong, but they have changed since they formed, and those changes can help you understand your own world.

1 Venus and Earth have outgassed about the same amount of CO_2, but Earth's oceans have dissolved most of Earth's CO_2 and converted it to sediments such as limestone. If all of Earth's sedimentary carbon were dug up and converted back to CO_2, our atmosphere would be much like Venus's.

Because Venus was warmer when it formed, it had little if any liquid water to dissolve CO_2, and that produced a greenhouse effect that made the planet even warmer. The planet could not purge its atmospere of CO_2, and as more was outgassed, Venus was trapped in a runaway greenhouse effect.

NASA

Only 0.7 AU from the Sun, Venus receives almost twice the solar energy per square metre as Earth does. Moved to Venus's orbit, Earth's surface would be 50°C hotter.

VENUS

2 Lava covers Venus in layers of basalt, and volcanoes are common. Some of those volcanoes may be active right now while others are dormant. Traces of past lava flows show up in radar images, including long, narrow valleys cut by moving lava.

UV image

Even its thick atmosphere cannot protect Venus from larger meteorites, yet it has few craters. That must mean the surface is not old.

Baltis Vallis (arrows), at least 6800 km (4200 mi) long, is the longest lava flow channel in the solar system.

Radar map

Radar map

NASA/JPL

NASA/JPL

2a The crust of Venus must be no older than 0.5 billion years. One hypothesis is that an earlier crust broke up and sank in a sea of magma as fresh lava flows formed a new crust. Such resurfacing events might occur periodically on a hot, volcanic planet like Venus.

What could cause a resurfacing event? Models of the climate on Venus show that an outburst of volcanism could increase the greenhouse effect and drive the surface temperature up by as much as 100°C. This could soften the crust, increase the volcanism, and push the planet into a resurfacing episode. This type of catastrophe may happen periodically on Venus, or the planet may have had just one resurfacing event about half a billion years ago.

Even if bodies of water existed when Venus was young, they could not have survived long.

NASA/JPL

Mars: Runaway Refrigerator

3 When Mars was young, water was abundant enough to flow over the surface in streams and floods, and may have filled oceans. That age of liquid water ended over 3 billion years ago. The climate on Mars has changed as atmospheric gases and water were lost to space and as water was frozen into the soil as permafrost.

MARS

The northern lowlands of Mars and the Hellas Basin may once have been filled with water.

Hellas Basin

NASA

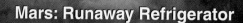

Evidence of surface water erosion on Mars

Visual-wavelength image

NASA/JPL/Malin Space Science Systems

4 Early in the history of Mars when its crust was thin, convection in the mantle could have pushed up volcanic regions such as Tharsis and Elysium, and limited plate motion could have produced Valles Marineris, but Mars cooled too fast, and its crust never broke into moving tectonic plates as did Earth's crust.

As its crust thickened, volcanism abated, and Mars lost the ability to replenish its waning atmosphere.

4a Mars has very large volcanoes, and their size shows that the crust has grown thick as the little planet has lost its heat to space. A thinner crust could not support such large volcanoes.

Olympus Mons volcano on Mars

If the crust of Mars were made up of moving plates, its volcanoes could not have grown so big.

Computer enhanced image

NASA/Goddard Space Flight Center

CHAPTER 13 Comparative Planetology of the Terrestrial Planets

2. Venus is highly volcanic, with a crust made up of lava flows that have covered over any older crust.

3. Mars is significantly smaller than Earth, with gravity too weak to prevent much of its atmosphere from leaking away. There is strong evidence of past water, but whatever is left is frozen in the soil or polar caps.

4. Mars is small and cooled quickly. Its crust has grown thick, and volcanism has dropped to such a low level that it cannot replenish the gases lost to space.

The history of Mars is a case of arrested development. The planet began by differentiating into a crust, mantle, and core. Measurements from orbiting spacecraft reveal that it has a dense core but no planetwide magnetic field. The core must have cooled quickly and shut off the dynamo effect that would have produced a field.

The crust of Mars is now quite thick, as shown by the mass of the Olympus Mons volcano (Figure 13.13), but it was probably thinner in the past. Cratering may have broken or at least weakened the crust, triggering lava flows that flooded some basins. Mantle convection may have pushed up the Tharsis and Elysium volcanic regions and broken the crust to form Valles Marineris, but moving crustal plates never dominated Mars. There are no folded mountain ranges on Mars and no sign of plate boundaries. As the planet cooled, its crust grew thick and immobile.

For Mars, the last stage of planetary development has been one of slow decline. Volcanoes may still occasionally erupt, but the little planet has lost much of its internal heat, and most volcanism occurred long ago. At some point in the history of Mars, water was abundant enough to flow over the surface in great floods and may have filled an ocean, but the age of liquid water must have ended more than 3 billion years ago. The climate on Mars changed as the atmosphere gradually became thinner. Atmospheric gases and water were lost to space, and the volcanic activity that could have replaced them has nearly stopped. LH 84001 is the name (identifier) given to a 1.93-kg meteorite discovered in 1984 in Antarctica. Following considerable analysis, it is commonly thought to have originated from Mars, possibly from the Valles Marineris canyon. More importantly, however, is that the analysis appears to show that the meteorite formed during a period when liquid water existed on Mars, and the meteorite exhibits features possibly resembling microbial fossils. The debate continues whether or not this is evidence of extraterrestrial life, although there is strong evidence that Mars was once hospitable to life.

The water remaining on Mars today is frozen in the polar caps or in the soil. However, note that water is the first necessity of life, so its presence long ago on Mars is exciting. Someday an astronaut may scramble down an ancient Martian streambed, turn over a rock, and find a fossil.

13.7 The Moons of Mars

Unlike Mercury or Venus, Mars has moons. Small and irregular in shape, Phobos (28 × 23 × 20 km in diameter) and Deimos (16 × 12 × 10 km) are almost certainly captured asteroids (see Figure 13.17). These moons are so small they cannot pull themselves into spherical shape. Phobos and Deimos are not just small; they are tiny. And an athletic astronaut who could jump 2 m high on Earth could jump almost 3 km on Phobos. However they formed, these moons are so small that any interior heat would have leaked away very quickly, and there is no evidence of any internally driven geologic activity on either object.

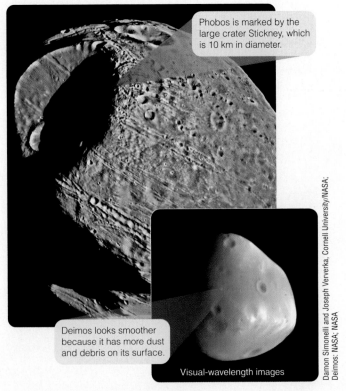

Phobos is marked by the large crater Stickney, which is 10 km in diameter.

Deimos looks smoother because it has more dust and debris on its surface.

Visual-wavelength images

Damon Simonelli and Joseph Ververka, Cornell University/NASA; Deimos: NASA; NASA

Figure 13.17 The moons of Mars are too small to pull themselves into spherical shape. The two moons, shown here to scale, were named for the mythical attendants of the god of war, Mars. Phobos was the god of fear, and Deimos was the god of dread.

Some futurists suggest that the first human missions to Mars may not land on the planet's surface but instead could build a colony on Phobos or Deimos. These plans involve speculation that these moons and other asteroids may have water in deep interior rocks that colonists could use.

What Are We? Comfortable but Curious

Humans have intense curiosity about their world. We want to know how things work, we want to know what happened in the past, and we want to know what the future might be like. We have a longing to explore other worlds, but leaving Earth is difficult for two reasons. First, to achieve escape velocity you need a powerful, expensive rocket. Second, we face evolutionary challenges. If you leave Earth, you have to take the Earthly environment with you.

On the Moon, astronauts' spacesuits provided them with air to breathe, water to drink, and climate control. Their spacesuits could not provide artificial gravity, and medical tests show that low-gravity conditions cause serious deterioration of bones and muscles unless difficult preventive measures are taken. It would be hard to stay healthy away from Earth for long periods of time. The Terrestrial planets and moons are the only ones in our solar system that you might reasonably expect to visit, and few are welcoming. Visiting Venus would require a deep-sea submersible. To explore Mercury you would need a superpower cooling system. Mars, the friendliest, is only somewhat more hospitable than the Moon. Even Titan, the moon that seems to have some Earth-like characteristics would be a very hostile place to explore.

Many planets in the universe probably look like the Moon and Mercury—small, airless, and cratered. Some are made of stone, others are made mostly of ices because they formed farther from their star, and many others are more like our Jovian planets. If you randomly visited a Terrestrial planet anywhere in the universe, you would probably stand on a moonscape.

Earth is unique in our solar system but probably not rare within our galaxy. The Milky Way Galaxy contains more than 100 billion stars, and more than 100 billion galaxies are visible throughout the universe with existing telescopes. Most of those stars probably have planets, and although many planets may look like our Moon or Mercury, there must be plenty of Earth-like worlds.

As you look around where you live, you can feel comfortable living on such a beautiful planet, but this was not always the case. The craters on the Moon and the rocks returned by astronauts show that the Moon formed with a sea of magma. Mercury seems to have had a similar history, so Earth may have formed the same way. Its surface was once a seething ocean of liquid rock swathed in a hot, thick atmosphere, torn by eruptions of more rock, explosions of gas from the interior, and occasional impacts from space. The Moon and Mercury assure you that Terrestrial planets began in this way. Earth has evolved to become your home world, but never forget that Mother Earth has had a violent past.

Review Questions

1. Why would you include the Moon in a comparison of the Terrestrial planets?
2. In what ways is Earth unique among the Terrestrial planets?
3. How do you know that Earth differentiated?
4. How are earthquakes in Hawaii different from those in southern California?
5. What characteristics must Earth's core have in order to generate a magnetic field?

6. How do island chains located in the centres of tectonic plates such as the Hawaiian Islands help you understand plate tectonics?
7. What has produced the oxygen in Earth's atmosphere?
8. How does the increasing abundance of CO_2 in Earth's atmosphere cause a rise in Earth's temperature?
9. Why would a decrease in the density of the ozone layer cause public health problems?
10. Why doesn't Earth have as many craters as the Moon?
11. Discuss the evidence and hypotheses concerning the origin of Earth's moon.
12. What evidence indicates that plate tectonics does not occur on Venus? On Mars?
13. What evidence suggests that Venus has been resurfaced within the last half billion years?
14. Why are the atmospheres of Venus and Mars mostly carbon dioxide? Why is the atmosphere of Venus very dense, but the atmosphere of Mars is very thin?
15. Why did Venus suffer from the runaway greenhouse effect, but Earth has avoided it so far?
16. What evidence indicates that there has been liquid water on Mars?
17. Why do astronomers conclude that the crust on Mars must be thicker than Earth's crust?
18. **How Do We Know?** Why is heat flow the key to understanding a planet's surface activity?
19. **How Do We Know?** How is solving a crime that had no witnesses similar to figuring out what happened to Venus and Mars's oceans?

Discussion Questions

1. If you orbited a planet in another solar system and discovered oxygen in its atmosphere, what might you expect to find on its surface?
2. If liquid water is rare on the surface of planets, most Terrestrial planets must have CO_2-rich atmospheres. Why?
3. If you visited a planet in another solar system and discovered that it was heavily cratered, but its small moon was nearly crater free, why would that be a surprise? Speculate about what might have happened to those objects.

Learning to Look

1. Look at the globe of Earth (following), and look for volcanoes scattered over the Pacific Ocean. What is producing these volcanoes?

National Geographical Data Center

2. Olympus Mons on Mars is a very large volcano. In this image you can see multiple calderas superimposed at the top. What do those multiple calderas and the immense size of Olympus Mons indicate about the geology of Mars?

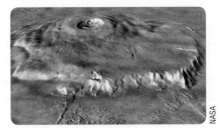

NASA

3. In what ways is the photo below a typical view of the surface of planet Earth? How is it unusual among planets in general?

William K. Hartmann/Planetary Science Institute

4. What do you see in the photo below that suggests heat is flowing out of Earth's interior?

USGS

5. In the photo below, Astronaut Alan Bean works at the *Apollo 12* lander *Intrepid*. Describe the surface you see. What kind of terrain did they land on—for this, the second human landing on the Moon?

NASA

STUDY TOOLS

IN THE BOOK

- Tear out the Review Card for Chapter 13

ONLINE

Visit CENGAGENOW™ for ASTRO, 2Ce at www.nelson.com/student

- eBook
- Interactive Quizzing
- Animations
- Tutorials

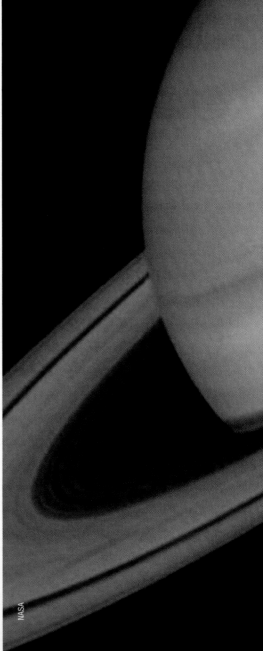

14

The Outer Solar System

CHAPTER OUTLINE

GUIDEPOST

In the previous chapter, you studied how Earth and the other Terrestrial planets evolved to their present forms. In this chapter, the Jovian (Jupiter-like) planets will challenge your imagination. They are such alien worlds that they would be unbelievable if we didn't have direct observational evidence to tell us what they are like. In contrast, Pluto and the other bodies in the Kuiper belt are not planets but intriguing clues about the planet-forming process.

As you explore, you will find answers to four important questions:

- **What are the properties of the Jovian planets?**
- **What is the evidence that some moons in the outer solar system have been geologically active?**
- **How are planetary rings formed and maintained?**
- **What do Pluto and the other Kuiper belt objects tell us about the formation of the solar system?**

In Chapters 13 and 14 you learn about the individual planets and see some patterns emerge. In Chapter 12 you learned about a comprehensive theory for the formation of the solar system. That theory explains the overall characteristics of the planets as well as the meteoroids, asteroids, and comets that also orbit the Sun, and it predicts that planetary systems should be common around other stars. In fact, you learned that astronomers have found hundreds of such systems.

The worlds of the outer solar system can be studied from Earth, but much of what astronomers know has been radioed back to Earth from

NASA

Space exploration is the ultimate tool for international cooperation.

Adriana Ocampo,
NASA planetary geologist who helped discover the
impact crater of the asteroid that wiped out the dinosaurs

space probes. The *Pioneer* and *Voyager* probes flew past the outer planets in the 1970s and 1980s, the *Galileo* probe orbited Jupiter in the late 1990s, and the *Cassini* orbiter and *Huygens* probe arrived at Saturn in 2004. The *New Horizons* probe will pass Pluto in 2015 and then sail deeper into the Kuiper belt. This chapter includes images and data returned by these robotic explorers.

14.1 A Travel Guide to the Outer Planets

You are about to study four worlds that are truly unearthly. This travel guide helps you anticipate what to expect.

The Outer Planets

The outermost planets in our solar system are Jupiter, Saturn, Uranus, and Neptune. They are often called the Jovian planets, meaning they resemble Jupiter (named after a Roman god known as Jove). In fact, each of these planets has its own attributes. Figure 14.1 compares these four worlds. Jupiter is the largest of the Jovian planets, over 11 times the diameter of Earth. Saturn is slightly smaller, and Uranus and Neptune are quite a bit smaller than Jupiter but still four times Earth's diameter. Pluto, smaller than Earth's moon, was considered a planet from the time of its discovery in 1930 until a decision by the International Astronomical Union (IAU) in 2006 that reclassified Pluto as a dwarf planet. You will learn about Pluto's characteristics, and reasons for the IAU decision, later in this chapter.

The other feature to notice immediately is Saturn's rings. They are bright and beautiful and composed of billions of ice particles. Jupiter, Uranus, and Neptune also have rings, but they are not easily detected from Earth and are not visible in Figure 14.1. As you study these worlds you will be able to compare four different sets of planetary rings.

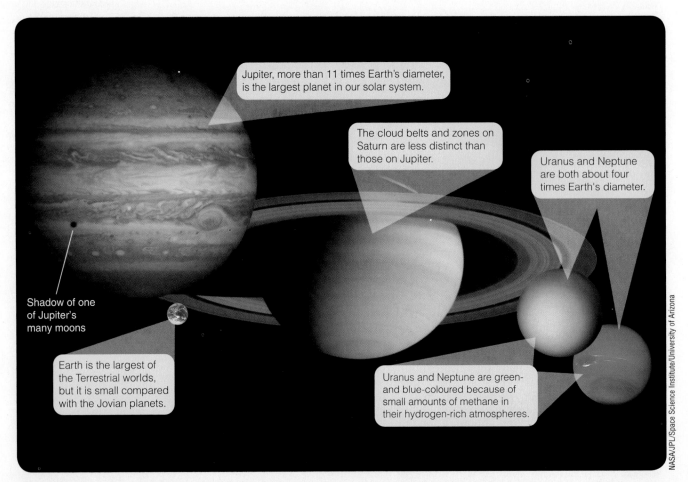

Jupiter, more than 11 times Earth's diameter, is the largest planet in our solar system.

The cloud belts and zones on Saturn are less distinct than those on Jupiter.

Uranus and Neptune are both about four times Earth's diameter.

Shadow of one of Jupiter's many moons

Earth is the largest of the Terrestrial worlds, but it is small compared with the Jovian planets.

Uranus and Neptune are green- and blue-coloured because of small amounts of methane in their hydrogen-rich atmospheres.

NASA/JPL/Space Science Institute/University of Arizona

Figure 14.1 The four Jovian planets are massive, low-density worlds that have no solid surface on which to stand.

Atmospheres and Interiors

The four Jovian worlds have hydrogen-rich atmospheres filled with clouds. The atmospheres of the Jovian planets are not very deep; for example, Jupiter's atmosphere makes up only about 1 percent of its radius. On Jupiter and Saturn, the clouds form stripes that circle each planet. Traces of these types of features are visible, but not very distinct, on Uranus and Neptune.

Models based on observations indicate that below their atmospheres Jupiter and Saturn are mostly liquid, so the old-fashioned term for these planets, the *gas giants*, should probably be changed to the *liquid giants*. Uranus and Neptune are sometimes called the *ice giants* because they are rich in water in both solid and liquid forms. Near their centres the Jovian planets have cores of dense material with the composition of rock and metal. None of the Jovian worlds has a definite solid surface on which you could walk.

Recall from Chapter 12 that the Jovian planets have low density because they formed in the outer solar nebula where water vapour could freeze to form ice particles. The ice accumulated into protoplanets with densities lower than the rocky Terrestrial planets and asteroids. Once the Jovian planets grew massive enough, they could draw in even lower-density hydrogen and helium gas directly from the nebula by gravitational collapse.

Satellite Systems

You can't land a spaceship on the Jovian planets, but you might be able to land on their moons. All the outer solar system planets have extensive moon systems. In many cases the moons interact gravitationally, mutually adjusting their orbits and also affecting the planetary ring systems. Some of the moons are geologically active now, while others show signs of past activity. Since geological activity requires heat flow from the interior, you might wonder what is heating the inside of these small objects.

oblateness The flattening of a spherical body, usually caused by rotation.

14.2 Jupiter

Jupiter can be very bright in the night sky, and its cloud belts and four largest moons can be seen through even a small telescope. Jupiter is the largest and most massive of the Jovian planets, containing 71 percent of all the planetary matter in the entire solar system. In Chapter 13, Earth was used as the basis for comparison with the other Terrestrial planets; here, Jupiter is the standard for the comparative study of the other Jovian planets.

The Interior

Jupiter is only 1.3 times denser than water. Comparatively, Earth is more than 5.5 times denser than water. This gives astronomers a clue about the average composition of the planet's interior. Jupiter's shape also gives information about its interior. Jupiter and the other Jovian planets are all slightly flattened. A world with a large rocky core and mantle would not be flattened much by rotation, but an all-liquid planet would flatten significantly. Jupiter's **oblateness**, the fraction by which its equatorial diameter exceeds its polar diameter, combined with its average density, helps astronomers model the interior.

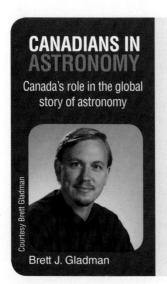

CANADIANS IN ASTRONOMY
Canada's role in the global story of astronomy

Courtesy Brett Gladman

Brett J. Gladman

Brett J. Gladman

Canadian astronomer, Brett J. Gladman, is a professor at the University of British Columbia's Department of Physics and Astronomy in Vancouver. He holds the Canada Research Chair in Planetary Astronomy and the chair of the Science Advisory Council of the Canada-France-Hawaii Telescope on Mauna Kea in Hawaii.

Gladman's best-known work is in the area of dynamical astronomy in the solar system: planet formation, transport of meteorites between planets, the delivery of meteoroids from the main asteroid belt, and the possibility of the transport of life via this mechanism, known as panspermia. He is discoverer or co-discoverer of many astronomical bodies in the solar system: asteroids, Kuiper belt comets, and many moons of the giant planets. Gladman was awarded the H. C. Urey Prize by the Division of Planetary Sciences of the American Astronomical Society in 2002. Asteroid 7638 Gladman is named in his honour.

Jupiter orbits the Sun at a distance of 5.2 AU, completing each orbit in about 11.9 years—which means that it goes through each zodiacal region per year, more or less. Despite the fact that Jupiter is the most massive of all the planets, its sidereal rotation period is merely 10 hours, making its spinning rate the fastest of all the planets. Consult the **Celestial Profiles** in Appendix C for more data about Jupiter.

Models indicate that the interior of Jupiter is mostly liquid hydrogen. However, if you jumped into Jupiter carrying a rubber raft expecting an ocean, you would be disappointed. The base of the atmosphere is so hot and the pressure is so high that there is no sudden boundary between liquid and gas. As you fell deeper and deeper through the atmosphere, you would find the gas density increased around you until you were sinking through a liquid, but you would never splash into a distinct liquid surface because the transition from gas to liquid takes place very gradually.

Under very high pressure, liquid hydrogen becomes **liquid metallic hydrogen**—a material that is a very good conductor of electricity. Most of Jupiter's interior is composed of this material. That large mass of conducting liquid, stirred by convection currents and spun by the planet's rapid rotation, drives the dynamo effect and generates a powerful magnetic field. Jupiter's field is over 10 times stronger than Earth's. A planet's magnetic field deflects the solar wind and dominates the volume of space around the planet called the **magnetosphere**.

The strong magnetic field around Jupiter traps charged particles from the solar wind in radiation belts a billion times more intense than the similar Van Allen belts that surround Earth. The spacecraft that have flown through these regions received over 1000 times the radiation that would have been lethal for a human being.

At Jupiter's centre, a so-called rocky core contains heavier elements, such as iron, nickel, and silicon. With a temperature four times hotter than the surface of the Sun and a pressure 50 million times Earth's air pressure at sea level, this material is unlike any rock on Earth. The term *rocky core* refers to the chemical composition, not to the properties of the material.

Careful infrared measurements of the heat flowing out of Jupiter reveal that the planet emits about twice as much energy as it absorbs from the Sun. This energy is understood to be heat left over from the formation of the planet. In Chapter 12, you saw that Jupiter should have grown very hot when it formed, and some of that heat remains in its interior.

Jupiter's Complex Atmosphere

Study **Visualizing Astronomy 14.1, Jupiter's Magnetosphere and Complex Atmosphere**, and notice four important ideas:

1. Jupiter's extensive magnetosphere is responsible for auroras around the magnetic poles. Interactions between Jupiter's magnetic field and the solar wind generate electric currents that flow around the planet's magnetic poles.

2. Jupiter's rings, discovered in 1979 by the *Voyager I* space probe, are relatively close to the planet.

3. The pattern of coloured cloud bands circling the planet, like stripes on a child's ball, is called **belt–zone circulation**. This pattern is related to the high- and low-pressure areas in Earth's atmosphere.

4. The positions of the cloud layers are at certain temperatures within the atmosphere where ammonia (NH_3), ammonium hydrosulphide (NH_4SH), and water (H_2O) can condense.

Jupiter's Rings

Astronomers have known for centuries that Saturn has rings, but Jupiter's ring system was not discovered until 1979, when the *Voyager 1* spacecraft sent back photos. Less than 1 percent as bright as Saturn's icy rings, Jupiter's rings are very dark and reddish, indicating that the rings consist of rocky material rather than being icy.

Astronomers conclude that the ring particles are mostly microscopic. Photos of the rings show that they are very bright when illuminated from behind—in other words, they are scattering light forward. Large particles do not scatter light forward: A ring filled with basketball-size particles would look dark when illuminated from behind. The **forward scattering** of visible light indicates that the rings are mostly made of tiny grains with diameters approximately equal to the wavelengths of visible light, about the size of particles in cigarette smoke.

liquid metallic hydrogen A form of liquid hydrogen that is a good electrical conductor, inferred to exist in the interiors of Jupiter and Saturn.

magnetosphere The volume of space around a planet within which the motion of charged particles is dominated by the planetary magnetic field rather than the solar wind.

belt–zone circulation The atmospheric circulation typical of Jovian planets in which dark belts and bright zones encircle the planet parallel to its equator.

forward scattering The optical property of finely divided particles to preferentially direct light in the original direction of the light's travel.

Figure 14.2 Colour-enhanced visual-wavelength image of Jupiter's Galilean moons.

The rings orbit inside the **Roche limit**, the distance from a planet within which a moon cannot hold itself together by its own gravity. If a moon comes inside the Roche limit, tidal forces overcome the moon's gravity and pull the moon apart. Also, raw material for a moon cannot coalesce inside the Roche limit. The Roche limit is about 2.4 times the planet's radius, depending somewhat on the relative densities of the planet and the moon material. Jupiter's rings, as well as those of Saturn, Uranus, and Neptune, lie inside the respective Roche limits for each planet.

Now you can understand why Jupiter has dusty rings. If a dust speck gets knocked loose from a larger rock inside the Roche limit, the rock's gravity cannot hold the dust speck. For the same reason, the billions of dust specks in the ring can't pull themselves together to make a moon because of the tidal forces inside the Roche limit.

You can be sure that Jupiter's ring particles are not old. The pressure of sunlight and the planet's powerful magnetic field alter the orbits of the particles. Images show faint ring material extending down toward the cloud tops; this is evidently due to dust grains spiralling into the planet. Dust is also destroyed by the intense radiation around Jupiter that grinds the dust specks down to nothing in a century or so. Therefore, the rings you see today can't be material left over from the formation of Jupiter; instead they must be continuously resupplied with new dust. Observations made by the *Galileo* spacecraft provide evidence that the source of ring material is the micrometeorites that erode small moons orbiting near or within the rings.

The rings around Saturn, Uranus, and Neptune are also known to be short lived, and they also must be resupplied by new material, probably eroded from nearby moons. Besides supplying the Jovian rings with particles, moons confine the rings, keep them from spreading outward, and alter their shapes.

Jupiter's Family of Moons

Jupiter has four large moons and at least 63 smaller moons. Larger telescopes and modern techniques are rapidly finding more small moons orbiting each of the Jovian planets. Most of the small moons are probably captured asteroids. In contrast, the four largest moons (Figure 14.2), called the Galilean moons after their discoverer, Galileo, are clearly related to each other and probably formed with Jupiter.

The outermost Galilean moons, Ganymede and Callisto, are about the size of Mercury, one and a half times the size of Earth's moon. In fact, Ganymede is the largest moon in the solar system. Ganymede and Callisto have low densities of only 1.9 and 1.8 g/cm^3, respectively, meaning they must consist roughly of half rock and half ice. Observations of their gravitational fields by the *Galileo* spacecraft reveal that both moons have rocky and metallic cores and lower-density icy exteriors, so they both have differentiated. Both moons interact with Jupiter's magnetic field in a way that shows they probably have mineral-rich layers of liquid water 100 km or more below their icy crusts.

Callisto's surface and most of Ganymede's surface appear old because they are heavily cratered and very dark. The continuous blast of micrometeorites evaporates surface ice, leaving behind embedded minerals to form a dark skin like the grimy crust on an old snowbank—so surfaces get darker with age. More recent impacts dig up cleaner ice and leave bright craters, as on Callisto (see Figure 14.2). Ganymede has some younger, brighter grooved terrain believed to be systems of faults in the brittle

Roche limit The minimum distance between a planet and its satellite so that the satellite can hold itself together by its own gravity. If a satellite's orbit brings it within its planet's Roche limit, tidal forces will pull the satellite apart.

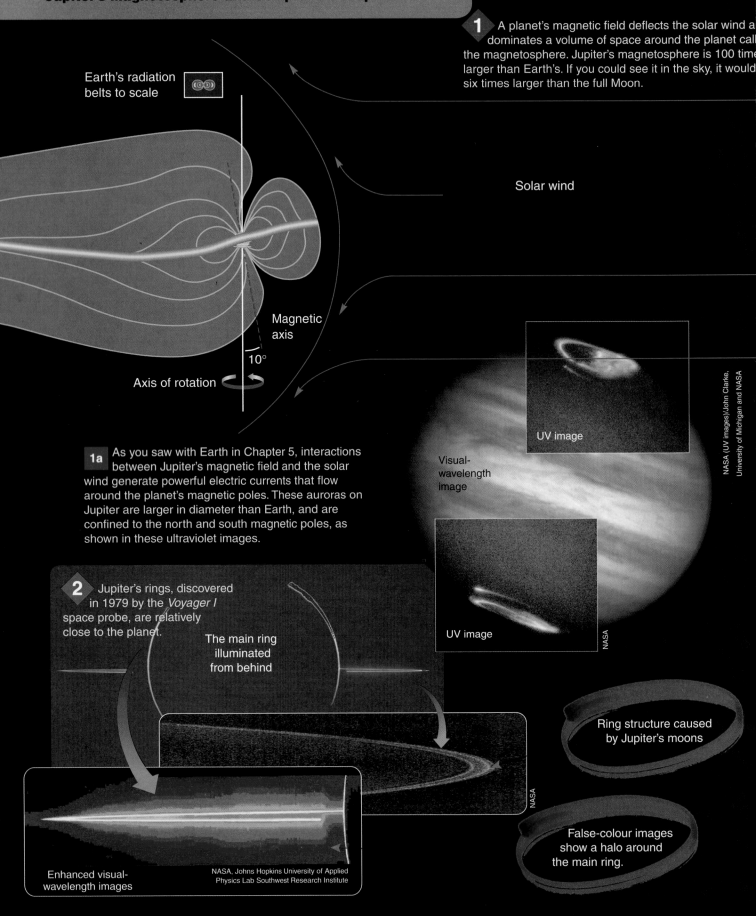

VISUALIZING ASTRONOMY 14.1
Jupiter's Magnetosphere and Complex Atmosphere

1 A planet's magnetic field deflects the solar wind a[nd] dominates a volume of space around the planet call[ed] the magnetosphere. Jupiter's magnetosphere is 100 time[s] larger than Earth's. If you could see it in the sky, it would [be] six times larger than the full Moon.

Earth's radiation belts to scale

Solar wind

Magnetic axis

10°

Axis of rotation

1a As you saw with Earth in Chapter 5, interactions between Jupiter's magnetic field and the solar wind generate powerful electric currents that flow around the planet's magnetic poles. These auroras on Jupiter are larger in diameter than Earth, and are confined to the north and south magnetic poles, as shown in these ultraviolet images.

UV image

Visual-wavelength image

UV image

NASA (UV images)/John Clarke, University of Michigan and NASA

NASA

2 Jupiter's rings, discovered in 1979 by the *Voyager I* space probe, are relatively close to the planet.

The main ring illuminated from behind

Ring structure caused by Jupiter's moons

NASA

False-colour images show a halo around the main ring.

Enhanced visual-wavelength images

NASA, Johns Hopkins University of Applied Physics Lab Southwest Research Institute

NASA/JPL

Great
Red Spot

3 The visible clouds are not at the top of the atmosphere; an upper atmosphere of clear hydrogen and helium extends far above the cloud tops. Jupiter's atmosphere makes up only 1 percent of its radius. Major spots on Jupiter, like the Great Red Spot, are embedded, circulating storms. They can remain stable for decades or even centuries.

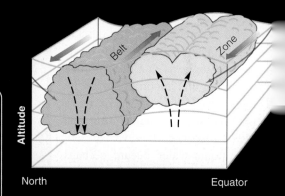

3a Cloud belts and zones circle Jupiter like stripes on a ball. This form of atmospheric circulation is belt-zone circulation. The poles and equator on Jupiter are about the same temperature, perhaps because of heat rising from the interior. Because of that, and also because of Jupiter's rapid rotation, instead of wave-shaped winds as on Earth, Jupiter's high- and low-pressure areas are stretched into belts and zones parallel to the equator. Zones are brighter than belts because rising gas forms clouds high in the atmosphere where sunlight is stronger and reflected back to outside viewers.

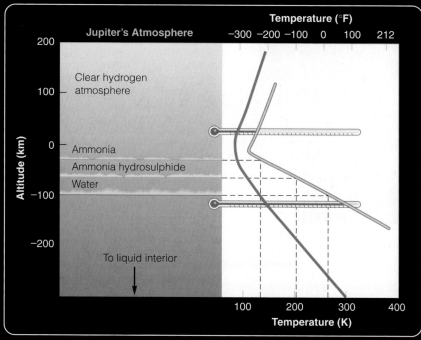

North   Equator

4 Jupiter's cloud layers lie at certain temperatures within the atmosphere where ammonia (NH_3), ammonium hydrosulphide (NH_4SH), and water (H_2O) can condense into droplets. If you could put thermometers into the different levels of the atmosphere, you would discover that the temperatures rise as you descend beneath the uppermost clouds, represented for Jupiter by the solid orange line. Because Saturn is further from the Sun, its temperature is colder, shown by the green line. The cloud layers on Saturn form at the same temperature as the cloud layers on Jupiter, but they are deeper in Saturn's hazy atmosphere.

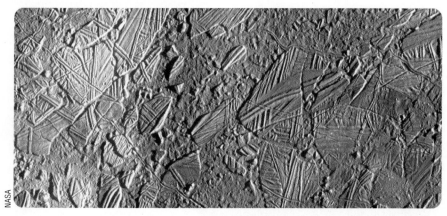

Figure 14.3 Like icebergs on the Arctic Ocean, blocks of crust on Europa appear to have floated apart. The blue icy surface is stained brown by mineral-rich water venting from below the crust. White areas are ejecta from the impact that formed the nearby crater Pwyll.

tidal heating The heating of a planet or satellite because of friction caused by tides.

crust. Some sets of grooves overlap other sets of grooves, suggesting extended episodes of geological activity.

The density of the next moon inward, Europa, is 3 g/cm³, high enough to mean that the moon is mostly rock with a thin icy crust. The visible surface is very clean ice, contains very few craters, has long cracks in the icy crust, and has complicated terrain that resembles blocks of ice in Earth's Arctic Ocean (Figure 14.3). The lack of craters tells you that Europa is an active world where craters are quickly erased. The pattern of folds on its surface suggests that the icy crust breaks as the moon is flexed by tides (see Chapter 3). Europa's gravitational influence on the *Galileo* spacecraft reveals there is a liquid-water ocean, perhaps 200 km deep, below the 10- to 100-km-thick crust.

Images from spacecraft reveal that Io, the innermost of the four Galilean moons, has over 150 volcanic vents on its surface (see Figure 14.4). The active volcanoes throw sulphur-rich gas and ash high above the surface; the ash falls back to bury the surface at a rate of a few millimetres a year. This explains why you see no impact craters on Io—they are covered up as fast as they form.

Io's density is 3.6 g/cm³, which indicates it does not consist of ice, but rather rock and metal. Its gravitational influence on the passing *Galileo* spacecraft revealed that it is differentiated into a large metallic core, a rocky mantle, and a low-density crust.

The activity we see in the Galilean moons must be driven by energy flowing outward, yet these objects are too small to have remained hot from the time of their formation. Io's volcanism seems to be driven by **tidal heating**. Io follows a slightly eccentric orbit caused by its interactions with the other moons. Jupiter's gravitational field flexes Io with tides, and the resulting friction heats its interior. That heat flowing outward causes the volcanism. Europa is not as active as Io, but it too must have a heat source, presumably tidal heating. Ganymede is no longer active, but when it was younger it must have had internal heat to break the crust and produce the grooved terrain.

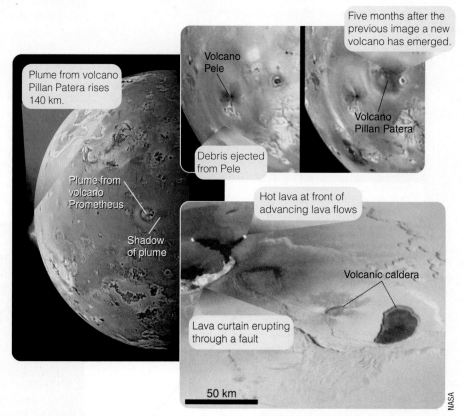

Plume from volcano Pillan Patera rises 140 km.

Plume from volcano Prometheus

Shadow of plume

Volcano Pele

Debris ejected from Pele

Five months after the previous image a new volcano has emerged.

Volcano Pillan Patera

Hot lava at front of advancing lava flows

Volcanic caldera

Lava curtain erupting through a fault

50 km

Figure 14.4 These colour images of volcanic features on Io were produced by combining visual and near-infrared images and then digitally enhancing the colour. To human eyes, most of Io would look pale yellow and light orange.

A History of Jupiter

Creating a logical argument from evidence and hypotheses is the ultimate goal of planetary astronomy. Can you put all the evidence together and explain the history of Jupiter?

Jupiter formed far enough from the Sun to incorporate large numbers of icy planetesimals, and it must have grown rapidly. Once it became about 10 to 15 times more massive than Earth, it could begin to grow further by gravitational collapse (see Chapter 12), capturing gas directly from the solar nebula. Consequently, it grew rich in hydrogen and helium from the solar nebula. Its present composition resembles the composition of the solar nebula and is also quite Sunlike. Jupiter's gravity is strong enough to hold on to all of its gases, even hydrogen.

The large family of moons may be mostly captured asteroids, and Jupiter may still encounter a wandering asteroid or comet now and then. Some of these are deflected, some captured into orbit, and some, like comet fragments in 1994 (Figure 12.14) and an unidentified object in 2009, actually strike the planet. Dust blasted off the inner moons by micrometeorites settles into the equatorial plane to form Jupiter's rings.

The four Galilean moons are large and seem to have formed like a mini-solar system in a disk of gas and dust around the forming planet. The innermost, Io, is densest, and the densities of the others decrease as you move away from Jupiter, similar to the way the densities of the planets decrease with distance from the Sun. Perhaps the inner moons incorporated less ice because they formed closer to the heat of the growing planet. You can recognize that tidal heating also has been important, and the intense warming of the inner moons could have driven off much of their ice. Taken together, these two processes are probably responsible for the differences in compositions of the Galilean moons.

14.3 Saturn

The Roman god Saturn, protector of the sowing of seed, was once celebrated in a week-long Saturnalia at the time of the winter solstice in late December. Early Christians took over the holiday to celebrate Christmas.

Saturn is most famous for its beautiful rings, which are easily visible through the telescopes of modern amateur astronomers. Large Earth-based telescopes have explored the planet's atmosphere, rings, and moons. Saturn's orbital radius is almost twice that of Jupiter and Saturn takes almost 30 years to orbit the Sun.

Interestingly, Saturn's density is 0.69 g/cm³, meaning that it would float on Lake Superior—although the lake would have to be considerably larger than it is now. The two *Voyager* spacecraft flew past Saturn in 1979, and the *Cassini* spacecraft went into orbit around Saturn in 2004 on an extended exploration of the planet, its rings, and its moons. Consult the **Celestial Profiles** in Appendix C for more data.

In the opening illustration for this chapter the belt-zone circulation of Saturn appears only faintly, but images from *Voyager*, the Hubble Space Telescope, and *Cassini* show that the belts and zones are present and that the associated winds blow up to three times faster than on Jupiter. Belts and zones on Saturn are less visible than on Jupiter because they occur deeper in the cold atmosphere, below a layer of methane haze.

The low density of Saturn suggests that it is, like Jupiter, rich in hydrogen and helium. As many photographs show, Saturn is the most oblate of the planets, which tells you that its interior is mostly liquid and has a small core of heavy elements. Because its internal pressure is lower than that of Jupiter, Saturn has less liquid metallic hydrogen than Jupiter. Perhaps that is why Saturn's magnetic field is 20 times weaker than Jupiter's. Like Jupiter, Saturn radiates more energy than it receives from the Sun, and models predict that it has a very hot interior.

Saturn's Rings

Study **Visualizing Astronomy 14.2, The Ice Rings of Saturn**, and notice three things:

1. The rings are made up of billions of ice particles, each in its own orbit around the planet. The ring particles you observe can't be as old as Saturn. The rings must be replenished now and then by impacts on Saturn's moons or other processes. The same is true of the rings around the other Jovian planets.

2. The gravitational effects of small moons can confine some rings in narrow strands or keep the edges of rings sharp. Moons can also produce waves in the rings that are visible as tightly wound ringlets.

3. The ring particles are confined in a thin layer in Saturn's equatorial plane, spread among small moons and confined by gravitational interactions with larger moons. The rings of Saturn, and the rings of the other Jovian worlds, are created by and controlled by the planet's moons. Without the moons, there would be no rings.

1 The brilliant rings of Saturn are made up of billions of ice particles ranging from microscopic specks to chunks bigger than a house. Each particle orbits Saturn in its own circular orbit. Much of what astronomers know about the rings was learned when the *Voyager 1* spacecraft flew past Saturn in 1980, followed by the *Voyager 2* spacecraft in 1981. The *Cassini* spacecraft reached orbit around Saturn in 2004. From Earth, astronomers see three rings, which they have labelled A, B, and C. *Voyager* and *Cassini* images reveal over a thousand ringlets within the rings.

Saturn's rings can't be leftover material from the formation of Saturn. The rings are made of ice particles, and the planet would have been so hot when it formed that it would have vaporized and driven away any icy material. Rather, the rings must be debris from collisions between passing comets, or other objects, and Saturn's icy moons. Such impacts should occur every 100 million years or so, and they would scatter ice throughout Saturn's system of moons. The ice would quickly settle into the equatorial plane, and some would become trapped in rings. Although the ice may waste away due to meteorite impacts and damage from radiation in Saturn's magnetosphere, new impacts could replenish the rings with fresh ice. The bright, beautiful rings you see today may be only a temporary enhancement caused by an impact that occurred since the extinction of the dinosaurs.

Encke Gap

Cassini Division

A ring

B ring

C ring

As in the case of Jupiter's ring, Saturn's rings lie inside the planet's Roche limit where the ring particles cannot pull themselves together to form a moon.

Because it is so dark, the C ring was once called the crepe ring (crepe being a black-dyed fabric worn for mourning).

Earth to scale

Visual-wavelength image

NASA

1a An astronaut could swim through the rings. Although the particles orbit Saturn at high velocity, all particles at the same distance from the planet orbit at about the same speed, so they collide gently at low velocities. If you could visit the rings, you could push your way from one icy particle to the next. This artwork is based on a model of particle sizes in the A ring.

The C ring contains boulder-size chunks of ice, whereas most particles in the A and B rings are more like golf balls, down to dust-size ice crystals. Further, C ring particles are less than half as bright as particles in the A and B rings. Cassini observations show that the C ring particles contain less ice and more minerals.

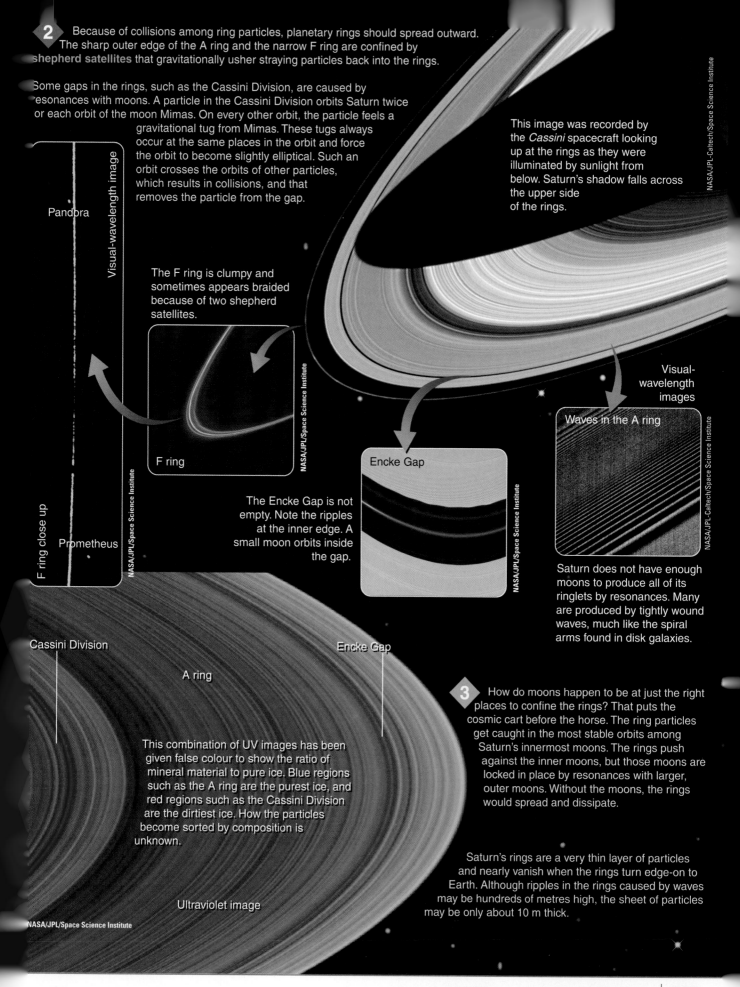

2 Because of collisions among ring particles, planetary rings should spread outward. The sharp outer edge of the A ring and the narrow F ring are confined by **shepherd satellites** that gravitationally usher straying particles back into the rings.

Some gaps in the rings, such as the Cassini Division, are caused by resonances with moons. A particle in the Cassini Division orbits Saturn twice or each orbit of the moon Mimas. On every other orbit, the particle feels a gravitational tug from Mimas. These tugs always occur at the same places in the orbit and force the orbit to become slightly elliptical. Such an orbit crosses the orbits of other particles, which results in collisions, and that removes the particle from the gap.

This image was recorded by the *Cassini* spacecraft looking up at the rings as they were illuminated by sunlight from below. Saturn's shadow falls across the upper side of the rings.

NASA/JPL-Caltech/Space Science Institute

Pandora

Visual-wavelength image

The F ring is clumpy and sometimes appears braided because of two shepherd satellites.

F ring

NASA/JPL/Space Science Institute

F ring close up

Prometheus

NASA/JPL/Space Science Institute

Visual-wavelength images

Waves in the A ring

NASA/JPL-Caltech/Space Science Institute

Encke Gap

The Encke Gap is not empty. Note the ripples at the inner edge. A small moon orbits inside the gap.

NASA/JPL/Space Science Institute

Saturn does not have enough moons to produce all of its ringlets by resonances. Many are produced by tightly wound waves, much like the spiral arms found in disk galaxies.

Cassini Division

A ring

Encke Gap

This combination of UV images has been given false colour to show the ratio of mineral material to pure ice. Blue regions such as the A ring are the purest ice, and red regions such as the Cassini Division are the dirtiest ice. How the particles become sorted by composition is unknown.

Ultraviolet image

NASA/JPL/Space Science Institute

3 How do moons happen to be at just the right places to confine the rings? That puts the cosmic cart before the horse. The ring particles get caught in the most stable orbits among Saturn's innermost moons. The rings push against the inner moons, but those moons are locked in place by resonances with larger, outer moons. Without the moons, the rings would spread and dissipate.

Saturn's rings are a very thin layer of particles and nearly vanish when the rings turn edge-on to Earth. Although ripples in the rings caused by waves may be hundreds of metres high, the sheet of particles may be only about 10 m thick.

Funding for Basic Research

Who pays for science? Obtaining new scientific knowledge can be expensive, and that raises the question of funding. In Canada, most university professors engage in fundamental research and publish their findings in scholarly journals. In many disciplines, especially in the sciences, university budgets can provide only limited financial support for such research, and faculty are expected to fund their research through external agencies. Some science has direct applications, and industry supports such research. For example, pharmaceutical companies have large budgets for scientific research that leads to the creation of new drugs. But with basic science, it is sometimes difficult to understand the immediate practical value, and commercial applications may develop much later and in unexpected ways.

During the 1950s physicists developed a device called a maser, the forerunner of the laser. This fundamental research quickly evolved into a highly viable commercial product. Where would we be today without lasers? Similarly, when Albert Einstein developed the theory of relativity few saw any value in such knowledge. Yet, without this fundamental research our GPS devices would not work properly. These are just a few examples of the unexpected applications of basic scientific research. However, who pays the bill?

In Galileo's time scientific research was simpler, and most researchers made their own equipment to support their endeavours. Today's astronomers require expensive and sophisticated tools as well as collaboration with colleagues who share interests. It falls to government institutions and private foundations to pay the bill for this kind of research. The Keck Foundation built two giant telescopes on Mauna Kea in Hawaii with no expectation of financial return. The National Science Foundation in the USA, the National Science and Engineering Research Council along with the Canadian Space Agency have funded thousands of astronomy research projects for the benefit of society.

Canada's contribution to NASA's Space Shuttle program came in the form of the Canadarm, raising the awareness of Canadians in space exploration. The production cost of this valuable equipment was about $100 million, about 30¢ for each Canadian. The ISS (International Space Station) is a collaboration of the United States, Russia, Europe, Japan and Canada. Building on its success in robotic manipulation, Canada built Canadarm2 at a cost of about $1.4 billion, successfully installed it on the ISS, and then used it to build the ISS in space.

The discovery of a new galaxy is of no great financial value, but such scientific knowledge is not worthless. Its value lies in what it tells us about the world we live in. Such scientific research enriches our lives by helping us understand what we are.

Ultimately, funding basic scientific research is a public responsibility that society must balance against other needs. There isn't anyone else to pick up the tab.

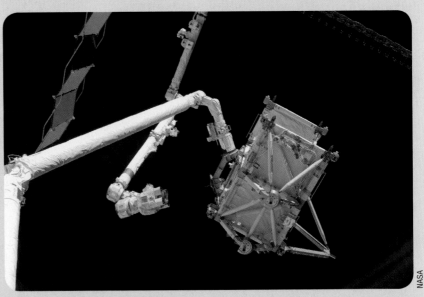

NASA

The Canadarm2 moves toward a P5 truss section, being held by *Discovery*'s Canadarm, in preparation for a hand-off during STS-116.

Saturn's Family of Moons

Saturn has more than 60 known moons, many of which are small, and all of them contain mixtures of ice and rock. Many are probably captured objects.

The largest of Saturn's moons is called Titan. Remarkably, Titan is a bit larger than the planet Mercury. Its density suggests it must contain a rocky core under a thick mantle of ice. Titan is so cold that its gas molecules do not travel fast enough to escape, so its atmosphere is about 1.5 times denser than Earth's; however, it is composed mostly of nitrogen, with traces of argon and methane. Sunlight converts some of the methane into complex carbon-rich molecules that collect into small particles and fills the atmosphere with orange smog (see Figure 14.5). These particles are understood to slowly settle down toward the surface in the form of dark, organic goo, meaning it is composed of carbon-rich molecules.

Titan's surface is mainly composed of ices of water and methane at −180°C. The *Cassini* spacecraft dropped the *Huygens* probe into the atmosphere of Titan, and it photographed dark drainage channels, suggesting that liquid methane falls as rain, washes the dark goo off the higher terrain, and drains into the lowlands. Such methane downpours may be rare, however. No direct evidence of liquid methane was detected as the probe descended, but later radar images made by the *Cassini* orbiter have detected what appear to be lakes, presumably containing liquid methane. One such lake, Ontario Lacus, has a surface area about 20 percent of its namesake (Lake Ontario) and a depth of less than 10 m, and it could be composed of methane, ethane, and propane—although recent measurements suggest it may be more like a mudflat. Infrared images suggest the presence of methane volcanoes that replenish the methane in the atmosphere, so Titan must have some internal heat source to power the activity.

Most of the remaining moons of Saturn are small and icy, have no atmosphere, and are heavily cratered. Most have dark, ancient surfaces. However, Enceladus,

Visual-wavelength images

Image recorded from 8 km above surface

Drainage channels were cut by flowing liquid.

Lakes of liquid methane and ethane look dark because they do not reflect radar waves.

At visual wavelengths, Titan's heavy atmosphere hides its surface.

False-colour Radar map

Icy grapefruit-size "rocks" on Titan are bathed in orange light from its hazy atmosphere.

Visual

ESA/NASA/JPL/USGS/University of Arizona; NASA

Figure 14.5 As the *Huygens* probe descended by parachute through Titan's smoggy atmosphere, it photographed the surface from an altitude of 8 km. Although no liquid was present, dark drainage channels were observed leading into the lowlands. Radar images reveal lakes of liquid methane and ethane around the poles. Once the *Huygens* probe landed on the surface, it radioed back photos showing a level plain and chunks of ice surrounded by a moving liquid.

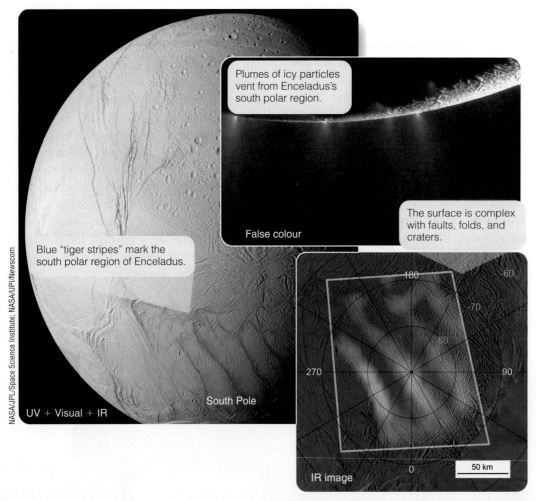

Blue "tiger stripes" mark the south polar region of Enceladus.

Plumes of icy particles vent from Enceladus's south polar region.

False colour

The surface is complex with faults, folds, and craters.

UV + Visual + IR

South Pole

IR image

180   -60

-70

-80

270   90

0   50 km

NASA/JPL/Space Science Institute; NASA/UPI/Newscom

Figure 14.6 Saturn's moon Enceladus is venting water, ice, and organic molecules from geysers near its south pole. A thermal infrared image reveals internal heat leaking to space from the "tiger stripe" cracks where the geysers are located.

Saturn's sixth-largest moon, remains geologically active due to tidal heating. Some parts of its surface contain up to 1000 times fewer craters than other regions, and infrared observations show that its south polar region is unusually warm. Furthermore, *Cassini* discovered water and ice-rich geyser-like jets venting from cryovolcanoes around the south pole (Figure 14.6). Analysis of these jets has revealed not only water vapour but other volatiles, including sodium chloride crystals. A portion of this material falls back onto the moon's surface as snow; the reminder escapes into space, feeding Saturn's E ring.

14.4 Uranus

After becoming familiar with the gas giants in our solar system, you will be able to appreciate the strangeness of the ice giants: Uranus and Neptune. Uranus, especially, seems to have forgotten how to behave like a planet.

Uranus was discovered in 1781 by the scientist William Herschel, a German expatriate living in England. He named it *Georgium Sidus*, George's Star, in honour of his patron English King George III. European astronomers, especially the French, refused to accept a planet named after an English king. They called it Herschel. Years later, German astronomer J. E. Bode suggested Uranus, the oldest of the Greek gods.

Uranus orbits the Sun at an average of 19.2 AU, almost twice as far away as Saturn; once again we see how greatly spaced are the Jovian planets compared to the Terrestrial planets. An interesting feature of Uranus's rotation is that it is inclined to the ecliptic at about 98°, meaning that it actually rotates backward while appearing to "roll" along its orbit.

Planet Uranus

Uranus is only one-third the diameter of Jupiter and only one-twentieth as massive, and, being about four times farther from the Sun, its atmosphere is almost 100°C colder than Jupiter's.

Recall that Uranus didn't grow massive enough to capture large amounts of gas from the nebula as Jupiter and Saturn did; so it has much less hydrogen and helium. Its internal pressure is low enough compared to Jupiter's that it should not contain any liquid metallic hydrogen. Models of Uranus based in part on its density and oblateness suggest that it has a small core of heavy elements and a deep mantle of partly solid water. Although referred to as ice, this material would not be anything like ice on Earth, given the temperatures and pressures inside Uranus. The mantle also contains rocky-composition material and dissolved ammonia and methane. Circulation in this electrically conducting mantle may generate the planet's peculiar magnetic field, which is highly inclined to its axis of rotation. Above this mantle lies a deep hydrogen and helium atmosphere.

As mentioned previously, Uranus rotates on its side, with its equator inclined about 98° to its orbit. With an orbital period of 84 years, each of the four seasons lasts 21 years, and the winter–summer contrast is extreme. During a season when one of its poles is pointed nearly at the Sun (a solstice), inhabitants of Uranus would never see the Sun rise or set. Compare this with seasons on Earth discussed in Chapter 2. Uranus's odd rotation may have been produced when it was struck by a very large planetesimal late in its formation, or by tidal interactions with the other giant planets as it migrated outward early in the history of the solar system (see Chapter 12).

Voyager 2 photos, like the one in Figure 14.7, show a nearly featureless ball. The atmosphere is mostly hydrogen and helium, but traces of methane absorb red light and thus make the atmosphere look blue or teal, depending on the image. There is no belt–zone circulation visible in the *Voyager 2* photographs, although extreme computer enhancement revealed a few clouds and bands around the south pole. In the decades since *Voyager 2* flew past Uranus, spring has come to the northern hemisphere of Uranus and autumn to the southern hemisphere. Images made by the Hubble Space Telescope as well as the most powerful Earth-based telescopes reveal changing clouds and cloud bands (Figure 14.8).

Infrared measurements show that Uranus is radiating about the same amount of energy that it receives from the Sun, meaning it has much less heat flowing out of its interior than Jupiter or Saturn (or Neptune). This may account for its limited atmospheric activity. Astronomers

Figure 14.7 No clouds were visible when *Voyager 2* flew past Uranus in 1986.

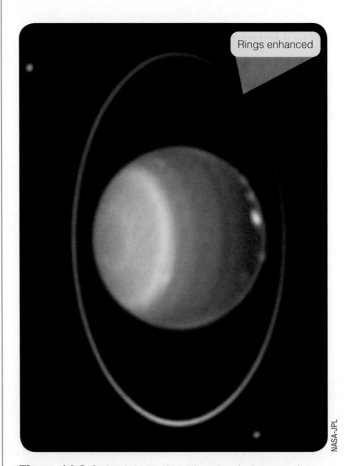

Figure 14.8 Spring in Uranus's northern hemisphere may have caused weather changes.

are not sure why Uranus differs in this respect from the other Jovian worlds.

The Uranian Moons

Until recently, astronomers could see only five moons orbiting Uranus. *Voyager 2* discovered 10 more small moons in 1986, and even more have been found in images recorded by new, giant telescopes on Earth: the total is now 27.

The five major moons of Uranus are smaller than Earth's moon and have old, dark, cratered surfaces. A few have deep cracks, produced, perhaps, when the interior froze and expanded. In some cases, liquid water "lava" appears to have erupted and smoothed over some regions. Miranda, the innermost moon, is only 14 percent the diameter of Earth's moon, but its surface is marked by grooves called **ovoids** (Figure 14.9). These may have been caused by internal heat driving convection in the icy mantle. By counting craters on the ovoids, astronomers conclude that the entire surface is old, and the moon is no longer active.

The Uranian Rings

The rings of Uranus are dark and faint, contain little dust, are confined by shepherd satellites, and must be continuously resupplied with material from the moons. They are not easily visible from Earth: The first hint that Uranus had rings came from **occultations**: the passage of the planet in front of a star. Most of what astronomers know about these rings comes from the observations of the *Voyager 2* spacecraft. Their composition appears to be water ice mixed with methane that has been darkened by exposure to radiation.

In 2006, astronomers found two new, very faint rings orbiting far outside the previously known rings of Uranus. The newly discovered satellite Mab appears to be the source of particles for the larger ring, and the smaller of the new rings is confined between the orbits of the moons Portia and Rosalind. Note that the International Astronomical Union (IAU) has declared that the newly discovered moons of Uranus are to be named after characters either in Shakespeare's plays or in Pope's "The Rape of the Lock." So far only Ariel, Umbriel, and Belinda have names from the latter; all the rest are names from Shakespearian literature.

ovoid The oval features found on Miranda, a satellite of Uranus.

occultation The passage of a larger body in front of a smaller body.

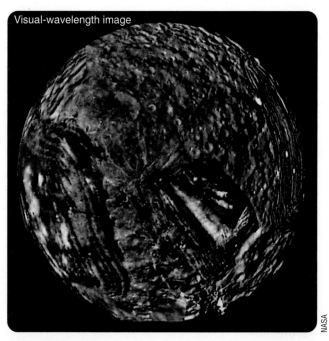

Visual-wavelength image

NASA

Figure 14.9 Geological activity on Uranus's moon Miranda. The face of Miranda is marked by ovoids, which are believed to have formed when internal heating caused slow convection in the ice of the moon's mantle. Note the 5-km-high cliff at the lower right edge of the moon.

14.5 Neptune

Travelling another 10 AU from Uranus, you reach the orbit of the outermost major planet in our solar system, Neptune. British astronomer John Couch Adams and French astronomer Urbain Le Verrier independently calculated the existence and location of Neptune based on irregularities they observed in the motion of Uranus. Since British observers were too slow to respond, Neptune was discovered in 1846, and the French astronomer got the credit. Neptune looks like a tiny blue dot with no visible cloud features. Because of its blue colour, astronomers named it after the god of the sea. In 1989, *Voyager 2* flew past and revealed some of Neptune's secrets.

Planet Neptune

Almost the same size as Uranus, Neptune is calculated to have a similar interior. It has a small core of heavy elements that lies within a slushy mantle of water, ices, and minerals (rock) beneath a hydrogen-rich atmosphere. Yet Neptune looks quite different; it is dramatically blue and has active cloud formations. Neptune has a dark blue tint because its atmosphere contains 1.5 times more methane than Uranus. Methane absorbs red photons better than blue and scatters blue photons better than red, giving Neptune a blue colour and Uranus a green-blue colour.

Atmospheric circulation on Neptune is much more dramatic than on Uranus. When *Voyager 2* flew by Neptune in 1989, the largest feature was the Great Dark Spot (see Figure 14.10). Roughly the size of Earth, the spot seemed to be an atmospheric circulation similar to Jupiter's Great Red Spot. Smaller spots were visible in Neptune's atmosphere, and photos showed they were circulating like hurricanes. More recently, the Hubble Space Telescope has photographed Neptune and found that the Great Dark Spot is gone, and new cloud formations have appeared. Evidently, the weather on Neptune is surprisingly changeable.

The atmospheric activity on Neptune is apparently driven by heat flowing from the interior as well as some contribution by dim light from the Sun, which is 30 AU away. Neptune may have more atmospheric activity than Uranus because it has more heat flowing out of its interior, for reasons that are unclear.

Like Uranus, Neptune has a highly inclined magnetic field that must be linked to circulation in the interior. In both cases, astronomers suspect that ammonia dissolved in the liquid water mantle makes the mantle a good electrical conductor and that convection in the water, coupled with the rotation of the planet, drives the dynamo effect and generates the magnetic field.

Neptune's Moons

Neptune has two moons that were discovered from Earth before *Voyager 2* flew past in 1989. The passing spacecraft discovered six more very small moons. Since then, a few more small moons have been found by astronomers using large Earth-based telescopes.

The two largest moons have peculiar orbits. Nereid, about one-tenth the size of Earth's moon, follows a large, elliptical orbit, taking about an Earth year to circle Neptune once. Triton, about 80 percent the size of Earth's moon, orbits Neptune backward—clockwise as seen from the north. These odd orbits suggest that the system was disturbed long ago in an interaction with some other body, such as a massive object.

Triton has an atmosphere of nitrogen and methane about 10^5 times less dense than Earth's, and a temperature of 36 K (–395°F). A significant part of Triton is ice, and deposits of nitrogen frost are visible at the southern pole (Figure 14.11). Many features on Triton suggest it has had an active past. It has few craters on its surface, but it does have long faults that appear to have formed when the icy crust broke, plus large basins that seem to have been flooded repeatedly by liquids from the interior. Even more interesting are the dark smudges visible in the southern polar cap; astronomers have interpreted these as sunlight-darkened deposits of methane that once erupted out of liquid nitrogen geysers.

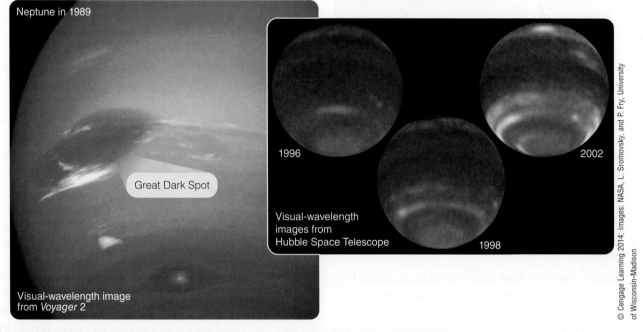

Neptune in 1989

Great Dark Spot

Visual-wavelength image from *Voyager 2*

1996

1998

2002

Visual-wavelength images from Hubble Space Telescope

© Cengage Learning 2014; Images: NASA, L. Sromovsky, and P. Fry, University of Wisconsin-Madison

Figure 14.10 Neptune's axis is inclined almost 29° to its orbit. It experiences seasons that each last about 40 years. Since *Voyager* visited in 1989, spring has come to the southern hemisphere, and the weather has clearly changed, which is surprising because sunlight at Neptune is 900 times dimmer than at Earth.

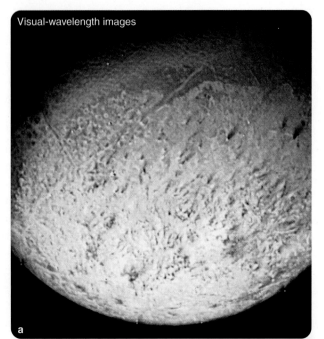

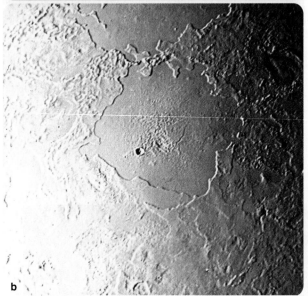

NASA

Figure 14.11 Visible-wavelength images of Neptune's moon Triton. (a) Triton's southern polar cap is formed of nitrogen frost. Note the dark smudges caused by organic compounds sprayed from nitrogen geysers, and the absence of craters. (b) These round basins on Triton appear to have been repeatedly flooded by liquid from the interior.

Neptune's Rings

Neptune's rings are faint and very hard to detect from Earth, but they illustrate some interesting processes of comparative planetology (Figure 14.12). Neptune's rings are similar to those of Uranus but contain more small dust particles. The gravitational influence of one of Neptune's moons causes the outermost ring to be concentrated

into short arcs. Neptune's ring system, like the others, is apparently resupplied during impacts on the moons, which scatter debris that then falls into the most stable places among the orbits of the moons.

14.6 Dwarf Planets

Beyond Neptune lies the Kuiper belt, a doughnut-shaped region extending from roughly 30 AU to 50 AU. This region consists of billions of icy planetesimals left over from the formation of the solar system. Sizes of these objects vary from small bits of ice and rock to large spheres with rocky cores and icy lithospheres more than 500 km in diameter. The largest of these planetesimals are known as the dwarf planets. To date, there are five official dwarf planets, four of which are found in the Kuiper belt, Pluto being the best known. The fifth official dwarf planet, Ceres, lies in the asteroid belt between Mars and Jupiter.

What Defines a Planet?

To understand why Pluto is no longer considered a planet, you need to know more about the Kuiper belt of small bodies. Since 1992, astronomers have discovered over a thousand icy bodies orbiting beyond Neptune. There may be as many as 100 million objects in the Kuiper belt larger than 1 km in diameter. As mentioned, some of the Kuiper belt objects are quite large, and one, named Eris, has about the same diameter as Pluto, but is 27 percent more massive. Three other Kuiper belt objects found so far—Sedna, Orcus, and Quaoar (pronounced kwah-o-wahr)—are half the size of Pluto, or larger. Some of these objects have moons of their own. In that way, they resemble Pluto and its moons.

A bit of comparative planetology shows that Pluto is not related to the Jovian or Terrestrial planets; it is obviously a member of a newfound family of icy worlds that orbit beyond Neptune. These bodies must have formed at about the same time as the eight classical planets of the solar system, but they did not grow massive enough to clear their orbital zones of remnant objects and remain embedded among a swarm of other objects in the Kuiper belt.

One of the criteria for planet status developed by the International Astronomical Union (IAU) is that an object must be large enough to dominate and gravitationally clear its orbital region of most or all other objects. Eris and Pluto, the largest objects found so far in the Kuiper belt, and Ceres, the largest object in the asteroid belt,

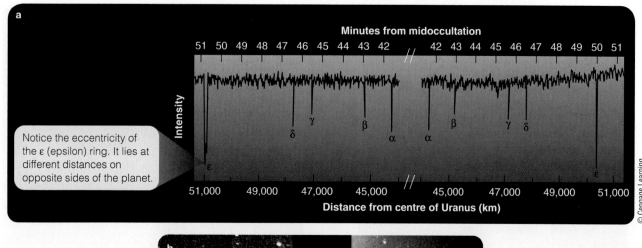

Figure 14.12 (a) The rings of Uranus were discovered in 1977, when Uranus crossed in front of a star. During this occultation, astronomers saw the star dim a number of times, both before and after the planet crossed over the star. The dips in brightness were caused by rings circling Uranus. (b) The bright disk of Neptune is hidden behind the black bar in this *Voyager 2* image. Two narrow rings are visible, and a wider, fainter ring lies closer to the planet. More ring material is visible between the two narrow rings. The rings are bright in forward-scattered light, indicating that the rings contain significant amounts of very small dust particles with short lifetimes. Like the rings of Uranus, the rings of Neptune reflect very little light and probably contain methane-rich ice darkened by radiation.

do not meet that standard. On the other hand, all three are large enough for their gravities to have pulled them into spherical shapes, so they are the prototypes of a new class of objects defined by the IAU as **dwarf planets**. Consequently, in 2006, the IAU voted to remove Pluto from the list of classical planets.

Pluto

Pluto is a very small, icy world. It is neither Jovian nor Terrestrial. Its orbit is highly inclined and so elliptical that Pluto actually comes closer to the Sun than Neptune at times. To understand Pluto's status, you must use comparative planetology to analyze Pluto in comparison with its neighbours.

Pluto is very difficult to observe from Earth. It has only 65 percent the diameter of Earth's moon. In Earth-based telescopes it never looks like more than a faint point of light, and even in Hubble Space Telescope images it shows little detail. Orbiting so far from the Sun, Pluto is cold enough to freeze most compounds you think of as gases, and spectroscopic observations have found evidence of nitrogen ice. Its thin atmosphere consists of nitrogen and carbon monoxide with small amounts of methane.

To date, five moons of Pluto have been discovered (Figure 14.13). Four of them

dwarf planet A body that orbits the Sun, is not a satellite of a planet, is massive enough to pull itself into a spherical shape, but is not massive enough to clear out other bodies in and near its orbit—for example, Pluto, Eris, and Ceres.

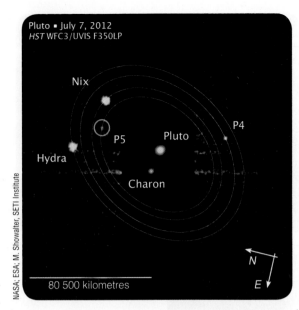

Pluto • July 7, 2012
HST WFC3/UVIS F350LP

NASA; ESA; M. Showalter, SETI Institute

Nix

P5

Pluto

P4

Hydra

Charon

N

E

80 500 kilometres

Figure 14.13 Hubble image of all five known moons of Pluto, with estimated orbits for the outer satellites. The brightness of Pluto and Charon is damped to bring out the dimmer moons.

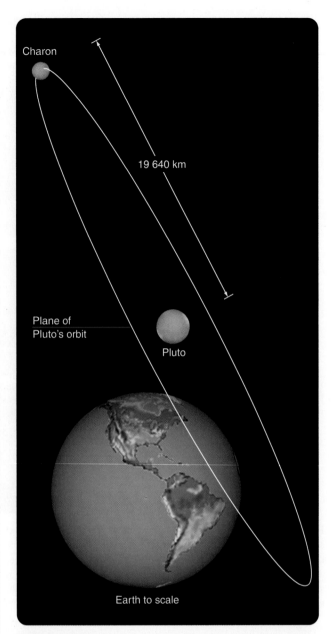

Charon

19 640 km

Plane of Pluto's orbit

Pluto

Earth to scale

Figure 14.14 The circular orbit of Pluto's moon Charon is seen here at an angle. The orbit is only a few times bigger than Earth and is tipped 118° to the plane of Pluto's orbit around the Sun.

are quite small, but the largest, Charon, has half the diameter of Pluto. Charon orbits Pluto with a period of 6.4 days in the same plane as the other moons, and the orbit is highly inclined to the ecliptic (Figure 14.14). Pluto and Charon are tidally locked to face each other, so Pluto's rotation is also highly inclined.

Charon's orbit size and period plus Kepler's third law reveal that the mass of the system is only about 0.002 Earth mass. Most of that mass is Pluto, which has about 12 times the mass of Charon. Knowing the diameters and masses of Pluto and Charon allows astronomers to calculate that their densities are both about 2 g/cm³. This indicates that Pluto and Charon must each contain about 35 percent ice and 65 percent rock.

The best photos by the Hubble Space Telescope reveal almost no surface detail, but we know enough about icy moons to guess that Pluto has craters and probably shows signs of tidal heating caused by interaction Charon. The *New Horizons* spacecraft will fly past Pluto in July 2015, and the images radioed back to Earth will certainly show that Pluto is an interesting world.

Pluto and the Plutinos

No, this section is not about a 1950s rock and roll band. It is about the history of the dwarf planets, and it will take you back 4.6 billion years to watch the outer planets form.

More than a hundred known Kuiper belt objects are caught with Pluto in a 3:2

plutino One of the icy Kuiper belt objects that, like Pluto, is caught in a 3:2 orbital resonance with Neptune.

resonance with Neptune. That is, they orbit the Sun twice while Neptune orbits three times. These Kuiper belt objects, named **plutinos**, formed in the outer solar nebula. But how did they get caught in resonances with Neptune? Recall from Chapter 12 that models of the formation of the planets suggest that Uranus and Neptune may have formed closer to the Sun, and sometime later gravitational interactions among the Jovian planets could have gradually shifted Uranus and Neptune outward. As Neptune migrated outward, its orbital resonances could have swept up small objects like a strange kind of snowplow. The plutinos are caught in the 3:2 resonance, and other

Kuiper belt objects are caught in other resonances. This appears to support the models that predict that Uranus and Neptune migrated outward.

The migration of the outer planets would have dramatically upset the motion of some of these Kuiper belt objects, and some may have been thrown inward where they could interact with the Jovian planets. Some of those objects may have been captured as moons, and astronomers wonder if moons such as Neptune's Triton started life as Kuiper belt objects. Other objects may have impacted bodies in the inner solar system and caused the late heavy bombardment episode that's especially evident on the surface of Earth's moon. The small frozen worlds on the fringes of the solar system hold clues to the formation of Earth and the other planets 4.6 billion years ago.

Ceres

Ceres, the only dwarf planet not found in the Kuiper belt, resides in the main asteroid belt between Mars and Jupiter. By far the largest asteroid, Ceres contains about a third of the total mass of this belt of rocky bodies. Giuseppe Piazzi discovered Ceres on the first day of the nineteenth century: January 1, 1801. A day on Ceres lasts just over nine hours but its orbital period is 4.6 years. It has an equatorial radius of about 490 km, but a mass of just 1.3 percent of Earth's moon; so its density is about 2 g/cm^3, the same as that of Pluto and Charon. With this density it must have an icy mantle, maybe as thick as 100 km, surrounding a rocky core. Cereian topography is largely unknown despite recent attempts by both the Hubble Space Telescope and the Keck telescope that have revealed several bright and dark but unresolved surface features. The darks areas are presumed to be craters. Recently, the Herschel space telescope discovered that Ceres has a tenuous atmosphere fed by water vapour due either to sublimation of surface water ice or to cryovolcanic mechanisms. We will know more about Ceres soon, as NASA's *Dawn* spacecraft is scheduled to arrive there in early 2015, when it will begin orbiting Ceres to examine its shape and elemental composition.

Other Dwarf Planets

The remaining three dwarf planets recognized by the IAU are Eris,

Haumea, and Makemake. Other candidates are known to exist (Sedna, Quaoar, and Orcus, for example) but have yet to be confirmed by the IAU. What this indicates is that the Kuiper belt may be teeming with objects massive enough to be in hydrostatic equilibrium and therefore largely spherical. It is, however, unlikely that they would outnumber the countless small, irregularly shaped bodies that constitute the Kuiper belt.

Eris was discovered in January 2005 by a team led by Mike Brown. Because of its size—initially determined to be somewhat larger than Pluto—the astronomical community considered Eris to be the tenth planet. However, it soon became clear that other objects existed of roughly the same size, and so a controversy over planetary status grew. The IAU quickly organized an investigation and, in August 2006, approved the now-famous resolution reducing the number of classical planets to eight and instituting the dwarf planet category. In a way, it was the discovery of Eris that led to Pluto's reduced status as a dwarf planet. The orbit of Eris is highly eccentric, having an aphelion distance of almost 100 AU and a perihelion distance of just under 40 AU—resulting in an eccentricity of 0.44 (Pluto's is 0.25) and an inclination of 43.9°. Its orbital period is 557 years. Eris has one known moon, Dysnomia.

Haumea and Makemake have similar orbital characteristics, with periods around 300 years and eccentricities of about 0.2. Haumea has an unusual ellipsoidal shape, with a major axis about twice as long as its minor axis (Figure 14.15). This shape may have resulted from a giant collision with another trans-Neptunian object,

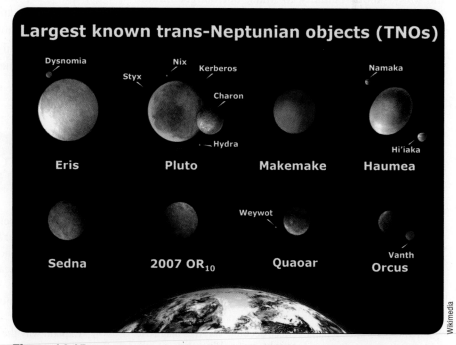

Figure 14.15 Largest known trans-Neptunian objects (TNOs).

which left Haumea as the largest remaining object along with its two captured moons. Makemake is distinctly spherical, with no known moons. It is currently 52.3 AU from the Sun and nearing its aphelion position. In spite of this distance, it is the second brightest Kuiper Belt Object (visually) after Pluto. Both the Spitzer Space Telescope and the Herschel space telescope have been used to determine that Makemake has an absolute visual magnitude of –0.44 that, when combined with its estimated diameter of about 1500 km and high albedo, suggests a surface temperature of about 35 K: bright but cold.

The Big Picture

What Are We? Trapped

The farthest anyone has been from Earth is the Moon. We have sent robotic spacecraft to visit most of the larger worlds in our solar system, and we have found them strange and wonderful places, but no human has ever set foot on any of them. We are trapped on Earth.

We lack the technology to leave Earth. Getting away from Earth's gravitational field is difficult and calls for very large rockets. America built such rockets in the 1960s and early 1970s. They could send astronauts to the Moon, but such rockets no longer exist. The best technology today can carry astronauts just a few hundred kilometres above Earth's surface to orbit above the atmosphere. The USA, Japan, India, and other nations are considering sending humans back to the Moon and eventually to Mars, but budget limitations have delayed specific plans. Does Earth's civilization have the resources to build spacecraft capable of carrying human explorers to other worlds? We'll have to wait and see.

Furthermore, we Earthlings have evolved to fit the environment on Earth. None of the planets or moons you explored in this chapter would welcome you. Lack of air, and extreme heat or cold, are obvious problems, but also Earthlings have evolved to live with Earth's gravity. Astronauts in space for just a few weeks suffer biomedical problems because they are no longer in Earth's gravity. Living in a colony on Mars or the Moon might raise similar problems. Just getting to the outer planets would take decades of space travel; living for years in a colony on one of the Jovian moons under low gravity and exposed to the planet's radiation belts may be beyond the capability of the human body. We may be trapped on Earth not because we lack large enough rockets but because we need Earth's protection.

It seems likely that we need Earth more than it needs us. The human race is changing the world we live on at a startling pace, and some of those changes could make Earth less hospitable to human life. All of our exploring of unearthly worlds serves to remind us of the nurturing beauty of our home planet.

Review and Discussion Questions

Review Questions

1. Why is Jupiter so much richer in hydrogen and helium than Earth?
2. How can Jupiter have a liquid interior and not have a definite liquid surface?
3. How does the dynamo effect account for the magnetic fields of Jupiter, Saturn, Uranus, and Neptune?
4. Why are the belts and zones on Saturn less distinct than those on Jupiter?
5. Why do astronomers conclude that none of the Jovian planets' rings can be left over from the formation of the planets?
6. How can a moon produce a gap in a planetary ring system?
7. Explain why the amount of geological activity on Jupiter's moons varies with distance from the planet.

8. What makes Saturn's F ring and the rings of Uranus and Neptune so narrow?

9. Why is the atmospheric activity of Uranus less than that of Saturn and Neptune?

10. Why do astronomers suspect that Saturn's moon Enceladus is geologically active?

11. What are seasons like on Uranus?

12. Why are Uranus and Neptune respectively green-blue and blue?

13. What evidence is there that Neptune's moon Triton has been geologically active recently?

14. How do astronomers account for the origin of Pluto and the plutinos?

15. What evidence indicates that catastrophic impacts have occurred in the solar system's past?

16. **How Do We Know?** Why would you expect research in archaeology to be less well funded than research in chemistry?

Discussion Questions

1. Some astronomers argue that Jupiter and Saturn are unusual, while other astronomers argue that all planetary systems should contain one or two such giant planets. What do you think? Support your argument with evidence.

2. Why don't the Terrestrial planets have rings? If you were to search for a ring among the Terrestrial planets, where would you look first?

Learning to Look

1. This photo shows a segment of the surface of Jupiter's moon Callisto. Why is the surface mostly dark? Why are some craters dark and some white? What does this image tell you about the history of Callisto?

NASA/JPL/University of Arizona

2. The *Cassini* spacecraft recorded this photo of Saturn's A ring and Encke's division. What do you see in this photo that tells you about processes that confine and shape planetary rings?

NASA/JPL/Space Science Institute

3. Two images are shown here of Uranus's northern hemisphere: one as it would look to the eye, and the other through a red filter that enhances methane clouds. What do the atmospheric features tell you about circulation on Uranus?

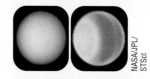

NASA/JPL/STScI

15
Life on Other Worlds

CHAPTER OUTLINE

GUIDEPOST

Astronomy is the study not only of the physical universe but also of your role as a living being in the evolution of the universe. Everything you have learned so far from this book has been preparation for this final chapter.

As you read this chapter, you will encounter four important questions:

- **What is life?**
- **How did life originate on Earth?**
- **Does life exist on other worlds?**
- **Can humans communicate with intelligent beings on other worlds?**

You won't get more than the beginnings of answers to those questions here, but often in science asking a question is more important than getting an immediate answer.

You have explored the universe from the phases of the Moon to the big bang, from the origin of Earth to the death of the Sun. Astronomy is meaningful, not just because it is about the universe but because it is also about you. Now that you know astronomy, you can see yourself and your world in a different way. Astronomy has changed you.

As a living thing, you have been promoted from darkness. The atoms of carbon, oxygen, and other heavy elements that are necessary components of your body did not exist at the beginning of the universe but were cooked up by successive generations of stars. The elements from which you are made are common everywhere in the observable universe, so it is possible that life began on other worlds and evolved to intelligence there as well. If so, perhaps those other civilizations will be detected from Earth. Future astronomers may discover distant alien species completely different from

The universe is a pretty big place. If it's just us, seems like an awful waste of space.

Carl Sagan,
Astronomer and author of Contact

astrobiology The study of the origin and evolution of life on Earth and the possibility of life on other worlds.

any life on Earth (see **How Do We Know? 15.1**). Your goal in this chapter is to try to understand truly intriguing puzzles—the origin and evolution of life on Earth and what that reveals about the possibility of life on other worlds, a field of study named **astrobiology**.

organism extracts energy from the surroundings, maintains itself, modifies the surroundings to foster its own survival and reproduction, and evolves into higher complexity and better adaptation to environment.

One very important observation is that all living things on Earth, no matter how apparently different, share certain characteristics in how they perform the processes of life.

15.1 The Nature of Life

What is life? Philosophers have struggled with this question for thousands of years, and it cannot be answered in a single chapter. A general definition of what living things do and how they are distinguished from non-living things could be as follows: Life is a *process* by which an

The Physical Basis of Life

The physical basis of life on Earth is the element carbon. Because of the way carbon atoms bond to each other and to other atoms, they can form long, complex, stable chains that are capable of storing and transmitting information. A large amount of information of some sort is necessary to maintain the forms and control the functions of living things.

HOW DO WE KNOW? 15.1

The Nature of Scientific Explanation

Must science and religion be in conflict? Science is a way of understanding the world around you, and at the heart of that understanding are explanations that science gives for natural phenomena. Whether you call these explanations stories, histories, hypotheses, or theories, they are attempts to describe how nature works based on evidence and intellectual honesty. While you may take these explanations as factual truth, you can understand that they are not the only explanations that describe the universe.

A separate class of explanations involves religion. For example, the Old Testament description of creation does not fit well with scientific observations, but it is a way of adding "who" and "why" to the scientific "how" and "when." Religious explanations are based partly on faith rather than on strict rules of logic and evidence, and it is wrong to demand that they follow the same rules as scientific explanations. In the same way, it is wrong to demand

that scientific explanations take into account religious beliefs. The so-called conflict between science and religion arises when people fail to recognize that science and religion are different ways of knowing about the universe.

Scientific explanations are quite compelling because science has been

Fair Use

Galileo's telescope gave him a new way to know about the universe.

so successful at producing technological innovations that have changed the world we live in. From new vaccines, to digital music players, to telescopes that can observe the most distant galaxies, the products of the scientific process are all around us. Scientific explanations have provided tremendous insights into the workings of nature. Many people are attracted to the suggestion, made by evolutionary biologist Stephen Jay Gould and others, that religious explanations and scientific explanations should be considered as "separate magisteria." In other words, religion and science are devoted to different realms of the mystery of existence.

Science and religion offer differing ways of explaining the universe, but the two ways follow separate rules and cannot be judged by each other's standards. The trial of Galileo can be understood as a conflict between these two ways of knowing.

Carbon may not be crucial to life. Science fiction authors have speculated that silicon could be substituted for carbon because the two elements share some chemical properties, but that seems unlikely because silicon chains are harder to assemble and disassemble than their carbon counterparts and can't be as lengthy. Even stranger life forms have been proposed, based on electromagnetic fields and ionized gas, and none of these possibilities can be ruled out. These hypothetical life forms make for fascinating speculation, but they can't be studied as systematically as the way that life on Earth can. This chapter is concerned with the origin and evolution of life as it is on Earth, based on carbon, not because of lack of imagination but because it is the only form of life about which we know anything.

In order to "build" carbon-based life from inorganic matter, we need several components: the building blocks of membranes; amino acids for making proteins; and constituents of nucleic acids, DNA and RNA, which store information in a genetic code. Various stellar processes have already produced these components and expelled them into interstellar matter. As Carl Sagan explained in his masterpiece book *Cosmos*: "The nitrogen in our DNA, the calcium in our teeth, the iron in our blood, the carbon in our apple pies were made in the interiors of collapsing stars. We are made of star stuff."[1]

Carbon-based life has its mysteries. What makes a lump of carbon-based molecules a living thing? An important part of the answer lies in the transmission of information from one molecule to another.

Information Storage and Duplication

Almost every action performed by a living cell is carried out by the chemicals it manufactures. Cells must store recipes for all these chemicals, use them when they need them, and pass them on to their offspring.

Study **Visualizing Astronomy 15.1, DNA: The Code of Life**, and notice three important points:

1. The chemical recipes of life are stored in each cell as information on DNA molecules, which resemble a ladder with rungs that are composed of chemical bases. The recipe information is expressed by the sequence of ladder rungs, providing instructions that guide chemical reactions within the cell.

2. DNA instructions normally are expressed by being copied into a messenger molecule called RNA,

which causes molecular units called amino acids to become connected into large molecules called proteins. Proteins serve as the cell's basic structural molecules or as enzymes that control chemical reactions.

3. The instructions stored in DNA are genetic information passed along to offspring. The DNA molecule reproduces itself when a cell divides so that each new cell contains a copy of the original information.

To produce viable offspring, a cell must be able to make copies of its DNA. Surprisingly, it is important for the continued existence of all life that not all the copies be exact duplicates.

Modifying the Information

Earth's environment changes continuously. To survive, species must change as their food supply, climate, or home terrain changes. If the information stored in DNA could not change life would quickly go extinct. The process by which life adjusts itself to its changing environment is called **biological evolution**.

When an organism reproduces, its offspring receives a copy of its DNA. Sometimes external effects such as radiation alter the DNA during the parent organism's lifetime, and sometimes mistakes occur in the copying process, so that occasionally the copy is slightly different from the original. Offspring born with random alterations to their DNA are called **mutants**. Most mutations make no difference, but some mutations are fatal, killing the afflicted organisms before they can reproduce. In rare but vitally important cases, a mutation can actually help an organism survive.

These changes produce variation among the members of a species. All of the squirrels in the park may look the same, but they carry a range of genetic variation. Some may have slightly longer tails or faster-growing claws. These variations make almost no difference until the environment changes. For example, if the environment becomes colder, a squirrel with a heavier coat of fur will, on average, survive longer and produce more offspring than its normal contemporaries. Likewise, the offspring that inherit this beneficial variation will also live longer and have more offspring of their own. These differing rates

biological evolution The processes of mutation, variation, and natural selection by which life adjusts itself to its changing environment.

mutant Offspring born with DNA that is altered relative to parental DNA.

[1]Carl Sagan, 1980, *Cosmos*, Random House, page 233.

of survival and reproduction are examples of **natural selection**. Over time, the beneficial variation becomes more common, and a species can evolve until the entire population shares the trait. In this way, natural selection adapts species to their changing environments by selecting, from the huge array of random variations, those that would most benefit the survival of the species.

It is commonly believed that evolution is random, but that is not true. The underlying variation within species is random, but natural selection is not random because progressive changes in a species are directed by changes in the environment.

15.2 Life in the Universe

It is obvious that the 4.5 billion chemical bases that make up human DNA did not just come together in the right order by chance. The key to understanding the origin of life lies in the processes of evolution. The complex interplay of environmental factors with the DNA of generation after generation of organisms drove some life forms to become more sophisticated over time, until they became the unique and specialized creatures on Earth today.

This means that life on Earth could have begun very simply, even in as simple a form as carbon-chain molecules that can copy themselves. Of course, this is a hypothesis for which you can seek evidence. What evidence exists regarding the origin of life on Earth?

natural selection The process by which the best genetic traits are preserved and accumulated, allowing the fittest organisms and species to survive and proliferate.

stromatolite A layered formation caused by mats of algae or bacteria combined with sediments.

chemical evolution The chemical process that led to the growth of complex molecules on primitive Earth. This did not involve the reproduction of exact molecules.

primordial soup The rich solution of organic molecules in Earth's first oceans.

The Origin of Life on Earth

All the oldest fossils are the remains of sea creatures, and this indicates that life began in the sea. However, identifying the oldest fossils is not easy. Fossils billions of years old are difficult to recognize because the earliest living things contained no easily preserved hard parts like bones or shells, and because the individual organisms were microscopic. Some rocks from Western Australia that are more than 3.4 billion

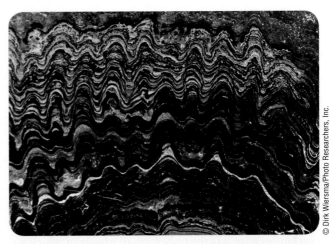

Figure 15.1 Cross-section of layers in a fossilized stromatolite. Layers are made of mineralized mats of bacteria covered repeatedly by sediment. Fossilized stromatolites have been found within rocks more than 3.4 billion years. This sample measures 300 millimetres across.

© Dirk Wiersma/Photo Researchers, Inc.

years old contain features that experts identify as fossil **stromatolites**: mineralized layers built up from deposits of single-celled organisms that lived in shallow water long ago (Figure 15.1). The evidence, though scarce, indicates that simple organisms lived in Earth's oceans 3.4 billion or more years ago, less than 1.2 billion years after Earth formed. Where did these simple organisms come from?

Greek philosophers Democritus, Plato, and Aristotle suggested that life appeared spontaneously out of non-life wherever conditions were appropriate, and that view persisted for centuries. Experiments aiming to synthesize organic molecules flourished in 18th and 19th centuries, and novel ideas arose. Charles Darwin wrote in 1871 about the possibility that life was conceived in a "warm little pond" from inorganic matter such as ammonia, phosphoric salts, light, heat, electricity. In the 1920s, Russian chemist Alexander Oparin and English geneticist John Haldane independently suggested the concept of **chemical evolution** in the early Earth's atmosphere as the basis for formation of life. In *Origin of Life* published in 1924, Oparin described the carbon found in hot stellar atmospheres as a component of hydrocarbons on Earth. He speculated that in waters of the primitive ocean, these substances formed more complex compounds such as proteins, improved structure, and "were finally transformed into primary living beings—the forebears of all life on Earth." Haldane called the early oceans and organic compounds the *prebiotic soup*: what today we call the **primordial soup**. Experimental confirmation of the theory of chemical evolution didn't arrive until the 1950s.

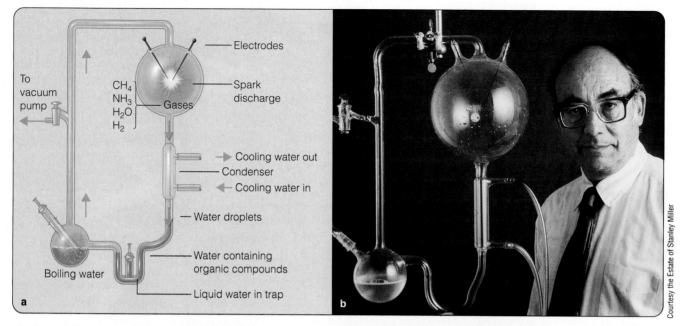

Figure 15.2 (a) The Miller-Urey experiment circulated gases through water in the presence of an electric arc. This simulation of primitive conditions on Earth produced many complex organic molecules, including amino acids, the building blocks of proteins. (b) Stanley Miller with the apparatus.

An important experiment performed by Stanley Miller and Harold Urey in 1952 sought to recreate the conditions in which life on Earth began. The **Miller-Urey experiment** consisted of a sterile, sealed, glass container holding water, hydrogen, ammonia, and methane. An electric arc inside the apparatus created sparks to simulate the effects of lightning in Earth's early atmosphere (Figure 15.2).

Miller and Urey let the experiment run for a week and then analyzed the material inside. They found that the interaction between the electric arc and the simulated atmosphere produced many organic molecules from the raw material of the experiment, including such important building blocks of life as amino acids. When other scientists later ran the experiment using different energy sources, such as hot silica to represent molten lava spilling into the ocean, similar molecules were produced. Even the amount of UV radiation present in sunlight is sufficient to produce complex organic molecules.

According to updated models of the formation of the solar system and Earth (see Chapters 12 and 13), Earth's early atmosphere probably consisted mostly of carbon dioxide, nitrogen, and water vapour instead of the mix of hydrogen, ammonia, and methane assumed by Miller and Urey. When gases corresponding to the newer understanding of the early Earth atmosphere are processed in a Miller apparatus, lower but still significant numbers of organic molecules are created.

The Miller-Urey experiment is important because it shows that complex organic molecules form naturally in a wide variety of circumstances. Lightning, sunlight, and hot lava pouring into the oceans are just some of the energy sources that can naturally rearrange simple common molecules into the complex molecules that make life possible. If you could travel back in time, you would expect to find Earth's first oceans filled with a rich mixture of organic compounds, the primordial soup.

Many of these organic compounds would have been able to link up to form larger molecules. Amino acids, for example, can link together to form proteins by joining ends and releasing a water molecule (Figure 15.3). It was initially thought that this must have occurred in Sun-warmed tidal pools where organic molecules were concentrated by evaporation. However, violent episodes of volcanism and catastrophic meteorite impacts would probably have destroyed complex molecules developing at the surface, so scientists now think that successful linkage of complex molecules might have taken place on the ocean floor, perhaps near the hot springs at mid-ocean rises (see **Visualizing Astronomy 13.1, The Active Earth**, and Figure 15.8).

These complex organic molecules were still not living things. Even though some proteins may have contained hundreds of amino acids, they did not reproduce; rather, they linked and broke apart at random. Because some molecules are more stable than others, and some bond together more easily than others,

Miller-Urey experiment An experiment that attempted to reproduce early Earth conditions and showed how easily amino acids and other organic compounds can form.

1 The key to understanding life is information—the information that guides all of the processes in an organism. In most living things on Earth, that information is stored on a long spiral molecule called **DNA (deoxyribonucleic acid)**.

1a The DNA molecule looks like a spiral ladder with rails made of phosphates and sugars. The rungs of the ladder are made of four chemical bases arranged in pairs. The bases always pair in the same way. That is, base A always pairs with base T, and base G always pairs with base C.

1b Information is coded on the DNA molecule by the order in which the base pairs occur. To read that code, molecular biologists have to "sequence the DNA." That is, they must determine the order in which the base pairs occur along the DNA ladder.

The Four Bases

A — Adenine
C — Cytosine
G — Guanine
T — Thymine

2 DNA automatically combines raw materials to form important chemical compounds. The building blocks of these compounds are relatively simple **amino acids**. Segments of DNA act as templates that guide the amino acids to join together in the correct order to build specific **proteins**, chemical compounds important to the structure and function of organisms. Some proteins called **enzymes** regulate other processes. In this way, DNA recipes regulate the production of the compounds of life.

The traits you inherit from your parents, the chemical processes that animate you, and the structure of your body are all encoded in your DNA. When people say "you have your mother's eyes" they are talking about DNA codes.

Vesna Milosevic-Zdjelar

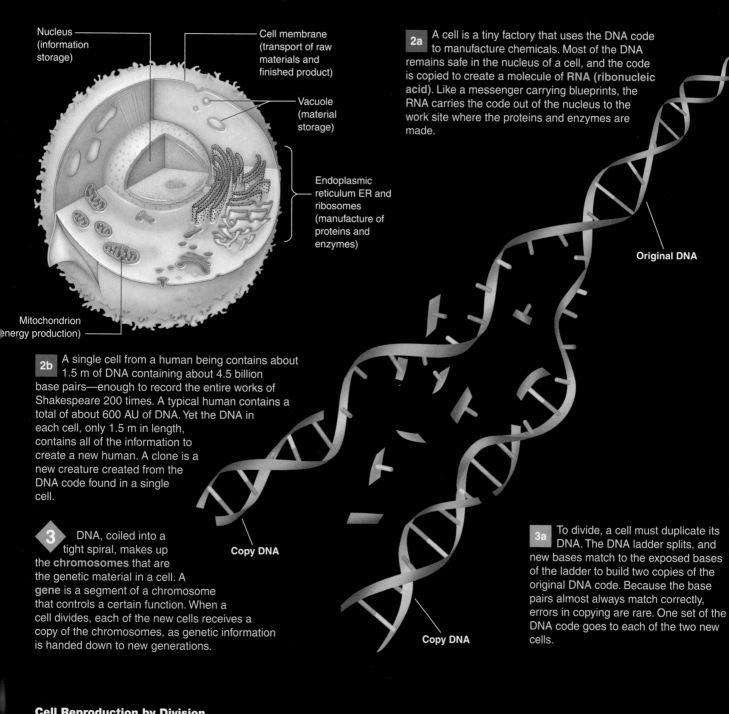

Nucleus
(information
storage)

Cell membrane
(transport of raw
materials and
finished product)

Vacuole
(material
storage)

Endoplasmic
reticulum ER and
ribosomes
(manufacture of
proteins and
enzymes)

Mitochondrion
(energy production)

2a A cell is a tiny factory that uses the DNA code to manufacture chemicals. Most of the DNA remains safe in the nucleus of a cell, and the code is copied to create a molecule of **RNA (ribonucleic acid)**. Like a messenger carrying blueprints, the RNA carries the code out of the nucleus to the work site where the proteins and enzymes are made.

Original DNA

2b A single cell from a human being contains about 1.5 m of DNA containing about 4.5 billion base pairs—enough to record the entire works of Shakespeare 200 times. A typical human contains a total of about 600 AU of DNA. Yet the DNA in each cell, only 1.5 m in length, contains all of the information to create a new human. A clone is a new creature created from the DNA code found in a single cell.

3 DNA, coiled into a tight spiral, makes up the **chromosomes** that are the genetic material in a cell. A **gene** is a segment of a chromosome that controls a certain function. When a cell divides, each of the new cells receives a copy of the chromosomes, as genetic information is handed down to new generations.

Copy DNA

Copy DNA

3a To divide, a cell must duplicate its DNA. The DNA ladder splits, and new bases match to the exposed bases of the ladder to build two copies of the original DNA code. Because the base pairs almost always match correctly, errors in copying are rare. One set of the DNA code goes to each of the two new cells.

Cell Reproduction by Division

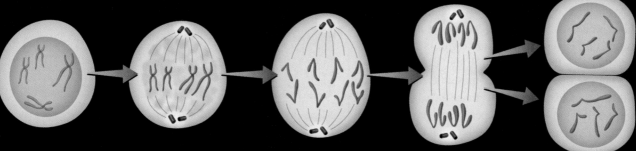

As a cell begins to divide, its DNA duplicates itself.

The duplicated chromosomes move to the middle.

The two sets of chromosomes separate, and . . .

the cell divides to produce . . .

two cells, each containing a full set of the DNA code.

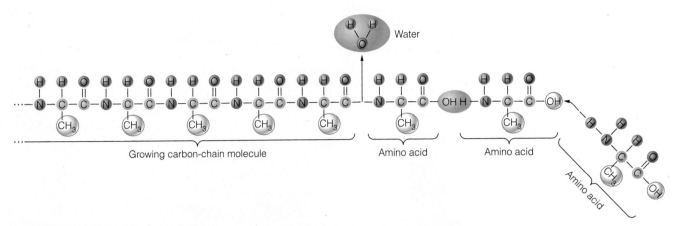

Water

Growing carbon-chain molecule   Amino acid   Amino acid   Amino acid

Figure 15.3 Amino acids can link together by releasing a water molecule to form long carbon-chain protein molecules. The amino acid in this hypothetical example is alanine, one of the simplest.

scientists hypothesize that a process of chemical evolution eventually concentrated the various smaller molecules into the most stable, larger forms. Eventually, according to this hypothesis, somewhere in the oceans, after sufficient time, a molecule formed that could copy itself. At that point, the chemical evolution of molecules became the biological evolution of living things.

The oldest fossils show that only 1.2 billion years passed from the formation of Earth to the emergence of living cells—an uncomfortably short period of time, since the nucleus in the cell required 2 billion years to form. An alternate theory for the origin of life, called panspermia (*pan* in Greek means "all" and *sperma* means "seed"), holds that molecules capable of reproducing may have arrived here from space. Radio astronomers have found a wide variety of organic molecules in the interstellar medium, and similar compounds have been found inside meteorites, such as the Murchison meteorite (Figure 15.4). The Miller-Urey experiment has shown how easy it is to create organic molecules in an environment with the right amount of hydrogen, so it is not surprising to find them in space.

Whether the first reproducing molecules formed here on Earth or in space, the important thing is that they formed by natural processes. Scientists know enough about these processes to feel confident about them, even though some of the steps remain unknown.

The details of the evolution of the first cells are unknown, but the first reproducing molecule to surround itself with a protective membrane must have gained an important survival advantage. Experiments have shown that microscopic spheres the size of cells containing organic molecules form relatively easily in water, so the evolution of cell-like structures is not surprising (see Figure 15.5).

The first cells must have been simple, single-celled organisms much like modern bacteria. Recall that these kinds of cells have been found preserved in

stromatolites, the mineral formations formed by layers of photosynthetic bacteria and shallow ocean sediments. Stromatolites are found in rocks with radioactive ages of 3.4 billion years, and they still form in some places today. Stromatolites and other photosynthetic organisms began adding oxygen, a product of photosynthesis, to Earth's

Figure 15.4 A piece of the Murchison meteorite. This piece of carbonaceous chondrite fell near Murchison, Australia, in 1969. Analysis of the interior of the meteorite reveals the presence of amino acids. Whether the first chemical building blocks of life on Earth originated in space is a matter of debate, but the amino acids found in meteorites illustrate how commonly amino acids and other complex organic molecules occur in the universe, even in the absence of living things.

early atmosphere (Figure 15.6). An oxygen abundance of only 0.1 percent would have created an ozone screen, protecting organisms from the Sun's ultraviolet radiation and later allowing life to colonize the land.

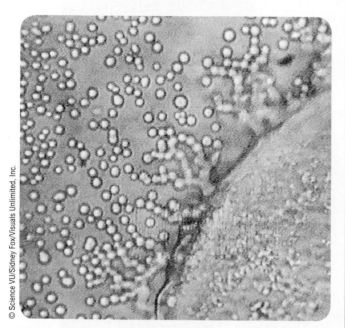

Figure 15.5 Single amino acids can be assembled into long protein-like molecules. When such material cools in water, it can form microspheres: microscopic spheres with double-layered boundaries similar to cell membranes. Microspheres may have been an intermediate stage in the evolution of life from complex molecules to living cells that have molecules capable of reproducing genetic information.

Over the course of eons, the natural processes of evolution gave rise to stunningly complex **multicellular** life forms with widely differing ways of life. A common misconception is that life is too complex to have evolved from such simple beginnings. However, it was possible because small variations accumulate, even though that accumulation requires huge amounts of time.

multicellular An organism composed of more than one cell.

Cambrian explosion A geologically brief period about 540 million years ago during which fossil evidence indicates life on Earth became complex and diverse. Cambrian rocks contain the oldest easily identifiable fossils.

The Cosmic Calendar Revisited: The Evolution of Life

Life has existed on Earth for at least 3.4 billion years, but there is no evidence of anything more than simple organisms until about 540 million years ago, when life suddenly branched into a wide variety of complex forms. This sudden increase in complexity is known as the **Cambrian explosion**, and it marks the beginning of the Cambrian period.

When the entire history of Earth is represented on a scale diagram as shown at the left of Figure 15.7, the Cambrian explosion appears near the top of the column. The period when most of today's familiar animals

Figure 15.6 Artist's concept of a Precambrian tidal scene on the young Earth, with mound-shaped stromatolites in the foreground.

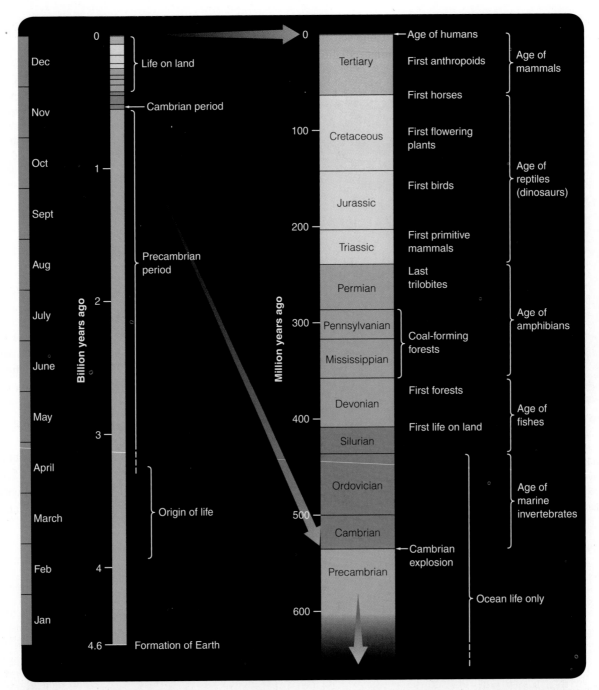

Figure 15.7 Complex life has developed on Earth only recently. If the entire history of Earth were represented in a timeline (left), you have to examine the end of the line closely to see details such as life leaving the oceans and dinosaurs appearing. The age of humans would still be only a thin line at the top of the diagram. If the history of Earth were a year-long videotape, humans would not appear until the last minutes of December 31.

emerged, including fishes, amphibians, reptiles, birds, and mammals, is crammed into the very top of the diagram, above the Cambrian explosion.

When this portion of the diagram is magnified, as shown on the right side of Figure 15.7, you can have a better idea of when these events occurred in the history of life. Humanoid creatures have walked the Earth for about 4 million years. This is a long time in terms of the standard human lifetime, but it makes only a narrow red line at the top of the diagram, and all of recorded history is represented as a microscopically thin line at the very top of the column.

To understand just how thin that line is in terms of the origin of the universe, look back to Figure 1.2, The Cosmic Year: A Timeline, in Chapter 1. Also, to gain perspective on the time scale of the rise of life, imagine the history of Earth as a year-long video. Figure 15.7 shows the

4.6 billion-year history of Earth as if compressed into a year-long video, and you began watching on January 1. According to this timeline, there are no signs of life until March or early April, and the slow evolution of the first simple forms takes the next six or seven months. Suddenly, in mid-November, you would see complex organisms of the Cambrian explosion.

Although no life of any kind appeared on land until November 28, once it appeared, it diversified quickly. By December 12 the dinosaurs were walking the continents, and by December 28th they were gone, and mammals and birds were on the rise. The first humanoid forms might have appeared by suppertime on New Year's Eve, and by late evening humans were making the first stone tools. Suddenly, things began to happen at lightning speed.

A tremendous amount of time was needed for the first simple living organisms to evolve in the oceans. But as life became more complex and as the problems of how

Canadian Space Agency

Canada has had an active space program for more than 40 years. In 1962, with the launch of *Alouette 1*, Canada became the third country after the USA and the former USSR to put a satellite in space, and a decade later it became the first country to establish a geostationary communication satellite network. These early successes as well as later projects and collaborations with NASA and other institutions led to the establishment of the Canadian Space Agency in 1989. The Agency oversees the Canadian space program and promotes the peaceful exploration and development of space through science. It partners with academic institutions, industry, and international organizations such as NASA on numerous projects related to space science and space exploration. Canadian astronauts have flown on missions aboard NASA's space shuttles as well as the Russian *Soyuz* spacecraft. One of Canada's main contributions to space technology is the Shuttle Remote Manipulator System, or Canadarm, a robotic arm deployed on the space shuttles to manoeuvre payloads into position in orbit. A second arm, called Canadarm 2, was used to assemble the International Space Station in orbit and is now used for general operations and maintenance on the space station. In 2012, astronaut Chris Hadfield became the first Canadian commander of the International Space Station. While on board the ISS, he shared his experiences via photos, videos, and tweets. His scientific demos, commentary, and his musical performances in space quickly made him one of the most popular astronauts of all time. By 2013, his Twitter account had over 1 million followers. He has received numerous awards after his return to Earth, and he continues to promote science and space exploration through books, lectures, and social media.

Astronaut Chris Hadfield

Canadian Space Agency

to reproduce, how to take energy efficiently from the environment, and how to move around were solved, new forms arose ever more quickly. Problems such as what to eat, where to live, and how to raise offspring were solved in different ways by different organisms, and this led to the diversity of life we see today.

Human intelligence—which appears to set humans apart from other animals—may have evolved as a unique solution to a problem that confronted our ancient ancestors. Because a smart animal can better escape predators, outwit its prey, and feed and shelter itself and its offspring, under certain conditions, evolution likely selected for intelligence. So you might ask, could intelligent life arise on other worlds? To try to answer this question, you need to estimate the chances of any type of life arising on other worlds and then assess the likelihood of that life developing intelligence.

Life in Our Solar System

Could there be carbon-based life elsewhere in our solar system? Liquid water seems to be a requirement of carbon-based life; it is necessary for vital chemical reactions and also as a medium to transport nutrients and wastes. It is not surprising that life developed in Earth's oceans and stayed there for billions of years before emerging in forms that could colonize the land.

Scientists are in agreement that any world harbouring living things must have significant quantities of some type of liquid. Water is a cosmically abundant substance. The most common molecule in the interstellar space is molecular hydrogen, and the next common is the water molecule. Several important properties of water that benefit life set it apart from other common molecules that exist in a liquid state at the temperatures on planetary surfaces. Water is peculiar solvent; it bonds with a variety of dissolved substances, fostering chemical combinations that would not occur in any other solvent. It also has a higher heat capacity than most other substances, which means it requires a higher amount of heat to raise its temperature by one degree; therefore, it has stable temperature over time. As a major component of living things, it reduces fluctuations in temperature, preventing excessive heating and cooling. Because it occurs as a liquid in a larger temperature range than most other substances, it prevents organisms from either freezing or boiling within a span of 100 degrees.

Many worlds in the solar system can be eliminated immediately as hosts for life because liquid water is not possible there. The Moon and Mercury are airless, and water would boil away into space immediately. Venus has traces of water vapour in its atmosphere, but it is too hot for liquid water to exist on the surface. The Jovian planets have deep

atmospheres, and at a certain level water condenses into liquid droplets. However, it seems unlikely that life could originate there as the Jovian planets do not have solid surfaces (see Chapter 14). Isolated water droplets could never mingle to mimic the rich primordial oceans of Earth, where organic molecules first grew and interacted. Additionally, powerful currents in the gas giants' atmospheres would quickly carry any of the reproducing molecules that did form there down into inhospitably hot regions of the atmosphere.

As you learned in Chapter 14, at least one of the Jovian satellites could potentially support life. Jupiter's moon Europa appears to have a liquid-water ocean below its icy crust (Figure 14.3), and minerals dissolved in the water could provide a source of raw material for chemical evolution. Europa's ocean is kept warm and liquid now by tidal heating. There also may be liquid water layers under the surfaces of Ganymede and Callisto. The idea of searching for potential life on Europa was prompted by the discovery in 1997 of volcanic vents, called *black smokers*, on the bottom of the Pacific ocean near the Galapagos Islands (see Figure 15.8). Mineral-rich water emerges from these

Figure 15.8 (a) A view of the "black smoker" hydrothermal vent captured by the deep-sea submarine. (b) Hot, black water is a source of chemicals that sustain the tubeworms and other organisms that thrive in this habitat without sunlight.

hydrothermal vents more than 3 km under the surface of the ocean. Life around the vents is abundant. About 350 new species were discovered living in the darkness and using the chemical energy of the vents instead of sunlight. Possibly, this mechanism could sustain life in Europa's ocean, under several kilometres of ice cover.

Observations of water venting from the south-polar region of one of Saturn's moons show that the moon Enceladus has liquid salty water below its crust (Figure 14.6). It is possible that life could exist in that water, but the moon is very small and has been warmed by tidal heating that may operate only occasionally. Enceladus may not have had enough liquid water for the length of time considered necessary for the rise of life.

Saturn's largest moon Titan is rich in organic molecules. Recall from Chapter 14 that sunlight converts the methane in Titan's atmosphere into organic smog particles that settle to the surface. The chemistry of any life that could have evolved from those molecules and survived in Titan's lakes of methane is unknown. It is fascinating to consider possibilities, but Titan's extremely low temperature of −180°C could make chemical reactions so slow that life processes would be unlikely.

Mars is the most likely place for life to exist in the solar system because, as you learned in Chapter 13, there is a great deal of evidence that liquid water once flowed on its surface. Even so, results from searches for signs of life on Mars are not encouraging. The robotic spacecrafts *Viking 1* and *Viking 2* landed on Mars in 1976 and tested soil samples for living organisms. Some of the tests had puzzling semi-positive results that scientists hypothesize were caused by non-biological chemical reactions in the soil. There is no clear evidence of life or even of organic molecules in the Martian soil.

In 1996, major stories in the news described chemical and physical traces of life on Mars that were discovered inside a Martian meteorite found in Antarctica (Figure 15.9). Scientists were excited by the announcement,

Figure 15.9 (a) Meteorite ALH 84001 is one of a dozen meteorites known to have originated on Mars. Its name means this meteorite was the first one found in 1984 near Antarctica's Allan Hills. (b) A research group studying ALH 84001 claimed that the meteorite contains chemical and physical traces of ancient life on Mars, including what appear to be fossils of microscopic organisms. This evidence has not been confirmed, and the claim continues to be tested and debated. (c) A map of Mars with colours representing the levels of methane concentration in the atmosphere measured by spectrographs on Earth-based telescopes. Methane is most abundant in locations other than volcanic regions, indicating the methane may be produced biologically.

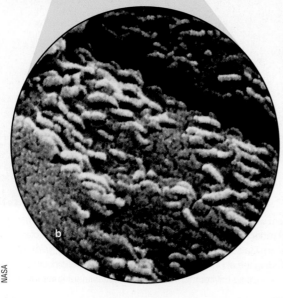

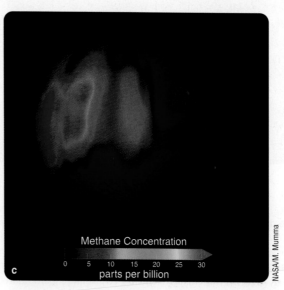

Methane Concentration

0   5   10   15   20   25   30
parts per billion

and immediately began testing the evidence. Their results suggest that the unusual chemical signatures in the rock may have formed by processes that did not involve life. Tiny features in the rock that were originally thought to be fossils of ancient Martian microorganisms could be non-biological mineral formations. This is the only direct evidence yet found regarding potential life on Mars, but it remains highly controversial. Conclusive evidence of life on Mars may have to wait until a geologist from Earth can scramble down dry Martian streambeds and crack open rocks looking for fossils.

There is no strong evidence for the existence of life elsewhere in the solar system. So your search will have to take you to distant planetary systems.

Life in Other Planetary Systems

Could life exist in other planetary systems? As a first step toward answering this question, try to identify the kinds of stars most likely to have stable planetary systems where life could evolve. You already know there are many different kinds of stars and many of these stars have planetary systems.

For a planet to be a suitable home for living things, it must be in a stable orbit around its sun. That is simple in a planetary system like our own, but most planet orbits in binary star systems are unstable, unless the component stars are very close together or very far apart. For binary systems with stars separated by distances of a few AU, astronomers can calculate that the planets should eventually be swallowed up by one of the stars or ejected from the system. Half the stars in the galaxy are members of binary systems, and many of them are unlikely to support life on planets.

Moreover, just because a star is single does not necessarily make it a good candidate for sustaining life. Earth required between 0.5 and 1 billion years to produce the first cells and 4.6 billion years for intelligence to emerge. Massive stars that live only a few million years do not meet this criterion. If the history of life on Earth is at all representative, the stars more massive and luminous than about spectral type F5 are too short-lived for complex life to develop. Main-sequence stars of types G and K, and possibly some of the M stars, are the best candidates.

The temperature of a planet is also important, and that depends on the type of star it orbits and its distance from the star. Astronomers have defined a **habitable zone** around a star as a region within which planets have temperatures that permit the existence of liquid water (Figure 15.10). The Sun's habitable zone extends from

Figure 15.10 (a) Stellar habitable zone—the zone within a stellar system where water can exist in a liquid state. In this diagram, habitable zones of various stars are shown (coloured green): The hotter the star, the wider and farther away the habitable zone is. In the solar system, Venus and Earth are within habitable zone, and Mars is on the outer edge. (b) Galactic habitable zone—the zone within the galaxy where emergence of life would be possible. Various factors are in play here, including the abundance of heavier elements—deficient in the outer part of the galaxy—and the rate of major catastrophes such as supernovae—too violent an environment close to the galactic centre. Coloured green is habitable zone in Milky Way Galaxy.

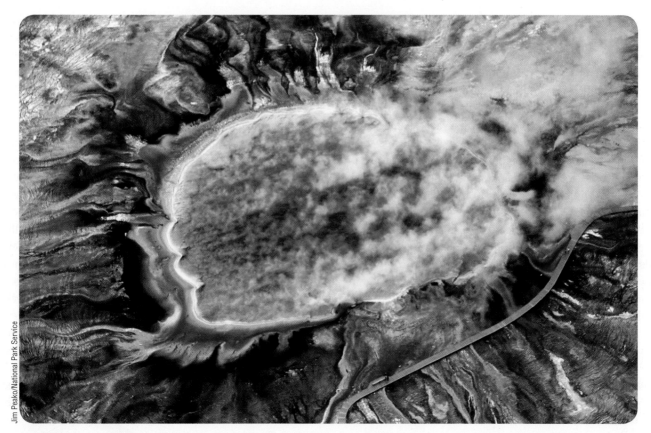

Figure 15.11 Organisms can live in environments that humans consider impossibly hostile. Colonies of thermophilic (heat-loving), single-celled organisms thrive around the edge of Yellowstone National Park's Grand Prismatic Spring at temperatures up to 72°C, producing the green pigments. The blue water in the centre of the pool is too hot even for thermophiles.

around the orbit of Venus to the orbit of Mars, with Earth right in the middle. A low-luminosity star has a small habitable zone, and a high-luminosity star has a large one. From 2009 to date, the *Kepler* mission space telescope discovered numerous Earth-like planets, many of which are orbiting within habitable zones around their stars (see Figure 12.18).

Scientists are finding life on Earth in places previously judged inhospitable, such as the bottoms of ice-covered lakes in Antarctica and far underground inside solid rock. Life has also been found in boiling hot springs with highly acidic water (Figure 15.11) and on cooling rods of nuclear reactors. As a result, it is difficult for scientists to pin down a range of environments and state with certainty that life cannot exist outside those conditions. You should also note that three of the environments listed as possible havens for life—Europa, Titan, and Enceladus—are in the outer solar system and lie far outside the Sun's conventional habitable zone. Stable planets inside the habitable zones of long-lived stars are the places where life seems most likely. However, given the tenacity and resilience of Earth's life forms, there might be other, seemingly inhospitable, places in the universe where life exists.

15.3 Intelligent Life in the Universe

For now, visiting extrasolar planets is impossible. Nevertheless, if other civilizations exist, humans might be able to communicate with them. Nature puts restrictions on such conversations. However, the main question is, What is the life expectancy of extraterrestrial civilizations?

Travel between the Stars

The distances between stars are almost incomprehensible. The space shuttle would take about 150 000 years to reach the nearest star. The obvious way to overcome these huge distances is with tremendously fast spaceships, but even the closest stars are many light-years away.

Nothing can exceed the speed of light, and accelerating a spaceship close to the speed of light would take a huge amount of energy. Even if you travelled more slowly, your rocket would require a massive amount of fuel. If you were piloting a spaceship with the mass of 100 tons (the size of a yacht) to the nearest star 4 ly away, and you wanted to travel at half the speed of light so as to arrive in eight years, the trip would require 400 times as much energy as Canada consumes in a year.

These limitations make it difficult not only for humans to leave the solar system, but also for aliens to visit Earth. Reputable scientists have studied "unidentified flying objects" (UFOs) and have never found any evidence that Earth is being visited or has ever been visited by aliens (see **How Do We Know? 15.2**). However, communication by radio across interstellar distances takes relatively little energy.

Radio Communication

Nature puts restrictions on travel through space, and it also restricts astronomers' ability to communicate with distant civilizations by radio. One restriction is due to basic physics. Radio signals are electromagnetic waves and travel at the speed of light. Due to the distances between the stars, the speed of radio waves would severely limit astronomers' ability to carry on normal conversations with distant civilizations. Decades could elapse between asking a question and getting an answer.

At the very start of 20th century, 50 years before the invention of a radio telescope, Nikola Tesla, the discoverer of radio and remote control, suggested that scientists could use a wireless electrical transmission system to receive and send radio waves and exchange messages with extraterrestrials. With the construction of the first radio telescopes in the 1950s, radio-astronomers started to conduct searches with the aim to detect any messages from potential extraterrestrial civilizations encoded in the frequency or amplitude of radio waves. This field of study is known as **SETI**, search for extraterrestrial intelligence. The first such project, Ozma (named after the queen of the Land of Oz from children stories), was organized and conducted by Frank Drake in 1960. His team analyzed radio waves from the direction of two nearby Sunlike stars. At the same time,

HOW DO WE KNOW? 15.2

UFOs and Space Aliens

If you conclude that there is likely to be life on other worlds, you might be tempted to use UFO sightings as evidence to test your hypothesis. Scientists don't do this for two reasons.

First, the reputation of UFO sightings and alien encounters does not inspire confidence that these data are reliable. Most people hear of such events in grocery store tabloids, daytime talk shows, or sensational "specials" on viewer-hungry cable networks. You should take note of the low reputation of the media that report UFOs and space aliens. Most of these reports, like the reports that Elvis is alive and well, are simply made up for the sake of sensation, and you cannot use them as reliable evidence.

Second, the few UFO sightings that are not made up do not survive

Flying saucers from space are fun to think about, but there is no evidence that they are real.

careful examination. Most are mistakes and unintentional misinterpretations of natural events or human-made objects, committed by honest people. Over many decades, experts have studied these incidents and found none that are convincing. In short, despite false claims to the contrary on TV shows, there is no dependable evidence that Earth has ever been visited by aliens.

That's too bad. A confirmed visit by intelligent creatures from beyond our solar system would answer many questions. It would be exciting, enlightening, and, like any real adventure, a bit scary. But there is not yet any direct evidence of life on other worlds.

Soviet scientists performed a number of wide-field sky searches with radio antennas in the hope of picking up powerful radio signals. In 1962, Iosif Shklovskii wrote the pioneering book in this field: *Universe, Life, Intelligence*. This book was expanded in collaboration with American astronomer Carl Sagan and published as *Intelligent Life in the Universe* in 1966.

Which channels should astronomers monitor? Wave-lengths longer than 100 cm would get lost in the background noise of the Milky Way Galaxy, while wavelengths shorter than about 1 cm are absorbed in Earth's atmosphere. Between those wavelengths is a radio window that is open for communication. Even this restricted window contains millions of possible radio-frequency bands and is too wide to monitor easily, but astronomers may have found a way to narrow the search. The 21-cm spectral line of neutral hydrogen and the 18-cm line of OH occur within this window (Figure 15.12). The interval between those lines has low background interference and is named the **water hole** because H plus OH yields water. Any civilizations sophisticated enough to do radio astronomy research must know of these lines and might appreciate their significance in the same way Earthlings do.

A group of astronomers led by Frank Drake and Carl Sagan decided in 1974 to broadcast a simple message of greeting toward the globular cluster M13, 26 000 ly away, using the Arecibo radio telescope (Figure 15.13). When the signal arrives 26 000 years in the future, alien astronomers may be able to decode it.

The Arecibo beacon is an anticoded message, meaning that it is intended to be decoded by beings about whom we know nothing except that they build radio telescopes. The message is a string of 1679 pulses and gaps. Pulses represent 1s, and gaps represent 0s (Figure 15.13a). The string can be arranged in only two possible ways: as 23 rows of 73 or as 73 rows of 23. The second arrangement forms a picture containing information about life on Earth (see panel b in Figure 15.13b).

Further interstellar radio messages were transmitted in 1999, 2001, 2003, and 2008 from the Evpatoria Planetary Radar—a radio telescope 70 m in diameter—at the Center for Deep Space Communications in Yevpatoria, Crimea. In addition to the usual function of a radio telescope receiver, this telescope has powerful transmitters that allow electromagnetic beams to be accurately targeted. On October 9, 2008, a high-powered, digital radio signal called A Message from Earth (AMFE) was sent toward Gliese 581 c—a large, terrestrial extrasolar planet orbiting the red dwarf star Gliese 581 and located approximately 20 ly away from Earth. Astronomers chose to send the message to this planet because they believed it may be capable of supporting life. Over a period of four-and-a-half hours, the telescope beamed a signal containing 501 messages (photos, drawings, and text messages) translated into binary format. This is the world's first digital time capsule with content selected by the public. The signal will reach the planet in early 2029. As of September 12, 2014, the message has travelled 56.05 trillion kilometres, which is 29.5 percent of the total 190 trillion kilometres from Earth to the Gliese 581 system. Science consultant for the transmission, Dr. Alexander Zaitsev—a radio astronomer and the SETI coordinator for Russia—suggests that the only way alien civilizations might find us is if we specifically make ourselves known.

Short-wave radio signals, such as TV and FM, have been leaking into space for about the last 50 years. Any civilization within 50 ly could already have detected Earth's civilization. That works both ways: Alien signals, whether intentional messages of friendship or the blather of their equivalent to daytime TV, could be arriving at Earth now. Astronomers all over the world are pointing radio telescopes at the most likely stars and listening for alien civilizations.

All these programs have the same aim—to detect a signal that looks like an intelligent one. For example,

water hole The interval of the radio spectrum between the 21-cm hydrogen emission line and the 18-cm OH emission line; wavelengths likely to be used in the search for extraterrestrial life.

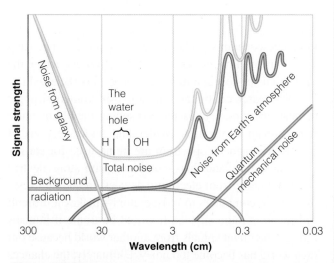

Figure 15.12 Radio noise from various astronomical sources makes it difficult to detect distant signals at wavelengths longer than 100 cm or shorter than 1 cm. In this range, radio emission lines from H atoms and from OH molecules mark a small wavelength range, named the water hole, that may be a likely channel for communication.

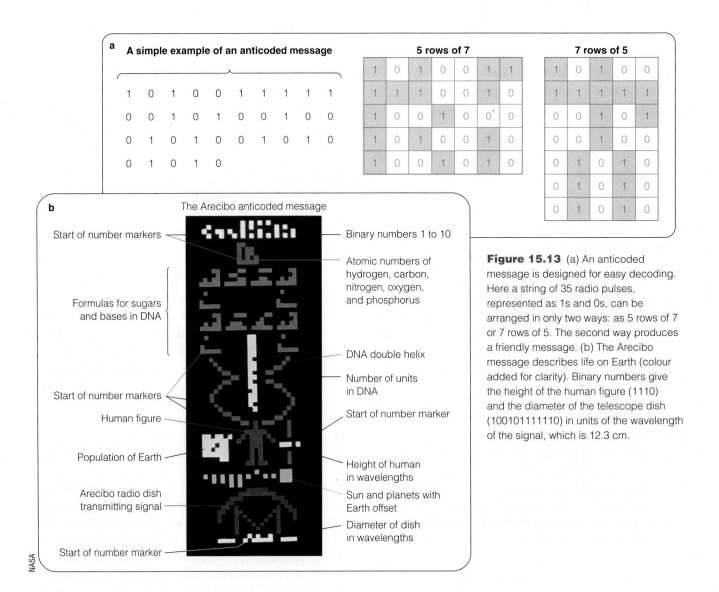

a A simple example of an anticoded message

1	0	1	0	0	1	1	1	1	1
0	0	1	0	1	0	0	1	0	0
0	1	0	1	0	0	1	0	1	0
0	1	0	1	0

5 rows of 7

7 rows of 5

b The Arecibo anticoded message

Start of number markers — Binary numbers 1 to 10

Atomic numbers of hydrogen, carbon, nitrogen, oxygen, and phosphorus

Formulas for sugars and bases in DNA

DNA double helix

Number of units in DNA

Start of number markers — Start of number marker

Human figure

Population of Earth

Height of human in wavelengths

Arecibo radio dish transmitting signal — Sun and planets with Earth offset

Diameter of dish in wavelengths

Start of number marker

NASA

Figure 15.13 (a) An anticoded message is designed for easy decoding. Here a string of 35 radio pulses, represented as 1s and 0s, can be arranged in only two ways: as 5 rows of 7 or 7 rows of 5. The second way produces a friendly message. (b) The Arecibo message describes life on Earth (colour added for clarity). Binary numbers give the height of the human figure (1110) and the diameter of the telescope dish (100101111110) in units of the wavelength of the signal, which is 12.3 cm.

a sequence of prime numbers (numbers only divisible by one and itself) could be considered a good candidate because it is impossible that any natural physical process would generate such a sequence. Steady pulses would not necessarily have to imply an intelligent sender. As you saw in Figure 8.14, the pulses could be of stellar origin, such as fast-rotating neutron stars with radio waves beaming toward us (pulsars).

There is even a way for you to help with searches. The Berkeley SETI team (note: they are separate from the SETI Institute), with the support of the Planetary Society, has recruited about 4 million owners of personal computers that are connected to the Internet. Participants download a screen saver that searches data files from the Arecibo radio telescope for signals whenever the owner is not using the computer. For further information, you can locate the seti@home project at http://setiathome.ssl.berkeley.edu.

The search continues, but radio astronomers struggle to hear anything against the worsening babble of noise from human civilization. Wider and wider sections of the electromagnetic spectrum are being used for earthly communication, and this—combined with stray electromagnetic noise from electronic devices, including everything from computers to refrigerators—makes it difficult to hear faint radio signals. It would be ironic if humans fail to detect faint signals from another world because our own world has become too noisy. Ultimately, the chances of success depend on the number of inhabited worlds in the galaxy.

The founders of SETI search using electromagnetic spectrum, Giuseppe Cocconi and Philip Morrison from Cornell University, concluded their pioneering paper from 1959—titled "Searching for Interstellar Communications"—with the following famous message: "The probability of success is difficult to estimate; but if we never search, the probability of success is zero."

How Many Inhabited Worlds?

Given enough time, the searches will find other worlds with civilizations, assuming that there are at least a few out there. If extraterrestrial intelligence is widespread, scientists should find signals relatively soon—within the next few decades. But if it is rare, it may take much longer.

Using simple arithmetic you can estimate the number of technological civilizations in the Milky Way Galaxy with which you might communicate: given the symbol N_c. The formula proposed for discussions about N_c is named the **Drake equation** after the radio astronomer Frank Drake, a pioneer in the search for extraterrestrial intelligence. The version of the Drake equation presented here is modified slightly from its original form:

$$N_c = N_* \times f_p \times n_{HZ} \times f_L \times f_I \times f_s$$

N_* is the number of stars in our galaxy, and f_P represents the fraction of stars that have planets. If all single stars have planets, f_P is about 0.5. The factor n_{HZ} is the average number of planets in each solar system suitably placed in the habitable zone. This factor actually means the number of planets possessing liquid water. Europa and Enceladus in our solar system show that liquid water can exist due to tidal heating outside the conventional habitable zone that in our system contains Earth's orbit. Therefore, n_{HZ} may be larger than had been previously thought. Furthermore, the recent discovery of multiple Earth-like planets

Table 15.1 The Number of Technological Civilizations per Galaxy

Variables		Estimates	
		Pessimistic	Optimistic
$N.$	Number of stars per galaxy	2×10^{11}	2×10^{11}
f_P	Fraction of stars with planets	0.1	0.5
n_{HZ}	Number of planets per star that lie in a habitable zone for longer than 4 billion years	0.01	1
f_L	Fraction of suitable planets on which life begins	0.01	1
f_I	Fraction of planets where life forms evolve to intelligence	0.01	1
f_S	Fraction of star's existence during which a technological society survives	10^{-8}	10^{-4}
N_c	Number of communicative civilizations per galaxy	2×10^{-4}	1×10^7

in habitable zones around a few stars will increase this estimate. The factor f_L is the fraction of suitable planets on which life begins, and f_I is the fraction of those planets where life evolved to intelligence.

The first five factors in the Drake equation can be roughly estimated, but the final factor, f_S, the fraction of a star's life during which an intelligent species is communicative, is extremely uncertain. If a society survives at a technological level for only 100 years, the chances of communicating with it are small. But a society that stabilizes and remains technological for a long time is much more likely to be detected. For a star with a lifespan of 10 billion years, f_S can range from 10^{-8} for extremely short-lived societies to 10^{-4} for societies that survive for a million years. Table 15.1 summarizes what many scientists consider a reasonable range of values for f_S and the other factors.

If the optimistic estimates are true, there could be a communicative civilization within a few tens of light-years of Earth. On the other hand, if the pessimistic estimates are true, Earth may be the only planet that is capable of communication within thousands of the nearest galaxies.

Drake equation The equation that estimates the total number of communicative civilizations in the Milky Way Galaxy.

The Big Picture

What Are We?

There are more than 4000 religions around the world, and nearly all hold that humans have a dual nature: We are physical objects made of atoms, but we are also spiritual beings. Science is unable to examine the spiritual side of existence, but it can tell us about our physical nature.

You are made of very old atoms. The matter you are made of appeared in the big bang and was cooked into a wide range of elements inside stars. Your atoms may have been inside at least two or three generations of stars. Eventually, your atoms became part of a nebula that contracted to form the Sun and the planets of the solar system.

Your atoms have been part of Earth for the last 4.6 billion years. They have been recycled many times through dinosaurs, stromatolites, fish, bacteria, grass, birds, worms, and other living things. Now you are using these atoms, but when you are done with them, they will be used again and again.

When the Sun swells into a red giant star and dies in a few billion years, Earth's atmosphere and oceans will be driven away, and at least the outer few kilometres of Earth's crust will be vaporized and blown outward to become part of the nebula around the white-dwarf remains of the Sun. Your atoms are destined to return to the interstellar medium and will become part of future generations of stars, planets, and perhaps living beings.

The message of astronomy is that humans are not just observers. We are participants, we are part of the universe. Among all the galaxies, stars, planets, planetesimals, and bits of matter, humans are objects that can think, and that means we can understand what we are.

Is the human race the only thinking species? If so, we bear the sole responsibility to understand and admire the universe. The detection of signals from another civilization would demonstrate that we are not alone, and such communication would end the self-centred isolation of humanity and stimulate a re-evaluation of the meaning of human existence. We may never realize our full potential as humans until we communicate with non-human intelligent life.

Review and Discussion Questions

Review Questions

1. If life is based on information, what is that information?
2. What would happen to a life form if the information handed down to offspring was always the same? How would that endanger the future of the life form?
3. How does the DNA molecule produce a copy of itself?
4. Give an example of natural selection acting on new DNA patterns to select the most advantageous characteristics.
5. What evidence do scientists have that life on Earth began in the sea?
6. Why do scientists think that liquid water is necessary for the origin of life?
7. What is the difference between chemical evolution and biological evolution?
8. What was the significance of the Miller-Urey experiment?
9. How does intelligence make a creature more likely to survive?
10. Why are upper-main-sequence (high-luminosity) stars unlikely sites for intelligent civilizations?
11. Why is it reasonable to suspect that travel between stars is nearly impossible?
12. How does the stability of technological civilizations affect the probability that Earth can communicate with them?
13. What is the water hole, and why would it be a good "place" to look for other civilizations?
14. The star cluster NGC 2264 contains cool red giants and main-sequence stars from hot blue stars all the way down to red dwarfs. Discuss the likelihood that planets orbiting any of these stars might be home to life. Don't neglect to estimate the age of the cluster.
15. How was the Arecibo message designed to be understood by extraterrestrial recipients?
16. **How Do We Know?** How do science and religion have complementary explanations of the world?
17. **How Do We Know?** Why are scientists confident that Earth has never been visited by aliens?

Discussion Questions

1. Do you expect that hypothetical alien recipients of the Arecibo message will be able to decode it? Why or why not?
2. How do you think the detection of extraterrestrial intelligence would be received by the public? Would it be likelier to upset, or confirm, humans' beliefs about themselves and the world?
3. What do you think it would mean if decades of careful searches for radio signals for extraterrestrial intelligence turn up nothing?

Learning to Look

1. The star cluster shown in the image below contains cool red giants and main-sequence stars from hot blue stars all the way down to red dwarfs. Discuss the likelihood that planets orbiting any of these stars might be home to life. (*Hint*: Estimate the age of the cluster.)

NASA

2. If you could search for life in the galaxy shown in the image below, would you look among disk stars or halo stars? Discuss the factors that influence your decision.

ESO

The aggregate of all our joys and sufferings, thousands of confident religions, ideologies and economic doctrines, every hunter and forager, every hero and coward, every creator and destroyer of civilizations, every king and peasant, every young couple in love, every hopeful child, every mother and father, every inventor and explorer, every teacher of morals, every corrupt politician, every superstar, every supreme leader, every saint and sinner in the history of our species, lived there on a mote of dust, suspended in a sunbeam.

Carl Sagan, American astrophysicist (1934–1996)

Our journey together is over, but before we part company let's ponder one more time the primary theme of this book: humanity's place in the universe. Astronomy helps us comprehend the workings of stars, galaxies, and planets, but its greatest value lies in what it teaches us about ourselves. Now that you have surveyed astronomical knowledge, you can better understand your own position in nature.

The word *nature* conjures up images of rabbits in a forest glade or blue-green oceans or windswept mountaintops. As diverse as these images are, they are all earthbound. Having studied astronomy, you can see nature as a beautiful mechanism composed of matter and energy interacting according to simple rules to

Earth photographed by *Voyager 1* from the edge of the solar system. The vertical beams are sunlight reflected inside the camera.

Earth →

form galaxies, stars, planets, mountaintops, ocean depths, forest glades, and people.

Perhaps the most important astronomical lesson is that humanity is a small but important part of the universe. Most of the universe is probably lifeless. The vast reaches between the galaxies appear to be empty of all but the thinnest gas, and stars are much too hot to preserve the chemical bonds that seem necessary for life to survive and develop. It seems that only on the surfaces of planets that are "just right," where temperatures are moderate, can atoms link together in special ways to form living matter.

Because life is special, intelligence is very precious. The universe may contain many planets devoid of life, planets where the wind has blown unfelt for billions of years. There may also exist planets where life has developed but has not become complex, planets on which the wind stirs wide plains of grass and rustles through dark forests. It is intelligence, human or non-human, that gives meaning to the landscape.

Science is the process by which Earth intelligence has tried to understand the physical universe. Science is not the invention of new devices or processes. It does not create home computers, cure the mumps, or manufacture plastic spoons; these are products of engineering and technology, the adaptation of scientific understanding for practical purposes. Science is the understanding of nature, and astronomy is that understanding on the grandest scale. Astronomy is the science by which the universe, through human intelligence, tries to understand its own existence.

As the primary intelligent species on this planet, we are the custodians of a priceless gift: a planet filled with living things. This is especially true if life is rare in the universe. In fact, if Earth is the only inhabited planet, our responsibility is overwhelming. We are the only creatures who can take action to preserve the existence of life on Earth, and, ironically, our own actions are the most serious hazards.

The future of humanity is not secure. We are trapped on a tiny planet with limited resources and a population growing faster than our ability to produce food. In our efforts to survive, we have already driven many organisms to extinction and now threaten others. But even if we control our population and conserve and recycle our resources, life on Earth is doomed. In 5 billion years, the Sun will leave the main sequence and swell into a red giant, incinerating Earth.

To survive, humanity must eventually leave Earth and search for other planets. Travel to the stars will perhaps be the greatest challenge we have ever faced, but throughout humanity's existence we have been explorers at heart, willing to set off toward uncharted territories undaunted by challenges. We do have a few billion years to prepare for this next great adventure, and a billion years is a fairly long time. Who can tell what future discoveries lie ahead in this most epic of quests! Perhaps we will finally answer that all-important question: are we alone?

But one thing is clear today. If we hope to survive and aim for the stars, we must do it together as one species, united in a common cause. This calls for drastic changes in our behaviour toward each other and other living things, and in our attitude toward our planet's resources. Our very survival requires us to become dependable custodians of our planet, preserving it, admiring it, and trying to understand it. Will we succeed? That depends on the choices we make. We are not perfect, but we have the gift of intelligence and that may be the most wonderful thing this planet has ever produced. The future of our planet, our very own spaceship in the cosmos, is in our hands. Let's guard it well.

The human brain now holds the key to our future. We have to recall the image of the planet from outer space: a single entity in which air, water, and continents are interconnected. That is our home.

David Suzuki, Canadian scientist and environmental activist

Units and Astronomical Data

The Metric System and SI Units

A system of measurement is based on the three fundamental units for length, mass, and time. By international agreement, there is a preferred set of metric units known as the *Système International d'Unités* (SI units) that is based on the metre, kilogram, and second.

Density should be expressed in SI units as kilograms per cubic metre, but no human hand can enclose a cubic metre, so that unit does not help you easily grasp the significance of a given density. Instead, this book refers to density in grams per cubic centimetre. A gram is roughly the mass of a paperclip, a cubic centimetre is the size of a small sugar cube, and a density of 1 g/cm³ equals the density of water, all tangible units.

The International System of Units has been adopted as the official system of weights and measures by all nations in the world except for Burma, Liberia, and the United States. This book expresses most quantities only in metric units. However, for conceptual purposes, occasionally some quantities are better expressed in more commonly used units. Instead of saying that the average person would weigh 133 N on the Moon, it might help some readers to see that weight described as 30 lb.

Temperature Scales

In astronomy, as in most other sciences, temperatures are expressed on the Kelvin scale, although the centigrade scale is also used. The centigrade scale is also called the Celsius scale after its inventor, the Swedish astronomer Anders Celsius (1701–1744). Temperatures on the centigrade scale are measured from the freezing point of water (0°C). Temperatures on the Kelvin scale are measured from absolute zero, the temperature of an object that contains no extractable heat (0 K, or −273 degrees centigrade). In practice, no object can be as cold as absolute zero, although laboratory apparatus have reached temperatures less than 10^{-6} K. The Kelvin scale is named after the Scottish mathematical physicist William Thomson, Lord

Kelvin (1824–1907). A one degree centigrade change is equal to a 1 Kelvin change.

The Fahrenheit scale fixes the freezing point of water at 32°F and the boiling point at 212°F. Named after the German physicist Gabriel Daniel Fahrenheit (1686–1736), who made the first successful mercury thermometer in 1720, the Fahrenheit scale is used routinely only in the United States.

Astronomy Units and Constants

Astronomy, and science in general, is a way of learning about nature and understanding the universe. To test hypotheses about how nature works, scientists use observations of nature. The tables that follow contain some of the basic observations that support science's best understanding of the astronomical universe. Of course, these data are expressed in the form of numbers, not because science reduces all understanding to mere numbers, but because the struggle to understand nature is so demanding that science must use every good means available. Quantitative thinking—reasoning mathematically—is one of the most powerful techniques ever invented by the human brain. Numbers and mathematical analysis can be used to recognize patterns and build models of nature as well as verify our growing understanding of the universe.

Table A.1 defines units of measure commonly used by astronomers. Table A.2 gives physical constants such as the speed of light, plus basic astronomical data such as the mass and luminosity of the Sun. Table A.3 presents the characteristics of different spectral types of main-sequence stars. Tables A.4 and A.5, respectively, list the 15 nearest and the 15 brightest stars with their individual properties. The fact that these two star lists have almost no overlap is an important truth about stars that you can read more about in Chapter 6. Table A.6 gives the physical and orbital properties of the major planets in our solar system. Table A.7 lists the larger moons of each planet and their characteristics. The outer planets have many smaller moons that are not listed here.

Table A.1 | Units Used in Astronomy

1 angstrom (Å)	$= 10^{-8}$ cm
	$= 10^{-10}$ m
	$= 10$ nm
1 astronomical unit (AU)	$= 1.50 \times 10^{11}$ m
1 light-year (ly)	$= 6.32 \times 10^{4}$ AU
	$= 9.46 \times 10^{15}$ m
1 parsec (pc)	$= 2.06 \times 10^{5}$ AU
	$= 3.09 \times 10^{16}$ m
	$= 3.26$ ly
1 kiloparsec (kpc)	$= 1000$ pc
1 megaparsec (Mpc)	$= 1\ 000\ 000$ pc

Table A.2 | Astronomical Constants

Velocity of light (c)	$= 3.00 \times 10^{8}$ m/s
Gravitational constant (G)	$= 6.67 \times 10^{-11}$ m^3/(s^{2}kg)
Mass of H atom	$= 1.67 \times 10^{-27}$ kg
Mass of Earth ($M_{\oplus}$)	$= 5.98 \times 10^{24}$ kg
Earth equatorial radius ($R_{\oplus}$)	$= 6.38 \times 10^{6}$ m
Mass of Sun ($M_{\odot}$)	$= 1.99 \times 10^{30}$ kg
Radius of Sun ($R_{\odot}$)	$= 6.96 \times 10^{8}$ m
Solar luminosity ($L_{\odot}$)	$= 3.85 \times 10^{26}$ J/s
Mass of Moon	$= 7.35 \times 10^{22}$ kg
Radius of Moon	$= 1.74 \times 10^{3}$ km

Table A.3 | Properties of Main-Sequence Stars

Spectral Type	Absolute Visual Magnitude (M_v)	Luminosity*	Temp. (K)	λ_{max} (nm)	Mass*	Radius*	Average Density (g/cm^3)
O5	−5.8	500 000	40 000	72.4	40.0	18.0	0.01
B0	−4.1	20 000	28 000	100	18.0	7.4	0.1
B5	−1.1	800	15 000	190	6.4	3.8	0.2
A0	+0.7	80	9900	290	3.2	2.5	0.3
A5	+2.0	20	8500	340	2.1	1.7	0.6
F0	+2.6	6.3	7400	390	1.7	1.4	1.0
F5	+3.4	2.5	6600	440	1.3	1.2	1.1
G0	+4.4	1.3	6000	480	1.1	1.0	1.4
G5	+5.1	0.8	5500	520	0.9	0.9	1.6
K0	+5.9	0.4	4900	590	0.8	0.8	1.8
K5	+7.3	0.2	4100	700	0.7	0.7	2.4
M0	+9.0	0.1	3500	830	0.5	0.6	2.5
M5	+11.8	0.01	2800	1000	0.2	0.3	10.0
M8	+16.0	0.001	2400	1200	0.1	0.1	63.0

*Luminosity, mass, and radius are given as multiples of the Sun's luminosity, mass, and radius.

Table A.4 | The 15 Nearest Stars

Name	Distance (ly)	Distance (pc)	Apparent Visual Magnitude (m_v)	Absolute Magnitude (M_v)	Spectral Type
Sun			−26.7	4.8	G2
Proxima Cen	4.2	1.3	11.0	15.5	M6
α Cen A	4.4	1.3	0.0	4.4	G2
α Cen B	4.4	1.3	1.3	5.7	K5
Barnard's Star	5.9	1.8	9.5	13.2	M4
Wolf 359	7.7	2.4	13.5	16.7	M6
Lalande 21185	8.3	2.5	7.5	10.5	M2
α CMa A (Sirius A)	8.6	2.6	−1.5	1.4	A1
α CMa B (Sirius B)	8.6	2.6	8.4	11.3	white dwarf
Luyten 726-8A	8.7	2.7	12.6	15.4	M6
Luyten 726-8B	8.7	2.7	12.0	14.9	M5
Ross 154	9.7	3.0	11.0	13.6	M3
Ross 248	10.4	3.2	12.2	14.8	M6
ε Eri	10.5	3.2	3.7	6.2	K2
Luyten 789-6	10.9	3.3	12.2	14.6	M6

Source: Data from the SIMBAD database, operated at CDS, Strasbourg, France.

Table A.5 | The 15 Brightest Stars

Star	Name	Apparent Visual Magnitude (m_v)	Distance (ly)	Absolute Magnitude (M_v)	Spectral Type
α CMa	Sirius	−1.47	8.6	1.4	A1
α Car	Canopus	−0.72	313	−5.6	F0
α Cen	Rigil Kentaurus	−0.29	4.3	4.1	G2
α Boo	Arcturus	−0.04	36	−0.3	K2
α Lyr	Vega	0.03	25	0.6	A0
α Aur	Capella	0.08	42	−0.5	G8
β Ori	Rigel	0.12	783	−6.8	B8
α CMi	Procyon	0.34	11	2.6	F5
α Eri	Achernar	0.50	144	−5.1	B3
α Ori	Betelgeuse	0.58	424	−5.0	M2
β Cen	Hadar	0.60	522	−5.4	B1
α Aql	Altair	0.77	17	2.2	A7
α Cru	Acrux	0.81	320	−4.2	B0
α Tau	Aldebaran	0.85	65	−0.7	K5
α Vir	Spica	1.04	261	−3.5	B1

Note: Data from the SIMBAD database, operated at CDS, Strasbourg, France.
For multiple star systems, the magnitude given is the combined light of all components; the spectral type is for the primary component.

Table A.6 | Properties of the Planets

PHYSICAL PROPERTIES (EARTH = ⊕)

Planet	Equatorial Radius (km)	Equatorial Radius (⊕ = 1)	Mass (⊕ = 1)	Average Density (g/cm³)	Surface Gravity (⊕ = 1)	Escape Velocity (km/s)	Sidereal Period of Rotation	Inclination of Equator to Orbit
Mercury	2440	0.38	0.055	5.43	0.38	4.3	58.65^d	0°
Venus	6052	0.95	0.815	5.20	0.90	10.4	243.02^d	177.3°
Earth	6378	1.00	1.00	5.52	1.00	11.2	23.93^h	23.4°
Mars	3396	0.53	0.107	3.93	0.38	5.0	24.62^h	25.2°
Jupiter	71 492	11.21	317.8	1.33	2.53	59.5	9.92^h	3.1°
Saturn	60 268	9.45	95.2	0.69	1.06	35.5	10.57^h	26.7°
Uranus	25 559	4.01	14.5	1.27	0.89	21.3	17.24^h	97.8°
Neptune	24 764	3.88	17.1	1.64	1.14	23.5	16.11^h	28.3°

h = hours; d = days

ORBITAL PROPERTIES

Planet	Semimajor Axis (AU)	Semimajor Axis (10⁶ km)	Orbital Period (years)	Orbital Period (days)	Average Orbital Velocity (km/s)	Orbital Eccentricity	Inclination to Ecliptic
Mercury	0.39	57.9	0.24	87.97	47.9	0.206	7.0°
Venus	0.72	108.2	0.62	224.68	35.0	0.007	3.4°
Earth	1.00	149.6	1.00	365.26	29.8	0.017	0° (by definition)
Mars	1.52	227.9	1.88	686.95	24.1	0.093	1.9°
Jupiter	5.20	778.5	11.9	4332.6	13.1	0.049	1.3°
Saturn	9.58	1433.4	29.5	10 760	9.7	0.056	2.5°
Uranus	19.23	2876.7	84.0	30 687	6.8	0.047	0.8°
Neptune	30.10	4503.4	164.8	60 190	5.4	0.009	1.8°

Table A.7 | Principal Satellites of the Solar System

Planet	Satellite	Radius (km)	Average Distance from Planet (10^3 km)	Orbital Period (days)	Orbital Eccentricity	Orbital Inclination
Earth	Moon	1738	384.4	27.32	0.055	5.1°
Mars	Phobos	14 × 12 × 10	9.4	0.32	0.018	1.0°
	Deimos	8 × 6 × 5	23.5	1.26	0.002	2.8°
Jupiter	Amalthea	135 × 100 × 78	182	0.50	0.003	0.4°
	Io	1820	422	1.77	0.000	0.3°
	Europa	1565	671	3.55	0.000	0.5°
	Ganymede	2640	1071	7.16	0.002	0.2°
	Callisto	2420	1884	16.69	0.008	0.2°
	Himalia	~85	11 470	250.6	0.158	27.6°
Saturn	Janus	110 × 80 × 100	151.5	0.70	0.007	0.1°
	Mimas	196	185.5	0.94	0.020	1.5°
	Enceladus	250	238.0	1.37	0.004	0.0°
	Tethys	530	294.7	1.89	0.000	1.1°
	Dione	560	377	2.74	0.002	0.0°
	Rhea	765	527	4.52	0.001	0.4°
	Titan	2575	1222	15.94	0.029	0.3°
	Hyperion	205 × 130 × 110	1484	21.28	0.104	~0.5°
	Iapetus	720	3562	79.33	0.028	14.7°
	Phoebe	110	12 930	550.4	0.163	150°
Uranus	Miranda	242	129.9	1.41	0.017	3.4°
	Ariel	580	190.9	2.52	0.003	0°
	Umbriel	595	266.0	4.14	0.003	0°
	Titania	805	436.3	8.71	0.002	0°
	Oberon	775	583.4	13.46	0.001	0°
Neptune	Proteus	205	117.6	1.12	~0	~0°
	Triton	1352	354.59	5.88	0.00	160°
	Nereid	170	5588.6	360.12	0.76	27.7°

~ signifies "approximately"

Observing the Sky

Observing the sky with the naked eye is as important to modern astronomy as picking up pebbles is to modern geology. Neglecting the beauty of the sky is equivalent to geologists neglecting the beauty of the minerals they study. It would be quite appropriate for you to regard the night sky as the first natural wonder of the world. This supplement to Chapter 2 will help you get started observing the night sky for yourself.

The brighter stars in the sky are visible even from the centres of cities that have air and light pollution. But in the countryside, only a few kilometres beyond the cities, the night sky is a velvety blackness strewn with thousands of glittering stars. From a wilderness location, far from the city's glare, and especially from high mountains, the night sky is spectacular.

Using Star Charts

The constellations are a fascinating part of our cultural heritage; however, they can be difficult to learn because of Earth's motion. The constellations that appear above the horizon change with the time of night and the seasons.

Because Earth rotates eastward, the sky appears to rotate westward around Earth, a fact you have known since childhood. A constellation that is visible shortly after sunset will appear to move westward, and in a few hours it will disappear below the western horizon. Other constellations will rise in the east, and so the sky changes gradually through the night.

In addition, Earth's orbital motion makes the Sun appear to move eastward among the stars. Each day the Sun moves about twice its own diameter, about one degree, eastward along the ecliptic. Consequently, each night at sunset, the constellations are about one degree farther toward the west.

For instance, Orion is visible in the evening sky in January, but as the days pass, the Sun moves closer to Orion. By March, Orion is difficult to see in the western sky soon after sunset. By June, the Sun is so close to Orion

that the constellation sets with the Sun and is invisible. Not until late July is the Sun far enough past Orion for the constellation to become visible rising in the eastern sky just before dawn.

Because of the rotation and orbital motion of Earth, you need more than one star chart to map the sky. Which chart you select depends on the month and the time of night. The charts printed on the next two pages show the evening sky for each season, as viewed from the northern hemisphere at a latitude typical of southern Canada or central Europe.

To use the charts, select the appropriate chart and hold it overhead as shown in Figure B.1. If you face south, turn the chart until the words southern horizon are at the bottom of the chart. If you face other directions, turn the chart appropriately. Note that hours are in Standard Time; for Daylight Savings Time (spring, summer, and the first half of fall in Canada) add one hour.

Figure B.1 To use the star charts in this book, select the appropriate chart for the season and time. Hold it overhead and turn it until the direction at the bottom of the chart is the same as the direction you are facing.

STAR CHARTS

NORTHERN HEMISPHERE SKY

February–March–April

February	midnight
March	10 PM
April	8 PM

Times are Standard Time; for Daylight Savings Time, add 1 hour.

Months along the ecliptic show the location of the Sun during the year.

Numbers along the celestial equator show right ascension.

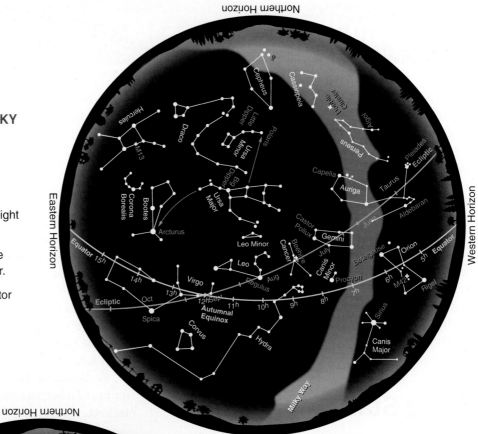

NORTHERN HEMISPHERE SKY

May–June–July

May	midnight
June	10 PM
July	8 PM

Times are Standard Time; for Daylight Savings Time, add 1 hour.

Months along the ecliptic show the location of the Sun during the year.

Numbers along the celestial equator show right ascension.

NORTHERN HEMISPHERE SKY

August–September–October

August	midnight
September	10 PM
October	8 PM

Times are Standard Time; for Daylight Savings Time, add 1 hour.

Months along the ecliptic show the location of the Sun during the year.

Numbers along the celestial equator show right ascension.

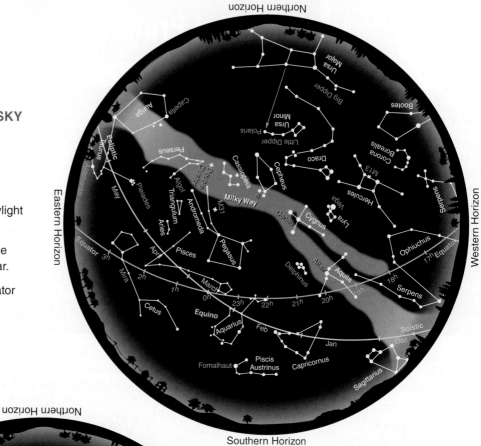

NORTHERN HEMISPHERE SKY

November–December–January

November	midnight
December	10 PM
January	8 PM

Times are Standard Time; for Daylight Savings Time, add 1 hour.

Months along the ecliptic show the location of the Sun during the year.

Numbers along the celestial equator show right ascension.

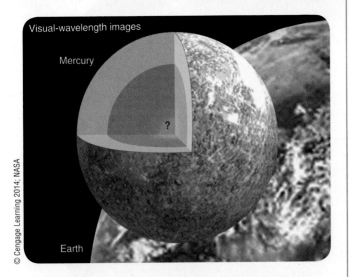

© Cengage Learning 2014; NASA

Mercury is slightly more than one-third the diameter of Earth. Its high density must mean it has a large iron core. The amount of heat it retains is unknown.

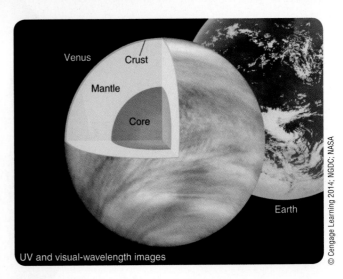

© Cengage Learning 2014; NGDC; NASA

Venus's diameter is 95 percent that of Earth. Its atmosphere is perpetually cloudy, and its surface is hot enough to melt lead. Whether it has a liquid metal core like Earth's is currently a matter of conjecture.

Mercury

Motion

Average distance from Sun	0.387 AU (5.79×10^7 km)
Eccentricity of orbit	0.206
Inclination of orbit to ecliptic	7.0°
Orbital period	0.241 y (88.0 d)
Period of rotation (sidereal)	58.65 d
Inclination of equator to orbit	0.0°

Characteristics

Equatorial diameter	4.89×10^3 km (0.383 $D_\oplus$)
Mass	3.30×10^{23} kg (0.0553 $M_\oplus$)
Average density	5.43 g/cm³ (5.4 g/cm³ uncompressed)
Surface gravity	0.38 Earth gravity
Escape velocity	4.3 km/s (0.38 $V_\oplus$)
Surface temperature	−170° to 430°C
Average albedo	0.12
Oblateness	0

Historical Point

Mercury lies very close to the Sun and completes an orbit in only 88 Earth days. For this reason, the ancients named the planet after Mercury, the fleet-footed messenger of the gods. The name is also applied to the element mercury, which is known as quicksilver because it is a heavy, quick-flowing silvery liquid at room temperatures.

Venus

Motion

Average distance from Sun	0.723 AU (1.08×10^8 km)
Eccentricity of orbit	0.007
Inclination of orbit to ecliptic	3.4°
Orbital period	0.615 y (224.70 d)
Period of rotation (sidereal)	243.0 d
Inclination of equator to orbit	177.3° (retrograde rotation)

Characteristics

Equatorial diameter	1.21×10^4 km (0.950 $D_\oplus$)
Mass	4.87×10^{24} kg (0.815 $M_\oplus$)
Average density	5.20 g/cm³ (4.2 g/cm³ uncompressed)
Surface gravity	0.90 Earth gravity
Escape velocity	10.4 km/s (0.92 $V_\oplus$)
Surface temperature	470°C
Albedo (cloud tops)	0.90
Oblateness	0

Historical Point

Venus is named for the Roman goddess of love, perhaps because the planet often shines so beautifully in the evening or dawn sky. In contrast, the ancient Maya identified Venus as their war god Kukulkan and sacrificed human victims to the planet when it rose in the dawn sky.

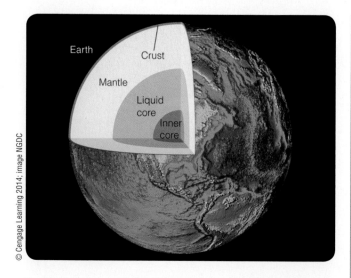

Earth's surface is marked by high continents and low seafloors. The crust is only 10 to 60 km thick. Interior to that are a thick mantle, liquid outer core, and solid inner core.

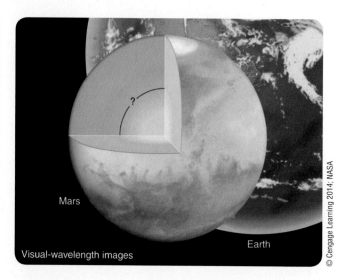

Mars has half the diameter of Earth and probably retains some internal heat, but the size and composition of its core are not well known.

Earth

Motion

Average distance from Sun	1.00 AU (1.50×10^8 km)
Eccentricity of orbit	0.017
Inclination of orbit to ecliptic	0° (by definition)
Average orbital velocity	29.8 km/s
Orbital period	1.0000 y (365.26 d)
Period of rotation	24.00 h (with respect to Sun)
Period of rotation	23.93 h (with respect to the stars)
Inclination of equator to orbit	23.4°

Characteristics

Equatorial diameter	1.28×10^4 km
Mass	5.97×10^{24} kg
Average density	5.52 g/cm³ (4.07 g/cm³ uncompressed)
Surface gravity	1.00 Earth gravity
Escape velocity	11.2 km/s
Surface temperature	−90° to 60°C
Average albedo	0.31
Oblateness	0.0034

Historical Point

The modern English word *Earth* comes from Old English *eorthe* and ultimately from the Indo-European root *er-*, meaning ground or dirt. *Terra* comes from the Roman goddess of fertility and growth: thus, *Terra Mater*, Mother Earth.

Mars

Motion

Average distance from Sun	1.52 AU (2.28×10^8 km)
Eccentricity of orbit	0.093
Inclination of orbit to ecliptic	1.9°
Orbital period	1.881 y (687.0 d)
Period of rotation (sidereal)	24.62 h
Inclination of equator to orbit	25.2°

Characteristics

Equatorial diameter	6.79×10^3 km (0.533 $D_\oplus$)
Mass	6.42×10^{25} kg (0.107 $M_\oplus$)
Average density	3.93 g/cm³ (3.3 g/cm³ uncompressed)
Surface gravity	0.38 Earth gravity
Escape velocity	5.0 km/s (0.45 $V_\oplus$)
Surface temperature	−140° to 15°C
Average albedo	0.25
Oblateness	0.009

Historical Point

Mars is named for the god of war. Minerva was the goddess of defensive war, but Bullfinch's *Mythology* refers to Mars's "savage love of violence and bloodshed." You can see the planet glowing reddish orange from Earth. Because of iron oxides in its soil, cultures throughout history have associated the red colour of Mars with blood.

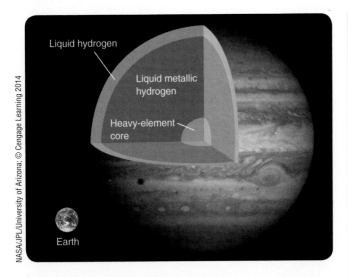

Jupiter is mostly a liquid hydrogen planet with a small core of heavy elements that is not much bigger than Earth.

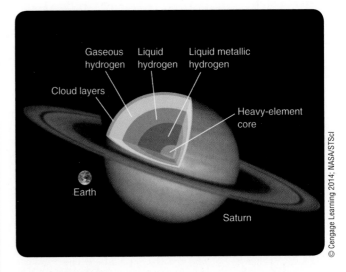

Density, oblateness, and gravity measurements made by planetary probes allow planetary astronomers to model Saturn's interior.

Jupiter

Motion

Average distance from Sun	5.20 AU (7.79 × 10⁸ km)
Eccentricity of orbit	0.049
Inclination of orbit to ecliptic	1.3°
Orbital period	11.9 y
Period of rotation	9.92 h
Inclination of equator to orbit	3.1°

Characteristics

Equatorial diameter	1.43×10^5 km (11.2 $D_\oplus$)
Mass	1.90×10^{27} kg (318 $M_\oplus$)
Average density	1.33 g/cm³
Gravity at cloud tops	2.5 Earth gravities
Escape velocity	59.5 km/s (5.3 $V_\oplus$)
Temperature at cloud tops	145°K
Albedo	0.34
Oblateness	0.065

Historical Point

Jupiter is named for the Roman king of the gods (the Greek Zeus), and it is the largest planet in our solar system. It can be very bright in the night sky, and its cloud belts and four largest moons can be seen through even a small telescope. Its moons are even visible with a good pair of binoculars mounted on a tripod.

Saturn

Motion

Average distance from Sun	9.58 AU (1.43 × 10⁹ km)
Eccentricity of orbit	0.056
Inclination of orbit to ecliptic	2.5°
Orbital period	29.5 y
Period of rotation	10.57 h
Inclination of equator to orbit	26.7°

Characteristics

Equatorial diameter	1.21×10^5 km (9.45 $D_\oplus$)
Mass	5.68×10^{26} kg (95.2 $M_\oplus$)
Average density	0.69 g/cm³
Gravity at cloud tops	1.1 Earth gravities
Escape velocity	35.5 km/s (3.2 $V_\oplus$)
Temperature at cloud tops	95°K
Albedo	0.34
Oblateness	0.098

Historical Point

The Greek god Cronus was forced to flee when his son Zeus took power. Cronus went to Italy where the Romans called him Saturn, protector of the sowing of seed. He was celebrated in a week-long Saturnalia festival at the time of the winter solstice in late December. Early Christians took over the holiday to celebrate Christmas.

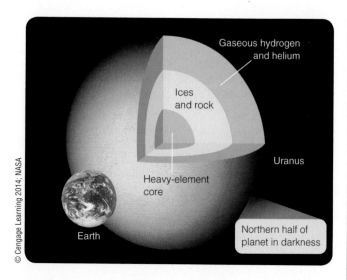

Uranus rotates on its side, and, when *Voyager 2* flew past in 1986, the planet's south pole was pointed almost directly at the Sun.

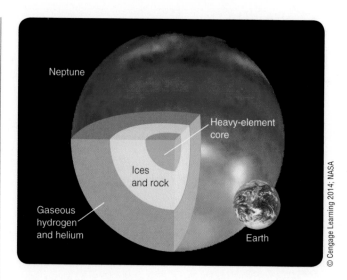

Neptune was tipped slightly away from the Sun when the Hubble Space Telescope recorded this image. The interior is much like that of Uranus, but Neptune has more heat flowing outward.

Uranus

Motion

Average distance from Sun	19.2 AU (2.88×10^9 km)
Eccentricity of orbit	0.047
Inclination of orbit to ecliptic	0.8°
Orbital period	84.0 y
Period of rotation	17.24 h
Inclination of equator to orbit	97.8° (retrograde rotation)

Characteristics

Equatorial diameter	5.11×10^4 km (4.01 $D_\oplus$)
Mass	8.68×10^{25} kg (14.5 $M_\oplus$)
Average density	1.27 g/cm³
Gravity	0.9 Earth gravity
Escape velocity	21.3 km/s (1.9 $V_\oplus$)
Temperature at cloud tops	55°K
Albedo	0.30
Oblateness	0.023

Historical Point

Uranus was discovered in 1781 by William Herschel, a German-born scientist who lived and worked most of his life in England. He named the new planet *Georgium Sidus*, meaning "George's Star" in Latin, after the English King George III. European astronomers, especially the French, refused to accept a planet named after an English king. Instead, they called the planet Herschel. Years later, German astronomer J. E. Bode suggested it be named Uranus after the oldest of the Greek gods.

Neptune

Motion

Average distance from Sun	30.1 AU (4.50×10^9 km)
Eccentricity of orbit	0.009
Inclination of orbit to ecliptic	1.8°
Orbital period	164.8 y
Period of rotation	16.11 h
Inclination of equator to orbit	28.3°

Characteristics

Equatorial diameter	4.95×10^4 km (3.88 $D_\oplus$)
Mass	1.02×10^{26} kg (17.1 $M_\oplus$)
Average density	1.64 g/cm³
Gravity	1.1 Earth gravities
Escape velocity	23.5 km/s (2.1 $V_\oplus$)
Temperature	55°K
Albedo	0.29
Oblateness	0.017

Historical Point

A British and a French astronomer independently calculated the existence and location of Neptune from its gravitational influence on the motion of Uranus. British observers were too slow to act on this information; Neptune was discovered in 1846, and the French astronomer got the credit. Because of its blue colour, astronomers named Neptune after the god of the sea.

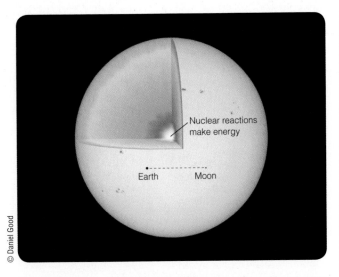

This visible image of the Sun shows a few sunspots and is cut away to show the location of energy generation at the Sun's centre. The Earth–Moon system is shown for scale.

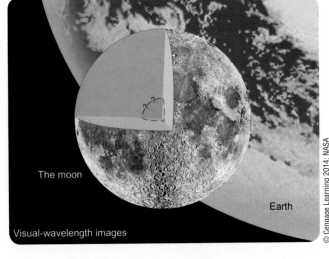

Earth's moon has about a quarter the diameter of Earth. Its low density indicates that it does not contain much iron. The size of its core, if any, and the amount of remaining heat are unknown.

The Sun

From Earth

Average distance from Earth	1.000 AU (1.496×10^8 km)
Maximum distance from Earth	1.017 AU (1.521×10^8 km)
Minimum distance from Earth	0.983 AU (1.471×10^8 km)
Equatorial angular diameter	0.533° (1920 arc seconds)
Period of rotation (sidereal)	24.5 days at equator
Apparent visual magnitude	−26.74

Characteristics

Radius	6.96×10^5 km
Mass	1.99×10^{30} kg
Average density	1.41 g/cm³
Escape velocity at surface	618 km/s
Luminosity	3.84×10^{26} J/s
Surface temperature	5780 K
Central temperature	15.7×10^6 K
Spectral type	G2 V
Absolute visual magnitude	+4.83

Historical Point

In Greek mythology, the Sun was carried across the sky in a golden chariot pulled by powerful horses and guided by the sun god Helios. When Phaeton, the son of Helios, drove the chariot one day, he lost control of the horses, and Earth was nearly set ablaze before Zeus smote Phaeton from the sky. Even in classical times, people understood that life on Earth depends critically on the Sun.

The Moon

Motion

Average distance from Earth	3.84×10^5 km (centre to centre)
Eccentricity of orbit	0.055
Inclination of orbit to ecliptic	5.1°
Average orbital velocity	1.02 km/s
Orbital period (sidereal)	27.3 d
Orbital period (synodic)	29.5 d
Inclination of equator to orbit	6.7°

Characteristics

Equatorial diameter	3.48×10^3 km (0.273 $D_\oplus$)
Mass	7.35×10^{22} kg (0.0123 $M_\oplus$)
Average density	3.35 g/cm³ (3.3 g/cm³ uncompressed)
Surface gravity	0.17 Earth gravity
Escape velocity	2.4 km/s (0.21 $V_\oplus$)
Surface temperature	−170° to 130°C
Average albedo	0.12
Oblateness	0

Historical Point

Lunar superstitions are common. The words *lunatic* and *lunacy* come from *luna,* the moon. Someone who is *moonstruck* is supposed to be a bit nutty. Because the moon affects the ocean tides, many superstitions link the moon to water, to weather, and to women's cycle of fertility. According to legend, moonlight is supposed to be harmful to unborn children, but on the plus side, moonlight rituals are said to remove warts.

INDEX

Magnitudes

Astronomers use a simple formula to convert between magnitudes and fluxes (brightness). If two stars have fluxes F_A and F_B, then the ratio of their fluxes is F_A/F_B. Magnitude scale is defined so two stars that differ by five magnitudes have a flux ratio of exactly 100. Therefore, two stars that differ by one magnitude must have a flux ratio that equals the fifth root of 100, $\sqrt[5]{100}$ or $100^{0.2}$, which equals 2.51; that is, the light arriving at Earth from one star must be 2.51 times brighter than from the other. Two stars that differ by two magnitudes will have a flux ratio of about 2.51×2.51, which is approximately 6.31, and so on (Table 1).

EXAMPLE A: Suppose star C is seventh magnitude, and star D is tenth magnitude. What is their brightness ratio? That is, what is the ratio of their fluxes?

SOLUTION: The magnitude difference is three magnitudes, and Table 1 shows the corresponding flux ratio is 15.8. Therefore, star C is 15.8 times brighter (has 15.8 times as much flux arriving at Earth) as star D.

A table is convenient, but for more precision you can express the relationship as a simple formula. The flux ratio F_A/F_B is equal to 2.51 raised to the power of the magnitude difference $m_B - m_A$:

$$\frac{F_A}{F_B} = (2.51)^{(m_B - m_A)}$$

In Example A, $(2.51)^{(10-7)} = (2.51)^3 = 15.8$

Table 1	Magnitude Differences and Flux Ratios
Magnitude Difference	**Corresponding Flux Ratio**
0.00	1.00
1.00	2.51
2.00	6.31
3.00	15.8
4.00	39.8
5.00	100
...	
10.0	10 000
20.0	100 000 000

On the other hand, when you know the flux ratio and want to find the magnitude difference, it is convenient to rearrange the previous formula which now includes the base 10 logarithm of the flux ratio (2.51 is rounded to 2.5).

$$m_B - m_A = 2.5 \log(F_A/F_B)$$

EXAMPLE B: The light from Sirius has 24.2 times as much flux—is 24.2 times brighter—compared to light from Polaris. What is their magnitude difference?

SOLUTION: The magnitude difference is 2.5 times the logarithm of 24.2, which is written $2.5 \log(24.2)$. Your calculator tells you the logarithm of 24.2 is 1.38, so the magnitude difference between Sirius and Polaris is 2.5×1.38, which equals 3.46 magnitudes.

Absolute Magnitude and Distance

Apparent visual magnitude tells you how bright a star looks, see the **Magnitudes** Math Reference Card. Absolute visual magnitude, M_V, the apparent visual magnitude the star would have if it were 10 pc away, tells you how luminous the star really is. If you know a star's apparent visual magnitude and its distance, you can calculate its absolute visual magnitude. The magnitude-distance formula that allows this calculation relates apparent visual magnitude, m_V, distance in parsecs, d, and absolute visual magnitude, M_V:

$$m_V - M_V = -5 + 5 \log(d)$$

Sometimes it is convenient to rearrange the equation if you are trying to find the distance:

$$d = 10^{(m_V - M_V + 5)/5}$$

EXAMPLE: The star Polaris is 133 pc from Earth and has an apparent magnitude of 2.0. What is its absolute visual magnitude?

SOLUTION: A calculator tells you that $\log(133)$ equals 2.12, so you substitute into the first equation to get

$$2.0 - M_V = -5 + 5(2.12)$$

Solving for M_V tells you that the absolute visual magnitude of Polaris is -3.6. If it were only 10 pc from Earth, it would dominate the night sky.

Newton's Laws of Motion and Gravitation

Newton discovered that the motion of an object is related to the forces (push or pull) exerted on the object. For an object of mass m, the acceleration, a, of the object is directly proportional to the net force, F, acting on the object.

$$F = ma$$

EXAMPLE A: How much force is required to increase the speed of a 1500 kg car from rest to 50.0 km/h in 10.0 seconds?

SOLUTION: Note that acceleration is the rate of change of velocity:

$$a = \frac{\Delta v}{\Delta t}$$

Δv is the change in velocity (final velocity minus initial velocity) and Δt is the time interval over which the change took place. In our example $\Delta v = 50.0$ km/h $= 13.9$ m/s and $\Delta t = 50.0$s. Therefore,

$$F = ma = m\frac{\Delta v}{\Delta t} = 1500 \text{ kg} \times \frac{13.9 \text{ m/s}}{10.0 \text{ s}} = 2080 \text{ N}$$

NOTE: we need to convert the speed from *km/h* to *metres/second* (m/s) in order to express the force in units of N (Newtons), which is the SI unit of force (see Appendix A).

Newton also discovered that all massive objects exert a force of attraction, called a gravitational force, on each other. The force of gravitation between any two objects with mass m_1 and m_2 is directly proportional to the products of the masses and inversely proportional to the square of the distance d between their centres of mass:

$$F_{12} = F_{21} = \frac{Gm_1m_2}{d^2}$$

G is the gravitational constant $G = 6.67 \times 10^{-11}$ Nm²/kg² The gravitational force between two objects is typically very small unless the objects are very massive such as, for example, planets or stars.

EXAMPLE B: What is the gravitational force between the Earth and a 1.0 kg object on the surface of the Earth?

SOLUTION: The distance d between the 1.0 kg object and the centre of the Earth is the radius of the Earth. Thus,

$$F_{12} = F_{21} = \frac{Gm_1m_2}{r^2}$$
$$= \frac{(6.67 \times 10^{-11}\text{ Nm}^2/\text{kg}^2)(M_{earth})(1.0 \text{ kg})}{(R_{earth})^2} = 9.8 \text{ N}$$

Note that we can also find the acceleration of the 1 kg object using the equation $F = ma$:

$$a = \frac{F}{m} = \frac{9.8 \text{ N}}{1.0 \text{ kg}} = 9.8 \text{ m/s}^2$$

This is, indeed, the acceleration due to Earth's gravity of all objects close to the surface of the Earth.

NOTE: The gravitational force is inversely proportional to the square of the distance between the two objects. For example, it decreases by a factor of 4 when the distance is doubled.

Circular Velocity

Circular velocity is the velocity a satellite must have to remain in a circular orbit around a larger body. If the mass of the satellite is small compared that of the central body, the circular velocity is given by

$$V_c = \sqrt{\frac{GM}{r}}$$

In this formula, M is the mass of the central body in kilograms, r is the radius of the orbit in metres, and G is the gravitational constant, 6.67×10^{-11} m³/s²kg. This formula is all you need to calculate how fast an object must travel to stay in a circular orbit.

For example, how fast does the Moon travel in its orbit? The mass of Earth is 5.98×10^{24} kg, and the Moon orbits 3.84×10^8 m from Earth's centre. The Moon's velocity is

$$V_c = \sqrt{\frac{6.67 \times 10^{-11} \times 5.98 \times 10^{24}}{3.84 \times 10^8}} = 1020 \text{ m/s}$$

This calculation shows that the moon travels 1.02 km along its orbit each second.

The Small-Angle Formula

Figure 1 shows the relationship among the linear diameter, angular diameter, and distance of an object, in this case the Moon. Linear diameter is simply the distance between an object's opposite sides. The average linear diameter of the Moon is 3470 km. The angular diameter of an object is the angle formed by lines extending toward you from opposite edges of the object, meeting at your eye. The farther away a given object is, the smaller its angular diameter.

To find the angular diameter of the Moon, you need to use the small-angle formula. It allows you to calculate the angular diameter of any object.

In the small-angle formula, you must always use the same units for distance and linear diameter. The version of the formula shown here has arc seconds as the unit of angular diameter.* You can use this formula to find any one of the three quantities involved (linear diameter, angular diameter, distance) if you know the other two, by cross-multiplying.

$$\frac{\text{angular diameter (in arc seconds)}}{2.06 \times 10^5} = \frac{\text{linear diameter}}{\text{distance}}$$

EXAMPLE: The Moon's linear diameter is 3470 km, and its average distance from Earth is 384 000 km. What is its angular diameter?

SOLUTION: Because the Moon's linear diameter and distance are both given in the same units, kilometres, you can put them directly into the small-angle formula:

$$\frac{\text{angular diameter}}{2.06 \times 10^5} = \frac{3470 \text{ km}}{384\,000 \text{ km}}$$

The resulting angular diameter is 1.86×10^3 arc seconds to three digits' precision, which equals 31 arc minutes—about 0.5°.

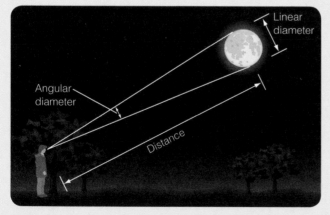

Figure 1 The three quantities related by the small-angle formula.
* When you divide by 2.06×10^5, you convert the angle from arc seconds into radians.

Wave Properties

When a wave travels through a medium, it is characterized by three properties. A wave is just a series of peaks and valleys (or ups and downs) and is one of two types, transverse or longitudinal. A transverse wave is when the particles being affected by the wave move perpendicularly to the direction in which the wave is moving (e.g., light); a longitudinal wave is when the particles move back and forth in the same direction in which the wave is moving (e.g., sound). The distance from one peak to the next peak (or valley to the next valley) is called the wavelength, usually denoted by λ, measured in metres. The number of waves passing any point in space is known as the frequency, f, measured in cycles/second. Finally, as the wave moves through the medium (air, glass, vacuum, etc.) it is characterized by its speed, v, measured in metres/second.

These quantities have a simple relationship:

$$v = f\lambda, \qquad \text{or} \qquad \lambda = v/f$$

Furthermore, if the wave phenomenon is light, then the energy, E, of a photon of light is proportional to the wavelength of the light, sometimes known as the Planck–Einstein relation:

$$E = hf$$

where h is Planck's constant, 6.626×10^{-34} joule seconds.

EXAMPLE A: Consider a sound wave travelling in air. The speed of the wave in air is 343.2 m/s and is independent of the frequency (pitch) of the sound. (This value is somewhat dependent on the air temperature so we have quoted a value for 20°C). What is the wavelength of middle C on the piano, $f = 261.2$ Hz (cycles/second)?

SOLUTION: $\lambda = \dfrac{v}{f} = \dfrac{343.2}{261.2} = 1.3$ m (metres)

EXAMPLE B: For light travelling through interstellar space the speed is 300 000 km/s or 3×10^8 m/s, usually denoted by c. Again, this speed is the same for all light whether it is visible light, X-rays, or radio waves. What is the frequency of H_α light (the red line in the Hydrogen Balmer series; see **Visualizing Astronomy 5.1**) whose wavelength is 656.3 nm (nanometres)?

SOLUTION: $f = \dfrac{c}{\lambda} = \dfrac{3 \times 10^8}{656.3 \times 10^{-9}} = 4.6 \times 10^{14}$ cycles/s

$$= 457 \text{ THz}$$

What is the energy of a photon of this frequency?

$$E = hf = \left(6.626 \times 10^{-34}\right) \times \left(4.6 \times 10^{14}\right)$$
$$= 3.05 \times 10^{-19} \text{ joules}$$

The Powers of a Telescope

The light-gathering power of a telescope is proportional to the area of the primary mirror or lens. A primary with a large area gathers a large amount of light. The area of a circular lens or mirror of diameter D is $\pi(D/2)^2$. To compare the relative light-gathering power *(LGP)* of two telescopes A and B, you can calculate the ratio of the areas of their primaries, which is the ratio of the diameters *(D)* squared:

$$\frac{LGP_A}{LGP_B} = \left(\frac{D_A}{D_B}\right)^2$$

EXAMPLE A: Suppose you compare a 4-cm telescope with a 24-cm telescope. How much more light will the larger telescope gather?

SOLUTION:

$$\frac{LGP_{24}}{LGP_4} = \left(\frac{24}{4}\right)^2 = 6^2 = 36 \text{ times more light}$$

EXAMPLE B: Your dark-adapted eye acts like a telescope with a diameter of about 0.8 cm, the maximum diameter of the pupil. How much more light can you gather if you use a 24-cm telescope, relative to your unaided eye?

SOLUTION:

$$\frac{LGP_{24}}{LGP_{eye}} = \left(\frac{24}{0.8}\right)^2 = 30^2 = 900 \text{ times more light}$$

The resolving power of a telescope is the angular distance between two stars that are just barely visible through the telescope as separate images. The resolving power α in arc seconds of a telescope with diameter D in metres and that is collecting light of wavelength λ in metres equals:

$$\alpha = 2.06 \times 10^5 \left(\frac{\lambda}{D}\right) \text{ arc seconds}$$

The multiplication factor of 2.06×10^5 is the conversion between radians and arc seconds (refer to The Small-Angle Formula Math Reference Card).

If the wavelength of light being studied is assumed to be 550 nm, in the middle of the visual band, then the above formula simplifies to

$$\alpha = \frac{0.113}{D} \text{ arc seconds}$$

EXAMPLE C: What is the resolving power of a 10-cm (= 0.10 m) diameter telescope observing at visual wavelengths?

SOLUTION:

$$\alpha = 2.06 \times 10^5 \left(\frac{550 \times 10^{-9}}{0.10}\right) = 1.13 \text{ arc seconds}$$

or, equivalently,

$$\alpha = \frac{0.113}{0.10} = 1.13 \text{ arc seconds}$$

In other words, using a 10-cm diameter telescope, if the lenses are of good quality, and if the seeing is good, you should be able to distinguish as separate points of light any pair of stars farther apart than about 1.1 arc seconds. Stars any closer together than that would be blurred together into a single image by the diffraction fringes.

The same formula can be applied to a radio telescope.

EXAMPLE D: What is the resolving power of a radio telescope with a dish (primary mirror) diameter of 100 m observing at a wavelength of 21 cm (0.21 m)?

SOLUTION:

$$\alpha = 2.06 \times 10^5 \left(\frac{0.21}{100}\right) = 430 \text{ arc seconds}$$

Note how poor the resolution of even a large radio dish is compared with optical telescopes. That resolution limit of 430 arc seconds corresponds to 1/4 the diameter of the full moon.

The magnification power M of a telescope is the ratio of the focal length of the primary lens or mirror F_p divided by the focal length of the eyepiece F_e:

$$M = \left(\frac{F_p}{F_e}\right)$$

EXAMPLE E: What is the magnification of a telescope with a primary mirror focal length of 80 cm if it is used with an eyepiece with a focal length of 0.50 cm?

SOLUTION: The magnification is 80 divided by 0.50, or 160 times.

Blackbody Radiation

Blackbody radiation is described by two simple laws that can be expressed in precise mathematical form. So many objects give off radiation as blackbodies that these two laws are important principles in the analysis of light from the universe.

Wien's law expresses quantitatively the relation between temperature and the wavelength at which a blackbody radiates the most energy: its wavelength of maximum intensity (λ_{max}). Written for conventional intensity units, the law is expressed as follows:

$$\lambda_{max} = \frac{2.90 \times 10^6}{T}$$

That is, the wavelength in nanometres of maximum radiation intensity emitted by a blackbody is inversely proportional to the blackbody's temperature on the Kelvin scale.

This law is a powerful aid in astronomy. For example, a cool star with a temperature of 2900 K emits most intensely at a wavelength of 1000 nm, which is in the near-infrared part of the spectrum. In contrast, a very hot star, with a temperature of 29 000 K, radiates most intensely at a wavelength of 100 nm, which is in the ultraviolet.

The Stefan–Boltzmann law, named after the two scientists who discovered it, relates the temperature of a blackbody to the total radiated energy. Recall that energy is expressed in units called joules (symbolized by capital J). The total radiation in units of joules per second given off by one square metre of the surface of the object equals a constant number, represented by sigma (σ), multiplied by the temperature raised to the fourth power:[*]

$$E = \sigma T^4 \ (\text{J/s/m}^2)$$

How does this help you understand stars? Suppose a star the same size as the Sun has a surface temperature twice as hot as the Sun's surface. Then each square metre of that star radiates not just twice as much energy, but 2^4, or 16, times as much energy. From this law you can see that a small difference in temperature between two stars can produce a very large difference in the amount of energy emitted from the stars' surfaces.

[*] For the sake of completeness, you can note that the constant σ equals 5.67×10^{-8} J/(s m² K⁴) (units of joules per second per square metre per degree Kelvin to the fourth power).

The Doppler Formula

Astronomers can measure radial velocity by using the Doppler effect. The "laboratory" wavelength λ_0 is the wavelength a certain spectral line would have if the source of the light is not moving relative to the spectrograph. In the spectrum of a star, this spectral line is shifted by some small amount, $\Delta\lambda$. If the wavelength is increased (a red shift), $\Delta\lambda$ is positive; if the wavelength is decreased (a blue shift), $\Delta\lambda$ is negative. The radial velocity, V_r, of the star is given by the Doppler formula:

$$\frac{V_r}{c} = \frac{\Delta\lambda}{\lambda_0}$$

That is, the radial velocity divided by the speed of light, c, is equal to $\Delta\lambda$ divided by λ_0. In astronomy, radial velocities are almost always given in kilometres per second, so c is expressed as 300 000 km/s.

For example, suppose the laboratory wavelength of a certain spectral line is 600.00 nm, and the line is observed in a star's spectrum at a wavelength of 600.10 nm. Then $\Delta\lambda$ is +0.10 nm, and the radial velocity is 0.10/600 multiplied by the speed of light, which equals 50 km/s. Because $\Delta\lambda$ is positive, you know the star is receding from you. The ratio of V_r/c is called "redshift" z and is used in Hubble law to determine the distance to the object.

Hydrogen Fusion

When four hydrogen nuclei fuse to make one helium nucleus, a small amount of matter seems to disappear. To see this, subtract the mass of a helium nucleus from the mass of four hydrogen nuclei:

$$
\begin{aligned}
4 \text{ hydrogen nuclei} &= 6.690 \times 10^{-27} \text{ kg} \\
-1 \text{ helium nucleus} &= 6.646 \times 10^{-27} \text{ kg} \\
\hline
\text{Difference in mass} &= 0.044 \times 10^{-27} \text{ kg}
\end{aligned}
$$

That mass difference, 0.044×10^{-27} kg, does not actually disappear but is converted to energy according to Einstein's famous equation:

$$
\begin{aligned}
E &= mc^2 \\
&= (0.044 \times 10^{-27} \text{ kg}) \times (3.0 \times 10^8 \text{ m/s})^2 \\
&= 4.0 \times 10^{-11} \text{ J}
\end{aligned}
$$

Recall that 1 joule is approximately equal to the energy of motion of an apple falling from a table to the floor.

The Mass–Luminosity Relation

You can estimate the luminosity of a main-sequence star based on the star's mass using a simple equation. A main-sequence star's luminosity in terms of the Sun's luminosity equals its mass in solar masses raised to the 3.5 power:

$$
L = M^{3.5}
$$

This is the mathematical form of the mass–luminosity relation. It is only an approximation, as shown by the red line in Figure 6.16, but it applies to most main-sequence stars over a wide range of stellar masses.

EXAMPLE: What is the luminosity of a main-sequence star with four times the mass of the Sun?

SOLUTION: The star is about 128 times more luminous than the Sun because

$$
L = M^{3.5} = 4^{3.5} = 128
$$

Parallax and Distance

To find the distance to a star from its measured parallax, astronomers use the same calculation as described in **The Small-Angle Formula** Math Reference Card. Imagine that you observe our solar system from the star. Figure 6.2 shows that the angular separation you would measure between the Sun and Earth equals the star's parallax, p. Recall that the small-angle formula relates an object's angular diameter, its linear diameter, and its distance. In this case, the angular diameter is the parallax angle p, and the linear diameter, the base of the triangle, is 1 AU. With the small-angle formula rearranged slightly, the distance, d, to the star in AU is equal to 2.06×10^5 divided by the parallax in arc seconds:

$$
d = \frac{2.06 \times 10^5}{p}
$$

The constant in the numerator is a conversion factor: the number of arc seconds in a radian.

Because the parallaxes of even the nearest stars are less than 1 arc second, the distances in AU are inconveniently large numbers. To keep the numbers manageable, astronomers have defined the parsec as their primary unit of distance in a way that simplifies the arithmetic. One parsec equals 2.06×10^5 AU, so the equation becomes

$$
d = \frac{1}{p}
$$

Thus, a parsec is the distance to an imaginary star whose parallax is 1 arc second.

EXAMPLE: The star Altair has a parallax of 0.194 arc second. How far away is it?

SOLUTION: The distance in parsecs (pc) equals 1 divided by 0.194, or 5.16 pc:

$$
d = \frac{1}{0.194} = 5.16 \text{ pc}
$$

One parsec equals about 3.26 light-years, so Altair is 16.8 ly away.

The Life Expectancies of Stars

You can estimate the amount of time a star spends on the main sequence—its life expectancy, τ—by estimating the amount of fuel it has and dividing by the rate at which it consumes that fuel:

$$\tau = \frac{\text{fuel supply}}{\text{rate of consumption}}$$

The amount of fuel a star has is proportional to its mass, M, and the rate at which it uses up its fuel is proportional to its luminosity, L. Thus, its life expectancy must be proportional to M/L. You can simplify this equation further because the luminosity of a star depends on its mass raised to the 3.5 power ($L = M^{3.5}$); see **The Mass–Luminosity Relation** Math Reference Card. So the life expectancy is

$$\tau = \frac{M}{M^{3.5}} = \frac{1}{M^{2.5}}$$

If you express the mass in solar masses, the lifetime will be in solar lifetimes.

EXAMPLE: How long can a 4-solar-mass star live?

SOLUTION:

$$\tau = \frac{1}{4^{2.5}} = \frac{1}{32} \text{ solar lifetimes}$$

Solar models show that the Sun, presently 5 billion years old, will last another 5 billion years. So a solar lifetime is approximately 10 billion years, and a 4-solar-mass star will last for about

$$\tau = \frac{1}{32} \times (10 \times 10^9 \text{ yr}) = 310 \times 10^6 \text{ years}$$

Luminosity, Radius, and Temperature

The luminosity, L, of a star depends on two things: its size and its temperature. Recall from the **Blackbody Radiation** Math Reference Card that the amount of energy emitted per second from each square metre of the star's surface is σT^4. Therefore, the star's luminosity can be written as its surface area in square metres times the amount it radiates from each square metre:

$$L = (\text{surface area}) \times \sigma T^4$$

Because a star is a sphere, you can use the formula for surface area, $4\pi R^2$. Then the luminosity is

$$L = 4\pi R^2\, \sigma T^4$$

If you express luminosity, radius, and temperature in proportion to the Sun, you get a simpler form:[*]

$$\frac{L}{L_\odot} = \left(\frac{R}{R_\odot}\right)^2 \left(\frac{T}{T_\odot}\right)^4$$

EXAMPLE A: How luminous is a star that has 10 times the Sun's radius but only half the temperature?

SOLUTION:

$$\frac{L}{L_\odot} = \left(\frac{10}{1}\right)^2 \left(\frac{1}{2}\right)^4 = \frac{100}{1} \times \frac{1}{16} = 6.25$$

This star is 6.25 more luminous than the Sun. You can also use this formula to find sizes of stars.

EXAMPLE B: What is the radius (relative to the Sun's radius) of a star whose absolute magnitude is 11 and whose spectrum shows it has twice the Sun's temperature?

SOLUTION: The star's absolute magnitude is four magnitudes brighter than the Sun. Recall from the **Magnitudes** Math Reference Card that four magnitudes is approximately a factor of 2.51^4, or about 40. The star's luminosity is therefore about $40\,L_\odot$. With the luminosity and temperature, you can find the radius:

$$\frac{40}{1} = \left(\frac{R}{R_\odot}\right)^2 \left(\frac{2}{1}\right)^4$$

Solving for the radius you get the following:

$$\left(\frac{R}{R_\odot}\right)^2 = \frac{40}{2^4} = \frac{40}{16} = 2.5$$

So the radius is $\dfrac{R}{R_\odot} = \sqrt{2.5} = 1.58$

The star is 58 percent larger in radius than the Sun.

---

[*] In astronomy, the symbols $\odot$ and $\oplus$ refer respectively to the Sun and Earth. Thus $L_\odot$ refers to the luminosity of the Sun, $T_\odot$ refers to the temperature of the Sun, and so on.

The Masses of Binary Stars

Johannes Kepler's third law of orbital motion worked only for the planets in our solar system. When Isaac Newton realized that mass produces the gravitational attraction that governs orbits, he made that law into a general principle. Newton's version of Kepler's third law applies to any pair of objects that orbit each other. The total mass of the two objects is related to the average distance, a, between them and their orbital period, P. If the masses are M_A and M_B, then

$$M_A + M_B = \frac{a^3}{P^2}$$

In this formula, a is expressed in AU, P in years, and the mass in solar masses.

Notice how this formula is related to Kepler's third law of planetary motion (refer to Table 3.1). Almost all the mass of the solar system is in the Sun. If you apply this formula to any planet in our solar system, the total mass is 1 solar mass. Then the formula becomes $P^2 = a^3$, which is Kepler's third law.

This formula lets you find the masses of binary stars. You must know the distance to the binary system to be able to convert the average angular separation between the two stars into AU. Using that and their orbital period in years, the sum of the masses of the two stars in solar units is just a^3/P^2.

EXAMPLE A: If you observe a binary system with a period of 32 years and an average separation of 16 AU, what is the total mass?

SOLUTION: The total mass equals $16^3/32^2$, which equals 4 solar masses.

EXAMPLE B: Let's call the two stars in the previous example A and B. Suppose star A is 12 AU away from the centre of mass, and star B is 4 AU away. What are the individual masses?

SOLUTION: The ratio of the masses must be 12:4, which equals a ratio of 3:1. What two numbers add up to 4 and have the ratio 3:1? Star B must be 3 solar masses, and star A must be 1 solar mass.

The Hubble Law

The apparent velocity of recession of a galaxy, V_r, in kilometres per second is equal to the Hubble constant, H_0, multiplied by the distance to the galaxy, d, in megaparsecs:

$$V_r = H_0 d$$

Astronomers use this equation as a way to estimate distance from a galaxy's apparent velocity of recession. Redshift $z = V_r/c$ is used in Hubble law to determine the distance to the object (refer to **The Doppler Formula** in Math reference Cards). Astronomers often refer to the distance to the object as "redshift".

EXAMPLE: If a galaxy has a radial velocity of 700 km/s, and H_0 is 70 km/s/Mpc,[*] then the distance to the galaxy equals the velocity divided by the Hubble constant, which is

$$d = \frac{(700 \text{ km/s})}{(70 \text{ km/s/Mpc})} = 10 \text{ Mpc}$$

Notice how the units in km/s cancel out to leave the distance in Mpc.

[*] H_0 has the units of a velocity divided by a distance. These are usually written as km/s/Mpc, meaning km/s per Mpc.

The Age of the Universe

Dividing the distance to a galaxy by the apparent velocity with which it recedes gives you an estimate of the age of the universe, and the Hubble constant simplifies your task further. The Hubble constant H_0 has the units km/s per Mpc, which is a velocity divided by a distance. If you calculate $1/H_0$, you have a distance divided by velocity. To finish the division and get an age, you need to convert megaparsecs into kilometres, and then the distances will cancel out and leave you with the age in seconds. To get years, divide by the number of units. Then the age of the universe in years is approximately 10^{12} divided by H_0 in its normal astronomical units, km/s/Mpc:

$$\tau_H = \frac{10^{12}}{H_0} \text{ years}$$

This estimate of the age of the universe is known as the Hubble time. For example, if H_0 is 70 km/s/Mpc, an estimated age for the universe is $10^{12}/70$, or 14 billion, years.

The Scale of the Cosmos: Space and Time

TOPIC SUMMARIES

1.1 From Solar System to Galaxy to Universe

Where is Earth in relation to the Sun, the planets, the stars, and the galaxies?

- We live on planet Earth, which orbits our star, the Sun, once a year.
- As Earth rotates once a day, we see the Sun rise and set.
- The other major planets in our solar system—Mercury, Venus, Mars, Jupiter, Saturn, Uranus, and Neptune—orbit our Sun in ellipses that are nearly circular.
- Our Sun is just one out of the billions of stars that fill our home galaxy, the Milky Way, which is a spiral galaxy.
- The Milky Way Galaxy is just one of billions of galaxies arranged in great clusters, clouds, walls, and filaments that fill the universe.

How do astronomers describe distances?

- Astronomers use scientific notation for very large or very small numbers.
- Astronomers have also invented new units of measure such as the astronomical unit (AU) and the light-year (ly). One AU is the average distance from Earth to the Sun. Mars, for example, orbits 1.5 AU from the Sun. The light-year (ly) is the distance light can travel in one year. The nearest star is 4.2 ly from the Sun.

Which of these objects are big relative to the others, and which are small?

- The Moon is only about one-fourth the diameter of Earth, but the Sun is about 110 times larger than Earth—a typical size for a star.
- Galaxies contain many billions of stars. We live in the Milky Way Galaxy, which is about 80 000 ly in diameter and contains over 100 billion stars.
- The largest things in the universe are the walls and long filaments containing many clusters of galaxies.

Are there other worlds like Earth?

- Planets as small as Earth are difficult to detect around other stars. Many stars have families of planets like our solar system, and some of those billions of planets may resemble Earth.

1.2 The Cosmic Calendar: Concepts of Time

Suppose you constructed a cosmic calendar spread over an average human lifetime (80 years) instead of over a calendar year. How would the timing of some of the important features of the universe's development change?

- The Milky Way gets created during your teen years.
- Our solar system is formed as you turn 50 years old.
- The dinosaurs roam Earth when you are about 79 years old.
- All of recorded history occurs in the last 6.6 seconds of your life.

Which timeframes are relatively large, and which are small?

- The oldest known entity is, in fact, the universe. Whether time even existed before the big bang is mere speculation.
- The Sun's age is about 5 billion years. It is assumed that it will last about another 5 billion years or so, at which time it will become a white dwarf, cooling down over millions of years and eventually becoming a black cinder of mostly carbon. It will stay in this form until the universe dies.
- The average sparrow lives for about three years.
- The half-life of the isotope beryllium-8 (^{8}Be) is about 70×10^{-18} seconds.

KEY TERMS

scientific notation The system of recording very large or very small numbers by using powers of 10. (p. 4)

field of view The area visible in an image, usually given as the diameter of the region. (p. 4)

astronomical unit (AU) Average distance from Earth to the Sun; 1.5×10^8 kilometres. (p. 5)

solar system The Sun and its planets, asteroids, comets, and so on. (p. 5)

planet A non-luminous body in orbit around a star, large enough to be spherical and to have cleared its orbital zone of other objects. (p. 5)

star A globe of gas held together by its own gravity and supported by the internal pressure of its hot gases, which generates energy by nuclear fusion. (p. 5)

light-year (ly) Unit of distance equal to the distance light travels in one year. (p. 8)

galaxy A large system of stars, star clusters, gas, dust, and nebulae orbiting a common centre of mass. (p. 8)

Milky Way The hazy band of light that circles our sky, produced by the glow of our galaxy. (p. 8)

Milky Way Galaxy The spiral galaxy containing our Sun, visible in the night sky as the Milky Way. (p. 8)

spiral arms Long spiral pattern of bright stars, star clusters, gas, and dust. Spiral arms extend from the centre to the edge of the disk of spiral galaxies. (p. 8)

supercluster A cluster of galaxy clusters. (p. 9)

User's Guide to the Sky: Patterns and Cycles

TOPIC SUMMARIES

2.1 The Stars

How do astronomers refer to stars?

- Astronomers divide the sky into 88 constellations with names that originated in Greek and Middle Eastern mythology. Modern constellations have been added to fill in spaces.
- Modern astronomers often refer to bright stars by a name composed of the constellation name plus a Greek letter assigned according to the star's brightness within the constellation.

How can you compare the brightness of stars?

- The magnitude system is the astronomer's brightness scale. First-magnitude stars are brighter than second-magnitude stars, which are brighter than third-magnitude stars, and so on.
- The magnitude you see when you look at a star in the sky is its apparent visual magnitude, which does not take into account its distance from Earth.

2.2 The Sky and Its Motions

How does the sky appear to move as Earth rotates?

- The celestial sphere is a model of the sky. The northern and southern celestial poles are the pivots on which the sky appears to rotate. The celestial equator, an imaginary line around the sky above Earth's equator, divides the sky in half.
- The angular distance from the horizon to the north celestial pole always equals your latitude. This is an important basis for celestial navigation.
- The gravitational forces of the Moon and Sun act on the spinning Earth and cause it to precess like a top. Earth's axis of rotation sweeps around in a circular motion with a period of 26 000 years, and consequently the celestial poles and celestial equator move slowly against the background of the stars.

2.3 The Cycle of the Sun

What causes the seasons?

- Because Earth orbits the Sun, the Sun appears to move eastward along the ecliptic. The inclination of the ecliptic means the Sun is in the northern hemisphere half the year and in the southern hemisphere the other half.
- In the summer, the Sun is above the horizon longer and shines more directly down on the ground. Both effects cause warmer weather.

2.4 The Cycles of the Moon

Why does the Moon go through phases?

- Because you see the Moon by reflected sunlight, its shape appears to change as it orbits Earth over a cycle of 29.53 days.

2.5 Eclipses

What is a solar eclipse?

- A total solar eclipse occurs if a new Moon passes directly between the Sun and Earth and the Moon's shadow sweeps over the part of Earth's surface where you are located. If you are outside the path of totality but the penumbra sweeps over your location, you see a partial eclipse.
- During a total solar eclipse, the bright disk of the Sun is covered, and you can see fainter features of the surrounding solar atmosphere.
- If the Moon is in the farther part of its orbit during a solar eclipse, it does not appear large enough to cover the solar disk, and you see only an annular eclipse.

What is a lunar eclipse?

- If a full Moon passes through Earth's shadow while you are on the night side of Earth, you see the Moon darken in a lunar eclipse.
- The totally eclipsed Moon looks copper-red because of sunlight refracted through Earth's atmosphere.

2.6 Stellar Coordinates

How do we locate the position of a star in the sky?

- The celestial sphere uses a coordinate grid similar to the longitude and latitude system used on Earth. Declination on the celestial sphere is identical to latitude, while right ascension is similar to longitude, with the zero of RA being the location of the vernal equinox on the celestial sphere.

2.7 Timekeeping

How do we determine the length of a day on Earth?

- There are two ways to measure the length of a day on Earth: one uses the time for successive crossings of the Sun on the meridian, called a solar day; the other uses the time for successive crossings of any particular star on the meridian, called a sidereal day. A sidereal day is shorter than a solar day by about four seconds.

KEY TERMS

constellation One of the stellar patterns identified by name, usually of mythological gods, people, animals, or objects; also the region of the sky containing that star pattern. (p. 16)

asterism A named grouping of stars that is not one of the recognized constellations. (p. 16)

magnitude scale The astronomical brightness scale; the larger the number, the fainter the star. (p. 17)

apparent visual magnitude (m_v) A measure of the brightness of a star as seen by human eyes on Earth. (p. 17)

flux A measure of the flow of energy out of a surface, usually applied to light. (p. 17)

celestial sphere An imaginary sphere of very large radius surrounding Earth and to which the planets, stars, Sun, and Moon seem to be attached. (p. 18)

scientific model A concept that helps one think about some aspect of nature, but is not necessarily true. (p. 19)

zenith The point in the sky directly above the observer. (p. 20)

nadir The point on the celestial sphere directly below the observer; the opposite of the zenith. (p. 20)

north, south, east, and west points The four cardinal directions; the points on the horizon in those exact directions. (p. 20)

precession The slow change in orientation of Earth's axis of rotation. One cycle takes nearly 26 000 years. (p. 22)

rotation Motion around an axis passing through the rotating body. (p. 22)

revolution Orbital motion about a point located outside the orbiting body. (p. 22)

ecliptic The apparent path of the Sun around the sky. (p. 23)

vernal equinox The place on the celestial sphere where the Sun crosses the celestial equator moving northward; also the beginning of spring. (p. 24)

summer solstice The point on the celestial sphere where the Sun is at its most northerly point; also the beginning of summer. (p. 24)

autumnal equinox The point on the celestial sphere where the Sun crosses the celestial equator going southward; also the beginning of autumn. (p. 24)

winter solstice The point on the celestial sphere where the Sun is farthest south; also the beginning of winter. (p. 24)

perihelion The orbital point of closest approach to the Sun. (p. 25)

aphelion The orbital point of greatest distance from the Sun. (p. 25)

solar eclipse The event that occurs when the Moon passes directly between Earth and the Sun, blocking our view of the Sun. (p. 30)

umbra The region of a shadow that is totally shaded. (p. 30)

penumbra The portion of a shadow that is only partially shaded. (p. 30)

annular eclipse A solar eclipse in which the solar photosphere appears around the edge of the Moon in a bright ring, or annulus. Features of the solar atmosphere cannot be seen during an annular eclipse. (p. 30)

lunar eclipse The darkening of the Moon when it moves through Earth's shadow. (p. 32)

Saros cycle An 18-year, 11⅓-day period, after which the pattern of lunar and solar eclipses repeats. (p. 33)

declination The angular distance of an object on the celestial sphere measured north (+) or south (–) from the celestial equator. (p. 33)

right ascension The angular east-west distance of an object on the celestial sphere measured from the vernal equinox, and measured in hours, minutes, and seconds, rather than angular degrees. (p. 33)

celestial equator The imaginary line around the sky directly above Earth's equator. (p. 33)

solar day The average time between successive crossings of the Sun on the local meridian (24 hours). (p. 34)

sidereal day The time between successive crossings of any star on the local meridian (23 hours, 56 minutes, 4.09 seconds). (p. 34)

synodic month The time for a complete cycle of lunar phases (about 29.5 days). (p. 34)

sidereal month The time for the Moon to orbit Earth once relative to any star (about 27.3 days). (p. 34)

sidereal year The time for Earth to complete one full orbit around the Sun relative to any star. (p. 34)

tropical year (solar year) The time between successive spring (or autumnal) equinoxes. (p. 34)

apparent solar time Time measured by the location of the Sun in the local sky such that noon occurs when the Sun crosses the meridian. (p. 34)

The Origin of Modern Astronomy

3.1 A Brief History of Ancient Astronomy

What did ancient civilizations achieve in astronomy?

- Ancient astronomers all over the world observed the sky and recognized patterns in the motion of the Sun, Moon, planets, and bright stars.
- The motions of celestial bodies were used for daily and monthly timekeeping, tracking seasons for agricultural purposes and for navigation. Many ceremonies and festivals grew around monthly and seasonal changes.
- The Greeks were among the first to develop models to explain what they observed in the universe.

What was the geocentric model?

- Ancient philosophers believed that the Earth was the unmoving centre of the universe
- Aristotle argued that the Sun, Moon, and stars were carried around Earth on circular spheres.
- Ptolemy gave mathematical form to Aristotle's model in about 140 CE. He kept the geocentric (Earth-centred) principle, but he added off-centre circles and variable speeds to better predict the motion of the planets.

3.2 Nicolaus Copernicus

How did Copernicus revise the geocentric model?

- Copernicus devised a heliocentric (Sun-centred) model. He preserved the principle of uniform circular motion, but he argued that Earth rotates on its axis and circles the Sun once a year. His theory was controversial because it contradicted Church teaching.
- Copernicus published his theory in his book *De Revolutionibus* in 1543, the year he died.

Why was the Copernican model gradually accepted?

- Because Copernicus kept the idea of uniform circular motion, his model did not predict the motions of the planets well, but it did offer a simple explanation of retrograde motion of planets without using large epicycles (circles on circles). He did have to include small epicycles to account for some observed planetary motions.
- The Copernican model was also more eloquent and straightforward. Venus and Mercury were treated the same as all the other planets, and the velocity of each planet was related to its distance from the Sun.

3.3 Tycho Brahe, Johannes Kepler, and Planetary Motion

How did Tycho Brahe and Johannes Kepler contribute to the Copernican Revolution?

- Tycho's great contribution was to compile the most precise and detailed naked-eye observations of the planets and stars ever made; his observations were later analyzed by Kepler.
- Kepler inherited Tycho's books of observations in 1601 and used them to uncover three laws of planetary motion. He found that the planets follow ellipses with the Sun at one focus, that they move faster when near the Sun, and that a planet's orbital period squared (in years) is proportional to its orbital radius cubed (in AU).

3.4 Galileo Galilei

Why was Galileo condemned by the Inquisition?

- Galileo used the newly invented telescope to observe the heavens, and he recognized the significance of what he saw there. His discoveries of the phases of Venus, the satellites of Jupiter, the mountains of the Moon, and other phenomena helped undermine the Ptolemaic model.
- Galileo based his analysis on observational evidence. In 1633, he was condemned before the Inquisition for refusing to obey an order to halt his defense of Copernicus's model.

3.5 Isaac Newton, Gravity, and Orbits

How did Isaac Newton change humanity's view of nature?

- Newton used the work of Kepler and Galileo to discover three laws of motion and the law of gravity.

These laws made it possible to understand such phenomena as orbital motion and the tides.

- Newton's laws gave scientists a unified way to think about the motion of all objects in the universe.
- The modern scientific method based on gathering evidence, creating models, and testing theories owes its origins to the efforts of Newton and his predecessors all the way back to our ancient ancestors.

KEY TERMS

first principle Something that seems obviously true and needs no further examination. (p. 48)

uniform circular motion The classical belief that the perfect heavens could move only by the combination of uniform motion along circular orbits. (p. 50)

parallax The apparent change in position of an object due to a change in the location of the observer. Astronomical parallax is measured in arc seconds. (p. 50)

retrograde motion The apparent backward (westward) motion of planets as seen against the background of stars. (p. 50)

epicycle The small circle followed by a planet in the Ptolemaic theory. The centre of the epicycle follows a larger circle (the deferent) around Earth. (p. 51)

geocentric universe A model of the universe with Earth at the centre, such as the Ptolemaic universe. (p. 52)

heliocentric universe A model of the universe with the Sun at the centre, such as the Copernican universe. (p. 53)

paradigm A commonly accepted set of scientific ideas and assumptions. (p. 56)

ellipse A closed curve around two points, called foci, such that the total distance from one focus to the curve and back to the other focus remains constant. (p. 56)

semi-major axis (*a*) Half of the longest diameter of an ellipse. (p. 56)

eccentricity (*e*) A number between 1 and 0 that describes the shape of an ellipse (how elongated it is); the distance from one focus to the centre of the ellipse, divided by the semi-major axis. (p. 57)

empirical Description of a phenomenon based only on observations, without explaining why it occurs. (p. 57)

hypothesis A conjecture, subject to further tests, that accounts for a set of facts. (p. 60)

theory A system of assumptions and principles applicable to a wide range of phenomena that has been repeatedly verified. (p. 60)

natural law A theory that has been so well confirmed that it is almost universally accepted as correct. (p. 60)

speed The rate at which an object moves (changes position); the total distance moved divided by the total time taken to move that distance. (p. 62)

velocity Both the speed and direction of travel of an object. (p. 62)

acceleration The rate of change of velocity with time. (p. 62)

mass A measure of the amount of matter making up an object. (p. 63)

weight The force that gravity exerts on an object. (p. 63)

inverse square relation A rule that the strength of an effect (such as gravity) decreases in proportion as the distance squared increases. (p. 63)

spring tide Ocean tide of large range that occurs at full and new moon. (p. 65)

neap tide Ocean tide of small range occurring at first- and third-quarter moon. (p. 65)

circular velocity The velocity an object needs to stay in orbit around another object. (p. 66)

geosynchronous satellite A satellite that orbits eastward around Earth with a period of 24 hours and remains above the same spot on Earth's surface. (p. 66)

centre of mass The balance point of a body or system of masses. The point about which a body or system of masses rotates in the absence of external forces. (p. 67)

closed orbit An orbit that repeatedly returns to the same starting point. (p. 67)

escape velocity The initial velocity an object needs to escape from the surface of a celestial body. (p. 67)

open orbit An orbit that carries an object away, never to return to its starting point. (p. 67)

Astronomical Telescopes and Instruments: Extending Humanity's Vision

TOPIC SUMMARIES

4.1 Radiation: Information from Space

What is light?

- Light is the visible form of electromagnetic radiation. The electromagnetic spectrum includes gamma rays, X-rays, ultraviolet radiation, visible light, infrared radiation, microwaves, and radio waves.
- You can think of a photon as a bundle of waves that acts sometimes as a particle and sometimes as a wave.
- The wavelength of visible light, usually measured in nanometres (10^{-9} m), ranges from 400 nm to 700 nm. Infrared and radio photons have longer wavelengths and carry less energy. Ultraviolet, X-ray, and gamma-ray photons have shorter wavelengths and carry more energy.

4.2 Telescopes

How do telescopes work? What are their capabilities and limitations?

- Astronomers use telescopes to gather light, see fine detail, and magnify images. Two of the three powers of a telescope—light-gathering power and resolving power—depend on the telescope's diameter. Consequently, astronomers strive to build telescopes with large diameters.
- Sometimes astronomical telescopes can be linked together to form an interferometer, which has a resolution equivalent to a telescope as large in diameter as the greatest separation between the individual telescopes.
- The third power of a telescope—magnifying power—is not an inherent property of a telescope but depends on which eyepiece is used.

4.3 Observatories on Earth: Optical and Radio

How are observatories built, and how are good locations chosen for them?

- Astronomers build optical observatories on high mountains for two reasons: the seeing is better in the calmer and dryer air, and the thinner air is more transparent, especially at infrared wavelengths.
- Radio telescopes consist of one or more large-dish reflectors, which record the intensity of the radio energy coming from a spot in the sky.
- Optical and radio telescopes need to be located where light pollution and human-made radio signals do not interfere with observations of faint cosmic sources.
- Telescopes on Earth must move continuously to compensate for Earth's rotation and stay pointed at celestial objects.

4.4 Astronomical Instruments and Techniques

What kinds of instruments and techniques do astronomers use to record and analyze light?

- For many decades, astronomers used photographic plates and photometers, but modern electronic array detectors such as CCDs have replaced them in most applications.
- Spectrographs using prisms or a grating can form a spectrum revealing information about the composition and motion of the object being studied.

4.5 Airborne and Space Observatories

Why do astronomers sometimes use X-ray, ultraviolet, and infrared telescopes, and why must these types of telescopes operate in the upper atmosphere or in orbit?

- X-ray, UV, and IR telescopes observe radiation from celestial objects at a wide range of temperatures and can also see through obscuring dust clouds in space.
- To observe wavelengths outside the visual window and the radio window permitted by our atmosphere, telescopes must go into the upper atmosphere or into space.
- Earth's atmosphere distorts and blurs images. Telescopes in orbit are above this seeing distortion and are limited only by diffraction fringes.

KEY TERMS

electromagnetic radiation Changing electric and magnetic fields that travel through space and transfer energy from one place to another; examples are light or radio waves. (p. 72)

wavelength The distance between successive peaks or troughs of a wave, usually represented by λ. (p. 72)

infrared (IR) The portion of the electromagnetic spectrum with wavelengths longer than red light, ranging from 700 nm to about 1 mm, between visible light and radio waves. (p. 73)

ultraviolet (UV) The portion of the electromagnetic spectrum with wavelengths shorter than violet light, between visible light and X-rays. (p. 74)

X-ray Electromagnetic waves with wavelengths shorter than ultraviolet light. (p. 74)

gamma rays The shortest-wavelength electromagnetic waves. (p. 74)

photon A quantum of electromagnetic energy that carries an amount of energy that increases proportionally with its frequency but decreases proportionally with its wavelength. (p. 74)

atmospheric window Wavelength region in which our atmosphere is transparent—at visual, radio, and some infrared wavelengths. (p. 74)

refracting telescope A telescope that forms images by bending (refracting) light with a lens. (p. 75)

reflecting telescope A telescope that forms images by reflecting light with a mirror. (p. 75)

primary lens In a refracting telescope, the largest lens. (p. 75)

primary mirror In a reflecting telescope, the largest mirror. (p. 75)

eyepiece A short-focal-length lens used to enlarge the image in a telescope; the lens nearest the eye. (p. 75)

focal length The focal length of a lens or mirror is the distance from that lens or mirror to the point where it focuses parallel rays of light. (p. 75)

optical telescope Telescope that gathers visible light. (p. 75)

radio telescope Telescope that gathers radio radiation. (p. 75)

light-gathering power The ability of a telescope to collect light; proportional to the area of the telescope's objective lens or mirror. (p. 76)

resolving power The ability of a telescope to reveal fine detail; depends on the diameter of the telescope objective. (p. 76)

diffraction fringe Blurred fringe surrounding any image, caused by the wave properties of light. Because of this, no image detail smaller than the fringe can be seen. (p. 76)

interferometer Separated telescopes combined to produce a virtual telescope with the resolution of a much larger-diameter telescope. (p. 76)

seeing Atmospheric conditions on a given night. When the atmosphere is unsteady, producing blurred images, the seeing is said to be poor. (p. 77)

adaptive optics A computer-controlled optical system in an astronomical telescope used to partially correct for seeing. (p. 77)

magnifying power The ability of a telescope to make an image larger. (p. 77)

sidereal tracking The continuous movement of a telescope to keep it pointed at a star as Earth rotates. (p. 79)

prime focus The point at which the objective mirror forms an image in a reflecting telescope. (p. 80)

secondary mirror In a reflecting telescope, a mirror that directs the light from the primary mirror to a focal position. (p. 80)

Cassegrain focus The optical design in which the secondary mirror reflects light back down the tube through a hole in the centre of the objective mirror. (p. 80)

photometer Sensitive astronomical instrument that measures the brightness of individual objects very precisely. (p. 83)

charge-coupled device (CCD) An electronic device consisting of a large array of light-sensitive elements used to record very faint images. (p. 83)

spectrograph A device that separates light by wavelengths to produce a spectrum. (p. 83)

spectrum A range of electromagnetic radiation spread into its component wavelengths (colours)—for example, a rainbow; also, representation of a spectrum as a graph showing intensity of radiation as a function of wavelength or frequency. (p. 84)

The Sun:
The Closest Star

5.1 The Sun: Basic Characteristics

How do you know the distance, size, mass, and density of the Sun?

- Observing the parallax shift of Venus in transit against the Sun's disk from opposite sides of Earth was the original method for finding the distance to the Sun. The diameter of the Sun can be calculated from its distance and its angular size.
- Newton's laws and the motion of the planets as they orbit the Sun allow the mass of the Sun to be determined. Its average density can be easily calculated from its mass and diameter.

5.2 Properties of Blackbody Radiation

How does matter produce light?

- Motion among charged particles in a solid, a liquid, or a dense gas causes the emission of blackbody radiation. Pure blackbody radiation is a continuous spectrum.
- The hotter an object is, the more energy it radiates and the shorter is its wavelength of maximum intensity, λ_{max}. This allows astronomers to estimate the temperature of the Sun and other stars from their colours.

5.3 The Sun's Surface

What do astronomers see when they observe the Sun?

- The photosphere is the level in the Sun from which visible photons most easily escape. Its temperature is about 5800 K.

- Energy flowing outward from the Sun's interior travels as rising currents of hot gas and sinking currents of cool gas in the convective zone just below the photosphere.
- The granulation of the photosphere is produced by convection currents of gas rising from below.

5.4 Light, Matter, and Motion

How does matter interact with light to produce spectral lines?

- Electrons in an atom may occupy various permitted orbits around the nucleus but not orbits in between. The size of an electron's orbit depends on the energy stored in the electron's motion.
- An electron may be excited to a higher orbit during a collision between atoms, or it may move from one orbit to another by absorbing or emitting a photon of the proper energy.
- A shift in the wavelength of features in spectra of the Sun and stars can occur due to their motion toward or away from Earth. This phenomenon, called the Doppler effect, reveals the radial velocity of the star, the part of its velocity directed toward Earth (blueshift) or away from Earth (redshift).

5.5 The Sun's Atmosphere

What can you learn from the Sun's spectrum?

- Because orbits of only certain energies are permitted in an atom, photons of only certain wavelengths can be absorbed or emitted. Each kind of atom has its own structure and therefore its own characteristic set of spectral lines.
- If light from a blackbody such as the Sun's photosphere passes through a low-density gas such as the

Sun's atmosphere on its way to your spectrograph, the gas can absorb photons of certain wavelengths, producing an absorption spectrum.

- The Sun's spectrum can tell you its chemical composition through the presence of spectral lines of a certain element. However, you must proceed with care because the strengths of lines also depend on the temperature of the gas.
- If you look at a low-density gas that is excited to emit photons, you see an emission spectrum.
- The solar atmosphere consists of two layers of hot, low-density gas: the chromosphere and the corona.
- The chromosphere is most easily visible during total solar eclipses. Its pink colour is caused by the Balmer emission lines in its spectrum. Filtergrams of the chromosphere reveal spicules and filaments.
- The corona is the Sun's outermost atmospheric layer. It is composed of a very-low-density, very hot gas extending far from the visible Sun. Astronomers have evidence that its high temperature—2 000 000 K or more—is maintained by effects of the magnetic carpet.
- Parts of the corona give rise to the solar wind.

5.6 Solar Activity

What is the solar cycle of activity, and how does that affect Earth?

- Sunspots seem dark because they are slightly cooler than the rest of the photosphere. The average sunspot is about twice the size of Earth and contains magnetic fields a few thousand times stronger than Earth's.

- Solar astronomers can study the motion, density, and temperature of gases inside the Sun through helioseismology.
- Astronomers can measure magnetic fields on the Sun by measuring the splitting of some spectral lines caused by the Zeeman effect.
- The average number of sunspots varies over a period of about 11 years and appears to be related to a magnetic cycle. Alternate sunspot cycles have reversed magnetic polarity, which is explained by the Babcock model.
- The sunspot cycle does not repeat exactly, and the Maunder minimum seems to have been a time when solar activity was very low and Earth's climate was slightly colder.
- The Sun rotates differentially, with regions far from the equator rotating slower than equatorial regions.
- Spectroscopic observations of other stars reveal that many have spots and magnetic fields that follow long-term cycles like the Sun's.
- Prominences occur in the chromosphere; their arched shapes show that they are formed of ionized gas trapped in the magnetic field.
- Flares are sudden eruptions of X-ray, ultraviolet, and visible radiation plus high-energy atomic particles produced when magnetic fields on the Sun interact and reconnect. Flares are important because they can have dramatic effects on Earth, such as communications blackouts and auroras.
- Spacecraft images show long streamers extending from the corona out into space. CMEs can produce auroras and other phenomena if they strike Earth.

KEY TERMS

spectral line A bright or dark line in a spectrum at a specific wavelength produced by the absorption or emission of light by certain atoms. (p. 92)

transits of Venus Rare occasions when Venus can be seen as a tiny dot directly between Earth and the Sun. (p. 92)

density Mass per volume. (p. 93)

atom The smallest unit of a chemical element, consisting of a nucleus containing protons and neutrons plus a surrounding cloud of electrons. (p. 93)

nucleus The central core of an atom containing protons and neutrons that carries a net positive charge. (p. 93)

proton A positively charged atomic particle contained in the nucleus of an atom. The nucleus of a hydrogen atom consists of a single proton. (p. 93)

neutron An atomic particle contained in the nucleus, with no charge and about the same mass as a proton. (p. 93)

electron Low-mass atomic particle carrying a negative charge. (p. 93)

molecule Two or more atoms bonded together. (p. 93)

heat Total energy stored in a material as agitation among its particles. (p. 93)

temperature A measure of the average agitation among the atoms and molecules of a material. (p. 93)

Kelvin temperature scale A temperature scale starting at absolute zero (−273°C). A one Kelvin change equals a one degree Celsius change. (p. 93)

absolute zero The theoretical lowest possible temperature at which a material contains no extractable heat energy. Zero on the Kelvin temperature scale. (p. 94)

blackbody radiation Radiation emitted by a hypothetical perfect radiator. The spectrum is continuous, and the wavelength of maximum emission depends on the blackbody's temperature. (p. 94)

wavelength of maximum intensity The wavelength at which a perfect radiator emits the maximum amount of energy; it depends only on the object's temperature. (p. 94)

Wien's law A law stating that the hotter a glowing object is, the shorter will be its wavelength of maximum intensity, inversely proportional to its temperature. (p. 94)

Stefan–Boltzmann law A law stating that hotter objects emit more energy than cooler objects of the same size, in proportion to the fourth power of temperature. (p. 94)

photosphere The bright visible surface of the Sun. (p. 95)

sunspot Relatively cooler, dark spot on the Sun that contains intense magnetic fields. (p. 96)

granulation The fine structure of bright regions (grains) with dark edges covering the Sun's surface. (p. 96)

convection Circulation in a fluid driven by heat. Hot material rises and cool material sinks. (p. 96)

Coulomb force The electrostatic force of repulsion between like charges or attraction between opposite charges. (p. 97)

ion An atom that has lost or gained one or more electrons. (p. 97)

ionization The process in which atoms lose or gain electrons. (p. 97)

binding energy The energy needed to pull an electron away from its atom. (p. 97)

quantum mechanics The study of the behaviour of atoms and atomic particles. (p. 97)

permitted orbit One of the unique orbits that an electron may occupy in an atom. (p. 97)

isotopes Atoms that have the same number of protons but a different number of neutrons. (p. 97)

energy level One of the rungs of the ladder of allowed energy states an electron may occupy in an atom. (p. 97)

excited atom An atom in which an electron has moved from a lower to a higher energy level. (p. 98)

ground state The lowest energy level an electron can occupy in an atom. (p. 98)

quantum leaps Jumps of electrons from one orbit or energy state to another. (p. 98)

Doppler effect The observed change in the wavelength of radiation due to a source moving toward or away from the observer. (p. 99)

blueshift A Doppler shift toward shorter wavelengths caused by a source approaching the observer. The faster the source approaches, the larger the blueshift. (p. 99)

redshift A Doppler shift toward longer wavelengths caused by a source receding from the observer. The faster the source recedes, the larger the redshift. (p. 99)

continuous spectrum A spectrum in which there are no absorption or emission lines. (p. 100)

absorption spectrum (dark-line spectrum) A spectrum that contains absorption lines. (p. 100)

absorption line A dark line in a spectrum produced by the absence of photons absorbed by atoms or molecules. (p. 100)

emission spectrum (bright-line spectrum) A spectrum produced by photons emitted by an excited gas. (p. 100)

emission line A bright line in a spectrum caused by the emission of photons from atoms. (p. 100)

Kirchhoff's laws A set of laws that describe the absorption and emission of light by matter. (p. 100)

transition The movement of an electron from one atomic energy level to another. (p. 101)

Lyman series Spectral lines in the ultraviolet spectrum of hydrogen, produced by transitions whose lowest energy level is the ground state. (p. 101)

Balmer series A series of spectral lines produced by hydrogen in the near-ultraviolet and visible parts of the spectrum. The three longest-wavelength Balmer lines are visible to the human eye. (p. 101)

Paschen series Spectral lines in the infrared spectrum of hydrogen produced by transitions whose lowest energy level is the third. (p. 101)

radial velocity (V_r) The component of an object's velocity that is directed directly away from or toward Earth. (p. 102)

chromosphere Bright gases just above the photosphere of the Sun. (p. 104)

corona The faint outer atmosphere of the Sun, composed of low-density, high-temperature gas. (p. 104)

filtergram A photograph (usually of the Sun) taken in the light of a specific region of the spectrum; for example, an H_α filtergram. (p. 105)

filament A solar eruption, seen from above, silhouetted against the bright photosphere. (p. 106)

spicule A small, flamelike projection in the chromosphere of the Sun. (p. 106)

coronagraph A telescope designed to capture images of faint objects, such as the corona of the Sun, that are near relatively bright objects. (p. 106)

magnetic carpet The network of small magnetic loops that covers the solar surface. (p. 106)

solar wind Rapidly moving atoms and ions that escape from the solar corona and blow outward through the solar system. (p. 107)

helioseismology The study of the interior of the Sun by the analysis of its modes of vibration. (p. 107)

differential rotation The rotation of a body in which different parts of the body have different periods of rotation. This is true of the Sun, the Jovian planets, and the disk of the galaxy. (p. 109)

dynamo effect The process by which a rotating, convecting body of conducting matter, such as Earth's core, can generate a magnetic field. (p. 109)

convective zone The region inside a star where energy is carried outward as rising hot gas and sinking cool gas. (p. 109)

Babcock model A model of the Sun's magnetic cycle in which the differential rotation of the Sun winds up and tangles the solar magnetic field. This is thought to be responsible for the sunspot cycle. (p. 109)

Maunder butterfly diagram A graph showing the latitude of sunspots versus time; first plotted by W. W. Maunder in 1904. (p. 110)

Zeeman effect The splitting of spectral lines into multiple components when the atoms are in a magnetic field. (p. 111)

Maunder minimum A period between 1645 and 1715 of less numerous sunspots and other solar activity. (p. 111)

active region A magnetic region on the solar surface that includes sunspots, prominences, flares, and the like. (p. 111)

prominence Eruption on the solar surface that is visible during total solar eclipses. (p. 114)

flare A violent eruption on the Sun's surface. (p. 115)

reconnection On the Sun, the merging of magnetic fields to release energy in the form of flares. (p. 115)

aurora The glowing light display that results when a planet's magnetic field guides charged particles toward the north and south magnetic poles, where they strike the upper atmosphere and excite atoms to emit photons. (p. 115)

coronal mass ejection (CME) Matter ejected from the Sun's corona in powerful surges guided by magnetic fields. (p. 115)

coronal hole An area of the solar surface that is dark at X-ray wavelengths; thought to be associated with divergent magnetic fields and the source of the solar wind. (p. 115)

The Family of Stars

TOPIC SUMMARIES

6.1 Star Distances

How far away are the stars?

- Distance is critical in astronomy. Finding the luminosities, diameters, and masses of stars requires first finding their distances.
- Astronomers can measure the distance to nearby stars by observing their parallaxes. Stellar distances are commonly expressed in light-years and parsecs. In this textbook we have chosen to use light-years because conceptually it is the simpler of the two options. A light-year (ly) is the distance light travels in one year. One parsec is 206 265 AU—the distance to an imaginary star whose parallax is 1 arc second.
- Stars farther away than about 550 ly have parallaxes too small to measure from ground-based observatories.

6.2 Apparent Brightness, Intrinsic Brightness, and Luminosity

How much energy do stars emit?

- Once you know the distance to a star, you can find its intrinsic brightness, which can be expressed as its absolute magnitude. The absolute magnitude of a star equals the apparent magnitude it would have if it were 33 ly away.
- The luminosity of a star, which can be found from its absolute magnitude, is a measure of the total energy radiated by the star. Luminosity can be expressed in watts, but luminosities of stars are often given in units of the luminosity of the Sun.

6.3 Star Temperatures

How can you tell a star's temperature using its spectrum?

- The hydrogen Balmer lines are weak in cool stars because atoms are not excited out of the ground state. In hot stars, the Balmer lines are weak because atoms are excited to higher orbits or are ionized. Only at intermediate temperatures are the Balmer lines strong.
- The strengths of many spectral lines in a star's spectrum can be used to tell you its temperature. Stars are classified in the temperature spectral sequence: O, B, A, F, G, K, M.
- Long after the spectral sequence was created, astronomers discovered L and T objects with temperatures even cooler than the M stars.

6.4 Star Sizes

How big are stars?

- The H–R diagram is a plot of luminosity versus surface temperature. It is an important graph in astronomy because it sorts the stars into categories by size.
- Roughly 90 percent of normal stars, including the Sun, fall on the main sequence, with the hotter main-sequence stars being more luminous. The giants and supergiants, however, are much larger and lie above the main sequence in the diagram. Some of the white dwarfs are hot stars, but they fall below the main sequence because they are so small.
- The large size of the giants and supergiants means their atmospheres have low densities. Giant stars, luminosity class III, have narrow spectral lines, and supergiants, class I, have extremely narrow lines. Class V main-sequence stars have relatively broad spectral lines.
- Stars so far away that their parallaxes are too small to measure can have their distances estimated by the technique of spectroscopic parallax.

6.5 Star Masses: Binary Stars

How much matter do stars contain?

- The only direct way you can find the mass of a star is by studying binary stars. When two stars orbit a common centre of mass, astronomers find their masses by observing the period and sizes of their orbits.
- Few binary star systems are easy to analyze; most are spectroscopic binaries in which the component stars

are known only by the alternating Doppler shifts of their spectral lines.

- Eclipsing binary star systems allow measurement not just of the component stars' masses but also independent checks on their temperatures and diameters.

6.6 Typical Stars

What is the typical star like?

- Given the mass and diameter of a star, you can find its average density. On the main sequence, the stars are about as dense as the Sun, but the giants and supergiants are very-low-density stars. Some are much thinner than air. The white dwarfs, lying below the main sequence, are tremendously dense.

- The mass–luminosity relation says that the more massive a main sequence star is, the more luminous it is. Giants and supergiants do not follow this relation in general, and white dwarfs not at all.

- A survey of stars in the neighbourhood of the Sun shows that giants and supergiants are rare and that red dwarfs, stars at the low-luminosity end of the main sequence, are the most common type, but also faint and hard to find.

KEY TERMS

stellar parallax (p) The small apparent shift in position of a nearby star relative to distant background objects due to Earth's orbital motion. (p. 120)

parsec (pc) The distance to a hypothetical star whose parallax is 1 second of arc. (p. 121)

intrinsic brightness A measure of the amount of light a star produces. (p. 122)

flux A measure of the flow of energy out of a surface; usually applied to light. (p. 122)

absolute visual magnitude (M_v) Intrinsic brightness of a star. The apparent visual magnitude the star would have if it were 33 ly away. (p. 122)

luminosity (L) The total amount of energy a star radiates per second at all wavelengths. (p. 123)

spectral class A star's position in the temperature classification system O, B, A, F, G, K, M, based on the appearance of the star's spectrum. (p. 124)

spectral sequence The arrangement of spectral classes (O, B, A, F, G, K, M) ranging from hot to cool. (p. 124)

brown dwarf A very cool, low-luminosity star whose mass is not sufficient to ignite nuclear fusion. (p. 125)

L dwarf, T dwarf Spectral classes of brown dwarf stars with lower surface temperatures and luminosities than M dwarfs. (p. 125)

Y dwarf A substellar object with temperature below 500 K, having inferred properties intermediate between brown dwarfs and Jovian planets. (p. 125)

Hertzsprung–Russell (H–R) diagram A plot of the intrinsic brightness versus the surface temperature of stars. It separates the effects of temperature and surface area on stellar luminosity. (p. 126)

main sequence The region of the H–R diagram running from upper left to lower right, which includes roughly 90 percent of all stars generating energy by nuclear fusion. (p. 127)

giant A large, cool, highly luminous star in the upper right of the H–R diagram, typically 10 to 100 times the diameter of the Sun. (p. 127)

supergiant An exceptionally luminous star whose diameter is 100 to 1000 times that of the Sun. (p. 127)

red dwarf A faint, cool, low-mass, main-sequence star. (p. 127)

white dwarf A dying star at the lower left of the H–R diagram that has collapsed to the size of Earth and is slowly cooling off. (p. 127)

luminosity class A category of stars of similar luminosity, determined by the widths of lines in their spectra. (p. 129)

spectroscopic parallax The method of determining a star's distance by comparing its apparent magnitude with its absolute magnitude as estimated from its spectrum. (p. 130)

binary stars Pairs of stars that orbit around their common centre of mass. (p. 130)

visual binary system A binary star system in which the two stars are separately visible in the telescope. (p. 132)

spectroscopic binary system A star system in which the stars are too close together to be visible separately. We see a single point of light, and only by taking a spectrum can we determine that there are two stars. (p. 132)

eclipsing binary system A binary star system in which the stars cross in front of each other as seen from Earth. (p. 133)

light curve A graph of brightness versus time commonly used in analyzing variable stars and eclipsing binaries. (p. 133)

mass–luminosity relation The more massive a main-sequence star is, the more luminous it is. (p. 134)

The Structure and Formation of Stars

TOPIC SUMMARIES

7.1 Stellar Structure

What are the insides of stars like?

- For a star to be stable, it must maintain hydrostatic equilibrium, and the deep layers must be hotter and denser and have higher pressure than the less-deep layers.
- Energy in a star must flow from the hot interior to the cool exterior by conduction, convection, or radiation. Conduction is not usually important inside stars.
- Much of what astronomers know about stars is based on detailed mathematical models of the interior of stars.

7.2 Nuclear Fusion in the Sun and Stars

How do stars generate energy?

- Stars generate energy near their centres, where conditions allow nuclear fusion reactions to combine hydrogen nuclei to make helium nuclei.
- Energy generated in a star's core flows outward either as photons moving through a radiative zone or as rising currents of hot gas and sinking currents of cool gas in a convective zone.
- Stars of the Sun's mass or less generate energy via the proton–proton chain; more massive main-sequence stars fuse hydrogen into helium in the CNO cycle.
- Observations of too few neutrinos coming from the Sun's core are now explained by the changing of neutrinos back and forth among three different types called "flavours." The neutrinos confirm that the Sun generates its energy by hydrogen fusion.
- The relationship between pressure and temperature, called the pressure–temperature thermostat, ensures that stars generate just enough energy to be stable.

7.3 Main-Sequence Stars

What determines the properties of main-sequence stars?

- The luminosity of a star depends on its mass. More massive stars have more weight to support, and their pressure–temperature thermostats must make more energy. That makes them more luminous.
- The main sequence has a minimum mass because objects less massive than 0.08 solar masses cannot get hot enough to begin hydrogen fusion.

How long can a star survive?

- The more massive a star is, the faster it uses up its hydrogen fuel. A 25-solar-mass star will exhaust its hydrogen and die in only about 7 million years.

7.4 The Birth of Stars

How are stars born?

- Stars form from the gas and dust of the interstellar medium.
- Astronomers know there is an interstellar medium because they can see emission nebulae, reflection nebulae, and dark nebulae. They can also detect interstellar absorption lines in the spectra of distant stars.
- The dust in the interstellar medium makes distant stars look fainter and redder than expected.
- Molecular clouds are sites of star formation. Such clouds can be triggered to collapse by collision with a shock wave that compresses and fragments the gas cloud, producing a cluster of protostars.

How do you know that theories of star formation are correct?

- A contracting protostar is cooler than a main-sequence star. The dust in the cocoon absorbs the protostar's light and re-radiates it as infrared radiation.

- As a protostar grows hot enough to begin hydrogen fusion at its core, it settles onto the main sequence.
- Very young star clusters contain large numbers of T Tauri stars.
- Some protostars have been found emitting jets of gas. Where these flows strike existing clouds of gas, astronomers can see Herbig–Haro objects. The jets are evidently focused by disks of gas and dust around the protostars.
- The Great Nebula in Orion is an active region of star formation. The bright stars in the centre of the nebula formed within the last few million years, and infrared telescopes detect protostars buried inside the molecular cloud behind the visible nebula.

KEY TERMS

conservation of mass One of the basic laws of stellar structure: The total mass of the star must equal the sum of the shell masses. (p. 144)

conservation of energy One of the basic laws of stellar structure: The total luminosity must equal the sum of energy generated in all of the layers. (p. 144)

hydrostatic equilibrium One of the basic laws of stellar structure: The weight on each layer must be balanced by the pressure in that layer. (p. 145)

energy transport One of the basic laws of stellar structure: Energy must move from hot to cool regions by conduction, radiation, or convection. (p. 145)

opacity The resistance of a gas to the passage of radiation. (p. 145)

stellar model A table of numbers representing the conditions in various layers within a star. (p. 146)

nuclear forces The two forces of nature that only affect the particles in the nuclei of atoms. (p. 148)

nuclear fission Reactions that break the nuclei of atoms into fragments. (p. 148)

nuclear fusion Reactions that join the nuclei of atoms to form more massive nuclei. (p. 148)

Coulomb barrier The electrostatic force of repulsion between bodies of like charge, commonly applied to atomic particles. (p. 149)

proton–proton chain A series of three nuclear reactions that builds a helium atom by adding together protons; the main energy source in the Sun. (p. 149)

deuterium An isotope of hydrogen in which the nucleus contains a proton and a neutron. (p. 150)

positron The antimatter equivalent of the electron; it has all the same properties as the electron except that its charge is positive instead of negative. (p. 150)

neutrino A neutral, nearly massless atomic particle that travels at or near the speed of light. (p. 150)

CNO (carbon–nitrogen–oxygen) cycle A series of nuclear reactions that use carbon as a catalyst to combine four hydrogen nuclei to make one helium nucleus plus energy; effective in stars more massive than the Sun. (p. 150)

zero-age main sequence (ZAMS) The location in the H–R diagram where stars first reach stability as hydrogen-burning stars. (p. 153)

interstellar medium (ISM) The gas and dust distributed between the stars. (p. 154)

interstellar dust Microscopic solid grains in the interstellar medium. (p. 155)

nebula A relatively dense cloud of interstellar gas and dust. (p. 155)

interstellar reddening The process in which dust scatters blue light out of starlight and makes the stars look redder. (p. 155)

emission nebula A cloud of glowing gas excited by ultraviolet radiation from hot stars. (p. 156)

HII region A region of ionized hydrogen around a hot star. (p. 156)

reflection nebula A nebula produced by starlight reflecting off dust particles in the interstellar medium. (p. 156)

dark nebula A cloud of gas and dust seen silhouetted against a brighter nebula. (p. 157)

molecular cloud A dense interstellar gas cloud in which atoms are able to link together to form molecules such as H_2 and CO. (p. 159)

shock wave A sudden change in pressure that travels as an intense sound wave. (p. 159)

star cluster A group of stars that formed together and orbit a common centre of mass. (p. 160)

stellar association A group of stars that formed together but are not gravitationally bound to one another. (p. 160)

protostar A collapsing cloud of gas and dust destined to become a star. (p. 160)

Bok globule Small, dark cloud only about 1 ly in diameter that contains 10 to 1000 solar masses of gas and dust, thought to be related to star formation. (p. 161)

Herbig–Haro object A small nebula that varies irregularly in brightness, evidently associated with star formation. (p. 161)

T Tauri star A young star surrounded by gas and dust, understood to be contracting toward the main sequence. (p. 161)

The Deaths of Stars

TOPIC SUMMARIES

8.1 Giant Stars

What happens to a star when it uses up the last of the hydrogen fuel in its core?

- As a star uses up the last of its hydrogen, the nuclear reactions die down, the core contracts, heats up, and forms a hydrogen-fusion shell. Energy flowing from the hydrogen-fusion shell swells the star into a cool giant or a supergiant.
- Eventually, contraction of the star's core ignites helium, first in the core and later in a shell. Massive stars can eventually fuse carbon and other elements.
- H–R diagrams demonstrate how stars in a cluster begin their evolution at the same time but evolve at different rates, depending on their masses.

8.2 The Deaths of Low-Mass Stars

How will the Sun and stars smaller than the Sun die?

- Red dwarfs less massive than 0.4 solar mass have very little hydrogen left when they die. They cannot become giant stars and will remain on the main sequence for a great amount of time.
- Medium-mass stars, up to about 4 solar masses, produce planetary nebulae and then become white dwarfs.

8.3 The Evolution of Binary Systems

What happens if an evolving star is in a binary star system?

- Mass can transfer in a binary system through accretion disks around receiving stars. Hot accretion disks can emit light and X-rays.
- Mass transferred onto a white dwarf can build and erupt as a nova explosion. As long as mass transfers form new layers of fuel, eruptions can occur repeatedly.

- A type Ia supernova can occur when mass transferred onto a white dwarf increases its mass above the Chandrasekhar–Landau limit, collapses, and immediately fuses its remaining nuclear fuel.

8.4 The Deaths of Massive Stars

How do massive stars die?

- The massive stars on the upper main sequence fuse nuclear fuels up to iron, then the iron core collapses, and this triggers a type II supernova.
- A type Ib supernova occurs when a massive star in a binary system loses its outer layers of hydrogen before exploding.

8.5 Neutron Stars

What are neutron stars, and how do you know they really exist?

- Theory predicts that a collapsing core cannot support itself as a white dwarf if its mass is greater than the Chandrasekhar–Landau limit. If its mass lies between 1.4 solar masses and about 3 solar masses, it can halt its contraction and form a neutron star.
- A neutron star is supported by degenerate neutron pressure. Theory predicts that a neutron star should spin very fast, have a surface temperature of millions of degrees K, and have a powerful magnetic field.
- Pulsars were discovered in 1967.
- Astronomers detect pulsars if their beams sweep across Earth as they spin.
- The pulsars found in binary systems allow astronomers to estimate the masses of neutron stars.
- Planets have been found orbiting at least one neutron star. They may be the remains of a companion star that was mostly devoured by the neutron star.

8.6 Black Holes

What are black holes, and how do you know they really exist?

- Black holes occur when the collapsing core of a supernova greater than 3 solar masses contracts to such a small size that no radiation can escape.
- There are two relativistic effects on an object falling into a black hole. Compared to the observer, the object's clock would slow and light would be redshifted. The object would heat and deform from powerful tidal forces.
- Binary star systems where mass flows into a compact object with mass greater than 3 solar masses and emits X-rays indicate possible black holes.
- Black holes and neutron stars at the centre of accretion disks can eject powerful beams of radiation and gas. Such beams have been detected.
- Gamma-ray bursts appear to be related to violent events involving neutron stars and black holes. The merging of binary compact objects or shifts in neutron star crusts may produce short bursts.

KEY TERMS

nova From the Latin, meaning "new," a sudden and temporary brightening of a star, making it appear as a new star in the sky; evidently caused by an explosion of nuclear fuel on the surface of a white dwarf. (p. 168)

supernova A "new star" in the sky that is roughly 4000 times more luminous than a normal nova and longer lasting; evidently the result of an explosion of a star. (p. 168)

giant star Large, cool, highly luminous star in the upper right of the H–R diagram, typically 10 to 100 times the diameter of the Sun. (p. 168)

supergiant star Exceptionally luminous star whose diameter is 100 to 1000 times that of the Sun. (p. 168)

horizontal branch The location in the H–R diagram of giant stars that are fusing helium. (p. 169)

planetary nebula An expanding shell of gas ejected from a medium-mass star during the latter stages of its evolution. (p. 171)

degenerate matter Extremely high-density matter in which pressure no longer depends on temperature due to quantum mechanical effects. (p. 172)

compact object One of the three final states of stellar evolution, which generates no nuclear energy and is much smaller and denser than a normal star. (p. 172)

Chandrasekhar–Landau limit The maximum mass of a white dwarf, about 1.4 solar masses. A white dwarf of greater mass cannot support itself and will collapse. (p. 173)

open cluster A cluster of 100 to 1000 stars with an open, transparent appearance, usually relatively young and located in the disk of the galaxy. The stars are not tightly grouped. (p. 174)

globular cluster A star cluster containing 100 000 to 1 million stars in a sphere about 75 ly in diameter, generally old, metal-poor, and found in the spherical component of the galaxy. (p. 174)

turnoff point The point in an H–R diagram at which a cluster's stars turn off the main sequence and move toward the red-giant region, revealing the approximate age of the cluster. (p. 174)

Roche lobe The volume of space a star controls gravitationally within a binary system. (p. 176)

angular momentum A measure of the tendency of a rotating body to continue rotating; mathematically, the product of mass, velocity, and radius. (p. 176)

accretion disk The rotating disk that forms in some situations as matter is drawn gravitationally toward a central body. (p. 177)

type II supernova A supernova explosion caused by the collapse of a massive star. (p. 181)

supernova remnant The expanding shell of gas and dust marking the site of a supernova explosion. (p. 181)

type I supernova A supernova whose spectrum contains no hydrogen lines. (p. 182)

neutron star A small, highly dense star, with radius about 10 km, composed almost entirely of tightly packed neutrons. (p. 183)

pulsar A source of short, precisely timed radio bursts, understood to be spinning neutron stars. (p. 185)

lighthouse model The explanation of a pulsar as a spinning neutron star sweeping beams of electromagnetic radiation around the sky. (p. 185)

general theory of relativity Einstein's theory that describes gravity as due to curvature of space-time. (p. 187)

gravitational radiation Expanding waves in a gravitational field that transport energy through space at the speed of light, as predicted by general relativity. (p. 187)

millisecond pulsar A pulsar with a pulse period of only a few milliseconds. (p. 187)

singularity An object of zero radius and infinite density. (p. 189)

black hole A mass that has collapsed to such a small volume that its gravity prevents the escape of all radiation. Also, the volume of space from which radiation may not escape. (p. 189)

event horizon The boundary of the region of a black hole from which no radiation may escape. No event that occurs within the event horizon is visible to a distant observer. (p. 190)

Schwarzschild radius (R_S) The radius of the event horizon around a black hole. (p. 190)

time dilation The slowing of moving clocks or clocks in strong gravitational fields. (p. 191)

gravitational redshift The lengthening of the wavelength of a photon as it escapes from a gravitational field. (p. 191)

gamma-ray burst A sudden, powerful burst of gamma rays. (p. 193)

hypernova Produced when a very massive star collapses into a black hole; a possible source of gamma-ray bursts. (p. 193)

The Milky Way Galaxy

TOPIC SUMMARIES

9.1 The Discovery of the Galaxy

How do you know you live in a galaxy?

- The hazy band of the Milky Way is our wheel-shaped galaxy seen from within, but its size and shape are not obvious. William and Caroline Herschel counted stars over the sky to show that it seemed to be shaped like a disk with the Sun near the centre, but they could not see very far into space because of interstellar gas and dust.
- In the early 20th century, Harlow Shapley calibrated Cepheid variable stars to find the distance to globular clusters and demonstrated that our galaxy is much larger than the part you can see easily and that the Sun is not at the centre.
- Modern observations suggest that our galaxy contains a disk component about 80 000 ly in diameter and the Sun is two-thirds of the way from the centre to the visible edge. The central bulge and an extensive halo that contains old stars and a small amount of gas and dust make up the spherical component.
- The mass of the galaxy can be found from its rotation curve. Kepler's third law tells astronomers the galaxy contains over 100 billion solar masses, and the rising rotation curve at great distance from the centre shows that the halo must contain much more mass. Because that material is not emitting detectable electromagnetic radiation, astronomers call it dark matter.

9.2 Spiral Arms and Star Formation

How do you know ours is a spiral galaxy, and what are the spiral arms?

- The most massive stars live such short lives that they don't have time to move from their place of birth. Because they are concentrated along the spiral arms, astronomers conclude that the spiral arms are sites of star formation.

- Spiral arms can be traced through the Sun's neighbourhood by using spiral tracers such as O and B stars; but to extend the map over the entire galaxy, astronomers must use infrared and radio observations to see through the gas and dust.
- The spiral density wave theory suggests that the spiral arms are regions of compression that move around the disk. When an orbiting gas cloud overtakes the compression wave, the gas cloud forms stars. Another process, self-sustaining star formation, may modify the spiral arms with branches and spurs; this happens when the birth of massive stars triggers the formation of more stars by compressing neighbouring gas clouds.

9.3 The Origin and History of the Milky Way

How did our galaxy form and evolve?

- The oldest open star clusters indicate that the disk of our galaxy is only about 9 billion years old. The oldest globular clusters appear to be at least 13 billion years old, so our galaxy must have begun forming at least 13 billion years ago.
- Stellar populations are an important clue to the formation of our galaxy. The first stars to form in our galaxy, termed population II stars, were poor in elements heavier than helium: elements that astronomers call metals. As generations of stars manufactured metals and spread them back into the interstellar medium, the metal abundance of more recent generations increased. Population I stars, including the Sun, are richer in metals than population II stars.
- Because the halo is made up of population II stars and the disk is made up of population I stars, astronomers conclude that the halo formed first and the disk later. The monolithic collapse model, that the galaxy formed from a single, roughly spherical cloud of turbulent gas and gradually flattened into a disk, has been amended to include mergers with other galaxies and later infalling gas contributing to the disk.

9.4 The Nucleus

What lies at the very centre of our galaxy?

- The nucleus of the galaxy is not visible at visual wavelengths, but radio, infrared, and X-ray radiation can penetrate the gas and dust in space. These wavelengths reveal crowded central stars and warmed dust.

- The very centre of the Milky Way Galaxy is marked by a radio source, Sagittarius A*. The source must be less than a few astronomical units in diameter, but the motion of stars around the centre shows that it must contain roughly 4.3 million solar masses. A supermassive black hole is the only object that could contain so much mass in such a small space.

KEY TERMS

Cepheid variable stars Variable stars with pulsation periods of 1 to 60 days and whose period of variation is related to their luminosity. (p. 199)

instability strip The region of the H–R diagram in which stars are unstable to pulsation. A star evolving through this strip becomes a variable star. (p. 199)

period–luminosity relation The relation between period of pulsation and intrinsic brightness among Cepheid variable stars. (p. 200)

proper motion The rate at which a star moves across the sky, measured in seconds of arc per year. (p. 200)

calibrate To make observations of reference objects, checks on instrument performance, calculations of unit conversions, and so on, needed to completely understand measurements of unknown quantities. (p. 201)

disk component All material confined to the plane of the galaxy. (p. 201)

spiral arms Long spiral pattern of bright stars, star clusters, gas, and dust. Spiral arms extend from the centre to the edge of the disk of spiral galaxies. (p. 202)

spherical component The part of the galaxy that includes all matter in a spherical distribution around its centre (the halo and central bulge). (p. 203)

halo The spherical region of a spiral galaxy, containing a thin scattering of stars, star clusters, and small amounts of gas. (p. 203)

central bulge The dense cloud of stars that surrounds the centre of our galaxy. (p. 203)

rotation curve A graph of orbital velocity versus radius in the disk of a galaxy. (p. 205)

dark halo The low-density extension of the halo of our galaxy, believed to be composed of dark matter. (p. 206)

dark matter Nonluminous matter that is detected only by its gravitational influence. (p. 206)

spiral tracer Object used to map the spiral arms—for example, O and B associations, open clusters, clouds of ionized hydrogen, and some types of variable stars. (p. 207)

density wave theory Theory proposed to account for spiral arms as compressions of the interstellar medium in the disk of the galaxy. (p. 207)

self-sustaining star formation The process by which the birth of stars compresses the surrounding gas clouds and triggers the formation of more stars. (p. 209)

population I star Stars rich in atoms heavier than helium, nearly always relatively young stars found in the disk of the galaxy. (p. 210)

population II star Stars poor in atoms heavier than helium, nearly always relatively old stars found in the halo, globular clusters, or the central bulge. (p. 210)

metals In astronomical usage, all atoms heavier than helium. (p. 210)

monolithic collapse model An early hypothesis that says that the galaxy formed from the collapse of a single large cloud of turbulent gas over 13 billion years ago. (p. 212)

Sagittarius A* The powerful radio source located at the core of the Milky Way Galaxy. (p. 216)

Galaxies

TOPIC SUMMARIES

10.1 The Family of Galaxies

What types of galaxies exist?

- Galaxies can be divided into three classes, and their subclasses specify details of the galaxy's shape.
- Elliptical galaxies contain little gas and dust and cannot make new stars. Consequently, they lack hot, blue stars and have a relatively red colour.
- Spiral galaxies contain more gas and dust and support active star formation. The massive, hot, and blue stars give these galaxies a blue colour.
- A spiral galaxy's halo and nuclear bulge usually lack gas and dust and contain little star formation, and so have a red colour.
- Irregular galaxies have no obvious shape but contain gas and dust and support star formation.

10.2 Measuring the Properties of Galaxies

How do astronomers measure the distances to galaxies, and how does that allow the sizes, luminosities, and masses of galaxies to be determined?

- Astronomers find the distance to galaxies using objects of known luminosity, such as Cepheid variable stars and type Ia supernovae explosions.
- Astronomers can estimate the distance to a galaxy by dividing its apparent rate of recession (its radial velocity) by the Hubble constant. Apparent rate of recession is related to distance by the Hubble law.
- Astronomers measure the masses of galaxies in several ways. The most precise is the rotation curve method, but this can be applied only to nearby galaxies.
- Observations show that galaxies contain 10 to 100 times more dark matter than visible matter. Signs of dark matter are more obvious in outer halos.
- Stars near the centres of galaxies are orbiting at high velocities, suggesting the presence of supermassive black holes in the centres of most galaxies.

10.3 The Evolution of Galaxies

Why are there different kinds of galaxies, and how do galaxies evolve?

- Rich clusters of galaxies contain fewer spirals than do poor clusters of galaxies, and that is evidence that galaxies evolve by collisions and mergers.
- When galaxies collide, tides twist and distort their shapes, and the resulting compression of gas clouds triggers star formation.
- There is clear evidence that our Milky Way Galaxy is devouring some of the small galaxies that orbit nearby and that it has consumed other small galaxies in the past.
- Shells of stars, counter-rotating parts of galaxies, streams of stars in the halos of galaxies, and multiple nuclei are evidence that galaxies can merge.
- The merger of two larger galaxies can scramble star orbits and drive bursts of star formation to use up gas and dust.
- Spiral galaxies have thin, delicate disks and appear not to have suffered mergers with large galaxies.
- A galaxy moving through the gas in a cluster of galaxies can be stripped of its own gas and dust and become an S0 galaxy.
- At great distances, astronomers see that galaxies were smaller, more irregular, and closer together. Also, there were more spirals and fewer ellipticals long ago.

10.4 Active Galaxies and Quasars

What is the energy source for active galaxies, what can trigger the activity, and what does that reveal about the history of galaxies?

- Seyfert galaxies are spirals with small, highly luminous cores. Spectra of Seyfert galaxy nuclei show that they contain highly excited, rapidly moving gas.
- Because the brightness of AGN can change noticeably in only a few minutes or hours, they must be smaller than a few AU in diameter.
- The lobes in double-lobed radio galaxies appear to be inflated by jets ejected from the nuclei of the galaxies.

- Quasars have very high redshifts, evidence of great distance. To be visible from so far, quasars must be ultraluminous and provide a window into the time when galaxies were just forming.
- The spectra of hazy objects near quasars and the spectra of quasar fuzz show that quasars are the active cores of very distant galaxies.
- Evidence is strong that AGN contain supermassive black holes into which matter is flowing through hot accretion disks. This can eject jets in opposite directions that push into the intergalactic medium and inflate radio lobes like balloons.
- The mass of a central black hole can be found by observing the velocity of stars orbiting the black hole or the rotational speed of its accretion disk.

- According to the unified model, what you see depends on the tilt of the accretion disk. Seen face-on, the core produces broad spectral lines. Seen edge-on, the core is hidden and the spectrum contains narrow lines.
- Many galaxies appear to contain dormant supermassive black holes at their centres. Only when a supermassive black hole is fed does it erupt.
- Matter flowing into a hot accretion disk around a black hole can eject high-energy jets of gas and radiation perpendicular to the disk.
- Interactions between galaxies can throw matter into the centre, feed the black hole, and trigger eruptions.
- Supermassive black holes powering AGN and quasars cannot have been formed by dying stars but may have formed as the nuclear bulges of their host galaxies began to form and contract.

KEY TERMS

Large Magellanic Cloud The larger of two irregular galaxies visible in the southern sky passing near the Milky Way Galaxy. (p. 222)

Small Magellanic Cloud The smaller of two irregular galaxies visible in the southern sky passing near the Milky Way Galaxy. (p. 222)

distance ladder The calibration used to build a distance scale extending from the size of Earth to the most distant visible galaxies. (p. 223)

elliptical galaxy A galaxy that is round or elliptical in outline and contains little gas and dust, no disk or spiral arms, and few hot, bright stars. (p. 224)

spiral galaxy A galaxy with an obvious disk component that contains gas, dust, hot bright stars, and spiral arms. (p. 224)

barred spiral galaxy A spiral galaxy with an elongated nucleus resembling a bar from which the arms originate. (p. 224)

irregular galaxy A galaxy with a chaotic appearance, large clouds of gas and dust, and both population I and II stars, but without spiral arms. (p. 225)

standard candle Object of known brightness that astronomers use to find distance—for example, Cepheid variable stars and supernovae. (p. 226)

Tully-Fisher relationship The linear relation between luminosity and the rotational rate of spiral galaxies used to determine the distance to spiral galaxies as standard candles. (p. 226)

look-back time The amount by which you look into the past when you look at a distant galaxy; a time that equals the distance to the galaxy in light-years. (p. 227)

Hubble law The linear relation between the distances to galaxies and the apparent velocity of recession. (p. 228)

Hubble constant A measure of the rate of expansion of the universe; the average value of the apparent velocity of recession divided by distance, about 70 km/s/Mpc. (p. 228)

rotation curve method A method of determining a galaxy's mass by observing the orbital velocity and orbital radius of stars in the galaxy. (p. 228)

rich galaxy cluster A cluster containing 1000 or more galaxies, usually mostly ellipticals, scattered over a volume only a few Mpc in diameter. (p. 232)

poor galaxy cluster An irregularly shaped cluster that contains fewer than 1000 galaxies, many of which are spiral, and no giant ellipticals. (p. 232)

Local Group The small cluster of a few dozen galaxies that contains our Milky Way Galaxy. (p. 232)

gravitational lensing The curving of light by a large mass when the light passes between the source and the observer. Multiple images of the source can be seen. (p. 232)

tidal tail A long streamer of stars, gas, and dust torn from a galaxy during its close interaction with another passing galaxy. (p. 235)

ring galaxy A galaxy that resembles a ring around a bright nucleus, resulting from a head-on collision between two galaxies. (p. 235)

starburst galaxy A galaxy undergoing a rapid burst of star formation. (p. 236)

active galaxy A galaxy whose centre emits large amounts of excess energy, often in the form of radio emissions. Active galaxies have massive black holes in their centres into which matter is flowing. (p. 239)

radio galaxy A galaxy that is a strong source of radio signals. (p. 239)

active galactic nuclei (AGN) The centres of active galaxies that are emitting large amounts of excess energy. (p. 240)

Seyfert galaxy An otherwise normal spiral galaxy with an unusually bright, small core that fluctuates in brightness. (p. 240)

double-lobed radio source A galaxy that emits radio energy from two regions (lobes) located on opposite sides of the galaxy. (p. 240)

quasar Small, powerful source of energy in the active core of a very distant galaxy. (p. 241)

unified model An attempt to explain the different types of active galactic nuclei using a single model viewed from different directions. (p. 243)

blazar A type of active galaxy nucleus that is especially variable and has few or no spectral emission lines. (p. 243)

Cosmology in the 21st Century

TOPIC SUMMARIES

11.1 Introduction to the Universe

Does the universe have an edge and a centre?

- Astronomers conclude that it is impossible for the universe to have an edge because this introduces logical inconsistencies. If the universe has no edge it cannot have a centre.
- The darkness of the night sky leads astronomers to the conclusion that the universe is not infinitely old. If it were infinite in extent and age, every spot on the sky would glow as brightly as the surface of a star. This problem, commonly known as Olbers's paradox, leads to the conclusion that the universe had a beginning.

11.2 The Big Bang Theory

How do you know that the universe began with a big bang?

- Edwin Hubble's 1929 discovery that the redshift of a galaxy is proportional to its distance is known as Hubble's law and indicates that the universe is expanding. Tracing this expansion backward in time brings you to an initial high-density, high-temperature state commonly called the big bang.
- The galaxies do not recede from a single point. They recede from each other as space expands between them.
- The CMB is blackbody radiation with a temperature of about 2.73 K uniformly spread over the entire sky. It is the light from the big bang, released from matter at the time of recombination and now redshifted by a factor of 1100.
- The background radiation is clear evidence that the universe began with a big bang.
- During the first three minutes of the big bang, nuclear fusion converted some of the hydrogen into helium but was unable to make many other heavy atoms because no stable nuclei exist with atomic weights of 5 or 8. Today, hydrogen and helium are common in the universe, but heavier atoms are rare.

11.3 Space and Time, Matter and Energy

How does the universe expand?

- In its major features, the universe is isotropic and homogeneous. It looks the same in all directions and in all locations.
- Isotropy and homogeneity together lead to the cosmological principle: the idea that there are no special places in the universe. Except for local differences, every place is the same.
- General relativity explains that cosmic redshifts are caused by the stretching of photon wavelengths as they travel through expanding space-time.
- Model universes with flat (uncurved) space-time are infinite and can expand forever. A flat universe would have an average density equal to what is called the critical density. Modern observations indicate that the universe is flat.
- The amounts of deuterium and lithium-7 show that normal baryonic matter can make up only about 5 percent of the critical density. Dark matter must be non-baryonic and makes up less than 30 percent of the critical density. For the universe to be flat, there must be another major component aside from baryonic matter and dark matter.

11.4 Modern Cosmology

How has the universe evolved, and what will be its fate?

- The inflationary theory proposes that the universe expanded dramatically a tiny fraction of a second after the big bang.
- Inflation solves the flatness problem because the sudden inflation forced the universe to become flat, just as a spot on an inflating balloon becomes flatter as the balloon inflates.
- Inflation solves the horizon problem because the part of the universe that is now observable was so small before inflation that energy could move and equalize the temperature everywhere.

- Observations of type Ia supernovae reveal that the expansion of the universe is speeding up. This is thought to be due to "dark energy."
- The nature of dark energy is unknown. It may be described by Einstein's cosmological constant, or it may change with time, in which case astronomers refer to it as quintessence.
- The observed value of the Hubble constant implies that the universe is 13.8 billion years old. The future fate of the universe depends on the nature of dark energy. If dark energy increases in strength with time, the universe could end in a big rip.
- The sudden inflation of the universe could have magnified tiny quantum mechanical fluctuations in space-time. These very large-scale but weak differences in gravity worked with dark matter to draw together baryonic (ordinary) matter and create the large-scale structure.
- Precise observations of irregularities in the CMB and in the large-scale structure of the universe confirm that the universe is flat and contains about 4.9 percent baryonic matter, 26.8 percent dark matter, and 68.3 percent dark energy.
- The Large Hadron Collider (LHC), the largest experiment in history, produces and smashes together beams of fundamental particles with energies high enough to recreate conditions of the big bang. The LHC experiments will give us insight into the fundamental forces, the origin of mass, extra dimensions of space, microscopic black holes, and the nature of dark matter.

KEY TERMS

cosmology The study of the nature, origin, and evolution of the universe. (p. 250)

Olbers's paradox The conflict between theory and evidence regarding the darkness of the night sky. (p. 252)

observable universe The part of the universe that you can see from your location in space and in time. (p. 253)

big bang The high-density, high-temperature state from which the expanding universe of galaxies began. (p. 255)

Hubble time The age of the universe, equivalent to 1 divided by the Hubble constant. The Hubble time is the age of the universe based on its expansion at a constant rate since the big bang. (p. 255)

cosmic microwave background (CMB) Radiation from the hot matter of the universe soon after the big bang. The large redshift makes it appear to come from a blackbody with a temperature of 2.7 K. (p. 256)

antimatter Matter composed of antiparticles, which upon colliding with a matching particle of normal matter, annihilates, converting the mass of both particles into energy. In comparison to the corresponding particles of normal matter, antiparticles have the same mass but opposite charge. (p. 258)

recombination The stage, within 400 000 years of the big bang, when neutral hydrogen formed and the gas became transparent to radiation. (p. 260)

dark age The period of time after the glow of the big bang faded into the infrared and before the birth of the first stars, during which the universe expanded in darkness. (p. 260)

reionization The stage in the early history of the universe when ultraviolet photons from the first stars ionized the gas that filled space. (p. 260)

isotropy The observation that, in its general properties, the universe looks the same in every direction. (p. 261)

homogeneity The observation that, on the large scale, matter is uniformly spread through the universe. (p. 261)

cosmological principle The assumption that any observer in any galaxy sees the same general features of the universe. (p. 261)

open universe A model of the universe in which space-time is curved in such a way that the universe is infinite. (p. 262)

closed universe A model of the universe in which space-time is curved to meet itself, and the universe is finite. (p. 262)

flat universe A model of the universe in which space-time is not curved. (p. 262)

critical density The average density of matter and energy in the universe needed to make its curvature flat. (p. 263)

nonbaryonic matter Proposed dark matter made up of particles other than protons and neutrons (baryons). (p. 263)

cold dark matter Dark matter that is made of slow-moving particles. (p. 263)

flatness problem The peculiar circumstance that the early universe must have contained almost exactly the right amount of matter to make space-time flat. (p. 264)

horizon problem The circumstance that the primordial background radiation seems much more isotropic than can be explained by the standard big bang theory. (p. 264)

inflationary big bang A version of the big bang theory, derived from grand unified theories of particle physics, that includes a rapid expansion when the universe was very young. (p. 264)

cosmological constant A constant in Einstein's equations of space and time that represents a force of repulsion. (p. 267)

quintessence A possible form of dark energy that can change in strength as the universe ages. (p. 267)

dark energy The energy believed to drive the acceleration of the expanding universe. (p. 267)

big rip The fate of the universe if dark energy increases with time, and galaxies, stars, and even atoms are eventually ripped apart by the accelerating expansion of the universe. (p. 268)

large-scale structure The distribution of clusters and superclusters of galaxies in filaments and walls enclosing voids. (p. 268)

The Origin of the Solar System

TOPIC SUMMARIES

12.1 The Great Chain of Origins

What theory explains the origin of the solar system?

- Modern astronomy reveals that the matter in our solar system was formed in the big bang, and the atoms heavier than helium were created in successive generations of stars. The Sun and planets evidently formed from a cloud of gas in the interstellar medium.
- Hot disks of gas and dust have been detected around young stars and are understood to be where planets could form.
- The solar nebula theory proposes that the planets formed in a disk of gas and dust around the protostar that became the Sun.

12.2 A Survey of the Planets

What observed properties of the solar system must be explained by the theory of its origin?

- The solar system is disk shaped. The orbital revolutions of the planets, as well as most of their axial rotations and most of the orbits of their moons, share a common direction of motion.
- The planets are divided into two types: Terrestrial planets and Jovian planets.
- The Jovian worlds have gaseous surfaces, ring systems, and large families of moons. The Terrestrial planets are denser, have rocky surfaces, and have no rings and few moons.

12.3 Space Debris: Asteroids, Comets, and Meteoroids

What are asteroids and comets and what are their connections to meteors and meteorites?

- Asteroids are rocky, irregular in shape and heavily cratered by collisions. Most asteroids lie in a belt between Mars and Jupiter, although some follow orbits that cross into the inner solar system.
- Comets are icy bodies that fall into the inner solar system along long elliptical orbits.

- A comet gas tail is ionized gas carried away by the solar wind. A comet dust tail is solid debris released from the nucleus and blown outward by the pressure of sunlight.
- Meteoroids that fall into Earth's atmosphere are vaporized by friction and become visible as meteors. Meteoroids that reach the ground are called meteorites.
- Evidence suggests that most meteorites are fragments of asteroids. The vast majority of meteors appear to be bits of debris from comets.

12.4 The Story of Planet Formation

How do planets form?

- The age of a rocky body can be found by radioactive dating. The oldest objects in our solar system are some meteorites that have ages of 4.6 billion years. This is taken to be the age of the solar system.
- Planets begin growing by accreting solid material. But once a planet approaches about 15 Earth masses, it can begin growing by gravitational collapse as it pulls in gas from the solar nebula.
- The condensation sequence explains that the Terrestrial planets formed in the inner solar system where only denser minerals could condense to form solids, while the Jovian planets formed farther out where ices could condense.
- The Terrestrial planets may have formed slowly from the accretion of planetesimals of similar composition and then differentiated later when radioactive decay heated the planet's interiors.
- Earth's first atmosphere was outgassed.
- The asteroids formed as rocky planetesimals between Mars and Jupiter, but Jupiter prevented them from forming a planet.
- Comets are the leftover icy planetesimals in the outer solar system; comets falling in from the Oort cloud become long-period comets.
- Other icy bodies in the outer solar system make up the Kuiper belt. Objects from the Kuiper belt can become short-period comets.

- All the old surfaces in the solar system were heavily cratered by an early bombardment of debris that filled the solar system when it was young.

12.5 Planets Orbiting Other Stars

What do astronomers know about other planetary systems?

- Debris disks appear to be produced by dust released during collisions among objects in other planetary systems, and they may contain planets.

- Planets orbiting other stars have been detected because they create small Doppler shifts in the stars' spectra. Planets have also been detected as they cross in front of their star and dim the star's light. Recently, planets have been directly imaged for the first time.
- The first extrasolar planets found were massive Jovian worlds. Lower-mass Terrestrial planets are harder to detect, but recently several promising candidates have been found.

KEY TERMS

solar nebula theory A theory of formation of the solar system consistent with our current observations that describes how a rotating cloud of gas and dust gravitationally collapsed and flattened into a disk around the Sun forming at the centre, from which the planets were formed. (p. 276)

asteroid Small, rocky world. Most orbit between Mars and Jupiter in the asteroid belt. (p. 278)

comet One of the small, icy bodies that orbit the Sun and produce tails of gas and dust when they approach the Sun. (p. 279)

Terrestrial planet An Earth-like planet—small, dense, rocky. (p. 280)

Jovian planet Jupiter-like planet with a large diameter and low density. (p. 280)

volatile Easily evaporated. (p. 282)

Kuiper belt The collection of icy planetesimals orbiting in a region from just beyond Neptune out to 50 AU or more. (p. 282)

Oort cloud The hypothetical source of comets, a swarm of icy bodies understood to lie in a spherical shell extending to 100 000 AU from the Sun. (p. 282)

meteor A small bit of matter heated by friction to incandescent vapour as it falls into Earth's atmosphere. (p. 284)

meteoroid A meteor in space before it enters Earth's atmosphere. (p. 284)

meteorite A meteor that survives its passage through the atmosphere and strikes the ground. (p. 284)

carbonaceous chondrite Stony meteorite that contains small, glassy spheres—called chondrules—and volatiles. These chondrites may be the least-altered remains of the solar nebula still present in the solar system. (p. 284)

meteor shower A display of meteors that appear to come from one point in the sky; understood to be cometary debris. (p. 285)

half-life The time required for half of the radioactive atoms in a sample to decay. (p. 285)

uncompressed density The density a planet would have if its gravity did not compress it. (p. 288)

ice line A boundary beyond which water vapour could freeze to form ice. (p. 288)

condensation sequence The sequence in which different materials condense from the solar nebula, depending on their distance from the Sun. (p. 288)

planetesimal One of the small bodies that formed from the solar nebula and eventually grew into a protoplanet. (p. 288)

condensation The growth of a particle by addition of material from surrounding gas, atom by atom. (p. 288)

accretion The sticking together of solid particles to produce a larger particle. (p. 288)

protoplanet Massive object, destined to become a planet, resulting from the coalescence of planetesimals in the solar nebula. (p. 289)

gravitational collapse The process by which a forming body such as a planet gravitationally captures gas rapidly from the surrounding nebula. (p. 289)

differentiation The separation of planetary material inside a planet according to density. (p. 289)

outgassing The release of gases from a planet's interior. (p. 290)

heavy bombardment The intense cratering that occurred sometime during the first 0.5 billion years in the history of the solar system. (p. 291)

NEO (near-Earth object) A small solar system body (asteroid or comet) with an orbit near enough to Earth that it poses some threat of eventual collision. (p. 292)

evolutionary theory An explanation of a phenomenon involving slow, steady processes. (p. 292)

catastrophic theory An explanation of a phenomenon involving special, sudden, perhaps violent, events. (p. 292)

heat of formation In planetology, the heat released by infalling matter during the formation of a planetary body. (p. 293)

debris disk A disk of dust around some stars, found by infrared observations. The dust is debris from collisions among asteroids, comets, and Kuiper belt objects. (p. 296)

extrasolar planet A planet orbiting a star other than the Sun. (p. 296)

Comparative Planetology of the Terrestrial Planets

TOPIC SUMMARIES

13.1 A Travel Guide to the Terrestrial Planets

How can comparison help you understand the Terrestrial planets?

- The Terrestrial worlds differ mainly in size, but they all have low-density rocky crusts, mantles of dense rock, and metallic cores.
- Comparative planetology alerts you to expect that cratered surfaces are old, that heat flowing out of a planet drives geological activity, and that the nature of a planet's atmosphere depends on both the size of the planet and its temperature.
- Earth's moon illustrates important principles such as cratering and flooding of basins by lava.

13.2 Earth: The Active Planet

What are the main features of Earth when viewed as a planet?

- Earth has passed through three evolutionary stages: (1) differentiation, forming a liquid metallic core that generates a magnetic field; (2) cratering and basin formation; and (3) continued slow surface evolution.
- Earth is dominated by plate tectonics, a process that breaks the crust into moving plates. This process is driven by heat flowing upward from the interior.
- Earth's primary atmosphere was probably mostly carbon dioxide, nitrogen, and water vapour. Most of the carbon dioxide dissolved in seawater and was added to ocean sediments, and plant life has added oxygen to the atmosphere, producing the current secondary atmosphere.
- The greenhouse effect can warm a planet if gases such as carbon dioxide in the atmosphere are transparent to light but opaque to infrared. Measurements of carbon isotope ratios and carbon dioxide versus oxygen abundances make it clear that the CO_2 added to the atmosphere since around 1800 is predominantly from the burning of fossil fuels. Observations and model calculations have eliminated other candidate causes for the current warming: for example, natural climate cycles or variations in the Sun's output.

13.3 The Moon

How does size determine the geological activity and evolution of a planetary body?

- Earth's moon formed in a molten state and partly differentiated, but it contains little metal and has a low density.
- Because it is a small world, Earth's moon has lost most of its internal heat and is no longer geologically active. Its old highlands are heavily cratered, but the lowland maria are filled with smooth lava flows that formed soon after the end of the heavy bombardment.
- The large-impact hypothesis suggests the Moon formed when an impact between Earth and a very large planetesimal ejected debris that formed a disk around Earth. The Moon formed from that disk.

13.4 Mercury

How does Mercury compare to Earth?

- Mercury is smaller than Earth but larger than Earth's moon. It is airless and has an old, heavily cratered surface.
- Mercury has a much higher density than Earth's moon and must have a large metallic core. When it was young, Mercury may have suffered a major impact that drove off some of its lower-density crust and mantle rock and left a metallic core that is larger than the condensation sequence would imply.
- Mercury has long curving ridges that were formed by compression of the crust when its large metallic core solidified and contracted.

13.5 Venus

How do distance from the Sun and planet size affect the properties of its atmosphere?

- Although Venus is almost as big as Earth, it has a thick, cloudy atmosphere of CO_2 that hides the surface. The surface can be studied by radar mapping.
- The CO_2 atmosphere drives an intense greenhouse effect, making Venus's surface hot enough to melt lead.

- Venus is slightly closer to the Sun than Earth and was too warm for liquid water oceans to persist and dissolve carbon dioxide from the atmosphere, so Venus suffered a runaway greenhouse effect.
- The hot crust of Venus is dominated by volcanism, but not by plate tectonics.

13.6 Mars

What is the evidence that surface conditions on Mars were originally more Earth-like than they are at present?

- Mars is about half the diameter of Earth; it has a thin atmosphere and has lost much of its internal heat.
- The loss of atmospheric gases depends on the size of a planet and its temperature. Mars is cold, but it is small and has a low escape velocity, and many of its lighter gases have leaked away.
- Some water may have leaked away because UV radiation from the Sun broke it into hydrogen and oxygen, but some water is frozen in the polar caps and in the soil. Orbiters have also measured large amounts of water frozen below the surface.
- Rovers have found clear signs that liquid water flowed over the surface in at least some places and therefore evidence that the Martian climate was different in the past. The northern lowlands may even have held an ocean once.
- Outflow channels and valley networks are visible from orbit, but water cannot now exist as a liquid on Mars because of its low temperature and low atmospheric pressure.
- The southern hemisphere of Mars is old, cratered terrain, but some large volcanoes lie in the north. The sizes of these volcanoes indicate that the crust does not have horizontal motions and plate tectonics.
- Some volcanism may still occur on Mars, but because the planet is small it has cooled and is not very active geologically.
- The two moons of Mars are probably captured asteroids.

KEY TERMS

comparative planetology Understanding planets by searching for and analyzing contrasts and similarities among them. (p. 302)

mantle The layer of dense rock and metal oxides that lies between the molten core and Earth's surface, or a similar layer in another planet. (p. 304)

primary atmosphere A planet's first atmosphere. (p. 307)

secondary atmosphere A planet's atmosphere that replaces the primary atmosphere—for example by outgassing, impact of volatile-bearing planetesimals, or biological activity. (p. 307)

plate tectonics The constant destruction and renewal of Earth's surface by the motion of sections of crust. (p. 308)

greenhouse effect The process by which a carbon dioxide atmosphere traps heat and raises the temperature of a planetary surface. (p. 310)

global warming The gradual increase in the surface temperature of Earth caused by human modifications to Earth's atmosphere. (p. 310)

maria (mare) Lunar lowlands filled by successive flows of dark lava; from the Latin for *sea*. (p. 312)

albedo The ratio of the amount of light reflected from an object to the amount of light received by the object. Albedo equals 0 for perfectly black and 1 for perfectly white. (p. 312)

ejecta Pulverized rock scattered by meteorite impacts on a planetary surface. (p. 312)

anorthosite Aluminum- and calcium-rich silicate rock found in the lunar highlands. (p. 312)

breccia Rock composed of fragments of older rocks bonded together. (p. 312)

large-impact hypothesis Hypothesis that the Moon formed from debris ejected during a collision between Earth and a large planetesimal. (p. 313)

magma ocean The exterior of the newborn Moon, a shell of molten rock hundreds of kilometres deep. (p. 314)

multiringed basin Large impact feature (crater) containing two or more concentric rims formed by fracturing of the planetary crust. (p. 314)

late heavy bombardment The sudden, temporary increase in the cratering rate in our solar system that occurred about 4 billion years ago. (p. 314)

micrometeorite Meteorite of microscopic size. (p. 314)

runaway greenhouse effect A greenhouse effect so dramatic that it amplifies itself, becoming stronger with time. (p. 318)

coronae On Venus, the large, round geological faults in the crust caused by the intrusion of magma below the crust. (p. 319)

permafrost Permanently frozen soil. (p. 321)

shield volcano Wide, low-profile volcanic cone produced by highly liquid lava. (p. 322)

outflow channel Geological features on Mars and Earth caused by flows of vast amounts of water released suddenly. (p. 323)

valley network A system of dry drainage channels on Mars that resembles the beds of rivers and tributary streams on Earth. (p. 323)

The Outer Solar System

TOPIC SUMMARIES

14.1 A Travel Guide to the Outer Planets

- The Jovian planets—Jupiter, Saturn, Uranus, and Neptune—are large, low-density worlds rich in hydrogen and helium.
- The atmospheres of the Jovian planets are marked by cloud belts parallel to their equators.
- Jupiter and Saturn, usually called "gas giants," are composed mostly of liquid hydrogen with liquid metallic hydrogen in deep regions close to their cores and might instead be called "liquid giants." Uranus and Neptune contain water in liquid and solid form and therefore are sometimes called "ice giants."
- All of the Jovian worlds have large systems of satellites and rings that have had complex histories.

14.2 Jupiter

- Jupiter's atmosphere contains three layers of clouds formed of hydrogen-rich molecules such as ammonia and water.
- The clouds are in bands parallel to the equator called zones and belts. Zones are high-pressure regions of rising gas, and belts are lower-pressure areas of sinking gas.
- Spots in Jupiter's atmosphere are circulating weather patterns.
- Models indicate that Jupiter has a core of heavy elements and a deep mantle of liquid metallic hydrogen in which the planet's magnetic field is generated.
- The magnetic field around Jupiter traps high-energy particles from the Sun to form intense radiation belts.
- Jupiter must be very hot inside because heat is flowing out of it.
- Jupiter's ring is composed of dark particles that strongly forward-scatter light, which means the particles are very small. They are probably composed of dust resulting from meteorite impacts on Jupiter's moons.
- Jupiter's ring, like all of the rings in the solar system, lies inside the planet's Roche limit, where moons would be torn apart or unable to form.
- Grooves on Ganymede, smooth ice and cracks on Europa, and active volcanoes on Io show that tidal heating has made these moons active.

14.3 Saturn

- Saturn is less dense than water and contains a small core and less metallic hydrogen than Jupiter.
- The cloud layers on Saturn occur at the same temperature as those on Jupiter, but, because Saturn is farther from the Sun and colder, the cloud layers are deeper in the hydrogen atmosphere below a layer of methane haze.
- Saturn's rings are composed of icy particles ranging in size from boulders to dust. In some regions the ice is purer than in other regions.
- Grooves and other features in the rings can be produced by resonances with moons or by waves that propagate through the rings.
- Narrow rings and sharp ring edges can be confined by shepherd satellites.
- The rings are short-lived. They cannot be as old as their planet and must be replenished now and then with material from meteorites and comets colliding with moons.
- Titan has a cold, cloudy nitrogen and methane atmosphere. Sunlight entering Titan's atmosphere can convert methane into complex carbon-rich molecules to form haze and particles that settle out to coat the surface with dark organic goo. Methane lakes may have been detected on Titan's surface in radar images made by the Cassini probe.
- Enceladus has a light surface with some uncratered regions. Geysers of water and ice spray from the south polar region and provide ice particles to the E ring.

14.4 Uranus

- Uranus is much less massive than Jupiter, and its internal pressure cannot produce liquid hydrogen. It has a heavy-element core and a mantle of slushy or solid ice and rock below a hydrogen-rich atmosphere.
- The atmosphere of Uranus is almost featureless at visual wavelengths with a pale green-blue colour.
- The larger moons of Uranus are icy and heavily cratered, with some signs of past geological activity.
- The rings of Uranus are narrow hoops confined by shepherd satellites. The particles appear to be ice with traces of methane darkened by radiation.
- Uranus rotates "on its side," with its axis nearly in the plane of its orbit, perhaps because of a major impact during its early history.

14.5 Neptune

- Neptune is an ice giant like Uranus with little or no liquid hydrogen in its interior.
- The atmosphere of Neptune, marked by faint patterns of belt–zone circulation, is rich in hydrogen and coloured blue by traces of methane.
- Neptune's satellite system is odd in that Nereid has an extremely elliptical orbit and Triton orbits backwards.
- Triton is icy with a thin atmosphere and frosty polar caps. Smooth areas suggest past geological activity, and dark smudges mark the location of active nitrogen geysers.

- The rings of Neptune are made of dark icy particles in narrow hoops. Neptune's rings contain arcs produced by the gravitational influence of one or more moons.

14.6 Dwarf Planets

- So far, five dwarf planets have been approved by the IAU: Eris, Haumea, Makemake, and Pluto in the Kuiper belt; and Ceres in the asteroid belt between Mars and Jupiter.
- The discovery in 2005 of Eris, about the same size as Pluto, forced the IAU to define planetary bodies, which resulted in the creation of the dwarf planet category. Pluto does not meet all the IAU's criteria to be classified as a planet: though spherical, it hasn't cleared its orbital zone of smaller objects, so it is now considered a dwarf planet.
- Pluto is a small, icy world with five moons, one of which is relatively large. The moons are in orbits highly inclined to Pluto's orbit around the Sun. Pluto has a thin atmosphere.
- Plutinos are other Kuiper belt objects caught in a 3:2 resonance with Neptune.
- Ceres, discovered in 1801, has similar characteristics to the other dwarf planets that have densities less than half that of Earth, compositions of ice and rock, and natural satellites.
- Haumea and Makemake have highly eccentric orbits inclined severely to the ecliptic plane.

KEY TERMS

oblateness The flattening of a spherical body, usually caused by rotation. (p. 335)

liquid metallic hydrogen A form of liquid hydrogen that is a good electrical conductor, inferred to exist in the interiors of Jupiter and Saturn. (p. 336)

magnetosphere The volume of space around a planet within which the motion of charged particles is dominated by the planetary magnetic field rather than the solar wind. (p. 336)

belt–zone circulation The atmospheric circulation typical of Jovian planets in which dark belts and bright zones encircle the planet parallel to its equator. (p. 336)

forward scattering The optical property of finely divided particles to preferentially direct light in the original direction of the light's travel. (p. 336)

Roche limit The minimum distance between a planet and its satellite so that the satellite can hold itself together by its own gravity. If a satellite's orbit brings it within its planet's Roche limit, tidal forces will pull the satellite apart. (p. 337)

tidal heating The heating of a planet or satellite because of friction caused by tides. (p. 340)

shepherd satellite A satellite that, by its gravitational field, confines particles to a planetary ring. (p. 343)

ovoid The oval features found on Miranda, a satellite of Uranus. (p. 348)

occultation The passage of a larger body in front of a smaller body. (p. 348)

dwarf planet A body that orbits the Sun, is not a satellite of a planet, is massive enough to pull itself into a spherical shape, but is not massive enough to clear out other bodies in and near its orbit—for example, Pluto, Eris, and Ceres. (p. 351)

plutino One of the icy Kuiper belt objects that, like Pluto, is caught in a 3:2 orbital resonance with Neptune. (p. 352)